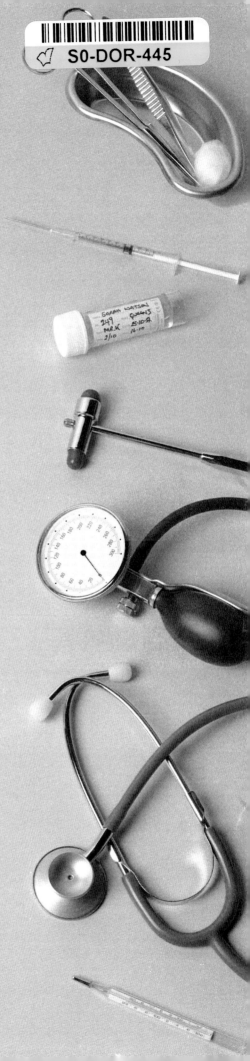

S0-DOR-445

ISBN: 978-0-9829321-8-6
Every precaution is taken to ensure the accuracy of the content of this publication; however, the publisher cannot accept responsibility for the correctness of the information supplied. At the time of publication, all Internet references (URLs) in this book were valid. However, these references are subject to change without notice.

Cover design by Karol A. Keane Design & Communications, karolkeanedesign.com.

Regulatory Affairs Professionals Society
5635 Fishers Lane
Suite 550
Rockville, MD 20852
USA

RAPS.org

Washington, DC ▪ Brussels ▪ Tokyo

Foreword

Global Medical Device Regulation is a compilation of chapters covering medical device regulation, adapted from the five books in RAPS' *Fundamentals of Regulatory Affairs* series. The chapters included here address everything from essential, broadly applicable regulatory information and concepts to the specific regulations governing medical devices and in vitro medical devices in several key global markets and internationally. The concept for this book arose from a request from faculty at Grace College in Winona Lake, IN, for material for a course on device regulations.

This book is intended as a single source of information on medical device regulations in the international arena, based largely on Global Harmonization Task Force and ISO requirements, and regulations in the US, EU, Canada and Japan. It is a handy compendium of regional regulatory requirements both for those who are new to the field and experienced professionals working in multiple markets.

The publication dates for the individual books from which these chapters are drawn are:
Fundamentals of International Regulatory Affairs ©2010
Fundamentals of US Regulatory Affairs ©2011
Fundamentals of EU Regulatory Affairs ©2011
Fundamentals of Canadian Regulatory Affairs ©2011
Fundamentals of Japanese Regulatory Affairs ©2010

Neither the chapters nor the web pages referenced (URLs) have been updated since their original publication in *Fundamentals*; they have merely been gathered into a single book. Therefore, some information and internet sources may have changed or been deleted after publication.

Pamela A. Jones
Senior Editor
Regulatory Affairs Professionals Society

Acknowledgements

The following authors from the RAPS Fundamentals Series contributed to this book. Please note that *Fundamentals of Japanese Regulatory Affairs* was written by RAPS Japan in cooperation with industry experts.

Richard Angelo, PhD
Director, Executive Consultant
Scientific Consulting
Beckloff Associates Inc.
Overland Park, KS, USA

Chas Burr, SM, MBA, FRAPS
Graduate Program Director
Regulatory and Clinical Research Management (RCRM)
Assistant Professor
Regis College
Winchester, MA, USA

Amber Yu-Pei Cheng, MSc
Regulatory Scientist
Scandinavian Health Limited
Taoyuan City, Taiwan

Vicky M. Cheng, PMP
Regulatory Scientist
Scandinavian Health Limited
Taoyuan City, Taiwan

John DeLucia
VP, Regulatory Affairs, Quality Assurance, and Clinical Affairs
ICAD Inc.
Nashua, NH, USA

Maria E. Donawa, MD
President
Donawa Lifescience Consulting Srl
Rome, Italy

Lea Epstein, JD, LLM
Barrister
Thornhill, ON, Canada

Caroline Freeman
Senior Consultant
Quintiles Consulting
Bracknell, UK

Estelle Geffard-Duchamp
MedPass International
Paris, France

Laila Gurney, MSc, RAC
Senior Director, Regulatory Affairs, Strategies, Standards and Processes
GE Healthcare
Toronto, ON, Canada

Susan K. Hamann, MS, MT(ASCP), RAC
Regulatory Affairs Manager
Perkin Elmer
Burlington, MA, USA

Merry Lane
Regulatory Affairs Associate
Optuminsight
Dundas, ON, Canada

Evangeline Loh, PhD, RAC
Vice President, Regulatory Affairs
Emergo Group
Austin, TX, USA

Salma Michor, PhD, MBA, CMgr, RAC
CEO and Principal Consultant
Michor Consulting e.U.
Vienna, Austria

Ludger Moeller
President
Medical Device Safety Service
Hannover, Germany

Richard Morroney, CQA, RAC
Director of Quality and Regulatory Affairs
VuCOMP Inc.
Dallas, TX, USA

Nandini Murthy, RAC
Regulatory Consultant
ENEM Consulting LLC
Lexington, MA, USA

Scott A. Oglesby, PhD
Director, Executive Consulting
Beckloff Associates
Hillsborough, NC, USA

RAPS Japan

Mika Reinikainen
Managing Director
Abnovo Ltd.
Novo Nordisk AB
Weybridge, UK

Kelly Rowland
Regulatory Affairs Specialist
Elekta Inc.
Maryland Heights, MO, USA

Nancy Ruth
Director, Medical Devices
Optuminsight
Dundas, ON, Canada

Sarah Sorrel
President
MedPass International SAS
Paris, France

Dirk Stynen, PhD
President
Qarad
Mol, Belgium

Jeremy J. Tinkler
Director, Regulatory Affairs
Medpass International SA
Paris, France

Michael Wienholt, RAC (US, EU)
Principal Consultant
d.b.a. Regulatory Consulting
Escondido, CA, USA

Table of Contents

TABLES

International Medical Device Regulation

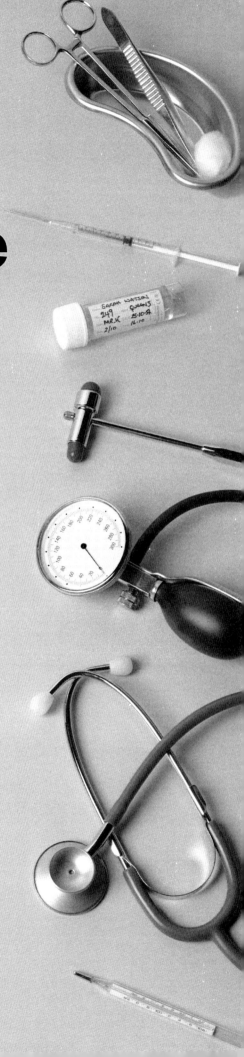

Chapter 1

Introduction to Regulatory Affairs

By Salma Michor, PhD, MBA, CMgr, RAC

OBJECTIVES

❑ Learn why healthcare regulations for medicinal products and devices were established

❑ Discover the key historical milestones leading to today's healthcare regulations

❑ Clarify the importance of global harmonization

LAWS, REGULATIONS AND GUIDELINES COVERED IN THIS CHAPTER

US

❑ The *Federal Food, Drug, and Cosmetic Act* of 1938 (*FD&C Act*), as amended by the *Food and Drug Administration Modernization Act* of 1997 (*FDAMA*) (Public Law 105-115)

EU

❑ Commission Directive 2003/32/EC introducing detailed specifications as regards the requirements laid down in Council Directive 93/42/EEC with respect to medical devices manufactured utilising tissues of animal origin

❑ Council Directive 93/42/EEC of 14 June 1993, concerning medical devices

❑ MEDDEV 2.12-1 rev 6., *Guidelines on a Medical Device Vigilance System* (December 2009)

❑ Regulation (EC) No. 1829/2003 of the European Parliament and of the Council of 22 September

2003 on genetically modified food and feed

ICH

❑ *Pharmacovigilance Planning E2E* (Current Step 4 version, November 2004)

GHTF

❑ SG2-N54R8:2006, *Medical Devices Post Market Surveillance: Global Guidance for Adverse Event Reporting for Medical Devices* (18 December 2006)

❑ SG5-N2R8:2007, *Clinical Evaluation*, May 2007 pp 4-12.

Introduction

The main aim of drug regulation is to keep unsafe products off the market. Drug regulation entails granting of marketing authorization licenses to place products (considered to be relatively safe) on the market after a thorough evaluation by Competent Authorities (CAs). It must be stressed, however, that no medicinal product is 100% safe. Tests carried out on a population of limited size, under controlled conditions during clinical trials may fail to identify critical issues and adverse events. When drugs are placed on the market for the first time, little is really known about side effects that may first come to light when used by millions in the population at large. Previously unknown adverse events may occur, or known adverse events may occur at a higher frequency than expected. Hence, regulations require medicinal product monitoring in the postauthorization and marketing phases. In addition to medicinal product regulation, most countries worldwide have enacted regulations for medical devices, food and food supplements and cosmetic products.

In some countries, such as the US and Canada, laws to regulate food and drug products were established in the 19th century. The evolution of modern healthcare in Canada began with the *British North American Act* of 1867, which gave individual provinces jurisdiction over most health services.[1] The *Vaccine Act* of 1813 was the first federal law in the US dealing with consumer protection and therapeutic substances.[2] Food regulations in the US and Europe have an even longer history, while regulations covering cosmetics and medical devices have been developed more recently. In the EU, healthcare regulations became firmly established during the second half of the 20th century.[3] Other regions, such as Asia and the Pacific, Middle East and Africa and the Americas have introduced drug and medical device regulations to greater or lesser extents and at various points.

In developing countries, drug regulations may be more difficult to implement and monitor; hence, the danger of drug and food adulteration may be higher there than in other regions of the world.

The history of medicinal product registration in much of the industrialized world has followed a similar pattern, which can be described as: "Initiation, Acceleration, Rationalization and Harmonization" (ICH).

The realization that it was important to have a critical evaluation of medicinal products by CAs before they are allowed on the market was reached at different times in different regions. The "initiation" of stricter controls was triggered by human disasters such as the tragic mistake in the formulation of a children's syrup in the 1930s in the US, which led to the introduction of the product authorization systems; in Europe, the trigger was the thalidomide tragedy of the 1960s.

Most countries saw a rapid increase ("acceleration") in laws, regulations and guidelines for reporting and evaluating safety, quality and efficacy data on new medicinal products in the 1960s and 1970s. Even though different regulatory systems were based on the same fundamental obligations of evaluating product quality, safety and efficacy, the detailed technical requirements diverged over time. This resulted in the duplication of effort involving time-consuming evaluations and expensive test procedures. Eventually, the rising costs of healthcare paved the way for "rationalization" and "harmonization" (ICH).[4]

It must be understood that many different stakeholders are involved in the regulatory process, including healthcare providers, industry and consumers. The aims of these interest groups may differ: providers and reimbursement bodies may aim to minimize costs; consumers crave a large variety of low-cost, good-quality medicines; while industry desires easy, inexpensive market access.

Before Regulations

Before regulations were in place, drugs and other critical products could be sold like any other consumer product. In the US, for example, medicines were initially patented to protect trade secrets. These medicines were uncontrolled products ranging from harmless mixtures to toxic combinations of narcotics and other substances.[5]

Lack of control not only allowed marketing of products that were not controlled or tested for efficacy, safety and tolerability, but also led to the possible sale of adulterated products. Adulteration was a problem in both the healthcare and food sectors, and governments began to impose laws and regulations to combat adulteration and ensure safety. Commonly adulterated foods included alcohol, milk and bread. Practices that make drugs and foods adulterated include using ingredients of inferior quality and making false claims on labels. Legislation designed to prevent the sale of unsafe or unwholesome food is one of the oldest forms of governmental or societal intervention in the food and agricultural system.[6]

Ethical considerations were also major contributors to stronger regulations.[7]

The need for ethical standards has its foundation in the inhumane practices of infamous Nazi physician, Josef Mengele, during the second world war. During World War II, doctors in Nazi Germany conducted horrifying research on prisoners in concentration camps, which resulted in the Nuremberg Code being created in 1948.[8]

Many unethical clinical research trials were also carried out in the US and the UK during the same period. President Franklin Roosevelt created an Office of Scientific Research and Development to combat diseases such as dysentery, influenza and malaria, and other diseases that commonly affect soldiers. Trials were carried out on orphans, mentally retarded individuals in institutions and prisoners, with the justification that it was necessary for some sacrifices to be made to benefit the whole of society. Negative publicity paved the way for healthcare regulations to protect public safety.

The introduction of stricter regulations in certain major economies has led the way to stricter regulations in other parts of the world.

Start of Regulation

Realization of the importance of drug evaluation was reached at different times in different regions.[9] The first food and drug laws aimed to prohibit commerce in misbranded and adulterated foods, drinks and drugs. In the US, initially, laws regulating product labeling rather than requiring a premarket assessment of safety or efficacy were implemented. The regulatory framework that evolved over the years imposed increasingly stricter control. Sulfanilamide is one example of a drug that was placed on the market without safety testing.[10] Following the introduction in 1937 of a liquid version of sulfanilamide that contained diethylene glycol (a poisonous solvent), 107 people in the US died from ingesting the elixir. The public outrage over the sulfanilamide tragedy led to the rapid passage of the *Federal Food, Drug, and Cosmetic Act* (*FD&C Act*) of 1938,[11] which required drugs to be cleared for safety before being introduced on the market.[12] In Japan, government regulations requiring all medicinal products to be registered for sale started around 1950.[13]

Stricter regulations came into force in the 1960s as a consequence of the thalidomide tragedy in Europe and Canada. Contergan, a product containing the active ingredient thalidomide, was used to treat morning sickness in pregnant women. The teratogenic potential of thalidomide was not adequately characterized during development. As a result, thousands of babies were born with a rare malformation known as phocomelia.[14]

Other cases calling for stricter regulations include the potential transmission of bovine spongiform encephalopathy (BSE, mad cow disease) and transmissible spongiform encephalopathy (TSE, Creutzfeldt-Jakob disease) to humans via medicinal products containing bovine-derived materials. The BSE/TSE crisis in the early 1990s led to stricter control of drugs containing or derived from bovine material (e.g., Commission Directive 2003/32/EC of 23 April 2003 introducing detailed specifications as regards the requirements laid down in Council Directive 93/42/EEC with respect to medical devices manufactured utilising tissues of animal origin in the EU[15]). Although the origins of such scandals have their roots in certain geographic regions, the impact has been felt worldwide. Other sectors, such as food, cosmetics and medical devices also came under closer scrutiny.

Globally, the 1960s and 1970s saw a rapid increase in laws, regulations and guidelines for reporting and evaluating the data on new medicinal products' safety, quality and efficacy. During this period, the industry was starting to become more international and globalization began. Registration of medicines, medical devices, cosmetic products and foods, however, remained a national responsibility in most cases. Although different regulatory systems were based on the same fundamental obligations to evaluate quality, safety and efficacy, the detailed technical requirements for each country and/or region were significantly divergent.

Harmonization

Nonharmonized registration regulations meant that it was necessary to duplicate efforts to obtain approvals in different regions, which was time-consuming and expensive. The drive to rationalize and harmonize regulations was impelled by concerns over rising healthcare costs, escalating R&D costs and the need to meet public expectations.[16] In addition, life-saving medicines need to reach patients with minimum delay.

Initiation of International Conference on Harmonisation (ICH)

Work on harmonizing regulatory requirements began in the 1980s. It was pioneered by the European Community (EC) with the aim of developing a single market for pharmaceuticals. The success achieved in Europe demonstrated that harmonization was feasible.[17] The desire to have international harmonized standards and trilateral discussions among the EC, Japan and the US led to specific plans for action during the World Health Organization (WHO) International Conference of Drug Regulatory Authorities (ICDRA) in Paris in 1989. The authorities of Europe, Japan and the US approached the International Federation of Pharmaceutical Manufacturers & Associations (IFPMA) to discuss a joint regulatory authority-industry initiative on international harmonization, and ICH was conceived. ICH was born at a meeting in Brussels in April 1990, hosted by the European Federation of Pharmaceutical Industries and Associations (EFPIA).

The Global Harmonization Task Force (GHTF)

GHTF was conceived in 1992 in an effort to achieve greater uniformity across national medical device regulatory systems.[18] As with ICH and pharmaceuticals, the main aim of GHTF is to enhance patient safety while increasing access to safe, effective and clinically beneficial medical technologies worldwide.

GHTF is comprised of five Founding Members—EU, US, Canada, Australia and Japan—and represents a partnership between regulatory authorities and industry.

Monitoring

Stricter regulation of drugs has continued from the 1960s through 2000 and beyond. This has been driven by a series of major adverse drug reactions. For example, subacute myelo-optic-neuropathy (SMON) was found to be caused by ciloquinol. While this drug was first marketed in the early 1930s, its side effects only became apparent in the 1970s when ciloquinol was linked to severe neurological reactions as a result of stricter pharmacovigilance and surveillance regulations.

Other examples include practolol, which after five years on the market was linked to oculomucocutaneous syndrome. In the 1980s, several drugs were linked to serious side effects: ticrynafen and benoxaprofen were found to cause deaths from liver disease. Zomepirac, a nonsteroidal anti-inflammatory drug, was associated with an increased risk of anaphylactoid reactions.[19]

The list goes on: suprofin was found to cause acute flank pain and reversible acute renal failure, and isotretinoin was almost removed from the US market because of its link to birth defects. Over the past few years, crises concerning the use of several drugs have arisen. Examples include allegations of ischemic colitis from alosetron; rhabdomyolysis from cerivastatin; arthralgia, myalgia and neurologic conditions from Lyme vaccine; multiple joint symptoms from anthrax vaccine; and heart attack and stroke from rofecoxib, to name a few.[20]

The results of such severe drug adverse events have in some instances led to recalls. In the US alone, more than 22 different prescription drug products have been removed from the market since the 1980s.[21]

Pharmacovigilance/Vigilance
Drugs

Vigilance requirements for both drugs and medical devices have increased in recent years. The decision to approve a drug is based on a satisfactory risk/benefit balance within the conditions specified in the product labeling.[22] The decision to approve a drug or device application is based upon information available at the time of approval. However, as noted above, tests carried out during the preclinical and clinical testing phases may fail to detect critical issues. A product's safety profile can change significantly through use in a much larger number of patients. Thus, it is vitally important that drugs and devices placed on the market be closely monitored, especially during the early postmarketing period.[23]

ICH has published the *Harmonised Tripartite Guideline Pharmacovigilance Planning E2E*.[24] Better and earlier planning of pharmacovigilance activities is needed before a product is approved or a license is granted. This guideline has been developed to encourage harmonization and consistency, and to prevent duplication of effort. The guideline could be of benefit to public health programs throughout the world as they consider new drugs in their countries.[25] The guideline recommends several pharmacovigilance activities including:

- passive surveillance
- stimulated reporting
- active surveillance
- comparative observational studies
- targeted clinical investigations
- descriptive studies

Medical Devices

In GHTF's *Medical Devices Post Market Surveillance: Global Guidance for Adverse Event Reporting for Medical Devices*, the objective of "vigilance" is described as:

"The objective of the adverse event reporting and subsequent evaluations is to improve protection of the health and safety of patients, users and others by disseminating information which may reduce the likelihood of, or prevent repetition of adverse events, or alleviate consequences of such repetition."[26]

Medical device manufacturers placing products on the market are required to notify regulatory authorities (RAs) of any adverse events. Different regions may implement more or less strict rules and each region may have regional and/or national guidelines and regulations. The EU, for example, has published *Guidelines on a Medical Device Vigilance System* (MEDDEV 2.12-1 rev. 6).[27]

For incidents/adverse events to be reportable to national CAs, the following are assumed:

- An event has occurred.
- The manufacturer's device is associated with the event.
- The event led to one of the following outcomes:
  o death of a patient, user or other person
  o serious injury of a patient, user or other person
  o no death or serious injury occurred, but the event might lead to the death or serious injury of a patient, user or other person if the event recurs

It is important that RAs communicate with counterparts in other countries to stay informed about incidents that have not occurred locally.[28] WHO follows standard operating procedures for issuing alerts among member states and may also work with GHTF to assist in disseminating information to countries as appropriate.

Foods, Food Supplements and Cosmetics

Less-critical products such as foods, food supplements and cosmetics do not require formal vigilance reporting, but follow regular monitoring via formal inspections. Food quality is becoming increasingly important and food manufacturers need to ensure strict hygiene and quality standards in their manufacturing facilities.

Stricter Authorization Requirements

Today, the drug and medical device approval processes in most countries require preclinical and clinical testing. In most developed countries, drug trials comprise preclinical testing followed by three phases of clinical testing:

- Phase 1—usually carried out by clinical pharmacologists on a small number of healthy volunteers to determine drug metabolism, a safe dosage range and tolerability
- Phase 2—also carried out by clinical pharmacologists on a small number of patients with the target disease; here, information about the drug's pharmacokinetic properties, safety and efficacy is gathered
- Phase 3—carried out by clinical investigators on a larger population to evaluate efficacy and to test for toxicity; at least one Phase 3 study needs to be a randomized clinical trial, in which some patients receive the trial drug and others receive a placebo or standard treatment[29]

For medical devices, the approach to clinical testing

(now also being applied to drugs) is to have the clinical evaluation as an ongoing process throughout the life of the device.[30] More emphasis is placed on collecting appropriate information via:

- literature reviews
- clinical experience
- clinical investigations

The manufacturer is responsible for identifying data relevant to the device and deciding what and how much data need to be collected during the investigation to prove the device's safety.

Other Products
Veterinary Products

Veterinary products are regulated in more or less the same manner as medicinal products for humans. The main difference is that drugs for animal populations need to conform to maximum residue limits since they may end up in the food chain. In the US, premarket approval is not required for medical devices intended for animal use; FDA does not require submission of a 510(k) or formal premarket approval for devices used in veterinary medicine.[31] In the EU, medical device law does not include veterinary products. That means such products as special drug delivery systems cannot be CE marked, and fall under drug regulations.

Abridged Applications

Less critical products, such as those of well-established use, traditional herbal medicinal products and generic drugs, may not require preclinical and clinical tests if their safety can be shown based on information in the public domain or by reference to originator products. Over-the-counter (OTC) products containing new chemical entities must be treated as full applications even though their active ingredients may not warrant prescription status.

Orphan Drugs

An "orphan drug" can be defined as a pharmaceutical agent that has been developed specifically to treat a rare medical condition, referred to as an "orphan disease."

In the US, a law regulating such drugs was enacted in 1983 (*Orphan Drug Act (ODA)*). The EU's definition of an orphan condition is broader than that of the US, in that it also covers some tropical diseases found primarily in developing nations.[32] Since financial incentives for manufacturing and marketing orphan drugs are low, many CAs have created initiatives and financial support for companies that engage in orphan drug research.

Food, Dietary Supplements and Cosmetics

In general, food, dietary supplements and cosmetic products do not need premarket controls. However, the manufacturer must be able to show that its products meet the minimum safety standards regarding composition, packaging and information. It is generally the manufacturer's responsibility to implement a market surveillance system both to ensure safety and in case the need for a batch recall arises.

Some countries require Genetically Modified Organisms (GMOs) entering the food chain to be closely monitored, and traceability needs to be ensured. For example, in the EU, clear systems for tracing and labeling GMOs (Regulation 1830/2003/EC) and for regulating the marketing and labeling of food and feed products derived from GMOs (Regulation 1829/2003/EC[33]) have been established.

Product Innovations

Technological advances have made many novel therapies available, including biologics, blood products and advanced therapy medicinal products (ATMPs). It is important that regulations evolve to keep abreast of advances in science and technology. Innovative product developers may both benefit from and exploit the existence of a "regulatory vacuum."[34] In such instances, manufacturers may be more informed than officials of the CA and could share their expertise by becoming involved in defining the regulatory framework for the new area, influencing public and agency opinion.[35]

Public Health and Economic Resources

Initially, science and public health protection were the motivating factors and primary drivers in healthcare regulation. In recent years, economic considerations have also begun impacting healthcare regulation development.[36,37]

In many countries, healthcare systems rely on products reimbursed by national health systems. In this respect, public health is highly dependent upon the availability of high-quality reimbursed products. It is in the interest of local governing bodies to have access to high-quality medicines at affordable prices, necessitating price controls. In countries where the healthcare costs are borne by individual consumers, access to affordable medicines is even more critical.

Stakeholders and the Availability of Information

In today's world of electronic media such as the Internet, it is almost impossible to hide any critical issues related to any product from the general public. Information is available to virtually anyone, even in very remote parts of the world. Industry must ensure that only safe products are placed on the market and act responsibly if any critical issues arise. To maintain public confidence in the healthcare system, timely and appropriate regulations that ensure medicinal/healthcare product(s) quality, safety and efficacy, and clear instructions for use, are necessary.[38]

Healthcare regulations must balance the interests of patients, manufacturers, RAs, insurance companies and others in a fast-moving and complex environment.[39] Such regulatory systems need to be robust and quickly adaptable in the face of advancing technology.

At the global level, it is imperative that laws regulating critical healthcare products and standards become more harmonized to ensure worldwide patient safety. Mutual Recognition Agreements between various geographical regions ensure that quality standards are harmonized, which also avoids duplication of efforts. In this respect, the work carried out by harmonization bodies such as ICH and GHTF is becoming increasingly important in defining and shaping the worldwide industry.

Last but not least, regulations continue to be a moving target. Regulatory professionals and the life science industry need to keep abreast of national, regional and global regulatory changes to ensure that safe, reliable and good-quality medicines reach patients at the right time.

References

1. Regulatory Affairs Professionals Society. Chapter 1, History of Canadian Regulatory Affairs. In: *Fundamentals of Canadian Regulatory Affairs.* Rockville, MD. 2006:1-8.
2. Regulatory Affairs Professionals Society. Chapter 1, History of US Regulatory Affairs. In: *Fundamentals of US Regulatory Affairs Fifth Edition.* Rockville, MD. 2007: 1-12.
3. Regulatory Affairs Professionals Society. Chapter 1, Why Have Regulations Become Necessary. In: *Fundamentals of EU Regulatory Affairs Fourth Edition,* Rockville, MD. 2008:1-16.
4. ICH, History and Future. ICH website. www.ich.org/cache/compo/276-254-1.html. Accessed 8 February 2010
5. Op cit 2.
6. Op cit 1.
7. Op cit 3.
8. Kiefer J. "The History and Importance of Informed Consent in Clinical Trials." Bryn Mawr website. http://serendip.brynmawr.edu/biology/b103/f01/web2/kiefer.html. Accessed 18 February 2010.
9. Op cit 4.
10. Grigg W. "1938–1988: The 50th Anniversary of the Federal Food, Drug and Cosmetic Act." *FDA Consumer.* January 1989: 28–32.
11. The *Federal Food, Drug and Cosmetic Act* of 1938, as amended by the *Food and Drug Administration Modernization Act.* 1997. Public Law 105-115.
12. Op cit 2.
13. Op cit 4.
14. Op cit 3.
15. Commission Directive 2003/32/EC of 23 April 2003 introducing detailed specifications as regards the requirements laid down in Council Directive 93/42/EEC with respect to medical devices manufactured utilising tissues of animal origin.
16. Op cit 4.
17. Ibid.
18. Global Harmonization Task Force website. www.ghtf.org/. Accessed 18 February 2010.
19. Op cit 15.
20. Ibid.
21. Ibid.
22. ICH, *Pharmacovigilance Planning E2E* (Current Step 4 version, November 2004).
23. Op cit 18.
24. Op cit 22.
25. Ibid.
26. GHTF (SG2-N54R8:2006), *Medical Devices Post Market Surveillance: Global Guidance for Adverse Event Reporting for Medical Devices* (December 2006).
27. MEDDEV 2.12-1 rev 6, *Guidelines on a Medical Device Vigilance System* (December 2009).
28. WHO, *Medical Device Regulation: Global Overview & Guiding Principles* (2003), pp 44-45.
29. Ibid.
30. GHTF, SG5-N2R8:2007, *Clinical Evaluation* (May 2007), pp 4-12.
31. US FDA, "How FDA Regulates Veterinary Devices." FDA website. www.fda.gov/AnimalVeterinary/ResourcesforYou/ucm047117.htm. Accessed [date].
32. "Definition of Orphan Disease." Medterms website. www.medterms.com/script/main/art.asp?articlekey=11418. Accessed 18 February 2010.
33. Regulation (EC) No. 1829/2003 of the European Parliament and of the Council of 22 September 2003 on genetically modified food and feed. Eurlex website. http://eurlex.europa.eu/LexUriServ/site/en/oj/2003/l_268/l_26820031018en00010023.pdf. Accessed 18 February 2010.
34. Op cit 3.
35. Ibid.
36. Ibid.
37. Strom BL. Chapter 1, What is Pharmacoepidemiology? In: Strom BL and Kimmel SE, eds. *Textbook of Pharmacoepidemiology.* Chicester, England: John Wiley & Sons, Ltd; 2006:3-11.
38. Op cit 3.
39. Ibid.

Chapter 2

International Medical Device Premarket Requirements

By Salma Michor, PhD, MBA, CMgr, RAC

OBJECTIVES

❏ Provide an overview of regulatory premarket requirements for marketing medical devices

❏ Review the *Essential Principles of Safety & Performance of Medical Devices*

❏ Review design and manufacturing requirements

❏ Describe the *Principles of Conformity Assessment for Medical Devices*

❏ Explain the *Principles of Medical Devices Classification*

❏ Examine the role of standards in the assessment of medical devices

REGULATIONS AND GUIDELINES COVERED IN THIS CHAPTER

GHTF

❏ SG1-N29R16:2005, *Information Document Concerning the Definition of the Term "Medical Device"* (May 2005)

❏ SG1-N41R9:2005, *Essential Principles of Safety & Performance of Medical Devices* (May 2005)

❏ SG1-N43:2005, *Labelling for Medical Devices* (June 2005)

❏ SG1-N40:2006, *Principles of Conformity Assessment for Medical Devices* (June 2006)

❏ SG1-N15:2006, *Principles of Medical Devices Classification* (June 2006)

❏ SG1-N44:2008, *Role of Standards in the Assessment of Medical Devices* (April 2008)

Introduction

The Global Harmonization Task Force (GHTF) has published the following harmonized definition of a medical device:

"Medical device means any instrument, apparatus, implement, machine, appliance, implant, in vitro reagent or calibrator, software, material or other similar or related article:

    a) intended by the manufacturer to be used, alone or in combination, for human beings for one or more of the specific purpose(s) of:

- diagnosis, prevention, monitoring, treatment or alleviation of disease,
- diagnosis, monitoring, treatment, alleviation of or compensation for an injury,
- investigation, replacement, modification or support of the anatomy or of a physiological process,
- supporting or sustaining life,
- control of conception,
- disinfection of medical devices,
- providing information for medical or diagnostic purposes by means of *in vitro* examination of specimens derived from the human body;

and

    b) which does not achieve its primary intended action in or on the human body by pharmacological, immunological or metabolic means, but which may be assisted in its intended function by such means"[1]

In vitro diagnostics may include reagents, calibrators, sample collection and storage devices and materials, control materials and related instruments or apparatuses. The way such products are regulated may differ from region to region. The approach used for regulating certain devices is still far from harmonized for certain product types including:
- aids for disabled/handicapped people
- devices for the treatment and/or diagnosis of diseases and injuries in animals
- accessories for medical devices
- disinfection substances
- devices incorporating animal and human tissues that may meet the requirements of the above definition but are subject to different controls

The way these devices are regulated at the national level may vary from jurisdiction to jurisdiction. In general, accessories are considered to be medical devices in their own right.

Essential Principles of Safety & Performance of Medical Devices

GHTF has published *Essential Principles of Safety & Performance of Medical Devices,* a document to assist in harmonization.[2] This document helps manufacturers design and manufacture a device and demonstrate its suitability for the intended use while reducing costs by eliminating differences between jurisdictions.

The document is based on six general safety and performance requirements that apply to all medical devices:
1. Medical devices should be designed and manufactured in such a way that, when used under the conditions and for the purposes intended and, taking into account the technical knowledge, experience, education or training of intended users, they will not compromise the clinical condition or the safety of patients, of users or, where applicable, other persons. This should be considered in the context of the risk/benefit ratio.
2. The solutions adopted by the manufacturer for the design and manufacture of the devices should conform to the most current safety principles and should address the issue of residual risk and risk reduction. The manufacturer is obliged to:
   - identify known or foreseeable hazards and estimate the associated risks arising from intended use/misuse
   - eliminate risks as much as possible
   - reduce remaining risks as far as is reasonably

practicable
   - inform users of any residual risks
3. Devices should achieve the performance intended by the manufacturer.
4. Device characteristics and performance should not be adversely affected to such a degree that the health or safety of the patient or the user is compromised during the lifetime of the device, under normal conditions of use.
5. The devices should be designed, manufactured and packed in such a way that their characteristics and performances are not affected under transport and storage conditions.
6. The benefits must be determined to outweigh any undesirable side effects for the performances intended.[3]

Design and Manufacturing Requirements
Chemical, Physical and Biological Properties

The choice of materials used in the manufacture of medical devices is very important, and special attention should be paid to toxicity and flammability. In addition, compatibility of the materials used with biological tissues, cells, body fluids and specimens is of significance. Devices should be designed, manufactured and packed in such a way as to minimize the risk posed by contaminants and residues.

Special attention needs to be paid to devices that incorporate, as an integral part, a substance which, if used separately, may be considered to be a medicinal product/drug as defined in the relevant legislation.

Infection and Microbial Contamination

Devices and manufacturing processes should be designed to eliminate or reduce the risk of infection to patients, users and, where applicable, other people. Especially for devices that incorporate substances of biological origin, the risk of infection must be reduced as much as is reasonably practicable and appropriate. This goal can be achieved by careful selection of donors and substances and validated inactivation coupled with strict controls.

In some jurisdictions, products incorporating tissues, cells and substances of non-human origin may be considered medical devices, while in others they are subject to drug laws. In either case, all claims made on the labels—such as "sterilized"—must be validated.

Manufacturing and Environmental Properties

If the device is intended for use in combination with other devices or equipment, the whole combination, including the connection system, should be safe. Devices should be designed and manufactured in such a way as to remove or reduce the risk of injury due to fire, explosion or any other environmental condition.

Devices With a Diagnostic or Measuring Function

Diagnostic devices with a measuring function, where inaccuracy could have a significant adverse effect on the patient, should ensure sufficient accuracy, precision and stability for their intended purpose, and the limits of accuracy should be indicated by the manufacturer. Values expressed numerically should be in commonly accepted standardized units understood by users. Diagnostic devices should be designed and manufactured to provide sufficient accuracy, precision and stability for their intended use, based on appropriate scientific and technical methods. Among other things, the design should address sensitivity, specificity, trueness, repeatability, reproducibility, control of known relevant interference and limits of detection, as appropriate.

Protection Against Radiation

Devices should be designed, manufactured and packaged in such a way as to minimize exposure of patients, users and other persons to any emitted radiation as far as is practicable and appropriate.

Requirements for Medical Devices Connected to or Equipped With an Energy Source

Devices incorporating electronic programmable systems, including software, should be designed to ensure these systems' repeatability, reliability and performance according to their intended use. Such systems should also be properly validated.

Protection Against Mechanical Risks

Devices should be designed and manufactured in such a way as to protect the patient and user against mechanical risks such as resistance to movement, instability and moving parts.

Protection Against the Risks Posed by Supplied Energy or Substances

Devices for supplying the patient with energy or substances should be designed and constructed so the delivered amount can be accurately set and maintained to ensure the safety of the patient and the user.

Protection Against the Risks Posed by Devices for Self Testing or Self Administration

Devices for self testing should be designed and manufactured to perform appropriately for their intended purpose, taking into account the skills and the means available to users. The information provided by the manufacturer for such devices is very critical and should be easy for the user to understand and apply.

Information Supplied by the Manufacturer

Users should be provided with clear instructions that can be easily understood. The instructions should include information needed to use the device safely and to ensure the intended performance, taking users' training and knowledge into account. To this end, GHTF published SG1-N009, *Labelling for Medical Devices* in February 2000. That document was superseded by SG1-N43,[4] *Labelling for Medical Devices* (revised), which added guidance on the labeling of in vitro devices, in June 2005.

According to this guidance,[5] device labeling must clearly inform the user of:

- the device's identity and intended use/purpose
- how the device should be used, maintained and stored
- any residual risks, warnings or contraindications

Manufacturers are encouraged to take intended users' technical knowledge, experience, education or training into consideration and to use symbols where possible. Harmonization is encouraged and the use of country-specific requirements should be avoided.

Performance Evaluation Including, Where Appropriate, Clinical Evaluation

Performance and clinical evaluations are still very much a national issue. All data generated should be obtained in accordance with the relevant requirements applicable in each jurisdiction and clinical investigations on human subjects should be carried out in accordance with the spirit of the Helsinki Declaration.[6]

Principles of Conformity Assessment for Medical Devices

To place medical devices on the market, manufacturers must demonstrate conformity to the minimum requirements for device safety and functionality. Conformity assessment elements include:[7]

- a quality management system
- a system for postmarket surveillance
- summary technical documentation
- a declaration of conformity
- the registration of manufacturers and their medical devices with the regulatory authority

These five elements are required for all device classes.

Quality Management System (QMS)

Manufacturers are obliged to have a QMS that meets internationally recognized standards to ensure medical devices will be safe and perform as intended by the manufacturer. Internationally recognized standards are those deemed to offer the presumption of conformity to specific essential principles of safety and performance.[8]

Further, medical devices must be manufactured in such a way that they consistently meet both customer and regulatory requirements. The scope and complexity of the QMS varies, depending upon the type of devices being manufactured, the size and the structure of the organization and specific regulatory requirements.

Activities carried out by third parties remain the responsibility of the manufacturer and are subject to control under the manufacturer's QMS. The adequacy of this control will be assessed by conformity assessment bodies and regulatory authorities during inspections.

In some jurisdictions, design and development activities may be excluded from the scope of the manufacturer's QMS. For example, some regional or country regulations may allow manufacturers to choose an alternate examination type to demonstrate conformity with the essential requirements of safety and performance. A full QMS is the preferred approach because it implements a full cycle of design and development controls that ensure medical devices comply with the relevant Essential Principles.[9]

Postmarket Surveillance (PMS)

As part of the QMS, prior to placing products on the market, manufacturers must have a functioning PMS system in place. This allows assessment of the continued conformity of the device to the Essential Principles through the postmarketing phase. This system comprises complaint handling, postmarket vigilance reporting and corrective and preventive actions (CAPA).[10]

Summary Technical Documentation (STED)

Manufacturers are required to prepare and keep detailed technical documentation that shows how each medical device was developed, designed and manufactured and the descriptions and explanations necessary to understand how the manufacturer ensures conformity of the device to the Essential Principles. The technical file provides the evidence used in the conformity assessment process. Part of the technical documentation generated comprising summary information on selected topics, detailed information on certain specific topics (controlled documents sufficient to communicate key relevant information), and an Essential Principles checklist (EP checklist) are either submitted to the regulatory authority (RA) or conformity assessment body (CAB), or kept on the manufacturer's premises ready for inspection. Not all documents relating to a device form part of the STED; many controlled documents are referenced in the EP checklist, but only some are contained within the STED. The EP checklist is created as part of the manufacturer's technical documentation. This is a controlled document within the manufacturer's QMS and provides a tabular overview of the Essential Principles and identifies those that are applicable to the device, while showing the chosen method of demonstrating that the device conforms to each relevant Essential Principle. The EP checklist references controlled documents that allow RAs and/or Competent Authorities (CAs) to request additional information as appropriate.

The depth and detail of the information contained in the STED will depend upon the classification of the device in question and the complexity of the subject device. This is discussed more fully in Chapter 3 where the proposed GHTF guidance document: *Summary Technical Documentation for Demonstrating Conformity to the Essential Principles of Safety and Performance of Medical Devices (STED)* is discussed in more detail.

Declaration of Conformity

A common approach to placing medical devices on the market involves the issuance of the Declaration of Conformity. This is a statement drawn up by the manufacturer attesting that the medical device placed on the market under its name fully complies with all applicable Essential Principles.

At minimum, the declaration should contain information attesting that each device subject to the declaration complies with the applicable Essential Principles, has been classified according to the classification rules and meets all applicable conformity assessment elements. In addition, both the manufacturer and the medical devices subject to the declaration must be clearly identifiable.

Other particulars include:
- the Global Medical Device Nomenclature (GMDN) code and term for the device
- the risk class allocated to the device
- which conformity assessment elements have been applied
- manufacturer name and address
- the date from which the Declaration of Conformity is valid
- the name, position and signature of the responsible person authorized to complete the Declaration of Conformity on the manufacturer's behalf

Registration of Manufacturers and Devices With the RA

Registration of manufacturers and their medical devices with the RA is the first step in exercising control over devices in the market. The registration system should be able to identify the device and the party responsible for the device within the particular jurisdiction, expediting any regulatory activity. The information must be filed with the RA by the manufacturer, its local distributor or its Authorized Representative (AR) before products are placed on the market.

Harmonized Conformity Assessment Procedures

GHTF recommends that each medical device be allocated to one of four risk classes, based on a set of rules (see below classification rules):

- lowest risk: Class A devices
- moderate to medium risk: Class B devices
- moderate to high risk: Class C devices
- highest risk: Class D devices

Tables 2-1–2-4[11] identify available conformity assessment elements and possible combinations of those elements. These elements may be applied to different classes of medical devices to construct a harmonized conformity assessment system that may be adopted as part of a global medical device regulatory model.[12]

Principles of Medical Device Classification

GHTF recommends the establishment of a global classification system based on four risk classes.[13] This in turn should be based on a set of rules related to device risk as explained below under "classification rules." It is important that any classification system also be capable of accommodating future technological developments. Device classification depends upon a number of factors, including the duration of device contact with the body, the degree of invasiveness, whether the device delivers medicinal products or energy to the patient, whether it is intended to have a biological affect on the patient and local versus systemic effects.[14]

Where one medical device is intended to be used together with another (from one or more manufacturers), the classification rules should apply separately to each device.

Classification Rules

The actual classification of each device depends upon the claims made by the manufacturer and its intended use.[15]

To properly classify a device, the manufacturer should decide whether the product falls under the definition of a medical device and determine its intended use. The classification should be made based upon the set of rules shown in **Tables 2-5–2-8**. In addition to the proposed 16 rules, manufacturers should determine whether the device is also subject to special national rules that apply within a particular jurisdiction.

Decision trees (**Figures 2-1–2-6**) are often used to demonstrate how the rules may be used to classify specific devices.[16] The determination of a risk class for a particular

Table 2-1. Class A Device

	Conformity Assessment Element	Manufacturer Responsibility	Regulatory Authority (RA)/ Conformity Assessment Body (CAB) Responsibility
Conformity assessment of the quality management system (QMS)	QMS	Establish and maintain a full QMS **or** a QMS without design and development controls	Regulatory audit normally not required except in special cases, e.g., assurance of sterility and of measuring function/s
	Postmarket surveillance	Establish and maintain an adverse event reporting procedure according to GHTF SG2 guidance	May audit postmarket to investigate specific safety or regulatory concerns
Conformity assessment of device safety and performance	Technical documentation	Prepare Summary Technical Documentation (STED) and have available for review by regulatory authority (RA) upon request	Premarket submission of STED normally not requested
	Declaration of Conformity	Prepare, sign and maintain	Submission normally not requested
Registration	Registration of manufacturers and their devices	Perform according to regulatory requirements	Maintain and verify as appropriate

Table 2-2. Class B Device

	Conformity Assessment Element	Manufacturer Responsibility	RA/CAB Responsibility
Conformity assessment of the QMS	QMS	Establish and maintain a full QMS or a QMS without design and development controls	Be satisfied that a current and appropriate QMS is in place, otherwise conduct a QMS audit prior to marketing authorization
	Postmarket surveillance	Establish and maintain an adverse event reporting procedure according to GHTF SG2 guidance	Be satisfied that a current and appropriate adverse event reporting procedure is in place as part of the QMS
Conformity assessment of device safety and performance	Technical documentation	Prepare STED and have available for review upon request	Not normally reviewed premarket; if submission is requested, receive and conduct a premarket review of the STED sufficient to determine conformity to Essential Principles.
	Declaration of Conformity	Prepare, sign and make available for review	Review and verify compliance with requirements
Registration	Registration of manufacturers and their devices	Perform according to regulatory requirements	Maintain and verify as appropriate

Table 2-3. Class C Device

	Conformity Assessment Element	Manufacturer Responsibility	RA/CAB Responsibility
Conformity assessment of the QMS	QMS	Establish and maintain a full QMS	Be satisfied that a current and appropriate QMS is in place, otherwise conduct a QMS audit prior to marketing authorization
	Postmarket surveillance	Establish and maintain an adverse event reporting procedure according to GHTF SG2 guidance	Be satisfied that a current and appropriate adverse event reporting procedure is in place as part of the QMS
Conformity assessment of device safety and performance	Technical documentation	Prepare and submit STED for review	Conduct a review, normally premarket, of the STED sufficient to determine conformity to Essential Principles
	Declaration of Conformity	Prepare, sign and submit	Review and verify compliance with requirements
Registration	Registration of manufacturers and their devices	Perform according to regulatory requirements	Maintain and verify as appropriate

Table 2-4. Class D Device

	Conformity Assessment Element	Manufacturer Responsibility	RA/CAB Responsibility
Conformity assessment of the QMS	Quality management system (QMS)	Establish and maintain a full QMS	Be satisfied that a current and appropriate QMS is in place, otherwise conduct a QMS audit prior to marketing authorization
	Postmarket surveillance	Establish and maintain an adverse event reporting procedure according to GHTF SG2 guidance	Be satisfied that a current and appropriate adverse event reporting procedure is in place as part of the QMS
Conformity assessment of device safety and performance	Technical documentation	Prepare and submit STED for review	Receive and conduct an in-depth premarket review of the STED to determine conformity to Essential Principles
	Declaration of Conformity	Prepare, sign and submit	Review and verify compliance with requirements
Registration	Registration of manufacturers and their devices	Perform according to regulatory requirements	Maintain and verify as appropriate

device should, however, be made by referring to the rules themselves, and not to the decision trees (see **Tables 2-5–2-8**).

The Role of Standards in the Assessment of Medical Devices

Standards also play an important role in harmonizing regulatory processes to assure the safety, quality and performance of medical devices. Standards represent the opinions of experts from all interested parties and stakeholders on a particular topic. Standards exist at different levels: international, such as the International Organization for Standardization (ISO) standards; regional, such as the European EN series; and national standards written and promoted by national standardization bodies, such as the American National Standards Institute (ANSI).

Standards are reviewed and updated on a regular and ongoing basis. The use of recognized standards is encouraged when designing and manufacturing medical devices.

The use of standards is voluntary. Manufacturers have the option of selecting alternative methods to demonstrate that their medical devices meet the relevant Essential Principles. In such cases, the manufacturer must demonstrate that the in-house or other methods used are at least equivalent to established standards in achieving conformity.

Conclusion

The basic concepts of medical device classification and conformity assessment have been accepted in many jurisdictions globally; however, regional differences still exist. For example, in the US, devices are classified based on risk, subject to the following different levels of controls:

Classes and Requirements:[17]
- Class I: General Controls
- Class II: General Controls and Special Controls
- Class III: General Controls, Special Controls and Premarket Approval

In the EU,[18] devices are classified based upon risk:
- Class I (nonsterile/no measuring function) —low risk
- Class I (sterile or with measuring function) —low risk
- Class IIa—medium risk
- Class IIb—high risk
- Class III—highest risk level

In Canada,[19] devices are classified as Classes I, II, III or IV, based on risk, essentially following the same principles as the EU.

The principles of safety and performance efficiency apply in all regions. Conformity to the Essential Requirements is a prerequisite in most regions. The requirements for design and manufacturing requirements, conformity assessment and medical device classification apply universally, and standards are widely used around the globe.

References

1. SG1-N29R16:2005, *Information Document Concerning the Definition of the Term "Medical Device"* (May 2005).

2. SG1-N41R9:2005, *Essential Principles of Safety and Performance of Medical Devices* (May 2005).

3. Ibid.

4. SG1-N43:2005, *Labelling for Medical Devices* (June 2005).

5. Ibid.

6. Op cit 2.

7. SG1-N40:2006, *Principles of Conformity Assessment for Medical Devices* (June 2006).

8. SG1-N44:2008, *Role of Standards in the Assessment of Medical Devices* (April 2008).

9. Op cit 7.

10. Ibid.

11. Ibid.

12. Ibid.

13. SG1-N15:2006, *Principles of Medical Devices Classification* (June 2006).

14. Ibid.

15. Ibid.

16. Ibid.

17. Regulatory Affairs Professionals Society. Chapter 18 Medical Device Submissions. In: *Fundamentals of US Regulatory Affairs Sixth Edition.* Rockville, MD. 2009:201–216.

18. Regulatory Affairs Professionals Society. Chapter 3 Overview of Authorisation Procedures for Medical Devices. In: *Fundamentals of EU Regulatory Affairs Fourth Edition.* Rockville, MD. 2008:pp 27–34.

19. Regulatory Affairs Professionals Society. Chapter 5 Medical Device Classification and Licensing In: *Fundamentals of Canadian Regulatory Affairs.* Rockville, MD. 2006:39–54.

Table 2-5 Noninvasive Devices

Rule	Examples
Rule 1. All noninvasive devices that come into contact with injured skin (Note: Devices covered by this rule are extremely claim sensitive.):	
are in Class A if they are intended to be used as a mechanical barrier, for compression or for absorption of exudates only, i.e., they heal by primary intent	Simple wound dressings; cotton wool
are in Class B if they are intended to be used principally with wounds that have breached the dermis, including devices principally intended to manage the microenvironment of a wound	Nonmedicated, impregnated gauze dressings
unless they are intended to be used principally with wounds which have breached the dermis and can only heal by secondary intent, in which case they are in Class C	Dressings for chronic ulcerated wounds; dressings for severe burns
Rule 2. All noninvasive devices intended for channeling or storing body liquids or tissues, liquids or gases for the purpose of eventual infusion, administration or introduction into the body (Note: Such devices are "indirectly invasive" in that they channel or store liquids that will eventually be delivered into the body.):	
are in Class A	Administration sets for gravity infusion; syringes without needles
unless they may be connected to an active medical device in Class B or a higher class, in which case they are in Class B	Syringes and administration sets for infusion pumps; anesthesia breathing circuits
unless they are intended for use of • channeling blood or • storing or channeling other body liquids or • for storing organs, parts of organs or body tissues in which case they are in Class B.	Tubes used for blood transfusion, organ storage containers
unless they are blood bags, in which case they are in Class C	Blood bags that do not incorporate an anticoagulant
Rule 3. All noninvasive devices intended for modifying the biological or chemical composition of blood, other body liquids or other liquids intended for infusion into the body (Note: Such devices are indirectly invasive in that they treat or modify substances that will eventually be delivered into the body.):	
are in Class C	Haemodializers; devices to remove white blood cells from whole blood
unless the treatment consists of filtration, centrifuging or exchanges of gas or of heat, in which case they are in Class B	Devices to remove carbon dioxide; particulate filters in an extracorporeal circulation system
Rule 4. All other noninvasive devices (Note: These devices either do not touch the patient or contact intact skin only.):	
are in Class A	Urine collection bottles; compression hosiery; noninvasive electrodes; hospital beds

Source SG1-N15:2006 Principles of Medical Devices Classification

Table 2-6. Invasive Devices

Rule	Examples
Rule 5. All invasive devices with respect to body orifices (other than those which are surgically invasive) and that are not intended for connection to an active medical device, or are intended for connection to a Class A medical device only:	
are in Class A if they are intended for transient use	Examination gloves; enema devices
are in Class B if they are intended for short-term use	Urinary catheters, tracheal tubes
unless they are intended for short-term use in the oral cavity as far as the pharynx, an ear canal up to the eardrum or a nasal cavity, in which case they are in Class A	Dentures intended to be removed by the patient; dressings for nose bleeds
are in Class C if they are intended for long-term use	Urethral stent; contact lenses for long-term continuous use (for this device, removal of the lens for cleaning or maintenance is considered part of the continuous use)
unless they are intended for long-term use in the oral cavity as far as the pharynx, an ear canal up to the eardrum or a nasal cavity and are not liable to be absorbed by the mucous membrane, in which case they are in Class B	Orthodontic wire, fixed dental prosthesis
All invasive devices with respect to body orifices (other than those which are surgically invasive) that are intended to be connected to an active medical device in Class B or a higher class, are in Class B.	Tracheal tubes connected to a ventilator; suction catheters for stomach drainage; dental aspirator tips
Rule 6. All surgically invasive devices intended for transient use are:	
in Class B	A majority of such devices fall into several major groups: those that create a conduit through the skin (e.g. syringe needles; lancets), surgical instruments (e.g., single-use scalpels; surgical staplers; single-use aortic punch); surgical gloves; and various types of catheter/sucker etc.
unless they are reusable surgical instruments, in which case they are in Class A	Manually operated surgical drill bits and saws
unless intended to supply energy in the form of ionizing radiation, in which case they are in Class C	Catheter incorporating/containing sealed radioisotopes
unless intended to have a biological effect or be wholly or mainly absorbed, in which case they are in Class C	Insufflation gases for the abdominal cavity
unless intended to administer medicinal products by means of a delivery system, if this is done in a manner that is potentially hazardous taking account of the mode of application, in which case they are in Class C	Insulin pen for self-administration
unless they are intended specifically for use in direct contact with the central nervous system, in which case they are in Class D	
unless intended specifically to diagnose, monitor or correct a defect of the heart or of the central circulatory system through direct contact with these parts of the body, in which case they are in Class D	Angioplasty balloon catheters and related guide wires; dedicated disposable cardiovascular surgical instruments
Rule 7. All surgically invasive devices intended for short-term use (Note: such devices are mostly used in the context of surgery or postoperative care, or are infusion devices or are catheters of various types.):	
are in Class B	Infusion cannulae; temporary filling materials; nonabsorbable skin closure devices; tissue stabilizers used in cardiac surgery
unless they are intended to administer medicinal products, in which case they are in Class C	

Rule	Examples
unless they are intended to undergo chemical change in the body (except if the devices are placed in the teeth), in which case they are in Class C	Surgical adhesive
unless they are intended to supply energy in the form of ionizing radiation, in which case they are in Class C	Brachytherapy device
unless they are intended to have a biological effect or to be wholly or mainly absorbed, in which case they are in Class D	Absorbable suture; biological adhesive **Note**: the "biological effect" referred to is an intended one rather than unintentional. The term "absorption" refers to the degradation of a material within the body and the metabolic elimination of the resulting degradation products from the body.
unless they are intended specifically for use in direct contact with the central nervous system, in which case they are in Class D	Neurological catheter
unless they are intended specifically to diagnose, monitor or correct a defect of the heart or of the central circulatory system through direct contact with these parts of the body, in which case they are in Class D	Cardiovascular catheters; temporary pacemaker leads; carotid artery shunts

Table 2-7. Active Devices

Rule	Examples
Rule 9(i). All active therapeutic devices intended to administer or exchange energy (Note: such devices are mostly electrically powered equipment used in surgery; devices for specialized treatment; and some stimulators.):	
are in Class B	Muscle stimulators; transcutaneous electrical nerve stimulation (TENS) devices; powered dental hand pieces; hearing aids; neonatal phototherapy equipment; ultrasound equipment for physiotherapy
unless their characteristics are such that they may administer or exchange energy to or from the human body in a potentially hazardous way, including ionizing radiation, taking account of the nature, the density and site of application of the energy, in which case they are in Class C	Lung ventilators; baby incubators; electrosurgical generators; external pacemakers and defibrillators; surgical lasers; lithotriptors; therapeutic x-ray and other sources of ionizing radiation
Rule 9(ii). All active devices intended to control or monitor the performance of active therapeutic devices in Class C, or intended directly to influence the performance of such devices:	
are in Class C	External feedback systems for active therapeutic devices
Rule 10(i). Active devices intended for diagnosis:	
are in Class B	Equipment for ultrasonic diagnosis/imaging, capture of physiological signals, interventional radiology and diagnostic radiology
if they are intended to supply energy that will be absorbed by the human body (except for devices used solely to illuminate the patient's body, with light in the visible or near infrared spectrum, in which case they are Class A)	Magnetic resonance equipment; diagnostic ultrasound in noncritical applications; evoked response stimulators
if they are intended to image *in vivo* distribution of radiopharmaceuticals	Gamma/nuclear cameras
if they are intended to allow direct diagnosis or monitoring of vital physiological processes	Electronic thermometers, stethoscopes and blood pressure monitors; electrocardiographs
unless they are specifically intended for: a) monitoring of vital physiological parameters, where the nature of variations is such that it could result in immediate danger to the patient, for instance variations in cardiac performance, respiration, activity of central nervous system or b) diagnosing in clinical situations where the patient is in immediate danger, in which case they are in Class C	Monitors/alarms for intensive care; biological sensors; oxygen saturation monitors; apnea monitors

Ultrasound equipment for use in interventional cardiac procedures |
Rule 10(ii). Active devices intended to emit ionizing radiation and intended for diagnostic and/or interventional radiology, including devices that control or monitor such devices, or those which directly influence their performance:	
are in Class C	Devices for the control, monitoring or influencing of the emission of ionizing radiation
Rule 11. All active devices intended to administer and/or remove medicinal products, body liquids or other substances to or from the body (Note: Such devices are mostly drug delivery systems or anesthesia equipment.):	
are in Class B	Suction equipment; feeding pumps; jet injectors for vaccination; nebulizer to be used on conscious and spontaneously breathing patients where failure to deliver the appropriate dosage characteristics is not potentially hazardous

Rule	Examples
unless this is done in a manner that is potentially hazardous, taking account of the nature of the substances involved, of the part of the body concerned and of the mode and route of administration, in which case they are in Class C	Infusion pumps; anesthesia equipment; dialysis equipment; hyperbaric chambers; nebulizer, where the failure to deliver the appropriate dosage characteristics could be hazardous
Rule 12. All other active devices	
are in Class A	Examination lamps; surgical microscopes; powered hospital beds and wheelchairs; powered equipment for the recording, processing, viewing of diagnostic images; dental curing lights

Source SG1-N15:2006 Principles of Medical Devices Classification

Table 2-8. Additional Rules

Rule	Examples
Rule 13. All devices incorporating, as an integral part, a substance that, if used separately, can be considered to be a medicinal product, and that is liable to act on the human body with action ancillary to that of the devices (Note: These medical devices incorporate medicinal substances in an ancillary role.):	
are in Class D	Antibiotic bone cements; heparin-coated catheters; wound dressings incorporating antimicrobial agents to provide ancillary action on the wound; blood bags incorporating an anticoagulant
Rule 14. All devices manufactured from or incorporating animal or human cells/tissues/derivatives thereof, whether viable or nonviable (Note: In some jurisdictions, such products are considered to be outside the scope of the medical device definition and may be subject to different controls.):	
are Class D	Porcine heart valves; catgut sutures
unless such devices are manufactured from or incorporate nonviable animal tissues or their derivatives that come in contact with intact skin only, in which case they are in Class A	Leather components of orthopedic appliances
Rule 15. All devices intended specifically to be used for sterilizing medical devices, or disinfecting as the end point of processing (Note: This rule does not apply to products that are intended to clean medical devices by means of physical action, e.g., washing machines.):	
are in Class C	Devices for disinfecting or sterilizing endoscopes; disinfectants intended to be used with medical devices
unless they are intended for disinfecting medical devices prior to end point sterilization or higher level disinfection, in which case they are in Class B	Washer disinfectors
unless they are intended specifically to be used for disinfecting, cleaning, rinsing or, when appropriate, hydrating contact lenses, in which case they are in Class C	In some jurisdictions, solutions for use with contact lenses: -are considered to be outside the scope of the medical devices definition -may be subject to different controls
Rule 16. All devices used for contraception or the prevention of the transmission of sexually transmitted diseases:	
are in Class C	Condoms; contraceptive diaphragms
unless they are implantable or long-term invasive devices, in which case they are in Class D	Intrauterine contraceptive device

Source SG1-N15:2006 Principles of Medical Devices Classification

Figure 2-1. Decision Tree Noninvasive Devices

Noninvasive Devices

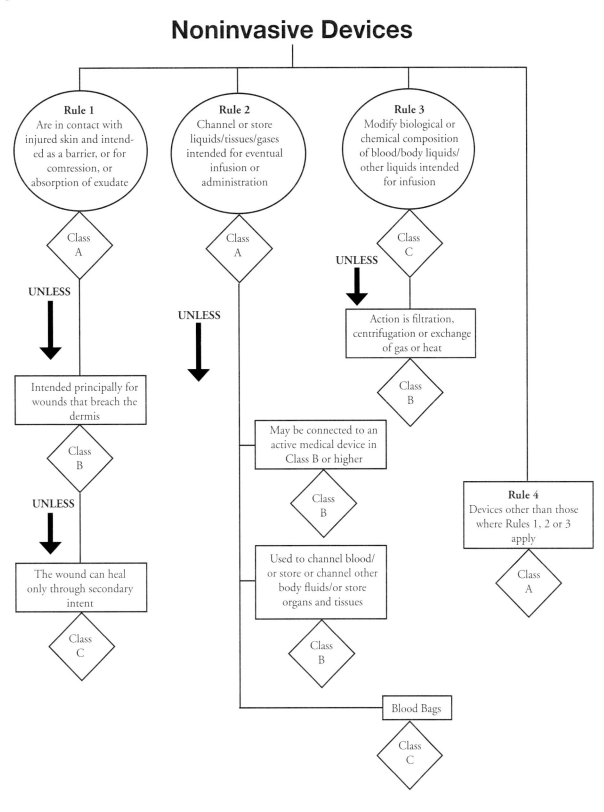

Source: GHTF: SG1-N15:2006

Figure 2-2. Decision Tree Invasive Devices

Invasive Devices

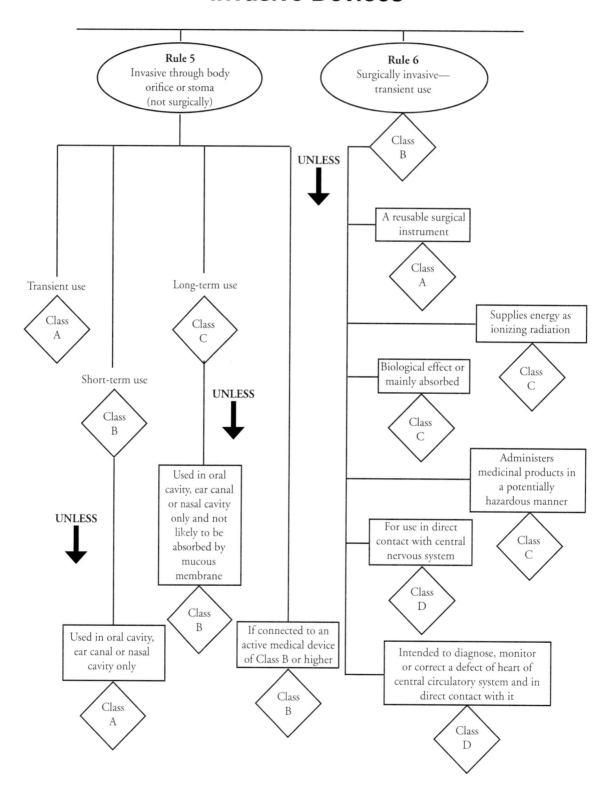

Source: GHTF: SG1-N15:2006

Figure 2-3. Decision Tree Invasive Devices

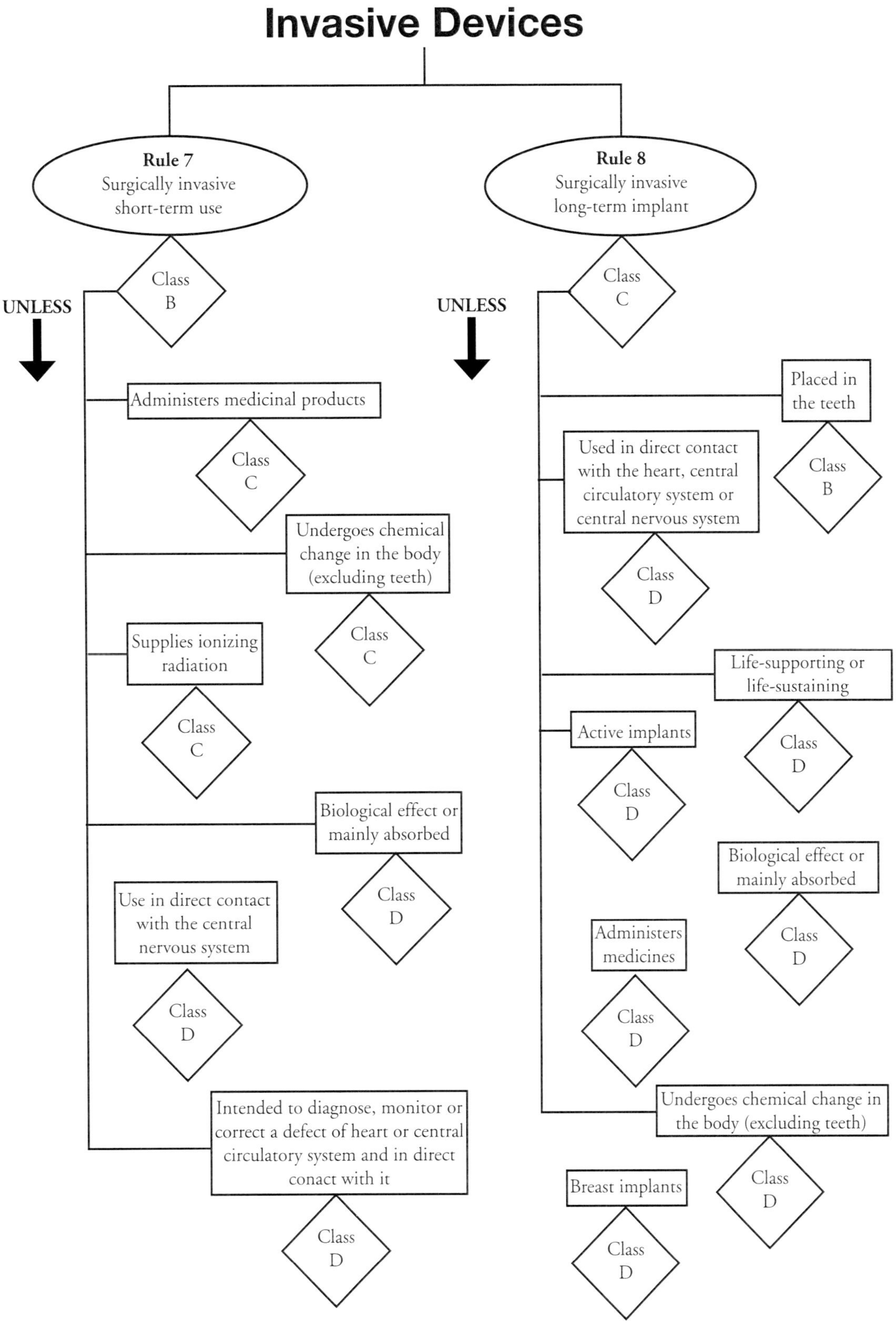

Invasive Devices

Rule 7
Surgically invasive
short-term use

Class B

UNLESS

Administers medicinal products

Class C

Undergoes chemical change in the body (excluding teeth)

Class C

Supplies ionizing radiation

Class C

Biological effect or mainly absorbed

Class D

Use in direct contact with the central nervous system

Class D

Intended to diagnose, monitor or correct a defect of heart or central circulatory system and in direct conact with it

Class D

Rule 8
Surgically invasive
long-term implant

Class C

UNLESS

Placed in the teeth

Class B

Used in direct contact with the heart, central circulatory system or central nervous system

Class D

Life-supporting or life-sustaining

Class D

Active implants

Class D

Biological effect or mainly absorbed

Class D

Administers medicines

Class D

Undergoes chemical change in the body (excluding teeth)

Class D

Breast implants

Class D

Source: GHTF: SG1-N15:2006

Figure 2-4. Decision Tree Active Devices

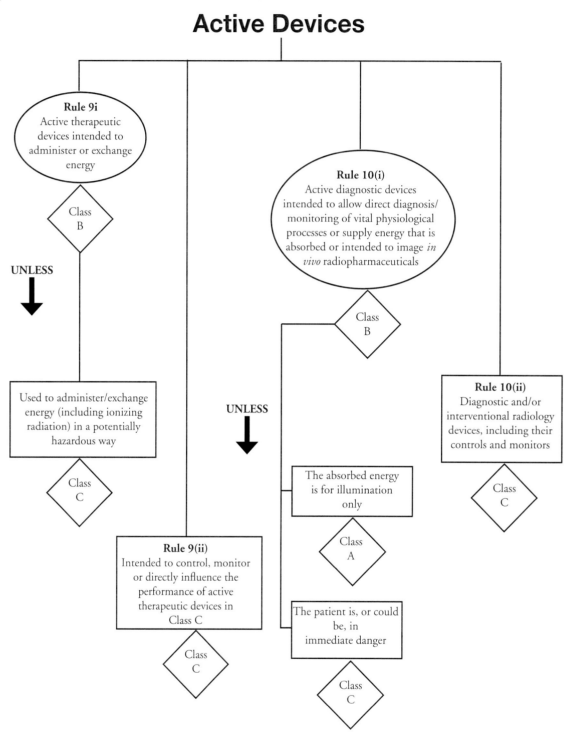

Source: GHTF: SG1-N15:2006

Figure 2-5. Decision Tree Active Devices

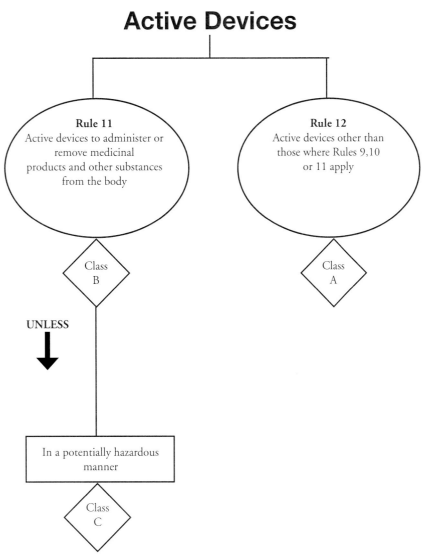

Source: GHTF: SG1-N15:2006

Figure 2-6. Decision Tree Additional Rules

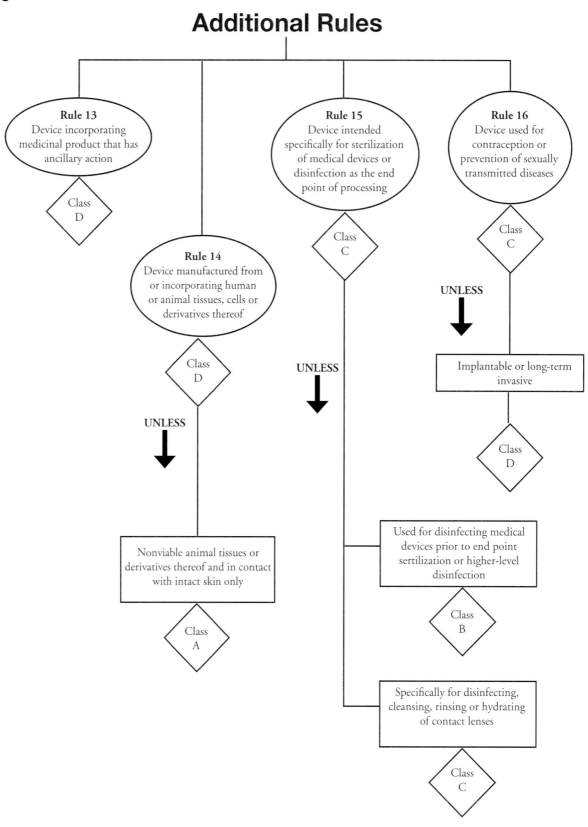

Source: GHTF: SG1-N15:2006

International Technical and Regulatory Requirements for Medical Devices

By Salma Michor, PhD, MBA, CMgr, RAC

OBJECTIVES

❏ Provide an overview of regulatory requirements for marketing medical devices

❏ Review the essential elements of a technical file (STED)

❏ Explain quality management systems (QMS) and risk management systems (RMS) for medical devices

REGULATIONS AND GUIDELINES COVERED IN THIS CHAPTER

GHTF

❏ SG1-N11:2008, *Summary Technical Documentation for Demonstrating Conformity to the Essential Principles of Safety and Performance of Medical Devices (STED)* (February 2008)

❏ SG1-N44:2008, *Role of Standards in the Assessment of Medical Device* (February 2008)

❏ SG5 Guidance documents

❏ SG1-N40:2006, *Principles of Conformity Assessment for Medical Devices* (June 2006)

❏ SG1-N55:2009, *Definition of the Terms Manufacturer, Authorised Representative, Distributor and Importer* (March 2009)

❏ SG3-N99-10 (Edition 2), *Quality Management Systems—Process Validation Guidance* (January 2004)

❏ SG3-N15R8:2005, *Implementation of Risk Management Principles and Activities Within a Quality Management System* (May 2005)

❏ SG3-N17R9:2008, *Quality Management System—Medical Devices—Guidance on the Control of Products and Services Obtained from Suppliers* (December 2008)

ISO
❏ EN ISO 14971 on Risk management.

Introduction

Legal requirements for the registration and marketing of medical devices differ from region to region. However, in most cases, manufacturers are expected to prepare and keep on their premises technical documentation that shows how each medical device was developed, designed and manufactured. For certain device classes, a design dossier must be submitted to the authorities for assessment before market entry. In either case, the manufacturer must ensure timely access to the technical documentation, either for assessment or during an audit, when the authorities carrying out the inspection may request access to certain documents.[1]

This technical documentation, typically controlled in the manufacturer's quality management system (QMS), is often extensive and sections may be held in different locations.[2] Usually, a subset of the technical documentation is prepared in the form of a technical file to be presented to the authorities responsible for assessing and inspecting the data. The availability of the Summary Technical Documentation

(STED) should help eliminate differences in documentation requirements between jurisdictions, decrease the cost of achieving regulatory compliance and allow patients earlier access to new technologies and treatments.[3]

Essential Technical File Elements

The technical file is a means for manufacturers of all device classes to demonstrate a product's conformity to the *Essential Principles of Safety and Performance of Medical Devices.* The technical documentation should show how each medical device was developed, designed and manufactured and should include descriptions and explanations necessary to understand the manufacturer's determination regarding conformity to the essential requirements. This technical documentation is a living document that must be updated regularly to reflect the device's current status, specifications and configuration.[4]

Premarket Phase

As noted above, the technical file for critical devices must be submitted to the regulatory authority for evaluation, while it is sufficient to have a copy of the files for less-critical devices readily available for inspection. The Global Harmonization Task Force (GHTF) has published the submission guidance shown in **Figure 3-1** for devices classified as A or B (lower risk), and C or D (critical devices).

Postmarket Phase

The regulatory authority (RA) may, at any time, request a copy of the technical file for Class A and B (lower risk) devices. The technical file must follow the lifecycle management (LCM) process in the postmarket phase. Changes that affect the QMS must be reported to the RA. At the same time, the technical file must be updated to reflect any changes. GHTF has published the submission guidance shown in **Figure 3-2** for the postmarket phase.

STED Content

The exact content of the technical file can differ from region to region. The STED gives guidance on which general information should be included to aid in an evaluation of the device and its intended use. Following is a brief overview of a technical file's contents using the STED format.

Device Description

The STED should contain the following descriptive information for the device:
1. general description of the device, including its intended use/purpose
2. intended patient population and medical condition to be diagnosed and/or treated and other considerations such as patient selection criteria
3. principles of operation

4. risk class and the applicable classification rule (see Chapter 2 on device classification)
5. explanation of any novel features
6. description of any accessories, other medical devices and other products intended to be used with the device
7. description or complete list of the various configurations/variants of the device that will be made available
8. general description of the device's key functional elements, including any parts, components, software, formulation, composition and functionality (may be presented via labeled pictorial representations)
9. description of the materials incorporated into key functional elements and those making either direct contact with a human body or indirect contact with the body, e.g., during extracorporeal circulation of body fluids[5]

Product Specification

Any product specifications made available to the end user in the form of brochures, catalogues, etc., should be included in the STED. Specifically, the STED should contain a list of the features, dimensions and performance attributes of the medical device and its variants and accessories.

Reference to Similar and Previous Generations of the Device

Information about the manufacturer's previous generation(s) of the device, if any, and/or any similar devices should be included in the technical file if it is relevant to demonstrating conformity to the Essential Principles.

Labeling

The STED should contain mock-ups of all labeling associated with the device. If the device is available on multiple markets, a list of language variants should be included. Labeling includes labels on the device and its packaging, instructions for use and promotional material.

Design and Manufacturing Information

This section of the file should include information to allow the reviewer to evaluate and understand the design stages applied to the device. In addition, the STED should contain sufficient information to allow the reviewer to obtain a general understanding of the manufacturing processes involved. The STED also should identify the sites where the design and manufacturing activities are performed. If there are any QMS certificates or the equivalent for these sites, they should be annexed to the STED.

Figure 3-1. Premarket Use of the STED

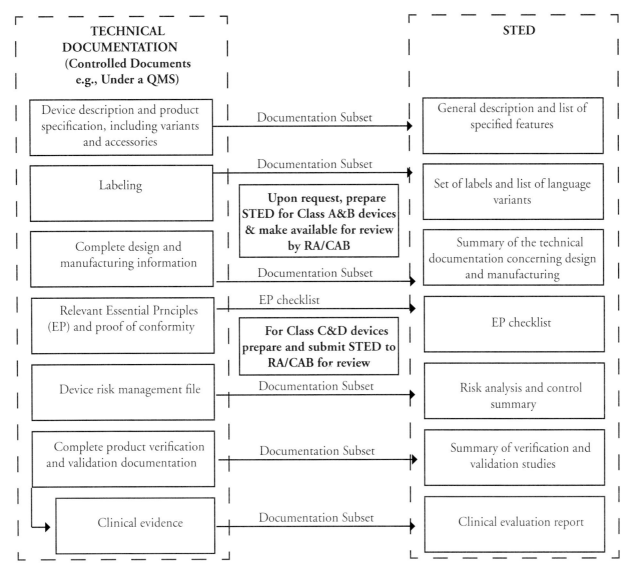

Source SG1-N11:2008

Essential Principles (EP) Checklist

It is customary for the STED to contain an EP checklist that identifies:

the Essential Principles

a) whether each Essential Principle applies to the device and if not, why not

b) method(s) used to demonstrate conformity with each applicable Essential Principle

c) reference (e.g., standard) for the method(s) employed

d) precise identity of the controlled document(s) that offers evidence of conformity with each method used[6]

The way in which conformity is achieved may differ; however, commonly used methods include: conformity with recognized or other standards;[7] conformity with a commonly accepted industry test method(s); conformity with an in-house test method(s); evaluation of preclinical and clinical evidence;[8] and comparison to a similar device already available on the market.

Risk Analysis and Control Summary

No technical file would be complete without a comprehensive summary of the risks identified and associated with the device and how these risks have been controlled to an acceptable level. The approach used should be based on internationally recognized standards or their equivalent and included in the manufacturer's risk management plan.

Product Verification and Validation

The STED should contain product verification and validation documentation. In general, the STED should summarize the results of verification and validation studies undertaken to demonstrate conformity of the device with the Essential Principles that apply. These results include outcomes of engineering tests; laboratory tests; simulated use testing; animal tests for demonstrating feasibility or proof of concept of the finished device; and any published literature regarding the device or substantially similar devices.

In addition, where applicable to the device, the STED should contain detailed information on biocompatibility; any medicinal substances incorporated into the device; biological safety of devices incorporating animal or human cells, tissues or their derivatives; sterilization; and software verification and validation. Animal studies that provide evidence of the device's safety and performance, especially when no clinical investigation of the device was conducted, and any clinical evidence should also be included.

Format of the STED

The format of the technical file is not specified, but following the general outline of the STED guidance makes it easier for regulatory reviewers to analyze the file and locate information.

Declaration of Conformity

The Declaration of Conformity is not part of the STED. However, it may be annexed to the STED once the conformity assessment process has been completed by the manufacturer.[9]

Definition of the Terms "Manufacturer," "Authorized Representative," "Distributor" and "Importer"

For medical device manufacturers, certain roles and functions carry specific legal obligations and responsibilities. Hence, the development of harmonized definitions for the main stakeholders in the medical device chain is vital to support global convergence of regulatory systems and offer significant benefits to RAs and organizations responsible for making and/or placing medical devices on the market.[10]

Manufacturer

"Manufacturer" means any natural or legal person with responsibility for the design and/or manufacture of a medical device with the intention of making the medical device available for use under his name, whether or not such a medical device is designed and/or manufactured by that person himself or on his behalf by another person(s).[11]

Authorized Representative

"Authorized representative" means any natural or legal person established within a country or jurisdiction who has received a written mandate from the manufacturer to act on his behalf for specified tasks with regard to the latter's obligations under that country's or jurisdiction's legislation.[12]

Distributor

"Distributor" means any natural or legal person in the supply chain who, on his own behalf, furthers the availability of a medical device to the end user.[13]

Importer

"Importer" means any natural or legal person in the supply chain who is the first in a supply chain to make a medical device, manufactured in another country or jurisdiction, available in the country or jurisdiction where it is to be marketed.[14]

QMS and Risk Management Systems (RMS) for Medical Devices

A functioning QMS is vital for medical device manufacturers. The components of a QMS include process validation, risk management and adequate controls. These system parts are subject to regulatory authority inspections.

QMS—Process Validation

GHTF has published a guidance document to assist manufacturers in understanding QMS requirements for process validation.[15] Qualification and validation processes go hand in hand. Qualification involves design qualification (DQ), installation qualification (IQ), operational qualification (OQ) and performance qualification (PQ).

Process validation uses objective evidence to prove that a process consistently produces a result or product meeting its predetermined requirements.[16] This evidence must be documented in a protocol explaining the different validation steps and test parameters. Process validation is only one element of validation and includes facility and equipment validation (DQ, IQ, OQ and PQ), in addition to cleaning validation, analytical validation and computer validation. All these activities are generally defined in a validation master plan.

Product development and manufacture involve diverse and complex steps. Adequate controls must be in place to ensure that products meet their declared specifications and that processes produce consistent results.

Inadequate process validation could result in critical process deviations at a later stage that may require corrective actions and revalidation and could raise compliance issues.

Figure 3-3 shows a process validation decision tree.

Such decision trees can help manufacturers determine whether a process needs to be validated, which is especially important for very complex processes. Software, even

Figure 3-2. Postmarket Use of the STED

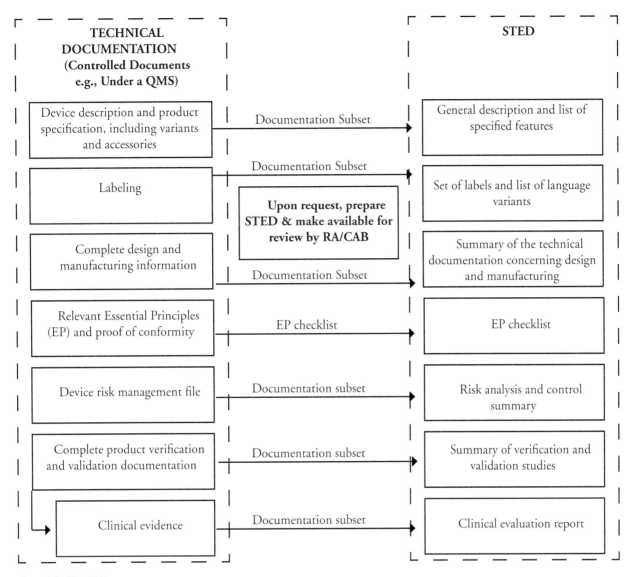

Source SG1-N11:2008

when used in verifiable processes, should also be validated.[17] Annex A of SG3-N99-10 (Edition 2) *Quality Management Systems—Process Validation Guidance* provides statistical methods and tools for process validation.

Practical steps involved in a validation process include:
- creating a validation master plan
- choosing team members from quality assurance, engineering, manufacturing, etc.
- developing a protocol to define which processes and devices need to be validated
- selecting statistical methods for data collection and analysis
- creating a maintenance plan and repair criteria
- developing criteria for revalidation

IQ, OQ and PQ

Facility and equipment validation relates to IQ, OQ and PQ and may include calibration and computer validation.
- IQ determines: Is the equipment installed correctly?
- OQ determines: Will the end product meet all defined requirements under all anticipated conditions of manufacturing, i.e., worst case testing?
- PQ determines: Will the process consistently produce acceptable product under normal operating conditions?
- All validation activities should be recorded in a final report. The validated state should be maintained by continuous monitoring and control. If

major changes are implemented, the process must be revalidated.

Validation Master Plan (VMP)

A VMP, although not mandatory, is useful; it is a document that outlines the principles involved in the qualification of a facility, defining the areas and systems to be validated.[18] The VMP, if available, forms the foundation for the validation program and should include process validation, facility and utility qualification and validation, equipment qualification, cleaning and computer validation. It provides a written program for achieving and maintaining a qualified facility with validated processes. The specific qualification and validation procedures/activities should be defined in specific SOPs covering both equipment and processes.

Examples of equipment-related SOPs:
- IQ
- OQ
- PQ
- calibration
- computer validation

Examples of process-related SOPs:
- process validation
- cleaning validation
- validation of analytical methods[19]

Risk Management Principles

The manufacture of medical devices requires the evaluation and control of risks. Risk management activities are normally recorded and referenced in various files such as the risk management file, design history file, technical file/technical documentation, design dossier, device master record, device history record and process validation files. Integrating risk management procedures, documents and records directly into the QMS is a good approach and makes the quality management process more manageable.[20] Care should be taken to ensure that all risk management aspects are covered.

Management should ensure that risk is properly assessed and controlled. Risk management activities may include:
- establishment of risk acceptability criteria
- risk analysis
- risk evaluation
- risk control and monitoring[21]

Management is responsible for ensuring that the company has sufficient resources to carry out risk management activities.

Outsourcing

A manufacturer may outsource one or several parts of the production process—e.g., sterilization, coating or design—or an entire product. However, the manufacturer is responsible for monitoring any outsourced activities and incorporating appropriate risk management activities to ensure product quality. After a device has been placed on the market, risk management activities should be linked to quality management processes, such as production and process controls, corrective and preventive actions (CAPAs), servicing and customer feedback, etc.

Risk management activities should also cover any outsourced activities or potential risks introduced by suppliers.

Design and Development and Planning

The objective of risk management is to reduce a device's risk to an acceptable level while maintaining the product's feasibility and functionality.[22] Risk-associated activities must be planned early in the development process and should cover the entire product lifecycle. Risk control measures are part of the design output and should be evaluated during design verification.

Risks in the development phase can be grouped by those arising during the design input phase and those occurring during the design output phase. Different risk assessment tools—e.g., failure modes and effects analysis (FMEA)—may be used to assess and reduce risks. The main principles of risk analysis and control are described in ISO 14971:2007,[23] *Application of risk management to medical devices*.

Design and development activities should also be verified and validated. Any changes occurring after the device is placed on the market should be monitored and captured using an appropriate change control system. Traceability forms an important part of any serious risk management system.

CAPAs

Corrective actions are planned in retrospect, whereas preventive actions can be planned before an incident occurs. CAPA reviews should reveal any previously unrecognized risks and the effectiveness of risk control measures.[24]

QMS—Medical Devices—Guidance on the Control of Products and Services Obtained from Suppliers

In today's complex manufacturing environment, medical device manufacturers rely heavily on suppliers for chemicals, parts, etc.

Typical services offered by suppliers include:
- off-the-shelf products
- parts and components made to a manufacturer's specifications
- services (e.g., sterilization, design, document archiving, transport)
- finished medical device

Although the term "manufacturer" may be defined differently in different jurisdictions, RAs ultimately hold one medical device "manufacturer" or entity primarily responsible for meeting regulatory quality management system

Figure 3-3. Postmarket Use of the STED

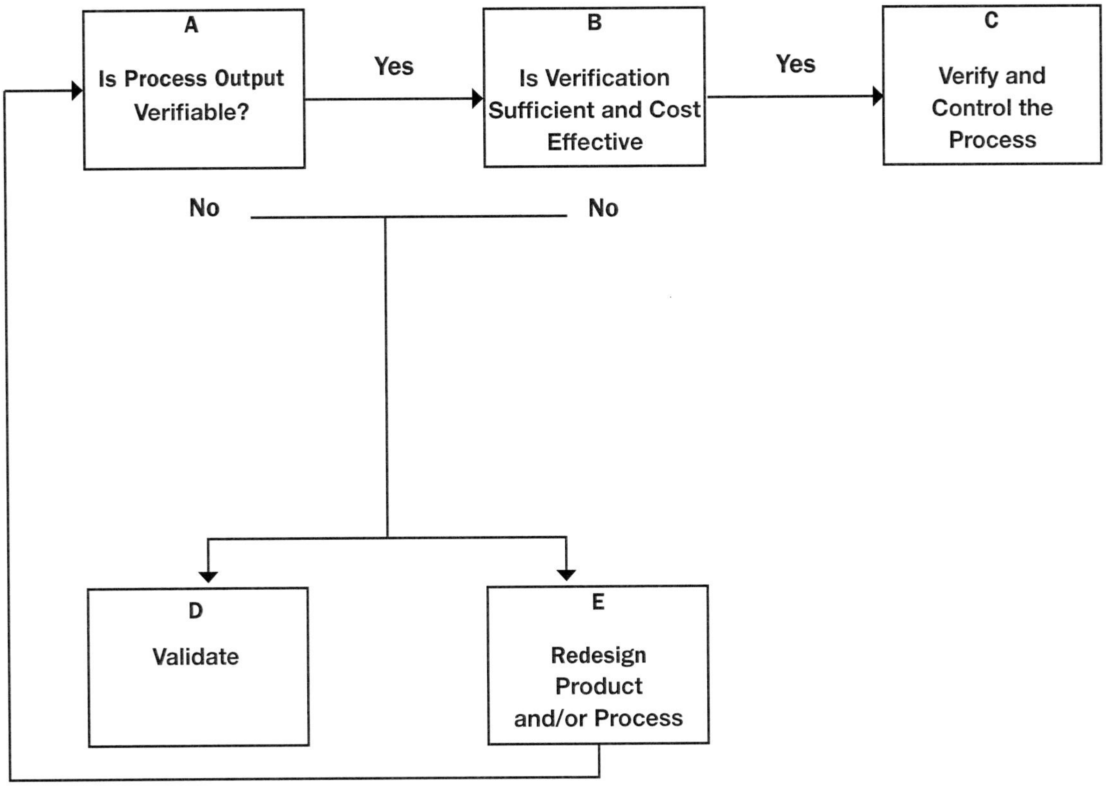

Source SG1-N11:2008

requirements.[25] If parts of the manufacturing process are outsourced, the responsibility for complying with QMS requirements lies with the manufacturer and cannot be delegated to any supplier of products and services.

Although some suppliers may undergo some form of oversight by either an RA or a third-party operating on behalf of an RA, this does not relinquish the manufacturer's responsibility to establish controls and provide evidence for products and services obtained from suppliers. This control typically comprises six phases:

- planning
- selection of potential supplier(s)
- supplier evaluation and acceptance
- finalizing controls
- delivery, measurement and monitoring
- feedback and communication, including the CAPA process[26]

Figure 3-4 shows key activities that a manufacturer should perform to help demonstrate its control over suppliers.

All products and services received from a supplier should be strictly controlled to ensure they meet the manufacturer's standards to enable the manufacturer to fulfill its legal obligations. Manufacturers should have a formal evaluation and

selection procedure to verify suppliers' capabilities. This may be a formal audit or, for less-important suppliers, ensuring ISO certification. Once selected, suppliers and contract manufacturers should be periodically inspected and reassessed at least once a year. Evidence of control over products and services from suppliers (on site or readily available) will normally be subject to inspection by RAs and/or third parties. Failure to demonstrate evidence of the controls associated with products and services from suppliers could result in the manufacturer's QMS being deemed noncompliant.[27]

Conclusion

Although the registration procedures for medical devices differ from region to region, GHTF has proposed a common technical file (STED) to comply with the requirements in most regions. This important document provides a way for manufacturers of all classes of devices to demonstrate conformity of their devices with the *Essential Principles of Safety and Performance of Medical Devices*. Manufacturers are required to present the results of preclinical and clinical testing as well as manufacturing information to gain market access. Technical documentation must be updated using a lifecycle management approach.

Figure 3-4. Key Activities for Supplier Control

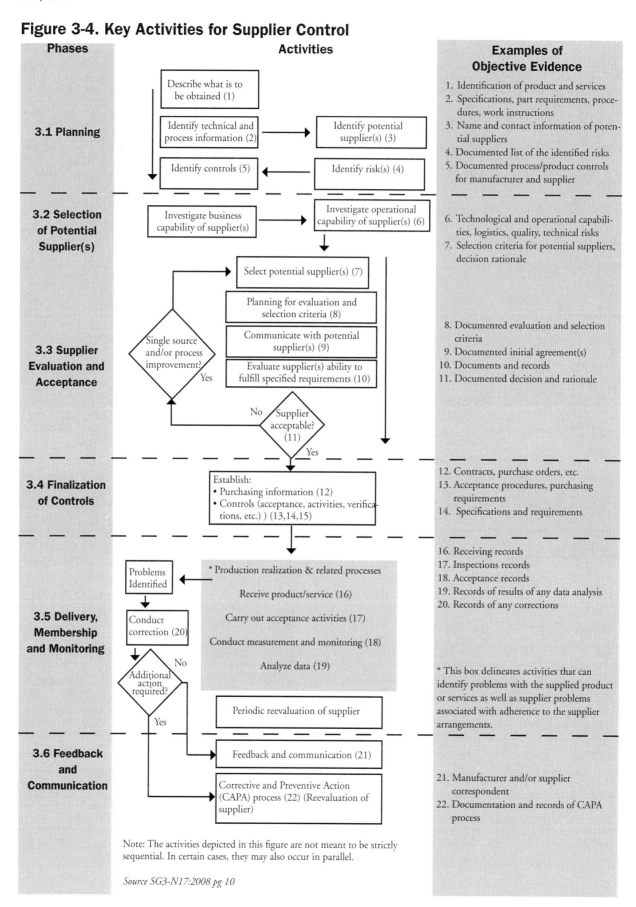

Note: The activities depicted in this figure are not meant to be strictly sequential. In certain cases, they may also occur in parallel.

Source SG3-N17:2008 pg 10

Quality and risk management play a vital role in the development and manufacture of medical devices. Medical device manufacturers ensure that risks are reduced to an acceptable level by initiating risk minimization activities, as necessary. Risk management can be integrated into the overall QMS to allow a comprehensive approach and simplify the control of documents.

References

1. SG1-N11:2008, *Summary Technical Documentation for Demonstrating Conformity to the Essential Principles of Safety and Performance of Medical Devices (STED)*, (February 2008).
2. Ibid.
3. Ibid.
4. Ibid.
5. Ibid.
6. Ibid
7. SG1-N044:2008, *Role of Standards in the Assessment of Medical* Devices (February 2008).
8. SG5 guidance documents
9. SG1-N40:2006, *Principles of Conformity Assessment for Medical Devices* (June 2006).
10. SG1-N55:2009, *Definition of the Terms Manufacturer, Authorised Representative, Distributor and Importer* (March 2009).
11. Ibid.
12. Ibid.
13. Ibid.
14. Ibid.
15. SG3-N99-10 (Edition 2), *Quality Management Systems—Process Validation Guidance* (January 2004).
16. Ibid.
17. Ibid.
18. http://www.validation-online.net/index.html. Accessed 29 January 2010.
19. *Biopharmaceutical Process Validation*, edited by Gail Sofer and Dane W. Zabriskie, ISBN: 0-8247-0249-2, Marcel Dekker Inc., New York: 2000.
20. SG3-N15R8:2005, *Implementation of Risk Management Principles and Activities Within a Quality Management System* (May 2005).
21. Ibid.
22. Ibid.
23. EN ISO 14971 on Risk management.
24. Ibid.
25. SG3-N17/2008, *Quality Management System—Medical Devices—Guidance on the Control of Products and Services Obtained from Suppliers* (February 2009)
26. Ibid.
27. Ibid.

Chapter 4

International Postmarket Requirements for Medical Devices

By Salma Michor, PhD, MBA, CMgr, RAC

OBJECTIVES

❏ Understand postmarket requirements for medical devices

❏ Understand vigilance reporting

❏ Understand postmarket surveillance (PMS)

❏ Understand field safety corrective actions (FSCAs)

❏ Understand medical device advertising rules

REGULATIONS AND GUIDELINES COVERED IN THIS CHAPTER

EC
❏ MEDDEV 2.12/1, *Guidelines on a Medical Devices Vigilance System* (rev. 5) (April 2007)

GHTF
❏ SG2-N8R4, *Guidance on How to Handle Information Concerning Vigilance Reporting Related to Medical Devices* (June 1999)

❏ SG2-N79R11:2009, *Medical Devices: Post Market Surveillance: National Competent Authority Report Exchange Criteria and Report Form* (February 2009)

❏ SG2-N54R8:2006, *Medical Devices Post Market Surveillance: Global Guidance for Adverse Event Reporting for Medical Devices* (November 2006)

❏ SG2-N47R4:2005, *Review of Current Requirements on Postmarket Surveillance* (May 2005)

❏ SG2-N57R8:2006, *Medical Devices Post Market Surveillance: Content of Field Safety Notices* (June 2006)

ISO
❏ ISO 13485:2003, *Medical devices—Quality management systems—Requirements for regulatory purposes*

❏ ISO 14971:2007, *Medical devices—Application of risk management to medical devices*

Introduction

A medical device manufacturer's regulatory obligations continue throughout the device's lifecycle,[1] and the postmarket phase is one of the most resource intensive. Departments involved in the postmarket phase include regulatory, vigilance, supply chain and marketing. Vigilance reporting, postmarket surveillance, the handling of customer complaints and recalls are among postmarket activities. Although national regulations may differ, the general postmarket requirements are similar at the global level. This chapter looks at some of the most important postmarket obligations for medical device manufacturers.

Vigilance Reporting

Manufacturers placing medical devices on the market must have a vigilance system in place for collecting and evaluating reported incidents and taking corrective action, if needed, to prevent the recurrence of such incidents. The main purpose of a medical device vigilance system is to improve protection of patients' and other users' health and safety by reducing the likelihood that a device incident will recur.[2] At a higher level, the vigilance system is an integral part of a postmarket surveillance (PMS) system.[3]

Reporting Adverse Events at the National Level

Reporting medical device adverse events to the national Competent Authorities (CAs) is an important element in a PMS system. It is worth noting, however, that reporting obligations differ among countries.[4] Reporting systems are compulsory in some regions and voluntary in others. The scope of the national or regional system will also vary. Currently, the trend in all systems is toward obligatory reporting by manufacturers of incidents related to their devices.

Manufacturers operating globally must ensure that they both meet local reporting requirements and have a system in place to gather all the necessary information on incidents to be reported at the national level in other regions. If third-party local distributors are part of the system, they should be trained on the relevant procedures to ensure that they understand their reporting obligations regarding the manufacturer's requirements and to complement the overall reporting system.

A good national and worldwide reporting system can be realized only if all parties have confidence in one another.[5] Data collected, especially any patient-related information, should come from trusted sources and should be treated confidentially.

The following criteria should be considered when disseminating national information on adverse events:

- What is the benefit or use of disseminating device-related information (e.g., issues related to device safety, possible risks, and information related to recalls)?
- Is the information relevant, and if yes, to whom: other authorities, manufacturers, distributors, hospitals, users, etc.?
- What is the traceability of persons or institutions who should receive vigilance-related information?

Disseminating information is the responsibility of the manufacturer or its representative. Dissemination should be supervised by the national CA, which should also assist in the process if necessary. In critical cases, the national CA may wish to disseminate the information itself.[6] In either case, before information is released, the relevance and benefit of its dissemination should be considered. Some useful questions to ask include:

- Does the public need this information and do they have the right to know?

- Will releasing such information benefit public health?
- Could releasing the information frighten or harm the public?

Distribution Records

If a critical event occurs, devices may have to be recalled from the market. Maintaining traceability of medical devices expedites their retrieval and removal during a product recall. Distribution records must contain sufficient information to permit devices to be recalled from the market completely and rapidly. Implanted devices must also be monitored and any information gathered must be recorded in the manufacturer's quality management system (QMS).[7]

NCAR Exchange Criteria and Report Form[8]

In February 2009, the Global Harmonization Task Force (GHTF) published SG2-N79R11:2009, *Medical Devices: Post Market Surveillance: National Competent Authority Report Exchange Criteria and Report Form*, guidance for exchanging medical device safety reports among national CAs. This guidance also can be used for the GHTF National Competent Authority Report (NCAR) exchange program, and includes:

- criteria to be used for deciding when to exchange information with other CAs and NCAR participants
- procedures to follow when exchanging information
- forms to use for exchanging information

The NCAR Secretariat is the organization that receives NCARs from reporting national CAs and distributes them to other NCAR participants.[9] "Active exchange" is a proactive exchange of information involving direct notification to nominated contact addresses via email and through the NCAR Secretariat. This form of exchange should be used for high-risk issues. For nonserious events, information should be entered into a database, website or other means for exchange participants to view at their discretion ("passive exchange").

An NCAR should only be sent if the issue is considered to be serious, in which case the information should be exchanged actively through the NCAR Secretariat. For example, an NCAR relating to an unexpected but nonserious event is unlikely to be exchanged actively. Whether the exchange is active or passive depends upon the seriousness of the issue.

The following criteria should be considered when determining whether an NCAR should be sent:[10]

- seriousness
- unexpectedness of the incident or event
- vulnerable population (pediatric/elderly patients)
- preventability (Can useful recommendations be made?)

Figure 4-1. CAs Reporting Flowchart

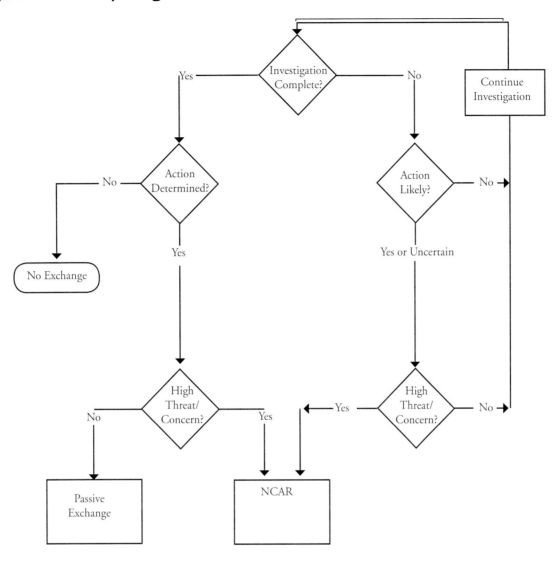

Source: SG2-N79R11:2009.

- public concern or outrage (e.g., lead aprons containing radioactive material)
- risk/benefit (Do benefits outweigh the risks? Are there any alternative, lower-risk approaches?)
- lack of scientific data (especially long-term effects)
- device problems that resurface (e.g., heating pads and operating room fires)
- written notifications from the national CA to the public (hospitals, physicians, etc.)
- if active exchange will help protect public health or if the manufacturer's actions have been sufficient

Information on high-risk issues is usually exchanged via email. A decision tree (**Figure 4-1**) can be used to determine whether an information exchange is necessary. GHTF's SG2-N79R11:2009 gives an example of what the NCAR form should look like and how it should be completed. Information on the form should be in English and of the highest quality possible in terms of both legibility and content. The person completing the NCAR is also responsible for determining the report's content, the appropriateness of submitting it and the scope of its distribution.

Decision Process

A reportable incident must meet three basic criteria:
- An event has occurred.
- The manufacturer's device is associated with the event.
- The event led to the death or serious injury of a patient, user or other person. The incident is also reportable if no death or serious injury occurred but a recurrence of the event might lead to the death or serious injury of a patient, user or other person.[11]

When there is doubt about the reportability of an event—even if the manufacturer has incomplete information—there should be a predisposition to report rather than not report.

According to GHTF's SG2-N54R8:2006, *Medical Devices Post Market Surveillance: Global Guidance for Adverse Event Reporting for Medical Devices*, events do not need to be reported if:
- the user found a deficiency in a device prior to patient use
- the adverse event was caused by patient conditions
- the event was caused by the device's service life or shelf life (i.e., when the only cause for the adverse event was that the device exceeded its service life or shelf life as specified by the manufacturer and the failure mode is not unusual, the adverse event does not need to be reported)
- malfunction protection operated correctly (i.e., adverse event did not lead to serious injury or death because a design feature protected against a malfunction's becoming a hazard)[12]
- there is negligible likelihood of occurrence of death or serious injury
- the event is an expected and foreseeable side effect
- the adverse event is described in an *Advisory Notice*
- There are reporting exemptions granted by a national CA

To Whom to Report

Adverse events must be reported to the CA as required by national legislation in each jurisdiction.

When to Report

As soon as a medical device manufacturer becomes aware of an incoming complaint, it must determine whether the incident is an adverse event.
- Any adverse event(s) that results in unanticipated death or unanticipated serious injury or represents a serious public health threat must be reported immediately by the manufacturer to the national CA.
- All other reportable events must be reported immediately, but no later than 30 elapsed calendar days after the date the manufacturer becomes aware of the event.[13]

PMS

All regulatory systems recognize that adverse event reporting alone cannot capture all risks related to medical devices in the postmarket phase.[14] For certain classes of products such as diagnostic devices, where false positives and/or false negatives may occur, long-term implantable devices and devices for home use, evaluating the device's performance from adverse event reports alone would not be sufficient. To address this requirement, PMS activities are mandated in most countries. Currently, requirements, definitions and understanding of PMS activities are not harmonized.[15] GHTF has been actively investigating whether harmonizing some aspects of PMS activities could benefit regulatory authorities and industry.

While the exact definition varies from country to country, PMS generally can be understood to be proactive activities carried out (by either the regulator or the manufacturer) to gain information about the quality, safety or performance of medical devices that have been placed on the market. Surveillance activities by CAs may involve testing, product review, inspections and other controlling measures. Information relating to PMS is also given in international standard ISO 13485:2003, *Medical Devices—Quality management systems—Requirements for regulatory purposes*.[16] This standard indicates that manufacturers should establish documented procedures for a feedback system to provide early warning of quality problems and input to the corrective and preventive action (CAPA) processes. These processes are, in turn, intended to detect and minimize risk, per ISO 14971:2007, *Medical Devices Application of risk management to medical devices*.[17]

The purpose of the PMS system is to implement and maintain a systematic procedure to review experience gained from devices in the postproduction/postmarket phase and apply any necessary corrective action(s).[18]

Typical sources of information on device experience include:
- customer surveys
- user surveys
- adverse events (vigilance system)
- user reports
- user feedback
- customer complaints
- customer requirements, contract information and market needs
- patient follow-up after clinical trials or investigations
- service and evaluation reports
- scientific papers in peer-reviewed journals
- reports on similar products by competitors
- compliance-related communications from regulatory agencies
- changes to relevant standards and regulations

Field Safety Corrective Action

Manufacturers placing medical devices on the market are obliged to put into place CAPA plans related to their products if those devices pose a risk to users or other individuals.[19] These plans include safety-related field corrective actions (FSCAs) taken by the manufacturer to reduce the risk of harm to patients, operators or others and/or to minimize chances the event will recur.

As defined in GHTF's SG2-N57R8:2006, *Medical Devices—Post Market Surveillance: Content of Field Safety Notices*, an FSCA is an action taken by a manufacturer to reduce the risk of death or serious deterioration in the state of health associated with the use of a medical device. The harmonized standard ISO 14971 presents a methodology to assess the need for an FSCA. Among the reasons for issuing an FSCA are:

- the return of a medical device to the manufacturer
- device modification
- device exchange
- device destruction
- advice given by the manufacturer regarding the use of the device (especially in the case of implants)

An FSCA should be sent in the official language of the recipient and, per SG2-N57R8:2006, should include:

- a clear title such as "Urgent Safety Notice" on the notice itself, on the envelope, if sent by mail in the subject line if sent by email or fax
- intended audience: a clear statement about the intended recipient of the notice
- concise description of subject device, including model, batch and/or serial number
- a factual statement explaining the reasons for the FSCA, including a description of the problem
- a clear description of the hazards associated with the device's specific failure and, where appropriate, the likelihood of occurrence, being mindful of the intended audience
- recommended action(s) to be taken by the recipient of the Field Safety Notice including people that have previously used or been treated by affected devices
- where appropriate, timeframes during which the action(s) should be taken by the manufacturer and user
- designated contact point for the recipient of the Field Safety Notice to obtain further information

Technical File Lifecycle Management (LCM)
Postmarket Phase

The content and description of the technical file for medical devices are covered in Chapter 3. In the postmarket phase, it is important to realize that the CA may request a copy of the technical file, even for lower-risk devices, at any time. Manufacturers of lower-risk medical devices are obliged to keep the technical file on their premises, while manufacturers of higher-risk devices must submit the technical file for review before placing the devices on the market. In the postmarket phase, manufacturers are obliged to have a functioning change control system in place that continuously updates the technical file. In general, changes that affect the quality system must be communicated to the authorities before implementation. For higher-risk devices, all changes that alter the information in the originally submitted technical file must be submitted for approval before implementation. In other words, the technical file must follow the LCM process in the postmarket phase.

Advertising

Medical device advertising should not impart false, misleading or deceptive information about the device that could give an erroneous impression of its design, construction, performance, intended use, quantity, character, value, composition, merit or safety. Advertising can create expectations and have a powerful influence on users; therefore, regulation plays an important role in preventing fraudulent and/or misleading advertising.[20] From the user's perspective, this may cause a delay in receiving appropriate treatment by the use of falsely advertised products making claims about performance. To save patients from such a situation, vendors must be properly controlled and regulated.

In addition, any claims made on product labeling should be supported by appropriate clinical evidence in the form of clinical investigations, performance evaluations or bibliographic literature.

Conclusion

Registering a medical device is but the first step in the device lifecycle. Manufacturers must ensure they fulfill their responsibilities in the postmarket phase. These include updating technical files regularly, reporting vigilance events, conducting any necessary FSCAs, maintaining a PMS system and abiding by national or regional advertising laws. Manufacturers also must update their quality systems, perform internal audits and ensure that device safety and performance levels are maintained. Failure to meet postmarket obligations could result in noncompliance, which in turn could lead to a batch recall or liability issues. It is worth noting that postmarket lifecycle management may well be the most resource-intensive phase for manufacturers placing medical devices on the market.

References

1. Regulatory Affairs Professionals Society. Chapter 8, Medical Device Postmarketing Activities. In: *Fundamentals of Canadian Regulatory Affairs.* Rockville, MD. 2006 p 75–81.

2. MEDDEV 2.12/1: *Guidelines on a Medical Devices Vigilance System* (rev 5) (April 2007)

3. Michor S. "Vigilance Reporting for Medical Devices in the EU," *Regulatory Affairs Focus*, September 2009.

4. SG2-N8R4 *Guidance on How to Handle Information Concerning Vigilance Reporting Related to Medical Devices*, 29 June 1999.

5. Ibid.

6. Ibid.

7. Op cit 1.

8. SG2-N79R11:2009 *Medical Devices: Post Market Surveillance: National Competent Authority Report Exchange Criteria and Report Form*, (February 2009)

9. SG2-N38R19:2009 *Application Requirements for Participation in the GHTF National Competent Authority Report Exchange Program* (July 2009).

10. Op cit 8.

11. SG2-N54R8:2006 *Medical Devices Post Market Surveillance: Global Guidance for Adverse Event Reporting for Medical Devices* (November 2006).

12. Ibid.

13. Ibid.

14. SG2/N47R4:2005 *Review of Current Requirements on Postmarket Surveillance* (May 2005).

15. Ibid.

16. International Organization for Standardization. EN ISO 13485:2003 *Medical devices–Quality management systems – Requirements for regulatory purposes.*

17. International Organization for Standardization. ISO 14971:2007 *Medical devices—Application of risk management to medical devices.*

18. Op cit 3.

19. SG2-N57R8:2006 *Medical Devices Post Market Surveillance: Content of Field Safety Notices* (June 2006).

20. WHO, *Medical device regulations: global overview and guiding principles*, ISBN 92 4 154618 2, copyright, World Health Organization 2003.

International In Vitro Diagnostic Medical Devices

By Salma Michor, PhD, MBA, CMgr, RAC

OBJECTIVES

❑ Understand the basic principles of in vitro diagnostic (IVD) medical devices

❑ Understand IVD classification

❑ Understand IVD classification rules

❑ Understand IVD conformity assessment (CA) procedures.

REGULATIONS AND GUIDELINES COVERED IN THIS CHAPTER

GHTF

❑ *Medical Devices Classification* (February 2008)

❑ SG1-N46:2008, *Principles of Conformity Assessment for In Vitro Diagnostic (IVD) Medical Devices* (July 2008)

❑ SG1-N41R9:2005, *Essential Principles of Safety and Performance of Medical Devices* (May 2005)

❑ SG1-N44:2008, *Role of Standards in the Assessment of Medical Devices* (March 2008)

❑ SG1-N11:2008, *Summary Technical Documentation for Demonstrating Conformity to the Essential Principles of Safety and Performance of Medical Devices (STED)* (February 2008)

❑ SG2-N47R4:2005, *Review of Current Requirements on Postmarket Surveillance* (May 2005)

Introduction

An "in vitro diagnostic (IVD) medical device" is defined as a device that, whether used alone or in combination, is intended by the manufacturer for the *in vitro* examination of specimens derived from the human body solely or principally to provide information for diagnostic, monitoring or compatibility purposes.[1] Examples include:

- reagents
- calibrators
- control materials
- specimen receptacles
- software and related instruments
- apparatus or other articles

IVD medical devices for self testing are intended by the manufacturer for use by lay people. In some jurisdictions, some classes of IVD medical devices may be covered by separate national regulations.

Principles of IVD Medical Device Classification

The interrelationship between device class and conformity assessment is critical in establishing a consistent approach to premarket approval across all countries/regions.[2] The Global Harmonization Task Force (GHTF) has published *Principles of In Vitro Diagnostic (IVD) Medical Devices Classification* (SG1-N45:2008) to help manufacturers assign in vitro diagnostic devices to the right risk class based upon their intended use. According to this guidance, the classification for IVDs depends upon the:

Figure 5-1. General GHTF Classification System for IVD Medical Devices

Class	Risk Level	Examples
A	Low Individual Risk and Low Public Health Risk	Clinical chemistry analyzer, prepared selective culture media
B	Moderate Individual Risk and/or Low Public Health Risk	Pregnancy self testing, anti-nuclear antibody, urine test strips
C	High Individual Risk and/or Moderate Public Health Risk	Blood glucose self testing, human leukocyte antigen (HLA) typing, prostate specific antigen (PSA) screening, Rubella
D	High Individual Risk and High Public Health Risk	HIV blood donor screening, HIV blood diagnostic

Source: SG1-N45:2008, p 9.

Figure 5-2. Regulatory Requirements Related to the Device Risk Class

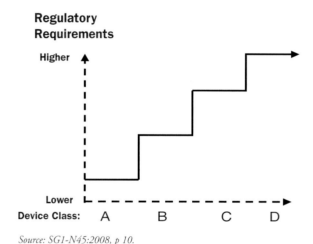

Source: SG1-N45:2008, p 10.

- intended use and indications for use as specified by the manufacturer
- technical, scientific and/or medical expertise of the intended user, including whether the user is a layperson or a healthcare professional
- importance of the information to the diagnosis, i.e., sole determinant or one of several
- impact the result (true or false) may have on the individual and/or on public health[3]

The exact rules for classification may differ slightly from one jurisdiction to another but are, in general, based upon a device's associated risk.

GHTF Proposed General Principles of Classification

GHTF proposes a four-class system as shown (see **Figure 5-1**). As the risk level increases from A (low risk) to D (very high risk), so do the regulatory requirements. Increasing requirements may include an operational quality system, a larger amount of clinical data, greater detail in the technical file and external audits. This escalation of requirements can be shown using a stepwise approach such as that in **Figure 5-2**.

Device Class and Classification Rules

Section 9 of GHTF SG1-N45:2008 proposes seven rules to help manufacturers classify their IVD devices correctly. It should be noted, however, that the exact classification should be based upon existing national laws and regulations. As a general rule, if more than one classification rule applies to the IVD medical device, or in borderline cases, the device should be assigned to the highest class indicated. The device class will have an effect on the conformity assessment procedure chosen. This, in turn, may affect the acceptability of such devices in various regions and countries. In such cases, the importing country may require the manufacturer to carry out additional tests to comply with local conformity assessment requirements. See **Tables 5-1** and **Table 5-2** for the seven rules proposed by GHTF.

Principles of Conformity Assessment for IVD Medical Devices

According to GHTF's *Principles of Conformity Assessment for In Vitro Diagnostic (IVD) Medical Devices* (SG1-N46:2008), such assessment can be defined as:[4]

"the systematic examination of evidence generated and procedures undertaken by the manufacturer, under requirements established by the Regulatory Authority, to determine that a medical device is safe and performs as intended

Table 5-1. Classification Rules for IVDs

Rule	IVD Medical Device Intended Purpose	Class	Example
1	1. Used to detect the presence of, or exposure to, a transmissible agent in blood, blood components, blood derivatives, cells, tissues or organs in order to assess their suitability for transfusion or transplantation 2. Devices intended to be used to detect the presence of, or exposure to, a transmissible agent that causes a life-threatening, often incurable, disease with a high risk of propagation	D	Examples include tests to detect infection by Human immnodeficiency virus (HIV), Hepatitis C (HCV), Hepatitis B (HBV), Human T-Lymphotropic (HTLV). The rule applies to first-line assays, confirmatory assays and supplemental assays
2	1. Intended to be used for blood grouping or tissue typing to ensure the immunological compatibility of blood, blood components, cells, tissue or organs that are intended for transfusion or transplantation, are classified as Class C, except for ABO system (A (ABO1), B (ABO2), AB (ABO3)) rhesus system (RH1 (D), RH2 (C), RH3 (E), RH4 (c), RH5 (e)) Kell system (Kell (K)), Kidd system (JK1 (Jka), JK2 (Jkb)) and Duffy system (FY1 (Fya), FY2 (Fyb)) determinations which are classified as Class D	C or D	Examples include HLA and the Duffy system (other Duffy systems except those listed in the rule as Class D are in Class C)
3	1. To detect the presence of, or exposure to, a sexually transmitted agent 2. To detect the presence in cerebrospinal fluid or blood of an infectious agent with a risk of limited propagation 3. To detect the presence of an infectious agent where there is a significant risk that an erroneous result would cause death or severe disability to the individual or fetus being tested 4. Used in prenatal screening of women in order to determine their immune status towards transmissible agents 5. To determine infective disease status or immune status, and where there is a risk that an erroneous result will lead to a patient management decision resulting in an imminent life-threatening situation for the patient 6. Used in screening for selection of patients for selective therapy and management, or for disease staging, or in the diagnosis of cancer 7. Used in human genetic testing 8. Used to monitor levels of medicines, substances or biological components, when there is a risk that an erroneous result will lead to a patient management decision resulting in an immediate life-threatening situation for the patient 9. Used in the management of patients suffering from a life-threatening infectious disease 10. Used in screening for congenital disorders in the fetus		1. Sexually transmitted diseases, such as Chlamydia trachomatis, Neisseria gonorrhoeae 2. Neisseria meningitis or Cryptococcus neoformans 3. diagnostic assay for CMV, Chlamydia pneumoniae, Methycillin Resistant Staphylococcus aureus 4. Immune status tests for Rubella or Toxoplasmosis 5. Enteroviruses, Cytomegaovirus (CMV) and Herpes Simplex (HSV) in transplant patients 6. Personalized medicine 7. Huntington's Disease, Cystic Fibrosis 8. Cardiac markers, Cyclosporin, Prothrombin time testing 9. HCV viral load, HIV Viral Load and HIV and HCV geno- and subtyping 10. Spina Bifida or Down Syndrome

Source: SG1-N45:2008, Section 9.

Table 5-2. Classification Rules for IVDs

Rule	IVD Medical Device Intended Purpose	Class	Example
4	1. IVD medical devices intended for self testing are classified as Class C, except those devices from which the result is not determining a medically critical status, or is preliminary and requires follow-up with the appropriate laboratory test, in which case they are Class B 2. IVD medical devices intended for blood gases and blood glucose determinations for near-patient testing would be Class C; other IVD medical devices that are intended for near-patient should be classified in their own right using the classification rules	C or B	1. Example for self testing Class C: Blood glucose monitoring, 2. Example for self testing Class B: Pregnancy self test, fertility testing, urine test strips.
5	1. Reagents or other articles that possess specific characteristics, intended by the manufacturer to make them suitable for in vitro diagnostic procedures related to a specific examination 2. Instruments intended by the manufacturer specifically to be used for in vitro diagnostic procedures 3. Specimen receptacles	A	Selective/differential microbiological media (excluding the dehydrated powders, which are not considered to be a finished IVD medical device), identification kits for cultured microorganisms, wash solutions, instruments and plain urine cups
6	IVD medical devices not covered in Rules 1 through 5 are classified as Class B	B	Blood gases, *H. pylori* and physiological markers such as hormones, vitamins, enzymes, metabolic markers, specific IgE assays and celiac disease markers
7	IVD medical devices that are controls without a quantitative or qualitative assigned value will be classified as Class B	B	

Source: SG1-N45:2008, Section 9.

by the manufacturer and, therefore, conforms to the *Essential Principles of Safety and Performance of Medical Devices (SG1/N041)*."[5]

Carrying out conformity assessment is the sole responsibility of the IVD medical device manufacturer; however, it must be done according to established regulatory requirements. In addition, except for very low-risk devices, conformity assessment conducted by the manufacturer is subject to further review by the Regulatory Authority (RA) and/or Conformity Assessment Body (CAB).

Conformity Assessment Elements

The main elements of a conformity assessment system are:
- a quality management system (QMS)
- a postmarket surveillance system (PMS)
- summary technical Declaration of Conformity
- a Declaration of Conformity
- registration of manufacturers and their IVD

medical devices with the RA[6]

The amount of detail needed for each of these elements to prove conformity for IVD medical devices is directly proportional to the device's associated risk. This requirement applies primarily to the level of detail in the clinical and/or performance data and details of the manufacturer's quality control release program included in the technical Declaration of Conformity.

QMS

As is the case with other medical devices, IVD manufacturers must have a suitable QMS in place. The purpose of the QMS (in combination with other conformity assessment elements) is to ensure that IVD medical devices will be safe and will perform as intended by the manufacturer. A QMS is usually based on internationally accepted standards.[7] The QMS ensures that the manufactured products consistently meet both customer and regulatory requirements.

Table 5-3. Class A Device

Conformity Assessment Element	Manufacturer Responsibility	RA/CAB Responsibility
QMS	Establish and maintain a full QMS or a QMS without design and development controls	Premarket regulatory audit not required
PMS	Establish and maintain an adverse event reporting procedure according to GHTF SG2 guidance	May audit postmarket to investigate specific safety or regulatory concerns
Technical Documentation	Upon request, prepare STED	Premarket submission of STED not required; may be requested to investigate specific safety or regulatory concerns
Declaration of Conformity	Prepare, sign and maintain.	On file with the manufacturer; available upon request
Registration of Manufacturers and Their Devices	Perform according to regulatory requirements	Maintain and verify as appropriate

Source SG1-N46:2008, pp 11–14.

The scope and complexity of the QMS needed depends upon the size of the organization and the type of products manufactured (i.e., high or low risk). Any outsourced processes must be properly controlled. For more information about QMS and outsourcing please see Chapter 3, under QMS and Risk Management Systems (RMS) for Medical Devices.

Except for the lowest-risk devices (Class A), the QMS will be subject to inspections by the RA and/or CAB.

PMS System

Prior to placing IVD devices on the market, manufacturers must have a system in place to collect and assess incoming complaints, perform vigilance reporting to the conformity assessment and carry out any corrective and/or preventive action (CAPA). For more information about vigilance reporting and PMS, please see Chapter 4, postmarket requirements. The PMS system will be inspected during the quality management inspections and periodically thereafter. It is worth mentioning here that the PMS system is of special significance for IVD device manufacturers, since vigilance alone cannot capture all risks related to the use of these devices. Examples include false positive and/or false negative results, and adverse events arising from use in the home, where it may be difficult or even impossible to evaluate the device's performance.[8]

Technical Declaration of Conformity

To demonstrate conformity, manufacturers must provide evidence in the form of technical Declaration of Conformity that the IVD medical device meets the required Essential Principles. Normally, the manufacturer establishes a subset of technical Declaration of Conformity, STED, that should either be submitted for evaluation and review before market entry (high-risk devices) or kept on the premises of the manufacturer to be reviewed during routine inspections. (For more information about STED requirements, please see Chapter 3, technical and regulatory requirements, and the GHTF guidance, *Summary Technical Declaration of Conformity for Demonstrating Conformity to the Essential Principles of Safety and Performance of Medical Devices (STED)* (SG1-N11:2008)).[9] The amount of detail required in the STED is directly related to the device's class and associated risk.

Declaration of Conformity (Declaration of Conformity)

The manufacturer of an IVD, like other medical devices, is responsible for issuing a written Declaration of Conformity that attests to the compliance of the IVD medical device with all applicable *Essential Principles of Safety and Performance of Medical Devices* (SG1-N41R9:2005). The Declaration of Conformity also confirms that the device has been properly classified[10] and has met all applicable conformity assessment elements.

The Declaration of Conformity must contain sufficient information to identify the device(s) to which it applies and the device's associated risk class. In addition, the Declaration of Conformity should clearly show which conformity assessment procedures have been applied and include other information such as the date from which

Table 5-4. Class B Device

Conformity Assessment Element	Manufacturer Responsibility	RA/CAB Responsibility
QMS	Establish and maintain a full QMS or a QMS without design and development controls	Be satisfied that a current and appropriate QMS is in place or conduct a QMS audit prior to marketing authorization
PMS	Establish and maintain an adverse event reporting procedure according to GHTF SG2 guidance	Be satisfied that a current and appropriate adverse event reporting procedure is in place as part of the QMS
Technical Documentation	Upon request, prepare STED	Premarket submission normally not required but if requested, receive and conduct a review of the STED to determine conformity to Essential Principles
Declaration of Conformity	Prepare, sign and submit	Review and verify compliance with requirements
Registration of Manufacturers and Their Devices	Perform according to regulatory requirements	Maintain and verify as appropriate

Source: SG1-N46:2008, pp 11–14.

the Declaration of Conformity is valid and the device manufacturer's name and address. The Declaration of Conformity must be signed by a responsible person who has been authorized to complete it on the manufacturer's behalf.[11]

Registration of Manufacturers and Their IVD Medical Devices With the RA

Prior to placing an IVD medical device on the market, the manufacturer, its local distributor or its authorized representative should register with the local RA. This helps the RA identify the IVD medical device and the party responsible for it within a particular jurisdiction, thereby

facilitating any necessary regulatory activity. It is the RA's responsibility to maintain this register and to initiate enforcement in case of noncompliance.

The Relationship Between Conformity Assessment and Device Classification

Based on GHTF's recommendation, IVD medical devices should be assigned to one of four classes (starting with lowest risk, A, to highest risk, D), using a set of rules as defined in *Principles of In Vitro Diagnostic (IVD) Medical Devices Classification*.[12] The level of manufacturer scrutiny from RAs and CABs is based upon the device's associated

Table 5-5. Class C Device

Conformity Assessment Element	Manufacturer Responsibility	RA/CAB Responsibility
QMS	Establish and maintain a full QMS	Be satisfied that a current and appropriate QMS is in place or conduct a QMS audit prior to marketing authorization
PMS	Establish and maintain an adverse event reporting procedure according to GHTF SG2 guidance	Be satisfied that a current and appropriate adverse event reporting procedure is in place as part of the QMS
Technical Documentation	Prepare and submit STED for review	Receive and conduct a premarket review of the STED to determine conformity to Essential Principles
Declaration of Conformity	Prepare, sign and submit	Review and verify compliance with requirements
Registration of Manufacturers and Their Devices	Perform according to regulatory requirements	Maintain and verify as appropriate

Source: SG1-N46:2008, pp 11-14.

Table 5-6. Class D Device

Conformity Assessment Element	Manufacturer Responsibility	RA/CAB Responsibility
QMS	Establish and maintain a full QMS	Be satisfied that a current and appropriate QMS is in place, or conduct a QMS audit prior to marketing authorization
PMS	Establish and maintain an adverse event reporting procedure according to GHTF SG2 guidance	Be satisfied that a current and appropriate adverse event reporting procedure is in place as part of the QMS
Technical Documentation	Prepare and submit STED for review; a STED for this class should contain more extended information such as full performance evaluation reports	Receive and conduct a premarket review of the STED to determine conformity to Essential Principles
Declaration of Conformity	Prepare, sign and submit	Review and verify compliance with requirements
Registration of Manufacturers and Their Devices	Perform according to regulatory requirements	Maintain and verify as appropriate

Source: SG1-N46:2008 pp 11–14.

risk. Although RA and CAB have the same responsibilities for Class C and D IVD medical devices, the amount of detail in the STED related to clinical and/or performance data and details of the manufacturer's QC release program will depend upon the risk level. **Tables 5-3–5-6** taken from GHTF SG1-N46:2008 illustrate this.

Conclusion

Incident reporting and vigilance may not be the most suitable way to monitor an IVD's performance after market entry. Therefore, for this class of devices, more emphasis is placed on an effective, functioning PMS system as compared with other device groups. In addition, clinical investigations generally are replaced by so-called "performance evaluations." However, for the most part, the regulatory requirements for IVD medical devices follow the same basic principles of performance and safety as those for other medical devices. GHTF has proposed seven classification rules and four device classes from A (low risk) to D (high risk). The route to achieving conformity assessment depends upon the device class. The complexity of established QMS and the detail needed in the accompanying technical Declaration of Conformity are directly proportional to the risk associated with the IVD medical device. In most jurisdictions, the internationally accepted guidance(s) published by GHTF must be read in conjunction with local regulations and restrictions to ensure compliance with national requirements.

References

1. SG1-N45:2008, *Principles of In Vitro Diagnostic (IVD) Medical Devices Classification* (February 2008), pp 5.
2. Ibid.
3. SG1-N45:2008, *Principles of In Vitro Diagnostic (IVD) Medical Devices Classification* (February 2008), pp 8.
4. SG1-N46:2008, *Principles of Conformity Assessment for In Vitro Diagnostic (IVD) Medical Devices* (July 2008), pp 7.
5. SG1-N41R9:2005, *Essential Principles of Safety and Performance of Medical Devices* (May 2005).
6. Op cit 4.
7. SG1-N44:2008, *Role of Standards in the Assessment of Medical Devices* (March 2008).
8. SG2-N47R4:2005, *Review of Current Requirements on Postmarket Surveillance* (May 2005).
9. SG1-N11:2008, *Summary Technical Declaration of Conformity for Demonstrating Conformity to the Essential Principles of Safety and Performance of Medical Devices (STED)* (February 2008).
10. Op cit 1.
11. SG1-N46:2008, *Principles of Conformity Assessment for In Vitro Diagnostic (IVD) Medical Devices* (July 2008) pp 9-10.
12. SG1-N46:2008, *Principles of Conformity Assessment for In Vitro Diagnostic (IVD) Medical Devices* (July 2008), pp 10-14.

International Glossary of Terms

A

Abridged application
An application for marketing authorization that, based on demonstration of essential similarity or by detailed references to published scientific literature, does not contain the results of pharmacological and toxicological tests or the results of clinical trials.

ACTD
ASEAN Common Technical Dossier

Active Pharmaceutical Ingredient
(API) Any drug component intended to furnish pharmacological activity or other direct effect in the diagnosis, cure, mitigation, treatment or prevention of disease; or to affect the structure or any function of the body of man or other animals.

ADME
Absorption, Distribution, Metabolism and Excretion

ADR
Adverse Drug Reaction

Adulterated
Product containing any filthy, putrid or decomposed substance; or prepared under unsanitary conditions; or not made according to GMPs; or containing an unsafe color additive; or does not meet the requirements of an official compendium.

ANDA
Abbreviated New Drug Application (US)

ANDS
Abbreviated New Drug Submission (Canada)

Annual Report
An annual periodic report or progress report that must be submitted to FDA. It must include new safety, efficacy and labeling information; preclinical and clinical investigation summaries; CMC updates; nonclinical laboratory studies; and completed unpublished clinical trials.

ANSI
American National Standards Institute

API
See Active Pharmaceutical Ingredient

AR
Authorized Representative

ARTG
Australian register of therapeutic goods

ASEAN
Association of Southeast Asian Nations. Comprised of Brunei Darussalam, Cambodia, Indonesia, Lao PDR, Malaysia, Myanmar, Philippines, Singapore, Thailand and Viet Nam.

ATMP
Advanced therapy medicinal product

B

BA
Bioavailability

BE
Bioequivalence

BGTD
Biologics and Genetic Therapies Directorate (Canada)

Biologic
Any virus, therapeutic serum, toxin, antitoxin or analogous product applicable to the prevention, treatment or cure of diseases or injuries in man.

Biosimilars
New versions of existing biologicals whose patents have expired. Also referred to as FOBs and SEBs.

BLA
Biologics License Application (US)

BSE
Bovine spongiform encephalopathy

C

CA
See Competent Authority

CAB
Conformity assessment body

CAC
Codex Alimentarius Commission

CADREAC
Collaboration Agreement between Drug Regulatory Authorities in EU Associated Countries

CAPA
Corrective and Preventive Actions

CAS
Chemical Abstracts Service

CBER
Center for Biologics Evaluation and Research (FDA)

CDER
Center for Drug Evaluation and Research (FDA)

CDRH
Center for Devices and Radiological Health (FDA)

Central Drugs Standard Control Organization
Primary regulatory body for healthcare products in India.

Centralised Procedure
(CP) A procedure to allow applicants to make an application directly to the European Medicines Agency, to be assessed by the CHMP or CVMP, to obtain a Marketing Authorisation (MA) that is valid throughout the EU. It is compulsory for medicinal products manufactured using biotechnological processes, but may also be used for other innovative products, on a voluntary basis. Centrally authorized products may be marketed in all Member States.

Certificate of Suitability
Certificate that the substance's quality is suitably controlled by the relevant monographs of the European Pharmacopoeia with, if necessary, an annex appended to the certificate. Can be granted for APIs or excipients and for substances or preparations with risk of transmitting agents of TSE.

CFR
Code of Federal Regulations (US)

CHMP
See Committee for Medicinal Products for Human Use

CIOMS
Council for International Organisations of Medical Sciences

CJD
Creuzfeldt-Jakob Disease

CMC
Chemistry, Manufacturing and Controls

CMS
Concerned Member State (EU)

Committee for Medicinal Products for Human Use
(CHMP) A scientific committee within the European Medicines Agency that provides scientific advice on questions relating to the evaluation of medicinal products for human use.

Committee for Veterinary Medicinal Products
(CVMP) A scientific committee within the European Medicines Agency that provides scientific advice on questions relating to the evaluation of veterinary medicinal products.

Competent Authority
(CA) A Competent Authority is the governmental authority responsible for the authorization and supervision of medicinal products.

Conformity assessment
A procedure to enable public authorities to ensure that industrial products, including medical devices, placed on the market conform to the requirements as expressed in the provisions of the directives, particularly regarding the health and safety of users and consumers.

CPP
Certificate of a Pharmaceutical Product

CRO
Contract research organization

CTA
Clinical Trial Application

CTD
Common Technical Document

CVM
Center for Veterinary Medicine (FDA)

CVMP
Committee for Medicinal Products for Veterinary Use (EU)

D

Decentralised Procedure
(DCP) Procedure that may be used for medicinal products for which there is no existing Marketing Authorisation in any EU Member State. The applicant can select the Reference Member State and list the Concerned Member States.

Declaration of Helsinki
Ethical principles for medical research involving human subjects. Trials conducted under Good Clinical Practice generally follow the Declaration of Helsinki.

DIN
Drug Identification Number (Canada)

Directive
An EC decision that is binding upon EC institutions and Member States, and must be transposed into national legislation. However, the way in which it is implemented is left to the discretion of each Member State.

DMF
Drug Master File

DQ
Design Qualification

DRI
Dietary Reference Intake

Drug
Any article intended for use in the diagnosis, cure, mitigation, treatment or prevention of disease in man.

Drug & Cosmetics Act
Primary law governing healthcare products in India.

DSHEA
Dietary Supplement Health and Education Act (US)

DTC
Direct-to-consumer

E

EC
European Community; also refers to European Commission

eCTD
Electronic Common Technical Document

EDMF
European Drug Master File

EDQM
See European Directorate for the Quality of Medicines

EEA
See European Economic Area

EEC
See European Economic Community

EFPIA
European Federation of Pharmaceutical Industries and Associations

EFTA
European Free Trade Association, composed of Iceland, Liechtenstein, Norway and Switzerland.

EP
Essential Principles

EPAR
See European Public Assessment Report

ERA
Environmental Risk Assessment

Essential Requirements
The technical requirements with which a medical device must comply in order to be CE marked.

EU
See European Union

European Commission
(EC) A body with powers of initiative, implementation, management and control. It is composed of 20 members, called commissioners, appointed to five-year terms by Member States after they have been approved by the European Parliament.

European Community
(EC) The collective body formerly designated as the European Economic Community (EEC). The plural term European Communities is also widely used.

European Council
The European Council is the Heads of State or Government of the European Union Member States, who meet regularly. It is another and the most senior manifestation of the Council of the European Union.

European Directorate for the Quality of Medicines
(EDQM) Part of the administrative structure of the Council of Europe. Its responsibilities include the Technical Secretariat of the European Pharmacopoeia Commission, certification for Ph. Eur.'s monograph suitability program, developing the European network of the Official Medicines Control Laboratories (OMCL) and providing the secretariat for this network.

European Economic Area
(EEA) A free-trade area, in all but agriculture, comprising the Member States of the EU plus Iceland, Liechtenstein and Norway. Previously called the European Economic Space.

European Medicines Agency
Agency responsible for coordinating the scientific evaluation of the safety, efficacy and quality of human and veterinary medicinal products that undergo the Centralised Procedure as well as for arbitration during the Mutual Recognition Procedure.

European Pharmacopoeia
(Ph. Eur.) Pharmacopée Européenne is a pharmacopoeia whose monographs are common to all concerned European countries.

European Public Assessment Report
(EPAR) The EPAR highlights CHMP's scientific conclusion at the end of the centralized evaluation process and summarizes the grounds for the CHMP Opinion regarding granting a marketing authorization for a specific medicinal product. It is made available by the European Medicines Agency for public information, after deletion of commercially confidential information.

European Union
(EU) The EU is composed of 27 Member States: Austria, Belgium, Bulgaria, Cyprus, Czech Republic, Denmark, Estonia, Finland, France, Germany, Greece, Hungary, Ireland, Italy, Latvia, Lithuania, Luxembourg, Malta, the Netherlands, Poland, Portugal, Romania, Slovakia, Slovenia, Spain, Sweden and the United Kingdom.

EWG
Expert Working Group

Excipient
An ingredient contained in a drug formulation that is not a medicinally active constituent.

F

F&DA
Food and Drugs Act. Primary law governing healthcare products in Canada.

F&EC
Facility and equipment controls

FAO
Food and Agriculture Organization

FD&C Act
Food, Drug, and Cosmetic Act. Primary law governing healthcare products in the US.

FDA
See US Food and Drug Administration

FIFARMA
Federación Latinoamericana de la Industria Farmacéutica

FMA
Foreign Manufacturing Authorization

FOB
Follow-on biologic (see biosimilars)

FSCA
Field safety corrective action

G

GCC-DR
Gulf Central Committee for Drug Registration. Comprised of Bahrain, Kuwait, Oman, Qatar, Saudi Arabia and the United Arab Emirates.

GCDMP
Good Clinical Data Management Practice

GCP
Good Clinical Practice

GDP
Good Distribution Practice

GDP
Good Documentation Practice

Generic Drug
Drugs manufactured and approved after the original brand name drug has lost patent protection.

Genetically Modified Organism
(GMO) An organism in which the genetic material has been altered in a way that does not occur naturally by mating and/or natural recombination.

GHTF
Global Harmonization Task Force

GLP
Good Laboratory Practice

GMDN
Global Medical Device Nomenclature

GMO
See Genetically Modified Organism

GMP
Good Manufacturing Practice

GP
General public (Canada)

GRASE
Generally recognized as safe and effective (US)

GSL
General Sales List (UK)

GxP
Good Pharmaceutical Practices

H

HACCP
Hazardous Analysis Critical Control Points

Hatch-Waxman Act
Enacted in 1984, this act forms the basis for generic drug approval in the US.

Health Canada
Primary regulatory body for healthcare products in Canada.

I

IB
Investigator's Brochure

IBD
International birth date

ICDRA
International Conference of Drug Regulatory Authorities

ICH
International Conference on Harmonisation of Technical Requirements for Registration of Pharmaceuticals for Human Use

ICSR
Individual case safety report

IFAH
International Federation for Animal Health

IFPMA
International Federation of Pharmaceutical Manufacturers & Associations

IGPA
International Generic Pharmaceutical Alliance

IND
Investigational New Drug

INN
International Nonproprietary Name

IQ
Installation Qualification

IRB
Institutional Review Board

ISO
International Organization for Standardization

IUPAC
International Union of Pure and Applied Chemistry

IVD
In vitro diagnostic medical device

L

LCM
Lifecycle management

M

MA
Marketing Authorization

MAD
Mutual acceptance of data

MAH
See Marketing Authorization Holder

Marketing Authorization
(MA) Authorization issued by a Competent Authority to place a medicinal product on the market.

Marketing Authorization Holder
(MAH) The person who holds the marketing authorization for placing a medicinal product on the market and is responsible for the product's marketing.

MEB
Medicines Evaluation Board (Netherlands)

MHLW
Ministry of Health, Labour and Welfare (Japan)

MHRA
Medicines and Healthcare products Regulatory Agency (UK)

MPA
Medicinal Product Agency (Sweden)

MRA
See Mutual Recognition Agreement

MRL
Maximum residue limit

MRP
See Mutual Recognition Procedure

MS
Member State

MUMS
Minor use, minor species

Mutual recognition agreement
(MRA) An international agreement by which two or more countries agree to recognize one another's conformity assessments.

Mutual Recognition Procedure
(MRP) The Mutual Recognition Procedure, which is applicable to most conventional medicinal products, is one licensing procedure in the EU based on the extension of national marketing authorizations to one or more additional MSs. Applicants may select the Reference Member State that conducts the assessment and applicable Concerned Member States where the product would be put on the market if approved.

N

NB
Notified Body

NCAR
National Competent Authority Report

NCE
New Chemical Entity

ND
Normative Documentation (Russia)

NDA
New Drug Application (US)

NDS
New Drug Submission (Canada)

NF
National Formulary (US)

NICPBP
National Institute of the Control of Pharmaceutical and Biological Products (China)

NIH
National Institutes of Health (US)

NME
New molecular entity

NOC
Notice of Compliance (Canada)

O

ODA
Orphan Drug Act

OECD
Organisation for Economic Cooperation and Development

OMCL
Official medicines control laboratory

OOPD
Office of Orphan Products and Development (FDA)

OQ
Operational Qualification

Orphan medicinal products
Drugs that cater to conditions with low prevalence and therefore lack commercial viability.

OTC
Over-the-counter (products available without a prescription)

P

P&PC
Production and process controls

PAHO
Pan American Health Organization

PAL
Pharmaceutical Affairs Law (Japan)

PD
Pharmacodynamics

Periodic Safety Update Report
(PSUR) A periodic report on a medicinal product's worldwide safety experience submitted at defined postauthorization times.

PIC
Pharmaceutical Inspection Convention. The PIC and the Pharmaceutical Inspection Co-operation Scheme (PIC Scheme) operate together as PIC/S.

PIL
Patient information leaflet

PK
Pharmacokinetics

PMDA
Pharmaceuticals and Medical Devices Agency (Japan)

PMF
Plasma Master File

PMS
See Postmarketing Surveillance

POM
Prescription only medicine (UK)

Postmarketing surveillance
(PMS) After placing a product on the market, the manufacturer must institute and update a systematic procedure that records, evaluates and reports any incidents, to proactively gather product experience in the postmarketing phase and to take any necessary corrective measures.

PQ
Performance Qualification

PSUR
See Periodic Safety Update Report

PV
Pharmacovigilance

Q

QA
Quality assurance

QMS
Quality management system

QOS
Quality overall summary

QP
Qualified Person

R

R&D
Research and development

RA
Regulatory authority

RDA
Recommended daily/dietary allowance

RMP
Reference medicinal product (EU)

RMP
Risk management plan

RMS
Reference Member State (EU)

RMS
Risk Management System

S

SAE
Serious adverse event

SEB
Subsequent entry biologic (Canada) (see biosimilars)

SFDA
State Food and Drug Administration (China)

SmPC
See Summary of product characteristics

SNDS
Supplementary New Drug Submission (Canada)

SOP
Standard operating procedure

SPC
See Supplementary Protection Certificates

Sponsor
Company, person, organization or institution conducting a clinical trial and/or filing for approval of a new medicinal product.

STED
Summary Technical Document

Summary of Product Characteristics
(SmPC) The definitive statement between the Competent Authority and the Marketing Authorization Holder regarding the medicinal or veterinary product. It contains all information a prescriber/supplier needs for proper use of the medicinal or veterinary product. The content must be approved by the Competent Authority, and cannot be changed without the approval of the originating Competent Authority.

Supplementary Protection Certificates
(SPC) An SPC protects intellectual property rights following patent expiration and is available in the EU for medicinal products and plant protection products. An SPC can come into force only after the corresponding

patent expires and for a maximum of five years, to grant a product not more than 15 years of market exclusivity. It is intended to compensate the holder for the extended period required for some products to be approved.

T

TBT
Technical Barriers to Trade

TGA
Therapeutic Goods Administration (Australia)

TPD
Therapeutic Products Directorate (Canada)

TSE
Transmissible spongiform encephalopathies

U

USP
US Pharmacopeia

V

VAERS
Vaccine Adverse Event Reporting System (US)

VAMF
Vaccine Antigen Master File

VICH
International Cooperation on Harmonisation of Technical Requirements for Registration of Veterinary Medicinal Products

W

WHA
World Health Assembly

WHO
World Health Organization

WSMI
World Self-Medication Industry

WTO
World Trade Organization

US Medical Device Regulation

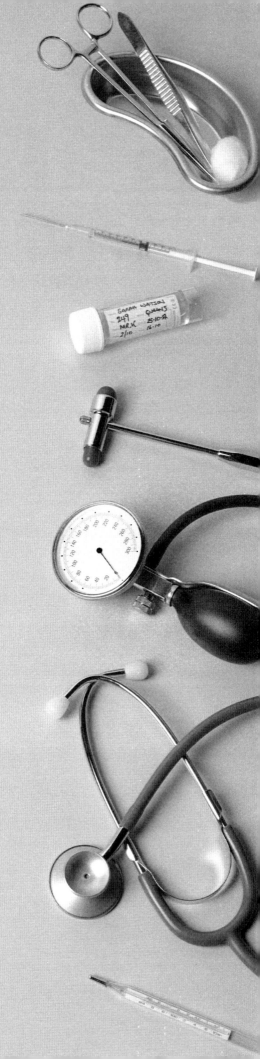

History of US FDA and Related Regulatory Agencies

By Richard Morroney, CQA, RAC and Nandini Murthy, RAC

Objectives

❏ Introduce the FDA and provide a history of the agency's evolution over more than a century and significant laws that guided FDA's growth

❏ Discuss the structure of FDA and its relationship with other US regulatory agencies

Laws, Regulations and Guidelines Covered in This Chapter

❏ *Food and Drug Act of 1906*

❏ *Federal Food, Drug and Cosmetic Act of 1938 (FD&C Act)*

❏ *Family Smoking Prevention and Tobacco Control Act of 2009*

❏ *Vaccine Act of 1813*

❏ *Federal Advisory Committee Act of 1972*

❏ *Federal Trade Commission Act of 1914*

❏ *Health Insurance Portability and Accountability Act of 1996*

❏ *Consumer Product Safety Act of 1972*

❏ *Occupational Safety and Health Act of 1970*

❏ *Federal Alcohol Administration Act of 1935*

❏ *Poultry Products Inspection Act of 1957*

❏ *Safe Drinking Water Act of 1974*

Introduction

Today, the US Food and Drug Administration (FDA) is part of the executive branch of government and falls under the jurisdiction of the US Department of Health and Human Services (DHHS). From its humble beginnings in 1862 as a laboratory that analyzed samples of food, fertilizers and agricultural substances, FDA has evolved over a century and a half, expanding its regulatory responsibility to include drugs, cosmetics and devices. Today, FDA regulates more than $1 trillion worth of consumer goods, about 25% of US consumer expenditures. This amount includes $466 billion in food sales, $275 billion in drugs, $60 billion in cosmetics and $18 billion in vitamin supplements.[1] Consistent with FDA's evolution, the agency's influence is likely to grow in the future.

FDA's Mission

FDA's current mission statement reads:

"FDA is responsible for protecting the public health by assuring the safety, efficacy, and security of human and veterinary drugs, biological products, medical devices, cosmetics, products that emit radiation and food supply. The FDA is also responsible for advancing the public health by helping to speed innovations that make medicines and foods more effective, safer, and more affordable. The FDA shares with the public accurate, science-based information they need to use medicines and foods to maintain and improve their health."

FDA's History

During the 19th century, states exercised principal control over domestically produced and distributed foods and drugs, while federal authority was restricted to imported foods and drugs. The *Vaccine Act* of 1813 was one of the first federal laws dealing with consumer protection and therapeutic substances. The Division of Chemistry, which became the Bureau of Chemistry in July 1901, began investigating the adulteration of agricultural commodities as early as 1867. Dr. Harvey W. Wiley, credited as the father of US food and drug law, and who eventually became chief chemist of the US Department of Agriculture, expanded the division's research in this area. He demonstrated his concern about chemical preservatives as adulterants in the highly publicized "poison squad" experiments, in which able-bodied volunteers consumed varying amounts of questionable food additives to determine their impact on health. Wiley also unified a variety of groups behind a federal law to prohibit the adulteration and misbranding of food and drugs, which was a rampant problem (e.g., arsenic in vinegar, sulfuric acid in pickles, woodchips in bread, alum and clay in wheat flour). Foods were also marketed with bold and unsubstantiated claims (e.g., as cures for cancer and the prevention of baldness). Upton Sinclair's description of the meatpacking industry in *The Jungle* was a precipitating force behind both a meat inspection law and a comprehensive food and drug law. On 30 June 1906, President Theodore Roosevelt signed the *Food and Drugs Act*, known simply as the *Wiley Act*. The *Federal Food, Drug, and Cosmetic Act (FD&C Act)* was passed in 1938.

Structure of FDA

FDA is an agency within the Department of Health and Human Services and consists of nine centers/offices:
- Office of the Commissioner (OC)
- Center for Biologics Evaluation and Research (CBER)
- Center for Devices and Radiological Health (CDRH)
- Center for Drug Evaluation and Research (CDER)
- Center for Food Safety and Applied Nutrition (CFSAN)
- Center for Tobacco Products (CTP)
- Center for Veterinary Medicine (CVM)
- National Center for Toxicological Research (NCTR)
- Office of Regulatory Affairs (ORA)

More information on FDA's organizational structure may be found at www.fda.gov/AboutFDA/CentersOffices/default.htm and www.fda.gov/AboutFDA/CentersOffices/OrganizationCharts/default.htm.

Office of the Commissioner (OC)

The Office of the Commissioner provides centralized agency-wide direction and management to support effective administration of all programs. It is responsible for the efficient and effective implementation of FDA's mission.

Among the offices reporting directly to OC are the Office of the Chief Counsel, the Office of the Chief Scientist, the Office of International Programs and the Office of Special Medical Programs.

For more information on the Office of the Commissioner, go to www.fda.gov/AboutFDA/CentersOffices/OC/default.htm.

Office of the Chief Counsel (OCC)

The Office of the Chief Counsel represents FDA in court proceedings, handling both civil and criminal enforcement cases and defending challenges to the *Food, Drug, and Cosmetic Act (FD&C Act)*. It also provides legal advice and policy guidance for FDA programs. The office drafts or reviews all proposed and final FDA regulations, performs legal research and gives legal opinions on regulatory issues, actions and petitions. OCC also acts as a liaison to the Department of Justice (DOJ) and other federal agencies for programs administered by FDA. In addition, FDA attorneys are involved in explaining agency programs to Congress, regulated industry and the public. For more information about the Office of the Chief Counsel, visit www.fda.gov/AboutFDA/CentersOffices/OC/OfficeoftheChiefCounsel/default.htm.

Office of the Chief Scientist

The Office of the Chief Scientist provides strategic leadership, coordination and expertise to support scientific excellence, innovation and capacity. It fosters the development and use of innovative technologies and provides cross-agency scientific coordination and supports the professional development of FDA scientists in all areas through the Commissioner's Fellowship Program, continuing education and scientific interaction with academia. In today's environment, the office supports science and public health activities to effectively anticipate and respond to counterterrorism and emerging deliberate and natural threats (e.g., chemical, biological, radiological and nuclear) to US and global health and security. Offices under the auspices of the Office of the Chief Scientist include:
- Office of Counterterrorism and Emerging Threats
- Office of Scientific Integrity
- Office of the Ombudsman
- Office of Science and Innovation
- Office of Critical Path Programs

More information about the Office of the Chief Scientist may be found at www.fda.gov/AboutFDA/CentersOffices/OC/OfficeofScientificandMedicalPrograms/default.htm

Office of International Programs

The Office of International Programs (OIP) is the focal point for all international FDA matters. It works in

Figure 7-1. US Food and Drug Administration Organizational Chart

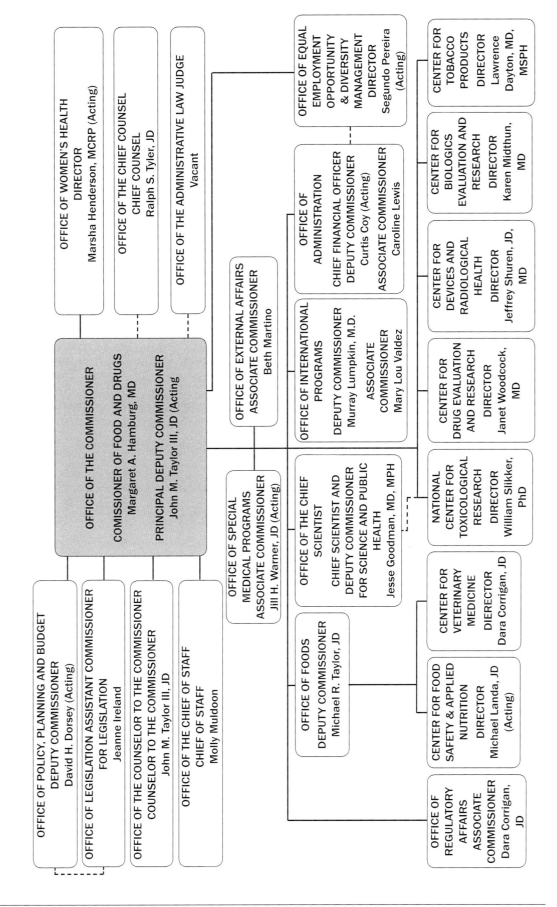

collaboration with international health and regulatory partners through ongoing communications, cooperation on health and regulatory issues, exchanges of information and documents, technical cooperation and training, personnel exchanges and certification of certain products exported to and from the US.

OIP activities include bilateral arrangements such as memoranda of understanding; formal arrangements with regulatory counterparts in other countries; participation in regional programs such as the Trilateral Cooperation (US/Canada/Mexico); multilateral organizations such as the World Health Organization and Pan American Health Organization; and taking part in harmonization and multilateral activities such as Codex Alimentarius and the International Conference on Harmonisation.

In addition, FDA has established a permanent presence in China, India, Europe and Latin America and there are ongoing efforts to establish a presence in the Middle East.

For more information about the Office of International Programs, see www.fda.gov/AboutFDA/CentersOffices/OC/OfficeofInternationalPrograms/ucm236581.htm.

Office of Special Medical Programs

The Office of Special Medical Programs serves as the agency focal point for special programs and initiatives that are cross-cutting and clinical, scientific and/or regulatory in nature.

According to the FDA website, The Office of Special Medical Programs provides for:
- coordinating internal and external review of pediatric science, safety, ethical and international issues as mandated by law and agency activities
- overseeing the implementation of the orphan products provisions of the *FD&C Act*
- executive leadership to the Office of Good Clinical Practice
- overseeing the functions of the Office of Combination Products as provided in the *FD&C Act*
- advisory committee oversight and management staff, working in close collaboration with all FDA centers to provide consistent operations and seek continuous improvements in the agency advisory committee program
- liaison with the Office of the Secretary, the DHHS Committee Management Office, all of FDA's center advisory committee support staff and other organizations/offices within FDA
- ensuring that all FDA committee management activities are consistent with the provisions of *Federal Advisory Committee Act*, departmental policies, and related regulations and statutes

The Office of Special Medical Programs includes the following offices:
- Office of Combination Products
- Office of Good Clinical Practice
- Office of Orphan Product Development
- Office of Pediatric Therapeutics

More information on the Office of Special Medical Programs can be found at www.fda.gov/AboutFDA/CentersOffices/OC/OfficeofScienceandHealthCoordination/default.htm.

Center for Drug Evaluation and Research (CDER)

CDER evaluates all new prescription and over-the-counter drugs before they are sold to ensure that they are safe and effective. The center routinely monitors television, radio and print drug ads to ensure they are truthful and balanced. CDER also plays a critical role in providing healthcare professionals and consumers with information on how to use drugs appropriately and safely. More information on CDER may be found at www.fda.gov/AboutFDA/CentersOffices/CDER/default.htm.

Center for Biologics Evaluation and Research (CBER)

CBER regulates biological products for disease prevention and treatment, including vaccines, protein-based products such as monoclonal antibodies and cytokines, and blood and blood products such as plasma, blood-derived proteins, tests used to screen blood donors and devices used to make blood products. More information on CBER, including the organizational structure, may be found at www.fda.gov/AboutFDA/CentersOffices/CBER/default.htm.

Center for Devices and Radiological Health (CDRH)

CDRH is tasked with ensuring that new medical devices are safe and effective before they are marketed. CDRH regulates medical devices and radiation-emitting products such as microwaves, television sets, cell phones and lasers to ensure they meet radiation safety standards. Many of these devices are the first of a kind. The center also monitors devices throughout the product lifecycle, including a nationwide postmarket surveillance system. More information on CDRH, including the center's organizational structure, may be found at www.fda.gov/AboutFDA/CentersOffices/CDRH/default.htm.

Center for Veterinary Medicine (CVM)

CVM helps ensure that animal food products are safe. CVM regulates the manufacture and distribution of food additives and drugs that will be given to animals. CVM

Table 7-1. CDER vs. CBER Product Oversight Responsibilities

CDER Oversight	CBER Oversight

• Small Molecule Drugs
• Therapeutic Biologics
   o Monoclonal antibodies
   o Cytokines
   o Growth factors
   o Enzymes and Interferons (including recombinant versions)
   o Proteins intended for therapeutic use derived from animals or microorganisms
   o Therapeutic immunotherapies
	• Vaccines
	• Blood products
	• Plasma expanders
	• Gene therapy
	• Products composed of human or animal cells or cell parts
	• Allergen patch tests and allergenic extracts
	• Antitoxins
	• Antivenins
	• Venoms
	• In vitro diagnostics
	• Toxoids/toxins intended for immunization

also evaluates the safety and effectiveness of drugs used to treat companion (pet) animals. More information on CVM may be found at http://www.fda.gov/AboutFDA/CentersOffices/CVM/default.htm.

Center for Food Safety and Applied Nutrition (CFSAN)

CFSAN is responsible for the safety of almost all food consumed in the US, with the exception of meat, poultry and some egg products, which are regulated by the US Department of Agriculture (USDA). CFSAN pioneered widespread use of the Hazard Analysis and Critical Control Point (HACCP) system, which places preventive controls at the most contamination-prone points in the production process. More information on CFSAN may be found at www.fda.gov/AboutFDA/CentersOffices/CFSAN/default.htm.

National Center for Toxicological Research (NCTR)

In partnership with other FDA entities, government agencies, industry and academia, NCTR conducts research and provides advice and training necessary for science-based decision making and developing sound regulatory policy. For example, in the areas of counterterrorism and food defense, NCTR scientists collaborate with scientists from other FDA centers and several federal and state agencies to evaluate the disease-causing potential of food-borne pathogens and to develop methods for rapid detection of bacterial pathogens. NCTR researchers, in collaboration with the National Institute of Child Health and Human Development (NICHD), initiated an animal study of a drug used to treat attention deficit disorder in children to assess whether this drug causes genetic alterations in children. More information about NCTR may be found at www.fda.gov/AboutFDA/CentersOffices/NCTR/default.htm.

Center for Tobacco Products (CTP)

CTP is responsible for overseeing the implementation of the *Family Smoking Prevention and Tobacco Control Act*, which became law on 22 June 2009. FDA responsibilities under the law include establishing performance standards, performing premarket review for new and modified risk tobacco products, reviewing labeling, and establishing and enforcing advertising and promotion restrictions. More information about CTP may be found at www.fda.gov/AboutFDA/CentersOffices/AbouttheCenterforTobaccoProducts/default.htm.

Office of Regulatory Affairs (ORA)

ORA advises and assists the FDA commissioner and other key officials on regulations and compliance matters. ORA evaluates and coordinates all proposed FDA legal actions to ascertain compliance with regulatory policy and enforcement objectives. It is the lead office for all FDA field activities and executes direct line authority over all agency field operations. It provides direction and counsel to FDA field offices in implementing FDA policies and operational guidelines. The Quality System Inspection Technique (QSIT) guide, which provides guidance to agency field staff on the inspectional process used to assess a manufacturer's compliance with the Quality System Regulation, was developed by ORA and CDRH staff. ORA also directs and coordinates the agency's emergency preparedness and civil defense programs. More information may be obtained at http://www.fda.gov/AboutFDA/CentersOffices/ORA/default.htm.

Agencies With Related Responsibilities
Federal Trade Commission (FTC)

FTC enforces the *Federal Trade Commission Act*, which prohibits unfair or deceptive acts or practices in or affecting commerce. The act prohibits the dissemination of any false advertisement for the purpose of inducing the purchase of food, drugs, devices, services or cosmetics. FTC is also empowered to seek monetary redress and other relief for conduct injurious to customers.

Per a 1971 memorandum of understanding (MOU), FDA has primary jurisdiction over advertising of prescription drugs and restricted devices, and over labeling of all products it regulates. FTC has primary jurisdiction over advertising of products other than restricted devices and prescription drugs. The two agencies cooperate in law enforcement efforts. For example, FTC and FDA both sent Warning Letters to website operators who were marketing coral calcium products claiming that coral calcium was an effective treatment or cure for cancer and/or other diseases.[2] While the FTC letter stated that such unsupported claims were false and deceptive and were unlawful under the *FTC Act*, FDA warned website operators that their products were in violation of the *FD&C Act* because of disease claims and unsubstantiated structure/function claims. FDA compliance and law enforcement personnel have access to FTC's secure, online complaint database, Consumer Sentinel, which receives thousands of complaints each year. More information on FTC may be found at www.ftc.gov/.

Center for Medicare and Medicaid Services (CMS)

CMS is a federal agency within DHHS. Formerly the Health Care Financing Administration (HCFA), CMS is responsible for Medicare, Medicaid and other programs. While FDA's focus is on safety and effectiveness, CMS evaluates whether new technologies are necessary and reasonable. CMS is not bound by FDA decisions and expects the clinical utility of new technologies to be proven in order to assign coding and reimbursement. Currently the two agencies review products serially. Per a DHHS announcement on 14 January 2005, FDA and CMS have agreed to work together in specific areas. At the request of the applicant and with the concurrence of both agencies, parallel review may be conducted to minimize delays between marketing approval and reimbursement. With respect to postmarket surveillance, FDA may make greater use of existing CMS mechanisms for collection of new data through the Medicare drug benefit. More information on CMS may be found at www.cms.hhs.gov/.

CMS has jurisdiction over the *Health Insurance Portability and Accountability Act* (*HIPAA*), which was enacted by Congress in 1996 to create a national standard for protecting the privacy of patients' personal health information. The regulation requires safeguards to protect the security and confidentiality of an individual's protected health information (PHI). The general rule is that healthcare entities may not use or disclose PHI without an individual's written authorization, with some exceptions as permitted or required by law. *HIPAA* allows for civil and criminal penalties for privacy and security violations. *HIPAA* also standardized the electronic exchange of health-related administrative information, such as claims forms. Where a healthcare entity conducts clinical research involving PHI, physician-investigators need to understand the Privacy Rule's restrictions on its use and disclosure for research purposes. More information on the impact of *HIPAA* as it relates to clinical research may be found at http://privacyruleandresearch.nih.gov/clin_research.asp.

Consumer Product Safety Commission (CPSC)

CPSC is responsible for ensuring the safety of consumer goods such as household appliances (excluding those that emit radiation), paint, child-resistant packages and baby toys. Tobacco, pesticides, motor vehicles and products subject to FDA jurisdiction are expressly exempt from regulation under the *Consumer Product Safety Act* (*CPSA*). FDA and CPSC work cooperatively for consumer protection. For example, articles employed in the preparation or holding of food that malfunction and cause contamination or spoilage (e.g., home canning equipment, pressure cookers, refrigerators, freezers and can openers) are subject to regulation as "consumer products" by CPSC under the *CPSA*. Under the *FD&C Act*, FDA may take action against manufacturers of food that has been contaminated or spoiled by such articles and shipped in interstate commerce.[3] More information on CPSC may be found at www.cpsc.gov/.

Securities and Exchange Commission (SEC)

SEC's primary mission is to protect the investing public and maintain the integrity of the securities market. FDA assists in SEC investigations of possible violations of federal securities laws. FDA also supports SEC staff in assessing the accuracy of statements by FDA-regulated firms in SEC filings, especially where such statements can have a powerful effect on stock prices. Under measures adopted in February 2004 to improve the sharing of information between the two agencies, a reporting process was established to allow any FDA employees who suspect erroneous or exaggerated public statements by a company to bring them to the attention of SEC staff as quickly and efficiently as possible. More information on SEC may be found at www.sec.gov/.

Occupational Safety and Health Administration (OSHA)

The *Occupational Safety and Health Act* (*OSH Act*) created OSHA at the federal level within the Department of Labor. OSHA's mission is to prevent work-related injuries, illnesses and deaths by issuing and enforcing rules (called standards) for workplace safety and health. FDA's statutory authority does not extend to the occupational safety and health responsibilities of OSHA. FDA has no workplace inspection program. However, the agencies coordinate their

Table 7-2. Selected Primary FDA Centers/Offices Involved in Sponsor Interface During the Development and Approval of Drugs and Devices

FDA Center/Office	Primary Responsibility
Office of the Commissioner • Office of Orphan Products Development (OOPD) • Office of Combination Products (OCP)	Review and adjudicate requests for orphan drug designation and review and award orphan drug grants
Center for Biologics Evaluation and Research (CBER) • Office of Biostatistics and Epidemiology • Office of Blood Research and Review • Office of Vaccines Research and Review • Office of Compliance and Biologics Quality • Office of Cellular, Tissue, and Gene Therapies	Evaluate and monitor the safety and effectiveness of biological products for disease prevention and treatment, including blood and blood products, vaccines, human gene therapy, xenotransplants, human tissues and cellular product and allergenics.

Center for Drug Evaluation and Research (CDER)
• Office of Compliance
  o Division of Compliance Risk Mgmt. and Surveillance (assigns NDC numbers)
• Office of Pharmacoepidemiology and Statistical Sciences
  o Office of Drug Safety
    □ Division of Drug Risk Evaluation (brand name review)
  o Office of Biostatistics (Biostats reviewers)
• Office of Clinical Pharmacology and Biopharmaceutics (Clin Pharm reviewers)
• Office of Medical Policy
  o Division of Drug Marketing, Advertising, and Communication (DDMAC)
• Office of New Drugs (includes OTC products)
• Office of Pharmaceutical Science
  o Office of Generic Drugs (OGD)
  o Office of New Drug Chemistry (CMC Reviewers and CMC Project Managers)
	Evaluate and monitor the safety and effectiveness of all prescription and over-the-counter drugs (including peptides and well-characterized proteins used for therapeutic purposes).

Center for Devices and Radiological Health (CDRH) • Office of Compliance • Office of Device Evaluation • Office of In Vitro Diagnostic Device Evaluation and Safety	Evaluate and monitor the safety and effectiveness of new medical devices for human use and assure that radiation-emitting products (e.g., microwave ovens, cell phones, x-ray machines) meet radiation safety standards.
Center for Veterinary Medicine (CVM) • Office of New Animal Drug Evaluation • Office of Surveillance and Compliance • Office of Minor Use and Minor Species	Evaluate and monitor the safety and effectiveness of new drugs for animals and the safety of animal food products.

efforts in cases of overlapping regulatory responsibility (e.g., unshielded syringes and natural rubber latex). More information on OSHA may be found at www.osha.gov/.

Tax and Trade Bureau (TTB)

The *Federal Alcohol Administration Act* (*FAAA*) provides for federal regulation of beer, wine and distilled spirits. It establishes requirements for packaging used to hold alcohol over and above those imposed by FDA for foods under the *FD&C Act*. The *FAAA* is administered by the Treasury Department's Alcohol and Tobacco Tax and Trade Bureau (TTB). TTB consults with FDA regarding the approval of ingredients in alcoholic beverages and the requirements of label disclosure. Under a 1987 MOU, FDA is directed to contact TTB when it learns or is advised that an alcoholic beverage is or may be adulterated. More information on TTB may be found at www.ttb.gov.

United States Department of Agriculture (USDA)

USDA's Food Safety and Inspection Service (FSIS) has oversight over dairy, poultry, fruit and meat products, except for shell eggs, for which FDA and USDA share jurisdiction. Egg processing plants (egg washing, sorting, egg breaking and pasteurizing operations) are under USDA jurisdiction. However, FDA is responsible for egg-containing products and other egg processing not covered by USDA, e.g., restaurants, bakeries, cake mix plants, etc. The *Poultry Products Inspection Act* (*PPIA*) defines the term "poultry" as any domesticated bird. USDA has interpreted the term "poultry" to include domestic ducks, domestic geese, chickens and turkeys. FDA is responsible for all non-specified birds, including wild turkeys, wild ducks and wild geese. FDA also regulates game meats such as venison and ostrich. FDA and USDA together published guidance on quality and environmental concerns for companies producing human and animal drugs from genetically modified plants. FDA has jurisdiction over labeling of genetically modified foods and food from cloned animals. More information on USDA may be found at www.usda.gov/wps/portal/usdahome.

Department of Commerce (DOC)

FDA operates a mandatory safety program for all fish and fishery products under the provisions of the *FD&C Act*. Seafood is one of the few FDA-regulated food groups further regulated under a system of risk prevention controls known as Hazard Analysis and Critical Control Points (HACCP). Under HACCP, domestic and foreign processors are required to prepare site- and product-specific plans that analyze potential safety hazards, determine where they are likely to occur during processing, identify control points and how they will be monitored, and study how hazards are being controlled.

The National Oceanic and Atmospheric Administration (NOAA) within DOC oversees fisheries management in the US. It has its own authority for the promulgation of grade standards and for inspection and certification of fish and shellfish. NOAA Fisheries administers a voluntary, fee-for-service seafood inspection program that exceeds FDA HACCP-based requirements by providing grading, certification, label review, laboratory testing, training and consultative services. Participants may use official marks on compliant products, indicating that they are federally inspected. More information may be found at www.nmfs.noaa.gov/.

Environmental Protection Agency (EPA)

The mission of EPA is to protect human health and the environment, which includes jurisdiction over the public water supply. In the past, FDA considered drinking water to be a food. However, both agencies have determined that the passage of the *Safe Drinking Water Act* (*SDWA*) in 1974 implicitly repealed FDA's authority under the *FD&C Act* over drinking water. EPA and FDA have a 1979 Memorandum of Agreement specifying that EPA regulates and develops national standards for the safety of drinking water from municipal water supplies while FDA regulates the labeling and safety of bottled water as a consumer beverage.

Antimicrobial surface solutions applied to counter tops, table tops, food processing equipment, cutlery, dishware or cookware, to sanitize such objects after they have been washed, meet the definition of "pesticide chemical" and therefore, are subject to regulation by EPA. However, any antimicrobial surface solutions used to sanitize food packaging materials are excluded from "pesticide chemical" classification and are considered food additives subject to regulation by FDA. Materials preservatives are sometimes incorporated into food-contact articles to protect the finished product from discoloration, degradation or decomposition due to microbiological activity, rather than to prevent microbial activity. These materials are regulated as food additives by FDA. Antimicrobials impregnated into food packaging to protect either the package, or to extend the shelf life of the food are also regulated as food additives by FDA. More information on EPA may be found at www.epa.gov/.

FDA, USDA and EPA share responsibility for regulating pesticides. EPA determines the safety and effectiveness of the chemicals and establishes tolerance levels for residues on feed crops, as well as on raw and processed foods. FDA and USDA are responsible for monitoring the food supply to ensure that pesticide residues do not exceed the allowable levels in the products under their jurisdictions.

Drug Enforcement Administration (DEA)

Illegal drugs with no approved medical use, such as heroin and cocaine, are under the jurisdiction of DEA. FDA assists DEA in deciding how stringent DEA controls should be on drugs that are medically accepted but that have a strong potential for abuse. DEA establishes limits on the amount of these prescription drugs that is permitted to be manufactured each year. More information on DEA may be found at www.usdoj.gov/dea/index.htm.

Tips for Obtaining Information

Information for consumers and industry can be obtained directly from FDA. Each agency division has its own website, containing a wide variety of information including laws and regulations, administrative information regarding FDA's organizational structure and staff contact information, news and events, problem reporting, guidance documents, forms and links to other national and international regulatory agencies. There also are databases of products cleared or approved for marketing, adverse event reporting and recalls. The websites and databases are fully searchable.

A network of FDA offices exists to help small businesses. The Commissioner's Office of the Ombudsman liaises with the Small Business National Ombudsman to resolve complaints and answer questions. Product-specific centers each have their own ombudsmen. Also, each of the five regional offices has a small business representative available to answer questions and provide training. The Division of Small Manufacturers, International, and Consumer Assistance (DSMICA) provides assistance to medical device manufacturers and consumers. A detailed directory identifies staff by area of expertise, and a toll-free number will connect you directly to staff members during normal business hours. Similarly, CDER and the other product-specific centers have staff members available to answer inquiries from small business owners and help explain the agency's structure and rules.

Information pertaining to the rulemaking process can be found at www.regulations.gov. This website facilitates public participation in the federal rulemaking process by enabling the public to view and comment on federal regulatory actions. Information may also be obtained through the Regulatory Affairs Professional Society (RAPS), which provides numerous resources to industry professionals. In addition to RAPS workshops and conferences, local RAPS chapters provide educational events for industry professionals.

Summary

FDA's regulatory responsibility has evolved over 150 years from being tasked with regulating foods to include drug, cosmetics, devices, biologics and tobacco products.

FDA is responsible for protecting the public health by assuring the safety, efficacy and security of human and veterinary drugs, biological products, medical devices, cosmetics, products that emit radiation and the food supply.

During the 19th century, states exercised principal control over domestically produced and distributed foods and drugs, while federal authority was restricted to imported foods and drugs. Dr. Harvey Wiley, the father of the food and drug laws, was concerned about the use of preservative chemicals as "adulterants" in food products. He organized various groups to support a federal law to prohibit the adulteration and misbranding of foods and drugs.

FDA is an agency within DHHS and consists of nine main centers/offices.

The Office of the Commissioner is responsible for the efficient and effective implementation of FDA's mission.

CDER evaluates all new prescription and over-the-counter drugs before they are sold to ensure that they are safe and effective.

CBER regulates biological products for disease prevention and treatment, including vaccines and blood and blood products such as plasma, blood-derived proteins,

tests used to screen blood donors and devices used to make blood products.

CDRH is tasked with ensuring that new medical devices are safe and effective before they are marketed.

CVM helps ensure that animal food additives and drug products are safe.

CFSAN is responsible for the safety of most food consumed in the US, with the exception of meat, poultry and some egg products, which are regulated by the USDA.

NCTR conducts research and provides advice and training necessary for science-based decision making and developing sound regulatory policy.

CTP is responsible for overseeing the implementation of the *Family Smoking Prevention and Tobacco Control Act*, which became law on 22 June 2009.

ORA advises and assists the FDA commissioner and other key officials on regulations and compliance matters and oversees all agency field operations.

Other agencies play a role or work with FDA in the regulation of food, drugs, cosmetics and devices. These agencies include: FTC, CMS, CPSC, SEC, OSHA, TTB, USDA, DOC, EPA and DEA.

References

1. www.nytimes.com/2008/11/02/magazine/02fda-t. html. Accessed 11 May 2011.
2. www.ftc.gov/opa/2003/06/trudeau.shtm. Accessed 11 May 2011.
3. www.fda.gov.

Recommended Reading

Grossman LA. "Food, Drugs and Droods: A Historical Consideration of Definitions and Categories in American Food and Drug Law." *Cornell Law Review.* Volume 93, pp. 1091–1148 (2008).

Burditt GM. "The History of Food Law." *Food and Drug Law Journal*, 50th Anniversary Special Edition, pp 197–201 (2009).

History of US Food, Drug and Cosmetic Laws

By Nandini Murthy, RAC and Richard Morroney, CQA, RAC

Objectives
❑ Provide an overview of the laws, regulations and regulatory agencies governing foods, drugs and medical products marketed in the US

❑ Discuss the historical context in which those laws were enacted

❑ Review the differences between laws, regulations and guidance documents

❑ Provide an overview of the rulemaking process

Laws, Regulations and Guidelines Covered in this Chapter
❑ *Pure Food and Drugs Act of 1906*

❑ *Federal Food, Drug, and Cosmetic Act of 1938*

❑ *Nutrition Labeling and Education Act of 1990*

❑ *Bioterrorism Act of 2002*

❑ *Food Allergen Labeling and Consumer Protection Act of 2004*

❑ *Color Additive Amendment of 1960*

❑ *Kefauver-Harris Amendments of 1962*

❑ *Controlled Substances Act of 1970*

❑ *Drug Price Competition and Patent Term Restoration Act of 1984 (Hatch-Waxman Act)*

❑ *Prescription Drug User Fee Act of 1992*

❑ *Food and Drug Administration Modernization Act of 1997*

❑ *Food and Drug Administration Amendments Act of 2007*

❑ *Medical Device Amendments of 1976*

❑ *Safe Medical Devices Act of 1990*

❑ *Medical Device User Fee and Modernization Act of 2002*

❑ *Durham-Humphrey Amendment of 1951*

❑ *Orphan Drug Act of 1983*

❑ *Prescription Drug Amendments of 1992*

❑ *FDA Export Reform and Enhancement Act of 1996*

❑ *Pediatric Research Equity Act of 2003*

Introduction
The history of modern food and drug law begins in the 20th century. During the 1800s, commerce in food and drugs was largely unregulated due to concerns about government interference with free trade and the inability of the individual states to control sales of products that were manufactured in other states.

This led to conditions such as those described in *The Jungle* by Upton Sinclair, published in 1906. Although it was presented as a work of fiction, the book's description of the unsanitary conditions in Chicago's meatpacking plants led to widespread public outrage and a demand for legislation.

In response, Congress passed the *Pure Food and Drugs Act* in 1906. This act prohibited interstate commerce of mislabeled and adulterated drugs and food.

Pure Food and Drugs Act of 1906

The 1906 *Pure Food and Drugs Act*, which the Bureau of Chemistry was charged to enforce, prohibited the interstate transport of unlawful food and drugs under penalty of seizure of questionable products and/or prosecution of responsible parties. The statute provided: "The term 'food,' as used herein, shall include all articles used for food, drink, confectionary, or condiment by man or other animals, whether simple, mixed or compound." The 1906 act defined "drug" as including "all medicines and preparations recognized in the United States Pharmacopoeia (USP) or National Formulary (NF) for internal or external use, and any substance or mixture of substances intended to be used for the cure, mitigation, or prevention of disease of either man or other animals." This "intended use" language, which was later also incorporated into the definition of "device," survives largely intact in the *Food, Drug, and Cosmetics Act* (*FD&C Act*) today.

The basis of the law rested on the regulation of product labeling rather than premarket approval. The food or drug label could not be false or misleading in any particular, and the presence and amount of 11 dangerous ingredients—including alcohol, heroin and cocaine—had to be listed. Specific variations from the applicable USP and NF standards for drugs were to be plainly stated on the label. Labels were not even required to state the weight or measure; only that any contents statement, if used, be truthful. If the manufacturer opted to list a food's weight or measure, the information had to be accurate. The law prohibited the addition of any ingredients that would substitute for the food, conceal damage, pose a health hazard or constitute a filthy or decomposed substance.

The law assumed that average consumers could avoid risks if they were made aware of same via product labeling; therefore, it relied upon consumer vigilance to assess labeling for deception or harm. Food manufacturers were not required to submit labeling for regulatory review. The Bureau of Chemistry was tasked with actively identifying violations and bringing legal action. The law enabled the government to prosecute manufacturers of illegal products but lacked affirmative requirements to guide compliance.

The Federal Food, Drug, and Cosmetic Act (FD&C Act) of 1938

The 1938 *FD&C Act* replaced the 1906 act and revised the misbranding standard for therapeutic claims in a way that helped further differentiate food labeling from drug labeling. The *Pure Food and Drugs Act*, as revised in 1912, stated that a drug was misbranded if its label contained a "false and fraudulent" statement regarding "curative or therapeutic effect." The requirement of demonstrating fraud made this a difficult standard for the US Food and Drug Administration (FDA) to satisfy. The 1938 act relaxed the standard from "false and fraudulent" to "false or misleading in any particular," a change that greatly eased FDA's burden in proving misbranding. The 1938 act also introduced premarket drug review, requiring the manufacturer of a "new drug" (defined as a drug not generally recognized as safe) to submit a New Drug Application (NDA) to FDA, setting forth the company's evidence of the drug's safety. It prohibited false therapeutic claims for drugs, while a separate law granted the Federal Trade Commission (FTC) jurisdiction over drug advertising. This act also brought cosmetics and medical devices under FDA's control and mandated legally enforceable food standards. In addition, tolerances for certain poisonous substances were addressed. The law formally authorized factory inspections and added injunctions to the enforcement tools at the agency's disposal.

The *FD&C Act* and its subsequent amendments remain the statutory framework under which FDA operates today. The *Durham-Humphrey Amendments* of 1951 clarified what constituted a prescription versus an over-the-counter drug. The *Kefauver-Harris Amendments* of 1962 mandated the establishment of efficacy as well as safety before a drug could be marketed, required FDA to assess the efficacy of all drugs introduced since 1938, instituted stricter agency control over drug trials (including a requirement that patients involved must give their informed consent), transferred regulation of prescription drug advertising from FTC to FDA, established Good Manufacturing Practice (GMP) requirements for the drug industry and granted FDA greater powers to access company production and control records to verify those practices.

Regulating Devices After the 1938 Act

While premarket approval in the 1938 *FD&C Act* did not apply to devices, for regulatory purposes, the new law equated them to drugs in every other sense. Issues facing FDA included increasing medical device quackery and a proliferation of medical technology in the post-World War II years. On the heels of a therapeutic disaster in which thousands of women were injured by the Dalkon Shield intrauterine device, Congress passed the 1976 *Medical Device Amendments*. This legislation established three classes of medical devices, each requiring a different level of regulatory scrutiny, up to premarket approval.

Regulating Foods After the 1938 Act

Significant amendments to the *FD&C Act* regarding the regulation of food include the *Nutrition Labeling and Education Act* of 1990, which requires manufacturers to provide standardized food labels and consistency in health claims and serving sizes. The *Dietary Supplement Health and Education Act* of 1994 was another significant amendment, classifying dietary supplements as foods and establishing a framework and requirements for labeling and GMPs, among other regulatory provisions.

The events of 11 September 2001 prompted a closer look at the food industry, leading to the *Bioterrorism Act* of 2002. This law and its implementing regulations were designed to improve the ability to trace the movement of foods through international and interstate commerce, to restrict the availability of certain biological agents and toxins and to improve the security of the drinking water supply.

In 2004, concerns regarding food allergies led to the passage of the *Food Allergen Labeling and Consumer Protection Act*, which requires food labels to include specific statements regarding the presence of eight major allergens.

Regulating Cosmetics After the 1938 Act

The *Color Additive Amendment* of 1960 requires manufacturers to establish the safety of color additives in foods, drugs and cosmetics, and was the source of the designation of colors as FD&C (safe for foods, drugs and cosmetics), D&C (safe for drugs and cosmetics) or Ext. D&C (for externally applied products only).

An important point worth noting is that some cosmetics are regulated as drugs based upon their labeling. For instance, cosmetics containing sunscreens are considered drugs because they are intended to affect the body's physiological response to solar radiation.

Current Trends in Drugs and Devices—Amending the FD&C Act
The Orphan Drug Act of 1983

The 1983 *Orphan Drug Act* originally defined the term "orphan drug" as "a drug for a disease or condition which is rare." In October 1984, the term "rare" was defined in an amendment as "any rare disease or condition which (a) affects less than 200,000 persons in the U.S. or (b) affects more than 200,000 persons in the U.S. but for which there is no reasonable expectation that the cost of developing and making available in the U.S. a drug for such disease or condition will be recovered from sales in the U.S. of such drug." The act guarantees the developer of an orphan product seven years of market exclusivity following FDA's approval of the product. Incentives also include tax credits for clinical research undertaken by a sponsor to generate data required for marketing approval.

The Drug Price Competition and Patent Term Restoration Act of 1984

Because the approval process for each new product required the submission of full safety and efficacy data, the economic pressures resulting from the lengthy review process led to the *Drug Price Competition and Patent Restoration Act* of 1984, also known as the *Hatch-Waxman Act*. This law established a process for the approval of drugs based upon comparison to an already approved product, and provided for exclusive marketing status for a period of time based upon the length of the approval process for new drugs or upon the patent status of the branded drug for generics.

This act included provisions for patent term extension, which gave certain patent holders the opportunity to extend patent terms by five years for human drug products, including antibiotics and biologics, medical devices, food additives and color additives. By giving inventors a portion of the patent term lost during federal regulatory review, Congress sought to restore some of the incentive for innovation to US domestic drug companies that was weakened as federal premarket approval requirements became more expensive and time-consuming. The *Hatch Waxman Act* authorized Abbreviated New Drug Applications (ANDAs) for generic drugs and specifically provided that FDA could require only bioavailability studies for ANDAs.

The *Safe Medical Devices Act* (*SMDA*) of 1990

The *SMDA* defined a "medical device" as "any instrument, apparatus, or other article that is used to prevent, diagnose, mitigate, or treat a disease or to affect the structure or function of the body, with the exception of drugs." It required user facilities and manufacturers to report certain adverse events to FDA, where a legally marketed medical device either had the potential to cause or contributed to a death, illness or injury. It instituted device tracking and postmarket surveillance requirements. It allowed FDA to temporarily suspend as well as withdraw approval of an application for premarket approval. The rule provided for civil penalties for violation of a requirement of the *FD&C Act* relating to devices. The act amended the *FD&C Act* to create an incentive for the development of orphan or humanitarian use devices (HUDs), defined as devices for use in the treatment or diagnosis of diseases or conditions affecting fewer than 4,000 patients in the US each year.

The *Prescription Drug User Fee Act* (*PDUFA*) of 1992

PDUFA authorized FDA to collect fees from companies that produce certain human drug and biological products and submit applications for FDA review. In addition, companies are required to pay annual fees for each manufacturing establishment and for each prescription drug product marketed. Previously, taxpayers paid for product reviews through budgets provided by Congress. In the new program, industry provides the funding in exchange for FDA's agreement to meet drug review performance goals, which emphasize timeliness.

The *Food and Drug Administration Modernization Act (FDAMA)* of 1997

FDAMA provided additional authority for monitoring the progress of drug and biologic postmarketing studies. The provisions in this act required FDA to issue regulations that allowed clinical study sponsors to modify any investigational device or study protocol by submitting to FDA a "Notice of Change" five days after instituting such a change, where such changes did not significantly affect the study design or patient safety. The law codified the expedited review policy for certain medical devices, amended and clarified the humanitarian device provisions of *SMDA* and allowed FDA to recognize international or other national standards. *FDAMA* also directed FDA to consider least-burdensome means of establishing substantial equivalence for certain device marketing applications. The act repealed the mandatory tracking requirements for some high-risk devices imposed by *SMDA*, and instead established requirements and a process under which FDA may order device tracking.

The *Medical Device User Fee and Modernization Act* of 2002 (*MDUFMA*)

MDUFMA established fees for premarket approval applications, supplements and 510(k) submissions. In return, FDA committed to strict performance goals for medical technology reviews.

The *Pediatric Research Equity Act (PREA)* of 2003

PREA gave FDA clear authority to require pediatric studies of drugs when other approaches are not sufficient to ensure that drugs are safe and effective for children. If the course of a disease and the effects of the drug treatment for that disease are "sufficiently similar in adults and pediatric patients," FDA may waive the requirement if it can be concluded that "pediatric effectiveness can be extrapolated from adequate and well-controlled studies in adults."

The *Food and Drug Administration Amendments Act (FDAAA)* of 2007

FDAAA reauthorized a number of key programs, including *PDUFA, MDUFMA* and *PREA. FDAAA* requires all clinical trials of drugs, biologics and devices—except Phase 1 clinical trials—to be registered in a clinical trial registry databank. ClinicalTrials.gov, established by the National Institutes of Health (NIH)/National Library of Medicine (NLM) in collaboration with FDA, meets *FDAAA* man-

dates. The results of clinical trials that serve as the basis for an efficacy claim or postmarketing studies are also required to be posted. *FDAAA* provides civil monetary penalties of as much as $10,000 for failure to comply with the registration requirements. If violations are not corrected within 30 days, additional penalties of up to $10,000 per day of violation may accrue. *FDAAA* permits FDA to require sponsors to submit direct-to-consumer (DTC) television advertisements for agency review no later than 45 days before dissemination of the advertisement, and permits FDA to impose penalties of as much as $500,000 for false and misleading DTC advertisements. In addition, civil penalties of as much as $10 million may be imposed for violations of postmarket studies, clinical trials or labeling changes required under *FDAAA*.

More information about the laws enforced by FDA can be obtained at www.fda.gov/RegulatoryInformation/Legislation/default.htm.

Other Food- and Drug-Related Laws

While the discussion above covers many of the laws that form the basis of current regulations, there are many others that affect foods, drugs and medical devices. **Table 8-1** lists some of these other laws.

Laws, Regulations and Guidance

Laws begin as legislation enacted by the US Congress. A bill is introduced by one house of Congress and is considered in committee where public hearings may be held. The bill is then amended as necessary and reintroduced into committee for debate and vote. Once approved, it becomes an act and goes through a similar process in the other house of Congress. The act is then submitted to the president. If the president signs the bill, it becomes a law. Laws establish general principles and clarify congressional intent. They can only be changed by Congress. Laws are enforced by regulations through an agency of the executive branch.

Regulations establish standards or requirements of conduct and provide details of how the law is to be followed. Regulations are both interpretive (they explain the meaning of the language of a section of the act) and substantive (they provide a specific scientific or technical basis). They are promulgated through the "rulemaking process" and have the force of law. Guidance documents and guidelines establish principles or practices that represent an agency's thinking. However, they do not go through the formal rulemaking process, and therefore do not have the force of law.

Rulemaking Process

Government agencies create regulations that are derived from statutes created through the legislative branch. Regulations define how FDA regulates products. Regulations are developed through the rulemaking process. Rulemaking is a transparent process that involves

Table 8-1 Other Laws, Regulations and Guidelines

• Federal Meat Inspection Act of 1906
• Poultry Products Inspection Act of 1957
• Egg Products Inspection Act of 1970
• Dietary Supplement Health and Education Act of 1994
• Public Health Service Act of 1944
• GMPs for the 21st Century (2004)
• Wheeler-Lea Act of 1938
• Food Additives Amendment of 1958
• Fair Packaging and Labeling Act of 1967
• Animal Drug Amendments of 1968
• Poison Prevention Packaging Act of 1970
• Infant Formula Act of 1980
• Generic Animal Drug and Patent Term Restoration Act of 1988
• Animal Medicinal Drug Use Clarification Act of 1994
• Food Quality Protection Act of 1996
• Animal Drug Availability Act of 1996
• Best Pharmaceuticals for Children Act of 2002
• Animal Drug User Fee Act of 2003
• Minor Use and Minor Species Animal Health Act of 2001
• Dietary Supplement and Nonprescription Drug Consumer Protection Act of 2006

the public. By law, anyone can participate in this process. Public comments are gathered through proposed rules or petitions. FDA carefully considers the public's comments when drafting final rules. Final rules become federal regulations upon codification in the Code of Federal Regulations. The *Administrative Procedure Act* of 1946 gave the public the right to participate in the rulemaking process by commenting on proposed rules. The public's rights were further extended through procedural rules that established a 60-day minimum public comment period for significant regulations. The enactment of the *Government in the Sunshine Act* of 1976 required advanced notice of rulemaking meetings, and required them to be open to the public. A regulatory agenda known as the Unified Agenda is published semi-annually and summarizes each agency's planned rulemaking activities for the following six months.

Proposed Rules

New regulations or revisions to existing regulations are announced in the *Federal Register*. A Notice of Proposed Rulemaking describes the rule and provides background information. A comment period is established that defines how long the agency will accept comments. The *Federal Register* announcement marks the beginning of the comment period.

Comment Period/FDA Action

Public comments may be submitted electronically through the regulations.gov website. Comments are logged,

numbered and placed in a file upon receipt by FDA. The comments become part of the public record and are available for anyone to read on the regulations.gov website or in the FDA Dockets Management Reading Room (Room 1061, 5630 Fishers Lane, Rockville, MD). Comment periods are generally at least 60 days including weekends and holidays, and can be as long as one year. Some comment periods may be shorter than 60 days. During the comment period, FDA carefully analyzes the public's comments. Upon the expiration of the comment period, FDA may perform one of three actions:

- promulgate interim or final rules
- extend the comment period
- abandon its intention to promulgate a rule

Rule Publication and Codification

Final rules are published in the *Federal Register*. Rules in the *Federal Register* are cited by volume and page number and are codified annually in the Code of Federal Regulations. Title 21 consists of nine volumes divided into two chapters. FDA regulations are provided in Chapter 1, which are contained in the first eight volumes. DEA regulations are provided in Chapter 2 in the ninth volume.

Petitions

Agency processes may be influenced through the petition process. Requests can be made to FDA to issue, change or cancel a regulation. Petitions must contain specific information:

- action requested
- statement of grounds
- environmental impact
- official certification statement
- petitioner identifying information

FDA may request economic impact information after reviewing the petition. FDA management will decide whether to grant or deny the petition after a review period.

Summary

Food and drug law, which provides the framework for regulatory practices, is closely linked to the larger historical context of the times in which the laws were enacted. Many laws, such as the *FD&C Act*, the *Kefauver-Harris Amendments* and the *Bioterrorism Act*, were enacted in response to specific events that called attention to the need for additional authorities or controls. Based on this history, it is likely that future such events will continue to shape food and drug law and regulation.

References

1. FDA websites:
    www.fda.gov. Accessed 11 May 2011.
    www.fda.gov/AboutFDA/Transparency/Basics/default.htm. Accessed 11 May 2011.
    www.fda.gov/RegulatoryInformation/Legislation/default.htm. Accessed 11 May 2011.
2. *Fundamentals of Law and Regulation,* Food and Drug Law Institute, Washington, DC, 1997.

Chapter 9

Overview of US Drug, Biologic and Device Regulatory Pathways

By Scott A. Oglesby, PhD

OBJECTIVES

❏ To provide an overview of US federal regulations and processes related to the development of drugs, biologics, devices and combination products and filing of a marketing application

❏ To provide an overview of the scientific questions and approaches that underpin the development process

❏ To provide a roadmap of the facts and related decisions that define how a drug, biologic, device or combination product needs to be developed to meet US federal regulations

LAWS, REGULATIONS AND GUIDELINES COVERED IN THIS CHAPTER

Regulations

❏ 21 CFR 511 New Animal Drugs for Investigational Use

❏ 21 CFR 514 New Animal Drug Applications

❏ 21 CFR 314.92 Drug products for which abbreviated applications may be submitted

❏ 21 CFR 314.93 Petition to request a change from a listed drug

❏ 21 CFR 314.54 Procedure for submission of an application requiring investigations for approval

of a new indication for, or other change from, a listed drug

❏ 21 CFR 310.3 Definitions and interpretations (new drugs)

❏ 21 CFR 316 Orphan Drugs

❏ 21 CFR 312 Subpart E Drugs intended to treat life-threatening and severely debilitating illnesses

❏ 21 CFR 314 Subpart H Accelerated approval of new drugs for serious or life-threatening illnesses

❏ 21 CFR 312 Investigational New Drug Application

❏ 21 CFR 312.50 General responsibilities of sponsors

❏ 21 CFR 312.60 General responsibilities of investigators

❏ 21 CFR 312.33 Annual reports (IND)

❏ 21 CFR 312.32 IND safety reports

❏ 21 CFR 312.23 IND content and format

❏ 21 CFR 312.38 Withdrawal of an IND

❏ 21 CFR 312.45 Inactive status (IND)

❑ 21 CFR 314 Applications for FDA Approval to Market a New Drug

❑ 21 CFR 207 Registration of Producers of Drugs and Listing of Drugs in Commercial Distribution

❑ 21 CFR 190.6 Requirement for premarket notification (dietary supplements)

❑ 21 CFR 3.2(e) Assignment of agency component for review of premarket applications—Definitions

❑ 21 CFR 328–358 OTC Monographs

❑ 21 CFR 330.11 NDA deviations from applicable monograph (OTC drugs)

❑ 21 CFR 10.30 Citizen petition

❑ 21 CFR 862–892 Device Classifications

❑ 21 CFR 807 Subpart E; Premarket notification procedures

❑ 21 CFR 812 Investigational Device Exemptions

❑ 21 CFR 814 Subpart H Humanitarian use devices

❑ 21 CFR 56 Institutional Review Boards

❑ 21 CFR 50 Protection of Human Subjects

❑ 21 CFR 54 Financial Disclosure by Clinical Investigators

❑ 21 CFR 814 Premarket Approval of Medical Devices

❑ 21 CFR 807 Establishment Registration and Device Listing for Manufacturers and Initial Importers of Devices

Guidance Documents

❑ *Guidance for Industry No. 185: Target Animal Safety for Veterinary Pharmaceutical Products VICH GL43 (April 2009)*

❑ *Guidance for Industry No. 104: Content and Format of Effectiveness and Target Animal Safety Technical Sections and Final Study Reports for Submission to the Division of Therapeutic Drugs for Non-Food Animals (July 2001)*

❑ *Guidance for Industry No. 3: General Principles for Evaluating the Safety of Compounds Used in Food-Producing Animals (July 2006)*

❑ *Guidance for Industry No. 149: Studies to Evaluate the Safety of Residues of Veterinary Drugs in Human Food: General Approach to Testing (March 2009)*

❑ *Guideline No. 24: Guidelines for Drug Combinations in Animals (October 1983)*

❑ *Guidance for Industry: Bioavailability and Bioequivalence Studies for Orally Administered Drug Products—General Considerations (March 2003)*

❑ *Guidance for Industry: Food-Effect Bioavailability and Fed Bioequivalence Studies (December 2002)*

❑ *Guidance for Industry: Bioanalytical Method Development (May 2001)*

❑ *Guidance for Industry: Statistical Approaches to Establishing Bioequivalence (January 2001)*

❑ *Guidance for Industry: 180-Day Exclusivity When Multiple ANDAs are Submitted on the Same Day (July 2003)*

❑ *Draft Guidance for Industry: Bioequivalence Recommendations for Specific Products (May 2007)*

❑ *Draft Guidance for Industry: Contents of a Complete Submission for the Evaluation of Proprietary Names (November 2008)*

❑ *Guidance for Industry: Formal Meetings Between the FDA and Sponsors or Applicants (May 2009)*

❑ *Draft Guidance for Industry: End-of Phase 2A Meetings (September 2008)*

❑ *Guidance for Industry: Special Protocol Assessment (May 2002)*

❑ *Guidance for Industry: Fast Track Drug Development Programs—Designation, Development, and Application Review (July 2004)*

❏ *Guidance for Industry M4: Organization of the CTD* (August 2001)

❏ *Guidance for Industry M4Q: The CTD—Quality* (August 2001)

❏ *Guidance for Industry M4S: The CTD—Safety* (August 2001)

❏ *Guidance for Industry M4S: The CTD—Safety Appendices* (August 2001)

❏ *Guidance for Industry M4E: The CTD—Efficacy* (August 2001)

❏ *Guidance for Industry M2 eCTD: Electronic Common Technical Document Specification* (April 2003)

❏ *Draft Guidance for Industry: Animal Models— Essential Elements to Address Efficacy Under the Animal Rule* (January 2009)

❏ *Guidance for Industry: Estimating the Maximum Safe Starting Dose in Initial Clinical Trials for Therapeutics in Adult Healthy Volunteers* (July 2005)

❏ *Draft Guidance: M3(R2) Nonclinical Safety Studies for the Conduct of Human Clinical Trials and Marketing Authorization for Pharmaceuticals* (July 2008)

❏ *Guidance for Industry: Immunotoxicology Evaluation of Investigational New Drugs* (October 2002)

❏ *Guidance for Industry: Nonclinical Evaluation of Pediatric Drug Products* (February 2006)

❏ *Guidance for Industry: Single Dose Acute Toxicity Testing for Pharmaceuticals* (August 1996)

❏ *Guidance for Industry: Dissolution Testing of Immediate Release Solid Oral Dosage Forms* (August 1997)

❏ *Guidance for Industry: CGMP for Phase 1 Investigational Drugs* (July 2008)

❏ *Draft Guidance for Industry: Analytical Procedures and Methods Validation Chemistry, Manufacturing, and Controls Documentation* (August 2000)

❏ *Guidance for Industry: Collection of Race and Ethnicity Data in Clinical Trials* (September 2005)

❏ *Guidance for Industry: Exposure-Response Relationships—Study Design, Data Analysis, and Regulatory Applications* (April 2003)

❏ *Draft Guidance for Industry: Drug-Induced Liver Injury: Premarketing Clinical Evaluation* (October 2007)

❏ *Guidance for Industry: S1C(R2) Dose Selection for Carcinogenicity Studies* (September 2008)

❏ *Draft Guidance for Industry: Drug Interaction Studies—Study Design, Data Analysis, Implications for Dosing and Labeling* (September 2006)

❏ *Guidance for Industry: Pharmacokinetics in Patients with Impaired Hepatic Function: Study Design, Data Analysis, and Impact on Dosing and Labeling* (May 2003)

❏ *Guidance for Industry: Pharmacokinetics in Patients with Impaired Renal Function: Study Design, Data Analysis, and Impact on Dosing and Labeling* (May 1998)

❏ *Guideline for Industry: Studies in Support of Special Populations: Geriatrics* (August 1994)

❏ *Draft Guidance for Industry: How to Comply with the Pediatric Research Equity Act* (September 2005)

❏ *Draft Guidance for Industry and Investigators— Safety Reporting Requirements for INDs and BA/BE Studies* (September 2010)

❏ *Draft Guidance for Industry: E2F Development Safety Update Report* (June 2008)

❏ *Draft Guidance for Industry and Review Staff: Target Product Profile—A Strategic Development Process Tool* (March 2007)

❏ *Guidance for Industry: Guideline for the Format and Content of the Nonclinical Pharmacology/ Toxicology Section of an Application* (February 1987)

❏ *Draft Guidance for Reviewers on the Integration*

Table 9-1. 21 CFR Parts Most Relevant to Drug and Device Development

21 CFR Parts	General Topics
1–100	Administrative Issues and Protection of Human Subjects
100s	Foods (not covered in this chapter except for dietary supplements)
200s	Labeling, CGMPs, Controlled Substances
300s	Drugs for Human Use
500s	Drugs for Animal Use
600s	Biologics
700s	Cosmetics (not covered in this chapter)
800s	Medical Devices
1000s–1400s	Contain many miscellaneous topics but 1270 Human Tissues Intended for Transplantation and 1271 Human Cells, Tissues and Tissue-Based Products are relevant

of Study Results to Assess Concerns about Human Reproductive and Developmental Toxicities (November 2001)

❏ Guidance for Industry and Review Staff: Recommended Approaches to Integration of Genetic Toxicology Study Results (January 2006)

❏ Draft Guidance for Industry: Statistical Aspects of the Design, Analysis, and Interpretation of Chronic Rodent Carcinogenicity Studies of Pharmaceuticals (May 2001)

❏ Guideline for the Format and Content of the Clinical and Statistical Sections of an Application (July 1988)

❏ Draft Guidance for Industry: Integrated Summary of Effectiveness (August 2008)

❏ Guidance for Industry: Premarketing Risk Assessment (March 2005)

❏ Guidance for Industry: Development and Use of Risk Minimization Action Plans (March 2005)

❏ Guidance for Industry: Good Pharmacovigilance Practices and Pharmacoepidemiologic Assessment (March 2005)

❏ Guidance for Industry: Submitting Separate Marketing Applications and Clinical Data for Purposes of Assessing User Fees (December 2004)

❏ Draft Guidance for Industry: Standards for Securing the Drug Supply Chain—Standardized Numerical Identification for Prescription Drug

Packages (January 2009)

❏ Draft Guidance for Industry: Forms for Registration of Producers of Drugs and Listing of Drugs in Commercial Distribution (April 2001)

❏ Draft Guidance for Industry: Applications Covered by Section 505(b)(2) (October 1999)

❏ Guidance for Industry: Structure/Function Claims Small Entity Compliance Guide (January 2002)

❏ The New 510(k) Paradigm—Alternate Approaches to Demonstrating Substantial Equivalence in Premarket Notifications—Final Guidance (March 1998)

❏ Guidance for Industry and FDA Staff: How to Write a Request for Designation (RFD) (August 2005)

❏ Guidance for Industry: Nonclinical Safety Evaluation of Drug or Biologic Combinations (March 2006)

Introduction

The development of drugs, biologics and devices in the modern era is a scientific process (hypothesis testing and the recognition and control of dependent and independent variables) in the context of objective and subjective interpretations of a product's potential or actual risks and benefits. The scope, interpretation and application of US federal regulations that must be met to market a drug, biologic or device have evolved over the past century and are documented in the Code of Federal Regulations (CFR). In practice, this translates into agency use of scientific review, standards, manufacturing and other inspections, advertising controls, conditional approvals, laboratory product testing and postmarketing pharmacovigilance activities. In the last quarter century, a plethora of US Food and Drug Administration (FDA) and International Conference on Harmonisation (ICH) guidelines have been issued to assist the regulatory professional in interpreting and defining the processes needed to successfully develop drugs and devices for marketing in a regulated industry. Although not enforceable as regulations, FDA guidelines (usually draft versions are available for public comment before finalization) provide an understanding of the agency's current thinking on any given topic.

This chapter provides an overview of the development and approval process for prescription drug, biologic, device and combination products in an environment regulated by the US government. Other chapters in this book provide details regarding many of the development and approval aspects touched on in this chapter. The purpose of this chapter is to tie the various topics together to provide a development context and roadmap.

Regulatory professionals must understand where regulations originate and how they are organized and updated. The difference between a law and a regulation is sometimes misunderstood. Only Congress can enact laws ("acts" of Congress). Federal executive departments and agencies such as FDA write the regulations to implement the authority of laws. The US Code (USC, which contains 19 "titles") is the official compilation of codified laws by subject, while the CFR is the official compilation of regulations. The CFR is updated annually (in April for food and drugs—Title 21) while the *Federal Register* is the daily supplement to the CFR. Thus, these two publications should be used together to find the latest version of a regulation. The original *Federal Food, Drug, and Cosmetic Act* of 1938 (*FD&C Act*) and its many subsequent amendments constitute the basic food and drug law of the US. A current version of this act can be found at www.fda.gov/RegulatoryInformation/Legislation/FederalFoodDrugandCosmeticActFDCAct/default.htm.

The CFR is divided into 50 titles that represent broad subject areas. Each title is divided into chapters, which usually bear the name of the issuing agency. Each chapter is further subdivided into parts that cover specific regulatory areas. Large parts may be subdivided into subparts. Finally, parts are divided into sections. Thus, the order for citations is: Title, CFR, Part, Section. For drugs and devices, Title 21 (Food and Drugs), and Chapter 1 (Food and Drug Administration) are the most relevant. There are 1,499 parts in Title 21 with the most applicable summarized in **Table 9-1**.

The CFR is accessible online, and the following FDA website is a convenient CFR research point for drugs and devices: www.accessdata.fda.gov/scripts/cdrh/cfdocs/cfcfr/

CFRSearch.cfm. The full CFR can be found and searched at www.access.gpo.gov/nara/cfr/cfr-table-search.html.

Although this book and the current chapter describe drug, biologic and device development and approval processes in the US, modern drug development is becoming more and more globalized. Hence, in any development program, consideration should be given to the impact of regulations in other world regions (for example, the usual requirement for a positive control in safety and efficacy trials of drugs in the EU).

Finally, this chapter touches on aspects of drug, biologic and device development to explain the relationships between different technical areas. Because chemistry, manufacturing and controls (CMC) relative to drugs and biologics involves a number of unique issues that are covered in detail in other chapters (including GMPs and Quality Systems), this aspect of drug development is not emphasized in this chapter.

Drug, Device or Combination?

FDA regulates more than 150,000 marketed drugs and medical devices. At any time, nearly 3,000 investigational new drugs are being developed. Organizationally, FDA is part of the Public Health Service (PHS) within the Department of Health and Human Services (DHHS). PHS also oversees the Centers for Disease Control and Prevention (CDC), the National Institutes of Health (NIH) and other agencies.

The workload described above is distributed across FDA's nine centers and offices with approximately 9,000 employees and 167 field offices. Since 1977, FDA centers have issued numerous guidances to increase the transparency of the development process and help move products through the process more rapidly. More recently, the Center for Drug Evaluation and Research (CDER) has developed a system of manuals of policies and procedures (MAPPs), which are written statements issued by CDER management to prescribe policies, responsibilities or procedures for the conduct of the center's work or daily operations. "MAPP 4000.1—Developing and Issuing Manuals of Policies and Procedures" (updated most recently in 2010) describes the guidance development process. All MAPPs can be accessed at www.fda.gov/AboutFDA/CentersOffices/CDER/ManualofPoliciesProcedures/default.htm. Several MAPPs regarding agency review processes are useful in understanding how FDA staff will use information from sponsors to make regulatory decisions, and can help sponsors prepare more reviewer-friendly documents. The Center for Biologics Evaluation and Research (CBER) has a similar system termed manuals of standard operating procedures and policies (SOPPs).

Figure 9-2 shows the decision tree regarding which regulations and FDA center or office will primarily govern development and approval of any given drug, device or combination product. Because the purpose of this flow diagram is to provide a simple overview for situations that require FDA premarket review, some complexities, such as the distinction between drugs and biologics and the development of combination products, OTC drugs and dietary supplements, are not highlighted but are addressed in the text of this chapter.

Drugs
Drugs for Veterinary Use

There has been a formal veterinary unit (currently the Center for Veterinary Medicine, CVM) at FDA since 1928.[1] The development and approval of drugs for animal use follows the same framework as for human drugs. For new drugs, the sponsor must file an Investigational New Animal Drug application (INAD, 21 CFR 511) and a New Animal Drug Application (NADA, 21 CFR 514). Under the *Generic Animal Drug and Patent Restoration Act* of 1988, generic veterinary drugs can be marketed under an approved Abbreviated New Animal Drug Application (ANADA). The Reference Listed Drugs (RLDs) for veterinary use are published in the *Green Book* (accessible at www.fda.gov/AnimalVeterinary/Products/ApprovedAnimalDrugProducts/ucm042847.htm). CVM oversees the veterinary drug development and approval process. However biologics for animal use (vaccines, bacterins, antisera and other products of biological origin) are overseen by the US Department of Agriculture, Animal and Plant Health Inspection Service, Center for Veterinary Biologics (CVB) on the basis of the *Virus Serum and Toxin Act* of 1902. More specifics are available on the CVB website, www.aphis.usda.gov/animal_health/vet_biologics.

Although the development of drugs for animal use has many of the same components and approaches as for human drugs, including Good Laboratory Practices (GLPs), Good Manufacturing Practices (GMPs), Good Clinical Practices (GCPs), study reports, characterization of dose-response relationships, adequate and well-controlled studies and even user fee), it does differ in a number of key aspects including:

- the ability to use known data from the development of a drug for use in humans or other animal species, as applicable
- the requirement of safety and efficacy studies for far smaller numbers of animals per group, compared to the hundreds of patients per group required for human drugs
- the relevance of species, class and breed of animals as well as geographic differences
- the distinction between drugs developed for the treatment of companion animals versus for animals (or their products) used for human food (e.g., cattle, poultry)

For the general development of drugs for veterinary use, safety aspects are covered in *Guidance for Industry No. 185: Target Animal Safety for Veterinary Pharmaceutical Products* (April 2009), as well as *Guidance for Industry No. 104: Content and Format of Effectiveness and Target Animal Safety Technical Sections and Final Study Reports for Submission to the Division of Therapeutic Drugs for Non-Food Animals* (July 2001). Although the latter guideline does address efficacy in a general fashion, a number of additional guidelines address therapeutic- and animal-specific efficacy issues.

For development of drugs for food-producing animals, two guidelines are helpful. The first, *Guidance for Industry No. 3: General Principles for Evaluating the Safety of Compounds Used in Food-Producing Animals* (July 2006), is very useful and provides links to seven additional guidelines for more in-depth coverage of specific topics. The second guideline (which should be read in conjunction with the first) is *Guidance for Industry No. 149: Studies to Evaluate the Safety of Residues of Veterinary Drugs in Human Food: General Approach to Testing* (March 2009).

Combining veterinary drugs into a single dosage form is addressed in *Guideline No. 24: Guidelines for Drug Combinations in Animals* (October 1983). Specifically, prior to approval of a drug combination, the sponsor must submit data to demonstrate that the combination provides a benefit that cannot be obtained by the use of each drug individually.

Finally, although slightly out of place in this section, it should be noted that for devices used in veterinary medicine, FDA does not require submission of a 510(k) or formal premarket approval application. Moreover, device manufacturers that exclusively manufacture or distribute veterinary devices are not required to register their establishments and list veterinary devices. However, FDA can take appropriate regulatory action if a veterinary device is misbranded, mislabeled or adulterated.

Generic Drugs for Human Use and the Abbreviated New Drug Application (ANDA)
Overview

In part as a result of the thalidomide tragedy, the *Kefauver-Harris Amendments* (*Drug Amendments*) to the *FD&C Act* were passed by Congress in 1962. These amendments required drug manufacturers to prove to FDA that their products were both safe and effective prior to marketing (only safety was required to be demonstrated in the original *FD&C Act*). The *Drug Amendments* also gave FDA control over prescription drug advertising and established GMPs and the requirement for informed consent of subjects in clinical trials. To comply, FDA contracted in 1966 with the National Academy of Sciences' National Research Council to study drugs that had been approved for safety only between 1938 and 1962 relative to the new requirement for demonstration of efficacy. The Drug

Efficacy Study Implementation (DESI) program evaluated more than 3,000 separate products and 16,000 therapeutic claims. One of the early effects of the DESI program was the development of the ANDA. ANDAs were accepted for reviewed products that required changes in existing labeling to be in compliance.[2]

The modern era of generic drugs was born in 1984 with passage of the *Drug Price Competition and Patent Term Restoration Act* (the *Hatch-Waxman Act*), which represented a compromise between the innovator pharmaceutical industry and the generic pharmaceutical industry. This act expedited the availability of less-costly generic drugs by permitting FDA to approve abbreviated applications after the patent of the innovator drug had expired. They are termed "abbreviated" applications because they are not required to include animal safety and clinical data to establish safety and effectiveness, but for oral dosage forms must scientifically demonstrate that the product is bioequivalent to the innovator drug (Reference Listed Drug (RLD)). In the case of products (usually steriles, otics and ophthalmics) that have a high solubility-high permeability rating (A/A rated), a waiver for *in vivo* bioequivalence testing can be obtained from FDA. To be bioequivalent, the generic drug product must deliver the same amount (within a range specified by FDA) of active ingredient into a subject's bloodstream over the same amount of time as the RLD. Specifically, a generic drug product is comparable to the innovator drug product in dosage form, strength, route of administration, quality, performance characteristics and intended use. All approved products, both innovator and generic, are listed in FDA's Approved Drug Products with Therapeutic Equivalence Evaluations (the *Orange Book*), which is accessible on FDA's website (www.accessdata.fda.gov/scripts/cder/ob/default.cfm). The *Orange Book* identifies the RLD and provides information on applicable patents and their expiration dates. A product approved under the ANDA process will have the same labeling as the RLD. Approximately 70% of the total drug prescriptions dispensed in the US are generic.

The ANDA is comprised of three primary components:
- chemistry, manufacturing and controls (CMC) information
- bioequivalence data
- administrative information (including labeling and patent certification information)

ANDA requirements for CMC information and manufacture under CGMPs are not significantly different from NDA requirements. A relatively recent initiative in FDA's Office of Generic Drugs (OGD) to streamline the review process for the CMC section is submission of the ANDA Quality Overall Summary in question-based review (QbR) format (versus a more traditional non-question based summary format). The QbR questions and answers are placed in Module 2 of the Common Technical Document

(CTD); therefore, QbR assumes the ANDA is submitted in the CTD format, which is not mandatory but strongly suggested. OGD has also developed a standard group of summary tables (termed Model Bioequivalence Data Summary Tables) consistent with the CTD format to ensure consistent and concise data are submitted in the applicable sections of the ANDA.

The design, conduct and analysis of clinical bioequivalence studies are covered in *Guidance for Industry: Bioavailability and Bioequivalence Studies for Orally Administered Drug Products: General Considerations* (March 2003) and *Guidance for Industry: Food-Effect Bioavailability and Fed Bioequivalence Studies* (December 2002). A third guideline, *Guidance for Industry: Bioanalytical Method Development* (May 2001), covers the requirements for validation of bioanalytical methods used to evaluate blood concentrations of the active ingredient, which also applies to drugs developed through the NDA route. OGD issued *Draft Guidance for Industry: Bioequivalence Recommendations for Specific Products* in May 2007, indicating how and where OGD will release bioequivalence recommendations for specific products in the future.

Generally, two-way crossover studies (sometimes preceded by pilot studies to determine variability and group sizes) of the generic drug product versus the RLD in the fasted state are performed. If the label of the RLD indicates a food effect, a second study in the fed state (using a standardized high-fat meal) is typically required. Additional studies may be needed to demonstrate bioequivalence of different strengths if the ratio of excipients to the active pharmaceutical ingredient in each dosage strength of the generic drug is not the same. As defined by FDA, the generic is deemed bioequivalent to the RLD in any of the above studies if the 90% confidence interval for the ratio of population geometric means between the two treatments, based on log-transformed data, is contained within the equivalence limits of 80%–125% for the area under the curve (AUC) and peak serum concentration (C_{max}). A common misinterpretation of this is that levels of the active ingredient in generic drugs may vary from minus 20% to plus 25% compared to the innovator. In fact, those numbers relate to a derived statistical calculation and do not represent the actual difference in the amount of active ingredient in a patient's bloodstream, which is generally similar to the variation between different batches of the same innovator drug. For those who are statistically minded, *Guidance for Industry: Statistical Approaches to Establishing Bioequivalence* (January 2001), describes how to conduct the above analysis. If the bioequivalance studies are being conducted to support an ANDA, they do not have to be conducted under an IND, but do need to be reviewed and approved (including an informed consent form) by a duly constituted Institutional Review Board (IRB).

An ANDA must contain a statement by the applicant

that one of the following patent certifications applies for the RLD:

- The patent information has not been filed (Paragraph I).
- The patent has expired (Paragraph II).
- The patent will expire on a specific date (Paragraph III) and the sponsor submitting the ANDA does not intend to market its product before that date.
- The patent is invalid or will not be infringed by the proposed drug product (Paragraph IV).

If the ANDA applicant certifies that the patent is invalid or will not be infringed (a Paragraph IV certification), the applicant is required to notify the NDA holder and patent owner. If the NDA holder brings an action for patent infringement within 45 days of this notification, FDA will not approve the ANDA for 30 months, or such shorter or longer period as a court may order, or until the date of a court decision (known as the 30-month stay). Originally, the 180-day exclusivity for generic drugs applied only to the first company to submit an ANDA with a Paragraph IV certification. However, the current approach to 180-day exclusivity (described in *Guidance to Industry: 180-Day Exclusivity When Multiple ANDAs are Submitted on the Same Day* (July 2003)) is applicable to all cases in which multiple ANDA applicants submit Paragraph IV certifications challenging the same listed patent or patents on the same first day. This provides a shared incentive for multiple companies willing to challenge a listed patent and possibly defend a patent infringement suit.

Although the development time for a generic is relatively short, ANDA review (several hundred applications each year) and approval times average approximately two years, and clearly impact the timeframe for moving generic products to the market. This suggests a proactive strategy of submitting ANDA applications well in advance of patent expiration date. A company with an approved ANDA is subject to the same postapproval reporting requirements as an NDA holder (21 CFR 314.80 Postmarketing reporting of adverse drug experiences and 21 CFR 314.81 Field alert reports and annual reports). The OGD website is also a good resource (www.fda.gov/AboutFDA/CentersOffices/CDER/ucm119100.htm).

Suitability Petitions

The regulations regarding ANDAs are contained in 21 CFR 314.92 and Section 505(j) of the *FD&C Act*. In addition, 21 CFR 314.92 cross-references the limits set forth in 21 CFR 314.93 for what characteristics a generic drug not identical to the RLD can possess and still potentially be submitted as an ANDA, subject to acceptance by FDA of a suitability petition. A suitability petition by the sponsor seeks permission to file an ANDA for the drug product and contains comparisons and contrasts between the generic drug and the RLD, forming the basis for approval. FDA is required to respond to the petition within 90 days. If a suitability petition is not accepted, an NDA under Section 505(b)(2) of the *FD&C Act* may be an option. Another route is a citizen petition. Details of this latter approach are beyond the scope of this chapter.

Branded and Authorized Generics

Recently, "branded" generics have become more prevalent. Branded generics are approved in the same manner as all generics, but the ANDA applicant also applies for and receives a brand (i.e., proprietary) name under the same process used for NDAs (*Draft Guidance for Industry: Contents of a Complete Submission for the Evaluation of Proprietary Names* (November 2008)). A brand name will allow the company to distinguish its generic from others if marketing activities are contemplated.

An "authorized generic" is a drug product for which there is a licensing agreement between the innovator company and a generic drug manufacturer. It allows the innovator company to obtain revenue through the generic process by licensing a manufacturer to market the RLD as a generic using a different "trade dress" while continuing to market the innovator drug under the original proprietary name. A list (updated quarterly) of authorized generics, including the original NDA applicant name, is available on the CDER OGD website (www.fda.gov/AboutFDA/CentersOffices/CDER/ucm126391.htm). The appeal of this approach is avoiding the ANDA review and approval process; instead, the generic can be added to the original NDA as a supplement or described in the NDA annual report.

In March 2010, the *Patient Protection and Affordable Care Act* was signed into law. This act contains a subtitle called the *Biologics Price Competition and Innovation Act* of 2009 (*BPCI Act*) that amends Section 351 of *Public Health Service Act* and other statutes to create an abbreviated approval pathway for biological products shown to be highly similar (biosimilar) to, or interchangeable with, an FDA-licensed reference biological product. FDA is currently soliciting input regarding the agency's implementation of the statute and considering how to deal with biosimilars that are regulated under Section 505 of the *FD&C Act* (well-characterized proteins and peptides). The approval process for biosimilars is more mature in the EU and further details of the biosimilar development approach, issues and examples can be reviewed on the relevant EU websites.

Table 9-2. Key Questions to be Addressed in a Drug Development Program

In Vitro—Animals—Adults—Children		
Safety **(Risk)**	**Pharmacokinetics** **(What the body does to the drug)**	**Pharmacodynamics/Efficacy** **(Benefit)**
How do you maximize the intellectual property aspect of the product?		
What is the known safety profile of other drugs like yours or the class of drugs in general? For a new class of drugs or mechanism of action this will not necessarily be known and hence associated with more risk.	Are there competitor drugs that have a less than ideal route of administration or pharmacokinetic profile (e.g., substrates, inhibitors or inducers of more commonly used cytochrome P [CYP] 450 isoenzyme pathways)?	What endpoints have been accepted by FDA for other drugs developed to treat the target disease, or is this a first-in-class drug?
What safety profile would provide a competitive advantage?	What pharmacokinetic (including route of administration) profile would provide a competitive advantage?	What is the potential breadth of the target indication(s)?
What do you want to say in your label? (This will drive the development of your product.)		
What are the target organs/systems for toxicity?	What exposure profiles produce target organ/system effects?	What are the target organs/systems for pharmacological effects?
What toxicity is observed acutely versus chronically?	How is the time course of the effects related to the time-concentration curves of the parent drug and its metabolites?	What is the time course and duration of pharmacological/ therapeutic effects?
Can the toxicities be monitored?	Are there potential or actual interactions with other drugs (especially those most commonly used by the target patient population)?	How do you measure the benefits?
Are the toxicities reversible?	What are the single-dose versus steady-state pharmacokinetics of the drug and its metabolites?	What happens to the therapeutic effects when you stop dosing?
What is the maximum tolerated dose and what are risks of overdose?	Is the pharmacokinetic profile linear?	What is the minimal effective dose and duration of treatment?
What are the frequency and severity of safety findings?	How variable (intra- and inter-subject) are drug concentrations (may be impacted by drug bioavailability or greater involvement of the more commonly used CYP isoenzyme systems)?	How reproducible and clinically relevant are the pharmacodynamic and/or efficacy endpoints (speaks to the validity of the endpoints)?

New Chemical Entities and the New Drug Application for a Marketing Application for Human Use (Section 505(b)(1) of the FD&C Act)

Overview of the Approach to Drug Development and Approval

A "drug" is defined as a product used in diagnosing, curing, mitigating, treating or preventing a disease or affecting a structure or function of the body (21 CFR 310.3). Under the same regulation, a drug is considered a new drug if:

- There is a new drug use of any substance (e.g., active ingredient, excipient, carrier, coating etc.) that composes the drug.
- There is a new drug use of a combination of approved drugs.
- The proportion of the ingredients in combination is changed.
- There is a new intended use for the drug.

- The dosage, method or duration of administration or application is changed.

Thus, the following are subject to FDA approval:

1. a drug containing a novel chemical compound as its active ingredient (new chemical entity (NCE))
2. a drug containing an existing active ingredient that has never been approved for use as a medicine in the US
3. a drug previously approved by FDA but now proposed for a new use or indication
4. a drug previously approved by FDA but in a dosage form, route of administration or other key condition of use different from what was originally approved

The distinction between a drug and a biologic is primarily based on historical issues. As a result of the St. Louis tetanus contamination due to infected serum and smaller occurrences of contaminated smallpox vaccine and diphtheria antitoxin, Congress passed the *Virus Serum and Toxin Act* (also known as the *Biologics Control Act*) in 1902. The act authorized the Hygienic Laboratory of the Public Health and Marine Hospital Service (which eventually became PHS) to issue regulations governing all aspects of commercial production of vaccines, serums, toxins, antitoxins and similar products with the objective of ensuring their safety, purity and potency. In 1934, the Hygienic Laboratory (renamed NIH in 1930 by the *Ransdell Act*) issued a regulation stating that licenses to manufacture new biologics would not be granted without evidence that the products were effective. The *Public Health Service Act of 1944* (*PHS Act*) saw the reorganization of PHS, with authority given to NIH to license, research and develop new biological products. Hence, one of the primary historical differences between biologics and drugs has been the inherent government research component of biologics as opposed to the testing and regulation emphasis for drugs.[3] In addition, because biologics are derived from living organisms, immunogenicity issues and how they are addressed in nonclinical and clinical studies often distinguish them from small-molecule drugs.

In 1972, the Division of Biological Standards (part of NIH and in turn part of PHS) was transferred to FDA and eventually became CBER. Although the *PHS Act* established the regulation of biologics licensure, biologics are classified as drugs under the *FD&C Act* and new biologic products require approval based upon safety and efficacy prior to marketing (through a Biologics License Application (BLA) as opposed to an NDA). Biologics are defined as substances derived from or made with the aid of living organisms. Review and approval of these products is conducted by CBER. As technology has evolved, CBER has reviewed more therapeutic proteins. To allow CBER to focus its expertise on vaccines, blood products and other, more-complex products such as gene therapy, FDA shifted the review and approval of biological therapeutics (primarily oncology products, peptides or well-characterized proteins) from CBER to CDER in 2003.

The intake of any exogenous substance that has pharmacological actions on the body presents some level of risk. Drug development consists of characterizing the safety profile (risk) and the efficacy profile (benefit) as it relates to the body's exposure to the drug (pharmacokinetic profile). The most successful drugs are those with minimal risk and maximum benefit. To align development with continuous evaluation of risk and benefit, it is often productive to consider questions and answers that affect decisions whether to continue a drug's development to the point of submitting a marketing application. The order and importance of these questions are different for each drug based upon aspects such as the product (formulation) chemical and physical characteristics, the route of administration, the target patient population, the medical need, the ability to monitor safety,

the ability to predict potential benefits from pharmacodynamic measures (surrogate endpoints) and the duration of treatment needed to demonstrate efficacy.

Table 9-2 lists some of the key questions FDA expects to be addressed as a drug is developed. Generally, due to risk, cost and time, evaluations are performed in the following order:

in vitro
live animals (juvenile if applicable)
adult humans (often in healthy subjects before patients)
children (if applicable)

However, as information is gained, new hypotheses may need to be tested. Therefore, drug development often is an iterative, dynamic process that involves ongoing effective communication between all the disciplines involved.

Table 9-2 identifies key questions to be addressed in a drug development program, i.e., how a company can maximize the market share of its product and realize the maximum return on investment with the least amount of risk. The sections below describe key aspects of the drug development process and regulatory tools and approaches to help reach these goals.

FDA Interface and Development Leverage Options

The relationship between FDA and an investigational drug product sponsor can begin very early in the process (before the sponsor submits an IND to test the product in humans) and extends through the typical IND development process (often defined as Phases 1, 2 and 3) to a marketing application and postapproval commitments, safety surveillance and product lifecycle management. It is important to structure the presentation to meet FDA expectations. To succeed, it is important to learn—through experience or interaction—the relevant review division's approach to issues under its purview. The most effective interfaces between sponsors and FDA are formal meetings and Special Protocol Assessment (SPA) requests.

FDA–Sponsor Meetings

Although sponsor meetings with FDA occurred prior to 1997, it was not until the reauthorization of the *Prescription Drug User Fee Act* in 1997 (*PDUFA 2*) that a formal process for meetings (with expectations and commitments from both parties) was established. Processes for the request and classification of meetings are covered in *Guidance for Industry: Formal Meetings Between the FDA and Sponsors or Applicants* (May 2009). Different kinds of meetings are categorized as Type A, B or C with different associated timelines (see aforementioned guidance). Meetings can be requested at any time for any valid reason, but FDA will decide if there is sufficient justification for a meeting (usually dictated by the product background and draft questions submitted in a written meeting request) or if a written response to questions and/or a teleconference would suffice. Most commonly, meetings are classified as either pre-IND, End-of-Phase 2 (*Draft Guidance for Industry: End-of Phase 2A Meetings* (September 2008)) or pre-NDA. For products that have been granted accelerated approval or fast track, an End-of-Phase 1 meeting generally will be granted.

For any meeting with FDA, it is important to submit clear and meaningful draft questions and a supporting pre-meeting package that is not merely a summary of what is known about a given drug (e.g., submission of only an Investigator's Brochure).

SPA

The SPA process is described in *Guidance for Industry: Special Protocol Assessment* (May 2002). Although prior to 1997, FDA reviewed draft protocols on a case-by-case basis, the process often took several months and did not always address all the issues. As a result of *PDUFA 2*, the SPA process was established. Within 45 days of receipt, FDA will evaluate certain protocols and related issues to determine whether they meet scientific and regulatory requirements identified by the sponsor (in the form of specific questions). Three types of protocols are eligible for an SPA under the *PDUFA* goals:

1. animal carcinogenicity protocols
2. final product stability protocols
3. clinical protocols for Phase 3 trials, the data from which will form the basis for an efficacy claim (i.e., a pivotal trial) if the trials were discussed at an End-of-Phase 2/Pre-Phase 3 meeting with the review division, or in some cases, if the division is aware of the developmental context in which the protocol is being reviewed and the questions are being posed

The clinical protocols for Phase 3 trials can relate to efficacy claims that will be part of an original NDA/BLA or an efficacy supplement to an approved NDA/BLA. Although the initial 45-day period is generally adhered to, depending upon FDA's responses to the questions, there could be several review/response cycles (that are no longer part of the timeframe) to reach a final understanding with the sponsor. If documentation of the final agreement is not provided by the FDA review division, the sponsor should request written communication from FDA acknowledging the final agreement.

In addition, sponsors have several available avenues to help focus FDA attention on the drug development program and expedite marketing application approval. These include orphan drug designation (when eligible) and, for drugs indicated for serious or life-threatening conditions, fast track development designation with opportunities for a "rolling NDA" and priority review. Sponsors may also seek accelerated NDA review based upon a surrogate endpoint

or an effect on a clinical endpoint other than survival or irreversible morbidity. Details are described in 21 CFR 314.510, Subpart H Accelerated Approval of New Drugs for Serious or Life-threatening Illnesses. Confirmatory studies are likely to be required if FDA approves an NDA under Subpart H.

Orphan Drug Designation

The *Orphan Drug Act* was signed into law in 1983 and, for the first time, provided incentives for development of drugs necessary, and often lifesaving, for patients with rare diseases but with minimal prospects for commercial return on investment. The *Orphan Drug Act* is codified in 21 CFR 316.

Since 1983, Congress has amended the act several times.

- The 1984 amendment redefined "rare disease or condition" as affecting fewer than 200,000 persons in the US at a given point or for which there is no reasonable expectation of recovering development costs through US sales.
- The 1985 amendment extended the marketing exclusivity to patentable as well as unpatentable drugs and allowed federal grants for the clinical evaluation of orphan-designated drugs.
- The 1988 amendment required industry sponsors to apply for orphan designation prior to submission of a marketing application.
- The *Food and Drug Administration Modernization Act* of 1997 (*FDAMA*) included a provision that exempted designated orphan drug products from paying new drug application fees (user fees). It also allowed sponsors to seek waivers of annual postapproval establishment and product fees on a case-by-case, year-by-year basis.

The *Orphan Drug Act* provides a number of specific incentives for sponsors:

- seven years of exclusive marketing rights for the designated indication once the drug receives FDA marketing approval
- a tax credit for up to 50% of qualified clinical research expenses incurred in developing a designated orphan product (This tax credit has a provision that allows the sponsor to carry the excess credit back one tax year if unable to use part or all of the credit because of tax liability limits, and then to carry forward any additional unused credit for up to 20 years after the year of the credit. The latter is important to start-up companies that may not make any profits until the drug is on the market. The US Internal Revenue Service administers the tax credit provisions of the *Orphan Drug Act*.)
- eligibility to apply for orphan drug grants

There is no formal application for orphan drug designation in the US; however, the European Medicines Agency (EMA) and FDA's Office of Orphan Products Development (OOPD) have developed a common application, benefitting sponsors seeking orphan drug designation in both regions. For US-only applications, the OOPD/EMA common application may be used or sponsors can produce a request consistent with the provisions of 21 CFR 316.20, which identifies the information to be included in a complete, signed and dated document. Essentially, it is a text document with appropriate literature references appended. References are provided to support the incidence statements and can increase the total size of the submission to approximately one to three volumes of paper (a volume is generally defined as between 250 and 350 pages).

An application for orphan drug designation generally includes:

- specific rare disease or condition for which designation is being requested
- sponsor contact, drug names and sources
- description of the rare disease or condition with a medically plausible rationale for any patient subset type of approach
- description of the drug and the scientific rationale for its use for the rare disease or condition
- summary of the drug's regulatory status and marketing history
- for a treatment indication, documentation that the disease or condition affects fewer than 200,000 people in the US (prevalence)
- for a prevention indication, documentation that the disease or condition affects fewer than 200,000 people in the US per year (incidence)
- alternatively, a rationale for why there is no reasonable expectation that costs of research and development for the indication can be recovered by US sales

Specifics on the submission format and other details are available on FDA's website (www.fda.gov/ForIndustry/DevelopingProductsforRareDiseasesConditions/default.htm). Once the request for designation has been received, OOPD will send a receipt letter, and a formal response will take one to three months. Upon notification of orphan drug designation, the sponsor's name and the proposed rare disease or condition will be published in the *Federal Register*.

Once an orphan drug designation has been granted by FDA, it can only be revoked if the application is found to contain false data or there is insufficient drug product to supply market needs. Notably, the designation cannot be revoked even if post-designation prevalence exceeds the original estimates. Finally, the sponsor must provide annual updates that contain a brief summary of any ongoing or completed nonclinical or clinical studies; a description of

the investigational plan for the coming year; as well as any anticipated difficulties in development, testing and marketing; and a brief discussion of any changes that may affect the product's orphan drug status.

Fast Track Designation

The fast track drug development program designation process is described in *Guidance for Industry: Fast Track Drug Development Programs—Designation, Development, and Application Review* (July 2004). FDA better defined the program (see 21 CFR 312 Subpart E) as a result of *FDAMA* in 1997. The fast track program is designed to facilitate the development and expedite the review of new drugs intended to treat serious or life-threatening conditions and that demonstrate the potential to address unmet medical needs. A disease is considered serious based upon the likelihood that if left untreated, it will progress from a less-severe to a more-severe condition (e.g., AIDS, Alzheimer's disease, heart failure and cancer, but also epilepsy, depression and diabetes). FDA defines "meeting an unmet medical need" as providing a therapy where none exists or that may be superior to existing therapy by either:

- showing superior effectiveness
- avoiding serious side effects of an available treatment
- improving the diagnosis of a serious disease where early diagnosis results in an improved outcome
- decreasing a clinically significant toxicity of an accepted treatment

Depending upon the stage of drug development, data that become available should support the drug's potential to address unmet medical needs, and the development plan should be designed to assess this potential. The agency will rely on summaries of available data to determine whether the potential to address unmet medical needs has been demonstrated and will provide a designation response within 60 days of receipt of the request. When fast track designation is no longer supported by emerging data or the designated drug development program is no longer being pursued, FDA may choose to send a letter notifying the sponsor that the product is no longer classified as fast track.

A sponsor may request fast track designation at any point in the development process. A product that is in a fast track development program is eligible for heightened interest by FDA in sponsor meetings, a greater probability of priority review of the marketing application (six months versus the standard 10 months), and piecemeal submission of portions (complete CTD modules—constituting a "reviewable unit") of a marketing application (referred to as a "rolling NDA"). Note that this latter provision is unique to fast track programs, but needs to be specifically requested. Moreover, the FDA review clock for the rolling

Figure 9-1 CTD Organization

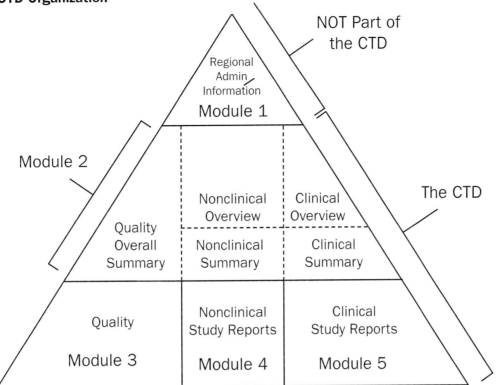

NDA does not start until the marketing application submission is complete.

ICH and FDA Guidelines and Their Relationship to the Development Process
ICH and the CTD Format

The International Conference on Harmonisation (ICH) was formed in 1990. It is a unique project that brings together the regulatory authorities of the EU, Japan and the US and experts from the pharmaceutical industry in the three regions to discuss scientific and technical aspects of product registration. ICH recommends ways to achieve greater harmonization in the interpretation and application of technical guidelines and requirements for product registration to reduce or avoid duplicating testing during the research and development of new drugs. The objectives are conservation of human, animal and material resources and elimination of unnecessary delays in global development and availability of new medicines, while safeguarding quality, safety and efficacy and protecting public health.

The ICH process has resulted in numerous guidelines in four major categories:

1. Quality—topics relating to chemical and pharmaceutical quality assurance including stability testing and impurity testing (approximately 24 guidelines)
2. Safety—topics relating to *in vitro* and *in vivo* nonclinical studies including carcinogenicity testing and genotoxicity testing (there are approximately 15 guidelines)
3. Efficacy—topics relating to clinical studies in human subjects including dose-response studies and GCPs (approximately 21 guidelines)
4. Multidisciplinary—topics covering cross-disciplinary issues or not uniquely fitting into one of the other categories, including *Medical Dictionary for Regulatory Activities* (*MedDRA*) terminology, the CTD and electronic CTD submissions (approximately 8 guidelines)

Copies of these guidelines and information on their history and status in the four-step review and consensus process are available at www.ich.org/products/guidelines. html. The majority of these guidelines have been accepted by FDA as reflecting current agency thinking (as documented in *Federal Register* announcements).

Two important aspects of the ICH endeavor are the CTD concept and *MedDRA*. The CTD is divided into five modules as shown in **Figure 9-1,** with a hierarchical structure with the most detail at the base leading to higher and higher level summaries and integration. *Guidance for Industry M4: Organization of the CTD* (2001) provides further details.

Module 1 is region-specific (US, EU, Japan). Modules 2, 3, 4 and 5 are intended to be common for all regions. For

US submissions, Module 1 will contain various FDA forms, draft labeling, Risk Evaluation and Mitigation Strategies (REMS) plans, key FDA correspondence (e.g., FDA meeting minutes), patent information and the Investigator's Brochure (IB) (important if the CTD format is used at the IND stage). Module 2 contains CTD summaries of the three technical areas:

- Module 3 Quality (see *Guidance for Industry M4Q: The CTD—Quality* (August 2001)) and corresponding summary in Module 2.3
- Module 4 Nonclinical/Safety (see *Guidance for Industry M4S: The CTD—Safety* (August 2001) and *Guidance for Industry M4S: The CTD—Safety Appendices* (August 2001)) and corresponding summaries in Module 2.4 Nonclinical Overview and 2.6 Nonclinical Written and Tabulated Summaries
- Module 5 Clinical (see *Guidance for Industry M4E: The CTD—Efficacy* (August 2001)) and corresponding summaries in Module 2.5 Clinical Overview and 2.7 Clinical Summary

Module 2 also has several sections, the goal of which is to provide a concise context for the reviewer and integrate key risk/benefit data. The above-cited guidelines contain not only information on their respective modules, but also what should be included in the related portions of Module 2. If submitting electronically, *Guidance for Industry M2 eCTD: Electronic Common Technical Document Specification* (April 2003) is a key starting point.

MedDRA, the currently accepted international medical terminology dictionary developed by ICH, is designed to support the classification, retrieval, presentation and communication of medical information throughout the regulatory cycle for drugs and medical devices. It is particularly important in the electronic transmission of adverse event reporting and the coding of clinical trial data. Further details are available at www.meddramsso.com/public_subscribe_meddra.asp. and in associated ICH *MedDRA* specific guidelines. *MedDRA* replaces the older *Coding Symbols for a Thesaurus of Adverse Reaction Terms* (COSTART) dictionary.

Guidance Documents

Collectively, CDER and CBER have issued more than 800 guidelines since 1977. These range from general topics addressing a number of the issues outlined in **Table 9-4** to drug-specific issues. They are not regulations, but do represent FDA's current thinking on a given topic. However, some guidelines are relatively old, so the definition of "current thinking" often needs to be validated by recent experience with the agency in the area covered by the guidance. Because they are guidance documents, they should not be blindly followed, but consideration should be given to their intent and applicability to a given development issue.

The Initial IND and the IND Amendment Process

Before initiating a clinical trial in the US (other than bioequivalence studies to support an ANDA), the drug product sponsor must submit nonclinical, CMC and previous human experience data (if applicable) to FDA in a notice of claimed investigational exemption for a new drug in the form of an Investigational New Drug Application (IND). The IND application requests permission to initiate clinical trials. IND regulations are detailed in 21 CFR 312.

The IND application is not a request for approval; rather, it is a request for exemption from federal law. Federal law requires that prior to transporting or distributing a drug in interstate commerce, an NDA or BLA must be approved by FDA. Because in most cases the drug product must be shipped to investigative sites across state lines to perform clinical trials, the sponsor must receive an exemption from this legal requirement.

After receipt of the initial IND application, FDA will send the sponsor a letter with the assigned IND number (note that an IND number with a "P" preface can be obtained at a pre-IND meeting, and the final IND number is the same minus this preface). The letter will indicate that the proposed clinical trial cannot begin until 30 calendar days after receipt of the IND. This 30-day safety review period gives FDA an opportunity to determine whether the data in the IND application support the safety of subjects in the proposed clinical trial. Following review, rather than providing formal approval, the agency will take action on the application as follows. If the proposed study is judged not to be reasonably safe for human subjects, FDA is required to inform the sponsor within 30 calendar days of receipt of the IND application that it may not begin the clinical trial (clinical hold). If the sponsor is not contacted by FDA within 30 days, approval to initiate clinical trials is implicit. In the latter case, it is advisable to contact the FDA project manager assigned to your IND to develop a relationship and to confirm the results of the review.

For the initial IND (the same is true for NDAs), FDA assigns a review team led by a regulatory project manager (RPM) that includes a medical reviewer and pharmacology/toxicology reviewer from the review division. Generally, a CMC reviewer from the Office of New Drug Chemistry is assigned. Depending upon the proposed study, a clinical pharmacologist from the Office of Clinical Pharmacology and a statistician from the Office of Biostatistics may be assigned as well. The team will generally meet the week that the 30-day review period ends and, with the division director, decide whether the proposed study may proceed. In some cases, the RPM may contact the sponsor to request additional information or to propose that the study may be initiated if certain amendments are made to the study protocol. In the latter case, or in the case of clinical hold, FDA

Table 9-3. IND Safety Reports Reporting Timeframes

SAE Outcome	Deadline for Reporting
Fatal or life-threatening	7 calendar days, by phone or facsimile, followed by a written report within 8 additional calendar days
All other outcomes	15 calendar days, in writing

will eventually issue a letter containing the details of any requested modifications to the protocol or supporting data.

If a pre-IND meeting was held with FDA, the assigned P-IND number becomes the IND number (the "P" is removed) and the initial submission is given a serial number (SN) 0000. Form FDA 1571 must accompany any submission (except a pre-IND meeting request) to the IND (termed an IND amendment) and each submission is given the next consecutive SN by the sponsor. This form is completed and signed by the sponsor or authorized representative to acknowledge sponsor responsibilities as codified in 21 CFR 312.50. Form FDA 1571 contains sponsor and drug product information and an indication of what the submission contains. Any initial IND submission must contain a clinical study protocol and at least one (if a multicenter study) completed Form FDA 1572. This form contains study site details and IRB name and address, as well as a signoff by the investigator acknowledging legal responsibilities as indicated on the form and in 21 CFR 312.60. The investigator's curriculum vitae, documenting qualifications to conduct the proposed study, is submitted with the Form FDA 1572. There is no 30-day review period for IND amendments.

Where previous clinical studies have not been conducted for an NCE, the initial IND is a major milestone because it summarizes the data that support moving a drug from in vitro and animal testing into evaluation in humans. There are a number of guidances (some in draft stage) on the content and issues relating to either first-in-human or IND clinical trials. These include:

- *Draft Guidance for Industry: Animal Models— Essential Elements to Address Efficacy Under the Animal Rule* (January 2009)
- *Guidance for Industry: Estimating the Maximum Safe Starting Dose in Initial Clinical Trials for Therapeutics in Adult Healthy Volunteers* (July 2005)
- *Draft Guidance: M3(R2) Nonclinical Safety Studies for the Conduct of Human Clinical Trials and Marketing Authorization for Pharmaceuticals* (July 2008)
- *Guidance for Industry: Immunotoxicology Evaluation of Investigational New Drugs* (October 2002)
- *Guidance for Industry: Nonclinical Evaluation of Pediatric Drug Products* (February 2006)
- *Guidance for Industry: Single Dose Acute Toxicity Testing for Pharmaceuticals* (August 1996)
- *Guidance for Industry: Dissolution Testing of*

Immediate Release Solid Oral Dosage Forms (August 1997)
- *Guidance for Industry: CGMP for Phase 1 Investigational Drugs* (July 2008)
- *Draft Guidance for Industry: Analytical Procedures and Methods Validation Chemistry, Manufacturing, and Controls Documentation* (August 2000)
- *Guidance for Industry: Collection of Race and Ethnicity Data in Clinical Trials* (September 2005)
- *Guidance for Industry: Exposure-Response Relationships—Study Design, Data Analysis, and Regulatory Applications* (April 2003)
- *Draft Guidance for Industry: Drug-Induced Liver Injury: Premarketing Clinical Evaluation* (October 2007)
- *Guidance for Industry: S1C(R2) Dose Selection for Carcinogenicity Studies* (September 2008)
- *Draft Guidance for Industry: Drug Interaction Studies—Study Design, Data Analysis, Implications for Dosing and Labeling* (September 2006)
- *Guidance for Industry: Pharmacokinetics in Patients with Impaired Hepatic Function: Study Design, Data Analysis, and Impact on Dosing and Labeling* (May 2003)
- *Guidance for Industry: Pharmacokinetics in Patients with Impaired Renal Function: Study Design, Data Analysis, and Impact on Dosing and Labeling* (May 1998)
- *Guideline for Industry: Studies in Support of Special Populations: Geriatrics* (August 1994)
- *Draft Guidance for Industry: How to Comply with the Pediatric Research Equity Act* (September 2005)

In addition, there are a number of other FDA guidelines specific to certain therapeutic indications that should be consulted where relevant.

The content and format of an initial IND are described in 21 CFR 312.23. Traditionally, the content follows the items listed in Section 12 of Form FDA 1571 and includes an IB, clinical protocol, CMC information, nonclinical pharmacology and toxicology information, and previous human experience information (the latter only if relevant). Although an initial IND can still be submitted in paper format (three copies of the submission are required), using the CTD format for the initial IND submission is becoming more common and is accepted by FDA. The advantage of this approach, especially when done electronically, is that it begins building a CTD for an eventual marketing application that is progressively updated during the course of drug development under the IND. The disadvantages are that the CTD structure in some areas (especially Module 1 and 2) does not easily fit the information available at an initial IND stage, and Section 12 of Form FDA 1571 (application contents) does not currently directly correlate with the CTD structure. The initial IND in CTD format can also be submitted electronically in the eCTD format (with the same considerations as for an electronically submitted NDA). However, once an IND is submitted electronically, all future IND submissions also must be submitted electronically.

For active INDs (an IND can be withdrawn (21 CFR 312.38) or considered inactive (21CFR 312.45)), sponsors are required to submit expedited safety reports for serious, unexpected adverse reactions to the IND (IND Safety Reports) as per the definitions provided in 21 CFR 312.32. A serious adverse event (SAE) is any untoward medical occurrence that results in death, is life-threatening, requires subject hospitalization or prolongation of existing hospitalization, results in persistent or significant disability/incapacity, or is a congenital anomaly/birth defect. Submission of IND safety reports to FDA is time sensitive. The date that the sponsor is notified of the SAE by the study site is considered Day 1, and all reporting timeframes are tied to this notification. **Table 9-3** summarizes these requirements. *Draft Guidance for Industry and Investigators—Safety Reporting Requirements for INDs and BA/BE Studies* (September 2010) provides further details and covers SAE reporting requirements for bioavailability (BA) and bioequivalence (BE) studies.

IND sponsors are required to submit annual reports to the IND within 60 days of the anniversary of the date the IND went into effect (21 CFR 312.33). The annual report focuses on safety signals (deaths or other SAEs, dropouts due to adverse events, and new nonclinical safety findings) and includes an outline of the development plan for the coming year. *Draft Guidance for Industry: E2F Development Safety Update Report* (June 2008) describes a new approach for annual safety reporting and is expected to replace the IND annual report with a comprehensive, harmonized safety summary that represents a common standard for the ICH regions.

Finally, FDA requires clinical trials to be registered with the Clinical Trials Data Bank (maintained by NIH's National Library of Medicine). This initiative began in 2001 with the posting of clinical studies for serious or life-threatening diseases and, under the *Food and Drug Administration Amendments Act* of 2007 (*FDAAA*), was expanded to include all controlled clinical trials in patients (i.e., other than Phase 1 studies). The Clinical Trials Data Bank can be accessed at www.clinicaltrials.gov. To date, the database has registered hundreds of thousands of trials in virtually every country in the world and can be a good resource for clinical study design information.

NDA and Risk/Benefit
General Considerations

The culmination of a drug or biologic development program is the preparation and submission of a marketing application (NDA or BLA). This is accomplished either through studies conducted by (or with a right of reference from) the sponsor (505(b)(1) approach) or by reference to FDA's finding of safety and effectiveness for a previously approved product (Section 505(b)(2) approach). Through frequent interactions with FDA during the development program, including a pre-NDA meeting (usually held no later than three months prior to the target filing date), sponsor and agency expectations should be reasonably well aligned. One tool suggested by FDA for late-stage discussions is the Target Product Profile (see *Draft Guidance for Industry: Target Product Profile—A Strategic Development Process Tool* (March 2007)). The marketing application should contain sufficient data for FDA to decide whether the drug's benefits outweigh its risks in the context of the sponsor's proposed label.

There are a number of key FDA guidances (some in draft stage) regarding the content and approaches to data organization in marketing applications. These include:

- *Guidance for Industry: Guideline for the Format and Content of the Nonclinical Pharmacology/Toxicology Section of an Application* (February 1987)
- *Draft Guidance for Reviewers on the Integration of Study Results to Assess Concerns about Human Reproductive and Developmental Toxicities* (November 2001)
- *Guidance for Industry and Review Staff: Recommended Approaches to Integration of Genetic Toxicology Study Results* (January 2006)
- *Draft Guidance for Industry: Statistical Aspects of the Design, Analysis, and Interpretation of Chronic Rodent Carcinogenicity Studies of Pharmaceuticals* (May 2001)
- *Guideline for the Format and Content of the Clinical and Statistical Sections of an Application* (July 1988)
- *Draft Guidance for Industry: Integrated Summary of Effectiveness* (August 2008)
- *Guidance for Industry: Premarketing Risk Assessment* (March 2005)

An NDA number for an application in paper format can be requested by contacting the Central Document Room at CDER by telephone. A number may be assigned directly over the phone upon provision of the review division name, sponsor's name, drug name, indication and your name and phone number. For electronic applications, there are specific instructions available on FDA's website for requesting a pre-assigned eCTD application number via secure email (www.fda.gov/Drugs/DevelopmentApprovalProcess/FormsSubmissionRequirements/ElectronicSubmissions/UCM085361).

Package Insert

Federal regulations pertaining to marketing applications are contained in 21 CFR 314. In addition to the study reports supporting the drug's safety and efficacy and the associated summaries, the core of the NDA is the draft package insert (or prescribing information, also referred to as simply the "label") which, since 2005, is required to be in structured product label (SPL) format in an XML (Extensible Markup Language) backbone in order to meet FDA filing requirements. SPL is a model-derived standard adopted for exchange of FDA-regulated product information in the content of the labeling, coded information from the content of the labeling (data elements) and a "wrapper" for electronic listing elements. In addition, most review divisions will request a copy of the label in Microsoft Word to be able to communicate in the label negotiation process using the track changes function. This should be confirmed either in the pre-NDA meeting or with the FDA project manager assigned to the NDA prior to filing. When a final label is agreed to, the sponsor will submit a revised copy of the label to the NDA in SPL format. Moreover, since 2006, new NDAs must follow the format required by the Physician Labeling Rule (PLR), which is made up of three parts: highlights (one page), contents and full prescribing information. The PLR format identifies and dates recent major changes to the prescribing information and includes the date of initial US approval for the active ingredient. Further information (including links to specific FDA guidelines on the content of different sections of the label) is available at www.fda.gov/Drugs/GuidanceComplianceRegulatoryInformation/LawsActsandRules/ucm084159.htm.

Electronic Submission

Since January 2008, sponsors submitting NDAs electronically have been required to use the eCTD format. Waivers are available for those who would like to submit electronically but are unable to do so in eCTD format. For further information, FDA maintains a useful Electronic Regulatory Submissions and Review website at www.fda.gov/Drugs/DevelopmentApprovalProcess/FormsSubmissionRequirements/ElectronicSubmissions/UCM085361. For an NDA, the content and format are dictated by the CTD format described above.

REMS

Evaluation of a product's risk potential has always been a difficult aspect of FDA drug approval. Generally, it is difficult to extrapolate from data derived from a few thousand patients exposed to the drug under relatively well-controlled conditions to millions of patients with much less oversight. FDA's mandate to mitigate potential risks of drugs throughout their development and marketing lifecycle led to the issuance of three draft guidances in 2004 (*Guidance*

for Industry: Premarketing Risk Assessment, Guidance for Industry: Development and Use of Risk Minimization Action Plans and *Guidance for Industry: Good Pharmacovigilance Practices and Pharmacoepidemiologic Assessment*). For drugs in development, FDA wanted to know how a sponsor planned to mitigate actual and potential risks (Risk MAP) if a marketing application was approved and how risk would be monitored postapproval. However, the agency did not have the statutory authority to require these assessments. This was rectified as part of *FDAAA,* which gave FDA the authority to require sponsors to submit a risk evaluation and mitigation strategy (REMS) plan prior to approval. A REMS may be as simple as inclusion of a medication guide with the package insert or as complex as a patient and pharmacist training program (additional elements to assure safe use). The REMS includes, at a minimum, a postapproval evaluation by the sponsor at 18 months, three years and seven years. However, given the newness of this requirement, only recently has more granularity on FDA expectations for these evaluations become available.

Proprietary Name

If not previously submitted, a request for review of the sponsor's proposed proprietary name(s) should be made to the review division under the IND (*Draft Guidance for Industry: Contents of a Complete Submission for the Evaluation of Proprietary Names* (November 2008)) or as a separate supplemental submission following submission of the initial NDA. Although the guidance states that this request may be submitted as early as at the end of Phase 2, FDA has begun to delay designating a proprietary name until close to the approval date. The review division will forward the proprietary name request to the Office of Postmarketing Drug Risk Assessment, Division of Drug Risk Evaluation, which will perform the primary review in consultation with the Division of Drug Marketing, Advertising, and Communication (DDMAC).

User Fees

Under the original *PDUFA* of 1992 (and subsequent amendments), user fees were levied on each "human drug application," including applications for:

- approval of a new drug submitted under section 505(b)(1) after 1 September 1992
- approval of a new drug submitted pursuant to section 505(b)(2) after 30 September 1992 for certain molecular entities or indications for use
- licensure of certain biological products under section 351 of the *PHS Act* submitted after 1 September 1992

PDUFA specifies different user fees for original applications depending upon whether they are accompanied by clinical data on safety and/or efficacy (other than BA or BE studies). The act also levies fees on supplements to human drug applications that require clinical data. Under the fee schedules provided in the act, original applications without clinical data and supplements that require clinical data are assessed approximately one-half the fee of original applications. Further details are provided in *Guidance for Industry: Submitting Separate Marketing Applications and Clinical Data for Purposes of Assessing User Fees* (December 2004). The user fee for a full submission has increased every year since it was implemented and is currently well over $1 million. FDA also levies annual establishment and product fees. Further information on these fees can be found at www.fda.gov/Drugs/DevelopmentApprovalProcess/SmallBusinessAssistance/ucm069943.htm. The Office of Regulatory Policy within CDER is responsible for all the above fees.

PAI

One of FDA's objectives in the NDA review process is to determine whether the methods used in manufacturing the drug and the controls used to maintain its quality are adequate to preserve the drug's identity, strength, quality and purity. In conjunction with this evaluation, FDA field inspectors conduct a CGMP preapproval inspection (PAI) of the drug product manufacturing site if it has not recently been inspected by FDA with a favorable outcome. A PAI can occur as early as 90 days after an NDA submission. An adequate PAI is generally required for NDA approval.

Periapproval Activities

There are a number of periapproval activities that should be part of the overall submission and approval plan. A safety update is required to be submitted as an amendment to the NDA within 120 days. In addition, approximately one month prior to the FDA action date, the FDA RPM will contact the sponsor and begin label negotiations. At this time (if not previously done), the sponsor should submit a request for a National Drug Code (NDC) assignment (*Draft Guidance for Industry: Standards for Securing the Drug Supply Chain—Standardized Numerical Identification for Prescription Drug Packages* (January 2009)). Historically, FDA has provided these NDC numbers months before approval of the application, but recently has limited this to the periapproval timeframe due to drug piracy concerns. Thus, the drug label, packaging artwork and labels and promotional material cannot be finalized until very close to the approval date.

In 1972, Congress passed the *Federal Advisory Committee Act*, which prescribed the formal use of Advisory Committees throughout the federal government. With the increasing complexity of risk benefit decisions, FDA has increasingly used Advisory Committees to provide independent advice that will contribute to the quality of the agency's regulatory decision making and lend credibility to

the product review process in cases where additional input is desired by FDA.

Establishment Listing

Under 21 CFR 207, FDA requires establishments (e.g., manufacturers, repackers and relabelers) upon first engaging in the manufacture, preparation, propagation, compounding or processing of human drugs, veterinary drugs and biological products, with certain exceptions, to register their establishments and submit listing information for all drugs and biological products in commercial distribution. Registrants are also required to submit, on or before 31 December each year, updates in registration information for their establishments. Form FDA 2656 is used for registration of the drug establishment (and also the labeler code assignment) and Form FDA 2657 is used for drug product listing purposes. In 2008, FDA began a pilot program to allow submission of the above information in an electronic format and, since 1 June 2009, all submissions are required to be completely electronic and in XML format, unless a waiver is granted. Further information is available in *Draft Guidance for Industry: Forms for Registration of Producers of Drugs and Listing of Drugs in Commercial Distribution* (April 2001) and at www.fda.gov/Drugs/GuidanceComplianceRegulatoryInformation/DrugRegistrationandListing/ucm084014.htm.

Patent Restoration

The passage of the *Hatch-Waxman Act* in 1984 represented a compromise between the innovator pharmaceutical industry and the generic pharmaceutical industry. It allowed the innovator pharmaceutical companies to apply for up to five years of additional patent protection for new drugs to make up for time lost while their products were going through the development and regulatory review process. The drug (animal or human), medical device, biologic or food or color additive must be the first commercial marketing or use of the product under the provision of the law for which regulatory review occurred. FDA assists the Patent and Trademark Office (PTO) in determining a product's eligibility for patent extension, but PTO is ultimately responsible for determining the period of patent extension. Similarly, up to three years of exclusivity is granted for a change in an approved drug product where approval requires new clinical investigations other than BA studies (e.g., new indication, strength, dosage form or route of administration). The following website provides further details on the patent term restoration program, www.fda.gov/Drugs/DevelopmentApprovalProcess/SmallBusinessAssistance/ucm069959.htm. Six months of pediatric exclusivity (FDA's incentive to conduct more studies of the use of the drug in pediatric populations) also can be requested; see www.fda.gov/Drugs/DevelopmentApprovalProcess/

Figure 9-2. Decision Tree for Drug and Device Delopment and Approval for Situations that Require FDA Premarket Review

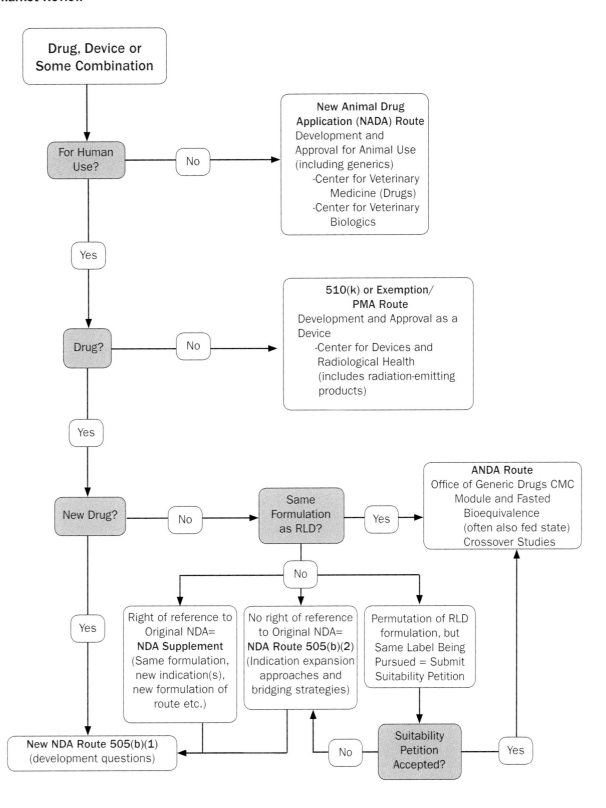

(ANDA, Abbreviated New Drug Application; CMC, Chemistry, Manufacturing, and Controls; NDA, New Drug Application; PMA, Premarket Approval; RLD, Reference Listed Drug (per *Orange Book*))

DevelopmentResources/UCM049867.htm for additional details.

NDA Amendments

Finally, an NDA amendment is submitted to change or add information to an unapproved NDA or NDA supplement. With the exception of the required 120-day safety update, sponsors should try to avoid initiating NDA amendments because they will potentially reset the review clock (especially if submitted in the final three months of the review period).

The 505(b)(2) NDA
Overview

The "paper" NDA approach was created after the 1962 passage of the *Drug Amendments* to the *FD&C Act*. It created a means by which duplicates (now known as generic drugs) of post-1962 drugs could be approved because the DESI program and the ANDA did not apply to drugs approved after 1962. The paper NDA policy allowed applicants to use published literature to satisfy the requirements for full reports of safety and effectiveness. The *Hatch-Waxman Act* eliminated the paper NDA policy because it provided a mechanism to approve duplicates of post-1962 drugs, including situations where the applicant did not have the right of reference to the original NDA submitted and approved under Section 505(b)(1) of the *FD&C Act*.

The 505(b)(2) NDA is a submission type that shares characteristics of both traditional NDAs and ANDAs and is named after the section of the *FD&C Act* that describes it. **Figure 9-2** outlines how this type of NDA potentially fits into the overall development and approval scheme for a drug. As with an NDA, a 505(b)(2) application is submitted under Section 505(b)(1) and is considered a complete application. Like a traditional NDA, it is approved under Section 505(c) of the act. Like an ANDA, a 505(b)(2) application may refer to FDA's finding of safety and effectiveness for a previously approved product, and its approval is subject to patent exclusivity limitations. The applicant may also rely on published literature. *Draft Guidance for Industry: Applications Covered by Section 505(b)(2)* (October 1999) provides additional details. The regulations for this type of application are codified in 21 CFR 314.54.

Bridging and Expansion Issues and Approaches

The most common uses of the 505(b)(2) route are for:
- change in drug product dosage form (including route of administration), formulation, strength and/or dosing regimen, including changes that were not accepted by OGD in a Suitability Petition
- change in active ingredient (different salt, acid or base)
- new combination product in which the active ingredients have been previously approved individually

- change from a prescription indication to an over-the-counter (OTC) indication
- indication that has not been previously approved for the active moiety
- NCE that is a prodrug or active metabolite of a drug approved in the US

If the applicant is the original NDA holder or has right of reference to that NDA from the holder, the above changes become supplements to the original NDA as outlined in **Figure 9-2**.

The data most commonly required in a 505(b)(2) approach provide a bridge between the data forming the basis for approval of the referenced NDA (and agreed to by FDA in the approved drug product label) and the different or additional claims in the 505(b)(2) NDA label. For active ingredient modifications, bridging centers on changes in impurity profiles and/or bioavailability and subsequent exposure. For drug product modifications, bridging centers on differences in the exposure profile. In both cases, a bridging toxicology program usually includes multiple-dose toxicology studies (between 14 and 90 days), with toxicokinetics in appropriate species, as well as mutagenicity and genotoxicity studies. The bridging program generally should not be initiated until agreement is reached with FDA in a formal meeting and the IND is in effect.

The above types of changes will also require additional bridging clinical pharmacokinetic studies. The product should be at least as bioavailable as the RLD unless it has some other advantage such as a smaller peak/trough exposure ratio. Moreover, the pattern of release of the proposed product, although different, should be at least as favorable as that of the RLD. Clinical studies conducted for a 505(b)(2) application generally should be performed under an IND. A 505(b)(2) application may itself be granted three years of exclusivity if one or more of the clinical investigations, other than BA/BE studies, was essential to approval and was conducted for or sponsored by the applicant. A 505(b)(2) application may also be granted five years of exclusivity if it is for an NCE.

Between 1996 and 2004, 126 Section 505(b)(2) applications were filed,[4] and this continues to be a productive approach for moving older drugs into new technology platforms and/or better characterized and understood therapeutic areas. Tuttle[5] provides a concise description of how the regulatory professional can research this development approach.

Dietary Supplements and Natural Health Products

A dietary supplement is a product taken by mouth that contains a "dietary ingredient" intended to supplement the diet. These dietary ingredients may be vitamins, minerals, herbs or other botanicals, amino acids or substances such as enzymes, organ tissues, glandulars and metabolites.

Until 1994, dietary supplements were subject to the same regulatory requirements as other foods. Based upon the belief in a positive relationship between sound dietary practices and health, Congress passed the *Dietary Supplement Health and Education Act (DSHEA)* in 1994, which amended the *FD&C Act* to create a new regulatory framework for the safety and labeling of dietary supplements (yet still under the regulatory umbrella of foods). Provisions of *DSHEA* define dietary supplements and dietary ingredients, and describe the proper use of statements of nutritional support. *DSHEA* also set forth new labeling requirements and required manufacturers of dietary supplements to notify FDA of new dietary ingredients (after 1994; 21 CFR 190.6) prior to marketing. Interestingly, it also authorized FDA to prescribe GMPs for the industry. A final rule on this latter aspect was not forthcoming until 2007. The *Final Rule on CGMPs in Manufacturing, Packaging, Labeling, or Holding Operations for Dietary Supplements* established dietary supplement CGMPs for all domestic and foreign companies that manufacture, package, label or hold these supplements, including those involved with testing, quality control, packaging and labeling and distribution in the US. The dietary supplement CGMPs bear a stronger resemblance to drug CGMPs than to the rather general food CGMPs; however, dietary supplement CGMPs do not require process validation, which is mandated for drug CGMPs.

Dietary supplements do not require premarket approval by FDA. The manufacturer is responsible for ensuring that a dietary supplement is safe before it is marketed. *DSHEA* places the burden on FDA to prove that a marketed dietary supplement is unsafe prior to any action to remove the product from the market. Because of this requirement and the fact that FDA received numerous reports of safety concerns for a number of products,[6] Congress passed the *Dietary Supplement and Nonprescription Drug Consumer Protection Act* in 2006. It mandates the same type of adverse event reporting for dietary supplements as for prescription drugs.

Dietary supplement claims allowed under *DSHEA* include:

- claims of benefits related to nutrient deficiencies (if the prevalence of the disease in the US is disclosed)
- claims describing the role of the dietary supplement's effects on structure or function in humans (e.g., "calcium builds strong bones")
- claims describing the mechanism of effects on structure or function (e.g., "fiber maintains bowel regularity")
- claims of general well being

Manufacturers cannot make an express or implied claim that a product will diagnose, mitigate, treat, cure or prevent a specific disease or class of diseases. Examples of prohibited statements include: "protects against the development of cancer" or "reduces the pain and stiffness associated with arthritis." Examples of allowable structure/function claims include: "helps promote urinary tract health," "helps maintain cardiovascular function," or "promotes relaxation." Further details can be found in *Guidance for Industry: Structure/Function Claims Small Entity Compliance Guide* (2002).

Over-the-Counter (OTC) Drugs

An OTC product is a drug product marketed for use by the consumer without the intervention of a healthcare professional. There are more than 80 therapeutic categories of OTC drugs, and more than 100,000 OTC drug products are marketed in the US, encompassing approximately 800 active ingredients. Oversight of OTC drugs is performed by the CDER's Office of Nonprescription Drugs.

The distinction between drugs that do and do not require a physician prescription dates back to the 1951 *Durham-Humphrey Amendment* to the 1938 *FD&C Act.*[7] FDA applied the principle of retrospective review to OTC drugs starting in 1972. The OTC review by panels of experts focused on active ingredients (initially, approximately 1,000 different moieties). The agency published the results as a series of monographs in 21 CFR 328–358, specifying the active ingredient(s), restrictions on formulations and labeling by therapeutic category for those drugs deemed appropriate for OTC use.

If the standards of the relevant monograph are met, marketing preclearance of an OTC is not required. An NDA 505(b)(2) can be used to request approval of an OTC drug that deviates in any respect from a monograph that has become final (21 CFR 330.11). However, a citizen petition (see 21 CFR 10.30) is an alternate route that bypasses the requirement of *PDUFA* user fees.

"Prescription-to-OTC switch" refers to over-the-counter marketing of a former prescription drug product for the same indication, strength, dose, duration of use, dosage form, population and route of administration. An efficacy supplement to an approved NDA for a prescription product should be submitted if the sponsor plans to switch a drug product covered under an NDA to OTC status in its entirety without a change in the previously approved dosage form or route of administration. An NDA under Section 505(b)(1) should be submitted if the sponsor is proposing to convert some, but not all, of the approved prescription indications to OTC marketing status. An original NDA ((505)(b)(1) or 505(b)(2)) needs to be submitted if the sponsor plans to market a new product whose active substance, indication or dosage form has never previously been marketed OTC.

FDA has approved the switch of a number of drugs from prescription to OTC status under NDAs:

Table 9-4. Summary of Device Classification System

Class	Required Controls			Exemptions	Examples
	General	Special	Premarket Approval		
I	X			Exempt = subject to limitations on exemptions covered under 21 CFR xxx.9, where xxx refers to Parts 862–892. Class I devices are usually exempt.	elastic bandages, examination gloves, hand-held surgical instruments
II	X	X		Nonexempt = 510(k) required for marketing	powered wheelchairs, infusion pumps, surgical drapes
III	X	X	X	Exempt if it is a preamendment device (i.e., on the market prior to the passage of the Medical Device Amendments in 1976, or substantially equivalent to such a device) and PMAs have not been called for. In that case, a 510(k) will be the route to market	heart valves, silicone gel-filled breast implants, implanted cerebellar stimulators

- antidiarrheals (loperamide)
- topical antifungals (clotrimazole, terbinafine)
- antihistamines (clemastine fumarate)
- vaginal antifungals (clotrimazole, miconazole nitrate)
- analgesics (ketoprofen, naproxen sodium)
- acid reducers (cimetidine, famotidine)
- hair growth treatments (minoxidil)
- smoking cessation drugs (nicotine polacrilex)

In allowing these drugs to be sold OTC, FDA considered safety and effectiveness, risk/benefit ratio and whether clear and understandable labeling could be written to enable consumers to safely self-medicate. In 21 CFR 201.66, the agency established standardized content and format for OTC drug product labeling. In addition, manufacturers commonly are required to conduct studies to determine whether consumers understand the proposed OTC labeling and can use the products in a safe and effective manner.[8] OTC product labeling has always contained usage and safety information for consumers. With the introduction of the "Drug Facts" label regulation in 1999, the information became more uniform and easier to read and understand. Patterned after the Nutrition Facts food label, the Drug Facts label uses simple language and an easy-to-read format to help people compare and select OTC medicines and follow dosage instructions. The following information must appear in the indicated order:

- product's active ingredients, including the amount in each dosage unit
- purpose of the product
- product uses (indications)
- specific warnings, including when the product should not be used under any circumstances, and when it is appropriate to consult with a doctor or

pharmacist; this section also describes possible side effects and substances or activities to avoid
- dosage instructions—when, how and how often to take the product
- inactive ingredients, to help consumers avoid ingredients that could cause an allergic reaction

Medical Devices
Overview and Medical Device Classification

A "device" is defined by FDA as an instrument, apparatus, implement, machine, contrivance, implant, in vitro reagent or other similar or related article, including a component part, or accessory which is:

- recognized in the official *National Formulary* or the *United States Pharmacopoeia* or any supplement to them
- intended for use in the diagnosis of disease or other conditions, or in the cure, mitigation, treatment or prevention of disease, in man or other animals
- intended to affect the structure or any function of the body of man or other animals, and which does not achieve any of its primary intended purposes through chemical action within or on the body of man or other animals and which is not dependent upon being metabolized for the achievement of any of its primary intended purposes

Devices first became subject to regulation under the *FD&C Act* (which also defined medical devices for the first time). As a result of the increasing hazards that could result from new, more-complicated devices that were being introduced in the 1960s and 1970s (e.g., pacemakers, kidney dialysis machines, replacement heart valves), Congress passed the *Medical Device Amendments* in 1976 and heralded the modern age of device regulation. These amendments included the following major provisions:

- redefined medical devices to make them more distinct from drugs and expanded the definition to include diagnostics for conditions other than disease
- established safety and efficacy requirements for devices
- established premarket review by FDA
- established the medical device classification system
- created two routes to market (premarket notification and premarket approval) and established Investigational Device Exemptions (IDEs)

A second milestone in device regulation was the passage of the *Safe Medical Device Act* (*SMDA*) in 1990. This act included the following major provisions:

- extended adverse device incident reporting to user facilities including hospitals, ambulatory surgical facilities and nursing homes (This was a landmark event because FDA had never extended its jurisdiction so broadly. When a user facility receives information regarding a death caused by a device, it must report it to FDA and the manufacturer. If a user facility receives information about a serious injury or illness caused by a device, it must report it to the manufacturer. A user facility must also submit to FDA an annual summary of its reports to the agency.)
- required device tracking requirements for high-risk devices
- defined substantial equivalence
- required that submitters of 510(k)s receive clearance by FDA prior to marketing
- gave FDA the authority to regulate combination products
- defined the humanitarian device exemption
- gave FDA recall authority

These regulatory milestones gave rise to most of the modern components of the regulations used by FDA's Center for Devices and Radiological Health (CDRH) to fulfill its responsibilities for regulating firms that manufacture, repackage, relabel and/or import medical devices sold in the US.

Because medical devices vary widely in complexity and risks or benefits, they do not all require the same degree of regulation. Thus, FDA places medical devices into one of three regulatory classes based upon the level of control necessary to assure safety and effectiveness. Device classification depends upon intended use as well as indications for use. In addition, classification is based upon the risk the device poses to the patient and/or the user. Class I includes devices with the lowest risk and Class III includes those with the greatest

risk. The class to which a device is assigned determines the type of premarketing submission/application required for marketing. **Table 9-4** summarizes this system.

General controls for all classes include:

1. establishment registration of companies required to register under 21 CFR 807.20, such as manufacturers, distributors, repackagers and relabelers; foreign establishments, however, are not required to register with FDA
2. medical device listing with FDA
3. manufacturing devices in accordance with GMP in 21 CFR 820
4. labeling devices in accordance with labeling regulations in 21 CFR 801 or 809
5. submission of a premarket notification (510(k)) (unless exempt) before marketing a device

Special controls may include special labeling requirements, mandatory performance standards and postmarket surveillance.

Premarket approval is the required process of scientific review to ensure the safety and effectiveness of Class III devices, the most stringent regulatory category. Class III devices are those for which insufficient information exists to assure safety and effectiveness solely through general or special controls. They usually support or sustain human life, are of substantial importance in preventing impairment of human health or present a potential, unreasonable risk of illness or injury.

FDA has established classifications for approximately 1,700 different generic types of devices and grouped them into 16 medical specialties, referred to as "panels." Classification of a device can be obtained through the CFR or the CDRH database.

CBER reviews marketing and investigational device submissions (510(k)s, PMAs and IDEs) for medical devices associated with blood collection and processing procedures, as well as those associated with cellular therapies and vaccines. Although these products are reviewed by CBER, the medical device laws and regulations still apply.

It is important for the regulatory professional to ensure that a general product definition is available for new devices. Responses to the following questions will help to guide this effort:

1. What will the device do? (intended use)
2. For what clinical conditions or patient population will the device be used? (indications for use)
3. How does the device work? (principles of operation)
4. What are the features of the product? For example, is it electronic versus mechanical, controlled by software or other mechanism, invasive or noninvasive, implanted versus not, sterile versus nonsterile, disposable versus reusable? (product characteristics)

5. What are the risks inherent in the use of the device? (risks)

A designation similar to that for an orphan drug provides an incentive for the development of devices for use in the treatment or diagnosis of diseases affecting small populations. A Humanitarian Use Device (HUD) is intended to benefit patients by treating or diagnosing a disease or condition that affects or is manifested in fewer than 4,000 individuals in the US per year. A request for HUD designation (21 CFR 807) needs to be submitted to FDA; if so designated, the device is eligible for a humanitarian device exemption (HDE). An HDE submission is similar in both form and content to a premarket approval (PMA) application, but is exempt from the effectiveness requirements of a PMA.

An approved HDE authorizes marketing of the HUD. However, an HUD may only be used in facilities that have established a local IRB to supervise clinical testing of devices and after the IRB has approved the use of the device to treat or diagnose the specific disease. The device labeling must state that it is a humanitarian use device and that, although authorized by federal law, its effectiveness for the specific indication has not been demonstrated.

The CDRH website has a number of useful, searchable databases including one for device classifications, one for 510(k)s, a similar one for PMAs, and one for registrations and listings. There is also Device Advice (www.fda.gov/MedicalDevices/DeviceRegulationandGuidance/default.htm), which is very helpful, and a relatively new CDRH Learn site (www.fda.gov/MedicalDevices/ResourcesforYou/Industry/ucm126230.htm) that provides both visual and audio components. Finally, Chapters 10, 11, 12 and 13 of this book are devoted to devices and provide more detailed coverage.

Premarket Notification 510(k) and Exemptions

A sponsor wishing to market a Class I, II or III device intended for human use in the US, for which a PMA is not required, must submit a 510(k) exemption to FDA unless the device is exempt from those requirements and does not exceed the limitations of exemptions in the CFR device classifications as detailed below.

FD&C Act Section 513(d)(2)(A) authorizes FDA to exempt certain generic types of Class I devices from the premarket notification (510(k)) requirement. FDA has exempted more than 800 generic types of Class I devices and 60 Class II devices from the requirement. It is important to confirm the exempt status and any limitations that apply with 21 CFR 862–892, the CDRH Product Code Classification Database or subsequent *Federal Register* announcements on Class I or II exemptions. The 510(k) exemption has certain limitations, which are so noted in ".9" of each chapter of the regulation.

There is no 510(k) form; however, 21 CFR 807 Subpart E describes requirements for a 510(k) submission. This premarket submission to FDA demonstrates that the device to be marketed is as safe and effective as (i.e., substantially equivalent to) a legally marketed predicate device that is not subject to PMA. A predicate device can be:

1. a preamendment device (a currently marketed device that was on the market prior to 1976)
2. a device reclassified from Class III to Class II or I
3. a device found to be substantially equivalent to a device in the one of the above two categories

A device is substantially equivalent if, in comparison to a predicate, it:
- has the same intended and the same technological characteristics as the predicate

or

- has the same intended use as the predicate and different technological characteristics and the information submitted to FDA
  o does not raise new questions of safety and effectiveness
  o demonstrates that the device is at least as safe and effective as the legally marketed device

A claim of substantial equivalence does not mean that the new device and the predicate device must be identical. Substantial equivalence is established with respect to intended use, design, energy used or delivered, materials, performance, safety, effectiveness, biocompatibility, standards and other applicable characteristics (e.g., sterility).

FDA determines substantial equivalence, usually within 90 days. If the device is determined to be substantially equivalent, it can be marketed in the US when the submitter receives a letter from the agency (and the sponsor has complied with the general controls provisions). If FDA determines that a device is not substantially equivalent, the applicant may:
- resubmit another 510(k) with new data
- request a Class I or II designation through the *de novo* process
- file a reclassification petition
- submit a PMA

A 510(k)'s content and complexity can vary significantly depending upon the amount of information needed to establish substantial equivalence to the predicate. A typical 510(k) is between 15 and 100 pages. There are three subtypes of 510(k)s: a traditional 510(k), described in 21 CFR 807; a special 510 (k); and an abbreviated 510(k) The latter two are described in *The New 510(k) Paradigm—Alternate Approaches to Demonstrating Substantial Equivalence in Premarket Notifications: Final Guidance* (March 1998).

Investigational Device Exemption (IDE) and Premarket Approval (PMA) Process

An IDE (21 CFR 812) allows the investigational device to be used in a clinical study to collect safety and effectiveness data required to support a PMA application or a Premarket Notification (510(k)) submission to FDA. Clinical studies are most often conducted to support a PMA. Only a small percentage of 510(k)s require clinical data to support the application. Investigational use also includes clinical evaluation of certain modifications or new intended uses of legally marketed devices. All clinical evaluations of investigational devices, unless exempt, must have an approved IDE before the study is initiated. The IDE is similar in content and organization to an IND. The sponsor may begin clinical trials 30 days after FDA receives the IDE, unless the agency objects.

Clinical evaluation of devices that have not been cleared for marketing requires:

- an IDE approved by an IRB; if the study involves a significant risk device, the IDE must also be approved by FDA
- informed consent from all patients
- labeling for investigational use only
- study monitoring
- records and reports

An approved IDE permits a device to be shipped lawfully for the purpose of conducting investigations without complying with other requirements of the *FD&C Act* that apply to devices in commercial distribution. Sponsors need not submit a PMA or Premarket Notification 510(k), register their establishment or list the device while it is under investigation. IDE sponsors are also exempt from the Quality System Regulation (QSR) except for the requirements for design control.

In an industry of 15,000 manufacturers, where half have fewer than 10 employees, the planning and conduct of a clinical study can take a significant proportion of resources. For significant risk devices, where trials can be relatively complex and expensive, following the types of processes used for industry-sponsored drug trials is advisable to protect the validity of the company's investment. This should include the use of clinical study protocols, informed consent forms that meet FDA regulations (21 CFR 50) and are reviewed by duly constituted IRBs (21 CFR 56), source documents at the investigational sites, clinical study reports and well-written investigator agreements that include not only financial aspects (see 21 CFR 54), but also compliance with the study protocol and IDE responsibilities.

Premarket approval is FDA's review process to evaluate the safety and effectiveness of Class III medical devices. Due to the level of risk associated with Class III devices, FDA has determined that general and special controls alone are insufficient to assure their safety and effectiveness. Therefore, these devices require a PMA application (21 CFR 814).

A PMA is the most stringent type of device marketing application required by FDA. The applicant must receive FDA approval of its PMA application prior to marketing the device. Approval is based upon a determination by FDA that the PMA contains sufficient valid scientific evidence to assure that the device is safe and effective for its intended use(s). An approved PMA is, in effect, a private license granting the applicant (or owner) permission to market the device. The PMA owner, however, can authorize use of its data by another.

The PMA application is similar in content and organization to a traditional (non-CTD format) NDA application, although with much less clinical data required. FDA has observed problems with study designs, study conduct, data analyses, presentations and conclusions. Sponsors should always consult all applicable FDA guidance documents, industry standards and recommended practices. Numerous device-specific FDA guidance documents are available. Although FDA has 180 days to review the PMA, in reality this usually takes longer, due to the frequent involvement of an Advisory Committee.

Establishment Registration and Medical Device Listing

Establishments involved in the production and distribution of medical devices intended for marketing or leasing (commercial distribution) in the US are required to register with FDA. This process is known as establishment registration. Registration provides FDA with the location of medical device manufacturing facilities and importers. An establishment is defined as any place of business under one management at one physical location at which a device is manufactured, assembled or otherwise processed for commercial distribution. The "owner/operator" is defined as the corporation, subsidiary, affiliated company, partnership or proprietor directly responsible for the activities of the registering establishment. The owner/operator is responsible for registering the establishment.

The regulations for establishment registration are provided in 21 CFR 807. As of 1 October 2007, all establishment registrations and listings must be submitted electronically using FDA's Unified Registration and Listing System (FURLS), unless a waiver has been granted. Congress also authorized FDA to implement a user fee for certain types of establishment registrations processed after 30 September 2007 (for 2011 this fee is $2,179). Registration of an establishment is not an approval of the establishment or its products by FDA. That is, it does not provide FDA clearance to market. Unless exempt, premarketing clearance or approval is required before a device can be placed into commercial distribution in the US.

Most medical device establishments required to register

with FDA must also identify the devices they have in commercial distribution, including those produced exclusively for export. This process is known as medical device listing and is a means of keeping FDA advised of the generic category(s) of devices an establishment is manufacturing or marketing. The regulations for medical device listing are also provided in 21 CFR 807.

Quality Systems for Manufacturing

The CGMP requirements set forth in the QSR require domestic or foreign manufacturers to have a quality system for the design, manufacture, packaging, labeling, storage, installation and servicing of finished medical devices intended for commercial distribution in the US. The regulation requires:

- various specifications and controls to be established for devices
- devices to be designed under a quality system to meet these specifications
- devices to be manufactured under a quality system
- finished devices to meet these specifications
- devices to be correctly installed, checked and serviced
- quality data to be analyzed to identify and correct quality problems
- complaints to be processed

FDA monitors device problem data and inspects the operations and records of device developers and manufacturers to determine compliance with the GMP requirements in the QSR.

The QSR is contained in 21 CFR 820. It covers quality management and organization, device design, buildings, equipment, purchasing and handling of components, production and process controls, packaging and labeling control, device evaluation, distribution, installation, complaint handling, servicing and records.

Combination Drug-Device and Drug-Drug Products

Combination products (i.e., drug-device, drug-biologic and device-biologic products, formally defined in 21 CFR 3.2(e)) have been regulated for decades. Prior to 1990, FDA regulated such products on a case-by-case basis. Generally, the sponsor and FDA negotiated an ad hoc regulatory approach without explicit statutory guidance. As combination products multiplied and increased in complexity, the ad hoc approach was no longer satisfactory, and in 1990, Congress enacted the *SMDA*. This provision required the agency to designate a center (CDER, CBER or CDRH) with primary jurisdiction based upon the product's primary mode of action. FDA issued intercenter agreements between the three centers in 1991; however, there were still a number of problems with this approach.[9]

As part of the *Medical Device User Fee and Modernization Act* of 2002 (*MDUFMA*), Congress established the Office of Combination Products (OCP) within FDA's Office of the Commissioner to ensure prompt assignment of combination products to FDA centers and oversee coordination of the development and approval processes.

By submitting a Request for Designation (RFD), a company may obtain a formal agency determination of a combination product's primary mode of action and assignment of the lead center for the product's premarket review and regulation. OCP will make a determination within 60 days of receipt of the RFD. *Guidance for Industry and FDA Staff: How to Write a Request for Designation* (August 2005) provides more specifics.

In recent years, in part as pharmaceutical companies strive to reduce the inherent risks of drug development, drug-drug combinations have become increasingly common. Combination drug products are convenient and can improve dosing compliance, especially in polypharmacy scenarios. Moreover, by combining drugs with different mechanisms of action, lower doses can be used, which may decrease adverse effects (e.g., diuretics combined with angiotensin-converting enzyme (ACE) inhibitors, angiotensin receptor blockers or beta-adrenergic blockers for the treatment of hypertension, or some antiretroviral agents combining up to three drugs in one dosage form).

The type of development program for drug-drug combinations will depend upon whether one, both or neither component of a two-drug (or greater) combination product has been previously approved. From a nonclinical perspective, FDA has issued *Guidance for Industry: Nonclinical Safety Evaluation of Drug or Biologic Combinations* (March 2006). Similar principles would apply to the clinical portion of the development program. However, in both cases, proposed development approaches should be discussed with FDA in the early stages.

Summary

The development of drugs and devices is a scientific process in the context of objective and subjective interpretations of a product's potential or actual risks and benefits. The scope, interpretation and application of US federal regulations that must be met to market a drug or device have evolved over the past century and are documented in the CFR. This translates into agency use of scientific review, standards, manufacturing and other inspections, advertising controls, conditional approvals, laboratory product testing and postmarketing pharmacovigilance activities. Over the last 25 years, a plethora of FDA and ICH guidelines have been issued to assist in interpreting and defining the processes needed to successfully develop drugs, biologics and devices for marketing in a regulated industry.

FDA is part of the PHS within DHHS and comprises nine centers/offices.

There has been a formal veterinary unit at FDA since 1928. CVM oversees the veterinary drug development and approval process. However biologics for animal use (vaccines, bacterins, antisera and other products of biological origin) are overseen by the US Department of Agriculture, Animal and Plant Health Inspection Service, CVB.

The modern era of generic drugs was born with passage of the *Hatch-Waxman Act*. This act expedited the availability of less-costly generic drugs by permitting FDA to approve abbreviated applications after the patent of the innovator drug had expired. These abbreviated applications generally are not required to include animal safety and clinical data to establish safety and effectiveness. Specifically, a generic drug product is comparable to the innovator drug product in dosage form, strength, route of administration, quality, performance characteristics and intended use.

A "drug" is defined as a product used in diagnosing, curing, mitigating, treating or preventing a disease or affecting a structure or function of the body. A "biologic" is defined as a substance derived from or made with the aid of living organisms. Drug development consists of characterizing the safety profile (risk) and the efficacy profile (benefit) as it relates to the body's exposure to the drug (pharmacokinetic profile). The most successful drugs are those with minimal risk and maximum benefit.

The relationship between FDA and an investigational drug product sponsor can begin very early in the process (before the sponsor submits an IND) and extends through the typical IND development process (often defined as Phases 1, 2 and 3) to a marketing application and postapproval commitments, safety surveillance and product lifecycle management. Meetings with FDA are an important component of the IND process. Meetings can be requested at any time for any valid reason, but FDA will decide whether there is sufficient justification for a meeting (usually dictated by the product background and draft questions submitted in a written meeting request) or if a written response to questions and/or a teleconference would suffice.

Sponsors can submit a request for a Special Protocol Assessment (SPA). Within 45 days of receipt, FDA will evaluate certain protocols and related issues to determine whether they meet scientific and regulatory requirements identified by the sponsor. Three types of protocols are eligible for an SPA under the *PDUFA* goals—animal carcinogenicity protocols, final product stability protocols and clinical protocols for Phase 3 trials whose data will form the basis for an efficacy claim (i.e., a pivotal trial).

The *Orphan Drug Act*, for the first time, provided incentives for development of drugs necessary, and often lifesaving, for patients with rare diseases (defined as a US prevalence of less than 200,000 patients) but with minimal prospects for commercial return on investment.

The fast track program is designed to facilitate the development and expedite the review of new drugs intended to treat serious or life-threatening conditions and that demonstrate the potential to address unmet medical needs. A disease is considered serious based upon the likelihood that if left untreated, it will progress from a less-severe to a more severe condition. FDA defines "meeting an unmet medical need" as providing a therapy where none exists or that may be superior to existing therapy by meeting a number of conditions. A sponsor may request fast track designation at any point in the development process. A product in a fast track development program is eligible for heightened interest by FDA in sponsor meetings, a greater probability of priority review of the marketing application and piecemeal submission of portions (complete CTD modules) of a marketing application ("rolling NDA").

ICH was formed in 1990. It brings together the regulatory authorities of the EU, Japan and the US and experts from the pharmaceutical industry in the three regions to discuss scientific and technical aspects of product registration. ICH recommends ways to achieve greater harmonization in the interpretation and application of technical guidelines and requirements for product registration to reduce or avoid duplicating testing during the research and development of new drugs.

The ICH process has resulted in numerous guidelines in four major categories—quality, safety, efficacy and multidisciplinary. Two important aspects of the ICH endeavor are the CTD concept and *MedDRA*.

Before initiating a clinical trial in the US (other than bioequivalence studies to support an ANDA), the sponsor must submit nonclinical, CMC and previous human experience data (if applicable) to FDA in the form of an IND. The IND application requests permission to initiate clinical trials. It is not a request for approval; rather, it is a request for exemption from federal law requiring an approved NDA or BLA prior to transporting or distributing a drug in interstate commerce. For an NCE, the initial IND is a major milestone because it summarizes the data that support moving a drug from *in vitro* and animal testing into evaluation in humans. Sponsors are able to initiate their proposed clinical trial if they have not received any communication from the FDA within 30 days of FDA receipt of the initial IND application.

The culmination of a drug or biologic development program is the preparation and submission of a marketing application (NDA or BLA). This is accomplished either through studies conducted by (or with a right of reference from) the sponsor (505(b)(1) approach) or by reference to FDA's finding of safety and effectiveness for a previously approved product (Section 505(b)(2) approach). Through frequent interactions with FDA during the development program, including a pre-NDA meeting, sponsor and agency expectations should be reasonably well aligned.

Items to be considered when preparing a marketing application include package inserts (labeling), electronic submissions, Risk Evaluation and Mitigation Strategies (REMS), proprietary names, user fees, preapproval inspections (PAIs), establishment listings, patent restoration, other periapproval activities and NDA amendments and supplements.

A dietary supplement is a product taken by mouth that contains a "dietary ingredient" intended to supplement the diet. *DSHEA* created a new regulatory framework for the safety and labeling of dietary supplements (yet still under the regulatory umbrella of foods). Provisions of *DSHEA* define dietary supplements and dietary ingredients, and describe the proper use of statements of nutritional support. *DSHEA* set forth new labeling requirements and required manufacturers of dietary supplements to notify FDA of new dietary ingredients prior to marketing. It also authorized FDA to prescribe GMPs for the industry. Dietary supplements do not require premarket approval by FDA. The manufacturer is responsible for ensuring that a dietary supplement is safe before it is marketed. *DSHEA* places the burden on FDA to prove that a marketed dietary supplement is unsafe (including noncompliance with CGMPs) prior to any action to remove the product from the market.

An OTC product is a drug product marketed for use by the consumer without the intervention of a healthcare professional. There are more than 80 therapeutic categories of OTC drugs, and more than 100,000 OTC drug products are marketed in the US, encompassing approximately 800 active ingredients. Oversight of OTC drugs is performed by CDER's Office of Nonprescription Drugs. In allowing drugs to be sold OTC, FDA considers safety and effectiveness, risk/benefit ratio and whether clear and understandable labeling can be written to enable consumers to safely self-medicate.

A "device" is defined as an instrument, apparatus, implement, machine, contrivance, implant, in vitro reagent or other similar or related article, including a component part or accessory that meets a number of conditions.

FDA places medical devices into one of three regulatory classes based upon the level of control necessary to assure safety and effectiveness. Device classification depends upon intended use as well as indications for use, and the risk the device poses to the patient and/or user. Class I includes devices with the lowest risk and Class III includes those with the greatest risk. The class to which a device is assigned determines the type of premarketing submission/application required for marketing.

A sponsor wishing to market a Class I, II or III device intended for human use, for which a PMA is not required, must submit a 510(k) exemption to FDA unless the device is exempt from those requirements and does not exceed the limitations of exemptions in the CFR device classifications. A 510(k)'s content and complexity can vary significantly

depending upon the amount of information needed to establish substantial equivalence to the proposed predicate.

Premarket approval is the required process of scientific review to ensure the safety and effectiveness of Class III devices. Class III devices are those for which insufficient information exists to assure safety and effectiveness solely through general or special controls. They usually support or sustain human life, are of substantial importance in preventing impairment of human health or present a potential, unreasonable risk of illness or injury. An IDE allows the investigational device to be used in a clinical study to collect safety and effectiveness data required to support a PMA application or a Premarket Notification (510(k)) submission.

Establishments involved in the production and distribution of medical devices intended for commercial distribution in the US are required to register with FDA (establishment registration). In addition, the QSR requires domestic or foreign manufacturers to have a quality system for the design, manufacture, packaging, labeling, storage, installation and servicing of finished medical devices intended for commercial distribution in the US.

Combination products are defined as drug-device, drug-biologic and device-biologic products. As part of *MDUFMA*, Congress established OCP to ensure prompt assignment of combination products to FDA centers and oversee coordination of the development and approval processes. By submitting an RFD, a company may obtain a formal agency determination of a combination product's primary mode of action and assignment of the lead center for the product's premarket review and regulation.

References
1. www.fda.gov/AboutFDA/WhatWeDo/History/FOrgsHistory/CVM/default.htm
2. Ibid.
3. www.fda.gov/AboutFDA/WhatWeDo/History/FOrgsHistory/CBER/ucm135758.htm
4. Tuttle ME. "Researching the 505(b)(2) Application." *Regulatory Affairs Focus*, May 2004; pp. 12–14.
5. Ibid.
6. Jiang T and Zhang S. "Stringent Laws and Regulations for Dietary Supplements." *Drug Information Journal*, Vol. 43; No. 1. pp. 75–81. (2009)
7. Op cit 1.
8. Hellbusch SJ. "Involving the End User in the Development of Label Wording." *Regulatory Affairs Focus*, May 2004, pp. 48–51.
9. Kahan JS and Shapiro JK. "FDA's Regulation of Combination Products: The Road Ahead." *Regulatory Compliance Newsletter*. November 2003, pp. 37–40.

US Medical Device Submissions

By Chas Burr, SM, MBA, FRAPS and John DeLucia, MS, RAC

Objectives

❑ Discuss the types of submissions made to the Center for Devices and Radiological Health (CDRH)

❑ Explain how medical devices are classified and how the classification affects the types of submissions required

❑ Describe the IDE (Investigational Device Exemption) requirements for clinical device studies

❑ Review the types of 510(k) Premarket Notification submissions, when 510(k) submissions are needed and what information is required

❑ Review the types of PMA (Premarket Approval) submissions, when PMA submissions are needed and what information is required

❑ Discuss when Expedited Review should be requested

❑ Explain when an HDE (Humanitarian Device Exemption) is appropriate and what information is required.

❑ Provide an overview of the nature and status of current proposals for change based on recommendations from the August 2010 reports on the 510(k) program and CDRH's use of science in its decision-making.

Laws, Regulations and Guidelines Covered in This Chapter

❑ *Federal Food, Drug, and Cosmetic Act* of 1938

❑ 21 CFR 807 Establishment registration and device listing, premarket notification

❑ 21 CFR 812 Investigational Device Exemptions

❑ 21 CFR 814 Premarket approval

❑ 21 CFR 860 Medical device classification procedures

Introduction

Medical devices were first regulated by the *Federal Food, Drug, and Cosmetic Act* of 1938 (*FD&C Act*). It is enforced by the US Food and Drug Administration (FDA). Under the act, devices were examined for adulteration and misbranding but no provision was made for review of their safety or effectiveness prior to marketing. In the late 1960s, FDA started to concentrate on devices that posed problems with safety and effectiveness, requiring recalls and replacements.

The *FD&C Act* was amended in 1976 to include premarket review of medical devices. Under the act's amendments, FDA was authorized to set standards, with premarket clearance for some devices and premarket approval for others. Devices posing little or no risk to users or patients were exempted from standards and premarket clearance, but were not necessarily exempt from complying with parts of the Good Manufacturing Practice requirements for devices under 21 CFR 820, the Quality System Regulation (QSR).

FDA, primarily through the Center for Devices and Radiological Health (CDRH), is responsible for assuring that medical devices are safe and effective. Per the FDA Intercenter Agreement (31 October 1991), the Center for Biologics Evaluation and Research (CBER) has responsibility for devices related to blood and cellular products. The agency bears this responsibility through authority granted by the *FD&C Act*, which is carried out in accordance with the regulations found in Title 21 of the Code of Federal Regulations (CFR). Medical devices, referred to as "devices," are defined in Section 201(h) of the *FD&C Act*:

"The term "device" means an instrument, apparatus, implement, machine, contrivance, implant, in vitro reagent, or other similar or related article, including any component, part, or accessory, which is:

(1) recognized in the official *National Formulary*, or the *United States Pharmacopeia*, or any supplement to them,

(2) intended for use in the diagnosis of disease or other conditions, or in the cure, mitigation, treatment, or prevention of disease, in man or other animals, or

(3) intended to affect the structure or any function of the body of man or other animals, and which does not achieve its primary intended purposes through chemical action within or on the body of man or other animals and which is not dependent upon being metabolized for the achievement of its primary intended purposes."

Medical Device Classification (21 CFR 860)

Medical devices are regulated based upon a classification system that evaluates the risk posed by the product and the level of control needed to adequately assure safety. The device classification system has been modified by subsequent amendments, but generally remains as originally intended. The act defines three classes of medical devices according to increasing complexity and regulatory control:

- Class I—General Controls
- Class II—General Controls and Special Controls
- Class III—General Controls and Premarket Approval

Class I devices are generally low-risk devices, such as nonprescription sunglasses, for which safety and effectiveness can be assured by adherence to a set of guidelines or "general controls." General controls include compliance with the applicable portions of the QSR for manufacturing and recordkeeping; requirements for issuing notices about repair; replacing or refunding money for devices presenting an unreasonable risk of substantial harm; facility registration and product listing; adverse event reporting; and appropriate, truthful and non-misleading labeling, advertising and promotional materials. In rare circumstances,

some Class I devices also require premarket clearance by FDA through the 510(k) premarket notification process.

Class II devices are intermediate-risk devices, such as blood glucose test systems and infusion pumps, where general controls are not sufficient to ensure their safety and effectiveness. Class II devices are subject to "special controls," in addition to general controls. Special controls may include performance standards, FDA guidance documents, special labeling requirements, tracking of implantable devices, and other actions the agency deems necessary to assure safety and effectiveness. Most Class II devices are subject to premarket review and clearance by FDA through the 510(k) premarket notification process. At times, the review and requirements are just as rigorous as those for a Class III device.

Class III devices, such as life-sustaining, life-supporting or implantable devices, are considered by FDA to pose the greatest risk. Devices that have a new intended use or employ a unique, new technology that is not substantially equivalent to a legally marketed predicate device are also categorized as Class III. Class III devices are subject to the most rigorous controls, including general controls (like Class I and Class II devices), any relevant special controls (like Class II devices) and, in most cases, premarket approval, which requires the submission of evidence to establish reasonable assurance of the device's safety and effectiveness. Detailed manufacturing information may also be required. FDA may request a panel of outside experts to recommend the action to be taken on the Class III device. However, the agency is not compelled to take the panel's advice.

FDA uses Medical Device Classification Procedures described in 21 CFR 860 to determine device classifications. 21 CFR 862–892 contain resulting classification regulations. A device may be classified by its regulation and by a product code. Product codes may provide more specific designations within a classification regulation. Occasionally, FDA assigns a product code to a category of devices prior to the formal assignment of a regulatory classification. CDRH's Product Classification database[1] can be used to help determine classifications.

Reclassification

The rules and procedures for establishing a device's classification and requesting a change in device classification are contained in 21 CFR 860. Advantages of reclassifying a device from a PMA to a 510(k) route to marketing include reduced fees required by FDA to review the submission; often, reduced information requirements; and reduced requirements for submissions for changes. In Fiscal 2011, the PMA review fee is more than $230,000, while the 510(k) processing fee is approximately $4,300.

Since 1976, the primary reclassification activity has been geared toward down-classifying Class III devices into Class

II or I. Generating reclassification data requires considerable effort and resources. If successful, the reclassified device and any substantially equivalent device can be cleared for marketing through the less-burdensome 510(k) process.

It was the intent of Congress that reclassification play a potentially significant role in the medical device clearance process, although CDRH's interpretation of its mandate has not permitted the reclassification process to be utilized to a meaningful extent. A primary obstacle has been the high level of scientific information that CDRH requires to support a device's reclassification. A second obstacle has been difficulty in obtaining agreement among manufacturers whose products have already been cleared by PMAs. Removal of the PMA requirement may be seen as loss of a barrier to entry that limits competitors.

In 2009, FDA initiated the 515 Program Initiative[2] to facilitate reclassifications.

513(g) Request for Designation

It is sometimes unclear into which classification a device falls. A provision in Section 513(g) of the *FD&C Act* allows the device sponsor to request a classification determination from FDA. This requires a letter with a description of the device and a fee payment. The agency usually responds within 60 days with a classification assignment based on the material presented. More information is provided in a CDRHLearn training class.[3]

Exemptions

Most Class I devices, and some Class II devices, are exempt from 510(k) premarket notification requirements. However, they are not exempt from general controls. All medical devices must be manufactured under a quality assurance program, proven suitable for their intended use, appropriately packaged and properly labeled. The establishment and device must be registered and listed with FDA. Establishment registrations and listings are in the public domain. Some Class I devices are exempt from most GMP requirements, with the exception of complaint files and general recordkeeping.

Devices exempt from 510(k) are preamendment devices not significantly changed or modified and Class I and II devices specifically exempted by regulation.

A "preamendment device is one legally marketed in the US before May 28, 1976 that has not been significantly changed or modified and for which a regulation requiring a PMA application has not been published by FDA." Devices meeting this description are referred to as "grandfathered" and do not require a 510(k).

The *FD&C Act* authorizes FDA to exempt certain generic types of Class I devices from the premarket notification requirement. FDA has exempted more than 800 generic types of Class I devices and 60 Class II devices from the premarket notification requirement. Exemptions

occur on a periodic basis and are published in the *Federal Register*. The 510(k) exemption has certain limitations. Before deciding that a device is exempt, the sponsor must determine the device's classification status and limitations.

De Novo Process

The *Food and Drug Administration Modernization Act* of 1997 (*FDAMA*) created a process for the classification of certain low risk devices for which there is no predicate. Before *FDAMA*, such a device would automatically be designated Class III. Reclassification would be required to move the device to Class I or II. Under the de novo process, the sponsor of a device that has received a Not Substantially Equivalent determination can apply for a risk-based determination. The process has proven unwieldy and is rarely used. See the section of this chapter entitled Proposed Submission Changes, which provides details on FDA's plans to address problems in the de novo process.

Combination Products

Until 1990 and the introduction of the *Safe Medical Devices Act*, there was no formal process to establish which FDA center would regulate combination products, such as drug-device, device-biologic or biologic-drug products.

Regulations have now established that FDA makes a determination based on the primary mode of action of the combination product. By making this determination, the agency in effect decides whether the item is a drug, a device or a biologic. Then, FDA determines which center (Center for Drug Evaluation and Research (CDER), CBER or CDRH) is the primary reviewer. However, representatives of the other appropriate centers are included on the review committee.

If it is not clear whether the combination product is a device or drug, the manufacturer may file a Request for Designation with FDA. This compels the agency to classify the combination product and indicate which center which is the primary review group. The agency must respond within 60 days.

Investigational Device Exemption (IDE) (21 CFR 812)

The IDE regulations provide a means of distributing devices that are not cleared to be marketed (i.e., by 510(k), PMA or Class I exemption) for the purposes of clinical research or to gather clinical evidence of safety and effectiveness. Guidance is provided at *Device Advice: Investigational Device Exemption (IDE)*.[4]

Quoting the regulations (21 CFR 812.1):

"An IDE approved under 812.30 or considered approved under 812.2(b) exempts a device from the requirements of the following sections of the Federal Food, Drug, and Cosmetic Act and regulations issued thereunder: Misbranding under section 502 of the act, registration, listing, and premarket notification under section 510, performance standards under section 514, premarket approval under section 515, a banned device regulation under section 516, records and reports under section 519, restricted device requirements under section 520(e), good manufacturing practice requirements under section 520(f) except for the requirements found in 820.30, if applicable (unless the sponsor states an intention to comply with these requirements under 812.20(b)(3) or 812.140(b)(4)(v)) and color additive requirements under section 721."

FDA regulation and guidance often use the terms, "significant risk" device and "non-significant risk" (NSR) device. In practice, FDA considers the risk of the study, not of the device. For example, a Class III device, depending upon the nature of the study, may be in a significant risk study or a non-significant risk study, or in a study that is exempt from IDE requirements. The rest of this section uses FDA's terminology, e.g., "significant risk device."

A "significant risk device" must comply with full IDE requirements, including FDA approval of an IDE submittal. NSR devices must comply with abbreviated IDE requirements as described in 21 CFR 812.2(b). Abbreviated IDE requirements do not require FDA approval, but do require approval by Institutional Review Boards (IRBs). Abbreviated requirements also include informed consent and some reporting and recordkeeping (see **Table 10-1**). FDA IDE approval is presumed for NSR devices.

A "significant risk" device, per 21 CFR 812.3(m), is:
- intended as an implant and poses a serious risk to patient health
- purported or represented to be of use in supporting or sustaining life and presents a serious risk to patient health
- of substantial importance for diagnosing, curing, mitigating or treating disease or preventing impairment of health and poses a serious risk to patient health
- otherwise presents a potential for serious risk to patient health

A device is exempt from the IDE requirements if it is:
- a device in commercial distribution prior to 28 May 1976
- a device, other than a transitional device, "introduced into commercial distribution on or after May 28, 1976, that FDA has determined to be substantially equivalent to a device in commercial distribution immediately before May 28, 1976, and that is used or investigated in accordance with the indications in the labeling FDA reviewed under

subpart E of part 807 in determining substantial equivalence"
(Note that a "transitional device" is one that FDA considered to be a new drug before 28 May 1976)
- a diagnostic device that:
  ○ is noninvasive
  ○ does not require a significant risk invasive sampling procedure
  ○ does not intentionally introduce energy into a subject
  ○ is not used for a diagnostic procedure without confirmation by another established procedure
- a device undergoing consumer preference testing, if the testing is not for determining safety and effectiveness or puts the subject at risk
- a device for veterinary use or research on animals
- a custom device unless it is being used to establish safety and efficacy for commercial distribution

An IDE application includes:
1. sponsor name and address
2. a complete report of prior investigations of the device and an accurate summary of those sections of the investigational plan described in 812.25(a)–(e) or, in lieu of the summary, the complete plan; a complete investigational plan and a complete report of prior investigations of the device if no IRB has reviewed them, if FDA has found an IRB's review inadequate or if FDA requests them
3. a description of the methods, facilities and controls used for the manufacture, processing, packing, storage and, where appropriate, installation of the device, in sufficient detail that a person generally familiar with Good Manufacturing Practices can make a knowledgeable judgment about the quality control used in the manufacture of the device
4. an example of the agreements to be entered into by all investigators to comply with investigator obligations, and a list of the names and addresses of all investigators who have signed the agreement
5. a certification that all investigators who will participate in the investigation have signed the agreement, that the list of investigators includes all who are participating in the investigation, and that no investigators will be added to the investigation until they have signed the agreement
6. a list of the name, address and chairperson of each IRB that has been or will be asked to review the investigation and a certification of the action concerning the investigation taken by each such IRB
7. name and address of any institution at which a part of the investigation may be conducted that has not been identified in accordance with the regulations
8. if the device is to be sold, the amount to be charged

Table 10-1. Abbreviated IDE Requirements, per 21 CFR 812.2(b)

Requirements	Additional Reference
An investigation of a device other than a significant risk device, if the device is not a banned device.	
Device is labeled per 21 CFR 812.5.	21 CFR 812.5
IRB approves after sponsor presents the IRB with a brief explanation of why the device is not a significant risk device.	
Investigators obtain informed consent from each subject.	
Sponsor monitors investigators and promptly secures compliance or takes appropriate measures if investigators fail to meet requirements.	21 CFR 812.46(a)
Sponsor immediately evaluates unanticipated adverse device effects and takes appropriate action, including termination of the study if there is an unreasonable risk to subject. A terminated study may not be resumed without IRB approval.	21 CFR 812.46(b)
Sponsor keeps records: • basic study information per 21 CFR 812.140(b)(4) • records concerning adverse device effects	21 CFR 812.140(b)(4) and (5)
Investigators keep records: • each subject's documents evidencing informed consent.	21 CFR 812.140(a)(3)(i)
Sponsor reports: • to FDA and IRBs, unanticipated adverse device effects • to FDA and IRBs, any withdrawal of IRB approval • to IRBs, withdrawal of FDA approval • to IRBs, progress reports and final report • to FDA and IRBs, recall and device disposition • to FDA, any report of a failure to obtain informed consent • to FDA, any IRB's determination that a device is a significant risk device • upon request of FDA or IRB, any aspect of the investigation	21 CFR 812 150(b)(1)-(3) and (5)-(10)
Investigator reports • to sponsor and IRB, unanticipated adverse device effects • to sponsor, withdrawal of IRB approval • to sponsor and IRB, any device use without informed consent • upon request of IRB or FDA, any aspect of the investigation	21 CFR 812.150(a)(1), (2), (5), (7)
Sponsor complies with prohibitions against promotion.	21 CFR 812.7

and an explanation of why sale does not constitute commercialization of the device; the submitter will also need to demonstrate cost recovery if sale is approved

9. a claim for categorical exclusion under 21 CFR 25.30 or 25.34 or an environmental assessment under 25.40
10. copies of all device labeling
11. copies of all forms and informational materials to be provided to subjects to obtain informed consent
12. any other relevant information FDA requests for review of the application
    a. additional information—FDA may request additional information concerning an investigation or revision in the investigational plan. This constitutes a clinical hold. The sponsor may treat such a request as a disapproval of the application for purposes of requesting a hearing.
    b. Information previously submitted—information

previously submitted to CDRH need not be resubmitted, but may be incorporated by reference.

FDA requires a risk analysis under 21 CFR 812.25 Investigational Plan. This is a description and analysis of increased risks to which subjects will be exposed by the investigation; the manner in which these risks are minimized; a justification for the investigation; and a description of the patient population, including the number, age, sex and condition.

When considering an IDE application, FDA reviews background information, such as animal testing, bench testing and the clinical protocol, to determine whether the product is safe for testing in humans and whether efficacy can be shown based upon the protocol requirements.

Supplemental IDE Submissions

Supplemental submissions are required for changes in the investigational plan, informed consent or other substantive information. Supplemental IDE submissions include:

- an IDE supplement, which is any additional submission to an IDE after approval of the IDE
- an IDE amendment is any additional submissions to an IDE before approval of the IDE

Institutional Review Board (IRB) Approval

Per 21 CFR 812.42, IRB approval is necessary before an investigation begins. For further information on IRB regulations and consent forms, see 21 CFR 50 and 56, respectively.

Pre-IDE Meeting

Sponsors are encouraged to contact FDA to obtain further guidance prior to the submission of an IDE application. (Pre-IDE Meetings may also be used to obtain guidance on 510(k) submissions even though no clinical data are required.) Early interaction with the agency should help increase the sponsor's understanding of FDA requirements, regulations and guidance documents, and allows FDA personnel to familiarize themselves with the new technologies. Communication with FDA may take the form of a Pre-IDE Meeting and/or a Pre-IDE Submission.

Informal Guidance Meeting

Sponsors are encouraged to meet with the Office of Device Evaluation (ODE) reviewing division so the division can provide advice that can be used to develop supporting preclinical data or the investigational plan. These meetings may take the form of telephone conference calls, video conferences or face-to-face discussions. The sponsor should contact the reviewing division directly or may contact the IDE staff for assistance.

Formal Guidance Meetings

There are two types of formal guidance meetings, a Determination Meeting and an Agreement Meeting.

For a Determination Meeting, a sponsor anticipating the submission of a PMA submits a written request to discuss the types of valid scientific evidence necessary to demonstrate that the device is effective for its intended use. This meeting focuses on the broad outline of clinical trial design. The request and summary information for a meeting should be submitted as a Pre-IDE Submission and identified as a Determination Meeting request. FDA's determination is provided to the applicant in writing within 30 days following the meeting.

For an Agreement Meeting, a sponsor submits a written meeting request to reach an agreement with FDA regarding the agency's review of an investigational plan (including a clinical protocol). The request and summary information

should be submitted as a pre-IDE submission and identified as an Agreement Meeting request. This meeting should take place no later than 30 days after receipt of the request. The written request should include a detailed description of the device, a detailed description of the proposed conditions of use of the device, a proposed plan (including a clinical protocol) for determining whether there is a reasonable assurance of effectiveness, and, if available, information regarding the expected performance of the device. If an agreement is reached between FDA and the sponsor or applicant regarding the investigational plan (including a clinical protocol), the terms of the agreement are put into writing and made part of the administrative record by FDA.

To request a formal guidance meeting, use the format in, *Early Collaboration Meetings Under the FDA Modernization Act (FDAMA), Final Guidance for Industry and CDRH Staff.*[5]

It is important to establish a good working relationship with the FDA project officer. The project officer may expedite meeting requests and can also provide clarification, ideas and suggestions.

510(k) Premarket Notification

A 510(k) submission is made for a new or modified device for which the product classification requires a 510(k). Some Class I products, most Class II products and a small number of Class III products require a 510(k). Product families, such as catheters of various sizes or patient monitor systems of varying configurations, can be cleared on a single 510(k) if the intended uses, technological characteristics and issues of safety and effectiveness are essentially the same within the family.

The purpose of a 510(k) is to demonstrate that a new or modified device is "substantially equivalent" in intended use, safety and effectiveness as a "predicate device." A predicate device is a legally marketed device that was cleared onto the market by a 510(k).

The content of 510(k) premarket notifications, described in 21 CFR 807.87, includes: the device name and class, an establishment registration number, an "Indications for Use Statement," a 510(k) summary, proposed labeling, substantial equivalence comparison with the predicate device, supporting performance data and a statement that all data and information submitted are truthful and accurate and that no material fact has been omitted. In particular, the Indications for Use Statement provides the specific indications, clinical settings, target population, anatomical sites, device configuration and other information critical to how the device is intended to be used clinically.

The format and amount of information in a 510(k) varies depending upon the intended use, technology, issues of safety and effectiveness, reliance on standards and special controls and, for modified devices, on the nature of the modification.

For more detail, see *Device Advice: Premarket Notification.*[6] This webpage and three linked guidances provide advice on content and links to required forms. Using the recommended format for 510(k) submissions helps reviewers find required information. Companies preparing 510(k)s help ensure the completeness of the submittal when they combine the preparation guidance with product- and technology-specific guidances.[7] (Note: Refer to the CBER website for guidances specific to 510(k)s reviewed by CBER.[8])

Often, clinical studies are not required for 510(k) devices. However, clinical studies may be necessary if the 510(k) device cannot be shown to be as safe and effective as the predicate device using laboratory tests, such as biocompatibility, engineering, bench performance, design verification and voluntary standards tests.

The required truthful and accurate statement, which must be signed by a designated and accountable person within the company requesting market clearance, is defined in 21 CFR 807.87(k) as:

"A statement that the submitter believes, to the best of his or her knowledge, that all data and information submitted in the premarket notification are truthful and accurate and that no material fact has been omitted."

The truthful and accurate statement carries significant legal implications and should be taken seriously by the individual signing it. It essentially amounts to a certification and, should FDA subsequently determine that false information or misstatement of material facts were included in the submission, or that material facts were omitted, judicial action could be taken against the person who signed the statement. It is prudent to conduct a formal audit of the information in the 510(k), including pertinent development information, documentation and raw data, prior to signing this statement.

Modifications to 510(k) Devices

A new 510(k) application is required for changes or modifications to an existing device when the modifications could significantly affect the device's safety or effectiveness, or if the device is to be marketed for a new or different indication.

When a 510(k) holder decides to modify an existing device, it must determine whether the proposed modification(s) requires submission of a new 510(k). Changes in indications for use, including a switch from prescription status to over-the-counter availability, require the submission of a 510(k).

Examples of modifications that may require a 510(k) submission include, but are not limited to:
- sterilization method
- structural material
- manufacturing method

- operating parameters or conditions for use
- patient or user safety features
- sterile barrier packaging material
- stability or expiration claims
- design

More detail is provided in the guidance, *Deciding When to Submit a 510(k) for a Change to an Existing Device (K97-1).*[9]

Not all changes to a device require a new submission to FDA. The sponsor must determine whether the submission criteria are met and proceed accordingly. It is good practice for a sponsor to document and file the review of the changes and the decision that a 510(k) is not required.

If a modification requires a 510(k), but the indication for use and the fundamental technology of the device are not affected, a Special 510(k) may be submitted.

Traditional 510(k)

See the guidance, *How to Prepare a Traditional 510(k).*[10] The traditional 510(k) format is the default format. Alternatives are the Abbreviated 510(k) and the Special 510(k).

Abbreviated 510(k)

See the guidance, *How to Prepare an Abbreviated 510(k).*[11] An Abbreviated 510(k) relies on the use of guidance documents, special controls and standards (particularly FDA recognized consensus standards). An Abbreviated 510(k) submission must include required elements. Under certain conditions, the submitter may not need to include test data.

Device sponsors may choose to submit an Abbreviated 510(k) when:
- a guidance documents already exists
- a special control has already been established
- FDA has recognized a relevant consensus standard

In an Abbreviated 510(k) submission, sponsors provide summary reports on the use of guidance documents and/or special controls or Declarations of Conformity to recognized consensus standards to expedite submission review.

An Abbreviated 510(k) that relies on a guidance document should include a summary report that describes the way in which the relevant guidance document was employed. It should also note how the guidance was used during device development and testing. The summary report should include information regarding the sponsor's efforts to conform to the guidance and outline any deviations.

Special controls are a way of providing reasonable assurance of a Class II device's safety and effectiveness. Special controls are defined as those controls (such as performance standards, postmarket surveillance, patient registries, development and dissemination of guidelines, recommendations and other appropriate actions) that establish reasonable assurance of the device's safety and effectiveness. The device classification regulations list special controls for the device, if any.

An Abbreviated 510(k) that relies on a special control(s) includes a summary report that describes adherence to the special control(s). It also notes how the special control(s) was used during device development and testing, including how it was used to address a specific risk or issue. The summary report includes information regarding the sponsor's efforts to conform to the special control(s) and should outline any deviations.

Recognized consensus standards may be cited in guidance documents or individual policy statements, or established as special controls that address specific risks associated with a type of device. FDA has recognized more than 800 standards to which 510(k) submitters can declare conformity. The current list of FDA recognized consensus standards is available in CDRH's standards database.[12]

A submitter may suggest a standard that is not yet recognized by FDA. The submitter should discuss such a strategy with FDA prior to submitting an Abbreviated 510(k) based on an unrecognized standard.

An Abbreviated 510(k) that relies on a standard must include a Declaration of Conformity to the standard.

If FDA determines that an Abbreviated 510(k) does not meet eligibility requirements, the reviewer notifies the sponsor of this decision and offers the option of having the document converted to a traditional 510(k) or withdrawing it for future submission. If the 510(k) is withdrawn and a new one submitted, a new user fee applies. If the 510(k) is converted, the original receipt date remains as the start of the review period. Sponsors should be aware that, in most cases, additional information is necessary for converted submissions.

In the Abbreviated 510(k) process, a sponsor must assess the device's conformance to a recognized consensus standard. Once the assessment is satisfactorily completed, the sponsor may submit the Abbreviated 510(k). Under certain conditions, conformance test data are not required to be submitted in the 510(k). To be sure, consult with the reviewing branch.

The sponsor may use a third party to assess conformance to the recognized consensus standard. The third party performs a conformance assessment with the standard for the sponsor and provides the sponsor with a statement to this effect. For example, a third party may be used to assess conformance to the standard for electromagnetic interference testing and shock hazards, IEC 60601-1-2.

The Abbreviated 510(k) should include a Declaration of Conformity signed by the sponsor, while the third party's statement should be maintained in the Device Master Record (DMR) and Design History File (DHF) (21 CFR 820.30).

Declarations of Conformity to recognized consensus standards should include the following:

- identification of applicable recognized consensus standards met
- statement, for each consensus standard, that all requirements were met except inapplicable requirements or deviations
- identification, for each consensus standard, of any way(s) in which it may have been adapted for application to the device under review (e.g., identification of an alternative series of tests that were performed)
- identification, for each consensus standard, of any requirements not applicable to the device
- specification of any deviations from each applicable standard that were applied
- specification of the differences that may exist, if any, between the tested device and the device to be marketed and a justification of the test results in these areas of difference
- name and address of any test laboratory and/or certification body involved in determining the device's conformance with applicable consensus standards and a reference to any of those organizations' accreditations

Special 510(k)

See the guidance, *How to Prepare a Special 510(k)*.[13] If a 510(k) is needed for a device's modification and if the modification does not affect the device's intended use or alter its fundamental scientific technology, summary information resulting from the design control process can serve as the basis for clearing the application along with the required elements of a 510(k).

Modifications to the indications for use or any labeling change that affects the device's intended use are not accepted as a Special 510(k). Special 510(k) sponsors should highlight or otherwise prominently identify changes in the proposed labeling that may result from modifications to the legally marketed device. It should be clearly stated in the Special 510(k) that the intended use of the modified device has not changed as a result of the modification(s). Note that a labeling change from prescription to over-the-counter use, or vice versa, is considered a change in intended use and is not eligible for a Special 510(k) submission.

Special 510(k)s are not accepted for modifications that alter the device's fundamental scientific technology. Such changes include modifications to the device's operating principle(s) or mechanism of action. Specific examples that illustrate types of changes that alter the fundamental scientific technology and should not be submitted as Special 510(k)s include:

- a change in a surgical instrument that uses a sharpened metal blade to one that cuts with a laser
- a change in an in vitro diagnostic device (IVD) that uses immunoassay technology to one that

uses nucleic acid hybridization or amplification technology
- incorporation of a sensing mechanism in a device to allow it to function "on demand" rather than continuously

Device modifications that should be appropriate for review as Special 510(k)s include:
- energy type
- environmental specifications
- performance specifications
- ergonomics of the patient-user interface
- dimensional specifications
- software or firmware
- packaging or expiration dating
- sterilization

A sponsor may make changes to the device that do not change the intended use or alter the technology and may not require a 510(k) submission. These changes may be minor but do require appropriate change control in the DMR and DHF.

Third Party Review

See the "Device Advice" guidance *Third Party Review.*[14] *FDAMA* established the Accredited Persons Program. Accredited Persons, which may be companies or individuals, are authorized to perform 510(k) reviews for certain Class II devices. The product classification database includes for each classification, what Accredited Persons, if any, are authorized to perform third party reviews for the device classification. Third party reviews are not subject to an FDA user fee. However, the fee paid to the third party reviewer is usually higher than the FDA 510(k) user fee. Advantages of third party reviews typically include:
- shorter review times
- responsiveness to questions
- expertise in testing, standards and international requirements
- local service, depending upon the location of the third party reviewer's office

Premarket Approval (21 CFR 814)

Premarket Approval (PMA) is the FDA process of scientific and regulatory review to evaluate the safety and effectiveness of Class III medical devices. A PMA is the most stringent type of device marketing application required by FDA. PMA approval is based on a determination by FDA that the PMA contains sufficient "valid scientific evidence" to assure that the device is safe and effective for its intended use(s).

There are essentially two types of PMA Applications:
- Traditional PMA
- Product Development Process

FDAMA introduced other Premarket Approval options:
- Modular PMA
- Streamlined PMA
- Humanitarian Device Exemption

See *PMA Application Methods.*[15]

Traditional PMA

The information required in a PMA is detailed in 21 CFR 814.20(b). In addition to voluntary completion of the applicable sections of a cover sheet, other required information includes:
1. table of contents showing the volume and page number for each item
2. summary of information in the submission, including:
   a. general description of the indications for use
   b. explanation of how the device functions, the scientific concepts upon which the device is based, general physical and performance characteristics, and a brief description of the manufacturing process, if it aids understanding
   c. generic, proprietary and trade name of the device
   d. description of existing alternative practices and procedures for which the device is intended
   e. brief description of the device's foreign and US marketing history by the applicant and/or any other person, including a list of the countries in which it has been marketed and from which marketing was withdrawn because of adverse safety and effectiveness experiences
   f. summary of studies and reports submitted with the PMA, including:
      i. nonclinical laboratory studies
      ii. human clinical investigations, other data, information or reports relevant to an evaluation of the device's safety and effectiveness from any source, known or that reasonably should be known to the applicant
      iii. discussion demonstrating that data and information in the submission constitute valid scientific evidence providing reasonable assurance of the device's safety and effectiveness, and conclusions drawn from the studies with a discussion of risk/ benefit considerations and adverse effects
3. complete description of:
   a. device, including photos, drawings and schematics
   b. each functional component and/or ingredient
   c. device properties relative to its specific indications for use

d. principles of operation

e. methods, facilities and controls used to manufacture, process, package, store and, if appropriate, install the device

4. references to any performance standard in effect or proposed at the time of submission and any voluntary standard relevant to the device's safety or effectiveness, including adequate information to demonstrate compliance with the applicable standards and an explanation of any deviation from the standards

5. technical sections containing data and information in sufficient detail to enable approval or disapproval of the application, including results of:

    a. nonclinical laboratory studies in a separate section, including a statement that each study was conducted in accordance with Good Laboratory Practices (21 CFR 58)

    b. human clinical investigations in a separate section, including a statement that each study was conducted in accordance with IRB rules (21 CFR 56), informed consent rules (21 CFR 50) and IDE rules (21 CFR 812)

6. bibliography of all published reports that are known or reasonably should be known concerning the device's safety or effectiveness not submitted under number 5 above:

    a. identification, analysis and discussion of any other data, information and reports relevant to the evaluation of the device's safety and effectiveness from any source that are known or reasonably should be known

    b. copies of all reasonably obtainable published and unpublished reports described in 3d and 3e, if requested by FDA or an FDA Advisory Committee

7. samples of the device and its components, if requested by FDA, submitted or available at a named location if impractical to submit

8. copies of all proposed labeling including labels, instructions for use, installation, maintenance and servicing, and any information, literature and/ or advertising that constitutes labeling (Section 201(m) of the *FD&C Act* and 21 CFR 801 or 809)

9. environmental assessment in accordance with 21 CFR 25.20(n) or justification for categorical exclusion under 21 CFR 25.30 and 25.34

10. disclosure of any financial arrangements between the sponsor and clinical investigators who performed studies included in the submission, or a certification on Form FDA 3454 attesting to the absence of any financial arrangements (21 CFR 54)

11. any other information requested by FDA

Omission of any required information must be identified

and justified in a statement attached as a separate section of the PMA. A DMF or other applicable information in FDA files may be incorporated by reference. However, if this information was not submitted by the PMA applicant, the applicant must receive permission from the filer of the information for it to be reviewed by FDA.

The sponsor is required to periodically update a pending PMA with new or newly learned safety and effectiveness information that could reasonably affect the device's evaluation and labeling (21 CFR 814.20(e)). To ensure adherence to all content and format requirements, manufacturers should carefully review the regulations in 21 CFR 814.20(a)–(h), as well as FDA's guideline on the arrangement and format of a PMA.

Traditional PMA Review Process

The PMA review is performed by an FDA team generally consisting of a medical officer, engineer, biologist, statistician, labeling expert and manufacturing expert. A decision to approve or not approve must be made by FDA within 180 calendar days following receipt of a complete PMA, although, in reality, reviews take much longer.

During the review process, FDA will order an inspection of the sponsor's manufacturing facility to provide evidence that the manufacturer complies with GMP requirements set forth in the QSR (21 CFR 820).

Often, PMAs for important or new technologies will also be reviewed by FDA advisory panels consisting of experts in the medical specialty (e.g., MDs, PhDs, engineers) and consumer and industry representatives. Advisory personnel are not regular employees of FDA, but are paid as "special government employees" for the days they participate as members of a panel. The panel members' recommendation is not binding, however FDA generally follows their advice.

The FDA review process can result in the following outcomes:

- Approval—The PMA substantially meets the requirements of the applicable part of the regulations and the device is safe and effective for its intended use(s).

- Not Approvable—The PMA has major deficiencies and review issues remain that stand in the way of approval (specifically identified in a letter to the applicant). This requires submission of a PMA amendment(s) by the applicant to respond to issues, and results in additional review cycle.

- Denial—The PMA does not meet the requirements of the applicable part of the regulations and the device is not safe and effective for its intended use(s).

PMA Amendments—21 CFR 814.37

Changes or revisions to the original PMA submission are submitted to FDA in the form of amendments.

Amendments are also submitted to FDA for changes to PMA supplements.

PMA Supplements

When a significant change to the device approved under a PMA affects the device's safety or effectiveness, a supplement to the original PMA is required. This became law when the *FD&C Act* was amended by Section 515(d)(6).

PMA supplements that are required include:
- new indication for use of the device
- labeling changes
- the use of a different facility or establishment to manufacture, process, sterilize or package the device
- changes in manufacturing facilities, methods or quality control procedures
- changes in sterilization procedures
- changes in packaging
- changes in the performance or design specifications, circuits, components, ingredients, principles of operation or physical layout of the device
- extension of the device's expiration date based on data obtained under a new or revised stability or sterility testing protocol that has not been approved by FDA (If the protocol has been previously approved by FDA, a supplement is not submitted but the change must be reported to FDA in the postapproval periodic reports as described in the Section 814.39(b).)

Supplements that are pending can also be amended with more information.

There are several ways of filing a PMA supplement:

PMA Supplement (180 days)—21 CFR 814.39(a)

The PMA Supplement is for significant changes that affect the device's safety and effectiveness and will require an in-depth review and approval by FDA before implementing the change. This may also require review by an advisory panel.

Special PMA Supplement—Changes Being Effected (CBE)—21 CFR 814.39(d)

The CBE is generally used when the change enhances or increases the device's safety. It does not require FDA approval before making the change. Examples are labeling changes that add more relevant information and increased quality control testing.

30-day Notice and 135 PMA Supplement—21 CFR 814.39(f)

A 30-day Notice is used for modifications to manufacturing procedures or methods that affect the device's safety and effectiveness. If FDA does not respond within 30 days after notification, the change can be made to the device and it can be marketed accordingly. If FDA finds the 30-day Notice is not adequate, but contains data meeting appropriate content requirements for a PMA supplement, the 30-day Notice will become a 135-day PMA Supplement.

PMA Manufacturing Site Change Supplement

When the manufacturing site is changed, a supplement needs to be filed. The site must have received a Quality System/GMP inspection within the last two years. If requirements are not met, a 180-day PMA Supplement must be submitted.

Annual (Periodic) Report or 30-day Supplements—21 CFR 814.39(e)

Changes can also be reported in the Annual Report instead of in a formal supplement. However, to use this approach, a sponsor should seek an advisory opinion from FDA.

"Real-Time" Review Program for PMA Supplements

In April 1996, ODE implemented a pilot program for "Real-Time" reviews of PMA supplements where the sponsor and the FDA review team meet to discuss any concerns FDA may have. Results of the pilot program demonstrated that faster review times for manufacturers and efficient use of FDA staff time were achieved. Because this type of review is not available for all supplements, a sponsor is advised to contact its FDA reviewer to understand the criteria established for the "Real-Time" review program within a particular branch and division within ODE.

The Product Development Protocol (PDP)

The PDP was authorized several years ago as an alternative to the IDE and PMA in *FD&C Act* Section 515(f). For Class III devices subject to premarket approval, the successful completion of a PDP results in market clearance and essentially is a PMA approval.

One intent of the *Medical Device Amendments* of 1976 was to create an alternate pathway for device approval and marketing by having the sponsor and FDA agree early in the development process on items needed for the successful analysis of a Class III device's safety and efficacy.

Once agreement is reached, the PDP contains all the information about design and development activities and acceptance criteria. A project timeline is established and information is furnished to FDA to review in a sequential fashion.

The PDP consists of:
- a description of the device and any changes that may be made to the device
- a description of the preclinical trials, if any
- a description of the clinical trials, if any
- a description of the manufacturing methods, facilities and controls

- a description of any applicable performance standards
- specimens of proposed labeling
- any other information "relevant to the subject matter of the protocol"

Upon completion of clinical studies, reports are furnished to FDA, which has 120 days to act on a PDP. Currently, the PDP approval approach is rarely utilized.

Modular PMA

The *Medical Device User Fee and Modernization Act (MDUFMA)* amended Section 515(c) of the *FD&C Act* to allow early FDA review of PMA information submitted in separate modules. Though the Modular PMA has the same content requirements as the Traditional PMA, the sponsor must meet with FDA to come to an agreement with the agency on the content of the PMA "Shell," a framework of modules that identifies the information necessary to support the filing and approval. Generally, this occurs during a pre-IDE submission meeting.

Each module is submitted to FDA as it is completed. The target FDA review period is 90 days for each module or amendment submitted in response to an agency deficiency letter. Upon receipt of the final module, a PMA number is assigned and a 180-day review clock will start. The entire PMA User Fee is due with the submission of the first module.

The Modular PMA is particularly useful for devices at an early stage of development, rather than for devices that are far along in the development process.

Advantages of the Modular PMA may include:
- allows more efficient use of resources
- potentially reduces PMA application review time
- creates ongoing open dialogue between FDA and the sponsor

Disadvantages may include:
- can cost more money and lengthen time to approval
- the need to establish a plan prior to approaching FDA about utilizing the modular approach

To file a Modular PMA, follow FDA's guidance document, *Premarket Approval Application Modular Review* (3 November 2003).[16]

Streamlined PMA

A Streamlined PMA is designed for devices using well-known technologies for well-known disease processes. A PMA may qualify as streamlined if: the device has a review guidance; four or more previous PMAs have been approved for the same type of device; or the device has a study protocol jointly developed by the manufacturer and FDA. The

Manufacturing Facility Inspection may be deferred if FDA completed a GMP inspection within past two years. The review time is the same as for Traditional PMAs (180 days).

Humanitarian Device Exemption (HDE)—21 CFR 814 Subpart H

A Humanitarian Use Device (HUD) is intended to benefit patients by treating or diagnosing a disease or condition that affects or is manifested in fewer than 4,000 individuals in the US per year. The number of patient contacts with a device may exceed one per patient, but the total number of patients treated or diagnosed with the device is fewer than 4,000 per year.

The HUD regulation provides a financial incentive for the development of devices for these small populations because manufacturer's research and development costs far exceed market returns for diseases or conditions affecting small patient populations.

A sponsor must receive Humanitarian Use status by submitting a Request for HUD Designation to FDA's Office of Orphan Products Development (OOPD).

The request should include:
- a statement that the applicant is requesting a HUD designation for a rare disease or condition
- the applicant's name and address
- a description of the rare disease or condition for which the device is to be used
- a description of the device
- documentation, with appended authoritative references, to demonstrate that the device is designed to treat or diagnose a disease or condition that affects or is manifested in fewer than 4,000 people in the US per year

A Humanitarian Device Exemption Application (HDE) is similar in both form and content to a Traditional PMA application, however it is exempt from the effectiveness requirements of a PMA. An HDE is not required to contain the results of scientifically valid clinical investigations demonstrating that the device is effective for its intended purpose. An HDE must contain sufficient information for FDA to determine that the device does not pose an unreasonable or significant risk of illness or injury, and that the probable benefit to health outweighs the risk of injury or illness from its use, taking into account the probable risks and benefits of currently available devices or alternative forms of treatment. Finally, the applicant must demonstrate that no comparable devices are available to treat or diagnose the disease or condition, and that they could not otherwise bring the device to market.

The agency has 75 days from the date of receipt to review an HDE. This includes a 30-day filing period during which the agency determines whether the HDE is sufficiently complete to permit substantive review. If

FDA notifies the sponsor that the HDE is incomplete and cannot be filed, the 75 day timeframe resets upon receipt of any additional information.

When approved by FDA, an HUD may only be used in facilities that have established a local institutional review board (IRB) to supervise clinical testing of devices and have obtained IRB approval for the use of the device to treat or diagnose the specific disease.

HDE amendments and supplements are subject to the same regulations as those for Traditional PMAs; however, the review timeframe for HDE amendments and supplements is 75 days, the same as for HDE originals.

Expedited Review
Devices Appropriate for Expedited Review

FDA considers a device or combination product containing a device appropriate for expedited review if the device or combination product:

1. is intended to treat or diagnose a life-threatening or irreversibly debilitating disease or condition
2. addresses an unmet medical need, as demonstrated by one of the following:
   a. The device represents a breakthrough technology that provides a clinically meaningful advantage over existing technology. Breakthrough technologies should be demonstrated to lead to a clinical improvement in the treatment or diagnosis of the life-threatening or irreversibly debilitating condition.
   b. No approved alternative treatment or means of diagnosis exists.
   c. The device offers significant, clinically meaningful advantages over existing approved alternative treatments. The device should provide a clinically important earlier or more accurate diagnosis, or offer important therapeutic advantages in safety and/or effectiveness over existing alternatives. Such advantages may include demonstrated superiority over current treatments for effects on serious outcomes, the ability to provide clinical benefit for those patients unable to tolerate current treatments, or the ability to provide a clinical benefit without the serious side effects associated with current treatments.
   d. The availability of the device is in the best interest of patients. That is, the device provides a specific public health benefit or meets the need of a well-defined patient population. This may also apply to a device that was designed or modified to address an unanticipated serious failure occurring in a critical component of an approved device for which there are no alternatives, or for which alternative treatment would entail substantial risk of morbidity for the patient.

Proposed Submission Changes

In 2009, CDRH established two committees—the 510(k) Working Group and the Task Force on the Utilization of Science in Regulatory Decision Making—to address challenges and explore opportunities to improve the 510(k) process. The Institute of Medicine is conducting an independent evaluation. In addition, CDRH has conducted public meetings and "town hall meetings" to gather input from sponsors and other constituencies affected by the device approval processes.

The Working Group and the Task Force issued 55 recommendations. CDRH reported that in public comments, 28 recommendations were supported, 12 were supported with caveat or modification, and 15 received significant concern. In 2011, CDRH is focusing on implementing the 40 recommendations that received support or support with modification. Recommendations to be implemented include:

- issuing more guidances for the 510(k) program
- increasing and improving training for FDA and industry
- improving CDRH business processes
- streamlining the de novo process

Of the 15 recommendations, seven were referred to the Institute of Medicine, four will be implemented on a case-by-case basis, and one was dropped (with clarification through training). The remaining three will be implemented with significant modifications to address the concerns.

In 2011 and 2012, there will be many changes—hopefully improvements—in CDRH's processes, particularly the 510(k) process. Sponsors should continually review plans and progress online at *CDRH Plan of Action for 510(k) and Science.*[17]

Summary

- FDA regulations for devices comprise sets of rules that classify devices that require agency clearance or approval. Devices may be classified into Class I, II or III. Reclassification or the de novo process allow classifications to be changed, but are complex. Classes I and II may require 510(k) Notification or may be 510(k)-exempt. Except for a small and decreasing number, Class III devices require a PMA. The exceptions require a 510(k).
- Significant risk clinical studies require FDA approval of an IDE.
- Pre-IDE meetings provide a mechanism for sponsors

to discuss proposals for submission strategies, as well as clinical trials, with FDA.

- CDRH is implementing a large number of changes to the 510(k) and related device approval and business processes.

References

1. CDRH Product Classification Database, www.accessdata.fda.gov/scripts/cdrh/cfdocs/cfPCD/PCDSimpleSearch.cfm. Accessed 11 April 2011.
2. 515 Program Initiative, www.fda.gov/AboutFDA/CentersOffices/CDRH/CDRHTransparency/ucm240310.htm. Accessed 11 April 2011.
3. CDRHLearn class regarding 513(g) Requests for Determination, www.fda.gov/MedicalDevices/ResourcesforYou/Industry/ucm127147.htm. Accessed 11 April 2011.
4. *Device Advice: Investigational Device Exemption* (IDE), www.fda.gov/MedicalDevices/DeviceRegulationandGuidance/HowtoMarketYourDevice/InvestigationalDeviceExemptionIDE/default.htm. Accessed 11 April 2011.
5. *Early Collaboration Meetings Under the FDA Modernization Act (FDAMA), Final Guidance for Industry and CDRH Staff*, www.fda.gov/MedicalDevices/DeviceRegulationandGuidance/GuidanceDocuments/ucm073604.htm. Accessed 11 April 2011.
6. *Device Advice: Premarket Notification*, www.fda.gov/MedicalDevices/DeviceRegulationandGuidance/HowtoMarketYourDevice/PremarketSubmissions/PremarketNotification510k/default.htm. Accessed 11 April 2011.
7. *Device Advice: Device Regulation and Guidance*, www.fda.gov/MedicalDevices/DeviceRegulationandGuidance/default.htm. Accessed 11 April 2011.
8. *Guidance, Compliance & Regulatory Information (Biologics)*, www.fda.gov/BiologicsBloodVaccines/GuidanceComplianceRegulatoryInformation/default.htm. Accessed 11 April 2011.
9. *Deciding When to Submit a 510(k) for a Change to an Existing Device (K97-1)*, www.fda.gov/MedicalDevices/DeviceRegulationandGuidance/GuidanceDocuments/ucm080235.htm. Accessed 11 April 2011.
10. *How to Prepare a Traditional 510(k)*, www.fda.gov/MedicalDevices/DeviceRegulationandGuidance/HowtoMarketYourDevice/PremarketSubmissions/PremarketNotification510k/ucm134572.htm. Accessed 11 April 2011.
11. *How to Prepare an Abbreviated 510(k)*, www.fda.gov/MedicalDevices/DeviceRegulationandGuidance/HowtoMarketYourDevice/PremarketSubmissions/PremarketNotification510k/ucm134574.htm. Accessed 11 April 2011.
12. CDRH's Standards database, www.accessdata.fda.gov/scripts/cdrh/cfdocs/cfStandards/search.cfm. Accessed 11 April 2011.
13. *How to Prepare a Special 510(k)*, www.fda.gov/MedicalDevices/DeviceRegulationandGuidance/HowtoMarketYourDevice/PremarketSubmissions/PremarketNotification510k/ucm134573.htm. Accessed 11 April 2011.
14. *Device Advice: Third Party Review*, www.fda.gov/MedicalDevices/DeviceRegulationandGuidance/HowtoMarketYourDevice/PremarketSubmissions/ThirdParyReview/default.htm. Accessed 11 April 2011.
15. *PMA Application Methods*, www.fda.gov/MedicalDevices/DeviceRegulationandGuidance/HowtoMarketYourDevice/PremarketSubmissions/PremarketApprovalPMA/ucm048168.htm. Accessed 11 April 2011.
16. *Premarket Approval Application Modular Review November 3, 2003*, www.fda.gov/MedicalDevices/DeviceRegulationandGuidance/GuidanceDocuments/ucm089764.htm. Accessed 11 April 2011.
17. *CDRH Plan of Action for 510(k) and Science*, www.fda.gov/AboutFDA/CentersOffices/CDRH/CDRHReports/ucm239448.htm. Accessed 11 April 2011.

US Medical Device Compliance and Postmarketing Activities

By Richard Angelo, PhD

Objectives

❏ Develop a basic understanding of FDA regulations that establish compliance and postmarketing requirements for manufacturers and importers of devices marketed in the US

❏ Learn how to prepare and file establishment registrations and device listings with FDA

❏ Review FDA's Quality System Regulation (QSR) for medical devices, as well as FDA's approach to medical device manufacturer inspections

❏ Understand postmarketing requirements for medical device reports (MDRs), corrections and removals (recalls) and medical device tracking

❏ Review US requirements for importing and exporting devices

Laws, Regulations and Guidelines Covered in This Chapter

❏ *Pure Food and Drugs Act* of 1906

❏ *Federal Food, Drug, and Cosmetic Act* of 1938 *(FD&C Act)*

❏ *FD&C Act* as amended by the *Food and Drug Administration Modernization Act* of 1997 *(FDAMA)*

❏ Chapter III—Prohibited Acts and Penalties

❏ Chapter V—Drugs and Devices

❏ Section 501—Adulterated Drugs and Devices

❏ Section 502—Misbranded Drugs and Devices

❏ Section 506A—Manufacturing Changes

❏ Section 506B—Reports of Postmarketing Studies

❏ Section 518(e)—Recall Authority

❏ Section 519(e)—Device Tracking

❏ Section 522—Postmarket Surveillance

❏ Chapter VIII—Imports and Exports, Sections 801–803

❏ 21 CFR Part 7 Enforcement Policy—Voluntary recalls

❏ 21 CFR Part 803 Medical device reporting

❏ 21 CFR Part 806 Medical devices; reports of corrections and removals

❏ 21 CFR Part 807 Establishment registration and device listing for manufacturers and initial importers of devices

❏ 21 CFR Part 810 Medical device recall authority

❏ 21 CFR 814.82(a)(2) Condition of approval studies

- ❏ 21 CFR Part 820 Quality system regulation

- ❏ 21 CFR 821 Medical device tracking requirements

- ❏ 21 CFR 822 Postmarket surveillance

- ❏ *Guidance for Industry and FDA Staff: Implementation of Medical Device Establishment Registration and Device Listing Requirements Established by the Food and Drug Administration Amendments Act of 2007* (October 2009)

- ❏ "How-To" Guide: Device Facility User Fee Process (October 2008)

- ❏ *Frequently Asked Questions on Recognition of Consensus Standards* (September 2007)

- ❏ *Guidance for Industry and FDA Staff: Recognition and Use of Consensus Standards* (September 2007)

- ❏ *Quality System Information for Certain Various Premarket Application Reviews; Guidance for Industry and FDA Staff* (February 2003)

- ❏ *Design Control Guidance for Medical Device Manufacturers* (March 1997)

- ❏ *Do It By Design: An Introduction to Human Factors in Medical Devices* (January 1997)

- ❏ *Medical Device Quality Systems Manual: A Small Entity Compliance Guide* (December 1996)

- ❏ *Guidelines on General Principles of Process Validation; Final Guidance for Industry and FDA Staff* (January 2002)

- ❏ Comparison Chart: 1996 Quality System Regulation Versus 1978 Good Manufacturing Practices Regulation Versus ANSI/ISO/ASQC Q9001 and ISO/DI 13485

- ❏ Compliance Program Guidance Manual 7382.845: *Inspection of Medical Device Manufacturers* (2 February 2011)

- ❏ *Guide to Inspections of Quality Systems: Quality System Inspection Technique* (August 1999)

- ❏ *Inspection by Accredited Persons Under the*

- ❏ *Medical Device User Fee and Modernization Act of 2002 and the FDA Amendments Act of 2007; Accreditation Criteria* (August 6, 2009)

- ❏ *Draft Guidance for Industry, User Facilities and FDA Staff: eMDR: Electronic Medical Device Reporting* (August 2009)

- ❏ *Medical Device Reporting—Remedial Action Exemption; Guidance for FDA and Industry* (September 2001)

- ❏ *Medical Device Reporting—Alternative Summary Reporting (ASR) Program* (October 2000)

- ❏ *Medical Device Reporting: An Overview* (April 1996)

- ❏ *Instructions for Completing FDA Form 3500A (MedWatch)* (July 2009)

- ❏ *Regulation of Medical Devices: Background Information for International Officials* (April 1999)

- ❏ *Guidance for Industry: Exports and Imports Under the FDA Export Reform and Enhancement Act of 1996* (July 2007)

- ❏ *Guidance for Industry: Exports Under the FDA Export Reform and Enhancement Act of 1996* (July 2007)

- ❏ *Compliance Policy Guide for FDA Staff*, Section 110.100 Certification of Exports (CPG 7150.01)

- ❏ *Medical Device Tracking; Guidance for Industry and FDA Staff* (January 2010)

- ❏ *Guidance for Industry: Product Recalls, Including Removals and Corrections* (November 2003)

- ❏ *Guidance for Industry and FDA Staff: Procedures for Handling Post-Approval Studies Imposed by PMA Order* (June 2009)

- ❏ *Guidance for Industry and FDA Staff: Postmarket Surveillance Under Section 522 of the Federal Food, Drug and Cosmetic Act* (April 2006)

- ❏ *General Principles of Software Validation; Final Guidance for Industry and FDA Staff:* (January 2002)

❏ *Final Guidance for Industry, FDA Reviewers and Compliance on Off-the-Shelf Software Use in Medical Devices* (September 1999)

❏ *Computerized Devices/Processes Guidance: Application of the Medical Device GMP to Computerized Devices and Manufacturing Processes* (February 1997)

❏ *Design Control Guidance for Medical Device Manufacturers* (March 1997)

Introduction
History of FDA Medical Device Regulations

All US medical device regulations are codified under 21 CFR Parts 800–899. However, the heritage of these regulations begins with the *Pure Food and Drugs Act* of 1906. This act was the true beginning of federal food and drug legislation intended to protect Americans from harmful substances and the deceptive practices that were becoming more and more common. Medical devices were not represented in the act, in large part because contemporary devices, such as stethoscopes and scalpels, were relatively simple and their corresponding risks, if any, were conspicuous. Although medical devices were considered helpful tools, they bore no significant weight and did not play a crucial role in mediating a caregiver's ability to diagnose or treat patients—medical devices neither gave life nor sustained it. It would soon become apparent, however, that medical devices represented fertile ground for new and far-reaching technological achievements, along with their accompanying risks. Medical device technology, much like a burgeoning youth, would continue to outgrow its regulatory wardrobe over the next century, requiring federal regulations to expand and change at a pace commensurate with the industry.

The modernization of the *Pure Food and Drugs Act* was driven, in part, by the recognized need to introduce a definition of medical devices into federal law. This modernization initiative resulted in the enactment of the *Federal Food, Drug, and Cosmetic Act (FD&C Act)* of 1938, which was the first law to mandate requirements for exporting unapproved devices. For the next 25 years, medical devices were subject only to the discretionary vigilance activities of the US Food and Drug Administration (FDA), whose charge it was to unilaterally determine whether a device was safe and effective, in the absence of any premarket testing, review or approval process. Accordingly, the agency was further empowered to bring federal charges against manufacturers of products or materials found to be either adulterated (e.g., defective, unsafe or unsanitary), or misbranded (e.g., false or misleading statements, designs or labeling).

In the early 1960s, President Kennedy advocated changes

to the ways medical devices entered the US market; however, the changes he sought were not realized until the mid-1970s. As the US prepared to celebrate the bicentennial anniversary of its founding, new legislation was enacted that established the ground rules and standards to which all US medical device manufacturers and importers must now adhere: the 1976 *Medical Device Amendments* to the *FD&C Act*. The new law applied safety and effectiveness safeguards to new devices and required FDA to establish, for the first time: regulations concerning establishment registration and device listing; Good Manufacturing Practices (GMPs) for medical devices; medical device reporting (MDR); and guidelines on policy, procedures and industry responsibilities for field corrections and removals.

Numerous changes to device laws and regulations have been implemented via various amendments to the *FD&C Act* over the years. Three of the most notable changes, mandated by the *Safe Medical Devices Act* of 1990 (*SMDA*) and the *Medical Device Amendments* of 1992, were:
- introduction of the Humanitarian Device Exemption (HDE), the medical device equivalent of orphan drug designation, providing limited exemptions from the law for devices intended to treat or diagnose rare diseases or conditions affecting fewer than 4,000 persons
- promulgation of the Quality System Regulation, resulting in substantial revisions that essentially harmonized US GMPs for medical devices with the European quality system regulations in EN 46001 and ISO 9001,[1] and added design controls to the GMP regulation, bringing product development under FDA scrutiny for the first time
- establishment of a regulatory requirement (previously an FDA request) that manufacturers and distributors promptly report field corrections and removals to FDA within 10 days after their initiation
- promulgation of the first device tracking regulation

The *FD&C Act* underwent additional change and reform as a result of the *Food and Drug Administration Modernization Act* of 1997 *(FDAMA)*. *FDAMA* empowered FDA to restrict the marketing of products for which the manufacturing processes are so deficient that use of the products could present a serious health hazard. The agency was given authority to take appropriate action if a device manufacturer advocates an off-label use of its product that may be potentially harmful. *FDAMA* further enhanced FDA's risk-based approach to medical device regulation, allocating FDA resources and diligence to the oversight of medical devices presenting the greatest risks to patients. For example, the law exempts from premarket notification Class I devices not intended for a use that is of substantial importance in preventing impairment of human health or that do not present a potential unreasonable risk of illness or injury. The law also directs FDA to focus its postmarket surveillance on higher-risk devices and allows the agency to implement a reporting system that concentrates on a representative sample of user facilities—such as hospitals and nursing homes—where patients may experience deaths and serious illnesses or injuries linked with the use of devices.

In addition, *FDAMA* expanded an ongoing pilot program under which FDA accredits outside (third-party) experts to conduct the initial review of all Class I and low-to-intermediate risk Class II device applications. The act, however, prohibits any accredited person from reviewing devices that are permanently implantable, life-supporting, life-sustaining or for which clinical data are required.

The *Medical Device User Fee and Modernization Act (MDUFMA)*, signed into law 26 October 2002, further amended the *FD&C Act* to include provisions that affect the compliance regulations. Under *MDUFMA*:

- Establishment inspections may be conducted by accredited persons (third parties) under carefully prescribed conditions.
- New labeling requirements were established for reprocessed single-use devices.
- The submission of validation data for some reprocessed single-use devices is required. On 30 April 2003, FDA identified the types of devices subject to this requirement (see 68 FR 23139).

MDUFMA made several other significant changes to the law that involve FDA postmarket surveillance appropriations, combination product review, electronic labeling, electronic registration, devices intended for pediatric use and breast implant reports. Additionally, it requires manufacturer identification on the device itself, with certain exceptions.

Background information, reference materials and additional information about *MDUFMA* can be found on the website of FDA's Center for Devices and Radiological Health (CDRH) (www.fda.gov/MedicalDevices/DeviceRegulationandGuidance/Overview/MedicalDeviceUserFeeandModernizationActMDUFMA/default.htm). *MDUFMA* also imposed various user fees. On 28 September 2007, as part of the *Food and Drug Administration Amendments Act* (*FDAAA*), user fees were reauthorized through Fiscal 2012. New fees include:

- a fee for each 30-day notice submitted to FDA
- a fee for each 513(g) request for classification information submitted to FDA
- an annual fee for periodic reporting made under a condition of approval for a Class III device
- an annual fee for the registration of each medical device establishment

Small businesses may qualify for reduced fees through an application process. However, there is no discount for small businesses on the annual establishment registration fee.

Establishment Registration and Product Listing

Registration and listing information provides FDA with the locations of medical device establishments and what devices are manufactured at each site. Knowing where devices are manufactured increases FDA's ability to prepare for and respond to public health emergencies.

A US establishment owner or operator that initiates or develops medical device specifications; manufactures, assembles, processes, repackages or relabels medical devices for domestic human use; or is an initial importer of medical devices (distributor for a foreign manufacturer), must register the establishment annually with FDA and submit medical device listing information, including activities performed on those devices, for all such devices in commercial distribution. Note that if a device requires a premarket submission (e.g., 510(k), Premarket Approval (PMA), Product Development Protocol (PDP) or HDE) for clearance, the owner or operator should also submit the FDA premarket submission number.

There is a fee for annual registration for some establishment types. On 1 October 2008, FDA instituted a new payment process for those establishments required to pay the device establishment user fee. This process involves first visiting the Device Facility User Fee website (DFUF) to pay the user fee and obtain a Payment Identification Number (PIN). Once the payment has been received and processed, the owner or operator will be notified by email. The email will include directions to return to the DFUF website to obtain the Payment Confirmation Number (PCN) for the order. The PIN and PCN are required as proof of payment before the facility can be registered using the FDA Unified Registration and Listing System (FURLS). Detailed information regarding registration and listing can be found at www.fda.gov/MedicalDevices/DeviceRegulationandGuidance/HowtoMarketYourDevice/RegistrationandListing/default.htm.

Changes brought about by *FDAMA* require foreign manufacturers of devices intended for US commercial distribution to also register with FDA and list their products. Additionally, foreign manufacturers are required to designate a US agent to act as the official correspondent responsible for, among other things, submitting establishment registration, device listing and medical device reports (MDRs). This requirement had been indefinitely stayed in July of 1996, but was later reinstated effective 11 February 2002.[2] The responsibilities of US agents are described at http://www.fda.gov/MedicalDevices/DeviceRegulationandGuidance/HowtoMarketYourDevice/RegistrationandListing/ucm053196.htm. For domestic and foreign registration and listing requirements, see **Tables 11-1** and **11-2**, respectively.

The initial registration and listing must be submitted within 30 days prior to starting any operations at the establishment toward the production and/or commercial distribution of finished devices (see **Table 11-3**). A device family with variations in physical characteristics should be

Table 11-1. Domestic Establishment Registration and Listing Requirements

Establishment Activity	Register	List	Pay Fee
Manufacturer	Yes 807.20(a)	Yes 807.20(a)	Yes
Manufacturer of a custom device	Yes 807.20(a)(2)	Yes 807.20(a)(2)	Yes
Manufacturer of accessories or components that are packaged or labeled for commercial distribution for health-related purposes to an end user	Yes 807.20(a)(5)	Yes 807.20(a)(5)	Yes
Manufacturer of components that are distributed only to a finished device manufacturer	No 807.65(a)	No	No
US manufacturer of export-only devices	Yes 807.20(a)(2)	Yes 807.20(a)(2)	Yes
Relabeler or repackager	Yes 807.20(a)(3)	Yes 807.20(a)(3)	No
Contract manufacturer that commercially distributes the device for the specifications developer	Yes 807.20(a)(2)	Yes 807.20(a)(2)	Yes
Contract manufacturer that does not commercially distribute the device for the specifications developer	No	No	No
Contract manufacturer of a subassembly or component, contract packager or labeler	No	No	No
Contract sterilizer that commercially distributes the device	Yes 807.20(a)(2)	Yes 807.20(a)(2)	Yes
Contract sterilizer that does not commercially distribute the device	No	No	No
Kit assembler	Yes 807.20(a)	Yes 807.20(a)	Yes
Domestic distributor	8007.20(c)(3)	No	No
Specification developer	Yes 807.20(a)(1)	Yes 807.20(a)(1)	Yes
Specification consultant only	No	No	No
Initial distributor/importer	Yes 807.40(a)	No Enforcement Discretion Used for 807.22(c)	No
Device being investigated under TDE	No	No 807.40(c)	No
Reprocessor of single-use devices	Yes 807.20	Yes 807.20	Yes
Remanufacturer	Yes	Yes	No

considered a single device for listing purposes, provided the function or intended use does not differ within the family. All subsequent establishment registration and product listing information must be updated annually between 1 October and 31 December, even if no changes have occurred. Failure of an establishment to register or maintain its registration can render its commercial medical device products misbranded and subject to regulatory actions.

After 30 September 2007, *FDAAA* mandated that all registration and listing information be submitted electronically via the FURLS Device Registration and Listing Module (DRLM), unless a waiver has been granted. This electronic registration and listing process replaced the previously used Forms FDA 2891 and 2891a, "Registration of Device Establishment," and Form FDA 2892 "Medical Device Listing." All owners or operators can access FURLS at any time throughout the year to update their registration and listing information as changes occur. Examples of changes to listings include:

- another device being introduced into commercial distribution
- a change to a previously listed device, such as where it is manufactured
- a previously listed device is removed from commercial distribution or commercial distribution is resumed

The information required for registering an establishment

Table 11-2. Foreign Establishment Registration and Listing Requirements

Establishment Activity	Register	List	Pay Fee
Foreign manufacturer	Yes 807.40(a)	Yes 807.40(a)	Yes
Foreign exporter of devices located in a foreign country	807.40 (a)	807.40 (a)	No
Contract manufacturer whose device is shipped to US by the contract manufacturer	Yes 807.40(a)	Yes 807.40(a)	Yes
Contract sterilizer whose sterilized device is shipped to the US by the sterilizer	Yes 807.40(a)	Yes 807.40(a)	Yes
Reprocessor of single-use device	807.20(a)	807.20(a)	Yes
Custom device manufacturers	807.20(a)(2)	807.20(a)(2)	Yes
Relabeler or repackager	Yes 807.20(a)(3)	Yes 807.20(a)(3)	No
Kit assembler	Yes 807.20(a)	Yes 807.20(a)	Yes
Device being investigated under IDE	No 812.1(a)	No 812.1(a) 807.40(c)	No
Specification developer	Yes	Yes	Yes
Remanufacturer	Yes	Yes	No
Manufacturer of components that are distributed only by a finished device manufacturer	No 807.65(a)	No	No
Maintains complaint files as required under 21 CFR 820.198 (Note: register as a manufacturer if physical manufacturing taking place at site, Otherwise register as a specification developer)	Yes	Yes	Yes

and listing medical device products is provided in 21 CFR 807.25 and is clearly cued during the electronic registration process. A permanent establishment registration number will be assigned to each registered device establishment.

FDA requires any person or entity that initiates and develops device specifications and commercially distributes that device to register and list any such medical device products (21 CFR 807.20(a)). A person or entity that only manufactures devices according to another's specifications and does not commercially distribute the devices is not required to register. Registration and listing also are not required of contract sterilizers that do not commercially distribute the devices (21 CFR 807.20 (c)(2)). *FDAMA* repealed the previous requirement in 21 CFR 807.20(c) to eliminate the registration and listing requirements for distributors who are not importers, effective 19 February 1998.

As amended by *FDAMA*, 21 CFR 807 asserts that entities that reprocess single-use devices for reuse in human patients are considered manufacturers; therefore, owners and operators of such establishments also must comply with registration and listing requirements. The FDA guidance, *Enforcement Priorities for Single Use Devices Reprocessed by Third Parties and Hospitals*[3] provides additional information about this requirement. *MDUFMA* added new

regulatory requirements for reprocessed single-use devices that primarily affect premarket submissions for reprocessed devices, "Information on the *Medical Device User Fee and Modernization Act (MDUFMA)* of 2002" (www.fda.gov/ MecicalDevices/DeviceRegulationandGuidance/Overview/ MedicalDeviceUserFeeandModernizationActMDUFMA/ default.htm).

Quality System Regulation

The Quality System Regulation (QSR), codified under 21 CFR Part 820, went into effect on 18 December 1978, and defined FDA current Good Manufacturing Practice (CGMP) requirements for medical devices and in vitro diagnostic products. Accordingly, the QSR and CGMP for medical devices should be regarded as synonymous.

Over the next 18 years, only three minor changes[4] would be made to the QSR. However, a substantive revision of the QSR, as authorized by the *SMDA*, was undertaken to add design controls, and to harmonize CGMP and quality system regulations with applicable international standards, such as the International Organization for Standards (ISO) 9001:1994 *Quality Systems—Model for Quality Assurance in Design, Development, Production, Installation and Servicing*, and, at the time, the ISO committee draft (CD) revision

Table 11-3. Registration and Listing Timelines

Information	Due Date
Establishment name and address	Annually between 1 October and 31 December, and anytime throughout year, but within 30 days of change
Owner/operator name and address	Annually between 1 October and 31 December, and anytime throughout year, but within 30 days of change
Official correspondent name and address	Annually between 1 October and 31 December, and anytime throughout year, but within 30 days of change
Trading name(s)	Annually between 1 October and 31 December, and anytime throughout year, but within 30 days of change
US agent (see foreign establishments)	Anytime throughout year, but within 30 days of change
Owner/operator	Anytime throughout year, but within 30 days of change
Proprietary name	Anytime throughout year, but within 30 days of change
Premarket submission number (for nonexempt devices)*	Annually between 1 October and 31 December, and anytime throughout year, but within 30 days of change
Product code (for exempt devices only)	Annually between 1 October and 31 December, and anytime throughout year, but within 30 days of change
* = For devices requiring 510(k) clearance or PMA approval, examples of change to the premarket submission number may be due to a new 510(k) or PMA supplement submitted for design change of a device.	

of ISO/CD 13485 *Quality Systems—Medical Devices—Supplementary Requirements to ISO 9001*. These QSR revisions went into effect 1 June 1997.

FDA has long been a staunch advocate of the international harmonization of medical device standards and regulations, with a shared goal of mutual recognition of CGMP inspections among major global medical device regulatory authorities. FDA's movement toward harmonization and mutual recognition of medical device CGMP inspections, or Quality System Conformity Assessments, was further galvanized through its collaboration with the Global Harmonization Task Force (GHTF) to develop a final rule that incorporates the harmonized quality system requirements, which are today recognized around the world.

GHTF is a voluntary, international group of representatives from medical device regulatory authorities and trade associations comprising the EU and European Free Trade Association (EFTA), the US, Canada, Japan and Australia. Since its inception in 1992, GHTF has pursued international consensus on medical device regulatory controls and practices. FDA, as one of the founding members of GHTF, has enjoyed a central role in this international collaboration to globally harmonize medical device regulations, standards and practices. This partnership has produced more than 30 voluntary guidance documents in pursuit of its pledge to develop a global regulatory model for medical devices. The GHTF Study Groups are focused

in these areas: Study Group 1, Premarket Evaluation; Study Group 2, Postmarket Surveillance/Vigilance; Study Group 3, Quality Systems; Study Group 4, Auditing; and Study Group 5, Clinical Safety/Performance. The GHTF website provides substantial information regarding its mission, charter and study groups, and its final guidance documents may be conveniently downloaded (www.ghtf.org/). In March 2011, GHTF announced its decision to reorganize. The new entity will be comprised solely of the regulatory authorities from the member countries and will focus on finding the optimum ways to achieve harmonization at an operational level in such areas as new science and technologies, information and resource sharing and increased opportunities for technical expert interchanges.

The amended QSR also includes:
- management responsibility and review controls (21 CFR 820.20)
- design controls (21 CFR 820.30)
- purchasing controls (21 CFR 820.50)
- process validation requirements (21 CFR 820.75)
- more robust requirements for corrective and preventive action (21 CFR 820.100)
- service recordkeeping and review requirements (21 CFR 820.200)

Although the original medical device GMPs of 1978 distinguished between requirements for critical and noncritical

Figure 11-1. Quality System Elements

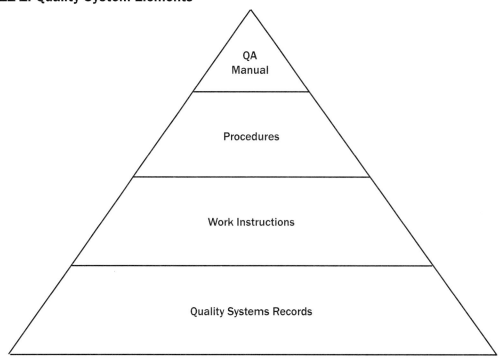

components and devices, this distinction has since disappeared from the QSR, and all medical devices are now subject to common requirements for specifications, acceptance criteria, identification, supplier agreements and records. As stated in 21 CFR 820.30(a), design controls apply to Class III, Class II and certain Class I devices, as listed.

If a device's failure to perform can result in a significant injury, the QSR requires procedures that allow the identification (21 CFR 820.60) and traceability (21 CFR 820.65) of each unit, lot or batch of finished devices, and, where appropriate, components, during all stages of receipt, production, distribution and installation. This is accomplished through the use of a control number intended to aid in any necessary corrective action. This medical device identification is to be documented in the Device History Record (DHR). Traceability generally applies to the manufacturing process of all eligible devices. This differs from medical device tracking (21 CFR 821), wherein the manufacturer must be capable of tracking (e.g., locating) certain devices from the device manufacturing facility to the actual person for whom the device was indicated. Effective tracking of devices from the manufacturing facility, through the distributor network, to the patient, is necessary in the event that patient notifications or device recalls are necessary. Device tracking requirements for certain devices are further discussed later in this chapter.

The CDRH *Medical Device Quality Systems Manual: A Small Entity Compliance Guide* contains more than 400 pages of detailed guidance information, illustrations and examples of QSR compliance that manufacturers should consider when designing, manufacturing and distributing medical devices.[5] The manual is available on CDRH's website, and each of the 18 chapters and two appendices is available as a separate document that can be downloaded in text format (www. fda.gov/MedicalDevices/DeviceRegulationandGuidance/ PostmarketRequirements/QualitySystemsRegulations/ MedicalDeviceQualitySystemsManual/default.htm). The manual explains each of the QSR's major provisions and includes a variety of model procedures and example forms. It can assist manufacturers in establishing or upgrading a quality system that will meet the QSR's intent. Quality system elements are traditionally represented by the following documentation (see **Figure 11-1**):

- The quality manual is a document that states the corporate quality policy, describes quality system components and how the system is implemented, and assigns authority and responsibilities. Quality system components typically are linked by specific reference to quality procedures.
- Quality procedures describe how specific quality system operating processes and controls are implemented. The strength of a set of quality procedures lies in cross-functional and interdepartmental linkages among associated processes and controls.
- Detailed work instructions specify the individual, intradepartmental steps necessary to consistently and reliably perform specific activities, such as those involved in component procurement, inspections, fabrication, assembly and testing, labeling, final

Figure 11-2. Relationship of Medical Device Records

acceptance, packaging, shipping, installation, maintenance and servicing of a device.

- Records, forms and reports provide evidence of how the system is functioning.

An important provision of the QSR requires manufacturers to establish and maintain specific records. These records are subject to the document control provisions of 21 CFR 820.40, including change control. Approved device master records (DMRs) as described in 21 CFR 820.181, and Chapter 8 of the CDRH manual, must be maintained. A DMR is analogous to the master batch record in drug manufacturing, and represents the template or stepwise procedure for manufacturing a medical device in accordance with the regulated and validated environment under which it was cleared. For each member (e.g., significant variant) of a family of medical devices being manufactured, there must be a corresponding DMR. Typically a DMR contains, but is not limited to:

- approved component and finished device specifications and drawings, and a complete printout of approved device software code
- production equipment, process and environmental specifications, methods and procedures
- quality assurance procedures and specifications including acceptance criteria and quality assurance equipment, tools and fixtures
- packaging and labeling specifications
- installation, maintenance and servicing procedures

Ideally, a DMR would comprise all of the aforementioned components localized and maintained in a single, physical repository (e.g., a notebook, a server domain, a file drawer, etc.). Alternatively, the DMR, at the very least, must refer to the individual locations of these informational components.

The QSR (21 CFR 820.184) also requires manufacturers to maintain device history records (DHRs). The DHR is simply a copy of the DMR that has been completed (e.g., values entered, process steps checked-off, initials/signatures applied, etc.) during the manufacture of a batch, lot or unit quantity of medical device product to document the production. The DHR is, therefore, comparable to an individual batch record in drug manufacturing. The DHR includes completed forms and reports for each manufactured batch, lot or unit, and demonstrates that devices were manufactured in accordance with the DMR. The DHR shall include, or refer to the location of, the following information:

- dates of manufacture
- quantity manufactured
- quantity released for distribution
- acceptance records that demonstrate that the device is manufactured in accordance with the DMR
- primary identification label and labeling used for each production unit
- device identification(s) and control number(s) used

The QSR (21 CFR 820.30(j)) also requires manufacturers to establish and maintain a design history file (DHF) for each type of device. The DHF shall contain or reference the records necessary to demonstrate that the design was developed in accordance with the approved design plan and the general requirements of design control. All approved changes to a cleared device should be appropriately chronicled in the DHF.

From a quality perspective, consider that all device properties and specifications as documented in the DHR representing a specific batch of product must reconcile with those details as documented in the DMR. Furthermore, all design properties and specifications as documented in the DMR must reside in the DHF (see **Figure 11-2**).

FDA Facility Inspection Programs

A major provision of *MDUFMA* authorizes FDA-accredited third parties to inspect qualified manufacturers of Class II and Class III devices. This initiative is intended to facilitate a greater focus of FDA's inspectional resources on higher-risk devices and provide greater efficiency in scheduling multiple inspections for medical device firms operating in global markets. Certain conditions must apply for a facility to be eligible for third-party inspections, including:

- The most recent inspection must have been classified as "no action indicated" or "voluntary action indicated."
- The establishment must notify FDA of the third

Table 11-4. Summary of Reporting Requirements for Manufacturers

Reporter	What to Report	Report Form Number	To Whom	When
Manufacturer	30 day reports of deaths, serious injuries and malfunctions.	Form FDA 3500A	FDA	Within 30 calendar days from becoming aware of an event.
Manufacturer	Five day reports on events that require remedial action to prevent an unreasonable risk of substantial harm to the public health and other types of events designated by FDA.	Form FDA 3500A	FDA	Within five working days of becoming aware of an event, or whenever FDA makes a written request for the submission a 5 day report.
Manufacturer	Follow-up or supplemental reports on previously reported events—information required under 21 CFR 803 that was not initially provided because it was not known or was not available when the initial report was submitted	Form FDA 3500A	FDA	Within 30 calendar days of becoming aware of the information

party it intends to use, and FDA must agree to the selection.

- The establishment must market a device in the US and must market a device "in one or more foreign countries."
- The third party must be certified, accredited or otherwise recognized by one of the countries in which the device is to be marketed.
- The establishment must submit a statement that one of the countries in which the device is to be marketed "recognizes an inspection of the establishment by [FDA]."

On 28 April 2003, FDA published a *Federal Register* notice providing criteria for the accreditation of third parties to conduct inspections. Commencing 26 October 2003, FDA has maintained a list of firms accredited to conduct third-party inspections on its website (www.accessdata.fda.gov/scripts/cdrh/cfdocs/cfthirdparty/accredit.cfm). An establishment is permitted to select any accredited person to conduct an inspection regarding an eligible medical device product in lieu of an FDA inspection.

A Quality Systems Inspections Technique (QSIT) was validated and subsequently implemented by FDA in July 1999, after the agency determined that it allows more focused and efficient inspections of medical device manufacturers. A QSIT inspections handbook was developed and issued in August 1999 and can be downloaded from the FDA website (www.fda.gov/ICECI/Inspections/InspectionGuides/UCM074883).

The QSIT inspectional approach segments the QSR into seven major subsystems:
1. Corrective and Preventive Action
2. Design Controls
3. Production and Process Controls
4. Management Controls

5. Records/Documents/Change Controls
6. Material Controls
7. Facility and Equipment Controls

QSIT inspections focus on the first four subsystems because they are the primary indicators of QSR compliance, and FDA believes that discrepancies in the last three subsystems will become evident through diligent review of the first four.

An additional resource is FDA's compliance program, which provides guidance manuals to its FDA field and center staff for inspection, administrative and enforcement activities related to the QSR, MDR, medical device tracking regulation (21 CFR Part 821), corrections and removals regulation (21 CFR Part 806), and the registration and listing regulation (21 CFR Part 807). *Compliance Program Manual 7382.845 Inspection of Device Manufacturers* spans five regulations for inspecting medical device firms and provides specific guidance for each. The compliance manual can be downloaded at www.fda.gov/MedicalDevices/DeviceRegulationandGuidance/GuidanceDocuments/ucm072753.htm.

Medical Device Reporting

Medical device manufacturers and importers were first required to report all device-related deaths, serious injuries and certain malfunctions beginning in 1984. In subsequent years, government studies showed that despite full implementation of the MDR regulation, less than 1% of problems occurring in hospitals were being reported to FDA. As a result, the scope of the MDR regulation was extended to require device user facilities to report deaths to both FDA and the manufacturer, and to report serious injuries to the manufacturer. The MDR regulations were amended by the *Medical Device Amendments* of 1992, with a final rule published in 1995, establishing a single reporting standard for

Table 11-5. Summary of Reporting Requirements for User Facilities and Importers

Reporter	What to Report	Report Form Number	To Whom	When
User Facility	Death	Form FDA 3500A	FDA and manufacturer	Within 10 working days after first becoming aware of the event
User Facility	Serious injury	Form FDA 3500A	Manufacturer; FDA only if manufacturer unknown	Within 10 working days after first becoming aware of the event
Importers	Death or serious injury	Form FDA 3500A	FDA and manufacturer	Not more than 30 calendar days after first becoming aware of the event
Importers	A device malfunction that would likely cause or contribute to a death or serious injury if the malfunction were to recur	Form FDA 3500A	Manufacturer	Not more than 30 calendar days after first becoming aware of the event

device manufacturers, initial importers, domestic distributors and user facilities. The 1995 rule was revised in April 1996 and subsequently amended in March 1997. The *FDAMA* changes to MDR became effective on 19 February 1998. On 26 January 2000,[6] changes to the implementing regulations were published in the *Federal Register*, including:

- Medical device manufacturers, importers and distributors are no longer required to submit an annual certification statement.
- Domestic distributors no longer have to submit MDR reports, but they must continue to maintain records of adverse events and product complaints.
- Importers continue to be subject to the remaining requirements of the MDR regulation, 21 CFR 803.
- User facilities now submit a report annually instead of semi-annually.

The MDR Rule changes became effective 27 March 2000. Additional information about these updated MDR reporting requirements is available on the CDRH Device Advice webpage (www.fda.gov/MedicalDevices/DeviceRegulationandGuidance/default.htm). The MDR Rule was further amended effective 27 October 2008 to eliminate the requirement for submission of baseline reports, and the use of Form FDA 3417, as the information was considered largely redundant with information provided in individual reports (www.federalregister.gov/articles/2008/06/13/E8-13349/medical-devices-medical-device-reporting-baseline-reports-companion-to-direct-final-rule).

FDA places high priority on compliance with MDR requirements during manufacturing facility inspections. Observed deficiencies are frequently cited on Form FDA 483 and, depending upon their seriousness, can lead to the issuance of a Warning Letter. Adherence to documented procedures that encompass MDR activities, as well as complaints and nonconforming product, is necessary to avoid citations. **Table 11-4** summarizes reporting and recordkeeping requirements for manufacturers and initial importers, and **Table 11-5** provides MDR requirements, including reporting timeframes, for user facilities and domestic distributors. More detailed information regarding reporting requirements is contained in MDR guidance manuals, available on CDRH's website (www.fda.gov/MedicalDevices/DeviceRegulationandGuidance/GuidanceDocuments/default.htm).

Recalls, Corrections and Removals

FDA defines a "recall" as correction or removal of a product that is defective, could be a risk to health, or is in violation of the rules administered by the agency. Recalls are classified into a numeric designation (I, II or III) by FDA to indicate the relative degree of health hazard presented by the recalled product. Health hazard evaluation is a key determinant of whether a product should be recalled and includes an assessment of the disease or injury associated with the product, seriousness of the risk posed by the product, likelihood of occurrence and consequences (immediate and long-term). FDA uses the health hazard evaluation as the basis for its recall classification:

- Class I—a situation presenting a reasonable probability that the use of, or exposure to, a violative product will cause serious adverse health consequences or death
- Class II—a situation in which use of, or exposure to, a violative product may cause temporary or medically reversible adverse health consequences or where the probability of serious adverse health consequences is remote
- Class III—a situation in which use of or exposure to a violative product is not likely to cause adverse health consequences

On 19 May 1997, FDA issued a final rule implementing

provisions under the *SMDA* that made medical device correction and removal (recall) reporting mandatory instead of voluntary. The new rule was applicable to manufacturers, initial importers and domestic distributors but, because of administrative delays in the Office of Management and Budget (OMB), its effective date was delayed until 18 May 1998.[7] A *FDAMA* provision, which was to be effective 19 February 1998, repealed the requirement for reporting any device removal or correction by domestic distributors.[8] However, FDA's final rule eliminating the requirement for distributor reporting did not become effective until 22 February 1999 due to administrative delays. Recall regulations include:

- 21 CFR 7, Enforcement Policy, Subpart C, Recalls—which covers voluntary removal of medical device(s)
- 21 CFR 806, Medical Device Corrections and Removals—which covers mandatory notification of correction or removal of a medical device(s)
- 21 CFR 810, Medical Device Recall Authority—which describes the procedures that FDA will follow in exercising its medical device recall authority under section 518(e) of the *FD&C Act*

Device manufacturers and importers for domestic distribution are required to report to FDA any correction or removal undertaken to reduce the risk to human health posed by a device's use. They also are required to report any action taken to remedy an *FD&C Act* violation caused by a device's risk to human health that would cause FDA to act if the manufacturer did not do so voluntarily. Reports of corrections and removals are required for Class I and Class II recalls. Under 21 CFR 806, Class III recalls need not be reported; only recordkeeping requirements would apply. However, FDA has an expectation that all recalls will be reported so that it may review the risk to health and render a final determination on the most appropriate classification.

Information required in such a report is detailed in 21 CFR 806.10(c)(1)–(13) and includes, but is not limited to:

- recalling firm name, address and telephone number
- batch, lot or unit identification numbers and quantity of affected devices manufactured or distributed
- consignee names, addresses and telephone numbers
- copies of all recall-related communications
- names and addresses of recall information recipients

The report must be submitted to the recalling firm's local FDA district office within 10 working days of initiating the recall. Reporting requirements regarding deaths and serious injury apply in accordance with MDR timeframes (see **Table 11-5**). Exemptions from these reporting requirements are provided in 21 CFR 806.1(b)(1)–(4) and include:

- manufacturer's actions to improve a device's performance or quality, which do not reduce a health risk or remedy a violation of the *FD&C Act*
- market withdrawal, defined as a recall of a distributed device that involves a minor or no violation of the *FD&C Act* and would not be subject to legal action by FDA (21 CFR 806.2(h))
- routine servicing, defined as regularly scheduled device maintenance, including the replacement of parts at the end of their normal life expectancy (21 CFR 806.2(k))
- stock recovery, defined as a recall of a device that has not yet been marketed or left the manufacturer's direct control

The recall reporting regulation does not indicate what actions FDA may take upon receiving the report. However, it may be anticipated that the enforcement policy guidelines in 21 CFR 74 would apply, involving periodic progress reports and permitting recall termination only when the agency determines that all reasonable efforts have been taken to recall the affected devices in accordance with the recall strategy and plan. The regulation further clarifies which records must be maintained if a recall is not required to be reported (21 CFR 806.20), as well as information about possible FDA actions to publicly disclose submitted recall reports. Under enforcement, FDA also has the authority to impose a mandatory recall on manufacturers (21 CFR 810).

As noted above, FDA has the authority to impose a mandatory recall on manufacturers under 21 CFR 810. If, after providing the appropriate person with an opportunity to consult with the agency, FDA finds there is a reasonable probability that a device intended for human use would cause serious, adverse health consequences or death, the agency may issue a cease distribution and notification order requiring the person named in the order to immediately:

- cease distribution of the device
- notify healthcare professionals and device user facilities of the order
- instruct these professionals and device user facilities to cease use of the device

The person named in the order will have an opportunity for a regulatory hearing or to provide a written request to FDA asking that the order be modified, vacated or amended. FDA may later amend the order to require a recall of the device.

Additional information concerning recalls, including guidance on recall procedures, effectiveness checks, model press releases, 510(k) requirements during firm-initiated recalls and the FDA recall database, may be found on FDA's website under CDRH Device Advice. In addition, Chapter 7 of the FDA *Regulatory Procedures Manual* provides information on internal FDA procedures used in handling regulatory and enforcement matters for domestic and imported devices.

Exports

Approved or Cleared Devices

There are no export restrictions, approvals, notifications or other requirements for medical devices approved or cleared for marketing in the US, and these may be exported anywhere in the world without prior FDA notification or approval. Although FDA does not place any restrictions on the export of these devices, certain countries may require written certification that a firm or its devices are in compliance with US law. In such instances, FDA will accommodate US firms by providing a Certificate for Foreign Government (CFG). Formerly referred to as a Certificate for Products for Export or Certificate of Free Sale, the CFG uses self-certification to speed the processing of requests, and the certificate is provided on counterfeit-resistant paper bearing an embossed gold foil seal. CDRH requires a fee for the initial certificate and for any additional certificates issued for the same product(s) in the same letter of request.

Requests for a CFG are submitted on Form FDA 3613 and questions regarding the CFG should be directed to the Office of Compliance, Export Certificate Team, at +1 301 796 7400 or via email (exportcert@cdrh.fda.gov). Additional information about certificate fees for device exports can be found at www.fda.gov/MedicalDevices/DeviceRegulationandGuidance/ImportingandExportingDevices/default.htm.

Unapproved or Uncleared Devices

It is only when a device has not been approved or cleared for domestic marketing and is, hence, considered investigational, that legal export provisions become applicable. The basis for the regulation of imports and exports is contained in Chapter VIII of the *FD&C Act*, because there are no regulations in the Code of Federal Regulations (CFR) that cover export requirements, with the exception of 21 CFR 812.18(b) regarding the export of investigational devices. That provision requires a person exporting an investigational device to obtain prior FDA approval as required by Section 801(e) of the act, or to comply with Section 802 of the act.

The export of devices has been regulated since the *FD&C Act* was enacted in 1938. The 1976 *Medical Device Amendments* tightened the rules, requiring a determination by FDA that exporting the device would not pose a public health and safety hazard (essentially an FDA approval to export) and was approved by the recipient country. Despite US medical device firms' positive balance of trade, industry felt the statute's export approval requirements hindered the

ability of US manufacturers to enter and compete in foreign markets. Addressing industry concerns, Congress enacted the *Food and Drug Export Reform and Enhancement Act* of 1996 *(FDERA)*.[9] In contrast to other *FD&C Act* provisions applicable to medical devices, no regulations have been codified to establish how FDA should manage unapproved device export requirements, except 21 CFR 812.18 regarding the export of investigational devices.

Following is a simplified and abridged summary of unapproved device export requirements. The rules are complex, and this summary is not intended to be inclusive of the requirements applicable to all devices or to any specific device. The statute and guidance documents should be consulted for specific requirements (www.fda.gov/MedicalDevices/DeviceRegulationandGuidance/ImportingandExportingDevices/ucm050521.htm#procedures).

Because the export rules apply to devices that are not approved or cleared for domestic distribution, these devices ordinarily would be considered adulterated, misbranded or both. Essentially, *FDERA* made certain regulatory changes that provide manufacturers with compliance options. When the minimum requirements of Section 801(e)(1) and either Section 801(e)(2) or one or more of the choices under Section 802 of the *FD&C Act* are met, FDA shall deem the devices to be not adulterated or misbranded for the purpose of export.

There are two principal scenarios governing the export of investigational medical devices: a) exportation of Class I and/or Class II devices, and b) the exportation of Class III and/or banned devices. Both scenarios require, at a minimum, that the investigational devices to be exported meet the basic provisions of the *FD&C Act*, as now amended in Section 801(e)(1). These provisions require that the device:

- meet the foreign purchaser's specifications
- not be in conflict with the importing country's laws
- be labeled, "intended for export only" on the outside of the shipping package
- not be sold or offered for sale in domestic commerce

Assuming the device a manufacturer wishes to export complies with these provisions, the remaining regulatory obligations include:

Exportation of Class I and/or Class II Devices

The only additional requirement for exportation is that the manufacturer reasonably believes that the device it is to export could obtain 510(k) marketing clearance in the US if reviewed by FDA. If the investigational device represents a Class I device that is exempt from premarket notification, then this requirement does not apply. However, if the device represents a Class I or Class II device that is subject to the requirements of premarket notification, then the manufacturer's belief that it would be cleared for marketing must be based upon it being similar in design, construction and intended use to one or more existing, cleared Class I or Class II devices, or it must be a reasonable belief that the investigational device would be regarded as "substantially equivalent" to one or more existing, cleared Class I or Class II devices. Therefore, if this belief of "approvability" is indeed reasonable, the manufacturer can anticipate securing authorization to export the investigational device solely under Section 801(e)(1) of the *FD&C Act*. Certification is required to complete the process.

FDA has implemented a new certification process referred to as a Certificate of Exportability (COE) in an effort to facilitate the export of a medical device under Section 801(e)(1). Persons exporting an article under Section 801(e)(1) must maintain records demonstrating that the investigational product does indeed comply with the four provisions of Section 801(e)(1) listed above. Retention requirements for these records mirror those for GMP documents, or any such quality systems records that apply to the exported product.

Manufacturers applying for a COE are required to sign a statement attesting that they meet the four criteria of Section 801(e)(1). False statements, in such circumstances, are considered violations of United States Code Title 18, Chapter 47, Section 1001. Penalties for a false statement include up to $250,000 in fines and up to five years imprisonment. CDRH requires an initial fee per certificate, and a subsequent nominal fee for each additional certificate issued for the same product(s) in the same letter of request. Original certificates will be provided on special counterfeit-resistant paper with an embossed gold foil seal. CDRH will issue the certification within 20 days upon the firm's demonstration that the product meets the applicable requirements. Requests for a COE are filed on Form FDA 3613a, Supplementary Information Certificate of Exportability Requests. Questions regarding the COE should be directed to the Office of Compliance, Export Certificate Team, at +1 301 796 7400. (exportcert@cdrh.fda.gov).

By meeting the four provisions of Section 801(e)(1) described above—ensuring that records substantiate that compliance, and obtaining a COE—the manufacturer may legally export the investigational device, without FDA permission, in accordance with Section 801(e)(1).

Exportation of Class III and/or Banned Devices

Along with the four basic requirements of Section 801(e)(1), additional provisions found either under Section 801(e)(2) or Section 802 of the *FD&C Act* allow a manufacturer to export unapproved Class III devices and devices otherwise required to meet a performance standard under Section 514 of the *FD&C Act* (currently, electrode lead wires and patient cables (21 CFR 898) are the only devices with an FDA performance standard under Section 514 of the *FD&C Act*). These devices include investigational devices, that would not be able to obtain Premarket Approval (PMA) or for which a PMA has not been approved, and banned devices (at present, only synthetic hair fibers intended for implant).

Via Section 801(e)(2), a manufacturer electing to comply with Section 801(e)(2) must apply for FDA approval to export and must submit:

- a complete device description
- the device's status in the US
- evidence from the importing foreign governmental authority that the device is not in conflict with its laws (or a notarized certification from a responsible company official in the US that the product is not in conflict with the foreign country's laws),[10] the device's US status is known and the import is permitted
- basic safety data pertaining to the device

Recordkeeping requirements as described above apply for devices exported according to Section 801(e)(2).

An alternative to export under Section 801(e)(2) involves a number of choices under Section 802, which do not require FDA approval but do require the exporter to submit a Simple Notification per 802(g) and maintain substantiating records, should FDA request them. The basic requirements, listed in Section 802(f), call for the devices to:

- satisfy the requirements of Section 801(e)(1)
- be manufactured in acceptable compliance either with US QSR (no deficiencies or satisfactory correction of deficiencies following the most recent FDA inspection) or with an international quality system standard recognized by FDA (currently, none is recognized)
- not be adulterated, other than lack of marketing approval
- not be the subject of a notice by the Department of Health and Human Services that reimportation would pose an imminent hazard nor pose an imminent hazard to the receiving country
- not be mislabeled, except that they must meet the importing country's labeling requirements

Records (Section 802(g), in addition to the requirements per Section 801(e)(1)) must also be maintained for devices exported under Section 802, and other requirements may apply. Even though FDA does not require a firm to obtain written permission prior to export under Section 802, a foreign purchaser may request proof of compliance with US law prior to export. FDA will provide a COE to the exporter under Section 802 to facilitate export of a medical device. Exporting manufacturers should consult Section 802 of the *FD&C Act* for further details specific to their devices.

Imports

Foreign establishments that manufacture medical devices and/or products that emit radiation must comply with applicable US regulations before, during and after importing into the US. These products must meet all applicable FDA regulatory requirements, because FDA does not recognize regulatory approvals from other countries.

Foreign Manufacturers

All foreign manufacturers must meet applicable US medical device regulations to import devices into the US, even if the product is authorized for marketing in another country. These requirements include establishment registration, device listing, manufacturing in accordance with the QSR, medical device reporting of adverse events and a 510(k) or PMA, if applicable. Foreign manufacturing sites are subject to FDA inspection. In addition, the foreign manufacturers must designate a US agent.

Initial Importers

An initial importer is any importer who furthers the marketing of a device from a foreign manufacturer to the person who makes the final delivery or sale of the device to the ultimate consumer or user, but does not repackage or otherwise change the container, wrapper or labeling of the device or device package. The initial importer of the device must register its establishment with FDA. Initial importers are also subject to regulations governing MDR, reports of corrections and removals and medical device tracking, if applicable. Under the MDR regulations, importers are required to report incidents in which a device may have caused or contributed to a death or serious injury, as well as report certain malfunctions. The importers must maintain an MDR event file for each adverse event. All product complaints, MDR and non-MDR events must be forwarded to the manufacturer. Under medical device tracking requirements, certain devices must be tracked through the distribution chain.

Responsibilities of the initial importer, beyond those noted above, may include:[11]

- acting as official correspondent (although this is not required)
- assisting FDA in communications with the foreign establishment and responding to questions concerning the foreign establishment's products that are imported or offered for import into the US
- assisting FDA in scheduling inspections of the foreign establishment if unable to contact the foreign establishment directly or expeditiously; FDA may provide information or documents to the US agent, and such an action shall be considered equivalent to providing the same information or documents to the foreign establishment

All medical devices imported into the US must meet Bureau of Customs and Border Protection (CBP) requirements in addition to those of FDA. A product that does not meet FDA regulatory requirements may be detained upon entry. Additional information about importing medical devices into the US is available at www.fda.gov/MedicalDevices/DeviceRegulationandGuidance/ImportingandExportingDevices/default.htm.

Medical Device Postmarket Activities

Following market clearance of a medical device, manufacturers and other establishments involved in their commercial distribution must adhere to various postmarketing requirements and applicable regulations. These activities are primarily intended to ensure ongoing monitoring and safety following market approval, and may include a wide array of statutory or voluntary activities for both industry and FDA. These include the use of tracking systems; the reporting of device malfunctions, serious injuries or deaths; and the registration of establishments where devices are produced or distributed.

Some compliance-related activities such as maintaining quality systems, inspections and import/export, although not strictly postmarket, are regarded as essential to the ongoing safety and effectiveness of marketed devices.

Postmarket requirements may also include postmarket surveillance studies required under Section 522 of the act, as well as postapproval studies required at the time of approval of a PMA, HDE or PDP application.

Postmarket activities initiated by FDA may include quality system inspections, monitoring of user reporting and public health notifications. FDA is also involved in disseminating accurate, science-based risk/benefit information for improving the public health.

Medical Device Tracking

Medical device tracking is intended to ensure that a manufacturer can promptly identify product distribution, notify patients and remove a device from the market if requested by FDA. *SMDA* provided for automatic, mandatory medical device tracking by creating a new Section 519(e) of the *FD&C Act*. Subsequently, the device tracking regulations (21 CFR 821) were amended by *FDAMA*, eliminating mandatory tracking and giving FDA discretion to require a manufacturer to adopt a method of tracking a Class II or Class III device. FDA most recently amended the device tracking regulations, effective 9 May 2002, with changes to 21 CFR 821 as follows:

- revising the existing scope and authority: the types of persons subject to tracking are no longer linked to registration requirements; as amended, the tracking requirements apply only to manufacturers that receive a tracking order from FDA

- modifying existing definitions of "importer" and "permanently implantable device"
- adding new patient confidentiality provisions[12]

Accordingly, the amended regulations specify certain devices to which tracking requirements apply. This includes devices, the failure of which would be reasonably likely to have serious adverse health consequences; devices that are intended to be implanted in the human body for more than one year; or devices that are life-sustaining, or life-supporting and are used outside a device user facility. FDA maintains a list of devices subject to tracking regulations.

Manufacturers of a tracked device must establish a written standard operating procedure (SOP), which includes a method for tracking the device throughout distribution, and a quality assurance program including audit procedures. Final distributors of these devices will be required to provide manufacturers with patient information. Device tracking is required for the useful life of the device.

Traceability is distinguished from medical device tracking in that traceability involves the identification of one or more device components or a finished device through the use of control numbers that may facilitate any warranted corrective actions. Therefore, traceability generally applies, and is limited to, the manufacturing stage for all devices. Device tracking, on the other hand, alludes to processes and methods that provide for the pursuit and location of devices that have since been distributed away from the manufacturing facility and may either be stored remotely or may have been prescribed and administered to a patient (e.g., implanted). Information to be maintained through tracking activities includes records concerning the patient and his or her whereabouts; the prescribing and treating physician(s); device identification numbers; and device shipment, treatment initiation and termination dates (21 CFR 821.25). For implants, the explant date and explanting physician information must be maintained. The regulation also requires distributors to provide the manufacturer with specified tracking information (21 CFR 821.30).

Device tracking information is available on CDRH's Device Advice website (www.fda.gov/MedicalDevices/DeviceRegulationandGuidance/default.htm). FDA issued *Medical Device Tracking: Guidance for Industry and FDA Staff* (25 January 2010) to provide manufacturers with more detailed information about device tracking requirements. This guidance can be found at www.fda.gov/MedicalDevices/DeviceRegulationandGuidance/GuidanceDocuments/ucm071756.htm.

Medical Device Postmarket Transformation Initiative

CDRH has made significant strides toward more robust monitoring of the safety and effectiveness of medical devices and radiation-emitting products in the postmarketing phase. In January 2006, CDRH created the Postmarket Transformation Leadership Team to evaluate current recommendations and to propose a prioritized implementation plan for a transformed postmarket process. The results of this initiative and the subsequent report published in November 2006 provided a vision and an action plan for changes to the medical devices postmarket program.

A key strategic goal of FDA toward the integration of postmarketing initiatives was the establishment and amplification of the interconnections found at all phases of the total product lifecycle (TPLC) (see **Figure 11-3**). This graphic illustrates the links between and interdependence of the regulatory process and lifecycle steps. The diagram further demonstrates the significance and magnitude of postmarketing activities, which comprise half of the critical steps of the TPLC (i.e., manufacturing, marketing, commercial use and obsolescence), and show the inherent balance and flexibility that exists between premarket and postmarket regulation.

As a result of this initiative, the following areas were designated for improvement. They are:

- Create a Culture of Collaboration—CDRH should transform its operations by adding a permanent matrix of cross-cutting, product-related groups over the current functionally based organizational structure to foster information sharing, collaboration and, ultimately, more effective public health promotion and protection. The cross-cutting matrix is designed to ensure that collaboration occurs not just in crisis situations, but also as a part of routine, day-to-day operations.
- Develop World Class Data Systems—Data input, mining, analysis and tracking systems should be strengthened, improved or created as needed for postmarket issues. Improvements to CDRH's critical medical device data and information systems, including the Manufacturer and User Facility Device Experience database (MAUDE) and the MDR system, are highlighted, and additional enhancements to CDRH's analysis and tracking capabilities are being pursued.
- Enhance Risk/Benefit Communication Efforts—CDRH should be a trusted, publicly identifiable source for safety information about medical devices and radiation-emitting products. To that end, an analysis of the communication needs of CDRH stakeholders should be performed. Clinical practitioners and professional communities should collaborate with the agency to develop a process for the dissemination of risk/benefit information.
- Collaborate on Enforcement Strategies and Outcomes—Both the quantity and quality of

Figure 11-3. Total Product Lifecycle

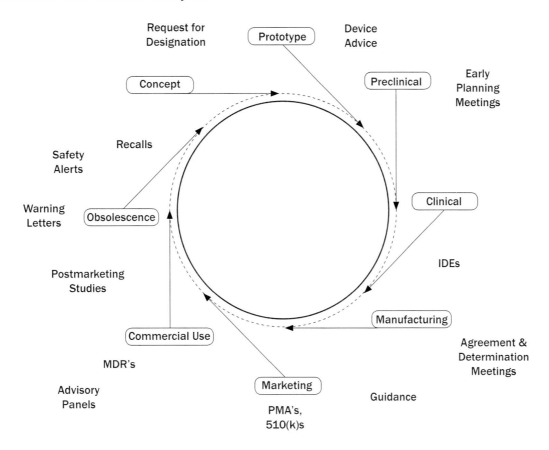

CDRH/Office of Regulatory Affairs (ORA) interactions should be transformed through increased collaboration among CDRH, ORA, and the Office of Chief Counsel. Postmarket data and information should be considered when prioritizing inspections and the inspection preparation process should include a review of recent postmarket data. CDRH should develop ways to leverage the audit results obtained by accredited third-party auditing bodies. Enforcement data systems should be updated and employees trained to use them. All available enforcement tools should be used, including civil money penalties.

Numerous priority actions within these four target areas for improvement were undertaken by FDA and significant accomplishments were realized, including the Medical Product Safety Network (MedSun), Unique Device Identification (UDI), safety news, issues, notifications and alerts.

Medical Product Safety Network (MedSun)

MedSun is an adverse event reporting program launched in 2002 by CDRH. Its primary goal is to work collaboratively with the clinical community to identify, understand and remedy problems associated with the use of medical devices. MedSun also serves as a powerful, two-way communications channel between CDRH and the clinical community.

MedSun participants are recruited from all regions of the country using the American Hospital Association (AHA) membership listing. Participants use an Internet-based system as an easy, secure way to report adverse medical device events. Each member facility has online access to the reports submitted to MedSun so that they can be tracked and reviewed at any time.

SMDA defines "user facilities" as hospitals, nursing homes and outpatient treatment and diagnostic centers. The facilities that comprise the MedSun participants are required to report medical device problems that result in serious illness, injury or death. They are also encouraged to voluntarily report other problems with devices, such as "close calls;" potential for harm and other safety concerns. By monitoring reports about problems and concerns before a more serious event occurs, FDA, manufacturers and clinicians work together to prevent serious injuries and death.

Once a problem is identified, MedSun researchers work with each facility's representatives to clarify and understand the issue. Reports and lessons learned are shared with the clinical community and the public, without facility and patient identification, so clinicians nationwide may take necessary preventive actions.

Additional information on MedSun can be found at www.fda.gov/MedicalDevices/Safety/MedSunMedicalProductSafetyNetwork/default.htm.

Unique Device Identification

FDAAA contains provisions granting FDA the express authority to propose and ultimately implement regulations requiring medical devices to display a UDI. This new system, when implemented, will require:

- the label of a device to bear a unique identifier, unless an alternative location is specified by FDA or an exception is made for a particular device or group of devices
- the unique identifier to be able to identify the device through distribution and use
- the unique identifier to include the lot or serial number if specified by FDA

The presence of a UDI on a medical device is intended to improve patient safety by reducing device-related medical errors, improving identification of specific devices in adverse event reports and facilitating more-effective device recalls. Additional information about the requirement of a UDI for medical devices is available at www.fda.gov/MedicalDevices/DeviceRegulationandGuidance/UniqueDeviceIdentifiers/ucm235962.htm.

In 2010, FDA continued to explore what the implementation of the UDI system will mean for various stakeholders. Labeling organizations continued to participate in informal feedback sessions, which included teleconference discussions and practical simulation exercises that provided FDA with a range of information that has further elucidated UDI system needs. Pilot activities conducted internally at FDA identified processes that are well equipped to handle UDI requirements, as well as those that will need to be modified. Fewer issues and questions now remain as FDA nears the release of the UDI regulation.

Safety News, Issues, Notifications, and Alerts

CDRH shares risk communication information with the public primarily through leaflets and Internet sites. Leaflets are mailed to individuals or made available at conferences. The website offers materials on a wide variety of topics of interest to consumers. Information relevant to particular age groups (e.g., children or the elderly) have been developed with those consumers' limitations in mind (e.g., reading level or accessibility needs). These communications are used to inform the public about what to look for in selecting medical devices and products, the availability of new medical devices, product recalls and safety information and how to report adverse events associated with the use of medical devices.

CDRH uses a variety of outreach tools including Urgent Alerts, multimedia outreach, technical publications, presentations and workshops to advise device users about potential risks. These tools utilize a variety of mechanisms, including broadcast media (press releases, talk papers, web-based news programs, websites and television interviews), public health notifications, patient notifications and public meetings to convey risk messages. In addition, staff presentations, CDRH workshops and technical publications, such as standards and guidance documents, convey important safety information to significant stakeholders. FDA's goal is to ensure that healthcare practitioners, industry and the public understand the risks and act appropriately to minimize them.

CDRH staff selects risk communication tools depending upon the urgency of the message, the intended target audience and the outreach goals. An Urgent Alert mechanism is used when the risk associated with a device problem is greatest. Multimedia outreach tools such as website linkages are readily available to keep the healthcare community informed about public health problems.

Urgent Alerts

When a postmarket assessment determines that a public health problem is an imminent hazard, CDRH utilizes experts from all parts of the center to develop Urgent Alerts to notify healthcare professionals and the affected population.

Preliminary Public Health Notification

The Preliminary Public Health Notification is an early alert issued to healthcare practitioners about a device risk. A key determination triggering the issuance of a Preliminary Public Health Notification is the urgency of providing the healthcare community with existing information to make informed clinical decisions about the use of a device or device type, even though information is often incomplete. Factors used to determine urgency include the severity of the potential risk, the population likely to be at risk, the likelihood that adverse events may occur and the need for information and feedback from the healthcare community. CDRH experts use their judgment to predict the impact of these factors. Often, the problem is being actively investigated by CDRH, the industry, another agency or some other reliable entity; hence, updates to the Preliminary Public Health Notification are provided when definitive new information becomes available.

The Preliminary Public Health Notification contains:
- current information on the problem
- analysis of the existing data with a preliminary finding
- preliminary or interim recommendations, usually general reminders (e.g., increase observation of

the patient, read the device labeling and/or report adverse events)

The decision to issue a Preliminary Public Health Notification often comes from a Postmarket Issue (PMI) action team or as the result of review of a recall by CDRH. CDRH publishes the Preliminary Public Health Notification on the CDRH and FDA websites and advertises on an office listserv, the MedWatch listserv and any other mechanism considered necessary to ensure that the target audience is made aware of its publication.

Preliminary Public Health Notifications are updated as frequently as necessary to keep the healthcare community aware of the problem. When the agency understands the problem and is able to provide recommendations to mitigate the risk, a Preliminary Public Health Notification will be replaced with a Public Health Notification.

Public Health Notification

Public Health Notifications are important messages about risks associated with the use of medical devices. They are placed on the CDRH and FDA websites and may be disseminated in additional ways to ensure the message reaches the target audience. Public Health Notification recommendations usually come from the PMI team, but in unusual circumstances the decision to issue a notification may be made without convening a PMI team.

Public Health Notifications are issued when:

- The information is important in order to make informed clinical decisions about the use of a device or device type.
- The information is not readily available to the affected target.
- CDRH recommendations will help healthcare practitioners mitigate or avoid the risk.

The decision to issue a Public Health Notification is dependent upon the quality of the information, the significance of the risk, the population at risk, the nature and frequency of adverse events, the urgency of the situation and the expectations of the public.

Press Releases

Press releases approved by CDRH are issued to the media by FDA's Office of Public Affairs whenever there is a need to alert the broader public to a potential health risk associated with an FDA-regulated product. In addition to Class I recalls, press releases are usually issued for seizures of medical devices. Press releases are distributed to a list of critical media nationwide via a listserv. They are also posted on the FDA and CDRH websites.

Multimedia Outreach

CDRH has established a number of methods for making information about public health concerns readily available to the healthcare community and the general public. For example, the Patient Safety News network disseminates information in video format through one of the center's website links. CDRH has also developed a number of relevant and consumer-friendly webpages addressing issues with commonly used medical devices.

Patient Safety News

CDRH leads the agency's production of FDA Patient Safety News (PSN), a monthly television news show distributed by CDRH. The show is broadcast each month on several medical satellite television networks that bring continuing education for healthcare professionals to more than 4,500 US hospitals and long-term care facilities. FDA PSN is a major vehicle for communicating safety messages about medical products to physicians, nurses, pharmacists, risk managers and educators across the nation. It incorporates stories from FDA's three medical product centers (Center for Drug Evaluation and Research (CDER), CDRH and Center for Biological Evaluation and Research (CBER)) on medical errors, patient safety, recalls and alerts and newly approved drugs, devices and biological products.

The show's website is www.accessdata.fda.gov/scripts/cdrh/cfdocs/psn/index.cfm.

Websites

CDRH communicates postmarket safety information through a variety of public websites.

- Medical Device Safety—This website presents a collection of medical device safety information (e.g., recalls, public health notifications, safety tips, "Dear Doctor" letters, etc.) for healthcare professionals. The site is updated regularly to feature high-priority risk messages. CDRH periodically conducts audience analysis and usability studies of this site to make it more accessible and understandable to practitioners (www.fda.gov/MedicalDevices/Safety/default.htm).
- CDRH Consumer Website—The CDRH consumer website provides information about specific devices and device issues for a patient/consumer audience. It includes links to postmarket safety information (including Class I recalls and Public Health Notifications), as well as information geared toward individuals who use devices in their homes. (www.fda.gov/ForConsumers/ConsumerUpdates/ucm149209.htm).
- Disease-Specific Websites (FDA Diabetes Information, Heart Health Online)—CDRH coordinates FDA's disease-specific websites on diabetes and heart disease. These websites are designed to educate patients and caregivers about the types of interventions involving medical devices

that prevent and treat disease. Each includes links to appropriate medical device patient labeling and postmarket safety information.

- Device-Specific and Topic-Specific Websites (i.e., LASIK, Phakic Lenses, Whole Body CT Scanning, Cochlear Implants, etc.)—CDRH's device-specific websites provide coordinated postmarket information about specific types of devices. These websites give patients and healthcare professionals easy access to descriptive information, indications for use, risks and precautions and specific safety information.

Postapproval Studies

A postapproval study (PAS), also known as a Condition of Approval study, under 21 CFR 814.82(a)(2), helps ensure the continued safety and effectiveness of an approved, marketed device. CDRH may require such a study, and FDA will state in the PMA approval order the reason or purpose for the requirement, the number of patients to be evaluated and the subsequent reports that must be submitted.

The last few years have seen a greater focus on PAS for FDA-regulated products. Both CDER and CBER now post the status of certain postmarketing studies on CDER's website (www.accessdata.fda.gov/scripts/cder/pmc/index.cfm). In 2005, the Institute of Medicine (IOM) completed a study entitled, "Safe Medical Devices for Children." Among its recommendations, the report urged FDA to establish a system for monitoring and publicly reporting the status of postmarket study commitments involving medical devices.

The new CDRH Postapproval Studies Program encompasses design, tracking, oversight and review responsibilities for studies mandated as a condition of approval of a PMA application. The program helps ensure that well-designed PAS are conducted effectively and efficiently and in the least burdensome manner. On 1 January 2005, oversight responsibility was transferred to CDRH's Office of Surveillance and Biometrics (OSB) and the PAS review functions were integrated into the medical device epidemiology program. This action enabled epidemiologists on the premarketing review teams to begin early planning regarding postmarketing concerns as the product moves through the approval process. In addition, industry is required to consider the design of its postmarketing studies during the approval process. Postmarketing studies are now a standard part of discussions with advisory panels, and products must have a protocol at the time of approval.

CDRH has an automated tracking system that efficiently identifies the reporting status of active PAS ordered since 1 January 2005. This system represents CDRH's effort to ensure all PAS commitments are fulfilled in a timely manner. The effective tracking system is based on study timelines incorporated in study protocols and agreed to by CDRH and the manufacturer. In addition

to this internal tracking system, CDRH launched a publicly available webpage (www.accessdata.fda.gov/scripts/cdrh/cfdocs/cfPMA/pma_pas.cfm?sb=dad) to keep all stakeholders informed of study progress. It displays not only PAS reporting status, but also the status (based upon protocol-driven timelines) of each PAS.

Postmarket Surveillance

Premarket review provides limited information on a device's performance, safety and effectiveness. However, it is generally recognized that quality and/or performance issues, along with newly emergent safety signals or efficacy outcomes, may arise after the device has been utilized by a more diverse population and under more varied conditions.

FDAMA modified postmarket surveillance requirements under Section 522 of the *FD&C Act*. Specifically, under the act, the agency may order a manufacturer to conduct postmarket surveillance for any Class II or Class III device, including a device reviewed under the licensing provisions of Section 351 of the *Public Health Service Act,* which meets any of the following criteria:

- The device's failure would be reasonably likely to have serious adverse health consequences.
- The device is intended to be implanted in the human body for more than one year.
- The device is intended to be a life-sustaining or life-supporting device used outside a device user facility.

There are various considerations given when establishing a postmarketing surveillance strategy for a particular device or type of device. A general approach by CDRH is to convene an expert review team within the center to establish the surveillance objective, the information needed to achieve this objective, appropriate sources and mechanisms for obtaining this information and necessary actions needed to address public health concerns. The postmarket surveillance plan will result in the collection of useful data that can reveal unforeseen adverse events, clarify the actual rate of expected adverse events and may provide other information necessary to protect the public health (21 CFR 822.2).

Postmarketing issues or signals may emerge at any point during the device lifecycle and can stem from a variety of sources, such as analysis of adverse event reports, a recall or corrective action, reports from other governmental authorities or the scientific literature. Once such an issue is identified, it is forwarded by the division director to the director of the Issues Management Staff (IMS) in OSB.

An expert review team will consider whether to impose a postmarket surveillance order under Section 522. The expert review team will develop the postmarket surveillance question(s) and the supporting rationale that will be part of the postmarket surveillance order. The questions focus on confirming the nature, severity or frequency of suspected problems. The OSB director will decide whether to order postmarket surveillance. Although postmarket surveillance will not be used in lieu of adequate premarket testing, it can serve to complement premarket studies.

Manufacturers who do not conduct postmarket surveillance in accordance with the approval plan may be subject to FDA enforcement actions, including civil money penalties (21 CFR 822.20). The results and status of the postmarket surveillance plan are available under the *Freedom of Information Act (FOIA)*, and the overall status of the surveillance, along with a brief description of the plan, may be available via the Internet.

Summary

- Both domestic and foreign medical device manufacturers are required to register their establishments with FDA and list the devices they distribute. The regulations are included in 21 CFR 807 and described in the FDA guidance, *Implementation of Medical Device Establishment Registration and Device Listing Requirements Established by the Food and Drug Administration Amendments Ace* of 2007 (8 October 2009).
- The Quality System Regulation in 21 CFR 820 defines FDA's current GMPs for medical devices. It was substantially augmented in 1996 and now includes premarket product development (design control), as well as installation and servicing.
- FDA's QSIT is an excellent model on which to base or prepare for quality system audits. The QSIT apportions the quality system into seven core subsystems, as follows:
  1. Corrective and Preventive Action
  2. Design Controls
  3. Production and Process Controls
  4. Management Controls
  5. Records, Documents and Change Controls
  6. Materials Controls
  7. Facility and Equipment Controls
  FDA's QSIT inspections generally focus on the first four subsystems because they are primary indicators of compliance.
- Regulations for MDRs in 21 CFR 803 and corrections and removals (recalls) in 21 CFR 806 require filing timely and accurate reports with FDA. The type and severity of adverse experiences occurring determine the timeframe in which these reports must be submitted.
- There are no restrictions for exporting medical devices already cleared or approved for marketing in the US. However, regulations for exporting unapproved or investigational devices can require careful consideration because they are driven by the device classification, degree of risk and similarity

in design, operation and intended use to existing predicate devices in US interstate commerce.
- Device tracking regulations in 21 CFR 821 provide for the post-manufacture identity, distribution, location and patient-specific use of certain eligible significant-risk devices. Traceability requirements in 21 CFR 820 provide for the identity of medical devices or certain components during and throughout the manufacture of the device.

References

1. International Organization for Standardization, ISO 13485:2003 *Medical devices: Quality management systems—Requirements for regulatory purposes.* ISO, Geneva, Switzerland, 2003.
2. US Food and Drug Administration. Foreign Establishment Registration and Listing. *Fed Reg* 27 November 2001, 66, 59138.
3. US Food and Drug Administration. *Enforcement Priorities for Single-Use Devices Reprocessed by Third Parties and Hospitals.* Center for Devices and Radiological Health, Rockville, MD, 14 August 2000. www.fda.gov/MedicalDevices/DeviceRegulationandGuidance/GuidanceDocuments/ucm107164.htm. Accessed 13 April 2011.
4. FDA, *Fed Reg* 21 December 1979, 44, 75628; *Fed Reg* 6 April 1988, 53, 11253; *Fed Reg* 27 March 1990, 55, 11169.
5. Division of Small Manufacturers Assistance (DSMA), *Medical Device Quality Systems Manual: A Small Entity Compliance Guide.* US Food and Drug Administration. Rockville, MD, 1997. www.fda.gov/cdrh/dsma/gmpman.html. Accessed 13 April 2011.
6. US Food and Drug Administration. "Medical Device Reporting: Manufacturer Reporting, Importer Reporting, User Facility Reporting, Distributor Reporting; Final Rule," *Fed Reg* 26 January 2000, 65, 4112.
7. US Food and Drug Administration. "Medical Devices; Reports of Corrections and Removals; Final Rule," *Federal Register* 62:27191 (19 May 1997).
8. US Food and Drug Administration. "Medical Devices; Reports of Corrections and Removals; Direct Final Rule." *Fed Reg* 7 August 1998, 63, 42232 (7 August 1998).
9. Public Law 104-134, as amended by Public Law 104 180.
10. US Food and Drug Administration. "Exports: Notification and Recordkeeping Requirements; Final Rule." *Fed Reg* 19 December 2001, 66, 65429.
11. US Food and Drug Administration. "Device Advice: Establishment Registration." Center for Devices and Radiological Health, Rockville, MD, 28 February 2002.
12. US Food and Drug Administration. "Medical

Devices; Device Tracking; Final Rule," *Fed Reg* 8 February 2002, 67, 5943.

Recommended Reading

Device Labeling Guidance # G91-1 (Blue Book Memo) http://www.fda.gov/MedicalDevices/ DeviceRegulationandGuidance/ GuidanceDocuments/ucm081368.htm. Accessed 20 April 2011.

FDA. Medical Devices; Current Good Manufacturing Practice Final Rule, Quality System Regulation. *Fed Reg* 7 October 1996, 61, 52602–52662. http://www.fda.gov/ medicaldevices/deviceregulationandguidance/ postmarketrequirements/qualitysystemsregulations/ ucm230127.htm. Accessed 13 April 2011.

FDA, Medical Devices, Device Tracking, New Orders to Manufacturers. *Fed Reg* 4 March 1998, 63, 10638–10640. http://www.federalregister.gov/ articles/1998/03/04/98-5520/medical-devices- device-tracking-new-orders-to-manufacturers. Accessed 13 April 2011.

Garcia DG. "Medtronic v. Lohr Decision Underscores Importance of Regulatory Compliance." *Med Device & Diag Ind.* March 1997, 97–101.

Gibbs JN. "Treatment IDEs: FDA Proposal Borrows from Treatment INDs." *Reg Aff Focus.* April 1997, 22–23.

Kahan JS. "FDA's New Approach to Export Regulation." *Med Device & Diag Ind.* September 1996, 68–72.

Kahan J. "The Reference List: A Legally Suspect, Dying Program." *Reg Aff Focus.* May 1997, 14–15.

Kingsley PA. (FDA). *Write It Right: Recommendations for Developing User Instruction Manuals for Medical Devices Used in Home Health Care.* FDA, Rockville, MD, FDA, August 1993. http://www.fda.gov/downloads/ MedicalDevices/DeviceRegulationandGuidance/ GuidanceDocuments/ucm070771.pdf. Accessed 13 April 2011.

Medtronic Inc. v. Lohr, 116 S. Ct. 2240; 1996. Spencer RL. Mandatory Device Recall Procedures. *RAPS News.* September 1994, 5–8.

Webster JL. "Medical Devices, Promotion, Labeling and Advertising." *Reg Aff Focus.* June 1997, 25–27.

Hooten WF. "FDA Makes Quality the Rule." *Med Device & Diag Ind.* January 1997, 114–128.

FDA Regulatory Procedures Manual, "Chapter 7. Recall Procedures" www.fda.gov/ICECI/ ComplianceManuals/RegulatoryProceduresManual/ default.htm. Accessed 13 April 2011.

Recall Procedures and Model Press Releases. www.fda. gov/Safety/Recalls/default.htm. Accessed 13 April 2011.

510(k) Requirements During Firm-Initiated Recalls, K95-1—Blue Book Memo. Issued 21 November 1995. www.fda.gov/

MedicalDevices/DeviceRegulationandGuidance/ GuidanceDocuments/ucm080297.htm. Accessed 13 April 2011.

FDA Recall Database/Medical Device Class I Recalls. www.fda.gov/MedicalDevices/Safety/ RecallsCorrectionsRemovals/ListofRecalls/. Accessed 13 April 2011.

Acknowledgements

The author wishes to acknowledge and thank Debra Jarvis-Ferguson for her support, contributions and diligence toward the completion of this chapter.

Chapter 12

US Advertising, Promotion and Labeling for Medical Devices and IVDs

Updated by Kelly Rowland

Objectives

❏ Understand the difference between "labels" and "labeling"

❏ Understand the basic regulatory requirements for labels and labeling for medical devices and in vitro diagnostics (IVDs)

❏ Understand the basic regulatory requirements for promotion and advertising.

❏ Explain the jurisdiction for promotion and advertising

❏ Understand the submission requirements for advertising and promotional materials

❏ Explain possible enforcement actions for violations of relevant laws and regulations

❏ Understanding medical device misbranding

Laws, Regulations and Guidelines Covered in This Chapter

❏ 21 CFR 801 (Subpart A) General labeling provisions

❏ 21 CFR 801 (Subpart C) Labeling requirements for over-the-counter (OTC) devices

❏ 21 CFR 801.119 In vitro diagnostic products

❏ 21 CFR 809 In vitro diagnostic products for human use

❏ 21 CFR 809.10 General labeling requirements on content of labeling for in vitro diagnostic products

❏ 21 CFR 809.20 General requirements for manufacturers and producers of in vitro diagnostic products

❏ 21 CFR 809.30 Restrictions on the sale, distribution and use of analyte-specific reagents

❏ 21 CFR 809.40 Restrictions on the sale, distribution, and use of OTC test sample collection systems for drugs of abuse testing

❏ 21 CFR 99 Dissemination of information on unapproved/new uses for marketed drugs, biologics, and devices

❏ 21 CFR 99.103 Mandatory statements and information

❏ *Guidance for Industry and FDA Staff: Use of Symbols on Labels and in Labeling of In Vitro Diagnostic Devices Intended for Professional Use* (November 2004)

❏ *Guidance for Industry: Alternative to Certain Prescription Device Labeling Requirements* (January 2000)

❏ *Guidance for Industry: User Labeling for Devices that Contain Natural Rubber (21 CFR §801.437); Small Entity Compliance Guide* (April 2003)

❑ *Guidance on Medical Device Patient Labeling; Final Guidance for Industry and FDA Reviewers* (April 2001)

❑ *Guidance for Industry: Designation of Special Controls for Male Condoms Made of Natural Rubber Latex (21 CFR 884.5300); Small Entity Compliance Guide* (January 2009)

❑ *Human Factors Principles for Medical Device Labeling* (September 1993)

❑ *Labeling Regulatory Requirements for Medical Devices* (August 1989)

❑ Device Labeling Guidance #G91-1 (Blue Book Memo) (March 1991)

❑ *Write it Right: Recommendations for Developing User Instruction Manuals for Medical Devices Used in Home Health Care* (August 1993)

❑ *Draft Guidance for Industry: Product Name Placement, Size, and Prominence in Advertising and Promotional Labeling* (January 1999)

❑ *Draft Guidance for Industry: "Help-Seeking" and Other Disease Awareness Communications by or on Behalf of Drug and Device Firms* (January 2004)

❑ *Draft Guidance for Industry and FDA: Consumer-Directed Broadcast Advertising of Restricted Devices* (February 2004)

❑ *Guidance for Industry: Good Reprint Practices for the Distribution of Medical Journal Articles and Medical or Scientific Reference Publications on Unapproved New Uses of Approved Drugs and Approved or Cleared Medical Devices* (January 2009)

❑ *Guidance for Industry: Accelerated Approval Products—Submission of Promotional Materials* (March 1999)

Label and Labeling

A "label," as defined under the *Federal Food, Drug, and Cosmetic Act (FD&C Act),*[1] is a display of written, printed or graphic material on the immediate container of any article (in this case a medical device). "Labeling" is a broader term and refers to any written, printed or graphic material on any article (medical device), on any of its containers or wrappers or on any material accompanying it. It includes any

form of publicity such as posters, tags, pamphlets, circulars, booklets, brochures, instruction or direction sheets, fillers, etc., as well as labeling intended to be used in promotional activities (sometimes referred to as promotional labeling), for example, on a company's website.

The above phrase "or any material accompanying it" was further defined by the Supreme Court in *Kordel v United States*, 335 U.S. 345 (1948).[2]

A more liberal interpretation meant that a physical association with the device was not necessary. Thus labeling is considered a wide variety of written, printed or graphic matter such as pamphlets, circulars, booklets, brochures, sales sheets, etc., that bear a textual relationship with a drug or device.

The US Food and Drug Administration (FDA) therefore recognizes two types of labeling for drugs and devices: FDA-approved labeling and promotional labeling. FDA-approved labeling is part of the submission process with a new drug application (NDA), a biologics license application (BLA) or a premarket approval application (PMA). For prescription medical device products, the FDA-approved labeling must be included in or within the package from which the drug or device is to be dispensed, or else the product is considered misbranded since it lacks adequate directions for use (*FD&C Act* Section 502(f) and 21 CFR 801.109(c)).

The 510(k) submission process provides draft labeling to the agency, but since this type of submission receives "clearance," the labeling is not FDA-approved. FDA does provide comment and request revisions to package insert labeling, and it is therefore implied that the labeling is cleared during the submission process.

The *FD&C Act* (Section 502(f)(1) and (2)) requires that device labeling bear adequate directions for use, proper operating and servicing instructions, warnings where its use may be dangerous to health or any information necessary to protect the user(s). All devices require directions for use unless specifically exempted by regulation.[3]

The basic outline for labels and/or labeling specific to medical devices includes the following (but is not limited to all label/labeling requirements):

- manufacturer, packer or distributor name and principal place of business
- device name, other required information
- description
- indications and usage
- contraindications
- warnings
- precautions
- use in specific patient populations (if applicable)
- adverse reactions (if applicable)
- prescription device statement or symbol[4]
- date of issue or latest revision of labeling bearing information for use

Additional labeling requirements for over-the-counter

(OTC) devices may be found in 21 CFR 801.60. Label/labeling requirements for Investigational Device Exemption (IDE) medical devices are located in 21 CFR 812.

In vitro diagnostic (IVD) products, according to 21 CFR 809.3, are reagents, instruments and systems intended for use in the diagnosis of diseases or other conditions, including a determination of the state of health, in order to cure, mitigate, treat, or prevent disease or its sequelae. IVD products are intended for use in the collection, preparation and examination of specimens taken from the human body. They are considered devices as defined in *FD&C Act* Section 201(h). IVDs are also covered under a separate FDA regulation (21 CFR 809). These devices have their own labels/labeling regulation within that part (809.10).

In addition to some of the basic items outlined above, there are specific requirements determined by the type of IVD:

Label

- proprietary name and established (common or usual) name, if applicable
- indications and usage
- manufacturer, packer or distributor name and place of business
- warnings/precautions per 16 CFR 1500
- IVD use statement and/or reagent use statement
- lot or control number

For a Reagent

- quantity of contents (i.e., weight or volume, numerical count or any combination of these or accurate indication of the package contents)
- proportion or concentration of each reactive ingredient
- storage conditions such as:
  - temperature
  - light
  - humidity
  - other pertinent factors as applicable
- statement of reagent purity and quality
- if reagent is derived from biological material, the source and a measure of its activity
- expiration date
- statement in reference to any observable indication of an alteration of product

Labeling (i.e., Package Insert, Instruction Manual)

- proprietary name and established (common or usual) name if any
- indication and usage
- type of procedure (qualitative or quantitative)
- warnings/precautions per 16 CFR 1500
- IVD use statement and/or reagent use statement

- summary and explanation of test (history of methodology)
- chemical, physical, physiological or biological principles of the procedure

For a Reagent

- declaration of quantity, proportion or concentration of reactive ingredient
- statement indicating the presence of and characterizing any catalytic or nonreactive ingredients (i.e., buffers, preservatives, stabilizers)
- instructions for reconstitution, mixing, dilution, etc. of reagent, if any
- storage conditions such as:
  - temperature
  - light
  - humidity
  - other pertinent factors as applicable
- statement of any purification or treatment required for use
- physical, biological or chemical indications of instability or deterioration

A labeling outline for an IVD instrument can be found in 21 CFR 809.10(b)(6). The following is an abbreviated list of the basic requirements for instrument labeling:

- use or function
- installation procedures
- principles of operation
- performance characteristics and specifications
- operating instructions
- calibration procedures, including materials and/or equipment to be used
- operational precautions and any limitations
- hazards
- storage, handling or shipping instructions
- list of all materials provided as well as those materials required but not provided
- calibration details
- details of quality control procedures and materials required (i.e., state if there are both positive and negative controls)
- expected values
- specific performance characteristics (i.e., accuracy, precision, specificity and sensitivity)
- bibliography

Additional labeling requirements for OTC IVDs may be found in 21 CFR 801.60. Analyte-specific reagents (ASRs) are considered restricted devices under the *FD&C Act* (Section 520(e)) and are defined and classified in 21 CFR 864.4020. The associated labeling is regulated by FDA (21 CFR 809.10(e) and 809.30). ASRs are defined as antibodies, both polyclonal and monoclonal; specific receptor proteins; ligands; nucleic acid sequences; and similar reagents that, through specific binding or chemical reaction with substances in a specimen, are intended for use in diagnostic application for identification and quantification of an individual chemical substance or ligand in biological specimens.[5] Although most are Class I devices, some more-complex ASRs require submission as Class II or III medical devices.

Unlike drug labels or labeling, there are no specific regulations establishing minimum requirements for key graphic elements, (e.g., bold type, bullet points, type size, spacing or use of vertical and horizontal lines) for medical devices and IVDs. Within the labeling requirements, it is recommended that instructions or any specific user-related information be clear, concise and understandable by the user—either a healthcare professional or lay person. Although there are no regulations for key graphic elements in medical device labeling, 21 CFR 801.15 does, in fact, reference some specific labeling format requirements for prescription medical devices. The labeling format for OTC medical devices is described in 21 CFR 801.60 and 801.61. Additionally, guidance documents are available to assist in developing such labels and labeling:

- *Guidance for Industry: Alternative to Certain Prescription Device Labeling Requirements* (January 2000)
- *Guidance on Medical Device Patient Labeling; Final Guidance for Industry and FDA Reviewers* (April 2001)
- Device Labeling Guidance #G91-1 (Blue Book Memo) (March 1991)
- *Write it Right: Recommendations for Developing User Instruction Manuals for Medical Devices Used in Home Health Care* (August 1993)
- *Human Factors Principles for Medical Device Labeling* (September 1993)
- *Guidance for Industry: User Labeling for Devices that Contain Natural Rubber (21 CFR 801.437); Small Entity Compliance Guide* (April 2003)

For IVDs

- *Guidance for Industry and FDA Staff: Use of Symbols on Labels and in Labeling of In Vitro Diagnostic Devices Intended for Professional Use* (November 2004)
- *Guidance for Industry and FDA Staff. Commercially Distributed Analyte-Specific Reagents (ASRs): Frequently Asked Questions* (September 2007)

Since most medical device labeling consists of instructions for using the device properly and safely and, where appropriate, any care instructions for the device, it would only be appropriate to evaluate and include human factors when developing and writing instructional labeling.

"Human factors," in this context is the study or evaluation of how people use technology, specifically the interaction of human abilities, expectations and limitations with work environments and system design. FDA's Center for Devices and Radiological Health (CDRH) has a webpage dedicated to human factors (http://www.fda.gov/MedicalDevices/DeviceRegulationandGuidance/PostmarketRequirements/HumanFactors/default.htm), which includes links to specific FDA guidance documents.

It is important that all medical devices contain complete and accurate labeling, as it is essential for the safe and reliable operation of that medical device, whether used by a customer in a home or by a professional in the hospital.[6] In addition to reviewing labeling requirements per 21 CFR 801 (medical devices) and 809 (ASRs and IVDs), two FDA guidance documents are available to manufacturers that contain examples of medical device labeling presentation, format and content. They are *Human Factors Principles for Medical Device Labeling* (September 1993), and *Write It Right, Recommendations for Developing User Instruction Manuals for Medical Devices Used in Home Health Care* (August 1993). These two guidance documents are important reference tools when developing and creating medical device labeling for both home and professional use.

Furthermore, manufacturers must be aware that if they modify any of their medical devices, the labels/labeling should also be reviewed to ensure that they reflect all current revisions and/or specifications. Therefore, a manufacturer's internal change control process should include a means to capture such label/labeling reviews.

Jurisdiction for Promotional Labeling and Advertising

The same agencies have jurisdiction over promotional labeling and advertising of medical devices, including IVDs, as over that for drug products. Healthcare product advertising is regulated by two federal agencies. First, it is regulated by the Federal Trade Commission (FTC) under the *Federal Trade Commission Act (FTC Act)*.[7] FTC utilizes three legal standards (represented as policy statements) related to the regulation of all advertising: substantiation, deception and fairness. The *FTC Act* prohibits advertising that makes deceptive claims, fails to reveal material information, is unfair, or makes objective claims for which there is not a reasonable basis before the claim was made. FTC has primary responsibility for the advertising of foods, cosmetics, OTC drugs, nonrestricted medical devices and other products whose safety, efficacy and labeling are regulated by FDA.

There is a Memorandum of Understanding (MOU) between FDA and FTC that establishes the division of responsibility between the two agencies with regard to advertising. Though FTC retains legal authority over some aspects of advertising, it generally defers to FDA's more specific authority.

Under the MOU, FDA has the primary responsibility for the labeling of foods, drugs, devices and cosmetics.

Each FDA center has its own division responsible for enforcing those regulations. Within the Center for Drug Evaluation and Research (CDER), the Office of Prescription Drug Promotion (OPDP) is responsible for the regulation of prescription drug promotion. In 1993, the Center for Biologics Evaluation and Research (CBER) formed the Advertising and Promotional Labeling Staff (APLS) within the Office of Compliance and Biologics Quality to review and monitor the promotion of biologic products. Because some of the regulations are open to interpretation, this can result in the application of different standards to drug and biologic products competing in the same therapeutic class. In 2003, CDRH's Office of Compliance (OC) assumed responsibility for the review and enforcement of restricted medical device advertising and promotional materials.

CDRH has a webpage with links to all guidance documents covering medical devices and radiation-emitting products (http://www.fda.gov/MedicalDevices/DeviceRegulationandGuidance/GuidanceDocuments/default.htm).

The 1976 *Medical Device Amendments* to the *FD&C Act* gave FDA authority over the promotion of restricted medical devices.[8] As defined in Section 520(e) of the act, "restricted medical devices" have the potential for harmful effect or require collateral measures for use. They have no implementing regulation. However, the approval order for a PMA or FDA's recommendations for many devices cleared for marketing via 510(k) may restrict the device's sale, distribution and use as a condition of approval. Under 21 CFR 801(D)(b)(1), labeling must bear the statement: "Caution: Federal law restricts this device to sale by or on the order of a (indicate type of practitioner and, if applicable, required training/experience, and facilities to which use is restricted)." Promotional labeling cannot make claims beyond the intended use for which the device was cleared.

FTC has authority for nonrestricted medical devices.

Promotional Labeling and Advertising

Both the term "advertising" and its regulations are somewhat vague. Generally, advertising is differentiated from promotional labeling simply by the practicality of supplying a copy of the complete prescribing information versus providing only a brief summary. Even though FDA does not specifically define advertising, the agency's interpretation of labeling is broad enough to cover most printed materials, which include most advertising. FDA's view of advertising also includes virtually all promotional activities.

Unlike FDA regulations for prescription drug advertising and promotional materials (21 CFR 202.1), the agency currently has no specific advertising and promotional regulations for medical devices. However, the medical device labeling regulation (21 CFR 801.109(a)

(2)) does discuss "other labeling," which FDA considers to be promotional labeling, and Section 502(r) of the *FD&C Act* addresses advertising for restricted devices.

There are three applicable guidance documents that provide current FDA thinking on promotional materials and activities: *"Help-Seeking" and Other Disease Awareness Communications by or on Behalf of Drug and Device Firms (Draft)* (January 2004); *Consumer-Directed Broadcast Advertising of Restricted Devices (Draft)* (February 2004); and *Good Reprint Practices for the Distribution of Medical Journal Articles and Medical or Scientific Reference Publications on Unapproved New Uses of Approved Drugs and Approved or Cleared Medical Devices (Final)* (January 2009).

FDA thus treats press releases, investor relations materials and exhibits as advertising, and these, therefore, are also considered labeling by definition. Additionally, information posted on the Internet is considered promotional labeling rather than advertising.

Misbranding

Section 502 of the *FD&C Act* (21 U.S.C. 352) contains misbranding provisions for prescription devices. A device is misbranded and considered in violation of the law under the act if the device labeling:

1. is false or misleading in any way, and
2. does not contain "adequate directions for use"

In the case of a restricted device, the labeling also must contain:

1. the device's established name printed in type at least half as large as the trade or brand name, and
2. a brief statement of the intended uses, relevant warnings, precautions, side effects and contraindications

The *Medical Device Amendments* expanded the authority of the *FD&C Act* over misbranded medical devices. The amendments contain further conditions under which a device is considered misbranded:

- The device's established name (if applicable), name in an official compendium, or common or usual name is not printed prominently in type at least half as large as used for any proprietary name.
- The device is subject to a performance standard and it does not bear the labeling requirements prescribed in that standard.
- There is a failure to comply with any requirement prescribed under the *FD&C Act* (Section 518, 21 U.S.C. 36h) on notification and other remedies; failure to furnish material or information requested by or under Section 518; or failure to furnish any materials or information requested by or under Section 519 of the act on records and reports.
- The device is commercially distributed without

FDA clearance on a 510(k) premarket notification submission.

Scientific Dissemination of Information

In parallel with the rules for drugs, FDA has traditionally objected to the dissemination of information that is not supported by the approved product labeling, typically referred to as "off-label" information. FDA does not prohibit physicians from prescribing drugs or devices off label, allowing for the appropriate exchange of scientific information. However, the agency historically has had a restrictive policy on off-label information dissemination, and this policy has been repeatedly challenged.

In response to the provisions outlined in the *Food and Drug Administration Modernization Act* of 1997 (*FDAMA*) regarding dissemination of information, FDA codified regulations under 21 CFR 99 entitled, "Dissemination of Information on Unapproved/New Uses for Marketed Drugs, Biologics, and Devices." Note that these regulations do not apply to a manufacturer's lawful dissemination of information that responds to a healthcare practitioner's unsolicited request for information. The regulations state that off-label information concerning the safety, efficacy or benefit of a use that is not included in the approved labeling for a drug or device approved/cleared by FDA may, conditionally, be disseminated to applicable individuals or institutions (healthcare practitioner, pharmacy benefit manager, health insurance issuer, group health plan or federal or state governmental agency). The information disseminated must:

- be about a drug or device that has been approved, licensed or cleared for marketing by FDA
- be in the form of an unabridged, peer-reviewed journal reprint (does not include letters to the editor or abstracts) or reference publication
- not pose a significant risk to public health
- not be false or misleading
- not be derived from clinical research conducted by another manufacturer without permission

The regulations (21 CFR 99.103) also require that the disseminated off-label information prominently display:

- the statement "This information concerns a use that has not been approved (additionally "or cleared" for devices) by the Food and Drug Administration"
- information on the research funding and the association of the authors and investigators with the manufacturer, and a statement, if applicable, if there are products or treatments that have been approved or cleared for the use being presented in the off-label information
- a copy of the approved labeling

- a bibliography of other relevant articles (supporting and not supporting the off-label information)
- any other information that will provide objectivity and balance to the information being presented

The regulations also require that the manufacturer submit the information 60 days before dissemination and eventually submit a supplemental application for the new use that is the subject of the disseminated information.

The requirements in these regulations have been legally challenged by claiming protection under the First Amendment's provisions for freedom of speech. In response to such challenges, FDA clarified that rather than defining the requirements, these regulations provide sponsors with a "safe harbor" to disseminate information on unapproved new uses for marketed drugs, biologics and devices under specific conditions without threat of enforcement action. It should be noted that this safe harbor allows for the dissemination of information regarding the safety, effectiveness or benefits of new uses of approved or cleared products but does not provide for statements about approved uses that FDA would otherwise find misleading. FDA stated that it reserves the right, on a case-by-case basis, to prosecute a manufacturer for misbranding its product if it can be shown that the company was promoting an unapproved use. The effects of these rulings/notices have not yet been tested, leaving this a gray area, open to various interpretations by most companies.

The provisions above are still found in 21 CFR 99, but did sunset in September 2006. In January 2009, the guidance entitled, *Good Reprint Practices for the Distribution of Medical Journal Articles and Medical or Scientific Reference Publications on Unapproved New Uses of Approved Drugs and Approved or Cleared Medical Devices* was issued. This set of draft guidelines is different from 21 CFR 99 in two important aspects:

1. manufacturers are no longer required to submit promotional materials for distribution to FDA for review
2. a new product submission is no longer required for the new use(s) being promoted

Much of this draft guidance originates from the regulations found in 21 CFR 99 and provides for:

- various types of reprints, articles and reference publications that are permitted to be distributed
- manner of the dissemination of scientific and medical information

Enforcement

FDA can enforce violations of the *FD&C Act* or agency regulations through a variety of mechanisms, including Notices of Violations (NOV) or "untitled letters," Warning Letters and, if the violation warrants, referring the issue for judicial action. With regard to devices, FDA will look at such things as a company website, videos, brochures, flyers/promotional flyers, advertisements in journals, bulk mailings, press releases and newsletters. FDA usually sends an NOV for the least violative practices that, in the agency's opinion, do not greatly jeopardize the public health. An NOV usually requires only that the company stop using materials that contain the claim the agency found to be violative. FDA may also issue a Warning Letter with or without a prior NOV letter. Warning Letters contain stronger language and generally are addressed to the company's CEO. In addition to requiring the company to cease using the violative materials, Warning Letters may require the company to provide corrective actions. For example, a company may be required to run a remedial advertisement to reach the same audience as the original violative advertisement or disseminate corrective information through the issue of a "Dear Healthcare Professional" letter as described in 21 CFR 200.5(c)(3). Warning Letters also frequently direct the sponsor to provide FDA with information on any other promotional items that contain similar messages. All FDA Warning Letters, regardless of issuing center or office, are available at www.fda.gov/ICECI/EnforcementActions/WarningLetters/default.htm.

If FDA is not satisfied by the sponsor's response to the actions, it may choose to recommend enforcement action in the form of injunctions, seizures and/or criminal prosecution. The judicial branch of the federal government carries out these activities. One possible outcome is that the company agrees to enter into an arrangement with the government, called a consent decree, that places severe restrictions on company operations to ensure the firm comes into compliance.

Actions That May be Brought by Competitors

The *Lanham Act*[9] of 1946 (*US Trademark Act*) allows private parties a course of action against false and misleading advertising. Trademarks themselves identify the source of a product. The *Lanham Act* prohibits the use of another's mark and false or unfair advertising and is administered by the Patent and Trademark Office (PTO). This act has been amended several times, including the *Trademark Law Revision Act* of 1988, which made it easier to register trademarks, and the *Trademark Dilution Act* of 1995, which prohibited the use of terms that would dilute a trademark (e.g., Buick aspirin). Although not often invoked in these cases, state laws covering false advertising, defamation and disparagement also can be applied to comparative advertising. FTC brings cases, primarily before administrative judges, against those companies it believes are making misleading statements in their promotions. In cases of fraud, FTC brings these into federal court. Many companies will settle out of court, agreeing to "cease and desist" while not admitting guilt.

Summary

- Labeling subject to FDA regulations includes the container label, the package insert used by the physician, patient labeling/medication guide and promotional labeling.
- FDA and FTC regulate healthcare product advertising. FDA regulates advertising for drugs (CDER, DDMAC) and restricted medical devices (CDRH, OC) under the *FD&C Act* and biologics (CBER, APLS) under the *PHS Act*. FTC regulates food, cosmetics, OTC drugs and nonrestricted medical devices under the *FTC Act*.
- Advertising and promotional materials must not be false or misleading, must present fair balance, and must reveal material facts.
- Advertising and promotional labeling are not allowed for unapproved products or unapproved uses of an approved product.
- FDA does, conditionally, allow for the appropriate exchange of scientific materials (unsolicited requests, scientific exhibits).
- FDA can enforce violations through Notices of Violation, Warning Letters, or judicial action (consent decrees, injunctions and seizures).

References

1. *Food, Drug, and Cosmetic Act* of 1938 (under Title 21 of the United States Code (U.S.C.)).
2. *Kordel v United States*, 335 U.S. 345 (1948) (available at http://supreme.justia.com/us/335/345/).
3. 21 CFR Part 801, Subpart D.
4. *Guidance for Industry: Alternative to Certain Prescription Device Labeling Requirements* (January 2000).
5. 21 CFR 864.4020(a)
6. *Human Factors Principles for Medical Device Labeling* (September 1993).
7. *Federal Trade Commission Act* of 1914 (*FTC Act*).
8. *Public Health Service Act* of 1944 (*PHS Act*), 42 USC Section 351 [262].
9. *Trademark Act* of 1946 (*Lanham Act*), 15 USC Chapter 22.

US In Vitro Diagnostics Submissions and Compliance

By Michael Wienholt, RAC (US, EU)

Objectives
❑ Know the definition of an in vitro diagnostic device (IVD)

❑ Understand the risk-based classification of IVDs

❑ Understand the regulatory submission types and their requirements

❑ Understand the labeling requirements for IVDs

❑ Know where to find additional information

Laws, Regulations and Guidance Documents Cited in This Chapter
❑ 21 CFR 50 Protection of human subjects

❑ 21 CFR 56 Institutional review boards

❑ 21 CFR 801 Labeling

❑ 21 CFR 809 In vitro diagnostic products for human use

❑ 21 CFR 812 Investigational device exemptions

❑ 21 CFR 814 Premarket approval of medical devices

❑ 21 CFR 820 Quality system regulation

❑ 21 CFR 862 Clinical chemistry and clinical toxicology devices

❑ 21 CFR 864 Hematology and pathology devices

❑ 21 CFR 866 Immunology and microbiology devices

❑ 42 CFR 493 Laboratory Requirements

❑ *Guidance for Industry and FDA Staff: In Vitro Diagnostic (IVD) Device Studies—Frequently Asked Questions* (June 2010)

❑ *Guidance for Industry and FDA Staff: Administrative Procedures for CLIA Categorization* (May 2008)

❑ *In Vitro Diagnostic Devices: Guidance for the Preparation of 510(k) Submissions* (January 1997)

❑ *New Section 513(f)(2)—Evaluation of Automatic Class III Designation, Guidance for Industry and CDRH Staff* (February 1998)

❑ *Guidance for the Content of Premarket Submissions for Software Contained in Medical Devices* (May 2005)

The Definition of an IVD
"In vitro diagnostics" (IVDs) are defined in Title 21 of the Code of Federal Regulations (CFR) Part 809.3 as "those reagents, instruments, and systems intended for use in the diagnosis of disease or other conditions, including a determination of the state of health, in order to cure, mitigate, treat, or prevent disease or its sequelae. Such products are intended

for use in the collection, preparation and examination of specimens taken from the human body."

The definition given in 21 CFR 809.3 also states that IVDs are devices as defined in Section 201(h) of the *Federal Food, Drug, and Cosmetic Act* (*FD&C Act*) and that they may also be biological products regulated under Section 351 of the *Public Health Service Act* (*PHS Act*). IVDs may be considered to be a subset of medical devices, the defining characteristic being the use of specimens taken from the human body. The US Food and Drug Administration's (FDA) classification rules define more than 500 different types of medical devices that meet the definition of an in vitro diagnostic product. Worldwide, the IVD industry accounts for more than $50 billion annually in diagnostic tests alone.

Additionally, the labeling regulation in 21 CFR 809.10 defines two other types of products: Research Use Only (RUO) and Investigational Use Only (IUO). Both RUO and IUO products are considered to be pre-commercial and, under specific circumstances, may be shipped without fully complying with the labeling requirements that apply to commercial IVDs.

RUO products are those "in the laboratory research phase of development, and not represented as an effective in vitro diagnostic product" (21 CFR 809.10(c)(2)(i)). Such products must be prominently labeled with the following statement: "For Research Use Only. Not for use in diagnostic procedures." RUO products are reagents, instruments or test systems that are under development and being evaluated for their potential use as IVDs, or are used in basic life science research and not intended for further development for a clinical diagnostic use.

IUO products are those "being shipped or delivered for product testing prior to full commercial marketing (for example, for use on specimens derived from humans to compare the usefulness of the product with other products or procedures which are in current use or recognized as useful)" (21 CFR 809.10(c)(2)(ii)). IUO products are reagents, instruments or test systems that are being used in a "clinical investigation or research involving one or more subjects to determine the safety and effectiveness of a device" (21 CFR 812.3(h)). Such products must be prominently labeled with the following statement: "For Investigational Use Only. The performance characteristics of this product have not been established."

Finally, the classification rules in 21 CFR 864 define two additional types of specimen preparation reagents: General Purpose Reagents (GPR), and Analyte Specific Reagents (ASR).

GPR products are chemical reagents having "a general laboratory application, that is used to collect, prepare, and examine specimens from the human body for diagnostic purposes, and that is not labeled or otherwise intended for specific diagnostic application" (21 CFR 864.4010(a)).

Importantly, GPRs are classified as Class I (general controls) and exempt from premarket notification, subject to the limitations described in 21 CFR 864.9. Such products must be labeled in accordance with 21 CFR 809.10(d) with basic identifying information, warnings and precautions, and the statement: "For Laboratory Use."

ASR products are "antibodies, both polyclonal and monoclonal, specific receptor proteins, ligands, nucleic acid sequences, and similar reagents which, through specific binding or chemical reaction with substances in a specimen, are intended for use in a diagnostic application for identification and quantification of an individual chemical substance or ligand in biological specimens" (21 CFR 864.4020(a)). Information on the classification of ASRs is given in 21 CFR 864.4020(b). ASRs are Class I and exempt from premarket notification except when they are used in blood banking tests that have been classified as Class II (e.g., cytomegalovirus serological reagents), and when they are intended to be used as components in Class III tests used in contagious fatal diseases (e.g., tuberculosis) or blood donor screening (e.g., blood group typing or hepatitis). ASRs must be labeled in accordance with 21 CFR 809.10(e)(1). Class I ASRs must bear the statement: "Analyte Specific Reagent. Analytical and performance characteristics are not established." Class II and III ASRs must bear the statement: "Analyte Specific Reagent. Except as a component of the approved/cleared test (Name of approved/cleared test), analytical and performance characteristics of this ASR are not established."

FDA Classification and Regulation of IVDs

As with all other medical devices, IVDs are regulated according to a risk-based classification scheme based upon the intended use. Factors that determine the classification of IVDs include whether the device is intended for diagnosis, monitoring or screening of a specific disease or condition; the patient population in which it will be used; the type of specimen to be tested; and the consequence of a false test result.

FDA classifies IVD products into Class I, II or III depending upon the level of control necessary to ensure that the devices are reasonably safe and effective when they are placed on the market. The classification determines the regulatory pathway to market. The CFR lists the classification of existing IVDs in 21 CFR 862 (clinical chemistry and toxicology devices), 864 (hematology and pathology devices) and 866 (immunology and microbiology devices).

Class I IVDs are the lowest risk category. Most are exempt from premarket review and are subject to General Controls only. (Some Class I IVDs do require submission of a premarket notification 510(k). These are termed "Reserved Devices" and include a total of 44 devices in 21 CFR 862, 864 and 866.) General Controls apply to all medical devices, regardless of class, and include establishment registration as a manufacturer, distributor, repackager or relabeler; listing the devices intended to be marketed with FDA; manufacturing in accordance with Good Manufacturing Practices (21 CFR 820), including maintenance of records and providing reports to FDA; and labeling in accordance with 21 CFR 801 and 809.

Approximately 50% of the IVDs currently marketed are regulated as Class I. Some examples of Class I IVDs include clinical chemistry tests for urine pH and osmolality, reagents and kits for immunohistochemistry stains, and serological reagents for immunology and microbiology.

Class II IVDs are those products that pose a moderate risk of harm due to a false test result. They are typically more complex in their design and mode of operation. Most Class II products require submission of a premarket notification 510(k) that includes evidence for a determination of "substantial equivalence" to a similar product already on the market. In addition to General Controls, Class II products require "Special Controls" to assure safety and effectiveness. Special Controls include certain mandatory performance standards, special labeling requirements and requirements for postmarket surveillance.

Approximately 42% of the IVDs currently marketed are regulated as Class II. Some examples of Class II IVDs include clinical chemistry tests for newborn screening for metabolic disorders, hematology tests for sickle cell hemoglobin and microbiology tests for pathogenic organisms that cause such diseases as meningitis.

Class III IVDs are those products that present a potential high risk of harm due to a false test result. These typically employ complex methodologies and algorithms for calculating a result and may be intended for diagnosis of serious infectious diseases. Class III products are those for which General Controls and Special Controls alone are not sufficient to provide assurances of safety and effectiveness. They are subject to the most rigorous premarket scrutiny, often requiring extensive clinical data. Class III products require submission of a Premarket Approval application (PMA) which includes a complete description of the manufacturing process and clinical evidence (diagnostic sensitivity and specificity) of safety and effectiveness in the intended use population.

Approximately 8% of the IVDs currently marketed are regulated as Class III. Some examples of Class III IVDs include tests for screening for various cancers (e.g., breast, prostate) and tests for screening the blood supply for infectious agents such as Hepatitis B and C.

Under an intercenter agreement that became effective in October 1991, two centers within FDA share responsibility for regulating IVDs—the Center for Devices and Radiological Health (CDRH) and the Center for Biologics Evaluation and Research (CBER). CDRH was assigned the lead role for policy development, procedural regulations, regulating all IVDs not assigned to CBER, small business assistance programs, registration and listing, GMP advisory activities and medical device reporting. CBER was assigned the lead role in regulating all IVDs for screening or confirmatory laboratory tests associated with blood banking operations, as well as those medical devices intended for use in collecting, processing, storing and administering blood products and their components. Each center retains authority for surveillance activities and compliance actions, issuing Special Controls guidance documents and performance standards, and for review of IDE, 510(k) and PMA submissions.

The Office of Blood Research and Review (OBRR) within CBER administers the premarket review and postmarket surveillance and compliance programs for IVDs assigned to the center. The Office of In Vitro Diagnostic Device Evaluation and Safety (OIVD) within CDRH administers the premarket review and postmarket surveillance and compliance programs for all other IVDs. OIVD is also responsible for making complexity categorization and waiver determinations under the *Clinical Laboratory Improvement Amendments* (*CLIA*) of 1988, which set standards and certification requirements for clinical laboratory tests. OIVD is organized into three principal divisions: the Division of Chemistry and Toxicology Devices (DCTD), the Division of Immunology and Hematology Devices (DIHD) and the Division of Microbiology Devices (DMD). On an annual basis, OIVD processes more than 1,000 premarket submissions and more than 2,000 *CLIA* determinations, and implements more than 150 compliance actions.

The Application of the *CLIA* to IVDs

As stated above, *CLIA* set standards and certification requirements for clinical laboratory tests. OIVD is responsible for the program for complexity categorization and waiver determinations of commercially marketed in vitro diagnostic tests under CLIA. Categorization is the process by which FDA assigns IVDs to one of three *CLIA* complexity categories based upon the potential risk to the public health. The categories are Waived, Moderate Complexity and High Complexity. FDA evaluates seven criteria to determine the complexity of an IVD and assigns a number score (1 = Low; 2 = Intermediate; 3 = High) to each. The evaluation criteria include: the scientific or technical knowledge required to perform the test; necessary training and experience; the complexity of the preparation of reagents and test materials; characteristics of the operational steps; the need for calibration, QC and proficiency testing; troubleshooting and maintenance; and the difficulty of interpreting the test results. The scores for each criterion are then totaled. Tests receiving scores of 12 or less are assigned Moderate Complexity. Tests receiving scores of 12 or higher are assigned High Complexity. Waived tests are those tests that were specified in the regulations that *CLIA* implemented (42 CFR 493) or tests that are granted a waiver by FDA following review of an application containing valid scientific data that demonstrates the test is simple to use, accurate and unlikely to pose a risk of harm to the patient if the test is performed inaccurately. Manufacturers apply for a CLIA categorization during the premarket review process. Further information can be found in *Guidance for Industry and FDA Staff: Administrative Procedures for CLIA Categorization.*

Premarket Submission Types for IVDs

As discussed above, the classification of an IVD determines the regulatory pathway to market. Class II IVDs require submission of a premarket notification 510(k) at least 90 days prior to placing the device on the market. The 510(k) must contain evidence that the device to be marketed is "substantially equivalent" to (i.e., as safe and effective as) to another device that is already legally marketed. This is termed the "predicate device." A predicate device is one that has a similar intended use and similar technological characteristics. Once FDA has determined that the new device is substantially equivalent (SE) to the predicate device, the new device is "cleared" for marketing in the US. If FDA determines that the new device has no predicate or that its performance is not equivalent to the predicate, then a "not substantially equivalent" (NSE) decision is rendered. The content and format of a 510(k) is given in *In Vitro Diagnostic Devices: Guidance for the Preparation of 510(k) Submissions.* The evidence establishing substantial equivalence to the predicate consists of nonclinical and clinical performance data. This includes analytical sensitivity and specificity, precision, reproducibility and reagent and sample stability. FDA recommends the use of standards published by the Clinical Laboratory Standards Institute (CLSI) to guide the evaluation of analytical performance. Additionally, a method comparison study showing similar clinical performance as the predicate device is also required. This is typically done by calculating the percent agreement between the two methods using retrospectively collected clinical samples. OIVD posts a summary of the 510(k) review on the FDA website that details the basis for the SE determination. These summaries provide manufacturers with valuable information on the choice of likely predicates and data requirements for establishing substantial equivalence to a predicate.

Class III IVDs require submission of a PMA. The required elements of a PMA are given in 21 CFR 814. PMAs are reviewed under a 180-day timeline. For most PMAs, a clinical study using prospectively collected samples is required to establish the device's safety and effectiveness. Such studies must be conducted in accordance with the informed consent regulations in 21 CFR 50 and the Institutional Review Board regulations in 21 CFR 56. If the device is the first of its kind, or if FDA's review of the PMA raises significant questions regarding safety and

effectiveness, FDA may seek advice or a determination of approvability of a PMA from an advisory panel comprised of external experts. In most cases, an inspection of the manufacturer's facility by FDA is required prior to approval of a PMA. FDA will often place postapproval requirements on manufacturers of Class III devices as a condition of approval. These may include additional studies of safety and effectiveness and periodic reporting of the results of such studies. Once a formal approval order is issued, FDA posts a Summary of Safety and Effectiveness Data (SSED) on the FDA website.

Another important premarket mechanism is the de novo reclassification. This was created by the *Food and Drug Administration Modernization Act* of 1997 (*FDAMA*) as a way of classifying new, lower risk devices that were automatically placed in Class III when the original classification rules were established. Such devices have no predicate, but are devices for which Special Controls would be an appropriate means of controlling risks and ensuring that the devices are reasonably safe and effective. De novo allows a manufacturer of an IVD that has been found NSE due to the lack of a predicate device to submit a petition to have a risk-based classification made for the device (often Class II) without submitting a PMA. The petition must include identification of the IVD's risks and benefits, the Special Controls the manufacturer believes will adequately control risks and ensure safety and effectiveness, and a recommendation as to whether the IVD should be placed in Class I or Class II. FDA will make a classification determination within 60 days. If the IVD is placed in either Class I or II, it may be legally marketed and will then become a predicate for any future device having the same intended use and technological characteristics. The de novo process is explained in detail in *New Section 513(f)(2)—Evaluation of Automatic Class III Designation, Guidance for Industry and CDRH Staff.*

The Pre-IDE Submission

In 1995, FDA issued a memorandum introducing the pre-IDE submission as a mechanism for sponsors of Investigational Device Exemption (IDE) applications under 21 CFR 812 to submit preliminary information to FDA prior to submitting an IDE. Since most IVDs are exempted from the IDE regulations, the pre-IDE has become an informal method for manufacturers to obtain advice and comment on the regulatory pathway and proposed studies prior to submission of a 510(k) or PMA. In fact, OIVD routinely requests that manufacturers submit a pre-IDE when a new device has novel performance characteristics or a new intended use. This is specifically designed for those devices that are likely to require a *de novo* petition, CLIA waiver application or complex 510(k) or PMA submission for multiplex tests or companion diagnostics. A pre-IDE may also be useful when a manufacturer is submitting its first ever premarket application. A pre-IDE should be submitted when the intended use (including the target patient population) has been defined and the manufacturer is ready to discuss the analytical and clinical performance studies that may be required for clearance or approval. The pre-IDE process begins with the submission of a written request to the Document Mail Center. The exchange of information between the submitter of a pre-IDE and FDA may take the form of written memoranda or in-person meetings or teleconferences. An important consideration regarding the pre-IDE is that it is nonbinding on both the manufacturer and the FDA.

The pre-IDE package consists of a cover letter with contact information, a brief device description, proposed intended use, predicate device (if known) and any specific questions the manufacturer has regarding the proposed analytical and clinical performance studies or regulatory pathway. Typically, FDA will respond to a pre-IDE submission within 60 days by returning a pre-IDE review memo to the submitter. This document will contain FDA's most current thinking regarding how the device is likely to be regulated and the data likely to be required in a 510(k) or PMA submission. A manufacturer may request a pre-IDE meeting with FDA in person, and vice versa.

Software Considerations for IVDs

Many IVDs employ software to control instrumentation and to calculate complex algorithms prior to providing the test result. As is the case for other medical devices, FDA regulates the software that is integral to the operation and safety of diagnostic test systems. Therefore, a certain amount of information related to the design and development of software must be included in premarket submissions. The extent of the documentation to be included in a 510(k) or PMA is based on the software "Level of Concern." FDA defines the Level of Concern as Minor, Moderate or Major depending upon the role of the software in causing, controlling or mitigating hazards that may result in injury to the patient or device operator. FDA classifies most IVD software as Moderate Level of Concern. Among the software documentation required to be submitted in premarket applications, the most important is a risk analysis. This must include the hardware and software hazards identified in the course of design and development, an assessment of their severity and the mitigations implemented to control them. To the extent that software plays a role in mitigating hazards associated with the laboratory examination of clinical specimens (e.g., user errors; incorrect or delayed diagnostic results), the hazard analysis must address the severity of the harm resulting from software failures. FDA defines these terms and the level of software verification and validation documentation required in *Guidance for the Content of Premarket Submissions for Software Contained in Medical Devices.*

Recent Trends in IVD Compliance— Laboratory Developed Tests (LDTs)

Recently, FDA has begun focusing attention on the marketing of so called "home brew" tests by clinical laboratories that have historically been regulated under *CLIA*. Since the passage of the *CLIA* regulations in 1988, diagnostic tests have reached the market in one of two ways: FDA clearance or approval of a premarket application submitted by a commercial manufacturer, or the offering of such tests directly to clinicians by *CLIA*-licensed laboratories. In a regulatory practice known as "enforcement discretion," FDA allowed the commercialization of such "laboratory developed tests" (LDTs) without premarket review. Over the past decade, FDA has become increasingly concerned with the lack of oversight of such tests, particularly a subset of molecular diagnostic tests that purported to predict the genetic risk of developing clinical diseases that were marketed on direct-to-consumer (DTC) websites. Specifically, FDA cited concerns over the apparent lack of clinical validation, absence of premarket review of diagnostic claims and the lack of postmarket surveillance and reporting. Beginning in 2000, FDA published a number of draft guidance documents related to the use of ASRs in the development of such tests, and began exercising its authority over ASRs and ROUs.

In June of 2010, FDA sent a number of regulatory letters to companies operating *CLIA*-certified laboratories offering DTC genetic tests. This was followed on 19–20 July 2010 by an unprecedented two-day public meeting in which FDA, industry and the public gave their perspectives on FDA oversight of LDTs. During the meeting, FDA stated its concerns that the *CLIA* regulations alone were insufficient to evaluate evidence of analytical and clinical validation of test performance of LDTs. FDA was further concerned about the lack of quality system requirements on ASRs, design controls (particularly with regard to validation of software) and postmarket surveillance (e.g., recalls and medical device reporting).

During the course of the FDA public meeting on LDTs, OIVD issued additional regulatory letters to manufacturers of genetic tests. Subsequently, on 22 July 2010 the Subcommittee on Oversight and Investigations of the US House of Representatives Committee on Energy & Commerce held a hearing on "Direct-To-Consumer Genetic Testing and the Consequences to the Public Health" where testimony was provided by representatives of CDRH, the General Accounting Office and several companies offering DTC genetic tests. Since then, FDA has been conducting an internal review prior to preparing further guidance on these matters.

FDA has stated that it will apply a risk-based classification to higher risk LDTs similar to the current regulations that apply to commercial IVDs. This would bring FDA oversight to tests intended for companion diagnostics associated with drug therapy, screening or diagnosis of cancer and other tests for potentially fatal communicable diseases.

Summary

IVDs are a subset of medical devices that are "intended for use in the collection, preparation, and examination of specimens taken from the human body." FDA's classification rules define more than 500 different types of medical devices that meet the definition of an IVD.

Research Use Only (RUO) and Investigational Use Only (IUO) products are considered to be pre-commercial, and under specific circumstances, may be shipped without fully complying with the labeling requirements that apply to commercial IVDs.

IVDs are regulated according to a risk-based classification scheme as either Class I, II or III, based upon their intended use. Factors that determine the classification of IVDs include whether the device is intended for diagnosis, monitoring or screening of a specific disease or condition; the patient population in which it will be used; the type of specimen to be tested; and the consequence of a false test result.

Most Class I IVDs are exempt from premarket review and are subject to General Controls only. Class II IVDs require submission of a premarket notification 510(k) at least 90 days prior to placing the device on the market. The 510(k) must contain evidence that the device to be marketed is "substantially equivalent" to (i.e., as safe and effective as) another device that is already legally marketed. This is termed the "predicate device." A predicate device is one that has a similar intended use and similar technological characteristics. Class III IVDs require submission of a PMA. For most PMAs, a clinical study using prospectively collected samples is required to establish the safety and effectiveness of the device. Such studies must be conducted in accordance with the Informed Consent regulations and the Institutional Review Board regulations.

General Controls apply to all IVD devices, regardless of class, and include establishment registration as a manufacturer, distributor, repackager or relabeler; listing the devices intended to be marketed with FDA; manufacturing in accordance with GMPs (21 CFR 820), including maintenance of records and providing reports to FDA; and labeling in accordance with 21 CFR 801 and 809.

The Office of In Vitro Diagnostic Device Evaluation and Safety (OIVD) website (www.fda.gov/MedicalDevices/ProductsandMedicalProcedures/InVitroDiagnostics/default.htm) is the primary source of information on IVD regulations, guidance documents, *CLIA* categorizations, relevant standards, assistance and guidance on pre- and postmarket issues and information on cleared or approved IVDs.

Sources of Additional Information

The Office of In Vitro Diagnostic Device Evaluation and Safety (OIVD) website (www.fda.gov/MedicalDevices/ProductsandMedicalProcedures/InVitroDiagnostics/default.htm) is the primary source of information on IVD regulations, guidance documents, CLIA categorizations, relevant standards, assistance and guidance on pre- and postmarket issues, and information on cleared/approved IVDs.

The Association of Medical Diagnostics Manufacturers (AMDM) website (http://amdm.org/) contains archived FDA presentations from public meetings and web links to FDA resources.

US Glossary of Terms

30-day hold
Time period between filing a protocol under an IND and FDA approval to proceed with enrollment. Also, the time period between when a company submits an IND and when it can initiate a protocol. This time line may be extended if FDA does not agree with the proposed protocol. (See "Clinical Hold.")

120-day Safety Report
Amendment to an NDA containing a safety update due 120 days after the NDA is filed.

510(k)
- Traditional 510(k): A premarket notification submitted to FDA to demonstrate that the medical device to be marketed is as safe and effective or "substantially equivalent" to a legally marketed device. 510(k) refers to the section of the *FD&C Act* authorizing the submission of the premarket notification.
- Special 510(k): For use where device modifications neither affect the intended use nor alter its fundamental scientific technology. FDA processing time is 30 days.
- Abbreviated 510(k): A type of 510(k) submission that is supported by conformance with guidance document(s), special controls or standards.

A

AABB
American Association of Blood Banks

ACE
Adverse Clinical Event

ACRP
Association for Clinical Research Professionals

ACS
American Chemical Society

Action Letter
Official communication from FDA informing NDA/BLA sponsor of an agency decision. Includes approvable, not approvable and clinical hold.

Active Ingredient
Any drug component intended to furnish pharmacological activity or other direct effect in the diagnosis, cure, mitigation, treatment or prevention of disease, or to affect the structure or any function of the body of man or other animals.

ADE
Adverse Drug Event or Adverse Drug Experience

ADME
Absorption, Distribution, Metabolism and Excretion

ADR
Adverse Drug Reaction

ADUFA
Animal Drug User Fee Act of 2003

ADUFA II
Animal Drug User Fee Amendments of 2008

Adulterated
Product containing any filthy, putrid or decomposed substance; or prepared under unsanitary conditions; or not made according to GMPs; or containing an unsafe color additive; or does not meet the requirements of an official compendium. (*FD&C Act*, SEC. 501 [351])

AdvaMed
Advanced Medical Technology Association

Advisory Committee
Committees and panels used by FDA to obtain independent expert advice on scientific, technical and policy matters.

AE
Adverse Event

AERS
Adverse Event Reporting System

AFDO
Association of Food and Drug Officials

AGDUFA
Animal Generic Drug User Fee Act of 2008

AHRQ
Agency for Healthcare Research and Quality

AIP
Application Integrity Policy. FDA's approach to reviewing applications that may be affected by wrongful acts that raise significant questions regarding data reliability.

AMDUCA
Animal Medicinal Drug Use Clarification Act of 1994

Amendment
Additions or changes to an ANDA, NDA, BLA, PMA or PMA supplement still under review. Includes safety updates. Any updates to an IND or an IDE prior to approval are also called amendments.

AMS
Agricultural Marketing Service (USDA)

ANADA
Abbreviated New Animal Drug Application

ANDA
Abbreviated New Drug Application. Used for generic drugs.

Animal Drugs@FDA
Database that allows users to search for approved animal drug products, suitability petitions, sponsors, the *Green Book*, CFR, *FR*, patents and exclusivity.

Annual Report
An annual periodic report or progress report that must be submitted to FDA. Depending on the type of application for which the report is submitted, it may include new safety, efficacy and labeling information; preclinical and clinical investigation summaries; CMC updates; nonclinical laboratory studies; and completed unpublished clinical trials.

ANPR
Advance Notice of Proposed Rulemaking

APhA
American Pharmacists Association

APHIS
Animal and Plant Health Inspection Service

API
Active Pharmaceutical Ingredient

APLB
Advertising and Promotional Labeling Branch (CBER)

Approved
FDA designation given to drugs, biologics and medical devices that have been granted marketing approval.

AQL
Acceptable Quality Level

ASTM
American Society of Testing and Materials

ASQ
American Society for Quality (formerly ASQC)

ASR
Analyte Specific Reagents

ATF
Bureau of Alcohol, Tobacco, Firearms and Explosives

AUT
Actual Use Trials

B
BACPAC
Bulk Actives Chemical Postapproval Changes

Banned Device
Device presenting a substantial deception, unreasonable risk of injury or illness, or unreasonable direct and substantial danger to public health.

BIMO
Bioresearch Monitoring Program

BIO
Biotechnology Industry Organization

Bioequivalence

The absence of a significant difference in the rate and extent to which the active ingredient or active moiety in pharmaceutical equivalents or pharmaceutical alternatives becomes available at the site of drug action when administered at the same molar dose under similar conditions in an appropriately designed study.

Biologic

A virus, therapeutic serum, toxin, antitoxin, vaccine, blood, blood component or derivative, allergenic product, protein (except any chemically synthesized polypeptide), or analogous product, or arsphenamine or derivative of arsphenamine (or any other trivalent organic arsenic compound), applicable to the prevention, treatment, or cure of a disease or condition of human beings.

BLA

Biologics License Application

Blinded Study

Clinical trial in which the patient (single-blind) or patient and investigator (double-blind) are unaware of which treatment the patient receives. Involves use of multiple treatment groups such as other active, placebo or alternate dose groups. Sometimes referred to as "masked."

BPCA

Best Pharmaceuticals for Children Act of 2002

BPCI Act

Biologics Price Competition and Innovation Act of 2009

BPDR

Biological Product Deviation Report

C

CAP

College of American Pathologists

CAPA

Corrective and Preventive Actions

CBE-30

Changes Being Effected in 30 days. A submission to an approved application reporting changes that FDA has identified as having moderate potential to adversely affect drug product identity, strength, quality, purity and potency. The supplement must be received by FDA at least 30 days before product distribution.

CBER

Center for Biologics Evaluation and Research

CBP

US Customs and Border Protection

CDC

Centers for Disease Control and Prevention

CDER

Center for Drug Evaluation and Research

CDRH

Center for Devices and Radiological Health

CF

Consent Form. Document used to inform a potential subject of the risks and benefits of a clinical trial per the Declaration of Helsinki. Sometimes referred to as ICF (Informed Consent Form) or ICD (Informed Consent Document).

CFG

Certificate to Foreign Government. Required by certain countries to prove that an exported product can be legally marketed in the US.

CFR

Code of Federal Regulations

CFSAN

Center for Food Safety and Applied Nutrition

CGMP

Current Good Manufacturing Practice

CH

Clinical Hold

CIR

Cosmetic Ingredient Review

Class I Device

Low-risk device requiring general controls to ensure safety and effectiveness.

Class II Device

Requires general and special controls to ensure safety and effectiveness. Special controls may include mandatory performance standards, patient registries for implantable devices and postmarket surveillance. Requires 510(k), unless exempted; may require clinical trials.

Class III Device
Requires general controls, special controls and premarket approval (PMA); includes devices that are life-sustaining, life-supporting or pose significant potential for risk to patient, or are not substantially equivalent to Class I or Class II devices. PMAs almost always require clinical trials.

Clearance
Devices that receive marketing permission through the 510(k) process based upon demonstrating substantial equivalence to a preamendment device or another device reviewed under section 510(k) of the *FD&C Act*.

CLIA
Clinical Laboratory Improvement Amendments of 1988

Clinical Hold
FDA order to delay proposed clinical investigation or suspend an ongoing investigation.

Clinical Investigator
A medical researcher in charge of carrying out a clinical trial's protocol.

ClinicalTrials.gov
A registry and results database of federally and privately supported clinical trials conducted in the US and around the world. Operated by NIH.

CLSI
Clinical and Laboratory Standards Institute (formerly National Committee for Clinical Laboratory Standards)

CMC
Chemistry, Manufacturing and Controls

CME
Continuing Medical Education

CMS
Centers for Medicare & Medicaid Services

COE
Certificate of Exportability. Required by certain countries for the export of unapproved devices not sold or offered for sale in the US; issued by FDA to the exporter.

Combination Product
Defined in 21 CFR 3.2(e) as a combination of two or more different types of regulated products, i.e.,
- a drug and a device
- a device and a biological product
- a drug and a biological product
- a drug, a device and a biological product

Commercial Distribution
Any distribution of a device intended for human use, which is offered for sale but does not include: internal or interplant transfer within the same parent, subsidiary or affiliate company any device with an approved exemption for investigational use.

Complaint
Any written, electronic or oral communication alleging deficiencies related to a product's identity, quality, durability, reliability, safety, effectiveness or performance after release for distribution.

Component
Any ingredient or part intended for use in the manufacture of a drug, device, cosmetic, biologic or IVD product, including those that may not appear in the finished product.

COOL
Country of Origin Labeling. Requirements for source labeling for food products (USDA)

Cosmetic
Articles intended to be rubbed, poured, sprinkled or sprayed on, introduced into or otherwise applied to the human body or any part thereof for cleansing, beautifying, promoting attractiveness or altering appearance; and, articles intended for use as a component of any such article; except that such term shall not include soap.

CPMP
Committee for Proprietary Medicinal Products (EU)

CPSC
Consumer Product Safety Commission

CRA
Clinical Research Associate

CRADA
Cooperative Research and Development Agreement (with a government agency such as NIH and FDA)

CRC
Clinical Research Coordinator

CRF
Case Report Form. Paper or electronic document used to record data collected in a clinical trial.

Critical Path Initiative

FDA's effort to stimulate and facilitate a national effort to modernize the scientific process through which a potential human drug, biological product or medical device is transformed from a discovery or "proof of concept" into a medical product.

CRO

Contract Research Organization

CSO

Consumer Safety Officer. Often the FDA contact person for sponsors. Also known as the regulatory project manager.

CTD

Common Technical Document

CTP

Center for Tobacco Products

Custom Device

A device that:
- deviates from devices generally available
- deviates from an applicable performance standard or PMA requirement in order to comply with the order of a physician or dentist
- is not generally available in finished form for purchase or dispensing by prescription
- is not offered for commercial distribution through labeling or advertising, is intended for use by an individual patient named in the order of a physician or dentist, and is to be made in a specific form for that patient
- is intended to meet the special needs of the physician or dentist

CVB

Center for Veterinary Biologics (USDA)

CVM

Center for Veterinary Medicine (FDA)

D

D&D

Design and Development Plan

DDMAC

Division of Drug Marketing, Advertising, and Communications

DDT

Drug Development Tools

DEA

Drug Enforcement Administration

Debarment

An official action in accordance with 21 CFR 1404 to exclude a person from directly or indirectly providing services in any capacity to a firm with an approved or pending drug/device product application. A debarred corporation is prohibited from submitting or assisting in the submission of any NDA or ANDA. Equivalent to disqualification for devices requiring a PMA submission.

Declaration of Helsinki

Ethical principles for medical research involving human subjects. Trials conducted under Good Clinical Practice generally follow the Declaration of Helsinki.

DESI

Drug Efficacy Study Implementation

DFUF

Device Facility User Fee

DHF

Design History File. Describes a finished device's design.

DHHS

Department of Health and Human Services

DHR

Device History Record. Contains a device's production history.

DIA

Drug Information Association

DMC

Data Monitoring Committee

DMEPA

Division of Medication Error Prevention and Analysis (CBER)

DMF

Drug Master File. Submission to FDA that may be used to provide confidential detailed information about facilities, processes or articles used in the manufacturing, processing, packaging and storing of one or more human drugs.

DMPQ

Division of Manufacturing and Product Quality (CBER)

DMR
Device Master Record. Compilation of records containing a finished device's procedures and specifications.

DNCE
Division of Nonprescription Clinical Evaluation

DRC
Direct Recall Classification

DRLS
Drug Registration and Listing System

Drug
Any article intended for use in the diagnosis, cure, mitigation, treatment or prevention of disease in man.

Drugs@FDA
A searchable database of brand-name and generic prescription and OTC human drugs and biological therapeutic products approved since 1939.

Drug Product
A finished dosage form (e.g., tablet, capsule, solution, etc.) that contains an active drug ingredient. It is generally, but not necessarily, also associated with inactive ingredients. This includes a finished dosage form that does not contain an active ingredient but is intended to be used as a placebo.

DSMICA
Division of Small Manufacturers, International, and Consumer Assistance (CDRH)

DSHEA
Dietary Supplement Health and Education Act of 1994

DTC
Direct-to-Consumer (advertising)

E
EA
Environmental Assessment

EC
European Commission, European Community or Ethics Committee

ECO
Emergency Change Order

eCTD
Electronic Common Technical Document

eBPDR
Electronic Biological Product Deviation Reports

EFTA
European Free Trade Association

EIR
Establishment Inspection Report

EMA
European Medicines Agency (formerly European Medicines Evaluation Agency)

Emergency Use IND
FDA authorization for shipping a drug for a specific emergency use for a life-threatening or serious disease for which there is no alternative treatment.

EPA
Environmental Protection Agency

ERS
Expedited Review Status. Program for veterinary products.

Establishment Listing and Registration
In accordance with 21 CFR 807, manufacturers (both domestic and foreign) and initial distributors (importers) of medical devices must electronically register their establishments with FDA. Manufacturers must also list their devices with FDA.

Excipient
An ingredient contained in a drug formulation that is not a medicinally active constituent.

Expected Life
Time a device is expected to remain functional after being placed into service.

Expiration Date
Date printed on product label indicating the end of the product's useful life. Expiration period length is determined by stability studies and negotiated with FDA.

ETASU
Elements to Ensure Safe Use

EU

European Union has 27 Member States: Belgium, Germany, France, Italy, Luxembourg, The Netherlands, Denmark, Ireland, the United Kingdom, Greece, Spain, Portugal, Austria, Finland, Sweden, Cyprus, the Czech Republic, Estonia, Hungary, Latvia, Lithuania, Malta, Poland, Slovakia, Slovenia, Bulgaria and Romania. EU policies also apply to members of the European Free Trade Association: Iceland, Norway, Switzerland and Liechtenstein.

F

FAR
Field Alert Report

Fast Track
FDA program to facilitate the development and expedite the review of new drugs intended to treat serious or life-threatening conditions that demonstrate the potential to address unmet medical needs. Accelerated NDA review.

FCA
False Claims Act

FCC
Federal Communications Commission

FD&C Act
Federal Food, Drug, and Cosmetic Act of 1938

FDA
Food and Drug Administration

FDAAA
Food and Drug Administration Amendments Act of 2007

FDA ESG
FDA Electronic Submissions Gateway. Enables the secure submission of regulatory information for review.

FDAMA
Food and Drug Administration Modernization Act of 1997

FDERA
Food and Drug Export Reform and Enhancement Act of 1996

FDLI
Food and Drug Law Institute

FALCPA
Food Allergen Labeling and Consumer Protection Act of 2004

FMECA
Failure Mode, Effects and Critical Analysis

FOIA
Freedom of Information Act

FPLA
Fair Packaging and Labeling Act

FR
Federal Register

FSMA
Food Safety Modernization Act of 2011

FTC
Federal Trade Commission

FURLS
FDA Unified Registration and Listing System for establishment registration of medical device operators and distributors.

G

GADPTRA
Generic Animal Drug and Patent Term Restoration Act of 1988

GAO
Government Accountability Office

GCP
Good Clinical Practice. Regulations and requirements with which clinical studies must comply. These regulations apply to the manufacturers, sponsors, clinical investigators and institutional review boards.

GDEA
Generic Drug Enforcement Act of 1992

GeMCRIS
Genetic Modification Clinical Research Information System. Allows public users to access basic reports about human gene transfer trials registered with NIH and to develop specific queries based on their own information needs.

Generic Drug
Drugs manufactured and approved after the original brand name drug has lost patent protection. Sponsor files Abbreviated New Drug Application (ANDA) for marketing approval.

GGP
Good Guidance Practice

GHTF
Global Harmonization Task Force. Comprised of five founding members: EU, US, Canada, Australia and Japan. Formed to encourage convergence in regulatory practices related to ensuring the safety, effectiveness/ performance and quality of medical devices, promoting technological innovation and facilitating international trade.

GLP
Good Laboratory Practice. Regulations governing the conduct of nonclinical laboratory studies that support or are intended to support applications for research or marketing applications.

GMP
Good Manufacturing Practice (for devices, see Quality System Regulation).

GPO
Government Printing Office

GPR
General Purpose Reagents

Grandfathered
Tacit approval of drugs marketed before 1938 and devices marketed before May 1976.

GRAS(E)
Generally Recognized as Safe (and Effective)

Green Book
FDA-published listing of all animal drug products approved for safety and effectiveness. Updated monthly.

GRP
Good Review Practice

GTP
Good Tissue Practice

Guidance
Documents published by FDA to provide current interpretation of regulations.

H
HAACP
Hazard Analysis and Critical Control Point (inspection technique)

Hatch-Waxman Act
Drug Price Competition and Patent Restoration Act of 1984

HCT/P
Human Cells, Tissues and Cellular and Tissue-Based Products

HDE
Humanitarian Device Exemption

HIPAA
Health Insurance Portability and Accountability Act of 1996, also known as the Privacy Rule, established the minimum federal requirements for protecting the privacy of individually identifiable health information.

HMO
Health Maintenance Organization

Homeopathic Drug
Any drug labeled as being homeopathic listed in the *Homeopathic Pharmacopeia of the United States* (*HPUS*), an addendum to it or its supplements. The practice of homeopathy is based on the belief that disease symptoms can be cured by small doses of substances which produce similar symptoms in healthy people.

HPCUS
Homeopathic Pharmacopoeia Convention of the United States

HPUS
Homoeopathic Pharmacopoeia of the United States

HUD
Humanitarian Use Device

I
IB
Investigator's Brochure

IC (ICF) (ICD)
Informed Consent (Form) (Document)

ICH
International Conference on Harmonisation of Technical Requirements for Registration of Pharmaceuticals for Human Use (participants include Europe, Japan and US; observers include Australia and Canada).

IDE
Investigational Device Exemption

IDMC
Independent Data Monitoring Committee

Inactive Ingredient
Any drug product component other than the active ingredient, such as excipients, vehicle and binders.

INAD
Investigational New Animal Drug (application)

IND
Investigational New Drug (application)

Information Amendment
Includes most submissions under an active IND, such as new protocols, final study reports, safety reports, CMC information, etc. The initial IND ends with 000; each serial amendment receives the next consecutive number.

INN
International Nonproprietary Names

Intended Use
Objective labeled use of a device.

Investigator IND
Protocol and IND submitted by an individual investigator instead of a manufacturer. A letter of authorization allows FDA to review the sponsor's DMF or cross-reference CMC information. The investigator, not the manufacturer, is responsible for maintaining the IND.

IOM
Investigations Operations Manual

IRB
Institutional Review Board or Independent Review Board

ISO
International Organization for Standardization

IUO
Investigational Use Only

IVD
In Vitro Diagnostic

L
Label
Any display of written, printed or graphic matter on the immediate container or package of, or affixed to, any article.

Labeling
All written, printed or graphic matter accompanying an article at any time while such article is in interstate commerce or held for sale after shipment in interstate commerce; includes user manuals, brochures, advertising, etc.

LDT
Laboratory developed test

LOA
Letter of Authorization. A letter from the holder of a Drug Master File to FDA, authorizing another party to reference the DMF (also Letter of Agreement).

M
Market Withdrawal
Firm-initiated removal or correction of a device, drug or biologic product involving a minor violation of the *FD&C Act*, not subject to legal action by FDA, or which involves no violation, e.g., normal stock rotation practices, routine equipment adjustments and repairs, etc.

MAF
Device Master File. Analagous to a drug master file; submission to FDA that may be used to provide confidential detailed information about a medical device or a component used in the manufacture of a medical device to FDA in support of another party's obligation.

MAPP
Manual of Policy and Procedures

MAUDE
Manufacturer and User Facility Device Experience database. Contains reports of adverse events involving medical devices.

MDR
Medical Device Reporting

MDUFMA
Medical Device User Fee and Modernization Act of 2002

Medical Device

An instrument, apparatus, implement, machine, contrivance, implant, in vitro reagent or other similar or related article, including any component, part or accessory that is:

- recognized in the official *National Formulary* or *US Pharmacopeia*, or any supplement to them
- intended for use in diagnosis of disease or other conditions, or in cure, mitigation, treatment or prevention of disease in man or other animals intended to affect the structure or any function of the body of man or other animals, and which does not achieve its primary intended purposes through chemical action within or on the body of man or other animals, and which is not dependent upon being metabolized for the achievement of its primary intended purposes. (*FD&C Act* Section 201(h))

MedDRA

Medical Dictionary for Regulatory Activities. Global standard international medical terminology designed to supersede or replace all other terminologies used within the medical product development process including COSTART and WHO-ART.

MedSun

Medical Product Safety Network. An adverse event reporting program for healthcare professionals launched in 2002 by CDRH.

MedWatch

FDA program for voluntary and mandatory reporting of AEs and product problems. (FDA Form 3500 or 3500A)

Misbranded

Designation given to a product that is incorrectly labeled (i.e., false or misleading or fails to include information required by law). Other violations may also render a product misbranded (e.g., failure to obtain a 510(k) for a device).

MMA

Medicare Prescription Drug, Improvement and Modernization Act of 2003

Modular PMA

Allows a company to file the completed portions or modules of a PMA for an ongoing review by FDA.

MOU

Memorandum of Understanding. An agreement between FDA and another country's regulatory authority that allows mutual recognition of inspections.

MSDS

Material Safety Data Sheet

MTD

Maximum Tolerated Dose

MUMS

Minor Use and Minor Species Animal Health Act of 2004

N

NADA

New Animal Drug Application

NAF

Notice of Adverse Findings

NAFTA

North American Free Trade Agreement

NAI

No Action Indicated. Most favorable FDA postinspection classification.

NCE

New Chemical Entity

NCTR

National Center for Toxicological Research

NDA

New Drug Application

NDA Field Alert

Report filed with FDA within three working days of obtaining information on any distributed drug product that has contamination, significant chemical or physical change, deterioration, batch failure or labeling causing mistaken identity.

NDC

National Drug Code. The first five digits identify establishment and last five digits identify drug name, package size and drug type.

NDF

New Dosage Form

NF

National Formulary (incorporated into the *USP-NF*)

NIDPOE

Notice of Initiation of Disqualification Proceedings and Opportunity to Explain Letter

NIH
National Institutes of Health

NLEA
Nutrition Labeling and Education Act of 1990

NLM
National Library of Medicine

NME
New Molecular Entity

NORD
National Organization for Rare Disorders

NOV
Notice of Violation letter

NRC
National Research Council or Nuclear Regulatory Commission

NSE
Not Substantially Equivalent. Designation for device that does not qualify for 510(k) clearance; generally requires a PMA.

NSR
Nonsignificant Risk

O

OAI
Official Action Indicated. Serious FDA postinspection classification.

OC
Office of the Commissioner (FDA)

OCBQ
Office of Compliance and Biologics Quality (CBER)

OCC
Office of the Chief Counsel (FDA)

OCI
Office of Criminal Investigation (FDA)

OCP
Office of Combination Products (FDA)

OCTGT
Office of Cellular, Tissue and Gene Therapies (CBER)

ODA
Orphan Drug Act of 1983

ODE
Office of Device Evaluation (FDA)

OECD
The Organization for Economic Cooperation and Development

Office of the Chief Scientist
Includes the following offices:
- Office of Counterterrorism and Emerging Threats
- Office of Scientific Integrity
- Office of the Ombudsman
- Office of Science and Innovation
- Office of Critical Path Programs

OGD
Office of Generic Drug Products (CDER)

OIG
Office of the Inspector General (FDA)

OIRA
Office of Information and Regulatory Affairs (OMB)

OIVD
Office of In Vitro Diagnostic Device Evaluation and Safety (FDA)

OIP
Office of International Programs (FDA)

OMUMS
Office of Minor Use & Minor Species Animal Drug Development (CVM)

ONADE
Office of New Animal Drug Evaluation (CVM)

OND
Office of New Drugs (CDER)

ONPLDS
Office of Nutritional Products, Labeling and Dietary Supplements (CFSAN)

OOPD
Office of Orphan Products Development (FDA)

OPA
Office of Public Affairs (FDA)

Open Label Study
A clinical trial in which subjects and investigators are aware of the treatment received.

ORA
Office of Regulatory Affairs (FDA); oversees FDA's field organization.

Orange Book
FDA-published listing of Approved Drug Products with Therapeutic Equivalence Evaluations generally known as generics (has an orange cover).

Orphan Drug
Drugs for a disease or condition that affects fewer than 200,000 persons in the US or occurs in more than 200,000 and for which there is no reasonable expectation that drug development and manufacturing costs will be recovered from US sales.

OSB
Office of Surveillance and Biometrics (CDRH)

OSHA
Occupational Safety Health Administration

OTC
Over-the-Counter. Nonprescription drugs receive this designation.

OTC Monograph
Rules for a number of OTC drug categories.

OVRR
Office of Vaccine Research and Review (CBER)

P

PAI
Preapproval Inspection

PAS
Prior Approval Supplement or Postapproval Study

PAT
Process Analytical Technology

PCPC
Personal Care Products Council (formerly Cosmetic, Toiletry and Fragrance Association)

PD
Pharmacodynamics. Study of the reactions between drugs and living structures.

PDA
Parenteral Drug Association

PDMA
Prescription Drug Marketing Act

PDP
Product Development Protocol (for medical devices) or Principal Display Panel (for product labels)

PDUFA
Prescription Drug User Fee Act of 1992

PGx
Pharmacogenomics. The study of variations of DNA and RNA characteristics as related to drug response

Pharmacovigilance
Adverse event monitoring and reporting

PhRMA
Pharmaceutical Research and Manufacturers of America

Phase I
Initial clinical safety studies in humans. May be as few as 10 subjects, often healthy volunteers, includes PK, ADME and dose escalation studies. Usually open label.

Phase II
Well-controlled clinical trials of approximately 100–300 subjects who have the condition of interest, includes PK, dose ranging, safety and efficacy.

Phase III
Larger, well-controlled clinical trials of hundreds to thousands of subjects, including both safety and efficacy data. Generally, two well-controlled studies are needed to establish efficacy for drug products.

Phase IV
Postmarket clinical trials performed to support labeling and advertising or fulfill FDA safety requirements noted at the time of NDA approval.

PHI
Protected Health Information

PHS
Public Health Service

PI
Package Insert (approved product labeling) or Principal Investigator

PK

Pharmacokinetics. The study of the processes of ADME of chemicals and medicines.

Placebo

A drug product fashioned to look like an active drug but containing no active ingredient. Used in clinical trials to blind or mask the patient, investigator or both as to the treatment received.

PLR

Physician Labeling Rule

PMA

Premarket Approval. Marketing application required for Class III devices.

PMN

Premarket Notification. A premarket notification is also called a 510(k).

PMOA

Primary Mode of Action. The single mode of action of a combination product that provides the most important therapeutic action of the combination product; used to assign a combination product to a lead FDA center.

PMS

Postmarketing Surveillance. Ongoing monitoring of the safety of approved medical products; may include Phase IV studies and AE reporting.

PNSI

Prior Notice System Interface. Used to provide prior notice for food products entering the US.

PPACA

Patient Protection and Affordable Care Act of 2010

PPI

Patient Package Insert

PPPA

Poison Prevention Packaging Act

PREA

Pediatric Research Equity Act of 2003

Preclinical Studies

Animal studies of PK and toxicity generally performed prior to clinical studies. These studies must comply with GLP.

Priority Review

FDA review category for drugs that appear to represent an advance over available therapy. NDA or BLA receives a faster review than standard applications.

Protocol

Document describing a clinical trial's objectives, design and methods. All GLP and GCP studies must follow a protocol.

PSUR

Periodic Safety Update Report

PTC

Points to Consider. Type of guidance published by FDA, usually by CBER.

PTCC

Pharmacology/Toxicology Coordinating Committee (CDER)

***Public Health Security and Bioterrorism Preparedness and Response Act* of 2002**

Also known as *Bioterrorism Act*

PWR

Pediatric Written Request. *BPCA* authorizes FDA (in consultation with NIH) to issue a written request for the conduct of pediatric studies to holders of approved NDAs and ANDAs for drugs on the NIH list.

Q

QA

Quality Assurance

QAU

Quality Assurance Unit

QC

Quality Control

QoL

Quality of Life

QSIT

Quality System Inspection Technique

QSR

Quality System Regulation (21 CFR 820). Identifies GMPs for medical devices.

R

R&D

Research and Development

RAC

Reviewer Affairs Committee (CDER) or Regulatory Affairs Certification

RAPS

Regulatory Affairs Professionals Society

RCT

Randomized Clinical Trial or Randomized Controlled Trial

Recall

A firm's removal or correction of a marketed product that FDA considers to be in violation of the laws it administers and against which the agency would initiate legal action, e.g., seizure. Recall does not include a market withdrawal or a stock recovery.

Recall Classification

Assigned by FDA and applicable to firm-initiated device recalls based upon reasonable probability and relative degree of health hazard.
- Class I: violative device would cause serious adverse health consequences.
- Class II: violative device may cause temporary or medically reversible adverse health consequences or such consequences are remote.
- Class III: violative device is not likely to cause adverse health consequences.

Regulation

Refers to Code of Federal Regulations

REMS

Risk Evaluation and Mitigation Strategy

RFR

Reportable Food Registry. An electronic portal used to report foods suspected of causing serious adverse health consequences.

Restricted Device

A device restricted, by regulation, to sale, distribution and/or use only upon the written or oral authorization of a licensed practitioner or other conditions prescribed by the commissioner.

RFD

Request for Designation. A written submission to OCP requesting designation of the center with primary jurisdiction for a combination or non-combination product.

RFR

Request for Reconsideration. A request that OCP reconsider an RFD determination.

RLD

Reference Listed Drug. Drug product listed in the Approved Drug Products with Therapeutic Equivalence Evaluations book (also known as the *Orange Book*).

Rolling NDA Submission

Allows a company to file the completed portions of an NDA for an ongoing review by FDA. Only permitted for drugs and biologics that have received Fast Track designation from FDA.

RTF

Refusal to File. Letter sent by FDA when incomplete NDA or ANDA is filed. FDA will not review the application until complete. Letter is sent within 60 days of submission.

RUO

Research Use Only

Rx

Prescription Use Only

S

SAE

Serious Adverse Event

SBA

Summary Basis of Approval

SC

Study Coordinator

SD

Standard Deviation

SE

Substantially Equivalent

S&E

Safety and Efficacy

Shelf Life
Maximum time a device will remain functional from the date of manufacture until it is used in patient care (See Expiration Date).

Significant Risk Device
An investigational device that:
- is intended as an implant
- is represented to be for use in supporting or sustaining human life
- is for a use of substantial importance in diagnosing, curing, mitigating, or treating disease or otherwise preventing impairment of human health and presents a potential for serious risk to the subject's health, safety or welfare

SMDA
Safe Medical Devices Act of 1990

SME
Significant Medical Event

SNDA
Supplemental New Drug Application

SoCRA
Society of Clinical Research Associates

SOP
Standard Operating Procedure

Source Documents
Original documents and records containing information captured in a clinical study. Case Report Forms are monitored against source documents. Includes office charts, laboratory results, x-rays, etc.

SPA
Special Protocol Assessment

SPL
Structured Product Label. Content of package insert in XML format.

SR
Significant Risk (device)

Sponsor
Company, person, organization or institution taking responsibility for initiating, managing or financing a clinical trial.

Standard Review (S)
FDA review category for drugs with therapeutic qualities similar to those already approved for marketing.

Subject
Clinical trial participant; may be a healthy volunteer or a patient.

Subpart E
21 CFR 312. Accelerated review for life-threatening and severely debilitating illness.

Subpart H
21 CFR 314.500. Approval based upon a surrogate endpoint or a product approved with restrictions and/or requirements for Phase IV trials.

Substantial Equivalence
Comparison of a new device to a legally marketed predicate device; substantial equivalence establishes a device is as safe and as effective as another 510(k) cleared device.

Suitability Petition
A request to FDA to submit an ANDA for a product that varies from a Reference Listed Drug in indication, strength, dosage form, route of administration, etc.

SUPAC
Scale Up and Post Approval Changes

Supplement (sNDA)
NDA submission for changes to an approved NDA, including SUPAC.

Supplement (sPMA)
PMA submission for changes to an approved PMA that affect the device's safety or effectiveness.

Surrogate Endpoint
A laboratory or physical sign that is used in trials as a substitute for a clinically meaningful endpoint that is a direct measure of how a patient feels, functions or survives and is expected to predict the effect of the therapy.

T

Target Product Profile (TPP)
A format for a summary of a drug development program described in terms of labeling concepts. A TPP can be prepared by a sponsor and then shared with the appropriate FDA review staff to facilitate communication regarding a particular drug development program.

Team Biologics
A group of specialized investigators who conduct routine and CGMP follow-up inspections of manufacturers of biological products regulated by CBER. Partnership program between ORA and CBER.

Third Party Review
Under *FDAMA*, FDA has accredited third parties that are authorized to conduct the primary review of 510(k)'s for eligible devices.

THOMAS
Public federal legislation database (Library of Congress)

TK
Toxicokinetics

TOPRA
The Organisation for Professionals in Regulatory Affairs

TPP
Target Product Profile

Treatment IND (tIND)
Allows limited use of an unapproved drug for patients with a serious or life-threatening disease.

Truthful Prescription Drug Advertising and Promotion (Bad Ad Program)
Educational outreach program to help healthcare providers recognize misleading prescription drug promotion and provide them with an easy way to report this activity to the agency.

U
UADE
Unexpected Adverse Device Effect. Any serious adverse effect on health or safety or any life-threatening problem or death caused by, or associated with, a device, if that effect, problem or death was not previously identified in nature, severity or degree of incidence in the investigational plan or application, or any other unanticipated serious problem associated with a device that relates to the rights, safety or welfare of subjects.

UDI
Unique Device Identification. Would require the label of a device to bear a unique identifier, unless an alternative location is specified by FDA or unless an exception is made for a particular device or group of devices.

Unexpected AE
An AE whose nature or severity is not described in the Investigator's Brochure (for an unapproved product) or in the package insert (for an approved product).

USAN
US Adopted Name

USANC
US Adopted Names Council

USC
US Code

USCA
US Code Annotated

USDA
US Department of Agriculture

User Fees
Fees authorized by Congress to fund various FDA activities. The fee schedule for different application types is published annually in the *Federal Register*. Initially established by the *Prescription Drug User Fee Act* and later extended to medical devices, generic drugs and animal drugs.

USP
United States Pharmacopeia

V
VA
Department of Veterans Affairs

VAERS
Vaccine Adverse Event Reporting System

VAI
Voluntary Action Indicated. Moderately serious FDA postinspection classification.

VCRP
Voluntary Cosmetic Registration Program. An FDA postmarket reporting system for use by manufacturers, packers and distributors of cosmetic products that are in commercial distribution in the US.

W
Warning Letter (WL)
Serious enforcement letter issued by FDA notifying a regulated entity of violative activity; requires immediate action within 15 days.

Warning Letter Database

Contains Warning Letters issued from November 1996 to the present. Searchable by company, subject, issuing office or date.

Well-Characterized Biologic

A biological product whose identity, purity, impurities, potency and quantity can be determined and controlled.

WHO

World Health Organization

EU Medical Device Regulation

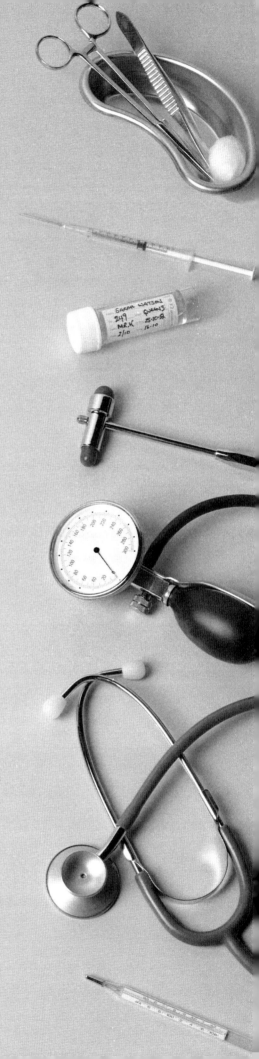

EU Regulatory Affairs—An Historic Perspective

Updated by Salma Michor, PhD, RAC

OBJECTIVES

❑ Learn why healthcare regulations for medicinal products and devices were established

❑ Discover the key historical milestones leading to today's healthcare regulations

❑ Understand the major regulations governing medicinal products and medical devices in the European Union (EU)

DIRECTIVES, REGULATIONS AND GUIDELINES COVERED IN THIS CHAPTER

❑ Council Directive 65/65/EEC of 26 January 1965 on the approximation of provisions laid down by law, regulation or administrative action relating to medicinal products, the first European medicinal product directive

❑ Directive 2001/83/EC of the European Parliament and of the Council of 6 November 2001 on the Community code relating to medicinal products for human use (*Medicinal Products Directive*)

❑ Council Directive 89/432/EEC of 12 June 1989 on the introduction of measures to encourage improvements in the safety and health of workers at work, the first European biologic product directive

❑ Regulation (EC) No 1394/2007 of the European Parliament and of the Council of 13

November 2007 on advanced therapy medicinal products and amending Directive 2001/83/EC and Regulation (EC) No 724/2004 (*ATMP Regulation*)

❑ Council Directive 81/851/EEC of 28 September 1981 on the approximation of the laws of the Member States relating to veterinary medicinal products, the first European veterinary product directive

❑ Council Directive 93/42/EEC of 14 June 1993 concerning medical devices (*Medical Devices Directive*)

❑ Council Directive 2007/47/EC of the European Parliament and of the Council of 5 September 2007 amending Council Directive 90/385/EEC on the approximation of the laws of the Member States relating to active implantable medical devices (*Active Implantable Medical Devices Directive*), Council Directive 93/42/EEC concerning medical devices (*Medical Devices Directive*) and Directive 98/8/EC concerning the placing of biocidal products on the market

Introduction

Every regulatory system's history provides insight into the circumstances that existed at the time it was established and sheds light on the system's current objectives. Compared to regulation of other industries, regulation of medicinal products in the EU is relatively recent. Medicinal product regulations and regulatory activities were not established until the second half of the 20th century. In common with other regions, the main goal of all European regulatory systems is keeping unsafe products out of the marketplace. Therefore, regulations were established to approve medicinal product Marketing Authorisation Applications (MAAs) and monitor those products in the postauthorisation stage.

A single EU market meets the various interests of healthcare providers, industry and consumers, although the involved parties' viewpoints may differ. Providers and reimbursement bodies focus on minimising healthcare costs, whereas consumers demand easy access to a broad range of safe and effective products and treatments without necessarily considering the cost implications. Industry prefers a regulatory system that enables an "approved once, accepted everywhere" approach to reduce the time and cost of multiple registrations resulting from heterogeneous national requirements; i.e., if a country approves a product on the basis of its regulatory system, then other countries should accept the product without further testing or application review.

This chapter simplifies the complex subject of EU medicinal product regulations. After briefly describing the history of EU healthcare regulations, it summarises those governing today's medicinal product industry.

Historic Factors in the Development of Medicinal Product Regulations

Healthcare regulations have their beginnings in ethics. Their main objective was to protect individuals against unethical and unsafe human trials. The need for ethical standards stemmed from the inhumane practices of infamous Nazi physician Josef Mengele during World War II. However, prior to those experiments, research-oriented physicians had conducted private clinical trials that exceeded the bounds of common ethical standards. For example, the first vaccine trials were performed without any regulatory supervision and the results were never published. Although these first human experiments were subject to internal ethical discussions by healthcare professionals, they were not regulated officially. Press reports about research incidents sensitised the public to the need for healthcare regulations to protect public safety. Therefore, by the early 20th century, the public increasingly viewed medicines and surgery not as treatments for illness but as sources of injury and failure if not used properly.

The first European healthcare regulations concerned the ethical treatment of human subjects and were promulgated midway through the 20th century. The *Helsinki Declaration* in 1964 set forth ethical standards for the first time. Subsequently, laws were passed regulating which products could be placed on the market and the claims manufacturers could make about those products. Today, medicinal product regulations not only target ethical, safety and efficacy concerns but also address economic issues, increased availability of information, continuing technological and product innovations, market structure changes and the groundswell of consumer activism.

Consequences of Unsafe Products

Certain safety incidents have been catalysts for medicinal product regulations. The thalidomide scandal in Europe and Canada was a milestone in the development of pharmaceutical product regulations. In the late 1950s, the German pharmaceutical company Grünenthal launched Contergan, a sedative containing thalidomide that also was used to treat morning sickness. Contergan was advertised by the company as supposedly "atoxic," "without danger" and "nonpoisonous." Soon after the product was introduced, thousands of babies were born with malformations, particularly to their limbs; the deformities soon were associated with thalidomide. In 1961, the turnover through Contergan reached its sales zenith with 1.3 million deutsche-mark per day. In 1961-62, the link to Contergan was officially established; this was the peak of the Contergan scandal. At the time, no premarket reproductive toxicity testing was legally required, so the teratogenic potential of new medicinal products was unknown prior to marketing authorisation.

Awareness of the potential transmission of bovine spongiform encephalopathy (BSE, also known as "mad cow disease") and transmissible spongiform encephalopathy (TSE) to humans during the 1990s led to heightened legislative activity to regulate medicinal products containing bovine-derived materials. In the early 1990s, cases of BSE were reported in the UK, as were a growing number of new forms of Creutzfeldt-Jakob disease (i.e., TSE), the human equivalent of BSE. Suspicions that these cases were associated with consuming BSE-infected beef led to dramatic export restrictions on British beef, resulting in significant economic impact on British farmers. The crisis led to amended medicinal products regulations because many products contain ingredients derived from bovine material (e.g., lactose, gelatine and magnesium stearate). One example of this type of regulation is Directive 2003/32/EC,[1] which is designed to reduce the risks of transmitting TSE to patients via medical devices manufactured with animal tissue under normal conditions.

Economic Issues

Although public health protection primarily drives healthcare regulation, economic considerations also began to have an impact in the second half of the 20th century. With the establishment of the first health insurance system, it became obvious that the growing availability and number of healthcare products would lead to increased costs for EU Member States because of higher medicinal product consumption and the subsequent rise in risks of side effects and misuse. The transfer of healthcare costs from individual consumers to private or public insurance systems necessitated product pricing transparency. It quickly became clear that limited economic resources had to be spent prudently. Awareness of healthcare's economic limits continues to build.

Availability of Information

Triggered by the media and supported by such worldwide communication systems as the Internet, medicinal product information is available almost immediately to virtually everyone. This information, both good and bad, can no longer be controlled or presented in an appropriate context by industry. For example, entering the word "Ritalin" into a common search engine may provide numerous hits, including some from anti-Ritalin activist groups fighting the drug's use for children with attention-deficit/hyperactivity disorder. In view of the extensive and often inaccurate material available to consumers, maintaining public confidence in the healthcare system necessitates timely and appropriate regulations that ensure medicinal product quality, safety and efficacy, and clear instructions for use.

Product Innovations

Tremendous technological advances have made many novel therapies available. Such new developments as biologics, blood products and in vitro diagnostics initially entered a market and a regulatory system that were not prepared for them. For example, the introduction of recombinant products led to implementation of the Concertation Procedure in 1987, in which Member States agreed to conduct a common MAA dossier assessment; this enabled Member States to collaborate across borders. This need to share expertise has driven the regulation development process.

Innovative product developers may both benefit from and exploit the existence of a "regulatory vacuum," as some areas still lack adequate regulations. Consequently, manufacturers can become involved in defining the regulatory framework of a new area and influence public and official opinion.

Changes in the Market Structure

Removal of trade barriers within the EU is another factor influencing healthcare regulations. The markets have been opened to products from many sources, and product quality control is an increasing concern. For example, importing single-use products (e.g., injection needles) signalled the need to include medical devices in existing medicinal product laws and regulations. Problems arose with imported products because manufacturers in the exporting countries were not fully governed by the importing country's product regulations. The range of European healthcare regulations—from practically none for certain products in some countries to well-defined frameworks in other countries—had to be brought under the same regulatory umbrella. This need led to a new product regulation approach.

Consumer Advocacy

Regulatory authorities consider safety to be of paramount importance. They ensure that adequate safety data are generated through clinical trials to support authorisation, and that these data are monitored throughout the product's postauthorisation lifecycle. They also promptly communicate any safety profile changes to the public when concerns arise—all while ensuring that products are available to patients in a timely manner.

Consumers' perceptions of health and healthcare have changed. The economic prosperity of most European countries has led to expectations for improved quality of life as well as improved survival rates and longevity. Demand for not only the treatment and prevention of illness but also improvement of consumers' general well-being is growing. This demand also drives new regulations.

Healthcare professionals who direct the use of healthcare products and the consumers of these products have divergent interests. Providers focus on reimbursement for services, whereas consumers want to protect their health by using products of maximum safety. Healthcare providers are subject to increased oversight by newly empowered consumers. Consumers are increasingly well educated and informed about health and health products and services, and are not afraid to challenge companies and regulatory and enforcement authorities.

Evolution of Current Regulations

Europe is the world's second-largest pharmaceutical market and is highly regulated. Since the adoption of the first pharmaceutical directive in 1965, European pharmaceutical legislation has consistently pursued two objectives: protection of public health and free movement of products among the Member States. The approval criteria and procedures for human medicines, as well as several other important aspects of pharmaceutical legislation, have been extensively harmonised within the EU. European pharmaceutical legislation now covers all industrially manufactured medicines, including vaccines, blood derivatives, biopharmaceuticals and homeopathic medicines.

The following legal framework for medicinal products for both human and veterinary use is available as a series of volumes entitled, *The Rules Governing Medicinal Products in the European Union,* published by the Office for Official Publications of the European Union:[2]
- pharmaceutical legislation (directives, regulations, decisions and other communications of the European Council and the European Commission)
- *Notice To Applicants* describing administrative procedures for marketing authorisations and the MAA dossier format including:
  o marketing authorisation submission procedures
  o dossier presentation and content (including CTD and eCTD)
  o regulatory guidelines
- guidelines on conducting recommended quality, safety and efficacy studies to support an MAA; the

subgroups are:
- o quality and biotechnology
- o safety, environment and information
- o efficacy (clinical guidelines)
- detailed Good Manufacturing Practice (GMP) guide
- detailed drug monitoring (pharmacovigilance) guide

The aforementioned legislation consists of directives, which are to be incorporated into each Member State's national laws; regulations that are directly applicable in each Member State; and notes for guidance, which are non-binding texts to help applicants fulfil regulatory approval obligations to place medicinal products on the market. National regulatory authorities frequently use the notes for guidance and other European nonbinding guidelines to interpret their own national laws.

Medicinal Products for Human and Veterinary Use

The first regulations governing medicinal products for human use came into force in the early 1960s. The Contergan catastrophe was the driving force for the first European medicinal product directive: Council Directive 65/65/EEC[3] (later codified into the unified Directive 2001/83/EC, as amended). For the first time, detailed marketing authorisation requirements for medicinal products for human use were described and applicable across the European Community. The directive reflects many of the requirements established by the US Food and Drug Administration (FDA). By the 1970s, the directive had been incorporated into the national laws of all Member States. The directive also regulated the registration of medicinal products already marketed in Member States.

Council Directive 75/318/EEC (later codified into the unified Directive 2001/83/EC in Article 8(3)(a)–(i) and Article 10a) defined legal requirements relating to MAA analytical, pharmacotoxicological and clinical documentation. Scientific and technological progress has been reflected in supplemental amendments to the directives such as the amendment involving requirements for minimising TSE contamination risks, among others.

In 1991, Directive 91/356/EEC[4] described GMP principles, which Member States incorporated into their regulations over the next 10 years. Prescription status (92/26/EEC, later codified into the unified Directive 2001/83/EC as Articles 70–75), medicinal product labelling and package leaflets (92/27/EEC, later codified into the unified Directive 2001/83/EC as Articles 54–69) and medicinal product advertising (92/28/EEC, later codified into the unified Directive 2001/83/EC as Articles 86–100) all were regulated somewhat later, in 1992. The national transition period in

some countries was rather long (e.g., package leaflets were not mandatory in the UK and Denmark before 1995).

At the end of 2001, the European Council adopted the *Medicinal Products Directive* (Directive 2001/83/EEC),[5] replacing all previous medicinal product directives. This huge project simplified the existing *Medicinal Products Directive*, unified recommendations that had diverged over time, clarified definitions of terms and enabled the repeal of directives that were no longer necessary. This made the regulatory environment clearer for authorities and industry.

Since then, the *Medicinal Products Directive* has been amended by:
- Directive 2002/98/EC,[6] setting standards of quality and safety for the collection, testing, processing, storage and distribution of human blood and blood components
- Directive 2003/63/EC,[7] establishing the analytical, pharmacotoxicological and clinical standards and protocols for medicinal product testing
- Directive 2004/24/EC,[8] regarding traditional herbal medicinal products
- Directive 2004/27/EC,[9] regarding GMP process requirements for Active Pharmaceutical Ingredients (APIs)
- Regulation (EC) No 1901/2006[10] regarding medicinal products for paediatric use and amendments
- Council Regulation (EC) No 1394/2007[11] on advanced therapy medicinal products
- Directive 2008/29/EC relating to medicinal products for human use, as regards the implementing powers conferred on the Commission

Directives 2004/24/EC and 2004/27/EC and a new Regulation (EC) 726/2004[12] regarding the European Agency for the Evaluation of Medicinal Products (EMA) were the result of a legislatively mandated review of EU pharmaceutical legislation that began in 2000 and was finalised in 2004, improving the EU medicinal product regulatory system. Directive 2004/27/EC introduced changes to labelling and packaging and the marketing authorisation ("Sunset Clause") and a "compassionate use" regulatory framework. Moreover, pharmacovigilance has been improved by implementing a database and an electronic notification system regarding adverse events.

Also in 2003, Directive 2003/94/EC[13] laid down further Good Manufacturing Practice principles and guidelines with respect to medicinal products and investigational medicinal products for human use.

Regulation (EC) No 1901/2006 established rules concerning the development of medicinal products for human use in order to meet the specific therapeutic needs of the paediatric population, without subjecting the paediatric population to unnecessary clinical or other trials and in compliance with Directive 2001/20/EC.[14]

In 1995, pursuant to Council Regulation (EEC) No 2309/93,[15] the EU implemented a pan-European registration system known as the "Centralised Procedure" and established the EMA. In 2004, Council Regulation (EC) No 2309/93 was superseded by Regulation (EC) No 726/2004[16] of the European Parliament and the Council of 31 March 2004. The regulation aimed to improve the authorisation procedure, amending certain administrative aspects. Further, the name of the European Agency for the Evaluation of Medicinal Products was changed to the European Medicines Agency, while retaining the acronym EMEA. This acronym was shortened to EMA in 2010.

This system enabled a single medicinal product marketing authorisation for the entire EU. The option of submitting an MAA through the Centralised Procedure also is available for biotechnology-derived products and products that are considered highly innovative. Moreover, Regulation (EC) No 726/2004 expanded application of the Centralised Procedure to orphan drugs (established by Regulation (EC) No 141/2000[17]) and products with new active substances dealing with acquired immune deficiency syndrome, cancer, neurodegenerative disorders, diabetes and, from 20 May 2008, autoimmune diseases and other immune dysfunctions and viral diseases.

Starting 30 December 2008, Regulation (EC) No 1394/2007 on advanced therapy medicinal products (ATMPs) expanded the applicability of Regulation (EC) No 726/2004 to advanced therapy medicinal products (such as gene and somatic therapy medicinal products as well as tissue-engineered products). This expansion has strengthened EMA by increasing its responsibilities and influence on the European pharmaceutical market.

EMA is headquartered in London and provides the administrative centre and support for MAA reviews.

One of five scientific committees conducts the technical review of all Centralised Procedure applications on the EU's behalf: the Committee for Medicinal Products for Human Use (CHMP); the Committee for Medicinal Products for Veterinary Use (CVMP); the Committee on Orphan Medicinal Products (COMP); the Committee on Herbal Medicinal Products (HMPC); and the Committee for Advanced Therapies (CAT).

CAT is responsible for reviewing ATMPs qualifying for the Centralised Procedure. COMP's role in reviewing orphan products is defined in Regulation (EC) No 141/2000. HMPC was established by Directive 2004/24/EC on traditional herbal medicine products. This directive also defines its role and duties. The roles of CHMP and CVMP in reviewing medicinal products for humans and animals, respectively, are defined in Regulation (EC) No 726/2004.

These committees are composed of regulatory agency representatives from each Member State. They meet at EMA's offices on a predefined schedule. The centralised

medicinal product review procedure and associated timelines are clearly defined in the *Notice to Applicants, Volume 2A.* Further information about this procedure is available from EMA.

Medicinal products that do not meet Centralised Procedure criteria may receive marketing authorisation through two mechanisms: national registration and decentralised mutual recognition (commonly referred to as mutual recognition). Marketing authorisation through the National Procedure is possible only for medicinal products that do not qualify for centralised approval and are intended for marketing in only one EU country. If these conditions apply, the requirements, review procedure and timelines are governed by the individual Member State's own process; reference should be made to the specific country's website for further information.

If, however, the intent is to market the product in more than one country, the MAA is reviewed through the Mutual Recognition Procedure. The Decentralised Procedure, a modified form of the Mutual Recognition Procedure, should be used for products for which no marketing authorisation exists. In essence, the MAA will be evaluated by one Member State (chosen by the sponsor) that will act as the Reference Member State (RMS). If marketing authorisation is granted by that state, other Member States (chosen by the sponsor, depending upon where the product will be sold), known as the Concerned Member States (CMS), are asked to "mutually recognise" the RMS approval. If the approval is recognised, a marketing authorisation will be granted in all the CMS.

Commission Regulation (EC) No 1234/2008 of 24 November 2008 (which is based on Commission Regulations (EC) 1084/2003[18] and (EC) No 1085/2003 of June 2003) concerning the examination of variations to the terms of marketing authorisations for medicinal products for human use and veterinary medicinal products uses a simplified approach to handling variations.

Biologics

In 1989, Council Directive 89/342/EEC[19] defined requirements for immunological medicinal products consisting of vaccines, toxins or sera, and allergens; Directive 89/381/EEC covers medicinal products derived from human blood or plasma. Council Directive 2001/18/EEC,[20] which replaced Council Directives 90/219/EEC and 90/220/EEC, regulates the use of genetically modified microorganisms and their deliberate release into the environment. This directive was amended by Regulation (EC) No 1830/2003,[21] establishing a clear EU system for tracing and labelling genetically modified organisms.

Biological medicinal product safety was increased by Directive 2003/63/EC, amending Annex I of Directive 2001/83/EC. Part III of Annex I now includes special biological pharmaceutical requirements. It established a new system that simplified approval and subsequent change procedures for human plasma-derived medicinal products. Moreover, it introduced a vaccine antigen master file (VAMF), which allows the pooling of national expertise and, through EMA coordination, a single evaluation of the concerned vaccine antigen.

The regulations and directives are complemented by various guidance documents that can be found on EMA's website.

Advanced Therapy Products

On 30 December 2007, Regulation (EC) No 1394/2007 on advanced therapy medicinal products (the *ATMP Regulation*) entered into force. The regulation included a "grandfather clause" with a transition period for products that were legally on the Community market when it came into force. Products new to the market had to comply with the regulation by 30 December 2008. "Grandfathered" products have to be in compliance by 30 December 2011, unless they are tissue-engineered products, in which case they must comply by 30 December 2012.

The regulation's purpose is to facilitate research, development and authorisation of advanced therapy products and to improve patient access to them. Advanced therapy products covered by the regulation are gene therapy medicinal products as defined in Part IV of Annex I to Directive 2001/83/EC, somatic cell therapy medicinal products as defined in Part IV of Annex I to Directive 2001/83/EC and tissue-engineered products as defined in the regulation itself.

Under this regulation, all advanced therapy medicinal products are required to have an EU-wide marketing authorisation as defined in Regulation (EC) No 726/2004. Moreover, it created centralised supervision and pharmacovigilance of ATMPs and a Committee for Advanced Therapies (CAT) within EMA. This provision combines expertise from different Member States to enable ATMP evaluation, and provides advice on the authorisation process, long-term follow-up of patients and risk management strategies for the postauthorisation phase. CAT is in charge of developing evaluation criteria and guidelines for these products.

A further effect of the *ATMP Regulation* was the applicability of the provisions of Directive 2001/83/EC governing GMP- and GCP-compliance, and ATMP advertising, labelling, classification and distribution.

The ATMP's regulations have been complemented recently by:

- Commission Directive 2009/120/EC of 14 September 2009 amending Directive 2001/83/ EC of the European Parliament and of the Council on the Community code relating to medicinal products for human use as regards advanced therapy medicinal products

- Commission Regulation (EC) No 668/2009 of 24 July 2009 implementing Regulation (EC) No 1394/2007 of the European Parliament and of the Council with regard to the evaluation and certification of quality and nonclinical data relating to advanced therapy medicinal products developed by micro, small and medium-sized enterprises

The regulations and directives are supported by a number of guidance documents that can be found on EMA's website.

Veterinary Products

The basic regulatory principles applied to human products also govern veterinary medicinal products. EU Directive 81/851/EEC[22] was the first Community directive regulating veterinary medicinal products and the analytical, pharmacotoxicological and clinical standards and protocols related to the testing of those products. A maximum residue limits regulation (Council Regulation (EEC) No 2377/90) and the *GMP Directive* (Directive 91/412/EEC) supplemented Directive 81/851/EEC in 1990 and 1991, respectively. Additional directives adopted during the 1990s recently have been codified into the unified Directive 2001/82/EC,[23] the Community code related to veterinary medicinal products.

Directive 2004/28/EC[24] of March 2004 amended Directive 2001/82/EC on veterinary medicinal products. As a result of scientific and technical progress in the animal health field, the definitions and scope of Directive 2001/82/EC needed to be clarified to meet high quality, safety and efficacy standards for veterinary medicinal products. Another aim of Directive 2004/28/EC was to eliminate remaining obstacles to free movement of these products within the European Community.

Directive 2006/130/EC[25] of 11 December 2006, laying down criteria for exempting certain veterinary medicinal products for food-producing animals from the requirement for a veterinary prescription, implements Directive 2001/82/EC.

Commission Directive 2009/9/EC of 10 February 2009 amended Directive 2001/82/EC on the Community code relating to medicinal products for veterinary use. It was introduced mainly to simplify current procedures for the assessment of veterinary vaccines, both for the granting of a first marketing authorisation and for subsequent changes due to modifications to the manufacturing process and testing of individual antigens involved in combined vaccines. A new system based on the concept of a master file (VAMF) should be introduced for vaccines which involve several antigens.[26]

Regulation (EC) 1950/2006[27] of 13 December 2006 established—in accordance with Directive 2001/82/EC on the Community code relating to veterinary medicinal products—a list of substances essential for the treatment of *equidae*.

Traditional Herbal Medicinal Products

In 2004, Directive 2004/24/EC amended Directive 2001/83/EC on traditional herbal medicinal products. Given the particular characteristics of these medicinal products—especially their long tradition—the European Commission established a special, simplified procedure for them. The Committee on Herbal Medicinal Products (HMPC) is responsible for reviewing registry documents and providing scientific opinions on traditional herbal medicines.

Medical Devices

To remove barriers to the free movement of goods, two innovative regulatory instruments regarding medical devices were developed in the EU: the New Approach to device regulation and the Global Approach to conformity assessment. The medical device regulations are the best-known examples.

New Approach directives describe a fast legislative pathway with a defined content and structure. Their legal basis is Article 95 of the *European Council Treaty*. The New Approach is not limited to healthcare devices; it also applies to toys, electromagnetic compatibility, lifts and radio and telecommunication equipment. Devices that are granted market access using the New Approach can be recognised by the European Conformity (CE) Mark. New Approach directives are harmonised across the EU; the Member States must repeal all contradictory national legislation and are not allowed to maintain or introduce more-stringent measures than those foreseen in the directives. When Member States incorporate the New Approach requirements, they may include additional provisions considered necessary to apply the requirements more effectively. These harmonised directives limit public intervention and enable industry to meet its obligations in a manner suitable to the specific situation or device without the need for a cumbersome regulatory approval process. About 20 New Approach directives came into force during the mid-1980s. As a result, the reduced regulatory burden for authorities enabled approval processes to advance much more quickly than before. In addition, the changes enabled the creation of a single European market for devices by December 1992—an objective of the *European Council Treaty*.

Council Directive 90/385/EEC[28] (June 1990), relating to active implantable medical devices, was the first application of the New Approach to the field of medical devices. The New Approach has not been applied in sectors where Community legislation was well advanced before 1985 or where provisions for finished products and hazards related to such products cannot be established. For instance, Community legislation on foodstuffs, chemical products and pharmaceutical products does not follow New Approach principles.

The Global Approach supplements the New Approach by defining the basis for Conformity Assessment Procedures within the New Approach directives. The Global Approach does not give conformity assessment details; those are described in the directives themselves. Its broader scope is to facilitate conditions to implement conformity assessment evidence when mutual recognition agreements are signed. Conformity assessments are to be found in regulatory and nonregulatory fields.

The *Guide to the Implementation of Directives Based on New Approach and Global Approach*, a detailed description of New Approach and Global Approach directives, is available from the European Commission.

The 1993 *Maastricht Treaty* introduced public health into the EU's areas of competence. The mission of the European Commission and, particularly, its Directorate-General for Health and Consumer Protection, is to ensure a high level of protection of consumers' health, safety and economic interests, as well as public health. Scientific advice for drafting and amending EU regulations is provided by a number of committees, including the Scientific Committee on Medicinal Products and Medical Devices. The Directorate-General for Enterprise promotes innovation, entrepreneurship, e-business, standardisation and New Approach EU regulations, which are of direct concern to the medical technologies and devices sector.

The medical devices definition is similar to the definition of medicinal products in Council Directive 65/65/EEC, and relevant medical device regulation sections were driven by pharmaceutical regulation experience. The difference between product groups is the mode of action. If the product's mode of action is primarily pharmacological, immunological or metabolic, it is classified as a medicinal product. In other cases—mainly, if the product acts by physical means—it is classified as a medical device. The heterogeneity of medical devices and the high degree of innovation in new product development, including software and such new technologies as chromatographic procedures, provide the rationale for establishing specific medical device regulations.

Interestingly, the *Medical Devices Directive (MDD)*[29] (93/42/EEC) regulates only products for human use. Therefore, medical devices for veterinary use, such as special drug delivery systems, are still under the medicinal products regulations. This situation may be a disadvantage for medical device manufacturers if the product is intended for use by both humans and animals. The products follow two different guidelines and must be labelled in two different ways, according to the intended use.

In Europe, medical devices are a €30 billion market. Recognising the growing need for international harmonisation of medical device regulatory control, senior government officials and regulated industry representatives in the EU, US, Australia, Canada and Japan are working to harmonise regulations through the medical device Global Harmonization Task Force (GHTF).

The EU has an open medical device regulatory system that is transparent and based upon harmonised standards, and spans all EU Member States. Medical devices sold within the EU must meet the health and safety requirements set forth in the EU medical devices directives. These directives, which are listed below, consolidate EU regulatory requirements under one system, meaning that if the device receives CE designation in one Member State, it can be sold in all EU Member States:

- *Active Implantable Medical Devices Directive (AIMDD)* (90/385/EEC) as amended
- *Medical Devices Directive (MDD)* (93/42/EEC) as amended
- Directive 2001/104/EC[30] amending Council Directive 93/42/EEC
- *In Vitro Diagnostic Devices Directive (IVDD)* (98/79/EC)
- *Clinical Trials Directive* (2001/20/EC)
- *Human Blood and Human Plasma Derivatives Directive* (2000/70/EC)[31]
- *Personal Protective Equipment Directive* (89/686/EEC)
- Directive 2003/12/EC on the reclassification of breast implants in the framework of Directive 93/42/EEC concerning medical devices
- Directive 2003/32/EC introducing detailed specifications regarding requirements laid down in council Directive 93/42/EEC on medical devices manufactured utilising tissues of animal origin
- Directive 2007/47/EC[32] amending Directive 90/385/EEC on the approximation of the laws of the Member States relating to active implantable medical devices, Directive 93/42/EEC concerning medical devices and Directive 98/8/EC concerning the placing of biocidal products on the market

The medical devices directives have been under revision by the European Commission. Directive 2007/47/EC of the European Parliament and of the Council of 5 September 2007 amending Directive 90/385/EEC on the approximation of the laws of the Member States relating to active implantable medical devices (*Active Implantable Medical Devices Directive (AIMDD)*), Directive 93/42/EEC concerning Medical Devices (*Medical Devices Directive (MDD)*) and Directive 98/8/EC concerning the placing of biocidal products on the market, was formally adopted and published on 21 September 2007.[33]

The most significant changes concern, *inter alia*, the expansion of the medical device definition to software products; clarification of the Essential Requirements and Requirements for Design Examinations; provision of a procedure of Scientific Advice on substance quality and safety for borderline products; conformity procedure and review of the validity of existing classifications; and clinical evaluation.

Moreover, in certain cases, additional regulations apply; for example, the statements on devices for special purposes required by Annex VIII of the *MDD* must also conform to regulations governing the field of human blood derivatives. However, the *In Vitro Diagnostic Medical Devices Directive (IVDD)*, Directive 98/79/EC, is not affected by Directive 2007/47/EC.

The new directive's key regulatory environment elements are:

- Legislative harmonisation is limited to essential requirements that devices must meet.
- Device technical specifications must meet the Essential Requirements. Harmonised standards can help determine conformance with these requirements. The application of harmonised or other standards remains voluntary, and the manufacturer may always apply other technical specifications to meet the requirements.

Although this directive does not apply to blood products, plasma or blood cells of human origin, or to human tissue-engineered products as such, provision has been made to bring devices with an ancillary human tissue-engineered product within its scope. This completes the *Regulation on Advanced Therapy Medicinal Products*[34] and thereby avoids a regulatory gap.

Member States adopted the laws, regulations and administrative provisions necessary to comply with this directive by 21 December 2008; it was implemented 21 March 2010.

To make the New Approach function reliably, conformity assessment conditions must build confidence through competence and transparency. Member States' obligation to ensure that only devices that do not endanger public safety and health or affect other public interests are placed on the market also entails market surveillance responsibility.

Essential Requirements are set forth in annexes to the directives and include all criteria necessary to achieve a directive's objective. When the manufacturer has not (or has only partially) applied national standards that incorporate harmonised standards, the measures taken and their adequacy must be documented to comply with the essential requirements.

Medical devices must fulfil the corresponding directive's Essential Requirements. They should provide patients, users and third parties with a high level of protection and attain the performance levels the manufacturer has ascribed to them. The Essential Requirements and other conditions, including those intended to minimise or reduce risk, must be interpreted and applied to take into account technology and practices in use at the time of design, as well as technical and economic considerations compatible with a high level of health and safety protection.

Before a manufacturer places a device on the Community market, the product must be subjected to the Conformity Assessment Procedure denoted in the applicable directive, with a view to affixing the CE Mark. For some device categories, third-party conformity assessment is carried out by so-called Notified Bodies, which have been designated by the Member States as fulfilling directive requirements and being established in their territory. Notified Bodies are public institutes or private companies; they are not Competent Authorities.

Devices in compliance with all of the directives' provisions concerning CE marking may bear the CE Mark. The mark is an indication that the products meet the essential requirements of applicable directives, have undergone a Conformity Assessment Procedure and, hence, may be placed on the market.

Member States are required to incorporate the directives' provisions into their national legislation. Five-year transition periods are typical. The Member States also must inform the Commission of measures taken. Member States must permit products that comply with regulations in force in their territory to be marketed when a directive is implemented.

For Conformity Assessment Procedures, medical devices are grouped into four product classes. The classification rules are based upon the human body's vulnerability and take into account potential risks associated with the device's technical design and manufacture. Manufacturers can carry out Conformity Assessment Procedures for Class I devices. However Class I devices that are sold in a sterile condition and devices that have a measuring function require the involvement of a Notified Body. Devices falling into Classes IIa, IIb and III, which have a high risk potential, require design and manufacture inspection by a Notified Body. Class III is set aside for the riskiest devices; explicit prior conformity authorisation is required before Class III devices can be placed on the market. Interestingly, hip, knee and shoulder joint replacements were reclassified as Class III devices by Directive 2005/50/EC. Reclassification by derogation to the classification rules set out in Annex IX to Directive 93/42/EEC is indicated where the shortcomings identified due to a product's specific characteristics will be more properly addressed under the Conformity Assessment Procedures corresponding to the new category.

Pursuant to Directive 2003/12/EC, breast implants also were reclassified as Class III medical devices.

Medical devices must bear the CE Mark to indicate their conformity with the provisions of the medical devices directives to enable them to move freely within the Community and be put into service in accordance with their intended purpose.

MEDDEV guidance documents are developed by representatives of the national Competent Authorities, European Commission, industry and other partners. The guidelines promote a common approach by the Competent Authorities charged with implementing the medical devices directives, as incorporated into national law. The guidelines are not legally binding. Because interested parties and Competent Authorities' experts participate in the development process, it is anticipated that these guidelines will be followed within the Member States and, therefore, ensure uniform application of relevant directive provisions.

Developments in both the US FDA's GMP regulations and the EU medical devices directives are part of a movement toward harmonising regulatory processes and requirements in an effort to diminish trade barriers. The EU and FDA have adopted a harmonised international management system standard for design, control and manufacturing (i.e., ISO 13485, which has minor variations in the US and EU).

Mutual Recognition Agreements (MRAs) between the EU and the US, Canada, Australia, New Zealand and Switzerland provide an improved way for foreign medical device manufacturers to enter the European market. The US/EU MRA began in 1998 with a three-year transition that was viewed as a "confidence-building" period. Its operational phase was postponed in 2002 when FDA and European regulators extended the medical device transition period for another two years to enable both sides to complete verification of conformity assessment bodies (CABs). This agreement recognises that certain CABs in the US can conduct product approval reviews and quality system evaluations that meet European regulatory requirements and are equivalent to those conducted by the EU. Similarly, the agreement recognises that EU CABs can conduct preliminary product approval reviews for listed medical devices and evaluations according to FDA requirements.

Funding of public health and health insurance programs relating directly or indirectly to devices is not subject to the regulations. Interpretation of EU legislation may vary in practice, as may the economic situation in Member States. Moreover, national authorities have an exclusive right to regulate many areas that directly or indirectly affect medical technology and device development—particularly reimbursing medical treatment expenses, encouraging research and development, and promoting patient access to new medical breakthroughs.

Blood Derivatives

In 2000, an amendment to the *MDD* through Directive 2000/70/EC passed the decision-making process. This amendment extended the *MDD*'s scope to include devices that incorporate stable derivates of human blood or blood products. Later, a mistranscription was found in the wording agreed to by the Council. To avoid confusion in interpreting the provisions, a new directive, 2001/104/EC, amending Council Directive 93/42/EEC, was published in the *Official Journal of the European Union* on 10 January 2002.

In 2003, Directive 2002/98/EC increased the quality

and safety requirements for human blood and blood components, also influencing blood derivative manufacturing. The directive set quality and safety standards for the collection, testing, processing, storage and distribution of human blood and blood components. The directive established a system that ensures traceability of blood and blood components through accurate donor, patient and laboratory identification procedures, record maintenance and an appropriate identification and labelling system. It also introduced surveillance procedures to collect and evaluate information on adverse or unexpected events or reactions resulting from the collection of blood or blood components to prevent similar or equivalent events or reactions.

Directive 2004/33/EC[35] implemented Directive 2002/98/EC regarding certain technical requirements for blood and blood components. Directive 2005/61/EC[36] and Directive 2005/62/EC[37] implemented Directive 2002/98/EC concerning traceability requirements and notification of serious adverse reactions and events, as well as Community standards and specifications relating to a quality system for blood collection establishments.

Cosmetics

In the early 1970s, the EU Member States decided to harmonise their national cosmetic regulations to enable the free circulation of cosmetic products within the European Community. After numerous discussions among experts from all Member States, Directive 76/768/EEC[38] was adopted in July 1976. The principles set forth in the *Cosmetics Directive* take into account the consumer's needs while encouraging commercial exchange and eliminating barriers to trade. One of the directive's main objectives was to give clear guidance on the requirements a safe cosmetic product must meet in order to freely circulate within the EU without national marketing authorisations. Cosmetic product safety relates to composition, packaging and information, which are the responsibility of the producer or EU importer, as is marketing liability. There are no cosmetic product premarket controls. Cosmetic product control within the EU, including a simple manufacturing and importing site notification and an in-market surveillance system, is the responsibility of the entity that places the product on the market.

Directive 95/17/EC[39] set forth detailed rules for the application of the basic *Cosmetics Directive* of 1976. The basic directive has already undergone several amendments and adaptations in response to technical progress.

Since its adoption, Directive 76/768/EEC has been amended several times; e.g., the sixth amendment (Directive 2003/15/EC[40]) provided, *inter alia,* more-detailed provisions on phasing out animal testing and introduced the "period-after-opening labelling." Moreover, the directive has been subject to numerous adaptations to adjust annex provisions to technical progress, for example, Directive

2005/80/EC.[41] The last amendments for the purpose of adapting Annexes II, III, IV and V to technical progress were the Commission Directives 2006/65/EC,[42] 2006/78/EC,[43] 2007/1/EC,[44] 2007/17/EC,[45] 2007/22/EC,[46] 2007/53/EC[47] and 2007/54/EC.[48]

The *Cosmetics Directive* has been recast into a regulation. On 30 November 2009, the new *Cosmetic Products Regulation,* Regulation (EC) No 1223/2009 of the European Parliament and of the Council of 30 November 2009 on cosmetic products, was adopted, replacing the *Cosmetics Directive.* The aim of the recast was a robust, internationally recognised regime that reinforces product safety, taking into consideration the latest technological developments, including the possible use of nanomaterials. Most of the provisions of this new regulation will be applicable from 11 July 2013.[49]

Food and Dietary Products

On 28 January 2002, the European Parliament and the Council adopted Regulation (EC) No 178/2002 laying down the general principles and requirements of food law.[50] Food and dietary supplements are also governed by this regulation.

The European Commission's horizontal legislation initially focused on additives, colours and materials intended to come into contact with foodstuffs. Directive 89/107/EEC addressed the approximation of Member States' laws concerning food additives authorised for use in foodstuffs intended for human consumption.

In 2000, Directive 2000/13/EC[51] combined all previous directives on foodstuff labelling. The directive was amended by Directive 2001/101/EC[52] on the approximation of the laws of the Member States relating to the labelling, presentation and advertising of foodstuffs, by Directive 2003/89/EC[53] as regards indication of the ingredients present in foodstuffs and by Directives 2006/107/EC[54] and 2006/142/EC.[55]

Two years later, Directive 2002/46/EC,[56] regulating food supplements, was adopted. Annex II to this directive has been amended by Directive 2006/37/EC[57] regarding the inclusion of certain substances.

In addition, several directives describe specific policies. Foods resulting from technological innovations as well as baby foods, sweeteners and dietary foods are subject to Commission regulations and directives. For example, European Council Directive 89/398/EEC concerns foodstuffs that, owing to their special composition or manufacturing process, are clearly distinguishable from foodstuffs for normal consumption. Such foodstuffs intended for particular nutritional uses are suitable for their claimed nutritional purposes and can be marketed in such a way as to indicate such suitability. These products may be characterised as "dietetic" or "dietary." Foodstuffs for normal consumption may not use the adjectives "dietetic" or "dietary" in labelling, presentation or advertising.

Following a series of food scares in the 1990s, the European Food Safety Agency (EFSA) was established. Provisionally organised in Brussels in 2002, it has been located in Parma, Italy, since 2003. EFSA deals with all matters related to food and feed safety, scientific advice on nutrition in relation to Community legislation and communication with the public.

In July 2003, the EU Council of Ministers formally adopted two European Commission proposals on genetically modified organisms (GMOs). The proposals establish a clear EU system for tracing and labelling GMOs (Regulation 1830/2003/EC) and for regulating the marketing and labelling of food and feed products derived from GMOs (Regulation 1829/2003/EC[58]).

More information can be found at http://ec.europa.eu/food/food/foodlaw/traceability/index_en.htm.

Future Issues

Healthcare regulations must balance the interests of patients, manufacturers, authorities, insurance companies and others in a fast-moving and complex environment. In Europe, the mechanisms for healthcare product review and approval must be robust enough to ensure patient safety throughout the Community. Those mechanisms, however, must be efficient and balance safety considerations with the need to make new therapeutics available to the public in a timely manner.

Advances in such novel therapies as cell technologies, tissue engineering and gene therapy led to a new proposal for a regulation by the European Parliament and Council on advanced therapy medicinal products. This proposal was adopted by the European Commission on 16 November 2005. It resolved the regulatory gap involving these innovative technologies by addressing such therapy products within a single, integrated and tailored framework. It covers the harmonisation and facilitation of market access and improves advanced therapy product safety by establishing a premarketing approval requirement.

Product classifications as we know them today (drugs, devices and biologics) are being redefined to include new technologies such as gene replacement therapy and the use of agricultural products as biofactories to produce human proteins.

Third-party inspections and self-certification programs may become more common and inspection standards will be harmonised globally. MRAs will increasingly allow nations' sovereignty over local industry to eclipse inspection by foreign regulatory authorities as the move toward transparency continues.

Biological research will partially fulfil its promise. The resulting new products, services and information will challenge current regulatory systems and push industry and

authorities into new discussions and debates concerning risks. New ethical and moral benchmarks will guide risk management. Oversight must continue to evolve as health and risk management knowledge expands, and as power and influence are redistributed within the global regulatory system.

Medical device regulations were revised by Directive 2007/47/EC. The growing number of medical devices on the market and the expansion of the EU have led to an increased need to coordinate activities of national authorities related to the *MDD* (93/42/EEC), involving a number of Member States and/or third countries. The majority of this directive's amendments are intended to clarify the process of bringing medical devices to market and monitoring them. Additionally, they seek to close certain gaps and update the framework for dealing with new developments, such as the increasing importance of software in medical devices. Moreover, safety is enhanced through the emphasis on clinical evaluation documentation included in the file, which Notified Bodies must now evaluate.

It remains to be seen whether the new *MDD* will indeed improve the safety of medical devices for users while ensuring the free movement of goods in the European Union, or if it simply means additional work for manufacturers.

References

1. Directive 2003/32/EC of 23 April 2003 introducing detailed specifications as regards the requirements laid down in Council Directive 93/42/EEC with respect to medical devices manufactured utilising tissues of animal origin.
2. European Commission, Eudralex. *The Rules Governing Medicinal Products in the European Union* (European Commission, April 1998).
3. Directive 65/65/EEC of 26 January 1965 on the approximation of provisions laid down by law, regulation or administrative action relating to medicinal products.
4. Directive 91/356/EEC of 13 June 1991 laying down the principles and guidelines of good manufacturing practice for medicinal products for human use.
5. Directive 2001/83/EC of the European Parliament and of the Council of 6 November 2001 on the Community code relating to medicinal products for human use.
6. Directive 2002/98/EC of the European Parliament and of the Council of 27 January 2003 setting standards of quality and safety for the collection, testing, processing, storage and distribution of human blood and blood components and amending Directive 2001/83/EC.
7. Directive 2003/63/EC of 25 June 2003 amending Directive 2001/83/EC of the European Parliament and of the Council on the Community code relating to medicinal products for human use (replacing Annex 1).
8. Directive 2004/24/EC of the European Parliament and of the Council of 31 March 2004 amending,

as regards traditional herbal medicinal products, Directive 2001/83/EC on the Community code relating to medicinal products for human use.

9. Directive 2004/27/EC of the European Parliament and of the Council of 31 March 2004 amending Directive 2001/83/EC on the Community code relating to medicinal products for human use.

10. Regulation (EC) 1901/2006 of the European Parliament and of the Council of 12 December 2006 on medicinal products for paediatric use and amending Regulation (EEC) 1768/92, Directive 2001/20/EC, Directive 2001/83/EC and Regulation (EC) 726/2004.

11. Regulation (EC) 1394/2007 of the European Parliament and of the Council of 13 November 2007 on advanced therapy medicinal products and amending Directive 2001/83/EC and Regulation (EC) 726/2004.

12. Regulation (EC) 726/2004 of the European Parliament and of the Council of 31 March 2004 laying down Community procedures for the authorisation and supervision of medicinal products for human and veterinary use and establishing a European Medicines Agency.

13. Commission Directive 2003/94/EC of 8 October 2003 laying down the principles and guidelines of good manufacturing practice in respect of medicinal products for human use and investigational medicinal products for human use.

14. Directive 2001/20/EC of the European Parliament and of the Council of 4 April 2001 on the approximation of the laws, regulations and administrative provisions of the Member States relating to the implementation of good clinical practice in the conduct of clinical trials on medicinal products for human use.

15. Council Regulation (EEC) 2309/93 of 22 July 1993 laying down Community procedures for the authorisation and supervision of medicinal products for human and veterinary use and establishing a European Agency for the Evaluation of Medicinal Products.

16. Regulation (EC) 726/2004 of the European Parliament and of the Council of 31 March 2004 laying down Community procedures for the authorisation and supervision of medicinal products for human and veterinary use and establishing a European Medicines Agency.

17. Regulation (EC) 141/2000 of the European Parliament and of the Council of 16 December 1999 on orphan medicinal products.

18. Commission Regulation (EC) 1084/2003 of 3 June 2003 concerning the examination of variations to the terms of a marketing authorisation for medicinal products for human use and veterinary medicinal products granted by a competent authority of a Member State.

19. Council Directive 89/342/EEC of 3 May 1989 extending the scope of Directives 65/65/EEC and 75/319/EEC and laying down additional provisions for immunological medicinal products consisting of vaccines, toxins or serums and allergens.

20. Directive 2001/18/EC of the European Parliament and of the Council of 12 March 2001 on the deliberate release into the environment of genetically modified organisms and repealing Council Directive 90/220/EEC.

21. Regulation (EC) 1830/2003 of the European Parliament and of the Council of 22 September 2003 concerning the traceability and labelling of genetically modified organisms and the traceability of food and feed products produced from genetically modified organisms and amending Directive 2001/18/EC.

22. Council Directive 81/851/EEC of 28 September 1981 on the approximation of the laws of the Member States relating to veterinary medicinal products.

23. Directive 2001/82/EC of the European Parliament and of the Council of 6 November 2001 on the Community code relating to veterinary medicinal products.

24. Directive 2004/28/EC of the European Parliament and of the Council of 31 March 2004 amending Directive 2001/82/EC on the Community code relating to veterinary medicinal products.

25. Commission Directive 2006/130/EC of 11 December 2006 implementing Directive 2001/82/EC of the European Parliament and of the Council as regards the establishment of criteria for exempting certain veterinary medicinal products for food-producing animals from the requirement of a veterinary prescription.

26. Commission Directive 2009/9/EC of 10 February 2009 amending Directive 2001/82/EC of the European Parliament and of the Council on the Community code relating to medicinal products for veterinary use

27. Commission Regulation (EC) 1950/2006 of 13 December 2006 establishing, in accordance with Directive 2001/82/EC of the European Parliament and of the Council on the Community code relating to veterinary medicinal products, a list of substances essential for the treatment of equidae.

28. Council Directive 90/385/EEC of 20 June 1990 on the approximation of the laws of the Member States relating to active implantable medical devices.

29. Council Directive 93/42/EEC of 14 June 1993 concerning medical devices.

30. Directive 2001/104/EC of the European Parliament and of the Council of 7 December 2001 amending Council Directive 93/42/EEC concerning medical devices.

31. Directive 2000/70/EC of 16 November 2000 amending Council Directive 93/42/EEC as regards

medical devices incorporating stable derivates of human blood or human plasma.

32. Directive 2007/47/EC of the European Parliament and of the Council of 5 September 2007 amending Council Directive 90/385/EEC on the approximation of the laws of the Member States relating to active implantable medical devices, Council Directive 93/42/EEC concerning medical devices and Directive 98/8/EC concerning the placing of biocidal products on the market.

33. Directive 2007/47/EC of the European Parliament and of the Council of 5 September 2007 amending Council Directive 90/385/EEC on the approximation of the laws of the Member States relating to active implantable medical devices, Council Directive 93/42/EEC concerning medical devices and Directive 98/8/EC concerning the placing of biocidal products on the market.

34. Regulation (EC) 1394/2007 of the European Parliament and of the Council of 13 November 2007 on advanced therapy medicinal products and amending Directive 2001/83/EC and Regulation (EC) 726/2004.

35. Commission Directive 2004/33/EC of 22 March 2004 implementing Directive 2002/98/EC of the European Parliament and of the Council as regards certain technical requirements for blood and blood components.

36. Commission Directive 2005/61/EC of 30 September 2005 implementing Directive 2002/98/EC of the European Parliament and of the Council as regards traceability requirements and notification of serious adverse reactions and events.

37. Commission Directive 2005/62/EC of 30 September 2005 implementing Directive 2002/98/EC of the European Parliament and of the Council as regards Community standards and specifications relating to a quality system for blood establishments.

38. Council Directive 76/768/EEC of 27 July 1976 on the approximation of the laws of the Member States relating to cosmetic products.

39. Commission Directive 95/17/EC of 19 June 1995 laying down detailed rules for the application of Council Directive 76/768/EEC as regards the non-inclusion of one or more ingredients on the list used for the labelling of cosmetic products.

40. Directive 2003/15/EC of the European Parliament and of the Council of 27 February 2003 amending Council Directive 76/768/EEC on the approximation of the laws of the Member States relating to cosmetic products.

41. Commission Directive 2005/80/EC of 21 November 2005 amending Council Directive 76/768/EEC, concerning cosmetic products, for the purposes of adapting Annexes II and III thereto to technical progress.

42. Commission Directive 2006/65/EC of 19 July

2006 amending Council Directive 76/768/EEC, concerning cosmetic products, for the purpose of adapting Annexes II and III thereto to technical progress.

43. Commission Directive 2006/78/EC of 29 September 2006 amending Council Directive 76/768/EEC, concerning cosmetic products, for the purposes of adapting Annex II thereto to technical progress.

44. Commission Directive 2007/1/EC of 29 January 2007 amending Council Directive 76/768/EEC, concerning cosmetic products, for the purposes of adapting Annex II thereof to technical progress.

45. Commission Directive 2007/17/EC of 22 March 2007 amending Council Directive 76/768/EEC, concerning cosmetic products, for the purposes of adapting Annexes III and VI thereto to technical progress.

46. Commission Directive 2007/22/EC of 17 April 2007 amending Council Directive 76/768/EEC, concerning cosmetic products, for the purposes of adapting Annexes IV and VI thereto to technical progress.

47. Commission Directive 2007/53/EC of 29 August 2007 amending Council Directive 76/768/EEC concerning cosmetic products for the purposes of adapting Annex III thereto to technical progress.

48. Commission Directive 2007/54/EC of 29 August 2007 amending Council Directive 76/768/EEC, concerning cosmetic products, for the purpose of adapting Annexes II and III thereto to technical progress.

49. Regulation (EC) No 1223/2009 of the European Parliament and of the Council of 30 November 2009 on cosmetic products (recast).

50. Regulation (EC) No 178/2002 of the European Parliament and of the Council of 28 January 2002 laying down the general principles and requirements of food law, establishing the European Food Safety Authority and laying down procedures in matters of food safety.

51. Directive 2000/13/EC of the European Parliament and of the Council of 20 March 2000 on the approximation of the laws of the Member States relating to the labelling, presentation and advertising of foodstuffs.

52. Commission Directive 2001/101/EC of 26 November 2001 amending Directive 2000/13/EC of the European Parliament and of the Council on the approximation of the laws of the Member States relating to the labelling, presentation and advertising of foodstuffs.

53. Directive 2003/89/EC of the European Parliament and of the Council of 10 November 2003 amending Directive 2000/13/EC as regards indication of the ingredients present in foodstuffs.

54. Council Directive 2006/107/EC of 20 November 2006 adapting Directive 89/108/EEC relating to

quick-frozen foodstuffs for human consumption and Directive 2000/13/EC of the European Parliament and of the Council relating to the labelling, presentation and advertising of foodstuffs, by reason of the accession of Bulgaria and Romania.

55. Commission Directive 2006/142/EC of 22 December 2006 amending Annex IIIa of Directive 2000/13/EC of the European Parliament and of the Council listing the ingredients which must under all circumstances appear on the labelling of foodstuffs.

56. Directive 2002/46/EC of the European Parliament and of the Council of 10 June 2002 on the approximation of the laws of the Member States relating to food supplements.

57. Commission Directive 2006/37/EC of 30 March 2006 amending Annex II to Directive 2002/46/EC of the European Parliament and of the Council as regards the inclusion of certain substances.

58. Regulation (EC) 1829/2003 of the European Parliament and of the Council of 22 September 2003 on genetically modified food and feed.

The European Medical Devices Legal System

By Mika Reinikainen

OBJECTIVES

❏ Gain insight into the European legislative process

❏ Understand the basic legal requirements for medical devices

❏ Become aware of the available guidance concerning the requirements for medical devices

LAWS, REGULATIONS AND GUIDANCE COVERED IN THIS CHAPTER

❏ Consolidated versions of the *Treaty on European Union* and the *Treaty on the functioning of the European Union*

❏ Decision No 768/2008/EC of the European Parliament and of the Council of 9 July 2008 on a common framework for the marketing of products, and repealing Council Decision 93/465/EEC

❏ Regulation (EC) No 765/2008 of the European Parliament and of the Council of 9 July 2008 setting out the requirements for accreditation and market surveillance relating to the marketing of products and repealing Regulation (EEC) No 339/93

❏ Council Directive 90/385/EEC of 20 June 1990 on the approximation of the laws of the Member States relating to active implantable medical devices

❏ Council Directive 93/42/EEC of 14 June 1993 concerning medical devices

❏ Directive 98/79/EC of the European Parliament and of the Council of 27 October 1998 on *in vitro* diagnostic medical devices

❏ Commission Decision of 19 April 2010 on the European Databank on Medical Devices (Eudamed) (2010/227/EU)

❏ Commission Decision of 7 May 2002 on common technical specifications for *in vitro* diagnostic medical devices (2002/364/EC)

❏ Commission Decision of 27 November 2009 amending Decision 2002/364/EC on common technical specifications for in vitro diagnostic medical devices (2009/886/EC)

❏ Commission Directive 2005/50/EC of 11 August 2005 on the reclassification of hip, knee and shoulder joint replacements in the framework of Council Directive 93/42/EEC concerning medical devices

❏ Commission Directive 2003/12/EC of 3 February 2003 on the reclassification of breast implants in the framework of Directive 93/42/EEC concerning medical devices

❏ Guidance from the Commission in the form of MEDDEV documents, consensus statements and interpretative documents

Table 16-1. European Council Weighted Votes

France	29	Germany	29	Italy	29	United Kingdom	29
Poland	27	Spain	27	Romania	14	Netherlands	13
Belgium	12	Czech Republic	12	Greece	12	Hungary	12
Portugal	12	Austria	10	Bulgaria	10	Sweden	10
Denmark	7	Finland	7	Ireland	7	Lithuania	7
Slovakia	7	Cyprus	4	Estonia	4	Latvia	4
Luxembourg	4	Slovenia	4	Malta	3		

❑ Guidance from the Notified Body Operations Group (NBOG)

Introduction

The European legal system has changed over the years through successive treaties. The last one of these, the *Treaty of Lisbon*, came into force on 1 December 2009. The basic principles of European law can be found in a consolidated version of the *Treaty on European Union* and the *Treaty on the functioning of the European Union,*[1] hereafter the "*Treaty,*" as amended by the *Treaty of Lisbon.*

Although the EU has many institutions similar to those of a sovereign state, its legal nature is nevertheless very different. Its members retain much more sovereignty than would be the case in a federation such as the US. These differences can be best understood in the context of the European legislative process and the interplay between European and national law.

Legislative Process

Article 288 of the *Treaty* defines the legal acts used in the EU. Regulations, directives and decisions are legally binding, whereas recommendations and opinions are not.

A "regulation" is directly applicable in all Member States.

A "directive" must be transposed into national law and administrative provisions. The Member State is free to decide on the nature and contents of the texts adopted

Table 16-2. New Approach Areas

Reference	Products Covered
87/404/EEC	Simple pressure vessels
88/378/EEC	Toys
89/106/EEC	Construction products
89/686/EEC	Personal protective equipment
90/384/EEC	Non-automatic weighing instruments
90/385/EEC	Active implantable medical devices
90/396/EEC	Appliances burning gaseous fuels
92/42/EEC	Hot-water boilers fired with liquid or gaseous fuels
93/15/EEC	Explosives for civil uses
93/42/EEC	Medical devices
94/9/EC	Equipment and protective systems intended for use in potentially explosive atmospheres
94/25/EC	Recreational craft
94/62/EC	Packaging and packaging waste
95/16/EC	Lifts
97/23/EC	Pressure equipment
98/79/EC	In vitro diagnostic medical devices
1999/5/EC	Radio equipment and telecommunications terminal equipment
2000/9/EC	Cableway installations designed to carry persons
2004/22/EC	Measuring instruments
2004/108/EC	Electromagnetic compatibility
2006/42/EC	Machinery
2006/95/EC	Low voltage equipment

Figure 16-1

The European Medical Devices Legal System

Figure 16-1. EU Legislative Process

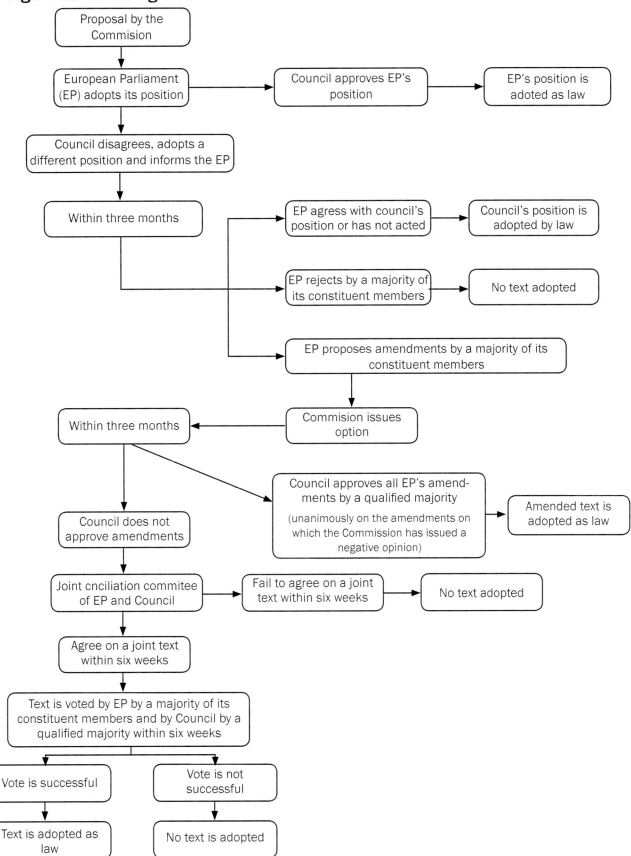

Table 16-3. MEDDEV Guidance Documents

Code	Title	Date
	2.1. Scope field of application definition	
MEDDEV 2.1/1	Definitions of "medical devices," "accessory" and "manufacturer"	April 1994
MEDDEV 2.1/2 rev. 2	Field of application of directive "active implantable medical devices"	April 1994
MEDDEV 2.1/2.1	Field of application of directive "active implantable medical devices	February 1998
MEDDEV 2.1/3 rev. 2	Interface with other directives—medical devices/medicinal products	July 2001
MEDDEV 2.1/3 rev. 3	Borderline products, drug-delivery products and medical devices incorporating, as an integral part, an ancillary medicinal substance or an ancillary human blood derivative—December 2009	December 2009
MEDDEV 2.1/4	Interface with other directives—Medical Devices Directive 89/336/EEC relating to electromagnetic compatibility and dDirective 89/686/EEC relating to personal protective equipment	March 1994
MEDDEV 2.1/5	Medical devices with a measuring function	June 1998
	2.2 Essential Requirements	
MEDDEV 2.2/1 rev. 1	EMC requirements	February 1998
MEDDEV 2.2/3 rev. 3	"Use by" date	June 1998
	2.4 Classification	
MEDDEV 2.4/1 rev. 9	Classification of medical devices	June 2010
	2.5 Conformity assessment procedure	
	General rules	
MEDDEV 2.5/3 rev. 2	Subcontracting quality systems related	June 1998
MEDDEV 2.5/5 rev. 3	Translation procedure	February 1998
MEDDEV 2.5/6 rev. 1	Homogenous batches (verification of manufacturers' products)	February 1998
	Conformity assessment for particular groups of products	
MEDDEV 2.5/7 rev. 1	Conformity assessment of breast implants	July 1998
MEDDEV 2.5/9 rev. 1	Evaluation of medical devices incorporating products containing natural rubber latex	February 2004
	2.7 Clinical investigation, clinical evaluation	
MEDDEV 2.7/1 rev. 3	Clinical evaluation: Guide for manufacturers and notified bodies	December 2009
Appendix 1:	Appendix 1: Clinical evaluation on coronary stents	December 2008
MEDDEV 2.7/2	Guide for Competent Authorities in making an assessment of clinical investigation; notification	December 2008
	2.10 Notified Bodies	
MEDDEV 2.10/2 rev. 1	Designation and monitoring of Notified Bodies within the framework of EC Directives on Medical devices & Annexes 1–4	April 2001
	2.11 Products using materials of biological origin	

MEDDEV 2.11/1 rev. 2	Application of Council Directive 93/42/EEC taking into account the Commission Directive 2003/32/EC for Medical Devices utilising tissues or derivatives originating from animals for which a TSE risk is suspected Annex 1	January 2008
	2.12 Market surveillance	
MEDDEV 2.12/1 rev. 6	Medical devices vigilance system Manufacturer Incident Report; Field Safety Corrective Action	December 2009
MEDDEV 2.12/2	Clinical Evaluation—Postmarket Clinical Follow-up	May 2004
	2.13 Transitional period	
MEDDEV 2.13 rev. 1	Commission Communication on the application of transitional provision of Directive 93/42/EEC relating to medical devices	August 1998
	2.14 IVD	
MEDDEV 2.14/1 rev. 1	Borderline issues	January 2004
MEDDEV 2.14/2 rev. 1	Research Use Only products	February 2004
MEDDEV 2.14/3 rev. 1	Supply of Instructions For Use (IFU) and other information for In-vitro Diagnostic (IVD) Medical Devices	January 2007
	Form for the registration of manufacturers and devices In Vitro Diagnostic Medical Device Directive, Article 10	January 2007
	2.15 Other guidance	
MEDDEV 2.15 rev. 3	Committees/Working Groups contributing to the implementation of the Medical Device Directives	December 2008

nationally, but it must achieve the results intended by the directive. Failure to do so may result in an infringement procedure against the Member State, which may lead to a judgement against it in the Court of Justice of the European Union (CJEU).

A "decision" applies to those to whom it is addressed.

Normally, regulations, directives and decisions are jointly adopted by the European Parliament and the Council based upon a proposal from the European Commission. This legislative procedure is defined in Article 294 of the *Treaty*. These joint acts can be used to delegate to the Commission the power to adopt legally binding acts in specific cases.

The ordinary legislative procedure is illustrated in **Figure 16-1**.

The basis upon which the Council will make its decisions is subject to a transitional period that ends in March 2017.[2]

Until 31 October 2014, for acts of the European Council and of the Council requiring a qualified majority, members' votes shall be weighted as shown in **Table 16-1**.

From 1 November 2014, the qualified majority is defined as at least 55% of the members of the Council, comprising at least 15 of them and representing Member States comprising at least 65% of the population of the EU. A blocking minority must include at least four Council members, failing which the qualified majority shall be deemed attained.

Between 1 November 2014 and 31 March 2017, when an

act is to be adopted by qualified majority, a member of the Council may request that it be adopted in accordance with the qualified majority as defined before 1 November 2014.

The "New Approach" Regulatory Philosophy

Medical device directives are based on the "New Approach" regulatory philosophy. In the early days of the European Communities, product-related directives contained much technical detail. The first directive on medicinal products (drugs)[3] in 1965 is a good example of such an approach and one that is still used for drug legislation.[4]

When the target of 1993 was set for creating a single market, a key challenge was drafting the needed product-oriented directives to eliminate technical barriers to trade. In order to speed this process, it was decided to abandon the approach of detailed technical legislation and use the so-called New Approach to legislation.

Table 16-2 illustrates the areas where the New Approach is used.[5]

All the key medical device directives can be found in this list, as well as some that may be jointly applicable (e.g., machinery).

The European Commission has issued a guidance document that explains the New Approach concepts in greater detail: the *European Commission Guide to the implementation*

Table 16-4. European Commission Consensus Statements

Guidance Notes for Manufacturers of Class I Medical Devices(December 2009)
Guidance Notes for Manufacturers of Custom-made Medical Devices (June 2010)
Guidance Document on Directive 2005/50/EC (December 2006)
IVD Trisomy 21 (December 2006)
IVE Rare Blood Groups (December 2003)

of directives based on the New Approach and the Global Approach (2000).

Key Principles of the "New Approach" Applied to Medical Devices

The following principles are applied in the main medical device directives.

Compliance

- The manufacturer must demonstrate that its products comply with the Essential Requirements. The key objective is to prove that the benefits to the patient outweigh the risks.
- The Essential Requirements are very general in content, but detailed technical explanations are found in voluntary harmonised standards.
- Demonstrated compliance with a harmonised standard creates a presumption of compliance with the corresponding Essential Requirements.

Verification of Compliance

- The manufacturer carries out conformity assessment procedures (technical file, quality systems).
- Depending upon their risk classification, some products and/or quality systems are certified by a Notified Body.

Compliance is attested by affixing the CE marking and by a Declaration of Conformity once the manufacturer is convinced of having achieved compliance.

No Member State can oppose the placing on its market of a CE-marked product unless it has reason to believe that the device is unsafe (principle of safeguard), is a threat to health and safety (precautionary principle) or the CE marking is wrongly affixed (failure to comply with the legal requirements).

It is important to understand that achieving CE marking is, in many cases, just the beginning of compliance, not an end point. Manufacturers have the obligation to monitor and collect information on the experience gained in the use of the device. Adverse incidents must be reported. More importantly, manufacturers must evaluate this usage experience by assessing whether the earlier determination of the risk/benefit relationship is still valid. If it is not, and no corrective action is taken, the CE marking would be invalid and the device would be on the market illegally.

The fundamentals of the New Approach have recently been revised by two key legal texts.[6] Their practical implication for the medical device industry is to tighten the accreditation of Notified Bodies and create special requirements for certain economic operators (distributors, importers and Authorised Representatives). The implementation of the new principles is likely to take several years before the potential of these texts to change the regulatory landscape is exhausted.

Medical Device Laws

The key directives that provide the bulk of European medical device law cover:

- active implantable medical devices (90/385/EEC)[7]

Table 16-5. Interpretive Documents Issued by the European Commission

Interpretation of the Customs Union Agreement with Turkey in the field of medical devices (11 February 2010)
Decision No 1/2006 of the EC-Turkey Association Council of 15 May 2006 on the implementation of Article 9 of Decision No 1/95 of the EC-Turkey Association Council on implementing the final phase of the Customs Union
Statement of Turkey-EC Customs Union Joint Committee on the implementation of Article 1 of Decision 1/2006
Interpretation of the relation between the revised Directives 90/385/EEC and 93/42/EEC concerning (active implantable) medical devices and Directive 2006/42/EC on machinery (21 August 2009)
Interpretation of the relation between the revised Directive 93/42/EEC concerning medical devices and Directive 89/686/EEC on personal protective equipment (21 August 2009)
Interpretative document of the Commission's services implementation of Directive 2007/47/EC amending Directives 90/385/EEC, 9342/EEC and 98/8/EC (5 June 2009)
Interpretation of the medical devices directives in relation to medical device own brand labellers (4 February 2008)

Table 16-6. NBOG Documents

Number	Title	Publication
NBOG BPG 2006-1	Change of Notified Body	November 2008
NBOG BPG 2009-1	Guidance on Design-Dossier Examination and Report Content	March 2009
NBOG BPG 2009-2	Role of Notified Bodies in the Medical Device Vigilance System	March 2009
NBOG BPG 2009-3	Guideline for Designating Authorities to Define the Notification Scope of a Notified Body Conducting Medical Devices Assessment	March 2009
NBOG BPG 2009-4	Guidance on Notified Body's Tasks of Technical Documentation Assessment on a Representative Basis	July 2009
NBOG BPG 2010-1	Guidance for Notified Bodies auditing suppliers to medical device manufacturers	March 2010
NBOG BPG 2010-2	Guidance on Audit Report Content	March 2010
NBOG BPG 2010-3	Certificates issued by Notified Bodies with reference to Council Directives 93/42/EEC, 98/79/EC, and 90/385/EEC	March 2010

NBOG Checklists

Number	Title	Publication
NBOG CL 2010-1	Checklist for audit of Notified Body's review of Clinical Data/Clinical Evaluation	**March 2010**

NBOG Forms

Number	Title	Publication
NBOG F 2009-1	Notification form—Directive 93/42/EEC	December 2009
NBOG F 2009-2	Notification form—Directive 90/385/EEC	August 2009
NBOG F 2009-3	Notification form—Directive 98/79/EC	August 2009
NBOG F 2010-1	Certificate Notification to the Commission and other Member States	March 2010

- medical devices (93/42/EEC)[8]
- in vitro diagnostic medical devices (98/79/EC)[9]

These are supplemented by several additional measures in the form of Commission directives and decisions.

Implementing Legislation
- Eudamed—European Databank on Medical Devices[10]
- Common Technical Specifications on IVDs[11]
- Medical devices manufactured utilising tissues of animal origin

Reclassification
- Reclassification of hip, knee and shoulder joint replacements[12]
- Reclassification of breast implants[13]

Interpretation of Medical Device Law
Interpretation by Courts

The Court of Justice of the European Union (CJEU) provides the ultimate interpretation of European law. At this point, however, there is very little case law to provide significant interpretation in the field of medical devices.

National courts may also interpret national and European medical device law. Occasionally, courts in different Member States may come to different conclusions on similar issues. Such conflicts of interpretation are not automatically brought to the attention of CJEU. At the time of this writing, the author is unaware of any case in which a conflict of interpretation between national court decisions has been brought to CJEU.

If the national court feels uncertain about a point of European law, it can request a preliminary ruling from CJEU.

Commission Guidance

The Commission provides interpretation in the form of guidance (MEDDEV documents),[14] consensus statements[15] and interpretative documents.[16]

The MEDDEV guidance documents are adopted by the Commission's Medical Device Expert Group (MDEG). MDEG is chaired by the Commission and its members are representatives of national Competent Authorities, standardisation bodies, European trade associations and Notified Bodies. MEDDEV documents are not legally binding, but they represent the consensus of the members of MDEG. Often they are prepared by working groups composed of various members of MDEG. The national Competent Authorities, therefore, generally accept compliance with

MEDDEV guidance as indicating compliance with the areas of directives that they cover.

Table 16-3 lists MEDDEV guidances from the Commission's website.[17]

The Commission has also issued statements, prepared by the Commission but endorsed by MDEG, which are listed in **Table 16-4**.

Table 16-5 lists interpretative documents issued by the Commission.

Additional guidance can be found from specific websites of certain MDEG working groups.

The Notified Body Operations Group (NBOG) issues guidance on Notified Bodies (see **Table 16-6**).[18]

The Commission as an Arbitrator

The Commission does not have any clear powers to make decisions in conflicts of interpretation. However, it does provide a forum for building consensus. MEDDEVs and consensus statements are one way of doing this. The Commission also holds closed meetings with representatives of national Competent Authorities where issues of interpretation are discussed. These meetings are confidential, so the outcomes of the discussions usually do not reach the public domain.

There is a quasi-informal process called the "Helsinki procedure." A national Competent Authority can request other national Competent Authorities to provide an opinion on a specific borderline or classification issue. If consensus is not reached in this manner, which is frequently the case, the matter is passed on for consideration to the Commission's Working Group on Classification and Borderline. This group draws its members from MDEG, so it also has representatives of industry and other stakeholders. When consensus is achieved within this group, the results are published in the Manual on Borderline and Classification.[19]

Guidance From Other Sources

Many European stakeholders provide guidance.

Notified Bodies are grouped in the European Association of Notified Bodies for Medical Devices (Team-NB), which issues guidance relevant to the operations of Notified Bodies. Team-NB has issued almost 200 guidance documents that can be found on its website.[20]

Trade associations often issue position papers that, in a sense, can be considered guidance, although there are no guarantees that such opinions would be accepted by Competent Authorities. Eucomed is the most prolific publisher of documents that provide an interesting perspective on European medical device law.[21]

Guidance From Member States

All national Competent Authorities have their own websites that, in most cases, provide links to national laws and regulations as well as guidance and often adverse incident- and enforcement-related information. The vast majority of the information available is in the Member State's national language, but English language content is increasing. The European Commission maintains a list of national Competent Authorities that includes links to the websites of most of them.[22] For the non-linguists, a useful site is that of the UK Competent Authority, the Medicines and Healthcare products Regulatory Agency (MHRA),[23] as it provides a wealth of guidance. However, there is no guarantee that the national Competent Authorities of other Member States would always agree with MHRA on everything.

Significance of Technical Standards

The Essential Requirements and some other requirements of the directives are very general, but for many of them solutions have been provided in harmonised technical standards. Compliance with such standards gives rise to a presumption of compliance with the corresponding requirements of the directives.

The general trend is to adopt international standards developed by the International Organization for Standardization (ISO)[24] and the International Electrotechnical Commission (IEC).[25]

European technical standards are adopted by the European Committee for Standardization (CEN)[26] and the European Committee for Electrotechnical Standardization (Cenelec),[27] if possible based on international standards and otherwise based purely on European work. These standards are made available through the national members of these organisations, e.g., the British Standards Institution.[28]

National Enforcement

The European Commission has no enforcement powers with respect to compliance with the medical device directives. Member States are responsible for enforcement, as stated, for instance, in Article 2 of Directive 93/42/EEC:

"Article 2 Placing on the market and putting into service Member States shall take all necessary steps to ensure that devices may be placed on the market and/or put into service only if they comply with the requirements laid down in this Directive when duly supplied and properly installed, maintained and used in accordance with their intended purpose."

Each Member State is free to carry out enforcement in the medical device area as it deems best. The texts transposing the requirements of the European directives into national law often set out how enforcement will be carried out and the penalties for violations of the law.

In practice, it is clear that many national Competent Authorities have only limited resources to carry out market surveillance and enforcement: for instance, Luxembourg cannot expend the same effort as France. Even the major Member States do not have unlimited resources. Market surveillance and enforcement efforts, therefore, tend to be more reactive than systematic. Adverse incidents and complaints by competitors tend to trigger action by national Competent Authorities. New information released by the US Food and Drug Administration or other non-European authorities may also be acted upon. In addition, there is increased interaction between the Member States, e.g., monitoring one another's websites and profiting from contacts made at European Competent Authority and expert meetings.

Evolution of the Legal System

The *Medical Devices Directive* was amended five times between 1993 and 2007. Most of the significant changes have been based on a better understanding of medical device safety and compliance dynamics. For instance, the role of clinical evaluation has increased considerably and more pressure has been put on the Notified Bodies to be stricter in their certification and periodic audits.

More effort is expended in trying to understand the impact of accelerating technological development on the regulatory framework. The Commission has set up a New & Emerging Technology Working Group to scan developments that might challenge the regulatory framework. The initial focus was on nanotechnology but, more recently, there has been a new focus on other potentially revolutionary technologies such as optogenetics and synthetic biology.

It is possible that the initiative taken by the Commission to recast the regulatory system for medical devices may bring about very significant changes around 2015. However, it is likely that the fundamentals will not change.

Summary

European laws are proposed by the Commission and debated and adopted by the Council (representing the Member State governments) and the European Parliament (representing the citizens). They take the form of directly applicable decisions and regulations as well as directives which must be transposed into national law.

Medical devices are mostly regulated by means of New Approach directives. These contain very general requirements that are explained in detail in harmonised technical standards. Compliance is denoted by CE marking, which allows the device to be placed on the market in all EU Member States and some other countries that have specific agreements with the EU.

A significant amount of guidance has been issued by the Commission and other key players. Competent Authorities of Member States are responsible for enforcing compliance. These enforcement actions as well as national court decisions provide further interpretation of the law. Ultimate

responsibility for interpretation of the law rests with the Court of Justice of the European Union.

References

1. The consolidated versions of these texts can be found at http://eur-lex.europa.eu/LexUriServ/LexUriServ.do?uri=OJ:C:2010:083:FULL:EN:PDF. *Official Journal of the European Union*, Volume 53. 30 March 2010. Eur-Lex website. Accessed 18 November 2010.
2. See protocol (no 36) on transitional provisions of the *Treaty.* European Commission website. Accessed 23 December 2010.
3. Council Directive 65/65/EEC of 26 January 1965 on the approximation of provisions laid down by law, regulation or administrative action relating to medicinal products.
4. Directive 2001/83/EC of the European Parliament and of the Council of 6 November 2001 on the Community code relating to medicinal products for human use.
5. Adapted from "New Approach Standardisation in the Internal Market" at http://www.newapproach.org/Directives/DirectiveList.asp. European Commission website. Accessed 18 November 2010.
6. Decision No 768/2008/EC of the European Parliament and of the Council of 9 July 2008 on a common framework for the marketing of products, and repealing Council Decision 93/465/EEC and Regulation (EC) No 765/2008 of the European Parliament and of the Council of 9 July 2008 setting out the requirements for accreditation and market surveillance relating to the marketing of products and repealing Regulation (EEC) No 339/93.
7. Council Directive of 20 June 1990 on the approximation of the laws of the Member States relating to active implantable medical devices (90/385/EEC). Eur-lex website. http://eur-lex.europa.eu/LexUriServ/LexUriServ.do?uri=CONSLEG:1990L0385:20071011:en:PDF. Accessed 18 November 2010.
8. Council Directive 93/42/EEC of 14 June 1993 concerning medical devices. Eur-lex website. http://eur-lex.europa.eu/LexUriServ/LexUriServ.do?uri=CONSLEG:1993L0042:20071011:en:PDF. Accessed 18 November 2010.
9. Directive 98/79/EC of the European Parliament and of the Council of 27 October 1998 on *in vitro* diagnostic medical devices. Eur-lex website. http://eur-lex.europa.eu/LexUriServ/LexUriServ.do?uri=CONSLEG:1998L0079:20090807:en:PDF. Accessed 18 November 2010.
10. Commission Decision of 19 April 2010 on the European Databank on Medical Devices (Eudamed) (2010/227/EU). Eur-lex website. http://eur-lex.europa.eu/LexUriServ/LexUriServ.do?uri=OJ:L:2010:102:0045:0048:en:PDF. Accessed 18 November 2010.

11. Commission Decision of 7 May 2002 on common technical specifications for *in vitro*-diagnostic medical devices (2002/364/EC). Eur-lex website. http://eur-lex.europa.eu/LexUriServ/LexUriServ.do?uri=OJ:L:2002:131:0017:0030:en:PDF and Commission Decision of 27 November 2009 amending Decision 2002/364/EC on common technical specifications for in vitro diagnostic medical devices (2009/886/EC). Eur-lex website. http://eur-lex.europa.eu/LexUriServ/LexUriServ.do?uri=OJ:L:2009:318:0025:0040:en:PDF. Accessed 18 November 2010.

12. Commission Directive 2005/50/EC of 11 August 2005 on the reclassification of hip, knee and shoulder joint replacements in the framework of Council Directive 93/42/EEC concerning medical devices. Eur-lex website. http://eur-lex.europa.eu/LexUriServ/LexUriServ.do?uri=OJ:L:2005:210:0041:0043:en:PDF. Accessed 18 November 2010.

13. Commission Directive 2003/12/EC of 3 February 2003 on the reclassification of breast implants in the framework of Directive 93/42/EEC concerning medical devices. Eur-lex website. http://eur-lex.europa.eu/LexUriServ/LexUriServ.do?uri=OJ:L:2003:028:0043:0044:en:PDF. Accessed 18 November 2010.

14. Guidance MEDDEVs. European Commission website. http://ec.europa.eu/consumers/sectors/medical-devices/documents/guidelines/index_en.htm. European Commission website. Accessed 18 November 2010.

15. Consensus Statements. European Commission website. http://ec.europa.eu/consumers/sectors/medical-devices/documents/consensus-statements/index_en.htm. European Commission website. Accessed 18 November 2010.

16. Interpretative Documents. European Commission website. http://ec.europa.eu/consumers/sectors/medical-devices/documents/interpretative-documents/index_en.htm. European Commission website. Accessed 18 November 2010.

17. Op cit 14.

18. Notified Body Operation Group website. http://www.nbog.eu/2.html. Accessed 18 November 2010.

19. *Manual on Borderline and Classification in the Community, Regulatory Framework for Medical Devices*, Version 1.7 (05-2010). European Commission website. http://ec.europa.eu/consumers/sectors/medical-devices/files/wg_minutes_member_lists/version1_7_borderline_manual_en.pdf. European Commission website. Accessed 18 November 2010.

20. Team-NB public documents. Team-NB website. http://www.team-nb.org/index.php?option=com_docman&task=cat_view&gid=17&Itemid=38. European Association of Notified Bodies for Medical Devices website. Accessed 18 November 2010.

21. Eucomed videos, images and documents. Eucomed website. http://www.eucomed.be/press/downloads.aspx. Eucomed website. Accessed 18 November 2010.

22. List of Contact Points Within the National Competent Authorities. European Commission website. http://ec.europa.eu/consumers/sectors/medical-devices/links/contact_points_en.htm. Accessed 18 November 2010.

23. Medicines and Healthcare products Regulatory Agency website. http://www.mhra.gov.uk/index.htm. Accessed 18 November 2010.

24. International Organization for Standardization website. http://www.iso.org/iso/home.htm. Accessed 18 November 2010.

25. International Electrotechnical Commission website. http://www.iec.ch/. Accessed 18 November 2010.

26. European Committee for Standardization website. http://www.cen.eu/cen/Pages/default.aspx. Accessed 18 November 2010.

27. European Committee for Electrotechnical Standardization website. http://www.cenelec.eu/Cenelec/Homepage.htm. Accessed 18 November 2010.

28. British Standards Institution website. http://www.bsigroup.com/. Accessed 18 November 2010.

Institutional Players on the EU Medical Device Regulatory Scene

By Mika Reinikainen

OBJECTIVES

❏ Gain awareness of the key players on the European regulatory scene

❏ Learn about EU institutions

❏ Understand the roles of the Member States and their Competent Authorities

❏ Gain insight into how industry interacts with institutional players

LAWS, REGULATIONS AND GUIDANCE COVERED IN THIS CHAPTER

❏ Consolidated versions of the *Treaty on European Union* and the *Treaty on the functioning of the European Union*

❏ Decision No 768/2008/EC of the European Parliament and of the Council of 9 July 2008 on a common framework for the marketing of products, and repealing Council Decision 93/465/EEC

❏ Regulation (EC) No 765/2008 of the European Parliament and of the Council of 9 July 2008 setting out the requirements for accreditation and market surveillance relating to the marketing of products and repealing Regulation (EEC) No 339/93

❏ Council Directive 93/42/EEC of 14 June 1993 concerning medical devices

Introduction

The European system within which medical device regulations are issued and applied is very complex. It comprises institutions of the EU, Member States, Notified Bodies, economic operators and various other stakeholders.

EU Institutions

The *Treaty on European Union* (Article 13) recognises seven institutions: the European Parliament, the European Council, the Council, the European Commission, the Court of Justice of the European Union, the European Central Bank and the Court of Auditors. The last two institutions are not directly relevant to the medical device industry and therefore will not be dealt with in this chapter.

The European Council is not to be confused with the Council of the European Union and even less with the Council of Europe.[1]

The European Council (Consilium Europaeum) has as its members the heads of the Members States, who determine overall policy. The Council of the European Union, officially the Council (Consilium) and commonly referred to as the Council of Ministers, has as its members the ministers of the Member States responsible for the specific matter being dealt with.

In terms of the legislative process, the European Commission proposes laws and the European Parliament and the Council adopt them. In terms of a typical structure of a parliamentary democracy, the Commission can be viewed as the EU's executive branch and the Council together with the European Parliament as the bi-cameral legislative arm, where the Council represents the Member States and the Parliament represents the citizens.

Table 17-1. National Representatives in the European Parliament[2]

Germany	96	France	74	United Kingdom	74	Italy	73
Spain	54	Poland	51	Romania	33	Netherlands	26
Belgium	22	Greece	22	Hungary	22	Czech Republic	22
Portugal	22	Sweden	20	Austria	19	Bulgaria	18
Denmark	13	Finland	13	Slovakia	13	Lithuania	12
Ireland	12	Latvia	9	Slovenia	8	Estonia	6
Cyprus	6	Luxembourg	6	Malta	6		

The European Parliament

The European Parliament is elected directly by the citizens of the EU Member States. The number of national representatives is correlated with national population figures (see **Table 17-1**), but there is a bias in favour of the smaller nations; for instance, Germany has one representative for approximately every 860,000 citizens, whereas Malta has one for every 66,000 citizens.

Parliament's powers have been strengthened by the *Lisbon Treaty*, and are as follows:

- Participates in the legislative process (see Chapter 16) and the budgetary process—Although it does not have a power of legislative initiative in these matters, it can block legislation.
- Elects the president of the Commission based upon a proposal from the European Council and may force the resignation of the Commission.[3]
- Plays a supervisory role—it can ask questions of the Commission and set up committees of enquiry.
- Elects an ombudsman who can receive and investigate complaints from any European citizen.[4]

The Council of the European Union

As noted above, the Council's primary role is legislative. The legislative process and the voting system are described in "Chapter 16 The European Medical Devices Legal System."

The preparatory work for the Council is carried out by the Committee of Permanent Representatives[5] (COREPER). The members are permanent representatives of the Member States. In practice, when legislation on medical devices is discussed, the COREPER meeting will include national civil servants responsible for medical devices.

The Council meets in pre-set configurations.[6] Currently these are:

- General Affairs (Genaff)
- Foreign Affairs (Foraff)
- Economic and Financial Affairs (Ecofin)
- Agriculture and Fisheries
- Justice and Home Affairs Council (JHA)

- Employment, Social Policy, Health and Consumer Affairs Council (EPSCO)
- Competitiveness
- Transport, Telecommunications and Energy
- Environment
- Education, Youth and Culture (EYC)

The European Commission

The European Commission is the EU's executive body and is responsible for proposing legislation and implementing decisions and for the general day-to-day running of the Union.[7]

The Commission is led by a president and 26 other commissioners appointed by the European Council and approved by the European Parliament.

The Commission has an administrative body of about 25,000 civil servants working in various directorates-general (DGs) and services (see Annex 1).

The department responsible for medical devices and medicinal products (drugs) is the Directorate-General for Health and Consumer Protection (also known as DG SANCO).[8]

The Commission has responsibility for monitoring the implementation of European law. It can start infringement procedures against a Member State, e.g., for failure to implement a directive. Such an infringement action can also arise from a complaint by an interested party.

However, enforcement of European legal requirements, including those related to medical devices, against enterprises and individuals is the responsibility of the Member States. There is one important exception to the Commission's lack of enforcement powers, namely competition law, where the Commission has significant powers to act.

The Court of Justice of the European Union

The Court[9] has one judge from each Member State and several advocates-general. It deals with alleged violations of European law and legal interpretations. A frequently used procedure is the "preliminary ruling." National courts can request the opinion of the European Court on a point of European law in a case before them. Thus, it would be possible for a case involving a medical device manufacturer challenging a restrictive decision by a national Competent Authority to end up in the Court of Justice of the European Union.

Other EU Agencies
European Medicines Agency

The European Medicines Agency (EMA)[10] is responsible for the scientific evaluation of medicines and thus plays a central role in the approval of pharmaceutical products in the EU. It is also responsible for the Committee for Advanced Therapies (CAT) that deals with advanced therapy medicinal products (e.g., tissue engineering products).

There is no equivalent institution for medical devices in the EU, although the Commission's recast strategy may lead to the creation of a European medical device authority within the next five years or so. It may even be a committee similar to CAT within the EMA structure.

Europol

The European Law Enforcement Agency[11] (Europol) provides analytical and coordinating assistance to combat organised crime across borders, including action against counterfeiting.

Member States and Other Relevant Countries

Member States must transpose the requirements of directives into their national laws and then enforce these requirements. The *Medical Devices Directive* states:

"Member States shall take all necessary steps to ensure that devices may be placed on the market and/or put into service only if they comply with the requirements laid down in this Directive when duly supplied and properly installed, maintained and used in accordance with their intended purpose."[12]

This general responsibility of enforcement also breaks down into specific responsibilities:
- centrally evaluate adverse incidents
- register manufacturers or their Authorised Representatives
- assess clinical trial applications
- act as a Competent Authority for Notified Bodies

The Member States typically carry out this responsibility through a national Competent Authority. Most often, there is a common authority for medicinal products (drugs) and devices (e.g., the Medicines and Healthcare products Regulatory Agency (MHRA) in the UK, Agence française de sécurité sanitaire des produits de santé (Afssaps) in France and the Irish Medicines Board (IMB) in Ireland), although the internal organisation may be split along drug and device lines.

There are very significant differences among the Member States due to availability of resources and historical experience. A small country like Malta or Luxembourg will typically embed the Competent Authority function in an institution that has much wider responsibilities than just medical devices.

Many countries will delegate some Competent Authority responsibilities to a regional level. Often, this is due to a pre-existing federalist approach to administration (e.g., the system of *Länder* in Germany, Autonomous Communities in Spain and cantons in Switzerland). Probably the most complex situation exists in Germany where the 16 *Länder* (states) may further assign responsibilities to the district level. It is estimated that, in reality, the German "Competent Authority" consists of some 80 different administrative units.

There are 27 Member States. To this total must be added the three countries of the European Economic Area (Iceland, Liechtenstein and Norway) that apply the medical device directives. Switzerland and Turkey have specific agreements with the EU that impact medical device regulatory compliance.

A list of these countries and their relevant Competent Authorities as well as their website addresses is provided in **Table 17-2** (the information is given in English and the country's official language(s)).

There are several countries being considered for membership in the EU: Bosnia-Herzegovina, Croatia, FYROM (Former Yugoslav Republic of Macedonia), Kosovo, Serbia and Turkey. Candidate countries often adopt regulations similar to those in the EU.

Notified Bodies (NBs)

NBs are certification organisations. They owe their official name to the fact that they are notified by the Member States to the Commission.

NBs are responsible for assessing manufacturers' compliance with the requirements of European medical device law, attesting to compliance by granting certificates and then monitoring it through periodic audits. The nature of an NB's involvement depends upon the class of the product. For instance, in the case of a Class III device, an NB will examine the product design and audit the quality system. An NB will not get involved in a Class I device unless it is sold sterile and/or has a measuring function, and then its scrutiny is limited to those aspects.

The control of the Member States over the NBs has gradually tightened. This is particularly evident in the New Approach laws issued in 2008[13] that set out specific requirements for the accreditation of NBs.

There are approximately 80 NBs in the EU. Many also have offices outside Europe (e.g., in the US) that carry out audit tasks and sales promotion. Most have prior histories as independent testing houses and a few are government institutions.

The Commission maintains a list of all NBs that also includes information on their areas of competence (http://ec.europa.eu/enterprise/newapproach/nando/).

Table 17-2. EU Member States and Affiliated Countries Competent Authorities

Member State	Competent Authority
Austria Österreich	**Austrian Federal Office for Safety in Health Care** **Medicines and Medical Devices Agency** Federal Ministry of Health Bundesamt für Sicherheit im Gesundheitswesen AGES PharmMed http://www.basg.at/medizinprodukte/
Belgium België/Belgique-	**MDD AIMDD** Federal Agency for Medicines and Health Products (Federaal Agentschap voor Geneesmiddelen en Gezondheidsproducten/ Agence Fédérale des Médicaments et des Produits de Santé) http://www.fagg-afmps.be/ **IVDMD** Scientific Institute Public Health, (Wetenschappelijk Instituut Volksgezondheid/Institut scientifique de Santé Publique) http://www.iph.fgov.be
Bulgaria България	Drug Agency http://www.bda.bg/
Czech Republic Česká republika	State Institute for Drug Control Státní **ústav** pro kontrolu léčiv (SÚKL) http://www.sifdc.eu
Cyprus Κύπρος	Cyprus Medical Devices Competent Authority http://www.moh.gov.cy
Denmark Danmark	Danish Medicines Agency Lægemiddelstyrelsen http://www.medicaldevices.dk
Estonia Eesti	Health Board, Medical Devices Department Terviseamet http://www.terviseamet.ee
Finland Suomi	Valvira - National Supervisory Authority for Welfare and Health Valvira - Sosiaali- ja terveysalan lupa- ja valvontavirasto http://www.valvira.fi/
France	French Health Products Safety Agency Agence française de sécurité sanitaire des produits de santé (AFSSAPS) http://www.afssaps.fr/

Germany Deutschland	Federal Institute for Drugs and Medical Devices Bundesinstitut für Arzneimittel und Medizinprodukte (BfArM) http://www.bfarm.de For some IVD aspects Paul-Ehrlich-Institute Paul-Ehrlich-Institut http://www.pei.de
Greece Ελλάδα	National Organization for Medicines http://eof1.eof.gr
Hungary Magyarország	Medical Device Department, Office of Health Authorisation and Administrative Procedures Orvostechnikai Főosztály, Egészségügyi Engedélyezési **és** Közigazgatási Hivatal http://www.eekh.hu
Ireland *Éire*	Irish Medicines Board Bhord Leigheasra na hÉireann http://www.imb.ie
Italy Italia	Ministry of Health, Directorate General of Medicines and Medical Devices Ministero della Salute Direzione Generale dei Farmaci e Dispositivi Medici http://www.salute.gov.it/dispositivi/dispomed.jsp
Latvia Latvija	State Agency of Medicines Zāļu valsts aģentūra http://www.zva.gov.lv
Lithuania Lietuva	The State Health Care Accreditation Agency under the Ministry of Health Valstybinė akreditavimo sveikatos priežiūros veiklai tarnyba prie Sveikatos apsaugos ministerijos (VASPVT) http://www.vaspvt.gov.lt/
Luxembourg	Health Ministry, Division for Therapeutic Medicine Ministère de la Santé, Division de la Médecine Curative http://www.ms.public.lu
Malta	Consumer and Industrial Goods Directorate Malta Standards Authority Awtorita' Maltija Dwar L-Istandards http://www.msa.org.mt/
Netherlands Nederland	Farmatec (e.g., device registrations) http://www.farmatec.nl Health Care Inspectorate (e.g. clinical investigations, vigilance) Inspectie voor de Gezondheidszorg (IGZ) http://www.igz.nl/
Poland Polska	Office for Registration of Medicinal Products, Medical Devices and Biocidal Products Urząd Rejestracji Produktów Leczniczych, Wyrobów Medycznych i Produktów Biobójczych http://en.urpl.gov.pl/

Portugal	Infarmed - National Authority of Medicines and Health Products INFARMED-Autoridade Nacional do Medicamento e Produtos de Saúde http://www.infarmed.pt
Romania România	Ministry of Health Ministerul Sănătății http://www.ms.ro/
Slovak Republic Slovenská republika	State Institute for Drug Control, Medical Devices Section **Štátny ústav** pre kontrolu liečiv, Sekcia zdravotníckych pomôcok http://www.sukl.sk
Slovenia Slovenija	Agency for Medicinal Products and Medical Devices of the Republic of Slovenia Javna agencija Republike Slovenije za zdravila in medicinske pripomočke – JAZMP http://www.jazmp.si
Spain España	Spanish Agency for Medicines and Medical Devices Agencia Española de Medicamentos y Productos Sanitarios http://www.aemps.es/
Sweden Sverige	Medical Products Agency Läkemedelsverket Web: http://www.lakemedelsverket.se/
United Kingdom	Medicines & Healthcare products Regulatory Agency (MHRA) http://www.mhra.gov.uk
EEA countries	
Iceland Island	Directorate of Health Landlæknisembættið http://www.landlaeknir.is/
Liechtenstein	Office of Public Health Amt für Gesundheit http://www.ag.llv.li/
Norway Norge	Health Directorate Helsedirektoratet http://www.helsedirektoratet.no/
Countries that have agreements with the EU with implications for medical devices	
Switzerland Suisse-Schweitz- Swizzera	Swissmedic – Swiss Agency for Therapeutic Products Institut suisse des produits thérapeutiques Schweizerisches Heilmittelinstitut Istituto svizzero per gli agenti terapeutici http://www.swissmedic.ch
Turkey Türkiye	Ministry of Health General Directorate of Pharmacy and Pharmaceuticals Sağlık Bakanlığı http://www.tibbicihaz.saglik.gov.tr/

The NBs have set up a collective organisation known as NB-MED. The Commission website describes the role of NB-MED:[14]

- to share experience and exchange views on application of conformity assessment procedures with the aim of contributing to a better understanding and consistent application of requirements and procedures
- to draft technical recommendations on matters relating to conformity assessment and build a consensus
- to advise the Commission, at its request, on subjects related to application of the medical device directives
- to consider, and if necessary, draft reports on ethical aspects of Notified Bodies' activities
- to ensure consistency with standardisation work at a European level
- to keep informed of harmonisation activities at a European level

Standardisation Organisations

There are three main standardisation organisations in Europe:

- The European Committee for Standardization (CEN) develops standards related to general compliance and specific nonactive (nonpowered) medical devices. See http://www.cen.eu.
- The European Committee for Electrotechnical Standardization (CENELEC) develops standards on electromedical devices. See http://www.cenelec.eu.
- The European Telecommunications Standards Institute (ETSI) develops standards for information and communications technologies. See http://www.etsi.org.

To the extent possible, international standards of the International Organization for Standardization (ISO) and the International Electrotechnical Commission (IEC) are adopted in Europe.

The Commission publishes lists of harmonised standards that provide a presumption of conformity with the requirements of the directives at http://ec.europa.eu/enterprise/policies/european-standards/documents/harmonised-standards-legislation/list-references/index_en.htm.

Economic Operators

The medical device directives provide definitions of manufacturers and Authorised Representatives and set out requirements for both. They do not mention importers and distributors; these, however, are identified in requirements set out in the texts on the New Approach.

Manufacturers

A "manufacturer" is defined as "the natural or legal person with responsibility for the design, manufacture, packaging and labelling of a device before it is placed on the market under his own name, regardless of whether these operations are carried out by that person himself or on his behalf by a third party"[15]

This definition permits all actual manufacturing operations to be delegated to a third party as long as the "legal manufacturer" retains responsibility and places the products on the market under its own name. This implies that distribution companies that sell third-party manufactured products under their own name may very well be considered legal manufacturers.

It is important to understand that despite the possibility of being able to delegate virtually all manufacturing tasks, the legal manufacturer is ultimately responsible for any noncompliance, even if it arises from the actions or failings of a subcontractor.

Authorised Representatives

An "Authorised Representative" is defined as:
"any natural or legal person established in the Community who, explicitly designated by the manufacturer, acts and may be addressed by authorities and bodies in the Community instead of the manufacturer with regard to the latter's obligations under this Directive"[16]

The exact responsibilities of the Authorised Representative are unclear and there are differences of interpretation among the Member States. These range from believing that the Authorised Representative has the same or similar responsibility for regulatory compliance as the manufacturer to considering the Authorised Representative a mere communications interface between the manufacturer and the Competent Authorities. The practical reality is somewhere between these two extremes. An Authorised Representative cannot fully assume the regulatory responsibilities of the manufacturer because that would imply it has powers of inspection and coercion that the manufacturer would never tolerate. It would also be very expensive for the manufacturer. However, the Authorised Representative must have sufficient regulatory expertise to be able to act on behalf of the manufacturer in compliance matters when so requested. There is also an implied duty to advise the manufacturer about potential noncompliance resulting from the manufacturer's decisions.

As the law stands today, there are no restrictions as to who can be an Authorised Representative. No authorisation is needed and no qualifications are required. Although there are many highly qualified and experienced

Table 17-3. European Commission Working Groups and Their Activities

Closed groups: European Commission services and national Competent Authorities participate (industry and Notified Bodies are normally excluded)

Competent Authority (CA) meetings
Chair: Member State holding the EU presidency
The Member State holding the rotating presidency of the EU traditionally organises a meeting at which the national Competent Authorities of the Member States, candidate countries and EFTA and the European Commission discuss policy issues.

Compliance and Enforcement Group (COEN)
Chair: Sweden
COEN focuses on the scope and coordination of the enforcement activities by Member States and considers how communications and cooperation between Member States can be made more effective and efficient.

Notified Body Operations Group (NBOG)
Chair: Germany
NBOG aims to improve the overall performance of NBs, primarily by identifying and promulgating examples of best practice to be adopted by both NBsand organisations responsible for their designation and control.
It reviews recommendations issued by the NB-MED group (in which all the EU NBs participate) and acts as a "Mirror Group" that follows GHTF work on certification bodies.
An NB representative can be invited to participate as appropriate, depending upon the issue discussed.

Open groups: Members are national Competent Authorities, industry (trade associations), NBs, standardisation bodies and Commission services.

Medical Devices Expert Group (MDEG)
Chair: European Commission
Umbrella group for other working groups in the field that also coordinates and oversees their activities. It adopts MEDDEV guidance documents.
MDEG meets also In closed session (with only Commission representatives and Member State Competent Authorities) to discuss confidential implementation issues.

Vigilance (adverse incidents)
Chair: European Commission
The group develops guidance, discusses actual cases, reviews current reporting practices and prepares input for the Eudamed database. The Vigilance group also acts as the GHTF-Study Group 2 Mirror Group.

Classification and Borderline
Chair: European Commission
The group discusses borderline (is a specific product a medical device?) and classification cases. Often this results in an entry into the Commission's *Manual on Borderline and Classification*.
The group typically uses an "Enquiry Template" to communicate questions to all Member States and gather responses. Responses are collated and presented at the meeting by the Member State originator, including its proposed consensus opinion based upon the responses.

IVD Technical Group
Chair: France
The group supplies to the Commission, MDEG and other working groups technical and specific input, for example by drafting CTS documents, and also provides input on the interpretation and implementation of the *IVDD*.

Working Group on Clinical Investigation and Evaluation (CIE)
Chair: Austria
The group develops and promotes homogenous interpretation and implementation of European requirements on clinical evaluation and investigation, including postmarket clinical follow-up (PMCF). It monitors the EU and international regulatory environment and technical standardisation in the clinical area. It serves as the European Mirror Group for GHTF SG 5.
Electronic Labelling Working Group
Chair: European Commission
It prepares guidance on the safe and appropriate use of electronic Instructions For Use (IFU), including any limitations and safeguards that should be applied. Such guidance will form the basis for possible Community measures on e-labelling.
New & Emerging Technologies Working Group (NET)
Chair: France
The group identifies new and emerging technologies that may challenge the adequacy of existing regulatory requirements for devices. Where shortcomings are identified, the group makes recommendations to MDEG about addressing these challenges by guidance or by regulatory changes. It also informs MDEG about relevant scientific trends.
Eudamed Working Group
Chair: European Commission
The group advises on all issues related to the implementation of the Eudamed database.

Authorised Representatives, there are also many who are not. Often, someone in the supply chain may provide this service, assuming naively that acting as an Authorised Representative is just a formality. The individual's ability to supply the service may quickly collapse the first time he or she receives a query from a Competent Authority relating to the manufacturer's compliance.

A guidance document on authorised representation is currently (2010) under preparation by a working group of the Commission (COEN) and should be adopted in 2011/2012. Although it will not offer any binding solutions to the current uneven quality of services offered, it should provide some clarity about the nature of responsibilities of Authorised Representatives. This will help Authorised Representatives decide whether they should really be in the business and also aid manufacturers in selecting an appropriate Authorised Representative. Perhaps more importantly, it will establish consensus among the Competent Authorities and the economic operators, in turn, creating favourable conditions for elements of the guidance to migrate into legislative proposals.

Importers and Distributors

European medical device law neither provides definitions of importers and distributors nor attributes any role in the compliance system to them. The New Approach texts identify them as economic operators with specific responsibilities, especially in the area of market surveillance, and provide the following definitions:

"'importer' shall mean any natural or legal person established within the Community who places a product from a third country on the Community market;"[17]

"'distributor' shall mean any natural or legal person in the supply chain, other than the manufacturer or the importer, who makes a product available on the market"[18]

The New Approach texts would, in particular, make importers, and to a lesser extent distributors, responsible for verifying that the products they handle are in compliance with European requirements. It is unclear to what extent these requirements are applicable in the medical device field. From a practical point of view, they would need to be implemented by appropriate measures. Some evidence of this can be found in national requirements. One would also expect that when the medical device directives are revised again, the role of the importer and distributor in market surveillance will be considered.

Healthcare Establishments

The medical device directives do not assign any clear responsibilities to healthcare establishments. This area is still regarded as the prerogative of national law. As medical technology becomes more complex, it is increasingly obvious that users have a significant burden of responsibility to learn how to operate, maintain and integrate modern devices into the systems of the healthcare establishment. Another trend is manufacturing of devices by healthcare establishments for their own use. New regulations are emerging in these areas at the national level.

Table 17-4. European Industrial Trade Associations

Trade association	Acronym	Website
European Coordination Committee of the Radiological, Electromedical and Healthcare IT Industry	COCIR	http://www.cocir.org
European Association of Authorised Representatives	EAAR	http://www.eaarmed.org/
European Diagnostic Manufacturers Association	EDMA	http://www.edma-ivd.be/
European Hearing Instrument Manufacturers Association	EHIMA	http://www.ehima.com
Eucomed		http://www.eucomed.be/
European Federation of Precision Mechanical and Optical Industries	EUROM	http://www.eurom.org/
European Federation of National Associations and International Companies of Contact Lens (and Lens Care) Manufacturers	EUROMCONTACT	http://www.euromcontact.org/
Federation of the European Dental Industry	FIDE	http://www.fide-online.org/

Institutional Cooperation and Consensus Building

The national Competent Authorities meet at least twice a year under the chairmanship of the Member State holding the presidency of the European Council (changes every six months).

Working Groups Established by the Commission

The Commission has established several working groups that develop guidance on European compliance requirements and related areas. These are described in Table 17-3.[19]

Representation of the Industry: European Trade Associations

There are many trade associations in Europe. Some are more active than others in the process of developing consensus among the Commission, the Member States, the Notified Bodies and industry regarding interpretation of regulatory requirements. **Table 17-4** lists the industry representatives in MDEG.

Eucomed is the largest of these trade associations and represents all areas of medical device technology except electromedical equipment and in vitro diagnostics. It is a federation of corporate members, European product-specific associations and national associations.

EUROM's membership extends beyond medical device manufacturers, which are placed in a sub-group—the EUROM VI committee.

Summary

The EU is similar in structure to a modern State, with its legislative, executive and judicial branches. However, a significant level of sovereignty is retained by its Member States. The EU also has many agencies, such as EMA.

Member States and their Competent Authorities are responsible for enforcing European medical device law. Independent Notified Bodies verify and certify manufacturers' compliance.

Manufacturers interact with the other players through expert working groups set up by the Commission and through their trade associations, and are thus able to influence the development of consensual interpretation of the law.

Annex I—Commission Services[20]

The Commission is divided into several departments (DGs) and services. This annex classifies each DG according to the policy for which it is responsible. Commission services deal with more-general administrative issues or have a specific mandate, for example fighting fraud or creating statistics.

Policy-specific Services

- Agriculture and Rural Development
- Budget
- Climate Action
- Competition
- Economic and Financial Affairs
- Education and Culture
- Employment, Social Affairs and Equal Opportunities
- Energy
- Enterprise and Industry
- Environment
- Executive agencies
- Home Affairs
- Maritime Affairs and Fisheries

- Mobility and Transport
- Health and Consumers
- Information Society and Media
- Internal Market and Services
- Justice
- Regional Policy
- Research
- Taxation and Customs Union
- Development

External Relations
- Enlargement
- EuropeAid–Co-operation Office
- External Relations
- Humanitarian Aid
- Trade

General Services
- Central Library
- Communication
- European Anti-Fraud Office
- Eurostat
- Historical Archives
- Joint Research Centre
- Publications Office
- Secretariat General

Internal Services
- Bureau of European Policy Advisers
- European Commission Data Protection Officer
- Human Resources and Security
- Informatics
- Infrastructures and Logistics—Brussels
- Infrastructures and Logistics—Luxembourg
- Internal Audit Service
- Interpretation
- Legal Service
- Office For Administration And Payment Of Individual Entitlements
- Translation

References

1. The Council of Europe is a separate organisation outside the European Union. It currently has 47 European countries as members (covering all of European subcontinent, including Russia and Turkey, but excluding Belarus). It deals with issues such as human rights and promotion of democracy (see http://www.coe.int/).
2. This is a slight increase from the members elected in 2009. The numbers given in this table are based on a decision of the European Council in June 2007 and will be fully implemented in 2014. (see http://wwweuroparl.europa.eu/sides/getDoc.do?type=IM-PRESS&reference=20070910BKG10267&language=EN).
3. Article 17 of the *Treaty on European Union.*
4. Article 228 of the *Treaty on the Functioning .of the European Union*
5. Article 13.7 of the *Treaty on European Union.*
6. Article 13.6 of the *Treaty on European Union*
7. Op cit 1.
8. Directorate-General for Health and Consumers. European Commission website. http://ec.europa.eu/dgs/health_consumer/index_en.htm. Accessed 10 December 2010.
9. Article 19 of the Treaty on European Union and articles 251 to 281 of the Treaty on the Functioning of the European Union
10. European Medicines Agency. EMA website. http://www.ema.europa.eu. Accessed 10 December 2010.
11. European Law Enforcement Agency. Europol website. http://www.europol.europa.eu/. Accessed 10 Decmeber 2010.
12. Article 2 of Council Directive 93/42/EEC of 14 June 1993 concerning medical devices (*MDD*).
13. Decision No 768/2008/EC of the European Parliament and of the Council on a common framework for the marketing of products, and repealing Decision 93/465/EEC, 23 June 2008; Regulation of the European Parliament and of the Council setting out the requirements for accreditation and market surveillance relating to the marketing of products, and repealing Regulation (EEC) No 339/93, 23 June 2008.
14. Working groups and taskforces. European Commission website. http://ec.europa.eu/consumers/sectors/medical-devices/dialogue-parties/working-groups/index_en.htm. Accessed 10 December 2010.
15. Article 1.2(f) of the *MDD*.
16. Article 1.2(j) of the *MDD*.
17. Article 2.5 of Regulation (EC) No 765/2008 of the European Parliament and of the Council setting out the requirements for accreditation and market surveillance relating to the marketing of products, and repealing Regulation (EEC) No 339/93, 23 June 2008.
18. Article 2.6 op cit.
19. Adapted from http://ec.europa.eu/consumers/sectors/medical-devices/dialogue-parties/working-groups/index_en.htm.
20. About the European Commission. European Commission website. http://ec.europa.eu/about/ds_en.htm. Accessed 10 December 2010.

Overview of EU Authorisation Procedures for Medical Devices

By Evangeline Loh, PhD, RAC

OBJECTIVES

❏ Provide a synopsis of the process to market medical devices in Europe

❏ Explain the role of the Competent Authorities, Notified Bodies and the European Commission

❏ Describe the three main medical device directives as well as considerations for obtaining CE marking for a medical device

❏ Describe the classification of medical devices and available conformity assessment routes

DIRECTIVES, REGULATIONS AND GUIDELINES COVERED IN THIS CHAPTER

❏ Council Directive 90/385/EEC of 20 June 1990 on the approximation of the laws of the Member States relating to active implantable medical devices (*Active Implantable Medical Devices Directive*)

❏ Council Directive 93/42/EEC of 14 June 1993 concerning medical devices (*Medical Devices Directive*)

❏ Directive 98/79/EC of the European Parliament and of the Council of 27 October 1998 on in vitro diagnostic medical devices (*In Vitro Devices Directive*)

❏ Council Directive 2007/47/EC of the European Parliament and of the Council of 5 September

2007 amending Council Directive 90/385/EEC on the approximation of the laws of the Member States relating to active implantable medical devices (*Active Implantable Medical Devices Directive*), the Council Directive 93/42/EEC concerning medical devices (*Medical Devices Directive*) and Directive 98/8/EC concerning the placing of biocidal products on the market

Introduction

The three main medical devices directives—*Active Implantable Medical Devices Directive (AIMDD)*, *Medical Devices Directive (MDD)* and *In Vitro Devices Directive (IVDD)*—impose a common regulatory structure on medical devices:

- Devices must be compliant with the relevant aspects of the directives to obtain CE marking.
- Directives must be transposed by each Member State into its national laws or regulations.
- The governmental Competent Authority appointed by each Member State is responsible for implementing respective national laws.
- Competent Authorities delegate certain tasks to third-party Notified Bodies (NBs).
- NBs are responsible for undertaking parts of the Conformity Assessment Procedures (CAPs) under commercial contracts with manufacturers.

Competent Authorities typically are the long-established health ministry departments of Member States. When differences of interpretation of the directives arise among Competent Authorities, they can communicate directly or through the Medical Devices Expert Group (MDEG) structure established by the European Commission. The MDEG also publishes guidance documents known as MEDDEVs, which are intended to help manufacturers and other parties reach a common interpretation of the directives across all Member States. Although these guidance documents have no specific legal status, they reflect current European expert consensus on specific matters. The guidances also provide details and explanation that expound upon some of the succinct text of the directives.

The *IVDD* is important to all medical devices because it contains Article 21, which modifies the previous *AIMDD* and *MDD*. Essentially, to discharge their duties effectively, Competent Authorities need to know what devices are being placed on their national markets. The *IVDD* amendment mandates establishment of a common, Europe-wide database that is accessible to all Competent Authorities and that requires extensive data regarding all medical device product manufacturers to be uploaded. The European Commission issued a decision (2010/227/EU) in 2010 that mandates the use of Eudamed, the databank for medical devices, by Competent Authorities as of 1 May 2011.

In 2004, the Competent Authorities established an informal consensus body, the Member States Operation Group (MSOG), which allows the Member States to congregate "privately" (i.e., without the presence of industry delegates). There are no public minutes, but the results usually serve to promote consensus among European Free Trade Association (EFTA) states (the 27 EU Member States plus Norway, Lichtenstein, Iceland and Switzerland).

Notified Bodies

Under previous national legislation, Competent Authorities may have routinely undertaken manufacturer assessment and device evaluation, but the device directives place most of this responsibility with NBs. NBs are impartial and independent third-party organisations specifically authorised to monitor and review the CAPs according to the device directives. The Member State's Competent Authority assesses any resident NB's organisational structure, operations policies and procedures and, particularly, the skills and competence of personnel involved in activities related to medical device authorisations. If an NB meets the necessary criteria, the Competent Authority recommends that the European Commission list that NB in the *Official Journal of the European Union (OJEU)*. Notification stipulates the specific directive areas in which the NB has been approved or "notified." It is not uncommon for this qualification to list specific product groups and CAPs for which the NB is approved. The Competent Authority is then responsible for monitoring the NBs periodically to ensure their continued operational compliance with standards.

Several hundred NBs exist in Europe, but only about 70 have activities in the medical devices industry (others may operate mainly or solely in other regulated industry sectors, such as personal protective equipment, recreational craft and telephone equipment). Once approved by their Competent Authority, NBs are free to operate in any country, subject only to their linguistic competence.

Under the new directives, NBs also needed a mechanism to foster dialogue on technical and interpretational issues. To that end, the Notified Body Operational Group (NBOG) formally meets three or four times per year to review matters with their members' respective Competent Authorities and manufacturers' trade associations. This group periodically publishes its own guidelines on specific matters as Medical Device Notified Body Recommendations, many of which form the foundation for subsequent MEDDEV development.

The primary role of medical device NBs may be in product testing or evaluating manufacturing quality and administrative systems. The *MDD* specifies various CAPs by which a manufacturer can demonstrate that a medical device complies with the applicable directive's Essential Requirements, depending upon perceived risk and other aspects of the device and its intended use.

Classification of Medical Devices

Rather than list products by specific classification categories (as the US Food and Drug Administration (FDA) does), the *MDD* (Annex IX) provides a classification criteria system that guides the manufacturer in determining a device's appropriate classification. Based upon the classification (Class 1 self-certified (low risk) to Class III (high risk)), Article 11 defines the available choices of CAPs that can be applied.

Essentially, the 12 general classification rules focus on the device's duration of intended use, level of invasiveness on or into the body and whether it is active. These general rules are supplemented by six special rules for particular products that, although covered by the directive, do not fit neatly into the general rules.

Conversely, the *IVDD* (Annex II) contains Lists A and B for risk categorisation, and devices explicitly delineated are classified as Annex II, List A or Annex II List B, as well as self-test in vitro diagnostic devices and all other devices, self-certified. Similar to the *MDD,* Article 9 defines the available choices of CAPs. The classification of in vitro diagnostic devices has been subject to some discussion as the Global Harmonization Task Force has proposed a risk- and rule-based classification scheme.

To determine a particular device's classification, the manufacturer should take the following steps:
- Ensure the product is covered by the correct directive. Although this may sound trivial, the incorrect application of a directive has led to many categorisation errors. Generally, Article 1 of a directive provides detailed definitions of its scope and clearly indicates products to which it does not apply.
- Document assumptions made about defining device parameters, such as intended use.

- Compare device parameters to all respective rules. Many devices are multifunctional and may be covered by more than one classification rule. The rule with the highest classification governs a device's final classification.
- Check the respective MEDDEV guidance document on classification as well as the manual of the Medical Device Expert Group on Borderline and Classification and guidances issued by trade or professional associations or even by the chosen NB.
- Keep a record of the determined classification.
- Review process and results periodically. Because classification is the basis of defining a manufacturer's route for compliance, it needs to be formally reviewed in light of any fundamental developments. Although classification rules are unlikely to change abruptly, the body of opinion behind the respective guidance documents has resulted in frequent changes.

CAPs

Article 11 of the *MDD* defines the available CAPs. As previously mentioned, the first critical step in the medical device authorisation process is to determine the device's classification according to its intended use and risk classification. Once this determination has been made, design control responsibility has been assigned, and means of demonstrating adequate production process control have been selected, the manufacturer has various options to demonstrate conformity to device directive requirements:

- Class I devices (nonsterile/no measuring function): Annex VII Declaration of Conformity
- Class I devices (sterile or with measuring function): Annex VII Declaration of Conformity with Notified Body assessment of Quality System according to Annex II, excluding Section 4, IV, V or VI
- Class IIa devices: Annex II Full Quality Assurance, excluding Section 4, or Annex VII Declaration of Conformity with Annex IV, V or VI Quality System assessment
- Class IIb Devices: Annex II Full Quality Assurance, excluding Section 4, or Annex III Type Examination with Annex IV, V or VI Quality System assessment
- Class III Devices: Annex II Full Quality Assurance, including Section 4, or Annex III Type Examination with Annex IV or Annex V Quality System assessment

For Class I devices (nonmeasuring, nonsterile) considered Class I self-certified, the manufacturer must comply with the Essential Requirements detailed in *MDD* Annex 1 and then follow Annex VII (including technical documentation

retention and adverse incident reporting arrangements) to issue its own Declaration of Conformity (DoC).

It is very important to understand that a DoC declares that on the date of signature, the manufacturer (not the NB or Competent Authority) of the product met the applicable directive's Essential Requirements. All products manufactured during that DoC's period of validity are permanently covered by it and, consequently, may be CE marked by the manufacturer. Conversely, abrogation of a DoC ends the legality of affixing subsequent CE markings. However, it does not invalidate CE markings prior to the abrogation (unless the DoC was never valid).

Because manufacturers of Class I products are not necessarily aligned with an NB (which also has a notification, monitoring and reporting role), they must also (Article 14) register specific details with the Competent Authority in the Member State where their European entity or their Authorised Representative is established. Following compliance with these requirements, a CE marking can be affixed (Article 17) to the device. No medical device may be placed on the market or put into use if it is not duly CE marked.

Involvement of an NB is required for all medical devices other than those that are Class I self-certified or those that are not custom-made or intended solely for clinical investigational purposes. The manufacturer must appoint an NB and agree upon the scope and nature of its involvement. Part of the NB's role is to advise its Competent Authority on details of all certificates granted or withdrawn. With the existence of Eudamed, information should be entered into the European database. However, in practice, most NBs will have insufficient information to populate all of the proposed database's fields and will require manufacturers to prepare an authorised list of devices.

Special Circumstances: Non-CE-marked Devices

Manufacturers of custom-made devices, a term specifically defined in *MDD* Article 1.2(d), must comply with the Essential Requirements for which they are responsible (a "duly qualified medical practitioner" will be responsible for other aspects beyond the control of the manufacturer) and, in compliance with Annex VIII, generate their statement concerning Devices for Special Purposes. Devices must not be CE marked but, as with the above, specific details must be registered with the Competent Authority. Directive 2007/47/EC also modified the *MDD* to require manufacturers of custom-made devices to possess a post-market surveillance system.

Devices intended solely for use as part of a regulated clinical investigation cannot, by definition, be deemed to comply with all Essential Requirements (because the principal purpose of all regulated clinical investigations is to determine a specific aspect of compliance). The manufacturer must follow Annex VIII to generate a statement concerning a Device for Special Purposes. Devices must not be CE marked but must be marked "exclusively for clinical investigation." Because the respective Competent Authority is already involved in approving the clinical investigation, there is no requirement for further registration of manufacturer details.

Clinical Evaluation and Clinical Investigations of Medical Devices

Directive 2007/47/EC modified the *MDD* to emphasize the requirement for clinical data and clinical evaluation for devices of all classes. MEDDEV 2.7/1 describes clinical evaluation as a review of (relevant) literature, a clinical investigation or a combination of these.

Where evidence is insufficient to demonstrate full compliance with one or more Essential Requirements, despite all reasonable *ex vivo* studies, a clinical investigation is necessary. Because such devices are incapable of being deemed fully compliant with the *MDD*, they must be deemed noncompliant and, therefore, as potentially presenting a risk to patients enrolled in such studies.

A principal role of each Competent Authority is to ensure that no subjects in its country are exposed to any foreseeable, undue risk. This is the basis upon which the Competent Authority regulates clinical investigations within its territory to prove *MDD* compliance.

Clinical investigations at any stage must comply with accepted ethical protocols, be conducted impartially and have statistical significance to be of any real value. In France, for instance, under the amended *Huriet-Secuslat Law*, all clinical investigations, whether pre- or post-market, are regulated. Most other countries rely upon a common standard, EN ISO 14155, accepted by most ethics committees.

Regulated clinical investigations require the study sponsor (and usually, but not necessarily, the manufacturer) to document the study protocol detailing the product's clinical merits, likely risks and benefits, intended enrolment criteria and statistical rationale and nature of the investigation, together with case review forms, patient informed consent forms and insurance and liability agreements.

These documents must be submitted for ethics committee review and approval, and then to the respective Competent Authority for study authorisation. In practice, most countries allow some parallel submissions, provided both are approved prior to commencement. Differences exist in each Member State regarding submission language, extent of insurance required, application documentation, review fees, review timelines and means of notification. Covering every Member State's precise terms, which often change depending upon the product and study, is beyond the scope of this chapter.

Adverse Incident Reporting for Medical Devices

All CAPs systems (Annexes II, V, VI and VII) require the manufacturer to institute and maintain a procedure to review experience gained during the device's postproduction phase and implement appropriate means to apply necessary corrective action. This requirement may be seen as extending normal complaint-handling requirements to provide a more proactive means of obtaining positive market feedback, less accurately but commonly known as postmarket surveillance (PMS).

"This undertaking must include an obligation for the manufacturer to notify the competent authorities of the following incidents immediately on learning of them:

(i)   Any malfunction or deterioration in the characteristics and/or performance of a device, as well as any adequacy in labelling or instructions for use which might lead or might have led to the death of a patient or user or to a serious deterioration in his state of health;

(ii)   Any technical or medical reason connected with the characteristics or the performance of device for the reasons referred to in subparagraph (i) leading to a systematic recall of devices of the same type by the manufacturer." MDD Annexes II, V, VI, and essentially VII. AIMDD Annex 2, 4, and 5. IVDD essentially Annex III, and as cross referenced by Annexes IV, VI, and VII."

What Needs to Be Reported?

MEDDEV Guidance Document 2.12/1 (Rev. 6, December 2009) provides details on how adverse incidents can be more precisely defined and gives a common format for initial and final reports. Some Member States use local report formats, but manufacturers should be safe using the Commission's report format for the initial submission and then following up with local formats.

Where Must It Be Reported?

Manufacturers are required to report adverse incidents to the Competent Authority of the Member State in which it occurred, immediately, without any delay that cannot be unduly justified. Competent Authority addresses are listed on the European Commission website.

The European Commission Consumer Affairs website lists vigilance contact points for EFTA countries' and Member States' national Competent Authorities that focus on the medical device industrial sector. When an incident outside Europe results in a field safety corrective action (FSCA) that will affect products in Member States, the FSCA needs to be reported to the relevant Competent Authorities.

The manufacturer also may have a contractual obligation

to inform its NB of adverse incidents or resultant changes to its quality system.

When Must It Be Reported?

The directive and many national transpositions require the manufacturer to report immediately upon becoming aware of an event (which may be through the sales or local office). The manufacturer must report in 10 elapsed calendar days when the event led to death or an unanticipated serious deterioration in the state of health; for others, 30 elapsed calendar days. However, it would be prudent to ensure there is no undue delay. For events deemed serious public health threats, the manufacturer has two days to report.

Why Must It Be Reported?

Competent Authorities have a duty to safeguard their populations and must assess which actions are the most appropriate. In evaluating the problem, Competent Authorities should work closely with the manufacturer to achieve optimum resolution. National laws vary, although all Competent Authorities indicate they adhere to the MEDDEV. However, in many cases, statutory penalties are imposed for failing to report and/or delaying reporting of adverse incidents. In some countries, statutes allow imprisonment for failing to report.

Authorised Representative

The *MDD* update and *IVDD* mandate the use of an Authorised Representative if the manufacturer has no establishment in Europe. Because the rules and regulations are so complex and, most importantly, due to the manufacturer's inherent conflict of interest with commercial objectives, distributors likely are unfit to serve as Authorised Representatives unless they have a dedicated and independent person or department dealing with these rather onerous and highly critical issues. Also, Directive 2007/47/EC modified the *MDD* to specify a single Authorised Representative. (The recital to Directive 2007/47/EC, which is explanatory material, indicates that this is for devices of the same model.)

Summary

In the EU, there are three main medical device directives: the *AIMDD*, *MDD* and *IVDD*. These directives are transposed by each Member State into its national laws or regulations. It is the obligation of the regulatory authority, the Competent Authority, in each Member State to implement the medical device laws or regulations. Competent Authorities delegate some of their device review to Notified Bodies.

The directives apply to active implantable medical devices, medical devices or in vitro diagnostic devices, respectively. Products that are medical devices must possess CE marking before they can be marketed in the EU, unless they are considered custom-made medical devices or products intended

for investigational use. The classification of the medical device determines the conformity assessment routes available to the manufacturer. CE marking can only be affixed after the manufacturer demonstrates compliance with the applicable elements of the directives. Certain classes of medical devices require Notified Body involvement, and the CE marking will reflect the Notified Body's four-digit number. Also, for higher-risk medical devices, there is a *de facto* expectation for the manufacturer to have a quality system certified to ISO 13485:2003. A manufacturer that is not established in the EU must appoint a European Authorised Representative.

In addition, a manufacturer, regardless of the classification of its devices, must have a postmarket surveillance procedure and a vigilance system in place.

EU Classification of Medical Devices

By Mika Reinikainen

OBJECTIVES

❑ Understand the difference between classes, categories and special devices

❑ Gain insight into the basic concepts and application of classification rules

❑ Learn how to find further guidance information

❑ Become aware of wider issues relating to classification

DIRECTIVES, REGULATIONS AND GUIDELINES COVERED IN THIS CHAPTER

❑ Council Directive 93/42/EEC of 14 June 1993 concerning medical devices

❑ *Classification of medical devices* (MEDDEV 2. 4/1 Rev. 9 June 2010)

❑ European Commission's *Manual on Borderline and Classification* (version 1.7 May 2010)

❑ *Borderline products, drug-delivery products and medical devices incorporating, as an integral part, an ancillary medicinal substance or an ancillary human blood derivative* (MEDDEV 2. 1/3 rev 3 December 2009)

Introduction

There are thousands of different types of medical devices presenting varying levels of risk to patients. It would not be feasible to implement the same high level of regulatory control over all of them. Since medical devices were first regulated, different attempts have been made to design systems of categorisation or classification to ensure that appropriate control mechanisms are applied based upon perceived risks and protection of public health. The solution adopted in the European Union is a rules-based system that gauges the increasing vulnerability of a human being to a device based upon factors such as the device's degree of invasiveness, its local or systemic effect and the duration of its use.

Categories and Classes

Although each of the key medical devices directives (see **Table 19-1**) applies varying requirements to the devices it covers on the basis of criteria that, in some cases, relate to risk, only the *Medical Devices Directive* (*MDD*) (Directive 93/42/EEC) contains a true classification system. This classification system is generally thought of as a three- or four-category system with subcategories. The full classification hierarchy can be listed as Class I, Class I (sterile), Class I (with a measuring function), Class IIa, Class IIb and Class III.

It is nevertheless useful to have some understanding of the special categories of devices outside the classification system. All three directives recognise certain categories of devices that are subject to requirements different from those for devices intended for CE marking and for placing on the market. These special categories and their definitions as they appear in the *MDD* are:

- "Custom-made device" defined as "any device specifically made in accordance with a duly qualified medical practitioner's written prescription which gives, under his responsibility, specific design characteristics and is intended for the sole use of a particular patient."[1]

Table 19-1. EU Medical Devices Directives

90/385/EEC	Active Implantable Medical Devices[i] (*AIMDD*)
93/42/EEC	Medical Devices (*MDD*)[ii]
98/79/EC	In Vitro Diagnostic Medical Devices[iii] (*IVDD*)

[i]*Council Directive of 20 June 1990 on the approximation of the laws of the Member States relating to active implantable medical devices (90/385/EEC)*
[ii]*Council Directive 93/42/EEC of 14 June 1993 concerning medical devices*
[iii]*Directive 98/79/EC of the European Parliament and of the Council of 27 October 1998 on in vitro diagnostic medical devices*

- "Device intended for clinical investigation" defined as: "any device intended for use by a duly qualified medical practitioner when conducting investigations as referred to in Section 2.1 of Annex X in an adequate human clinical environment."[2]
- Device authorised nationally "in the interest of protection of health." This category is not defined, but it is usually understood to be used in a situation where the device is not CE marked, but there is a real clinical need for it on compassionate grounds. Some of these devices may be orphan devices.

The same or similar concepts exist in the two other main directives (*AIMDD* and *IVDD*).

The *AIMDD* does not have a risk classification system, but products covered under it are subject to a compliance regime that is very close to the one applied in the *MDD* for Class III devices.

The *IVDD* differentiates between products for professional and patient use and defines the latter, called a "device for self-testing" as "any device intended by the manufacturer to be able to be used by lay persons in a home environment."[3] It also lists certain reagents and related materials thought to carry higher risks in its Annex II.

The Global Harmonization Task Force (GHTF) has proposed a rules-based classification system for in vitro diagnostic devices (IVDs) (see http://www.ghtf.org/documents/sg1/sg1final_n045.pdf), which probably will be taken into account in a future revision of the *IVDD*.

Why Is Classification Needed?

There are literally thousands of different types of medical devices on the market (the Global Medical Device Nomenclature lists over 20,000 generic medical device terms at the time of writing). As mentioned above, it would not be economically feasible to apply the same degree of regulatory control on all devices. Furthermore, equal control is not needed. A philosophy of proportionate control as applied in the EU is illustrated in **Table 19-2**.

These proportionate controls apply to the conformity assessment process (verification of compliance). However, compliance with Essential Requirements applies to all medical devices regardless of their classification. Devices in all classes also require clinical evidence, although

there are some class-related variances concerning clinical investigation.

Instructions for use can be omitted for devices in Class I or IIa if they can be used safely without any.[4]

The Classification Process

The legal requirements for classification can be found in *MDD* Annex IX.

The manufacturer determines the appropriate class for its device using the classification principles and rules contained in Annex IX and based upon the device's intended purpose . It is important to understand that anything said about the device by the manufacturer and its agents may be construed as forming part of the intended purpose. The *MDD* provides the following definition:[5]

"'intended purpose' means the use for which the device is intended according to the data supplied by the manufacturer on the labelling, in the instructions and/or in promotional materials"

Sometimes there can be a gap between the instructions for use and promotional materials that can result in Competent Authorities' questioning the classification applied by the manufacturer. Competent Authorities are known, for instance, to check product descriptions on the Internet.

Basic Principles of Application

Annex IX contains certain basic principles that need to be understood before applying the classification rules.

As indicated before, the intended purpose of a device is determinant in arriving at a correct classification decision. An alternative, off-label use not indicated by the manufacturer has no bearing on the determination of class.

The claimed intended purpose must be achieved by a describable mode of action supported by scientific evidence. All modes of action present must be considered. The manufacturer cannot pick and choose, e.g., ignore a specific mode of action of the device that contributes to the intended purpose in order to claim the device falls into a lower class than it should.

The manufacturer must consider all the rules. Often, two or more rules may apply to the device. In such a case, the highest possible classification applies. The same principle applies for devices that can be used on different parts

Table 19-2. Risk Class-based Conformity Assessment

Notified Body Verifies	Class I	Class IIa	Class IIb	Class III
Quality system used in manufacturing	Manufacturer verifies conformity (Annex VII)—No Notified Body intervention (except for sterilisation and measuring function)	YES (Annex V or VI), but also option to have product testing and technical documentation verified instead (using Annex IV)	YES (Annex V or VI), but also option to have product testing and technical documentation verified instead (using Annex IV)	YES (Annex II), but also option to have a type examination (Annex III) together with quality system assessment ((Annex V) or further product testing instead (Annex IV)
Product design		NO, but option for technical documentation assessment on sampled basis (Annex II)	Type examination (Annex III) or assessment of technical documentation on sampled basis (Annex II)	Design dossier approval (Annex II) or type examination (Annex III)

of the body or have multiple purposes, i.e., the application resulting in the highest possible class applies.

Individual devices that are used in a system—e.g., an extracorporeal blood circulation system containing an oxygenator, a pump and tubes—can be classified in their own right or the system can be classified as a whole, in which case the item that is in the highest class is used as the class for the whole system.

Key Concepts of Classification

The European classification system is based on an understanding of human vulnerability in terms of certain key characteristics of the device and its use: time period, degree of invasiveness, use of a source of energy, biological activity and incorporation of drugs. These concepts tend to have a common-sense relationship with risk, e.g., the more invasive a device and the longer it is used, the riskier it tends to be.

Time

The duration of use of the device is categorised in terms of "normally intended continuous use:"[6]

- transient use: less than 60 minutes
- short-term use: not more than 30 days
- long-term use: more than 30 days

These are time periods of use as envisaged by the manufacturer. If an individual decides to use a device beyond the time parameters defined by the manufacturer, this would not affect the device's classification.

The concept of "continuous use" has been subject to some confusion and has been recently defined as:[7]

"An uninterrupted actual use of the device for the intended purpose. However where usage of a device is discontinued in order for the device to be replaced immediately by the same or an identical device this shall be considered an extension of the continuous use of the device"

Invasiveness

Invasiveness obviously involves penetration of the body as confirmed by the general definition of an "invasive device:"[8]

"A device which, in whole or in part, penetrates inside the body, either through a body orifice or through the surface of the body."

There is a significant difference between invasiveness through a body orifice and surgical invasiveness, which involves piercing the body surface.

"Body orifice" is defined as:[9]

"Any natural opening in the body, as well as the external surface of the eyeball, or any permanent artificial opening, such as a stoma"

"Surgically invasive device" is defined as:[10]

"An invasive device which penetrates inside the body through the surface of the body, with the aid or in the context of a surgical operation.

For the purposes of this Directive devices, other than those referred to in the previous subparagraph and which produce penetration other than through an established body orifice, shall be treated as surgically invasive devices."

Table 19-3. Excerpt From MEDDEV 2. 4/1 Rev. 9
Classification of Medical Devices

Rule 6	Examples
All surgically invasive[1] devices intended for transient use are in Class IIa unless they are:	• Needles used for suturing • Needles of syringes • Lancets • Suckers • Single use scalpels and single-use scalpel blades • Support devices in ophthalmic surgery • Staplers • Surgical swabs • Drill bits connected to active devices • Surgical gloves • Etchants • Tester of artificial heart valves • Heart valve occluders, sizers and holders • Swabs to sample exudates • Single-use aortic punches (see note 2)
Intended specifically to control, diagnose, monitor or correct a defect[2] of the heart or of the central circulatory system[1] through direct contact with these parts of the body, in which case they are in Class III:	• Cardiovascular catheters (e.g., angioplasty balloon catheters, stent delivery catheters/systems, including related guidewires, related introducers and dedicated[4] disposable cardiovascular surgical instruments (e.g., electrophysiological catheters, electrodes for electrophysiological diagnosis and ablation) • Catheters containing or incorporating sealed radioisotopes, where the radioactive isotope is not intended to be released into the body, if used in the central circulatory system • Distal protection devices

Explanations of special concepts
Note 1: Terms such as "surgically invasive device", "central circulatory system", "central nervous system" and "reusable surgical instruments" are defined in Section I of Annex IX of Directive 93/42/EEC. In particular surgical instruments connected to an active device are not considered to be "reusable surgical instruments."
Note 2: The expression "correct a defect" does not cover devices that are used accessorily in heart surgery procedures, e.g., clamps, aortic punch instruments. The first indent of this rule does not apply to aortic punches and similar cutting instruments which perform a similar function to a scalpel.
Note 4: Dedicated means that the intended purpose of the device or accessory is to specifically control, diagnose, monitor or correct a defect of the heart or of the central circulatory system.

A surgically invasive device is not necessarily something that would involve surgery. For instance, needles used for injections are regarded as surgically invasive. Surgically invasive devices may be introduced through a temporary, surgically created opening, e.g., implants.

The classification system recognises two specific subtypes of surgically invasive devices: implants and reusable surgical instruments. This distinction has been made to separate implants, which are thought to be high risk and classified in Class IIb or III, from reusable surgical instruments, which are regarded as low risk and are therefore in Class I.

This illustrates an important principle of risk classification. A scalpel can cause significant trauma if used badly, but this is outside the manufacturer's control, whereas a patient can die from a poorly designed heart valve, something for which the manufacturer would bear responsibility. Risk classification therefore relates to risk factors that the manufacturer can influence, but not those that are outside the manufacturer's control.

An "implantable device" is defined as:[11]

"Any device which is intended:

—to be totally introduced into the human body or,

—to replace an epithelial surface or the surface of the eye,

by surgical intervention which is intended to remain in place after the procedure.

Any device intended to be partially introduced into the human body through surgical intervention and intended to remain in place after the procedure for at least 30 days is also considered an "implantable device."

"Reusable surgical instrument" is defined as an:[12]

"Instrument intended for surgical use by cutting, drilling, sawing, scratching, scraping, clamping, retracting, clipping or similar procedures, without connection to any active medical device and which can be reused after appropriate procedures have been carried out."

The classification system identifies two areas of the body that are regarded as particularly vulnerable: the central circulatory and nervous systems.

The "central circulatory system" is defined as:[13]

"arteriae pulmonales, aorta ascendens, arcus aorta, aorta descendens to the bifurcatio aortae, arteriae coronariae, arteria carotis communis, arteria carotis externa, arteria carotis interna, arteriae cerebrales, truncus brachiocephalicus, venae cordis, venae pulmonales, vena cava superior, vena cava inferior"

The "central nervous system" is defined as:[14]

"brain, meninges and spinal cord"

Use of Energy

Energy is regarded as a risk factor because of its potential for systemic effects and the difficulty in restricting the energy to a specific location. Thus the concept of "active device" was created, which is defined as:[15]

"Any medical device, the operation of which depends on a source of electrical energy or any source of power other than that directly generated by the human body or gravity and which acts by converting this energy. Medical devices intended to transmit energy, substances or other elements between an active medical device and the patient, without any significant change, are not considered to be active medical devices."

The critical element of this definition is the concept of conversion of energy, which must produce a significant change. Such a significant change is understood to occur when the nature, level and/or density of energy changes. The effect of resistance in a wire is not regarded as a significant change. The conversion can occur in the device itself, e.g., electrical energy converted to thermal energy, or at the interface between the device and tissue, e.g., the conversion produced by the electrical scalpel blade.

Biological Activity

If a device is intended to have a biological effect or is absorbed, this action tends to push a device into a higher class.

While absorption is generally accepted as normal for some types of devices, a biological mode of action is more difficult to understand as a medical device-like action as opposed to a medicinal (drug) mode of action. The following definition clarifies this point:[16]

"A material is considered to have a biological effect if it actively and intentionally induces, alters or prevents a response from the tissues that is mediated by specific reactions at a molecular level."

"Absorption" is defined as:[17]

"degradation of a material within the body and the metabolic elimination of the resulting degradation products from the body"

Drug/Device Combinations

Integration of a drug into a medical device for an ancillary purpose makes the device a drug/device combination in Class III in most cases. If, however, the manufacturer can demonstrate that the drug substance is not liable to act on the human body, then it does not become the determinant factor in the device's class. Such "pure device" drug/device combinations can even be in Class I.

Software

Software is classified in the same way as any other medical device or accessory, except for the following principles:

- Standalone software is considered an active medical device.
- Software that drives a device or influences the use of a device falls automatically into the same class. This can be true for both embedded and standalone software.

The European Commission is preparing a guidance document on the qualification (determination of legal status) and classification of standalone software, which should be published in 2011.

Classification Rules (Annex IX)

The *MDD* classification rules are grouped into sections as follows:

- Rules 1–4   noninvasive devices
- Rules 5–8   invasive devices
- Rules 9–12 additional rules for active devices
- Rule 13–18 other special rules
  - o devices incorporating ancillary action medicinal products and human blood derivatives
  - o devices used for contraception or the prevention of the transmission of sexually transmitted diseases
  - o devices intended specifically to be used for disinfecting, cleaning, rinsing
  - o devices specifically intended for recording X-ray diagnostic images
  - o devices manufactured utilising animal tissues or derivatives rendered nonviable
  - o blood bags

Following is a typical example of a classification rule "Rule 6

All surgically invasive devices intended for transient use are in Class IIa unless they are:

— intended specifically to control, diagnose, monitor or correct a defect of the heart or of the central circulatory system through direct contact with these parts of the body, in which case they are in Class III,
— reusable surgical instruments, in which case they are in Class I,
— intended specifically for use in direct contact with the central nervous system, in which case they are in Class III,
— intended to supply energy in the form of ionising radiation, in which case they are in Class IIb,
— intended to have a biological effect or to be wholly or mainly absorbed, in which case they are in Class IIb,
— intended to administer medicines by means of a delivery system, if this is done in a manner that is potentially hazardous taking account of the mode of application, in which case they are in Class IIb."

Guidance on Classification

The European Commission has issued guidance on classification. Although this is very helpful, it is important to remember that such guidance is not legally binding. The use of any concrete example to illustrate a classification rule should not be taken as definitive confirmation that all similar devices are in the same class. Often similar devices may have some specific features not present in the other devices that result in a different classification.

The main guidance document is the "Classification of medical devices," MEDDEV 2. 4/1 Rev. 9 June 2010 (http://ec.europa.eu/consumers/sectors/medical-devices/files/meddev/2_4_1_rev_9_classification_en.pdf).

This document is intended to cover all the basic principles and to provide clear and noncontroversial examples of typical devices falling under the specific rules. **Table 19-3** is an excerpt from the guidance document explaining part of Rule 6, above.

A Commission expert working group with members from the Competent Authorities and industry and certain other stakeholders meets three or four times a year to discuss specific classification problems. Decisions arising from this process can be found in the Commission's *Manual on Borderline and Classification*. It is frequently updated; at the time of writing, the most recent edition was version 1.7 dating from May 2010 (http://ec.europa.eu/consumers/sectors/medical-devices/files/wg_minutes_member_lists/version1_7_borderline_manual_en.pdf).

The manual often deals with complicated cases for which consensus is sometimes difficult to achieve. The solutions offered in the manual tend to provide criteria that

should be used in classifying a device rather than arriving at a definitive classification.

Following is an example of one of the simpler cases in this manual:

"8.16. Ethyl chloride spray for local refrigeration anaesthesia

- **Background**

A manufacturer of a spray for local anaesthesia containing ethyl chloride wants to place this product on the market as a medical device. Several other products with a similar intended use and mode of action are already placed on the market as medical devices but with some discrepancies regarding their classification.

In some countries, ethyl chloride is regulated as a medicinal product because of its toxicity and its narcotic properties.

Ethyl chloride is used as local anaesthetic in minor operative procedures and is used also to alleviate pain associated with bruises, contusions, etc…

The rapid vaporisation of ethyl chloride when applied as a spray to the skin produces freezing of superficial tissues to -20°C, which results in insensitivity of peripheral nerve endings and a local anaesthesia.

- **Outcome**

In the present case the principal mode of action of ethyl chloride is not pharmacological, immunological or metabolic and therefore this product could be qualified as a medical device.

As stated in MEDDEV 2.4/1 rev.9, medical devices using pre-stored gases and/or vacuum as a power source are regarded as active devices. Consequently, this product could be qualified as an active medical device and, according to Rule 9 of Annex IX of Directive 93/42/EEC, could be classified as Class IIa medical device."

The Commission's guidance on the borderline between medical devices and medicinal products contains useful information in particular for deciding if a product is a drug/device combination that falls automatically in Class III (MEDDEV 2. 1/3 rev 3 issued in December 2009, http://ec.europa.eu/enterprise/sectors/medical-devices/files/meddev/2_1_3_rev_3-12_2009_en.pdf).

Classification Disputes

The manufacturer initially determines the device's class using the classification rules. If the conformity assessment process requires the intervention of a Notified Body, the two parties must agree on the classification. If there is a disagreement that cannot be resolved between them, the Notified Body will normally go to its Competent Authority to request a solution.

A national Competent Authority may feel unsure about the classification of a specific device. It has the option of submitting its view to a review by the national Competent Authorities of other EU Member States (the so-called "Helsinki procedure"). Often, this results in diverging views expressed by the national Competent Authorities. Such cases are usually brought to the Commission's working group on borderlines and classification. If it is resolved, the solution is entered in the *Manual on Borderline and Classification.*

Classification decisions by Competent Authorities can be challenged by the manufacturer in the national courts. If the national court feels that the matter involves interpretation of a point of European law that should be resolved first, it can request a preliminary ruling from the Court of Justice of the European Union. At the time of writing, no such cases had occurred.

Reclassification Process

Although the classification rules have worked successfully since the initial adoption of the *MDD*, it is recognised that situations may arise when the rules do not produce an optimal classification result. The *MDD* contains a clause that allows changes that do not require a full legislative process:

"Where a Member State considers that the classification rules set out in Annex IX require adaptation in the light of technical progress and any information which becomes available under the information system provided for in Article 10, it may submit a duly substantiated request to the Commission and ask it to take the necessary measures for adaptation of classification rules. The measures designed to amend non-essential elements of this Directive relating to adaptation of classification rules shall be adopted in accordance with the regulatory procedure with scrutiny referred to in Article 7 (3)."[18]

Significant reclassification operations have taken place already in two areas:
- Reclassification of breast implants:
  http://eur-lex.europa.eu/LexUriServ/LexUriServ.do?uri=OJ:L:2003:028:0043:0044:en:PDF
- Reclassification of hip, knee and shoulder joint replacements:
  http://eur-lex.europa.eu/LexUriServ/LexUriServ.do?uri=OJ:L:2005:210:0041:0043:en:PDF

International Reach of the European Classification System

The GHTF has adapted the European rules-based system as a recommendation for the rest of the world (see http://www.ghtf.org/documents/sg1/SG1-N119-2006-Classification-FINAL.pdf). Several countries, e.g., Argentina, Australia, Brazil, Canada, Hong Kong and South Korea, have adopted a similar rules-based approach.

Although the US has a very different mechanism of classification, medical devices nevertheless tend to be placed in equivalent classes in both the EU and the US.

Summary

The medical device classification system adopted in the EU is based upon a set of rules and principles of application listed in Annex IX of the *Medical Devices Directive* (*MDD*). The manufacturer applies them to its own products, taking into account the intended purpose of each device. The resulting classification determines the conformity assessment options available to the manufacturer. There are 18 rules that assign devices into one of the risk classes: I, IIa, IIb and III.

References

1. Council Directive of 20 June 1990 on the approximation of the laws of the Member States relating to active implantable medical devices (90/385/EEC) (*AIMDD*).
2. Council Directive 93/42/EEC of 14 June 1993 concerning medical devices (*MDD*).
3. Directive 98/79/EC of the European Parliament and of the Council of 27 October 1998 on *in vitro* diagnostic medical devices (*IVDD*).
4. Article 1.2(d) *MDD*.
5. Article 1.2(e) *MDD*.
6. Article 1.2(d) *IVDD*.
7. *MDD* Annex I, Section 13.1.
8. Article 1.2(g) *MDD*.
9. Annex IX, Section 1.1 *MDD*.
10. Annex IX, Section 2.6 *MDD*.
11. Annex IX, Section 1.2 *MDD*.
12. Annex IX, Section 1.2 *MDD*.
13. Annex IX, Section 1.2 *MDD*.
14. Annex IX, Section 1.2 *MDD*.
15. Annex IX, Section 1.3 *MDD*.
16. Annex IX, Section 1.7 *MDD*.
17. Annex IX, Section 1.8 *MDD*.
18. Annex IX, Section 1.4 *MDD*.
19. MEDDEV 2. 4/1 Rev. 9, p.34.
20. MEDDEV 2. 4/1 Rev. 9, p.34.
21. Article 9.3 *MDD*.

Chapter 20

EU Clinical Evaluation of Medical Devices

By Maria E. Donawa, MD

OBJECTIVES

❑ Understand European clinical data requirements

❑ Understand European clinical evaluation requirements

❑ Learn about important European guidance documents for clinical evaluation

❑ Understand important aspects of the clinical evaluation process

❑ Understand elements of recommended clinical evaluation documentation

❑ Learn about checklists that Notified Bodies can use for checking clinical evaluation documentation

DIRECTIVES, REGULATIONS AND GUIDELINES COVERED IN THIS CHAPTER

❑ Council Directive 93/42/EEC of 14 June 1993 concerning medical devices (consolidated version incorporating amendments including those from Directive 2007/47/EC); also known as the *Medical Devices Directive* (93/42/EEC)

❑ Council Directive of 20 June 1990 on the approximation of the laws of the Member States relating to active implantable medical devices (90/385/EEC); also known as the *Active Implantable Medical Devices Directive* (90/385/EEC)

❑ Directive 2007/47/EC of the European Parliament and of the Council of 5 September 2007 amending Council Directive 90/385/EEC on the approximation of the laws of the Member States relating to active implantable medical devices, Council Directive 93/42/EEC concerning medical devices and Directive 98/8/EC concerning the placing of biocidal products on the market

❑ Clinical Evaluation: A Guide for Manufacturers and Notified Bodies, MEDDEV 2.7.1 Rev.3 (December 2009)

❑ Appendix 1: Clinical Evaluation of Coronary Stents, MEDDEV 2.7.1, December 2008

❑ Guidelines on Post Market Clinical Follow-Up, MEDDEV 2.12-2, May 2004

❑ Clinical Evaluation, Global Harmonization Task Force, Study Group 5 (May 2007)

❑ Clinical evidence–Key Definitions and Concepts, Global Harmonization Task Force, Study Group 5 (May 2007)

❑ Checklist for audit of Notified Body's review of Clinical Data/Clinical Evaluation, NBOG CL 2010-1 (March 2010)

Requirements for Clinical Data

The requirements for European clinical data and clinical evaluation are closely connected. Thus, to understand

European clinical evaluation requirements, it is necessary to be aware of the European requirements for clinical data, which were strengthened and clarified by the revised Directive 2007/47/EC. This directive amended the *Medical Devices Directive* (*MDD*) (Directive 93/42/EEC) and *Active Implantable Medical Devices Directive* (*AIMDD*) (Directive 90/385/EEC) to clarify existing requirements and, in some cases, to add new ones.

The amendments became mandatory on 21 March 2010 and apply not only to medical devices being placed on the market after that date, but also to those on the market before the effective date of the amendments. This is a critical point because some manufacturers may believe that medical devices already on the market when the amendments became mandatory are "grandfathered" and do not need to meet the amended requirements. This is not correct. All medical devices placed on the market under the *MDD* and *AIMDD* must meet the new requirements. Some of the most important amendments are related to clinical requirements, including clinical data and clinical evaluation. This means that the amended requirements under Annex X, Clinical Evaluation, of the *MDD* and Annex 7, Clinical Evaluation, of the *AIMDD*, which lay down the requirements for clinical data, must be met by any medical device that was placed on the market under the *MDD* or *AIMDD*.

Clinical data are typically required to support compliance with the general Essential Requirements described in Sections 1, 3 and 6 of Annex I of the *MDD* and Sections 1, 2 and 5 of Annex 1 of the *AIMDD*. These Essential Requirements are shown in **Table 6-1**. Specifically, Annex X of the *MDD* states that as a general rule, confirmation of conformity with the requirements concerning the characteristics and performances referred to in Sections 1 and 3 of Annex I, under the normal conditions of use of the device, and the evaluation of the side effects and of the acceptability of the risk/benefit ratio referred to in Section 6 of Annex I, must be based on clinical data. An analogous statement is made in Annex 7 of the *AIMDD* except that the relevant Essential Requirements are Sections 1, 2 and 5.

Therefore, with regard to the general Essential Requirements, clinical data are needed to:

- support claims that medical devices will not compromise the clinical condition or safety of patients or the safety and health of users or, where applicable, other persons, provided that any risks that may be associated with their intended use constitute acceptable risks when weighed against the benefits to the patient and are compatible with a high level of protection of health and safety
- demonstrate that devices perform as intended by the manufacturer and are suitable for one or more functions included in the definition of medical device in the *MDD* or *AIMDD*

- support the conclusion that any undesirable side effect constitutes an acceptable risk when weighed against the performances intended

Given the critical role played by clinical data in demonstrating compliance with the *MDD* and *AIMDD*, it is important to understand what constitutes clinical data. The *MDD* and *AIMDD* contain the following definition of "clinical data," which is found in Article 1(2)(k) of both directives:

"'clinical data' means the safety and/or performance information that is generated from the use of a device. Clinical data are sourced from: clinical investigation(s) of the device concerned; or clinical investigation(s) or other studies reported in the scientific literature, of a similar device for which equivalence to the device in question can be demonstrated; or published and/or unpublished reports on other clinical experience of either the device in question or a similar device for which equivalence to the device in question can be demonstrated"

The revising Directive 2007/47/EC introduced the definition of clinical data into the *MDD* and *AIMDD*, contributing to efforts to harmonise regulatory requirements regarding clinical data requirements, i.e., the new definition in the revised directives is virtually identical to the definition in the Global Harmonization Task Force (GHTF) guidance document on clinical evidence.

In addition to the need to base specific general Essential Requirements upon clinical data, other Essential Requirements regarding design and construction may also need to be based upon clinical data. For this reason, an evaluation of the need to base compliance on clinical data should be considered for all applicable Essential Requirements and not just those specified in Annex X of the *MDD* and Annex 7 of the *AIMDD*.

Annex X of the *MDD* and Annex 7 of the *AIMDD* clarify that the evaluation of clinical data is termed "clinical evaluation;" a process discussed in the next section of this chapter.

Clinical Evaluation Requirements

All devices subject to the *MDD* and *AIMDD* require a clinical evaluation, regardless of the device class, unless there is convincing justification otherwise. This requirement is in the Essential Requirement described in Section 6a of Annex I of the *MDD*, which states: "Demonstration of conformity with the Essential Requirements must include a clinical evaluation in accordance with Annex X." The same requirement is in Section 5a of Annex 1 of the *AIMDD*; however, reference is made to Annex 7. This means that all devices covered by the *MDD* and *AIMDD* require a clinical evaluation, regardless of the *MDD* device class; however, a possible exemption from this requirement is provided in Annex X of the *MDD* and Annex 7 of the *AIMDD*. This exclusion is discussed later.

Table 20-1. General Essential Requirements Usually Requiring Clinical Data

MDD Essential Requirements, Annex I I. General Requirements	AIMDD Essential Requirements, Annex 1 I. General Requirements
Section 1. The devices must be designed and manufactured in such a way that, when used under the conditions and for the purposes intended, they will not compromise the clinical condition or the safety of patients, or the safety and health of users or, where applicable, other persons, provided that any risks which may be associated with their intended use constitute acceptable risks when weighed against the benefits to the patient and are compatible with a high level of protection of health and safety. This shall include: • reducing, as far as possible, the risk of use error due to the ergonomic features of the device and the environment in which the device is intended to be used (design for patient safety), and • consideration of the technical knowledge, experience, education and training and, where applicable, the medical and physical condition of intended users (design for lay, professional, disabled or other users).	Section 1. The devices must be designed and manufactured in such a way that, when implanted under the conditions and for the purposes laid down, their use does not compromise the clinical condition or the safety of patients. They must not present any risk to the persons implanting them or, where applicable, to other persons.
Section 3. The devices must achieve the performances intended by the manufacturer and be designed, manufactured and packaged in such a way that they are suitable for one or more of the functions referred to in Article 1 (2) (a), as specified by the manufacturer.	Section 2. The devices must achieve the performances intended by the manufacturer, viz. be designed and manufactured in such a way that they are suitable for one or more of the functions referred to in Article 1 (2) (a) as specified by him.
Section 6. Any undesirable side effects must constitute an acceptable risk when weighed against the performances intended.	Section 5. Any side effects or undesirable conditions must constitute acceptable risks when weighed against the performances intended.

Both Annex X of the *MDD* and Annex 7 of the *AIMDD* are entitled "Clinical Evaluation" and both consist of Section 1, General provisions, and Section 2, Clinical investigation. The requirements for clinical evaluation are found in Section 1 of the directives and are briefly described in this chapter; however, the complete texts of Annex X of the *MDD* and Annex 7 of the *AIMDD* should be reviewed to gain a full understanding of the requirements.

Clinical evaluation must take into account, where appropriate, any relevant harmonised standards and must follow a defined and methodologically sound procedure. It can be based upon a critical evaluation of scientific literature, the results of all clinical investigations conducted on the device in question or a combination of clinical data from both these sources.

In practice, unless medical device technology is innovative and very little scientific literature exists related to the device, a literature search should always be conducted regardless of a manufacturer's intention to conduct one or more clinical investigations. In fact, a clinical evaluation

based upon the results of a properly conducted literature search, taking positive and negative clinical data into account, and the results of an analysis of preclinical data are critical factors that need to be considered in the design of the clinical investigation(s).

If clinical evaluation is based upon clinical data from scientific literature, specific requirements apply:
• scientific literature must be currently available
• scientific literature must relate to the device's safety, performance, design characteristics and intended purpose , where there is demonstration of equivalence of the device to the device to which the data relates
• data adequately demonstrate compliance with the relevant Essential Requirements

If a clinical evaluation is based upon clinical data from clinical investigations, all clinical investigations, regardless of the outcome, must be included in the clinical evaluation.

A clinical evaluation can also be based upon scientific

literature together with data from clinical investigations of the device that is the subject of the clinical evaluation.

Section 1.1a of Annex X of the *MDD* requires that, in the case of implantable devices and devices in Class III, clinical investigations shall be performed unless the manufacturer can duly justify relying on existing clinical data. Section 1.2 of Annex 7 of the *AIMDD* requires that clinical investigations shall be performed unless the manufacturer can duly justify relying on existing clinical data.

The clinical evaluation and its outcome must be documented and the documentation must be included and/or referenced in the device technical documentation.

The clinical evaluation and its documentation must be actively updated with data obtained from postmarket surveillance. Where postmarket clinical follow-up (PMCF) as part of the device's postmarket surveillance plan is not deemed necessary, this must be duly justified and documented.

As indicated previously, Annex X of the *MDD* and Annex 7 of the *AIMDD* allow for exclusion of the need to base conformity with the Essential Requirements on clinical data. This exclusion is described in Section 1.1d of Annex X of the *MDD* and Section 1.5 of Annex 7 of the *AIMDD*. These sections state that where demonstration of conformity with Essential Requirements based upon clinical data is not deemed appropriate, adequate justification for any such exclusion must be given based on risk management output and under consideration of the specifics of the device/body interaction, the clinical performances intended and the manufacturer's claims. In addition, the adequacy of demonstration of conformity with the Essential Requirements by performance evaluation, bench testing and preclinical evaluation alone must be duly substantiated.

Finally, Section 1.2 of Annex X of the *MDD* states that all data must remain confidential in accordance with the provisions of Article 20, whereas Section 1.6 of Annex 7 of the *AIMDD* states that all data must remain confidential unless it is deemed essential that they be divulged.

Clinical Evaluation Guidance Documents

The most important guidance document on how to comply with the European medical device requirements for clinical evaluation is, *Clinical Evaluation: A Guide for Manufacturers and Notified Bodies*. It replaces the previous version, which was issued in April 2003 and was only 19 pages. The current version is based almost entirely on the GHTF document, *Clinical Evaluation*, and is 46 pages. It is a more comprehensive document that not only explains the requirements for and importance of clinical evaluation, but also provides more-detailed advice on the clinical evaluation process.

The current guidance document includes an introduction and scope, references, definitions, general principles of clinical evaluation, sources of data/documentation used in a clinical evaluation (Stage 1), appraisal of clinical data (Stage 2), analysis of the clinical data (Stage 3), the clinical evaluation report and the role of the Notified Body in the assessment of clinical evaluation data. It also contains six appendices, which provide: a possible format for the literature search report, a possible methodology for documenting the screening and selection of literature within a literature search report, some examples to assist with the formulation of criteria, a possible method of appraisal, a possible format for a clinical evaluation report and a clinical evaluation checklist for Notified Bodies.

In addition to general European guidance on clinical evaluation, European guidance on the clinical evaluation of coronary stents was published as Appendix 1 of the previous version of the European clinical evaluation guidance document. This appendix is still considered in force even though its parent document is obsolete. The appendix is expected to be updated to refer to the current version of the European clinical evaluation guidance document. The purpose of the guidance is to assist manufacturers of coronary stents in their clinical investigations and the subsequent evaluation of all clinical data required under the *MDD*. It is also intended to assist Notified Bodies in conducting their design dossier reviews, type test certifications or evaluations of notifications of significant changes in coronary stents, and Member State Competent Authorities in their postmarket surveillance of coronary stents. The guidance document covers factors that should be considered during preclinical assessment, clinical investigations, clinical evaluation, PMCF and modifications to the stent or its indications for use.

Another important guidance document has been developed by the Notified Body Operations Group (NBOG): *Checklist for Audit of Notified Bodies Review of Clinical Data/Clinical Evaluation*. This guidance document is not directed to manufacturers, but is intended to act as a checklist for designating authorities when they evaluate the Notified Body's ability to assess clinical data and clinical evaluation documents. Nonetheless, it is useful for manufacturers because section B of the document indicates the types of documentation and activities that Notified Bodies should check during their clinical evaluation assessments. It is important to note that the items in the NBOG checklist are not identical to those in the European clinical evaluation guidance checklist.

Importance of Clinical Evaluation

As discussed in the European clinical evaluation guidance document, clinical evaluation is the assessment and analysis of clinical data pertaining to a medical device in order to verify its clinical safety and performance. It is a very important process, which is first conducted during the conformity assessment process leading to the marketing of the medical device, and then becomes an ongoing process that must be updated throughout the device's lifecycle.

Because of the need to periodically update the clinical evaluation, manufacturers need to have effective postmarket surveillance programs appropriate for the particular device and its intended use. The data from such programs may include adverse event reports, results from published literature, further clinical studies, formal postmarket surveillance studies or other resources. These data should be used to update the clinical evaluation, which is then fed into the ongoing risk analysis. Updating the risk analysis allows manufacturers to make appropriate decisions regarding device safety and performance claims.

Clinical Evaluation Process

The introduction of the guidance document states that to conduct a clinical evaluation, a manufacturer needs to:

- identify the Essential Requirements that require support from relevant clinical data
- identify available clinical data relevant to the device and its intended use
- evaluate data in terms of their suitability for establishing the device's safety and performance
- generate any clinical data needed to address outstanding issues
- bring all the clinical data together to reach conclusions about the device's clinical safety and performance

From a practical point of view, however, the actions that need to be taken in developing a clinical evaluation report are somewhat different from the steps listed above and include:

- ensuring that the Essential Requirements checklists for the devices concerned are accurate and up-to-date so that those requiring clinical data can be identified
- ensuring that relevant harmonised standards have been identified because conformity to these standards may be sufficient to demonstrate compliance with relevant Essential Requirements
- defining the scope of the clinical evaluation based upon the Essential Requirements that need to be addressed from a clinical perspective
- ensuring the adequacy of risk management documentation for the device concerned
- identifying relevant equivalent devices, which should be based upon clinical, technical and biological characteristics
- following the three stages of clinical evaluation as described in the European guidance on clinical evaluation, which are briefly described below

Stage I, Sources of Data/Documentation

During this stage, clinical data should be identified from literature searches, clinical experience and/or clinical investigation. It should also be kept in mind during this stage that conformity to harmonised standards may be sufficient to demonstrate compliance to relevant Essential Requirements. Each of these types of data sources is discussed briefly.

Clinical data from literature searches may relate to the device in question or to equivalent devices. A critical element is the development of a literature search protocol that includes the search strategy and methods. For many manufacturers, the development of such a protocol will be a new activity. Thus, it is important that people with the requisite training and/or experience develop these protocols and evaluate the selected papers. Otherwise, the usefulness of the resulting search could be questioned. A literature search report should include the protocol and note any deviations from it. The European clinical evaluation guidance document provides detailed advice on conducting the literature search, including a possible format for the literature search report in Appendix A of the guidance document and a possible methodology for documenting the screening and selection of literature within a literature search report in Appendix B.

Clinical experience is clinical data from clinical use other than clinical investigations and consists of published and unpublished reports. Some examples of clinical experience include manufacturer premarket or postmarket surveillance reports, registries, adverse events databases and details of clinically relevant field corrective actions. These data are considered valuable because they provide actual experience obtained in populations extending beyond the controlled environment of a clinical study. The European clinical evaluation guidance document provides additional information on the use of clinical experience in clinical evaluations.

Clinical investigations conducted by or on behalf of the manufacturer, where documentation on the study design, ethical and regulatory approvals, conduct and results and conclusions are available, allow much more information to be used in the clinical evaluation compared with a published paper on a clinical study. For this reason, well-designed clinical studies are one of the most valuable sources of clinical data for clinical evaluation purposes. Clinical investigations used for clinical evaluations should have been conducted under good clinical practices in accordance with applicable regulatory requirements. Any clinical investigation not in compliance with applicable ethical standards or regulations should be rejected and the reasons for rejection of the investigation should be noted in the clinical evaluation report.

Stage II, Appraisal of Clinical Data

This stage involves the appraisal of individual data sets for suitability and how their results contribute to the demonstration of safety and performance. Without the effective appraisal of identified data, the value of the resulting clinical evaluation is questionable. Therefore, manufacturers need to ensure that the people appraising clinical data are qualified to assess them for their quality and relevance to the device in question and its intended use.

The European clinical evaluation guidance document describes what should be covered by the appraisal. For example, the evaluator of the data should identify in advance the appropriate criteria for appraising each data set. Appendix C of the guidance document provides examples to assist with the formulation of criteria for appraising data from randomised controlled studies, cohort studies, case-controlled studies and case series. Appendix D provides a possible method of appraisal that includes sample criteria for suitability (of the data to address questions about the device) (Table D1) and for data contribution (of results to demonstrate safety and performance) (Table D2).

Stage III, Analysis of the Clinical Data

Once each data set has been appraised, it is necessary to determine if they collectively demonstrate the device's clinical safety and performance for its intended use. The European clinical evaluation guidance document explains that analysis methods are generally quantitative or qualitative. The document points out that because most devices are developed through incremental changes in device design with more reliance on literature and clinical experience than on clinical investigations, qualitative or descriptive methods are generally used to address the incremental changes. Data sets, which may be considered pivotal regarding conclusions of safety and performance, should be identified, as well as any inconsistencies across data sets in identified risks and device performance characteristics.

The final step in the analysis is a determination of whether the combined data support compliance with the Essential Requirements that were identified in the scope of the clinical evaluation. The European clinical evaluation guidance document discusses several factors to be taken into consideration during this final step, for example, the number of patients exposed to the device and the number and severity of adverse events. It also discusses the need to review device literature and instructions for use to ensure they are consistent with the data, and all hazards and other clinically relevant information have been appropriately identified.

Clinical Evaluation Report

The results of the clinical evaluation process are documented in a clinical evaluation report. The report, together with the clinical data on which it is based, serves as the clinical evidence that supports the safety and performance claims being made for the device. The clinical evidence and other design verification and validation documentation—device description, labelling, risk analysis and manufacturing information—are needed to demonstrate conformity with the Essential Requirements.

According to the European clinical evaluation guidance document, the clinical evaluation report should describe the scope and context of the evaluation; the clinical data; the appraisal and analysis stages; and conclusions about the safety and performance of the device in question. The guidance document also states that the report should contain sufficient information to be read as a standalone document by an independent party such as a regulatory authority or Notified Body. Therefore, the report should outline:

- the technology on which the medical device is based, the intended use of the device and any claims made about the device's clinical performance or safety
- the nature and extent of the clinical data that have been evaluated
- how the referenced information (recognised standards and/or clinical data) demonstrate the clinical performance and safety of the device in question

A suggested format for the clinical evaluation report is provided in Appendix E of the guidance document.

Notified Body Role and Assessment Checklist

The last section of the European guidance document on clinical evaluation is Section 10, The Role of the Notified Body in the Assessment of Clinical Evaluation Data. This section is also intended to serve as best practice guidance for Competent Authorities in their market surveillance activities. For these reasons, manufacturers should pay particular attention to this section of the guidance document because it can help them successfully prepare not only for Notified Body (NB) assessments of clinical evaluations but also for assessments by Competent Authorities conducting market surveillance checks.

This section describes the different roles of an NB, depending upon the classification of the device and the Conformity Assessment Procedure. It provides guidance on how the NB should examine clinical evaluation documentation submitted in a design dossier or type-examination dossier. This section also covers the examination by the NB of clinical evaluation procedures and documentation as part of the quality system, including the review of written procedures and the technical documentation of Class IIa and Class IIb devices.

Appendix F of the guidance document provides a checklist the NB should use when assessing clinical evaluation documentation. The checklist is 12 pages and is very detailed with regard to the documentation that should be examined. The first section of the checklist addresses the evaluation of a manufacturer's justification for demonstrating conformity to relevant Essential Requirements without clinical data. Each of the additional five sections contains multiple aspects of the clinical evaluation documentation that is to be checked.

Clinical Evaluation Procedures

The European clinical evaluation guidance document foresees documented procedures for the evaluation of clinical data. This is clearly stated in Section 10.2.1 of the document, Review of the Manufacturer's Procedures, which states that the NB must, as part of the review of the manufacturer's quality system, assess the establishment, maintenance and application of the manufacturer's documented procedures for the evaluation of clinical data. Furthermore, it states that the NB review should cover:

- the proper assignment of responsibilities to suitably qualified persons involved in the clinical evaluation, such as clinical evaluator(s), information retrieval expert(s) and clinical investigator(s)
- the integration of clinical evaluation into the quality system as a continuous process, to be specifically interrelated to, and informed by, preclinical evaluation and risk management
- Standard Operating Procedures to assure proper planning, conduct, evaluation, control and documentation of scope, identification of clinical data, literature searching, collection of clinical experience, clinical investigation and appraisal of clinical data
- analysis of clinical data, concluding, reporting and updating clinical evaluation, including PMCF (MEDDEV 2.12/2)
- document control as part of overall documentation of procedures, reporting, qualifications and technical documentation/design dossier(s)
- identification and evaluation of undesirable side effects and of clinical performance(s)

Thus, an important task for manufacturers is to ensure that appropriate quality system written procedures cover these activities.

Summary

Medical device manufacturers need to ensure that they fully understand European clinical evaluation requirements. Failure to do so is risky and can lead to nonconformities during quality system audits by NBs, problems during technical documentation reviews by NBs and/or compliance issues during Competent Authority marketing surveillance checks. Even more importantly, failure to adequately understand and comply with the requirements could result in a failure to develop sufficient clinical data to support device safety and performance claims, which can place patients and users in jeopardy and expose manufacturers to unnecessary product liability risks.

These problems can be avoided by carefully reviewing the European clinical evaluation guidance document, checking with the NB or qualified expert(s) where doubts in interpretation of the requirements exist, developing clear and easy-to-follow clinical evaluation procedures and ensuring that individuals with the needed expertise are involved in performing clinical evaluations.

EU Medical Device Clinical Investigations

By Sarah Sorrel and Estelle Geffard-Duchamp

OBJECTIVES

❑ Understand how medical device clinical investigations relate to CE marking

❑ Understand the applicable regulations for initiating and conducting clinical investigations in the EU

❑ Understand the documentation requirements

DIRECTIVES, REGULATIONS AND GUIDELINES COVERED IN THIS CHAPTER

❑ Council Directive 93/42/EEC of 14 June 1993 concerning medical devices, Article 15 and Annexes VIII and X

❑ Council Directive 90/385/EEC of 20 June 1990 on the approximation of the laws of the Member States relating to active implantable medical devices, Article 10 and Annexes 6 and 7

❑ Directive 2007/47/EEC of the European Parliament and of the Council of 5 September 2007 amending Council Directive 90/385/EEC on the approximation of the laws of the Member States relating to active implantable medical devices, Council Directive 93/42/EEC concerning medical devices and Directive 98/8/EC concerning the placing of biocidal products on the market

❑ Co-ordination of Notified Bodies Medical Devices (NB-MED) on Council Directives 90/385/EEC,

93/42/EEC and 98/79/EC, NB-Med 2.7/ Recital 3, Evaluation of Clinical Data, Clinical Investigations, Clinical Evaluation

❑ MEDDEV 2.7.1 Rev 3, Guidelines on Medical Devices, December 2009

❑ MEDDEV 2.12.2, Guidelines on Post Market Clinical Follow-up, May 2004

❑ ISO 14155-1:2010, *Clinical Investigations of medical devices for human subjects*

❑ Declaration of Helsinki, October 2008

KEY TERMS AND DEFINITIONS (ISO 14155)

❑ adverse device effect (ADE)—any untoward and unintended response to a medical device

❑ case report form (CRF)—document designed to record all information to be reported to the sponsor on each subject as required by the clinical investigation plan

❑ clinical investigation—any designed and planned systematic study in human subjects undertaken to verify the safety and/or performance of a specific device

❑ clinical investigation plan (CIP)—document that states the rationale, objectives, design and proposed analysis, methodology, monitoring, conduct and record-keeping of the clinical investigation

- ethics committee (EC)—independent and properly constituted competent body responsible for ensuring that the safety, well-being and human rights of the subjects participating in a clinical investigation are protected

- investigator—individual and/or institution responsible for the conduct of a clinical investigation and assuming clinical responsibility for the well-being of the subjects involved

- Investigator's Brochure (IB)—compilation of the clinical and nonclinical information on the device(s) under investigation relevant to human subjects

- monitor—individual appointed by the sponsor who is responsible for assessing the investigator's compliance with the clinical investigation plan and for verifying source data

- serious adverse event—adverse event that:

  o led to death
  o led to a serious deterioration in the health of the subject that
     ◊ resulted in life-threatening illness or injury
     ◊ resulted in a permanent impairment of a body structure or a body function
     ◊ required in-patient hospitalisation or prolongation of existing hospitalisation
     ◊ resulted in medical or surgical intervention to prevent permanent impairment to body structure or a body function
  o led to foetal distress, foetal death or a congenital abnormality or birth defect.

- sponsor—individual or organisation with responsibility for the initiation and/or implementation of a clinical investigation

Introduction

Pursuant to Directive 2007/47/EC of the European Parliament and of the Council of 5 September 2007, all medical devices are subject to clinical evaluation prior to CE marking. In cases where a medical device cannot be fully evaluated with respect to its safety, performance and favourable risk/benefit ratio without prospective clinical data, a clinical investigation is necessary. Furthermore, since this directive came into full force in March 2010, clinical investigations are now mandatory for CE marking of all implantable and Class III devices, unless duly justified by the manufacturer.

Clinical Investigations and CE Marking

Within the meaning of the European legislation on medical devices, clinical investigations are clinical trials that are carried out by or on behalf of a manufacturer specifically for the purposes of conformity assessment in accordance with the requirements for CE marking. Such clinical investigations are subject to the requirements of the medical devices directives, i.e., are generally expected to be designed, conducted and reported in accordance with EN ISO 14155:2010 or to a comparable standard and to comply with applicable national laws.

There is no requirement that clinical investigations for CE marking be carried out in full or in part within the EU insofar as the clinical data, wherever it is obtained, is relevant to the intended use of the device in Europe.

The standard for *Clinical investigations of medical devices for human subjects*, EN ISO 14155:2010 (which replaced the original EN 540:1993) was developed under the former *Medical Devices Directive* (*MDD*) and *Active Implantable Medical Devices Directive* (*AIMDD*) to describe the procedures that need to be followed in a clinical investigation to ensure its ethical conduct and the scientific validity of its results. In essence, EN ISO 14155:2010 is a Good Clinical Practice guideline for medical device clinical trials as it outlines, in particular, the respective roles and responsibilities of the clinical investigator, the sponsor and the monitor.

EN ISO 14155:2010 is a European harmonised standard. Therefore, any clinical study that meets its requirements is regarded as fulfilling the legal requirements of the *MDD* and *AIMDD*, i.e., there is a "presumption of conformity" of the results with the directives. However, as it is also an international standard and is intended to apply throughout the world, EN ISO 14155:2010 does not include any legal regulatory requirements for clinical investigations. It should be noted that EN ISO 14155:2010 does not apply to in vitro diagnostic devices, since their clinical performance can be established by an investigation that does not involve the use of the investigational device in the treatment of patients.

Clinical investigations are clinical trials that usually involve non-CE-marked devices. The directives clearly specify that the requirements for clinical investigations do not apply to clinical trials with CE-marked devices used within their intended use as specified in the labelling. Clinical trials of CE-marked devices may be performed in the postmarket phase as part of a postmarket surveillance program pursuant to the requirements in Directive 2007/47/EEC for postmarket clinical follow-up (PMCF).

Table 21-1. Key Elements for Clinical Investigation Regulatory Submissions*

Notification form, if applicable
Clinical Investigation Plan (CIP)
Case report form (CRF)
Patient informed consent
Curriculum vitae of Principal Investigator and co-investigators
Insurance certificates, if applicable
Investigator's Brochure (IB)
Notification fees, if applicable

AIMDD Annex 6 2.2, 3.2; MDD Annex VIII 2.2, 3.2; EN ISO 14155-1 section 7; National Transpositions

Regulatory Framework for Clinical Investigations

Regulatory Requirements for Clinical Investigations in the EU

Special requirements apply to non-CE-marked devices that are put into service for clinical investigation purposes in the EU. These requirements are set forth in the *MDD* and transposed into the national laws of each Member State.

First and foremost, according to the directives, clinical investigations should only be carried out for the purpose of conformity assessment and—before being placed under investigation—devices must meet all of the Essential Requirements of the directives except those that are subject of the clinical trial. Further, the manufacturer must sign a written statement to this effect, the Statement of Compliance, per Annex VIII of the *MDD*. Clinical investigations with non-CE-marked devices can only be undertaken for the purpose of verifying that, under normal conditions of use, the safety and performance of the devices meet the requirements of the directive.

The directives specify that clinical investigations shall have ethics committee approval prior to initiation and shall be notified to the Competent Authority (*AIMDD* Annex 7-2.2/*MDD* Annex X-2.2 and *AIMDD* Article 10.1/*MDD* Article 15.1, respectively). The key components of the ethics committee and Competent Authority submissions are outlined in **Table 21-1**.

The directives specify that the Competent Authority may apply a waiting period of up to 60 days before the clinical investigation can start. Examples of differences in timelines in national transpositions for several Member States are provided in **Table 21-2**.

Following are some points to consider regarding regulatory submissions in EU Member States:

Ethics committee submissions:
- Which ethics committee(s) should be consulted (local/national)?
- Who should submit (investigator/sponsor)?
- What specific form(s) is to be completed and what is the specific format for submission?
- What is the submission fee?

- What are the submission deadlines?
- What is the frequency of meetings?
- What is the time to approval?

Competent Authority Notifications:
- What specific form(s) is to be completed and what is the specific format for submission (same as ethics committee form or different)?
- Is prior ethics committee approval needed or is notification in parallel with ethics committee submission?
- Who performs notification and to which authority(ies)?
- What is the notification fee?
- What are the timeline and rules for review—does the clock stop or not?
- How is the "60 day waiting period" applied?

Moreover, the revised *MDD* requires that, during the course of the clinical investigation, notification of all serious adverse events—whether device- or procedure-related or not—must be provided to the Competent Authorities in all Member States where the clinical investigation is being conducted (*AIMDD* Annex 7 2.3.5/*MDD* Annex X 2.3.5). Competent Authorities and the European Commission have developed a summary reporting form that considerably simplifies this task. This form is accepted by all Competent Authorities, apart from Germany, which requires detailed reports for each serious adverse event that occurs in Germany. Other Competent Authorities reserve the right to require detailed information on individual incidents on a case-by-case basis, for example, when there are concerns about device-related effects or clinical practice at a particular clinical centre. A guidance document (MEDDEV) on this subject, which includes the summary reporting form, is under development by the Commission at the time of this writing.

All of these basic requirements have been transposed into the national laws of each Member State and therefore apply in one form or another in each EU country. However, there are significant differences in how the regulations are

Table 21-2. Overview of Regulatory Approval Timelines in Six EU Member States

Competent Authority Timelines for Approval	Belgium	France	Germany	Italy	The Netherlands	Spain
Submission in parallel with EC (Y/N)	No	Yes	Yes	No	No	Yes
Pre-checking (Y/N)	yes (20 days)	yes (5 days)	yes (10 days)	yes	No	Yes (10 days)
Review period	60 days	60 days	30 days	60 days	N/A	60 days
Clock stopped in case of questions (Y/N)	No	No	Yes	Yes	N/A	Yes

actually applied in each jurisdiction and these should be reviewed carefully on a country-by-country basis prior to conducting clinical investigations in the EU. Further, in many countries, additional regulations may apply on the national, regional or local level and these should be thoroughly researched. For example, national requirements for insurance coverage of clinical trials vary from no statutory requirement (UK) to highly specific requirements for minimum coverage per subject, per protocol and for a specified duration (France).

Finally, amendments to the clinical investigation plan and/or changes to the clinical investigation device, including amendments to the protocol or patient informed consent form or substantial changes to the device (i.e., where the change has an impact on the declaration of conformity, the risk analysis or conformity with the Essential Requirements) are also subject to the regulations. Depending upon the nature of the change, full review by the ethics committee and/or Competent Authority may be required. Changes may also have an impact on the insurance coverage.

Key Elements of EN ISO 14155:2010

As stated above, it is recommended that clinical investigations comply with the recently revised European harmonised standard ISO 14155:2010, *Clinical investigation of medical devices for human subjects*. Following are key elements of the revised standard and a brief description of the contents of each section.

Ethical Considerations

Clinical investigations should be conducted in accordance with the ethical principles laid down in the most recent revision of the Declaration of Helsinki. Communication should be established with an appropriate ethics committee

and a process, described in the protocol, should be followed for obtaining and documenting informed consent by subjects participating in a clinical investigation. The standard provides useful guidance on the consent process for vulnerable populations and for special circumstances such as emergency situations.

Clinical Investigation Planning

This section is central to the decision on whether or not to perform a clinical investigation. It places the clinical investigation of a medical device within the context of the general risk management process. It requires a full risk assessment in line with ISO 14971:2007, *Application of risk management to medical devices*, and consideration of risks associated with the clinical procedure in order to justify the decision to embark on a clinical investigation and to identify anticipated adverse device effects. It also requires a critical assessment of clinical and preclinical investigations pertaining to the device to justify the design of the clinical investigation. Furthermore, it sets forth detailed requirements for key study documents such as the clinical investigation plan, the Investigator's Brochure (IB), the case report forms, monitoring plan, investigator agreements, labelling and pre-study procedures such as investigation site selection and establishment of data monitoring committees.

Clinical Investigation Conduct

This section covers the key aspects of the conduct of a clinical investigation from clinical site initiation, monitoring and adverse event handling through documentation, confidentiality of data, data recording and control, accountability of investigational devices and subjects and, finally, auditing.

Suspension, Termination and Close-out of Clinical Investigation

Specific guidance and procedures regarding suspension or premature termination of a clinical investigation are given. This section also details the procedures for routine close-out and the requirements for clinical investigation reports and document retention.

Responsibilities of the Sponsor and Investigator

These sections provide detailed guidance on the respective roles and responsibilities of the sponsor, including monitoring the investigation, and for the Principal Investigator. These should be carefully integrated into study procedures and contracts.

Documentation for Clinical Investigations

Guidance on three key documents related to clinical investigations is provided as Annexes of ISO 14155.

Annex A: Clinical Investigation Plan (CIP)

The main purpose of the CIP is to describe precisely what is to be done in the study. Thus, it needs to describe clearly the hypothesis to be tested, study design, primary and secondary objectives and endpoints, study population, inclusion and exclusion criteria, statistical design, methodology, analytical procedures, etc. Although the IB (see next section) contains supporting technical and clinical data, the CIP should contain sufficient information to provide a justification for these aspects of study design. A carefully constructed CIP can optimise the scientific validity and value of study results.

The content of the CIP is specified in Annex A of ISO 14155 under the following headings:
- identification of the clinical investigation plan
- sponsor
- Principal Investigator, coordinating investigator and investigation site(s)
- overall synopsis of the clinical investigation
- identification and description of the investigational device
- justification for the design of the clinical investigation
- investigational device and clinical investigation risks and benefits
- objectives and hypotheses of the clinical investigation
- design of the clinical investigation, including investigational device(s) and comparator(s), procedures, monitoring plan
- statistical considerations
- data management
- amendments to the CIP
- CIP deviations
- device accountability

- statements of compliance
- informed consent process
- adverse events, adverse device effects and device deficiencies
- vulnerable population
- early termination or suspension of the clinical investigation
- publication policy
- bibliography

Any deviation from the CIP must be recorded, with an explanation. Deviations must be reported to the sponsor, who is responsible for analysing them and assessing their significance.

Annex B: Investigators Brochure (IB)

The purpose of the IB is to provide the investigator of a clinical investigation with sufficient safety and performance data from preclinical investigations and/or previous clinical investigations to justify human exposure to the specified investigational device. The IB should, therefore, contain a summary of the literature and preclinical and existing clinical data, with an evaluation justifying the device's intended use and the clinical investigation design.

The content of the IB is specified in Annex B of ISO 14155, under the following headings:
- identification of the IB
- sponsor/manufacturer
- preclinical testing
- existing clinical data
- risk management
- regulatory and other references

The IB should be updated throughout the course of the clinical investigation as significant new information becomes available. The revised brochure should be sent to Competent Authorities and ethics committees for approval and then distributed to all investigators.

Annex C: Case Report Forms (CRFs)

CRFs are used to record data collected during the study. The content of the CRFs is specified in Annex C of ISO 14155, under the following headings:
- overall considerations
- cover page/login screen
- header or footer/e-CRF identifier
- types of CRFs
- procedural issues

Annex D: Final Report

A final report is required upon completion of the clinical investigation, even if terminated prematurely. The final report must be presented in written form. It must be signed by the sponsor and the coordinating investigator (if appointed) and the principal clinical investigator(s) in each centre and made available, upon request, to all clinical investigators, the ethics committee(s) and the Competent Authority(ies).

The final report must include a thorough identification of the device(s), a description of the clinical investigation's methodology and design, any deviations from the CIP and data analysis with any statistical analysis and a critical appraisal in relation to the aims of the investigation. The final report should take into account all data from each investigation centre/site and all enrolled subjects. No subject should be identifiable either from the final report or published results. All clinical investigators must have the opportunity to review and comment on the final report.

The content of the clinical investigation report is specified in Annex D of ISO 14155, under the following headings:

- cover page
- table of contents
- summary
- introduction
- investigational device and methods
- investigational device description
- CIP
- results
- discussion and overall conclusions
- abbreviated terms and definitions
- ethics
- investigators and administrative structure of clinical investigation
- signature page
- annexes to the report

Summary

Under the medical devices directives, a clinical evaluation is necessary for all devices, regardless of their classification. A key component of the clinical evaluation is the results of a clinical investigation conducted in accordance with the standard EN ISO 14155. This chapter describes the regulatory requirements that are applicable to clinical investigations carried out for the purpose of CE marking both in the premarket and postmarket phases.

EU Conformity Assessment Procedures Quality Systems Requirements

By Ludger Möller

OBJECTIVES

❑ Understand the Conformity Assessment Procedures and the similarities between directives

❑ Understand the flexibility of the Conformity Assessment Procedures in relation to the risk classes

❑ Understand the involvement of Notified Bodies

❑ Understand the relationship of the Conformity Assessment Procedures to the quality system standard

DIRECTIVES, REGULATIONS AND GUIDELINES COVERED IN THIS CHAPTER

❑ Council Directive 90/385/EEC of 20 June 1990 on the approximation of the laws of the Member States relating to active implantable medical devices (*Active Implantable Medical Devices Directive*)

❑ Council Directive 93/42/EEC of 14 June 1993 concerning medical devices (*Medical Devices Directive*)

❑ Directive 98/79/EC of the European Parliament and of the Council of 27 October 1998 on *in vitro* diagnostic medical devices (*In Vitro Devices Directive*)

❑ Directive 2000/70/EC of the European Parliament and of the Council of the 16 November 2000 amending Council Directive 93/42/EEC as regards medical devices incorporating stable derivates of human blood or human plasma

❑ Directive 2002/98/EC of the European Parliament and of the Council of 27 January 2003 setting standards of quality and safety for the collection, testing, processing, storage and distribution of human blood and blood components and amending Directive2001/83/EC

❑ Commission Directive 2003/12/EC of 3 February 2003 on the reclassification of breast implants in the framework of Directive 93/42/EEC concerning medical devices

❑ Commission Directive 2005/50/EC of 11 August 2005 on the reclassification of hip, knee and shoulder joint replacements in the framework of Council Directive 93/42/EEC concerning medical devices

❑ Directive 2007/47/EC of the European Parliament and of the Council of 5 September 2007 amending Council Directive 90/385/EEC on the approximation of the laws of the Member States relating to active implantable medical devices, Council Directive 93/42/EEC concerning medical devices and Directive 98/8/EC concerning the placing of biocidal products on the market

- Decision 93/465/EEC Council Decision of 22 July 1993 concerning the modules for the various phases of the conformity assessment procedures and the rules for the affixing and use of the CE conformity marking, which are intended to be used in the technical harmonization directives

- Decision No 768/2008/EC of the European Parliament and of the Council and of 9 July 2008 on a common framework for the marketing of products, and repealing Council Decision 93/465/EEC

- EN ISO 13485 Medical Devices—Quality management systems—Requirements for regulatory purposes

Introduction

It must be understood that the European system relies upon medical device manufacturers' ability to comply with the requirements applicable to them and their products. The articles of each directive describe the requirements and the annexes may be considered the *a la carte* menu on how to apply the requirements. Article 9 of the *Active Implantable Medical Devices Directive* (*AIMDD*), Article 11 of the *Medical Devices Directive* (*MDD*) and Article 9 in the *In Vitro Devices Directive* (*IVDD*) outline the requirements of Conformity Assessment Procedures (CAPs) available to the manufacturer. Those articles refer to a specific annex or combination of annexes a manufacturer may apply based upon the medical device's classification. The CAPs include quality system- and product-related aspects. The selection of annexes allows the application of a specific CAP, which may emphasise one aspect over the other.

The overall goal of the various CAPs is to ensure that a medical device used under proper conditions and for its intended purpose will not compromise the patient's clinical condition or safety, provided that any risks are acceptable when weighed against the benefit of the device throughout its lifetime.

General Aspects

The *AIMDD*, *MDD* and *IVDD* provide a variety of CAP choices. However, the procedures are comparable due to the fact that they have been created based upon Council Decision 93/465/EEC of 22 July 1993 concerning the modules for the various phases of the conformity assessment procedures and the rules for the affixing and use of the CE conformity marking. This decision was replaced by Decision No 768/2008/EC of the European Parliament and of the Council of 9 July 2008 on a common framework for the marketing of products, which reinforces the Global Approach.[1] All directive updates will follow this new

decision. The description of the general CAPs still applies within this decision; therefore, we will see the same elements in the future.

Another aspect that makes the conformity assessment similar across the various directives is the so-called New Approach, which addresses technical barriers among Member States (Directive 98/34/EC of the European Parliament and of the Council of 22 June 1998 laying down a procedure for the provision of information in the field of technical standards and regulations).[2] This has led to the implementation of harmonised standards or common technical specifications. All New Approach directives use modules, which can be variously applied to demonstrate conformity assessment.

In general, all CAPs require the preparation of technical documentation that refers to, among other things, the Essential Requirements, which are described in the first annex of each directive.

Product-related aspects vary simply due to the type of products, but the quality system standard for medical devices is currently EN ISO 13485, which may be applied for all quality system-related requirements.

All CAPs require manufacturer vigilance and postmarket surveillance after the product has been delivered or installed.

At the time of writing, there are movements in the EU to combine the three medical devices directives into one regulation. This proposal seems to find support from the various stakeholders for the *AIMDD* and the *MDD* but not the *IVDD*. However, the combination of all directives is certainly possible, taking each speciality into consideration. An example of combining the legislations may be seen with the German transposition of all three directives in one law, the *Medizinproduktegestz* (*MPG*).

It is important for manufacturers that have different medical devices to relate the requirements of the directives to one another. For example, an in vitro medical device kit manufacturer may have to include a medical device within the kit and therefore the CAP selected by the manufacturer should satisfy the requirements of the *IVDD* and *MDD* CAP. However, understanding the *IVDD* requirement will allow a manufacturer to apply that knowledge to the *MDD*, taking particular differences into consideration.

CAPs in Relation to the Risk Class

The selection of the various CAPs is limited to those foreseen for a particular risk class.

The *AIMDD* was the first directive and covers a particular type of medical device, e.g., pacemakers, as indicated in directive's name. This directive also applies to all accessories for those products.

Due to the limited application to one type of medical device, the compliance routes described are particular for these types of high-risk products.

Figure 22-1. CAPs for Active Implantable Medical Devices

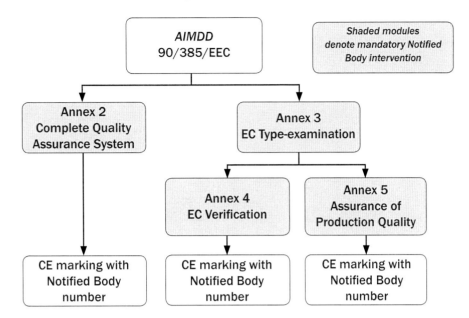

Medical devices covered under the *MDD* are divided into four different risk classes (I, IIa, IIb and III). In vitro diagnostics medical devices are also divided into four different risk classes (Annex II list A and B, devices for self-testing and all other devices). The higher the risk class, the more controls are applied and, therefore, the CAPs vary significantly from the lowest to the highest risk class. Certain aspects of the selected CAP must be reviewed by a Notified Body (NB), which issues a certificate of conformity on those aspects only.

CAP According to the *AIMDD*

As previously noted, the *AIMDD* is only applicable for particular types of high-risk medical devices. The CAPs outlined are very limited for these products and an NB is always involved. The European Conformity (CE) mark shall always show the NB number. **Figure 22-1** shows the three CAP choices available to a manufacturer.

The CAPs may be compared with those for *MDD* Risk Class III products. The terms vary slightly but the similarity is obvious when comparing **Figure 22-1** with **Figure 22-5**.

CAPs for the *MDD* and *IVDD*

In the two other medical device directives, a variety of products are covered with various compliance routes available to the manufacturer. The various CAPs are presented below according to the risk classes.

MDD Risk Class I (e.g., Wheelchairs, Orthoses)

A very limited assessment procedure according to Annex VII of the *MDD* is applied to Risk Class I devices. The technical documentation must be in place and available for

Competent Authority inspection. An NB is not involved and, therefore, no NB number will accompany the CE mark (**Figure 22-2**).

Stricter rules apply to Risk Class I devices that have a measuring function or are sterile. For those products, II, IV, V or VI. The manufacturer has the choice and shall involve an NB to certify only those specific aspects.

The 2007 update to the directive added Annex II to the choices. The requirements in Annex II were considered too strict for these low risk class products in the past, but a manufacturer had to apply another CAP (Annex IV, V or VI) if it applied Annex II to other products of higher risk classes. Today, for practical matters, a manufacturer is also able to apply Annex II for Risk Class I products that are sterile or have a measuring function.

It should be noted that the update of the directive in 2010 added the reference to clinical and preclinical data. Therefore, it is evident that clinical data, even for the lowest risk class of products, is a must.

MDD Risk Class IIa (e.g., Single-use Surgical Instruments)

Annex VII may be applied to Risk Class IIa products; in addition, the manufacturer shall apply Annex IV, V or VI (**Figure 22-3**). Annex IV refers to the verification of products, Annex V refers to production quality assurance and Annex VI refers to product quality assurance.

The manufacturer also may apply Annex II, full quality assurance system but without Annex II section 4. Section 4 is a design examination required only for Risk Class III products.

These choices allow the manufacturer to select the CAP

Figure 22-2. CAP for Risk Class I Medical Devices

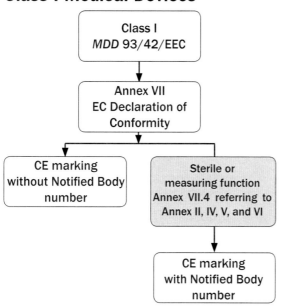

route it deems most appropriate. A manufacturer with very deep in-house production levels may select Annex II, while a manufacturer with very little production involvement may only apply Annex VII with Annex IV. Annex II relies on the manufacturer's ability to control all aspects of making the product and an NB will review the whole process. When Annex VII is applied in conjunction with Annex IV, an NB reviews "only" the medical device to the extent that products or a sample of products from a batch are being directly verified against the technical documentation. However, the NB may even test the product, applying harmonised standards. These two extremes of the CAP choices make it clear that the directive tries to take various business solutions into consideration. The manufacturer must involve an NB with all CAPs.

Since the last update in 2007, Annex II, V and VI refer to the obligation of an NB to assess the technical documentation "for at least one representative sample for each device subcategory for compliance with the provision with this directive." Due to the nature of Annex IV, where the NB will verify the product against the technical documentation, an additional technical file assessment is not foreseen for this CAP.

MDD Risk Class IIb (e.g., Defibrillator, Monitoring Equipment for Vital Physiological Processes)

The CAPs for Risk Class IIb (**Figure 22-4**) deviate only slightly from the one outlined for devices of Risk Class IIa (**Figure 22 3**). Annex II may be applied in the same manner but Annex IV, V or VI shall be combined with Annex III. Annex III refers to EC type-examination. This is the procedure where an NB reviews and may even test

the type in a very detailed manner. Additional aspects of Annex IV, V and VI ensure that subsequent products shall conform to the type examined by the NB. The NB is involved in all CAPs.

Since the last update in 2007, Annex II refers to the obligation of the NB to assess the technical documentation "for at least one representative sample for each generic device group for compliance with the provision of this directive." Due to the combination with Annex III type-examination, it is logical that the Annexes IV, V and VI do not refer to such an additional review within these CAPs.

The details for the selection of technical files as well the level of review conducted by the NB were heavily discussed among the stakeholders. Guidance was provided by the Notified Body Oversight Group (NBOG). At the time of writing this chapter, NBs may still deviate in regard to this review process. Therefore, it is recommended that manufacturers communicate with their NBs regarding this additional review level in advance.

MDD Risk Class III (e.g., Circulatory System and Central Nervous System Devices)

In reviewing **Figure 22-5** for Risk Class III products, two aspects are immediately obvious. For Risk Class III products, Annex VI cannot be applied in conjunction with Annex III. Also, Annex II must be applied in its entirety, including Annex II.4, which refers to the design dossier that requires NB review. The NB issues a separate certificate for this aspect.

For Risk Class III products that incorporate medicinal products or human blood derivatives, additional aspects must be considered. For products incorporating medicinal substances, the NB shall consult with one of the Competent Authorities or the European Medicines Agency (EMA). Only the EMA shall be involved when products incorporate human blood derivatives. These aspects should be carefully discussed with the NB. Approval depends upon a positive outcome of the consultation process between the NB and the agency. These aspects are described in Annex II and Annex III. This means that independent of the CAP selected, equal scrutiny is being applied to these aspects of the product.

IVDD In Vitro Diagnostic Devices (Except those listed in Annex II or devices for self-testing, e.g., HCG test for use in laboratory – professional use)

The annexes of the *IVDD* contain requirements similar to those of the *MDD* or *AIMDD*. For example, Annex IV refers to the full quality system, as do *MDD* Annex II and *AIMDD* Annex 2. Based upon the risk category, the manufacturer may have various choices to achieve compliance, as is the case with the *MDD* and *AIMDD*.

For all devices that are not listed in *IVDD* Annex II and are not for self-testing, the CAP is outlined in Annex

Figure 22-3. CAPs for Risk Class IIa Medical Devices

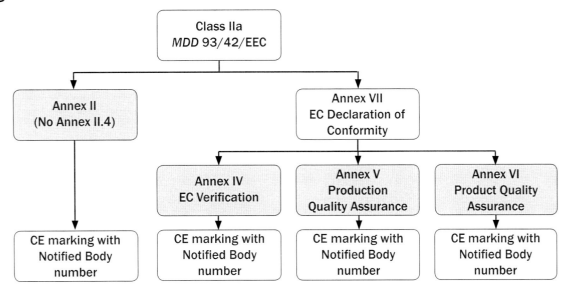

III (**Figure 22-6**). The CAP is similar to *MDD* Annex VII for Risk Class I products. However, more-specific quality system aspects are required. As is the case with *MDD* Annex VII, an NB is not involved. Therefore, those products are commonly referred to as Risk Class I, even though the *IVDD* does not utilise a risk class numbering system.

IVDD Self-Testing Products (e.g HCG test for the lay person)

Self-testing devices offer manufacturers the most choices from which to select (**Figure 22-7**). The manufacturer may apply Annex III in its entirety. Annex III.6 refers to a design dossier and the manufacturer must apply to an NB for the design examination.

Another choice is to apply a full quality assurance system as outlined in Annex IV. Annex IV sections 4 and 6 are not applied for this risk category. The last option the manufacturer has is to follow Annex V in combination with Annex VI or Annex VII. Annex V refers to the EC type-examination, similar to the procedure outlined in *MDD* Annex III. Annex VI and Annex VII are the procedures that verify that the products produced conform to the type examined by the NB, with Annex VII focusing more on quality aspects. In all instances, an NB is involved.

Products Listed in Annex II List B

The CAPs for Annex II List B (**Figure 22-8**) are similar to those for self-testing devices. However, Annex III is not allowed.

Products Listed in Annex II List A

The products in Annex II List A are considered to be of the highest risk category and, therefore, are scrutinised

the most. With the above outlined CAPs for the lower risk classes, certain parts of an annex were not applied. For this risk category, the complete annexes shall be applied (**Figure 22-9**). Furthermore, the choice of CAPs for these products is very limited. With Annex III already not allowed for List B products, now the combination of Annex V and Annex VI is also no longer an option.

The high level of concern regarding these products is made particularly clear by the fact that an NB approves each individual batch with both available CAPs. This may involve actual quality control testing by the NB and the review of manufacturing documentation.

Particulars of the CAPs

This section will outline the main aspects of each particular procedure. Furthermore, it will demonstrate the direct correlation of the three medical devices directives to one another and to Decision 768/2008/EC with regard to CAPs. However, in any case, each directive's particularities must be taken into consideration. Certain procedures from the decision were not considered appropriate for all directives and therefore were not applied. In each annex, various additional aspects may apply as outlined above. The decision provides eight assessment procedures or "modules" that cover the design and production phases:

- Module A: Internal production control
- Module B: EC type-examination
- Module C: Conformity to type based on internal production control (not applicable for the medical devices directives)
- Module D: Conformity to type based on quality assurance of the production process
- Module E: Conformity to type based on product quality assurance

Figure 22-4. CAPs for Risk Class IIb Medical Devices

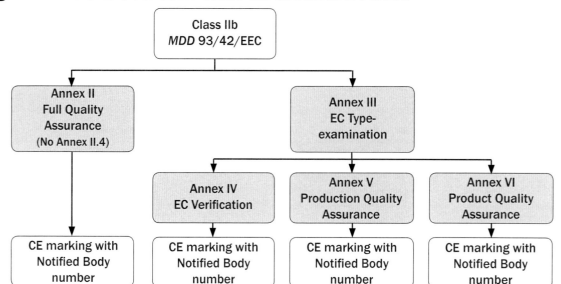

- Module F: Product verification
- Module G: Unit verification (Not applicable for the medical devices directives)
- Module H: Full quality assurance

Internal Production Control (Module A)

With the EC Declaration of Conformity, the main focus is on the technical documentation (**Table 22-1**). The *IVDD* describes further quality system aspects, but an NB is not involved.

EC Type-examination (Module B)

An EC type-examination is product-related, where an

NB examines the product and issues an EC type-examination certificate (**Table 22-2**). The device may even be tested directly by the NB. The goal is to verify that the design of the product meets the requirements of the applicable directive, mainly compliance with that directive's Essential Requirements. The EC type-examination procedure will always be applied with other procedures.

Production Quality Assurance (Module D)

The main goal of the production quality assurance procedure (**Table 22-3**) is to ensure that the products are in fact produced and conform to the type described in the EC

Figure 22-5. CAPs for Risk Class III Medical Devices

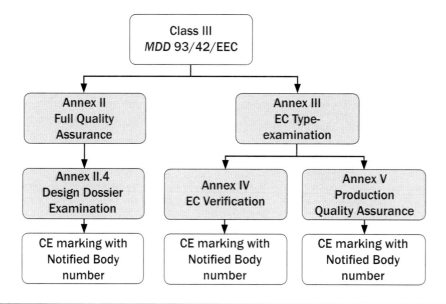

Table 22-1. Internal Production Control

Decision No 768/2008/EC	AIMDD 90/385/EEC	MDD 93/42/EEC	IVDD 98/79/EEC
Module A	NA	Annex VII	Annex III
Internal production control		EC Declaration of Conformity	EC Declaration of Conformity

Table 22-2. EC Type-examination

Decision No 768/2008/EC	AIMDD 90/385/EEC	MDD 93/42/EEC	IVDD 98/79/EEC
Module B	Annex 3	Annex III	Annex V
EC type-examination	EC type-examination	EC type-examination	EC type-examination

Table 22-3. Production Quality Assurance

Decision No 768/2008/EC	AIMDD 90/385/EEC	MDD 93/42/EEC	IVDD 98/79/EEC
Module D	Annex 5	Annex V	Annex VII
Conformity to type based upon quality assurance of the production process	Assurance of production quality	Production quality assurance	Production quality assurance

Table 22-4. Product Quality Assurance

Decision No 768/2008/EC	AIMDD 90/385/EEC	MDD 93/42/EEC	IVDD 98/79/EEC
Module E	NA	Annex VI	NA
Conformity to type based upon product quality assurance		Product quality assurance	

Table 22-5. Product Verification

Decision No 768/2008/EC	AIMDD 90/385/EEC	MDD 93/42/EEC	IVDD 98/79/EEC
Module F	Annex 4	Annex IV	Annex VI
Conformity to type based upon product verification	EC verification	EC verification	EC verification

Table 22-6. Full Quality Assurance System

Decision No 768/2008/EC	AIMDD 90/385/EEC	MDD 93/42/EEC	IVDD 98/79/EEC
Module H	Annex 2	Annex II	Annex IV
Conformity based upon full quality assurance	Complete quality assurance system	Full quality assurance system	Full quality assurance system

type-examination certificate. The production shall follow certain requirements that may be fulfilled with the application of the harmonised quality system standard, EN ISO 13485. Since not all aspects of the quality system need to be applied, the exemptions allowed in the standard may be utilised. The production quality assurance procedure is normally applied together with the EC type-examination. However, the *MDD* allows the application with Annex VII for Risk Class IIa products. In that case, the procedure shall ensure that the devices produced conform to the technical documentation. An NB is involved.

Product Quality Assurance (Module E)

The main goal of the product quality assurance procedure is to ensure, via final inspection and testing, that the products are in fact in conformity to the type described in the EC type-examination certificate (**Table 22-4**). This can be achieved with very limited quality system aspect. The harmonised standard, EN ISO 13485, may be utilised with exemptions not applicable to this procedure. The product quality assurance procedure is normally applied with the EC type-examination. However, the *MDD* allows the application with Annex VII for Risk Class IIa products. In that case, the procedure shall ensure that the devices conform to the technical documentation. An NB is involved. Please

Figure 22-6. CAP for All In Vitro Medical Devices
(Except devices listed in Annex II and devices for self-testing)

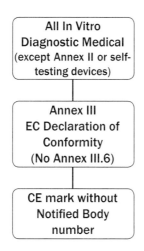

note that this procedure is not applicable for the *AIMDD* and the *IVDD*.

Product Verification (Module F)

The main goal of the product verification procedure (**Table 22-5**) by the NB is to ensure that the devices are in conformity with the type described in the EC Examination Certificate. The verification may be performed on each individual product or a batch of products. The procedure is normally applied with the EC type-examination. However,

the *MDD* allows the application with Annex VII for risk class IIa products. In that case, the procedure shall ensure that the devices conform to the technical documentation. The NB must carry out appropriate examinations and tests.

Full Quality Assurance System (Module H)

The main goal of this procedure is to ensure that the manufacturer applies a full quality assurance system, which includes all aspects of design, manufacture and final product inspection (**Table 22-6**). This may be achieved with the full application of EN ISO 13485. For higher risk classes, the procedure is extended with the examination of the design dossier by the NB. For IVD products, an additional product verification by the NB is being applied within the procedure.

Product Approach or Quality Approach

In reviewing the various procedures, it becomes obvious that a complete CAP may be more focussed on a quality system or on a product. With the EC type-examination, the focus is more product related, while with the full quality assurance system procedure, the focus is on a quality system approach. All CAPs for a particular risk class shall provide the same level of scrutiny to the products' compliance but, as outlined above, the manufacturer selects the procedure that best fits its business.

Quality System Requirements

The directives refer to certain quality assurance aspects. Those may be fulfilled with the application of harmonised standards. The directives do not stipulate a specific standard

Figure 22-7. CAPs for Self-testing In Vitro Medical Devices

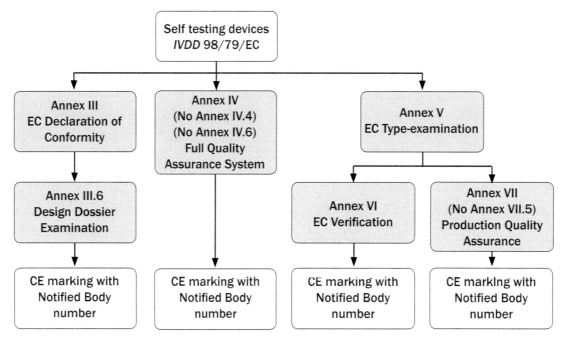

Figure 22-8. CAPs for Annex II List B In Vitro Medical Devices

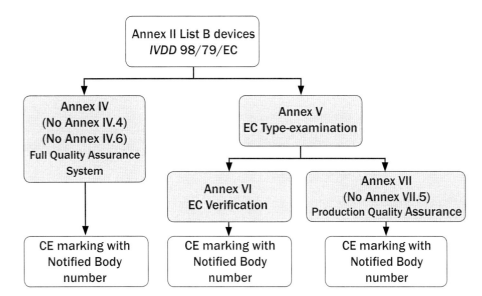

to use and standards are being developed independently of the directives. The standards harmonisation process is a faster process than actually updating a particular law in the EU. This ensures that technical aspects and quality system requirements are kept state-of-the-art.

The quality system standards have developed over time. The first standards harmonised and applied were the ISO 9000 series. Today, for medical devices, the EN ISO 13485 quality system standard is the most appropriate for manufacturers to apply. It is important to note that the application of this standard is not mandatory. The manufacturer may apply other quality system standards. However, the application of the harmonised standards conveys the presumption of conformity. In any case, the level of quality control as outlined in the directive shall be achieved. If a different standard is applied, the NB must accept this, but it may be more difficult for the review order to establish compliance with the requirements as outlined in the directives.

The exclusions, which are allowed in the EN ISO 13485 standard for certain quality system aspects, go along with the CAPs. For example, *MDD* Annex II refers to the full quality system, which would mean, in essence, that the complete EN ISO 13485 shall be applied. Annex V refers to the production quality system; this would then mean the manufacturer would exclude the particular clause from the standard that refers to design and development. Any exclusion should be carefully reviewed with the NB involved regarding the selected CAP.

NBs

NBs are involved in many stages of the conformity assessment. It is often said that an NB approves products

for CE marking. This is a misconception. It should be clearly understood that an NB might have only very limited involvement. However, the level of involvement increases with the risk associated with the product and most certainly a product shall not be marketed until the conformity assessment, including issuance of the appropriate certificates by the NB, is completed.

Figure 22-9. CAPs for Annex II List A In Vitro Medical Devices

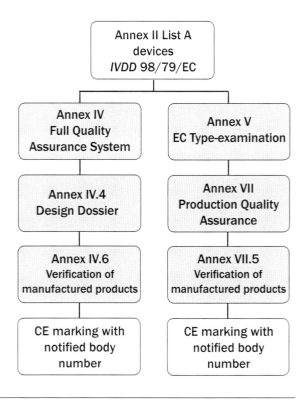

NBs have to fulfil requirements as outlined in the specific directive as well as any additional national requirements. They are approved to be NBs in their countries by their national Competent Authorities. Once approved, they are notified to the European Commission and are published with their scope in the *Official Journal of the European Union*. The national Competent Authorities then further monitor the NBs.

An NB may select the specific areas for which it is notified. For example, not all NBs are notified to the Commission for all directives or for all possible CAPs within a directive. Therefore, an NB might not be able to review all CAPs. A manufacturer should check the NBs to find one that can address its particular needs. On the other hand, an NB should not accept an application from a manufacturer for which it cannot provide the required service. The European Commission publishes lists of NBs with their scope on its website.

A manufacturer is free to select any NB for its products. Therefore, other relevant aspects may need to be considered, such as timing, price or overall customer service.

Summary

- The medical device directives follow the so-called Global and New Approach promoted for the EU.
- The goal of the various CAPs is to ensure compliance with the Essential Requirements.
- The medical devices directives allow the selection of various CAPs.
- The choice of CAPs is related to the risk class of the product.
- Based upon the selection, the CAPs may focus either on product- or quality system-related aspects.
- Compliance with the CAPs may be achieved with the application of harmonised standards.
- EN ISO 13485 is the harmonised standard to comply with the quality system requirements.
- NBs may be involved with various stages of the CAPs.
- NBs are notified to the EU with the scope for which they are allowed to be certified.
- The manufacturer may freely select an NB. Other aspects like cost or service may play a role with the selection of an NB.

References

1. Decision No 768/2008/EC of the European Parliament and of the Council of 9 July 2008 on a common framework for the marketing of products, and repealing Council Decision 93/465/EEC http://eur-lex.europa.eu/LexUriServ/LexUriServ.do?uri=OJ:L:2008:218:0082:0128:EN:PDF. Accessed 14 December 2010.
2. Directive 98/34/EC of the European Parliament and of the Council of 22 June 1998 laying down a procedure for the provision of information in the field of technical standards and regulations. Europa website. http://eur-lex.europa.eu/smartapi/cgi/sga_doc?smartapi!celexplus!prod!DocNumber&lg=en&type_doc=Directive&an_doc=98&nu_doc=34. Accessed 1 December 2010.

Technical Requirements for EU Conformity Assessment

By Jeremy Tinkler

OBJECTIVES

❏ Understand the technical requirements that need to be met in order to demonstrate conformity with the the Essential Requirements of the European medical device directives

❏ Understand the role of European and international standards in the conformity assessment process

❏ Understand how risk management principles and processes are fundamental to conformity assessment

❏ Understand documentation requirements

❏ Understand biocompatibility requirements

DIRECTIVES, REGULATIONS AND GUIDELINES COVERED IN THIS CHAPTER

❏ Council Directive 93/42/EEC of 14 June 1993 concerning medical devices

❏ Council Directive 90/385/EEC of 20 June 1990 on the approximation of the laws of the Member States relating to active implantable medical devices

❏ ISO 14971:2007 *Medical devices—Application of risk management to medical devices*

❏ ISO 10993-1:2009 *Biological evaluation of medical devices—Part 1: Evaluation and testing*

within a risk management process

❏ ISO/TR 15499 *Guidance on the conduct of biological evaluation within a risk management process*

❏ MHRA, Guidance Note 5, *Guidance on Biocompatibility Assessment*, January 2006

Essential Requirements

For CE marking of general or active implantable medical devices, it is necessary to demonstrate conformity with all relevant Essential Requirements contained in Annex I of the applicable European medical devices directive. Notified Bodies will expect to see a checklist, listing all the Essential Requirements and indicating, for each one, how conformity has been demonstrated or why it is not relevant. A checklist is also required for Class I devices that are self-certified and, in such cases, provides the assurance needed to underpin the certificate of conformity.

The Essential Requirements have been devised with care and attention to detail and are the result of a systematic approach to specifying necessary and appropriate regulatory requirements. They therefore demand an equally ordered approach by those who wish to demonstrate compliance. Only by showing systematically how each of the Essential Requirements has been met can a manufacturer declare conformity and affix the CE marking. Similarly, when a manufacturer has to make a compliance statement prior to commencing a clinical investigation (an "Annex VIII Statement"), an Essential Requirements checklist is indispensable in providing the signatory with the confidence that he or she is making a truthful declaration. Even prior to that point, the checklist is a valuable tool for gap analysis during design verification.

Table 23-1. Essential Requirement Check List:
Example (*MDD* (93/42/EEC, as amended)—Annex I)

	Requirements	A—N/A	Standard/Rationale	Reference to Documents
I.	General Requirements			
	The devices must be designed and manufactured in such a way that, when used under the conditions and for the purposes intended, they will not compromise the clinical condition or the safety of patients, or the safety and health of users or, where applicable, other persons, provided that any risks which may be associated with their intended use constitute acceptable risks when weighed against the benefits to the patient and are compatible with a high level of protection of health and safety. This shall include: <ul><li>reducing, as far as possible, the risk of use error due to the ergonomic features of the device and the environment in which the device is intended to be used (design for patient safety), and</li><li>consideration of the technical knowledge, experience, education and training and where applicable the medical and physical conditions of intended users (design for lay, professional, disabled or other users).</li></ul>	A	Risks to patients and users have been controlled through application of X-XXX, Risk management and analysis procedure, which complies with EN/ISO 14971-2007. A Clinical Evaluation was carried out in line with European Commission guidance document MEDDEV 2.7.1 Rev. 3	Risk Analysis report XXXX. Clinical Evaluation report XXXX.
2	The solutions adopted by the manufacturer for the design and construction of the devices must conform to safety principles, taking account of the generally acknowledged state of the art. In selecting the most appropriate solutions, the manufacturer must apply the following principles in the following order : <ul><li>eliminate or reduce risks as far as possible (inherently safe design and construction)</li><li>where appropriate take adequate protection measures including alarms if necessary, in relation to risks that cannot be eliminated</li><li>inform users of the residual risks due to any shortcomings of the protection measures adopted</li></ul>	A	Risk management procedure (X-XXX), which complies with EN/ISO 14971-2007 includes specification of safety requirements (safety by design, alarms, etc.) and labelling requirements for residual risks	Risk Analysis report XXXX .

Technical details should not be included in the Essential Requirements checklist, but standards for which compliance has been claimed should be cited and all documents providing evidence of conformity should be referenced. Such documents must be available in the Technical File (see below). An example of part of an Essential Requirements checklist is given in **Table 23-1**.

There are 13 Essential Requirements in Annex I of the *Medical Devices Directive* (*MDD*[1]); however, these are subdivided at several levels and the list runs to five pages. The Essential Requirements in the *Active Implantable Medical Devices Directive (AIMDD*[2]) are similar and need not be considered separately. In some way, all Essential Requirements address one of two issues: safety or performance. All the basic principles upon which the directives are based are summarised within the first three Essential Requirements. These principles are as follows:

- Devices must not compromise the clinical condition or safety of the patient or user.
- Risks must be acceptable when weighed against the benefits to the patient.
- Risks must be eliminated or minimised in line with the state of the art.
- Devices must perform as intended by the manufacturer.

These concepts are difficult to quantify, but the manufacturer needs to demonstrate that it has assessed the risks and benefits of its device and that the balance is appropriate.

The remaining Essential Requirements are permutations on this theme relevant to specific circumstances or device attributes. Following six (or seven, depending upon how you count them) general Essential Requirements, there are seven Essential Requirements covering various aspects of design and construction, each of them split into several parts. These are:

- chemical, physical and biological properties
- infection and microbial contamination
- construction and environmental properties
- devices with a measuring function
- protection against radiation
- devices connected to or equipped with an energy source
- information supplied by the manufacturer

Use of Standards

A standard is a consensus document. The Global Harmonization Task Force (GHTF) sees international consensus standards as a tool for harmonising regulatory processes to assure the safety, quality and performance of medical devices. The International Standards Organization (ISO) defines a "standard" as a document, established by consensus and approved by a recognised body, which provides, for common and repeated use, rules, guidelines or

characteristics for activities or their results, aimed at the achievement of the optimum degree of order in a given context. It further notes that standards should be based upon the consolidated results of science, technology and experience and aimed at the promotion of optimum community benefits.

The consensus described in the standard was reached by the members of the committee that wrote it, as influenced by the comments of those who participated in the consultation phases. The way standards writing bodies are constituted and carry out their tasks, therefore, affects the quality of a standard, which should be an important factor in the extent to which a particular standard is used. It is good practice to consider objectively the extent to which the use of a standard ensures compliance with Essential Requirements and identify any aspects of conformity assessment that need to be addressed by other means. This chapter, therefore, presents some general observations about the nature of standards and the way they are generated. First, however, it is important to consider the critical role that standards play in the European system of medical device regulation.

Regulatory Status of European Standards

The nature and role of standards in the regulatory process is explained in recitals at the beginning of the medical devices directives. Because the Essential Requirements of the directives are designed to cover a wide variety of aspects of safety and performance of a wide array of products, it is recognised that they cannot provide the level of technical detail required to address everything that is relevant to conformity assessment. It is the role of standards to provide this level of detail. The basis for this arrangement lies in the "New Approach" to European regulation, adopted in 1985, based upon the principle that the establishment of an internal European market with free movement of goods and services is critically dependent upon technical harmonisation. Dismantling the barriers to trade that previously existed within Europe required a mechanism to ensure technical equivalence of goods in terms of safety and critical performance. The European standards bodies were given the task of drawing up technical specifications to meet the Essential Requirements of the various New Approach directives. Inherent in the New Approach is the expectation that compliance with such specifications provides a presumption of conformity with the Essential Requirements.

In practice, this means that the European Commission "mandates" the European Standardization Committee (CEN) or Electrotechnical Commision (CENELEC) to develop the standards considered necessary for demonstrating compliance with Essential Requirements in one or more of the directives. CEN (or CENELEC) develops a relevant document, normally through cooperation with

ISO. Typically, an international standard is developed by a working group within an ISO technical committee and published by European national standards bodies as a dual EN/ISO standard. Not all European standards are harmonised, however. Once the standard has been approved for publication as a European standard, advisors to CEN review it to verify that it is adequate for the task of conformity assessment. If it is, a reference to the standard is published in the *Official Journal of the European Communities* (*OJ*). This process is termed "harmonisation" and the resulting document is known as a harmonised European standard. Lists of harmonised standards are available from the European Commission website (www.europa.eu) and are periodically published in the *OJ*.[3]

An annex in the European version of each harmonised standard indicates the Essential Requirements for which the standard is deemed relevant. By referencing such information and showing compliance with the requirements of the standard, a manufacturer can claim conformity with specific Essential Requirements. This should not be seen as a box-checking exercise; it is necessary to confirm that the standard is indeed appropriate and adequate for demonstrating full compliance. The process is set out in Article 5 of the *MDD*. In summary, a harmonised standard is deemed necessary and sufficient to carry the presumption of conformity with Essential Requirements of the relevant European directive.

It is not obligatory to use harmonised standards to demonstrate compliance with Essential Requirements. It is up to a manufacturer to show compliance through any means considered appropriate. Manufacturers may choose to use an ISO standard where no harmonised CEN standard exists. Alternatively, national or in-house standards (e.g., standard operating procedures (SOPs)) can be used. In any event, SOPs should contain a justification for the methods chosen and include references to the applicable standards, indicating the degree to which compliance with each standard is required. Wherever alternative routes to harmonised standards are used, questions from Competent Authorities and Notified Bodies can arise and a justification for the departure from the norm will be required. The justification should cover the reasons why a harmonised standard is not used and why the methods chosen are appropriate and adequate for the job.

The Nature of Consensus

The purpose of the standards writing process is to produce a document that is a clear statement of the technical state of the art, particularly with regard to expectations of safety and performance. It is not by accident, therefore, that participants in a working group are called "experts." They should be put forward for membership of the working group by their national standards body because of their high level of relevant expertise. Most of the necessary expertise resides within industry; therefore, it is not surprising that standards committees are dominated by industry representatives.

A criticism often levelled at the standards writing process is the inadequate or inappropriate level of input from regulatory agencies. Most European Competent Authorities rarely participate in ISO working groups. The comparative lack of relevant technical expertise within Competent Authorities is one reason; another is the perception that it is not the role of the regulatory agency to develop the consensus. It is, however, the agency's role to object when it considers a standard inadequate, and the means is provided by Paragraph 3 of Article 5 of the *MDD*. Where Competent Authorities do participate, they often help to direct the focus of a standard toward its role in conformity assessment. Conversely, US Food and Drug Administration (FDA) officials involved in standards writing often have a high level of technical expertise but participate with the understanding that their agency is not obliged to adopt the standard as a regulatory component. Officials from Japan, China and Korea tend to combine both technical expertise and reliance on standards in their regulations and are increasingly important players in the process.

As well as having technical expertise, therefore, the standards writer must have a keen appreciation of the role the standard will play in the regulatory process and the nuances of language used in standards. For example, there is a critical difference between a normative requirement (i.e., "shall") and guidance ("should"). There is a responsibility to ensure that the requirements are sufficient to ensure safety and essential performance but not unnecessarily onerous or restrictive. The wider purpose of a standard is to assist industry and commerce, so it is a delicate balancing act. The user of the standard should also appreciate these points.

In the 20 years since medical device standards were first written with a defined European regulatory purpose in mind, there have been, on the whole, significant improvements in the quality of the standards. In the past, there have been standards that were deemed unsuitable for harmonisation, but that situation should be less likely today. The process is monitored by national standards committees, Competent Authorities, industry groups and other interested and affected parties, and this oversight helps to identify problems and ensure that the product is fit for its purpose. Using a harmonised standard is thus the most convenient and safest way to demonstrate conformity with Essential Requirements.

Identifying and Referencing Applicable Standards

Generic standards, relevant to all devices or a wide range of product types, are termed "horizontal" (or Level 1) standards. Examples are standards on quality systems, risk management, biological safety and sterilisation. "Semi-horizontal" (Level 2) standards contain requirements applicable to a range of similar products, such as endovascular devices or surgical instruments. "Vertical" (Level 3) standards apply to single product types or a range of closely related products, such as vascular stents or surgical scalpels.

National standards bodies, from which standards can be purchased, provide searchable listings on their websites. These generally provide enough information to determine the scope of the standard cited. A list of harmonised standards can be found on the European Commission website (http://europa.eu). A search of these sources should reveal all the standards that may be applicable to a product.

There are a number of places within the technical documentation where it is necessary to list all standards that have been applied, in full or in part, to the product. This list is important in the Investigators Brochure for a premarket clinical investigation and for the Essential Requirements checklist. This requirement is often applied as an afterthought and interpreted as a simple list of all the standards that are relevant and to which some degree of compliance can be shown. A slap-dash approach here can lead to significant problems or delays in regulatory approval. However, the objective of this regulatory requirement is to allow a precise indication of the extent to which conformity with the Essential Requirements can be presumed through the application of harmonised standards. Unless the extent of compliance with a standard is clearly specified, conformity cannot be established in this way.

It makes sense to map out the way that conformity will be established early in the product development process. The Essential Requirements checklist is a good place to start such planning. The standards that are potentially relevant can be mapped against the checklist and reviewed to establish whether they are indeed applicable or whether alternative or additional means of conformity assessment are necessary. Whenever a standard is used for the presumption of conformity, any departure from complete compliance should be noted and its significance to compliance with the relevant Essential Requirements taken into account. The reports that are cited alongside references to the applicable standards in the Essential Requirements checklist should clearly indicate any aspect of noncompliance with a standard, the reasons for this and the alternative measures that have been taken to ensure full compliance with Essential Requirements.

Risk Management

Risk management is the systematic application of management policies, procedures and practices to the tasks of identifying, analysing, treating and monitoring risk. Its purpose is to enable organisations to minimise loss and maximise opportunity.[4]

All aspects of the design, manufacture and marketing of a medical device introduce or modify risks. The management of risk is, thus, an essential component of these activities. For every decision related to the provision of a medical device,

the consequences and probabilities of possible outcomes need to be considered, together with the cost implications of the proposed action. Adherence to a comprehensive and well-documented risk management plan is good business practice as well as a regulatory requirement.

The directives require that a manufacturer refrain from putting a device into service unless the hazards that could be associated with its use are known and the nature and likelihood of any undesirable consequences that could arise are understood. The ISO 14971:2007 standard, *Medical Devices—Risk Management*, sets out the method by which the design of a device should be analysed and the identified risks controlled effectively. Potential hazards need to be identified and the chances of the occurrence and the possible consequences of a hazardous situation analysed. Once the possibilities and probabilities associated with a risk have been established, risk control entails taking action to reduce or constrain the identified risks. A careful balance must be struck so that risks can be controlled in a way that achieves the desired degree of safety without undue cost. It should be noted, for example, that further risks can be introduced by increasing the cost of a product to a level that restricts the activities of the user. Any significant risks remaining after risk control measures have been taken need to be warned against in the product labelling (the instructions for use (IFU)). Finally, in order to show that risks are outweighed by benefits, it is also necessary to analyse the benefits expected as a result of the use of the device. Unfortunately, little guidance is given in ISO 14971 on this subject, but it can be treated in a way that is analogous to the treatment of risks.

ISO 14971 contains important definitions that need to be understood and the concepts described need to be used appropriately. This chapter does not attempt to recapitulate the process; instead it tries to provide insight into its application. It should, therefore, be read in conjunction with the standard. The different parts of the process need to be applied systematically. It is no good rushing into a detailed Failure Mode Effects Analysis (FMEA) without doing preparatory work and understanding the context within which this risk analysis tool is used. The normative part of the standard only contains the basic outline of the process, so without following the guidance given in the annexes, it is possible to end up with a risk analysis that does not actually comply with the standard. It is also important to ensure that the criteria chosen as a basis for judgements on the acceptability of risks are compatible with the first three Essential Requirements.

The starting point of a risk analysis is focussed brainstorming, through which all the characteristics of a device are considered in order to identify all aspects of design and use that can affect safety.[5] The object of this exercise is to identify all possible hazards and establish factors that limit their risk. A hazard is simply a potential source of harm, such as electricity or deep water. These remain hazardous under all circumstances; however, they cannot cause harm unless a hazardous situation arises (e.g., exposed bare wires or a baby left by a swimming pool). When treating a risk (i.e., taking risk control measures), you cannot do anything to change the ability of a hazard to cause harm or to reduce the severity of the harm that can be caused. Risk control action normally consists of the avoidance, recognition or treatment of hazardous situations. Thus, the brainstorming that informs the hazard analysis needs to be focussed on consideration of how harm could occur under a wide range of possible circumstances.[6]

ISO 14971 is widely accepted and even virtually insisted upon by medical device regulatory agencies throughout the world, including US FDA. As any standard should, it sets out what is normal. Neither ISO 14971 nor its predecessor, EN 1441, broke any new ground when published, but simply stated principles and processes that, over the past 30 years or so, have become accepted practice right across industry and government worldwide (with the possible exception of the medicinal product sector, whose regulations predate this period). The standard and the risk analysis techniques commonly used to inform the risk management process are predominantly engineering tools aimed at maximising safety through design. Thus, as with Essential Requirement 2 of the *MDD*, inherently safe design and production is a top priority. If inherent safety is not possible, the second and third lines of defence are protective measures and warnings, in that order. Like the Essential Requirements, the standard dictates the principles by which safety should be established and leaves the detail to be determined by the particular circumstances of the case in hand. Thus, ISO 14971 does not specify a particular risk analysis tool (such as FMEA, which is often used by device manufacturers) or schemes for estimating risks or judging acceptability; neither does it say how a risk management report or the "results of the risk analysis" should be written. While this lack of detail allows manufacturers freedom to choose the most appropriate techniques, it also carries the potential for risk management activities to be judged inappropriate by a Notified Body or Competent Authority. For this reason, such activities must be firmly grounded in the relevant Essential Requirements.

Some requirements of ISO 14971 relating to risk acceptability decisions are commonly overlooked by manufacturers. The first is for the company's top management to implement a policy for determining criteria for risk acceptability. This policy needs to be in line with the "current values of society," as evidenced by regulatory requirements, standards, the generally accepted state of the art and known stakeholder concerns. Thus, a manufacturer needs to be politically astute and include acquisition of relevant knowledge in routine surveillance activities. Then, the risk acceptability criteria, based on this policy (and thus in line with Essential

Requirements), need to be included in the risk management plan. When it comes to risk evaluation (i.e., judging the risk against the risk acceptability criteria), it is common to confuse the concepts of risk estimation and risk evaluation. It is normal practice to assign values to the severity of potential harm and the probability of its occurrence and, from these, to derive a risk value, often termed a risk priority number (RPN). This, however, is a risk estimate, not a risk evaluation. ISO 14971 does not allow risk estimates to be translated directly into judgements of acceptability without reference to the risk acceptability criteria. Not all risks are equal, so it is a simplification (but often practiced, and sometimes legitimate) to say that all risks over a certain level are unacceptable and all risks under a certain level are acceptable. The standard notes that there are some risks that are so low, it is not worth bothering about them. These can be classified as negligible or broadly acceptable. A decision can also be made that risks over a certain level are considered intolerable. However, there will be circumstances in healthcare where people are prepared to take virtually any risk to prolong or enhance life, so this is a level that varies with the circumstances. A more difficult question arises as to what to do with the risks that fall between these two levels. This is the ALARP region, where risks must be reduced to a level "As Low As Reasonably Practicable."[7] This is where the feasibility of further risk reduction and the risk/benefit balance need to be considered on a case-by-case basis, so a clear management policy and criteria for risk acceptability are indispensable.

Technical File

A number of terms are used to describe the collection of documents that describe how a manufacturer has demonstrated the conformity of its product with Essential Requirements. The directives speak of technical documentation as a generic term and mention the "design dossier" in the context of Notified Body review, where applicable (i.e., for devices requiring design examination, mainly Class III products). However, there is no definition of this term in the directives. Design dossier should be used to refer to those parts of the technical file that are put together and made available to the Notified Body for review. Technical documentation has to be kept available by the manufacturer or its Authorised Representative for review by the Competent Authority and there are a number of circumstances where the Notified Body has to examine it. ISO 14971 defines the "risk management file," which forms part of the technical file, as the set of records and other documents that are produced by risk management. The earlier version of the standard used a more informative definition, indicating this was not necessarily a discrete physical file, but its elements could be in a variety of formats and locations.

There are no rules about the format or location of the technical file, although the design dossier must be a defined set of documents prepared for a specific purpose. Any other rules about the technical file apply by inference because there are no explicit requirements. The documents that make up the technical file are relevant to regulatory compliance and are thus considered critical to product quality. They, therefore, need to be part of the manufacturer's controlled documentation system and comply with documentation requirements specified by ISO 13485 or ISO 9001.

Like their location, the contents of a technical file are indeterminate. As a minimum, the file must contain everything that can be referenced via the Essential Requirements checklist and anything else relevant to product design and regulatory compliance. This includes:

- identification of product and regulatory classification
- literature reviews
- design input assumptions and calculations
- design history
- design and manufacturing specifications
- quality plan and rationale for quality control measures
- process validation and design verification reports
- verification of packaging and product stability
- labelling (including information provided with the device)
- postmarket surveillance data and/or plan
- Essential Requirements checklist
- risk management file (including risk management plan and report)
- clinical evaluation report

Relevant SOPs and standards are also referenced by the Essential Requirements checklist and are important elements of conformity assessment. They show how compliance has been achieved and are of interest to assessors. Thus, although they do not contain results relevant to the product, they may be relevant to the technical file.

Guidance on the technical documentation needed to meet the requirements of the medical devices directives is provided by a "recommendation" document produced by the European Association of Medical Device Notified Bodies (NB-MED).[8] The primary purpose of this guidance is to document the consensus view of the Notified Bodies' Recommendations Group on appropriate Conformity Assessment Procedures. However, the document notes that it is also of relevance to Competent Authorities and manufacturers. Although published in 2000, this guidance is still definitive. However, in interpreting its contents, attention should be paid to more recent changes in conformity assessment expectations, for example in the area of clinical evaluation and postmarket clinical follow-up. The NB-MED recommendation contains information on the following topics which, where applicable, should be considered required components of the technical file:

- content of technical documentation
- general description of the device
- description of the device's intended use and operation
- devices incorporating a medicinal substance
- devices incorporating nonviable materials of animal origin
- devices requiring special consideration
- description of the methods of manufacture
- description of accessories, adaptors and other devices or equipment and other interfaces intended to be used in combination with the device
- classification of the device under the relevant directive
- identification of technical requirements
- solutions adopted to fulfil the Essential Requirements
- standards applied
- results of risk analysis
- specification of materials and manufacturing processes (including special processes)
- specifications, drawings and circuit diagrams for components, sub-assemblies and the complete product, including packaging
- specification of checks, tests and trials intended to be carried out as part of routine production
- performances and compatibilities intended by the manufacturer
- labelling, including any instructions for use
- identification of "shelf-life" reflected by any "use by" date, or other "lifetime" of the device
- bench testing results
- clinical data
- documentation and reporting of design changes
- Declaration of Conformity
- application for conformity assessment
- declaration that no other Notified Body is used in conformity assessment
- Notified Body decisions and reports
- manufacturer's undertaking on procedure to review postproduction experience
- recommended structure of the technical documentation
- availability of the technical documentation
- language of the technical documentation

Biological Safety Evaluation

This section looks briefly into the theoretical basis of biological safety assessment and describes how a biological safety evaluation programme should be put together. It explains how data from various sources should be selected and evaluated. The ultimate aim of the process is the assessment of the suitability of the materials for use in a particular product in terms of both toxicological risk and biocompatibility.

Biological Safety and Biocompatibility

Three basic types of information are required for a biological safety assessment. These are identified in Annex I of ISO 14971:2007:

- data characterising the chemical nature of the materials
- information on the prior use of the materials
- results of biological tests

The probability that an adverse effect will arise from exposure to a chemical depends upon the inherent toxicity of the chemical (the toxicological hazard) and the amount of the chemical to which the subject is exposed, which is influenced by the nature of exposure. "Toxicological hazard" can be defined as the potential for a compound or material to cause an adverse biological reaction, taking into account the nature of the reaction and the dose required to elicit it. Toxicology involves the elucidation of the nature of a toxic response on the target organs and the dose-response relationship.

Toxicological risk is a function of toxicological hazard and exposure. Biological safety assessment should, therefore, include an analysis of the inherent toxicity of the materials and the expected extent of tissue exposure, including an assessment of the leachability of components and degradation processes.

Since medical device materials or their component chemicals typically do not elicit toxic responses at realistic levels of exposure, this sort of analysis often is not possible. We can define "toxicological risk" more precisely as the probability of a specified degree of an adverse reaction occurring in response to a specified level of exposure. If the level of exposure is specified as that arising from the use of the device, toxicological risk can be seen as the probability that a toxic effect will occur as a result of device use. Medical device toxicology is thus characterised by analyses that allow a conclusion of safety, but with the higher levels of uncertainty that are associated with negative data.

Biocompatibility, on the other hand, is an altogether more constructive concept, but an elusive one. Usually defined as the ability of a material to perform with an appropriate host response in a specific application,[9] it expresses a dynamic equilibrium in which tissues interreact with biomaterials in a manner appropriate to the therapeutic need. This concept acknowledges that there is a complex interaction between the multitude of biological processes going on within cells or tissues and numerous factors relating to the biomaterial. The latter are mainly a function of surface chemistry and topography.

Biocompatibility can only be demonstrated for a particular material in relation to a defined set of circumstances, which include the purpose for which it is used and the tissues with which it comes into contact. The factors that influence biocompatibility include individual variation in tissue response, so it is possible for a device to show a suitable response in one patient and not in another. Biocompatibility is difficult to establish experimentally but, since it is by definition a desirable characteristic, it can be considered an indicator of biological safety.

Using ISO 14971 and ISO 10993 as a Basis for Toxicological Risk Assessment

The aim of a biological evaluation is to investigate the biological safety of a medical device. The risk management standard (ISO 14971) and the biological evaluation standard (ISO 190993-1) provide a framework around which to plan a safety assessment through a systematic and thorough risk analysis.[10]

Biological safety assessment does not fit the ISO 14971 model precisely. In practice, a biological safety evaluation will use both risk analysis and risk assessment techniques as necessary, until sufficient evidence has been collated to allow safety to be evaluated by identifying any toxicological hazards arising from the materials that come into patient contact and estimating the resultant risk associated with the intended use. An important development in biological evaluation standards is the development of two critical documents, a revised version of ISO 10993-1[11] and an ISO guidance document that provides additional advice on using the standard.[12] These documents correct a longstanding problem with the previous version of ISO 10993-1, i.e., that it has often been misinterpreted as suggesting that a biological evaluation consists of the conduct of certain tests that are listed in a matrix. In fact, ISO 10993-1 has never contained any test requirements at all; the only requirements in the 2003 version of the standard were the following:

- Ensure the biological evaluation is planned, carried out and documented by knowledgeable and experienced individuals capable of making informed decisions.
- As part of a structured assessment programme, make and document an informed decision that weighs the advantages and disadvantages of material and test procedure choices.
- Apply the general principles of evaluation and testing.
- Record the rationale for selection/waiving of tests.
- Base any tests on end-use applications.
- Consider appropriate tests listed in matrices.
- Use sensitive, precise and accurate test methods.
- Follow appropriate Good Laboratory Practices.
- Retain test data, complete to the extent that an independent analysis can be made.
- Consider the need for biological reevaluation.

The revised version of ISO 10993-1 presents the

same scientific principles of biological safety evaluation more clearly and emphasises that, where existing data are adequate, additional testing is not required. The standard includes an annex containing guidance on the relevant risk management process, describing it as a continuous process by which a manufacturer can identify the biological hazards associated with medical devices, estimate and evaluate the risks, control these risks, and monitor the effectiveness of the control. It concludes that the use of ISO 10993 as part of a risk management process offers scientific validity to the process of biological response evaluation, makes proper provisions for the ethical use of animals and offers greater reassurance to the public regarding the biological safety of medical devices.

The ISO guidance document, ISO/TR 15499, takes the approach described in ISO 10990-1:2009 and Annex I of EN/ISO 14971 further by setting out the role of different components of a biological evaluation in terms of the ISO 14971 risk management process. The technical report provides more-detailed guidance, intended to be helpful in the practical application of the standard. The adoption of these two documents marks the culmination of a slow and difficult process, initiated in 1996 within the ISO Technical Committee, designed to make it clear that the bureaucratic box-checking exercise that has been apparent in the past needs to be replaced by a scientifically valid risk evaluation. Since ISO 10993-1 is a harmonised standard, this method of assessment becomes, *de facto*, the method needed for conformity assessment in Europe.

The Biological Evaluation Process

The first stage in a biological safety evaluation should be the collection of all relevant data that are immediately available. ISO 14971 requires that relevant characteristics that could affect safety be listed and, from these, possible hazards identified. In general terms, relevant data comprise:

- data on the intended use of the device under consideration, which will be needed both to characterise the risks arising from identified hazards and to devise a suitable evaluation programme
- data relating to the materials, which will characterise the toxicological hazards and any risks apparent from previous clinical use or biological tests
- data on previous use of the materials in other medical device applications, which may allow conclusions to be drawn about their suitability in the proposed application
- data on biological testing that has previously been carried out on the materials to support their prior use, which can reduce the need for further testing

An initial review may suggest that biological safety is verifiable without further data, in which case a more thorough assessment can be carried out straight away. It is often the case that further data will be deemed necessary, and the purpose of the initial review is to define the type of data required as fully as possible. At this early stage of the assessment, the possibility of significant toxicity arising from the use of many materials can be entirely discounted from knowledge of their composition, the toxicity of their components and information on their prior use. This allows the conclusion that the biological safety of the material can be assured on the basis of the lack of any significant toxicological hazard. If, however, this sort of analysis identifies any hazardous chemicals with the potential to be present in the final device, further assessment is needed and the associated risks need to be controlled. Risk control can be achieved by defining appropriate limits to ensure that the level of exposure to a toxic residue in the device is lower than that at which harm to health would result., A method for managing such risks is provided within the ISO 10993 series.[13] This is the same approach that is used for the management of the toxicological risk associated with ethylene oxide, which is a potent carcinogen.[14]

Acceptable results from appropriate biological tests, of the sort described in the ISO 10993 series of standards, give a degree of reassurance that the risk of adverse reactions occurring during clinical use is low. These tests, commonly termed biocompatibility tests, differ from "classical" toxicity tests in that they typically attempt to mimic the conditions of clinical exposure to medical devices and thus provide an indication of the probability of adverse effects arising during use; i.e., they are used as an indicator of risk, rather than to identify hazards. As a result, they can be less sensitive than classical toxicity tests, in which exposure is maximised to elicit an effect. Biological test data should therefore be used to complement an assessment based on material and toxicological characterisation, rather than as a replacement for it.

Well-established and documented clinical use of materials or their chemical components in an analogous situation can provide an indication of their suitability for an intended purpose. It is common practice to evaluate biological safety primarily on the basis that the materials have been used before in comparable applications. This sort of evaluation requires sufficient information about the material or chemical to determine equivalence.[15] It also requires clinical evidence to demonstrate that the material or chemical has performed with a suitable biological response. This may be in the form of clinical investigation or marketing and adverse incident data. It is important to note that, because patients cannot be subjected to the sort of rigorous toxicological study that is a feature of animal or *in vitro* tests, clinical experience is an imprecise indicator of toxicity.

ISO 10993-1 speaks of conducting a structured biological evaluation programme within a risk management process. The standards available can guide a manufacturer

Table 23-2. Standards Relevant to Biological Safety Assessment

Biological Evaluation Principles	
ISO 14971	*Medical devices: Application of risk management to medical devices*
ISO 10993-1	*Evaluation and testing within a risk management process*
ISO/TR 15499	*Guidance on the conduct of biological evaluation within a risk management process*
Materials Characterisation	
ISO 10993-18	*Chemical Characterisation of Materials*
ISO 10993-19	*Physico-chemical, Morphological and Topographical Characterisation of Materials*
Degradation of Materials	
ISO 10993-9	*Framework for identification and quantification of potential degradation products*
ISO 10993-16	*Toxicokinetic study design for degradation products and leachables*
ISO 10993-13	*Identification and quantification of degradation products from polymeric medical devices*
ISO 10993-14	*Identification and quantification of degradation products from ceramics*
ISO 10993-15	*Identification and quantification of degradation products from metals and alloys*
General Principles for Testing	
ISO 10993-2	*Animal welfare requirements*
ISO 10993-12	*Sample preparation and reference materials*
Test Selection and Methods	
ISO 10993-3	*Genotoxicity, carcinogenicity, reproductive toxicity*
ISO 10993-4	*Selection of tests for interaction with blood*
ISO 10993-5	*Cytotoxicity*
ISO 10993-6	*Local effects after implantation*
ISO 10993-10	*Irritation and delayed-type hypersensitivity*
ISO 10993-11	*Systemic toxicity*
ISO 10993-20	*Principles and methods for immunotoxicology testing of medical devices*
Control Limits for Toxic Compounds	
ISO 10993-17	*Method for the establishment of allowable limits for leachable substances*
ISO 10993-7	*Ethylene oxide sterilization residuals*

through the process, although construction of the programme and assessment of the data should be carried out by someone with the relevant expertise. The relevant standards can be categorised as in **Table 23-2**.

The Biological Evaluation Report

The end result of a biological safety evaluation should be a report by a "knowledgeable and experienced individual" in which a judgement of safety is made. It is convenient to present this in the form of a short summary report, authorised by the assessor and those with responsibility for quality assurance. This allows Notified Bodies and Competent Authorities an immediate appreciation of the nature and result of the assessment, which should, in many cases, be sufficient for their purposes. Such a report should describe the basis of the judgement and verify that risks have been reduced to an acceptable level and that the data available are sufficient to demonstrate conformity with

the relevant Essential Requirements. The UK Competent Authority has published guidance setting out its expectations for the biological safety report provided with a clinical investigation notification dossier.[16] This document includes principles that are also relevant for CE marking.

Just as a report of a toxicity study needs to contain sufficient data to re-create the study, the summary of the evaluation should give the essential details necessary to indicate how the assessment was carried out. The report should include an outline of the evaluation programme and present the assessor's rationale for his decisions and at least reference the data upon which they were based. It should explain how risks have been identified, estimated and addressed and give references to supporting documentation, which must be available for inspection. Test reports need to be included with the technical documentation, and may be requested by regulatory bodies, but should not normally be included in an overall biological evaluation report or an Investigators

Brochure. The report should, in turn, be referenced by the risk analysis and the Essential Requirements checklist as an indication of how Essential Requirements relating to biological safety have been addressed.

Summary

For CE marking of general or active implantable medical devices, it is necessary to demonstrate conformity with all relevant Essential Requirements contained in Annex I of the applicable European medical devices directive. The many Essential Requirements follow the following basic principles:

- Devices must not compromise the clinical condition or safety of the patient or user.
- Risks must be acceptable when weighed against the benefits to the patient.
- Risks must be eliminated or minimised in line with the state of the art.
- Devices must perform as intended by the manufacturer.

Because the Essential Requirements of the directives are designed to cover a wide variety of safety and performance aspects for a broad range of products, it is recognised that they cannot provide the level of technical detail required to address everything that is relevant to conformity assessment. A harmonised European standard is one that is deemed necessary and sufficient to carry the presumption of conformity with Essential Requirements of the relevant European directive. While a manufacturer can show compliance through any means considered appropriate, harmonised standards represent the most efficient way of demonstrating compliance with Essential Requirements.

A checklist must be completed, indicating, for each Essential Requirement, how conformity has been demonstrated and which European or international standards, or other guidance documents have been applied. However, this should not be seen as a box-checking exercise; it is necessary to confirm that the standard is indeed appropriate and adequate for demonstrating full compliance. It is also necessary to indicate whether a standard has been applied in full or only partially.

Effective risk management by the manufacturer is an essential component of European regulatory requirements. ISO 14971 sets out the method by which risks associated with a device should be analysed and the identified risks controlled effectively to ensure the safety of the patient and others. As well as setting out an overall process for managing risks, ISO 14971 requires a company's top management to implement a policy for determining criteria for risk acceptability. Risk acceptability criteria, based on this policy need to be included in the risk management plan for a product. Since the policy must be based on Essential Requirements, the acceptability criteria must take into account at least the first three principles in the bulleted list above. Risk evaluation involves a judgement on risk acceptability in line with the established criteria.

The data showing how a manufacturer has demonstrated conformity with Essential Requirements is collated in the technical file. This must conform to ISO 9001 documentation requirements. While there is no defined format for the technical file, it must be made available to a Competent Authority upon request. Where required by the Conformity Assessment Procedure specified in the relevant directive, these data will be reviewed by the Notified Body as part of the CE marking process and a "design dossier" must be submitted for this purpose. The design dossier should be compiled in line with guidance prepared by the Notified Bodies' Recommendation Group

Requirements for biological safety assessment have often been subject to misinterpretation. The revised standard, ISO 10993-1:2009, and the accompanying guidance, ISO/TR 15499, present the scientific principles behind biological safety assessment within the context of risk management and explain how data relevant to biological safety can be obtained and presented effectively. The use of ISO 10993 as part of a risk management process offers scientific validity to the process of biological evaluation, makes proper provisions for the ethical use of animals and offers greater reassurance regarding the biological safety of medical devices.

References

1. Council Directive 93/42/EEC of 14 June 1993 concerning medical devices.
2. Council Directive 90/385/EEC of 20 June 1990 on the approximation of the laws of the Member States relating to active implantable medical devices.
3. For example: *Official Journal of the European Union*, C 183/15 - C 183/43; 7.7.2010.
4. IEC 56/629/CD Dependability management—Part 3-13: Application Guide—Project risk management. International Electrotechnical Commission, Geneva (1998).
5. See Annex C of ISO 14971:2007.
6. See Annexes D and E of ISO 14971:2007 for guidance and a discussion of the relevant concepts.
7. See Annex D.8 of ISO 14971:2007.
8. MB-MED/2.5.1/Rec5 Rev4: Technical Documentation.
9. Williams DF. "Fundamental aspects of biocompatibility." *Biocompatibility*, 1, CRC Press, 1980; and Williams DF. "Definitions in Biomaterials." *Progress in Biomedical Engineering:*, 4, 1-72, 1987.
10. Tinkler J J B. Biological safety and European medical device regulations.: Quality First International Press, London, England; 2000.
11. ISO 10993-1:2009 Biological evaluation of medical

devices: Evaluation and testing within a risk management process.

12. ISO/TR 15499 Guidance on the conduct of biological evaluation within a risk management process.

13. ISO 10993-17, Method for the establishment of allowable limits for leachable substances.

14. ISO 10993-7, Ethylene oxide sterilization residuals.

15. See Annex C of ISO 10993-18, Chemical characterization of materials.

16. MHRA *Guidance Note 5—Guidance on Biocompatibility Assessment*, 2006. Available from mhra.gov.uk.

Chapter 24

EU In Vitro Diagnostic Medical Devices

Dirk Stynen, PhD

OBJECTIVES

❑ Summarize the European *In Vitro Diagnostic Medical Devices Directive*

❑ Describe the regulatory process to be followed by IVD manufacturers

❑ Focus on the specific elements in this directive

DIRECTIVES, REGULATIONS AND GUIDELINES COVERED IN THIS CHAPTER

❑ Directive 98/79/EC of the European Parliament and of the Council of 7 December 1998 on *in vitro* diagnostic medical devices (*In Vitro Diagnostic Devices Directive (IVDD)*)

❑ Directive 93/42/EEC of the European Parliament and of the Council of 14 June 1998 concerning medical devices (*Medical Devices Directive (MDD)*)

❑ MEDDEV 2.14/2 rev.1, *IVD Guidance: Research Use Only products*, 2004

❑ MEDDEV 2.14/1 rev.1. *IVD Guidances: Borderline issues*, 2004

❑ MEDDEV 2.12/1 rev. 6. Medical Devices— Guidelines on a medical devices vigilance system, 2009

❑ Summary Technical Documentation (STED) for Demonstrating Conformity to the Essential

Principles of Safety and Performance of In Vitro Diagnostic Medical Devices, GHTF

❑ MEDDEV 2.14/3 rev. 1. 2007. *IVD Guidances: Supply of Instructions For Use (IFU) and other information for In-vitro Diagnostic (IVD) Medical Devices*

Introduction

Directive 98/79/EC of the European Parliament and of the Council of 7 December 1998 on *in vitro* diagnostic medical devices (*IVDD*) became the third in the series of directives on medical devices.[1] It laid out pan-European requirements for in vitro diagnostic medical devices (IVDs), replacing national regulations where they existed. Since 7 December 2003, the end of the transition period, all IVDs in the European Economic Area (EEA) and Switzerland also must comply with the requirements of the *IVDD* and carry the CE mark.

The *IVDD* has been transposed into the national legislation of each Member State. Although the national transpositions largely follow the *IVDD*, they do contain specific elements with which devices in the respective national territory must comply. The language requirements for IVDs for professional use are a good example of these national differences.

In order to gain a full understanding of the regulatory requirements for IVDs in Europe, other important documents should be consulted: harmonised standards, guidance documents and, if applicable, the Common Technical Specifications.

The *IVDD* shares many features with Directive 93/42/EEC of the European Parliament and of the Council of 14 June 1998 concerning medical devices (*MDD*). The *MDD* is treated in more detail in other chapters of this book and repetition is avoided as much as possible. This chapter focuses on the particularities of the *IVDD*.

At the time of writing, the European Commission had begun preparing the revision of the *IVDD*. A draft text of this revision is not yet available, but there are indications that the changes will be important.

The Scope of the IVDD

The *IVDD* (Art. 1.2.b) defines an *IVD* as follows:
"'in vitro diagnostic medical device' means any medical device which is a reagent, reagent product, calibrator, control material, kit, instrument, apparatus, equipment, or system, whether used alone or in combination, intended by the manufacturer to be used in vitro for the examination of specimens, including blood and tissue donations, derived from the human body, solely or principally for the purpose of providing information:
- concerning a physiological or pathological state, or
- concerning a congenital abnormality, or
- to determine the safety and compatibility with potential recipients, or
- to monitor therapeutic measures."

An assay must first meet the definition of a medical device. This excludes a number of assays, e.g., those intended by their manufacturers to be used for forensic purposes.

Specimen receptacles and accessories to IVDs are also included in the scope of the *IVDD*.

IVDs that are introduced in European laboratories in order to establish their performance characteristics are also subject to the *IVDD*. Such products cannot carry the CE mark because their performance characteristics have not yet been established, but otherwise should meet all the requirements. Annex VIII of the *IVDD* further details the documentation and notification requirements for performance evaluation of these devices.

Assays, intended for research purposes are not subject to the *IVDD*. These assays lack a clinical application and therefore are not medical devices. The *IVDD* neither explicitly defines "Research Use Only" nor defines any requirements for such products. Manufacturers of these reagents should not apply the CE mark, but clearly label them as "Research Use Only" and should ensure that all the labelling is consistent with their nonclinical purpose.

It is not unusual for clinical laboratories to develop and produce their own reagents. These "home brew" tests are not subject to the *IVDD*. However, to be exempt, these reagents must be manufactured and used within the same legal entity and in the same geographic location. Moreover, the tests can only be run on specimens from patients from the same health institution. Preamble 11 clearly brings home brew assays "intended to be used in a professional and commercial context" within the *IVDD*'s scope. As a consequence, biotech companies that are, for example, commercializing their often innovative assays as a testing service instead of selling the reagents to other laboratories, will also have to comply with the *IVDD*.

Guidance documents on "Research Use Only"[2] and borderline products[3] further clarify these subjects.

Process to be Followed by the Manufacturer
Short Overview of the Steps

An IVD manufacturer that wishes to place a product on the European market must do the following:
- define its product's classification
- ensure that the product meets the Essential Requirements, preferably complying with harmonised standards and, for Annex II List A products only, complying with the Common Technical Specifications
- ensure that its organization meets the quality system requirements
- implement vigilance procedures
- establish technical documentation, demonstrating compliance with the Essential Requirements and the applied harmonised standards
- draft labelling meeting national language requirements of the target countries
- appoint an Authorised Representative, if it is located outside the EEA or Switzerland
- execute an appropriate conformity assessment procedure, including Notified Body (NB) certification, if applicable
- sign the Declaration of Conformity and apply the CE mark to the device
- notify its product to the Competent Authorities in its home country and those in all other Member States where the product will be placed on the market (if the manufacturer is located outside Europe, this must be done by the Authorised Representative)

These points are described in more detail in this chapter and/or in other chapters of this book.

Classification of an IVD

The classification of an IVD determines the conformity assessment procedure to be followed and, hence, whether a Notified Body (NB) will be involved in the approval and certification of the product and the quality system. This has an impact on the cost and the time to market.

The current classification is risk-based, but instead of defining classification rules, as is the case in the *MDD*, the *IVDD* literally lists the high-risk products in Annex II. This annex contains two lists, List A and List B. List A mentions the highest-risk products. List B mentions the products considered to be high risk but less so than those in List A.

The *IVDD* does not speak of "Class I, Class II, etc." of products, which results in rather awkward denominations of the IVD classes. Based upon Annex II and Articles 1 and 9, the following categories are defined:

- "Annex II List A-products," covering the highest-risk products
- "Annex II List B-products," covering products with somewhat less risk
- "Devices for self-testing," covering products to be used by lay persons in their home environment
- "non-Annex II–products for professional use," covering all products not mentioned in the previous classes

Both the classification system and the actual classifications badly need modification to bring them in line with technological and medical advancements and also to accommodate future evolutions. Therefore, they will probably be substantially changed in the revised *IVDD*. In the meantime, assays for variant Creutzfeldt-Jakob Disease (vCJD) are likely to be integrated into List A of Annex II.

Following are the lists of highest-risk and high-risk products, as defined in Annex II of the current *IVDD*.

List A

- reagents and reagent products, including related calibrators and control materials, for determining the following blood groups: ABO system, rhesus (C, c, D, E, e) anti-Kell
- reagents and reagent products, including related calibrators and control materials, for the detection, confirmation and quantification in human specimens of markers of HIV infection (HIV 1 and 2), HTLV I and II and hepatitis B, C and D

List B

- reagents and reagent products, including related calibrators and control materials, for determining the following blood groups: anti-Duffy and anti-Kidd
- reagents and reagent products, including related calibrators and control materials, for determining irregular anti-erythrocytic antibodies
- reagents and reagent products, including related calibrators and control materials, for the detection and quantification in human samples of the following congenital infections: rubella, toxoplasmosis
- reagents and reagent products, including related calibrators and control materials, for diagnosing the following hereditary disease: phenylketonuria
- reagents and reagent products, including related calibrators and control materials, for determining

the following human infections: cytomegalovirus, chlamydia
- reagents and reagent products, including related calibrators and control materials, for determining the following HLA tissue groups: DR, A, B
- reagents and reagent products, including related calibrators and control materials, for determining the following tumoral marker: PSA
- reagents and reagent products, including related calibrators, control materials and software, designed specifically for evaluating the risk of trisomy 21
- the following device for self-diagnosis, including its related calibrators and control materials: device for the measurement of blood sugar

Essential Requirements, Harmonized Standards and Common Technical Specifications

Before signing the Declaration of Conformity and affixing the CE mark, the manufacturer must ensure that its product meets the Essential Requirements of Annex I of the *IVDD*.

Annex I consists of a long list of requirements that must be met, if applicable. The wording is often rather vague, but many Essential Requirements are supported by harmonised standards. These standards describe in more detail what the regulator expects for achieving compliance with the respective requirement. A manufacturer should carefully identify which Essential Requirements apply to its product and whether any harmonised standards have been published to support these requirements.

The high importance and relevance of applying harmonised standards are the same as for medical devices and are explained elsewhere in this book.

Several Essential Requirements and harmonised standards are generic and apply to IVDs and other medical devices alike. A typical and important example is the requirement to manage the risks associated with the use of the device, supported by the harmonised standard ISO14971.[4]

Other Essential Requirements and associated harmonised standards are specific for some IVDs, e.g., the Essential Requirements and harmonised standards for stability testing, for traceability of calibration for quantitative assays, for devices for self-testing and for labelling.

The Essential Requirements cover a variety of subjects, all somehow safety related. They include risk management, analytical and clinical performance, stability, chemical and physical properties, infection and microbial contamination, manufacturing and environmental properties, measuring functions, radiation, electronic safety and electromagnetic compatibility, protection against mechanical and thermal risks, risk for devices for self-testing and information supplied by the manufacturer (labelling).

The Common Technical Specifications (CTS)[5] are a specific set of requirements published in the *Official Journal of the European Union* and currently only applicable to the Annex II List A products. The name of the document is misleading, since they really contain performance specifications and not technical specifications. The CTS strictly define the minimum performance requirements for the various products in Annex II List A and also describe in detail how they should be established. They also include the batch release criteria for these products, as they have to be applied by the manufacturer and its NB in charge of batch release.

The purpose of the CTS is to ensure that NBs assess the performance of these highest-risk devices and the quality of the individual batches in a consistent way. The *IVDD* allows CTS to be established for Annex II List B products, too, but these have not yet been developed.

Quality System Requirements and Vigilance Procedures

The *IVDD* imposes quality system requirements on all IVD manufacturers, including those that only place non-Annex II products for professional use on the market.

ISO 13485[6] is the harmonised standard and should be chosen as the quality system model. However, certification against this standard is not mandatory. At the same time, an ISO 13485-certified quality system may show major nonconformities versus the requirements of the *IVDD*.

The quality system should include adequate procedures for handling field safety corrective actions and managing and reporting incidents and other postmarketing surveillance activities in agreement with the *IVDD* and the applicable guidance document.[7]

Technical Documentation and Design Dossier

The manufacturer must be capable of making technical documentation available for all CE-marked IVDs, regardless of the class. This technical documentation must demonstrate compliance with the applicable Essential Requirements and applied harmonised standards. *IVDD* Annex III lists items that should be part of the technical documentation. Not all items are applicable to each device and, conversely, the technical documentation of an IVD may also have to contain information that is not explicitly listed in Annex III.

For Annex II List A products, a design dossier must be submitted to the NB when the Annex IV conformity assessment procedure is chosen. Whereas technical documentation does not have to be one physical file, the design dossier is a single document that addresses all the items required for an effective NB assessment. NBs may make a proposal on the contents of the design dossier. The Summary Technical Documentation (STED) format, proposed by the Global Harmonization Task Force in a draft guidance document[8]

may become a model in the future, but its use for IVDs is currently not as widespread as for medical devices.

In practice, manufacturers applying for an NB certificate for Annex II List A or Annex II List B devices or devices for self-testing according to the Annex V conformity assessment procedure may also submit technical documentation structured as a design dossier.

Labelling, e-Labelling and Language Requirements

Annex I.B.8 spells out the labelling requirements for IVDs, further specified in the ISO 18113 series of harmonised standards.[9] Both sources primarily focus on the contents of the labels and the instructions for use.

The *IVDD* explicitly demands that the information provided to the users of devices for self-testing be in the national language(s) of the target market. However, for IVDs for professional use, the *IVDD* left the decision on languages to the individual Member States. The Member States published their language requirements in their national transpositions of the *IVDD*. The majority decided to impose their national language(s) for professional IVDs, too. In practice, an IVD manufacturer selling products in all 32 countries covered by the *IVDD* must make instructions for use available in about 15 languages.

To overcome some of the practical problems resulting from the language requirements, the European Commission published a guidance document[10] defining the conditions for the provision of instructions for use by means other than physically sending them with the product itself. Instructions can now be posted on a website. However, strict conditions apply to this "e-labelling" solution. The website must meet certain requirements and the manufacturer must make a free telephone number available so users can request a mailed or faxed copy.

Devices for self-testing and for point-of-care-testing are excluded from e-labelling. Special requirements apply to instrument manuals.

The language requirements also apply to labels. Use of the symbols from harmonised standard EN 980[11] mitigates the problem.

Conformity Assessment Procedures

The IVD manufacturer must assess the conformity of its products and quality system prior to signing the Declaration of Conformity and affixing the CE mark to the product. In the case of non-Annex II products for professional use, the manufacturer has sole responsibility for doing this. For other devices, the conformity assessment involves a third-party review by the NB.

In the case of Annex II products, the NB will inspect the product's quality and the conformity of the quality system. In the case of Annex II List A products, the NB also has to release each batch.

Devices for self-testing can be certified by the NB based

upon product documentation alone, although the manufacturer can also opt for conformity assessment procedures including quality system inspections.

Chapter 22 is dedicated to conformity assessment procedures.

Authorized Representative, Declaration of Conformity and Registration

Other chapters in this book describe the role of the Authorised Representative and the signing of the Declaration of Conformity.

After signing the Declaration of Conformity and prior to placing the product on the market, the manufacturer and the devices must be registered. The manufacturer, or its Authorised Representative in the case of non-European companies, informs the Competent Authorities in the country in which it is based about placing the device(s) on the market.

The registration of IVDs is different from the registration of medical devices.

The registration requirement applies to all IVD classes, not only to those that do not require NB involvement. Furthermore, the notification must be repeated in every country where a product is placed on the market, not only in the country in which the manufacturer or its Authorised Representative is based. The latter obligation will disappear when Eudamed, the European databank for medical devices, becomes operational.

Only general information is requested for non-Annex II products for professional use; however, information on the performance, NB certificates and labelling must be provided for devices in other classes.

In practice, the large majority of countries accept the "Form for the registration of manufacturers and devices, In Vitro Diagnostic Medical Device Directive, Article 10,"[12] available on the European Commission's website for this purpose. However, differences between the countries exist with respect to the information to be provided and costs.

The *IVDD*'s Revision

The *IVDD* is currently under revision. The new version is expected to be published by the end of 2011. A transition period of one to three years is likely to be defined.

No draft is available yet, but from the Public Consultation text,[13] one can conclude that changes are being considered in the following areas:

- the classification of IVDs, which will also impact conformity assessment procedures
- "home brew" or "in-house" testing
- diagnostic service laboratories
- genetic testing
- point-of-care testing
- demonstrating clinical validity and utility

Other Regulations

IVDs are exempt from other directives, such as those on biocides, machinery, electric safety and electromagnetic compatibility, often because the *IVDD* itself defines requirements that address the safety issues in these directives.

However, other regulations may apply. Relevant examples are:

- regulations on dangerous substances and preparations, which may have an impact on the labelling and may require the availability and distribution of material safety data sheets
- transport regulations
- Directive 2002/96/EC of the European Parliament and of the Council of 27 January 2003 on waste electrical and electronic equipment
- regulations on radioactive materials
- regulations on animal sourced raw materials

This list may not be complete.

Summary

- The *IVDD* shares many features with the *MDD*. The general concept of the regulation, the conformity assessment procedures and the requirements on postmarketing surveillance, vigilance, risk management and technical documentation are identical or very similar. The responsibilities of the manufacturer, the Competent Authorities, Notified Bodies and Authorised Representative are very similar to those defined in the *MDD*.
- Device classification is risk-based. The *IVDD* literally lists the high-risk products in Annex II. This annex contains two lists, List A and List B. Self-testing devices are in a separate category.
- Before signing the Declaration of Conformity and affixing the CE mark, the manufacturer must ensure that its product meets the Essential Requirements and, preferably, the requirements in the associated harmonised standards. The CTS are additional requirements, only applicable to Annex II, List A products.
- The *IVDD* is currently subject to revision. Significant changes are expected, e.g., in device classification.

References

1. Directive 98/79/EC of the European Parliament and of the Council of 27 October 1998 on *in vitro* diagnostic medical devices. Eudralex website. http://eur-lex.europa.eu/LexUriServ/LexUriServ.do?uri=CONSLEG:1998L0079:20031120:en:PDF. Accessed 8 October 2010.
2. MEDDEV 2.14/2 rev.1, 2004. *IVD Guidance: Research Use Only products*. European Commission

website. http://ec.europa.eu/consumers/sectors/
medical-devices/files/meddev/2_14_2_research_
only_product_en.pdf. Accessed 8 October 2010.

3. MEDDEV 2.14/1 rev.1. 2004. *IVD Guidances: Borderline issues*. European commission website. http://ec.europa.eu/consumers/sectors/medical-devices/files/meddev/2_14_ivd_borderline_issues_jan2004_en.pdf. Accessed 8 October 2010.

4. ISO 14971:2009. *Medical Devices—Application of risk management to medical devices*.

5. Commission Decision of 3 February 2009 amending Decision 2002/364/EC on common technical specifications for *in vitro*-diagnostic medical devices (2009/108/EC).

6. ISO 13485:2003. *Medical Devices—Quality management systems—Requirements for regulatory purposes*.

7. MEDDEV 2.12/1 rev. 6. 2009. *Guidelines on a medical devices vigilance system*. European Commission website. http://ec.europa.eu/consumers/sectors/medical-devices/files/meddev/2_12_1-rev_6-12-2009_en.pdf. Accessed 8 October 2010.

8. Summary Technical Documentation (STED) for Demonstrating Conformity to the Essential Principles of Safety and Performance of In Vitro Diagnostic Medical Devices. Study Group 1 of the Global Harmonization Task Force. 2009. Draft document.

9. ISO 18113:2009 (part 1–5). *In vitro diagnostic medical devices—Information supplied by the manufacturer (labelling)*. (5 parts have been published).

10. MEDDEV 2.14/3 rev. 1. 2007. *IVD Guidances: Supply of Instructions For Use (IFU) and other information for In-vitro Diagnostic (IVD) Medical Devices*. European Commission website. http://ec.europa.eu/consumers/sectors/medical-devices/files/meddev/2_14_ivd_borderline_issues_jan2004_en.pdf. Accessed 8 October 2010.

11. EN 980:2008. *Symbols for use in the labelling of medical devices*.

12. Form for the registration of manufacturers and devices, In Vitro Diagnostic Medical Device Directive, Article 10. European 'Commission website. http://ec.europa.eu/consumers/sectors/medical-devices/documents/guidelines/index_en.htm. Accessed 16 December 2010.

13. Revision of the Directive 98/79/EC of the European Parliament and of the Council of 27 October 1998 on *in vitro* diagnostic medical devices—Public Consultation. 2010.

Medical Device Compliance: EU Postmarket Requirements

Updated by Evangeline Loh

OBJECTIVES

❏ Obtain an overview of the mechanisms in place to ensure medical device compliance in the postmarket phase

❏ Review the requirements for manufacturers concerning postmarket surveillance procedures

❏ Understand the European vigilance system concerning medical devices and the requirements for incident reporting

❏ Review other measures that are used by the Competent Authorities of the Member States to control the medical device market

DIRECTIVES, REGULATIONS AND GUIDELINES COVERED IN THIS CHAPTER

❏ Council Directive 90/385/EEC of 20 June 1990 on the approximation of the laws of the Member States relating to active implantable medical devices (*Active Implantable Medical Devices Directive (AIMDD)*)

❏ Council Directive 93/42/EEC of 14 June 1993 concerning medical devices (*Medical Devices Directive (MDD)*)

❏ Directive 98/79/EC of the European Parliament and of the Council of 27 October 1998 on *in vitro* diagnostic medical devices (*In Vitro Diagnostic Devices Directive (IVDD)*)

❏ Directive 2001/95/EC of the European Parliament and of the Council of 3 December 2001 on general product safety

❏ MEDDEV 2.12/1 (Rev. 6). *Medical Devices— Guidelines on a medical devices vigilance system*, 2009

❏ MEDDEV 2.12/2 Medical Devices—Guidelines on post market clinical follow-up, 2004

❏ Commission Decision of 19 April 2010 on the European Databank on Medical Devices (Eudamed) 2010/227/EC

❏ Report on the Functioning of the Medical Devices Directive

❏ Commission Communication of 2 July 2003 to the Council and the European Parliament on Medical Devices

Introduction

In the application and enforcement of the European medical device directives, it is essential to have an effective system to collect, analyse and share information about issues concerning devices and any adverse incidents resulting from their day-to-day use. Having an effective information system makes it possible for all interested parties, particularly Member State Competent Authorities, to take action as needed to protect the public.

The medical device directives establish two principal mechanisms for providing feedback about medical devices. The first mechanism arises from the requirement for manufacturers to implement a systematic procedure to review postproduction phase device experience and implement appropriate means to apply any necessary corrective action. This mechanism is commonly referred to as postmarket surveillance. Directive 2007/47/EC of the European Parliament and of the Council of 5 September 2007, amending Council Directive 90/385/EEC on the approximation of the laws of the Member States relating to active implantable medical devices (*AIMDD*) and Council Directive 93/42/EEC concerning medical devices (*MDD*) indicated that postmarket surveillance data are also to be used to update the clinical evaluation report document.

The second mechanism stems from the requirements to notify Competent Authorities when so-called incidents, near incidents or a recall (Field Safety Corrective Action (FSCA) occur. An "incident or recall" is defined as:

a. any malfunction or deterioration in a device's characteristics and/or performance, as well as any inadequacy in the labelling or the instructions for use that might lead to or might have led to the death of a patient or user or a serious deterioration in his state of health

b. any technical or medical reason relating to a device's characteristics or performance for the reasons referred to in subparagraph (a), leading to a manufacturer's systematic recall of devices of the same type

The criteria and procedures used by manufacturers, Competent Authorities and all other interested parties to notify and handle incidents and FSCAs/recalls are collectively known as the Medical Devices Vigilance System.

Provisions regarding these two mechanisms are found in various sections of the medical device directives, as summarised in **Table 25-1.**

In each case, the objective is to provide feedback and analysis so that the manufacturer and or Competent Authority can put any subsequent measures into practice.

Relationship Between the General Product Safety Directive and the Medical Devices Directives

Other, less-obvious, horizontal directives, such as Directive 2001/94/EC of the European Parliament and of the Council of 3 December 2001 concerning general product safety (*General Product Safety Directive* or *GPSD*), also need to be considered. This directive is intended to ensure a high level of product safety for consumer products; it completes, complements and reinforces the medical device vigilance provisions found in the *AIMDD, MDD* and *In Vitro Devices Directive* (*IVDD*).

As regards the *MDD*, examples of products falling under the scope of the *GPSD* are adhesive bandages, crutches, condoms, glasses, contact lenses, hearing aids and in vitro

diagnostics for self-testing. Medical devices supplied to healthcare professionals and intended to be used by them— even if used on a consumer—generally do not qualify as consumer products. Examples include cardiovascular catheters, laboratory equipment, scalpels and x-ray equipment.

The *GPSD* uses the term "producer," and producers are responsible for placing safe products on the market. Producers are defined as follows: manufacturer of a product when established in the EU, entity presenting as manufacturer by affixing name or trademark, manufacturer's representative or importer of product, and other professionals in the supply chain whose activities may affect a product's safety.

The medical device directives cover most producer obligations specified in the *GPSD*. *GPSD* Articles 5.1 and 5.3 may, however, apply regarding producers' general obligation to follow up on product safety after placing devices on the market, and to inform Competent Authorities about dangerous products and actions to prevent risk related to custom-made devices, in those cases where they are considered consumer products. Additionally, the medical device directives have no provisions related to distributors' obligations, although the New Approach directives define economic operators: manufacturer, Authorised Representatives, importers, and distributors. Therefore, aspects of *GPSD* Article 5 relevant for distributors apply to medical device consumer products.

Postmarket Surveillance Procedures

As indicated in the corresponding directive articles, medical device manufactures are required to implement a systematic procedure to review device experience in the postproduction phase. This requirement affects all information concerning medical devices that have been appropriately CE marked and put into service. This system should be both proactive (seeking information) and reactive (collecting and assessing complaints). Possible sources of information and/or experience include:

- customer and user surveys
- adverse incidents (vigilance system)
- user reports and feedback on product aspects
- customer complaints
- customer requirements, contract information and market needs
- patient follow-up after clinical trials or investigations
- services and evaluation reports
- scientific papers in peer-reviewed journals
- reports on similar products by competitors
- compliance-related communications from regulatory agencies
- changes to relevant standards and regulations

The important point is that the manufacturer must

Table 25-1. Provisions for Providing Feedback About Medical Devices

Mechanism	AIMDD 90/385/EEC3	MDD 93/42/EEC4	IVDD 98/79/EC5
Postmarket surveillance by the manufacturer	Annex II.3.1 Annex IV.3 Annex V.3.1	Annex II.3.1 Annex IV.3 Annex V.3.1 Annex VI.3.1 Annex VII.4	Annex III.5
Medical Devices Vigilance System	Article 8 Annex II.3.1 Annex IV.3 Annex V.3.1	Article 10 Annex II.3.1 Annex IV.3 Annex V.3.1 Annex VI.3.1 Annex VII.4	Article 11 Annex III.5

AIMDD = Active Implantable Medical Devices Directive; MDD = Medical Devices Directive; and IVDD = In Vitro Devices Directive

implement procedures to collect and analyse this information, then handle and process it appropriately to determine whether any corrective or preventive action is necessary. If incidents, near incidents or FSCAs are detected through this procedure, or if the actions to be taken involve change or correction of devices already placed on the market, the Competent Authorities may need to be informed in accordance with the vigilance system. (It should be noted that "near incident" is not a term used in the current revision of the European guidance, MEDDEV, on the topic.)

Procedures for reviewing feedback also are mentioned in the standards for medical device quality assurance and management systems. For example, Section 8.2.1 of EN ISO 13485 states that the manufacturer, "shall establish a documented procedure for a feedback system to provide early warning of quality problems and for input to the corrective and preventive action processes" and that, "if national or regional regulations require the organisation to gain experience from the post-production phase, the review of this experience shall form part of the feedback system."

The system for gathering postmarket surveillance information has been identified by the Medical Devices Expert Group as a weak point in the medical device directives; the consensus is that further guidance is needed to promote manufacturer improvement of these systems.

Risk Management in the Medical Device Industry

Risk assessment, risk analysis and risk management are critical phases for any medical device in design, production and postmarket surveillance.

Regulatory bodies and standards development committees prefer a descriptive rather than a prescriptive approach during the standards development process. This seems a sensible way to move forward, as technology changes rather quickly and prescribing numeric values or specific details for compliance makes the existing standards' versions outdated in regard to any technological advance. Effectively, it means that the onus is on manufacturers to define their own risk-acceptance criteria in accordance with the relevant standards' described guidance to demonstrate compliance.

As part of postmarket surveillance activities, manufacturers need to review developments in regulations and standards. Currently, manufacturers are reasonably well

organised when it comes to generating the initial risk management file. However, they rarely revisit and update these documents from risk perspectives after product release; at times, these documents do not reflect the current status of known issues with which risks may be associated. If a new standard has been implemented, existing products are not necessarily considered unsafe. However, it could be questionable whether a product is still complying with the state-of-the-art principle, and Notified Bodies are likely to address this question in the context of certificate renewal. Implementing new or revised standards stresses the importance of a comprehensive risk management file and emphasises that the file should be a living document that reflects and documents all known product issues from all project phases, including postmarket surveillance. From risk perspectives, manufacturers usually react to a raised complaint or an issue and then try to address the problem. It would be advisable to have a combination of proactive and reactive strategies for managing risks throughout the product lifecycle.

Additionally, clinical evaluation and its documentation must be actively updated. In general, postmarket clinical follow-up (PMCF) is deemed necessary, as premarket data do not necessarily enable the manufacturer to detect infrequent complications or problems that become apparent only after long-term use. Where PMCF is deemed unnecessary as part of the device's postmarket surveillance plan, this must be duly justified and documented. All of this information should be included in the risk assessment, which is part of the technical file/design dossier.

Medical Devices Vigilance System

Competent Authorities are responsible for establishing and operating a medical devices vigilance system within each Member State. Under *AIMDD* Article 8, *MDD* Article 10 and *IVDD* Article 11, Competent Authorities are responsible for taking all necessary steps to ensure that information concerning incidents is centrally recorded and evaluated. This central coordination will also be facilitated when Eudamed, the European database, becomes operational (European Commission decision, effective May 2011).

It is intended that information and data collected and recorded in this manner be shared among Competent

Authorities, thereby facilitating corrective action earlier than if data were evaluated on a state-by-state basis. This gives the vigilance system considerable relevance for protecting the health and safety of patients, users and third parties. On the basis of the information collected and evaluated, Competent Authorities may decide to disseminate information within the market to prevent incidents.

Extensive guidance on interpreting the directives' requirements concerning vigilance is provided in MEDDEV 2.12/1 (Rev. 6, December 2009). There were significant modifications from Rev. 4 (April 2003) to Rev. 5 (April 2007). Although not legally binding, this guidance is the result of a general consensus among Competent Authorities, European Commission services and industry representatives. It is expected, therefore, that the document's recommendations will be closely followed in many Member States.

MEDDEV 2.12/1 (Rev. 6) describes the medical devices vigilance system as a vehicle for adverse incident notification and evaluation. It covers the activities of the European Commission, Competent Authorities, manufacturers, Authorised Representatives, users and others concerned with continued medical device safety. Moreover, the vigilance guidelines clarify actions to be taken once a manufacturer or Competent Authority receives information concerning an incident. The guidelines are intended to apply equally to the *AIMDD*, *MDD* and *IVDD*. The procedures are intended to be the same for all the directives with respect to the vigilance system and refer to incidents that occur within EU Member States and those within the European Economic Area (EEA) and Switzerland regarding devices bearing the CE mark. The guidance also applies to incidents involving devices that do not bear the CE mark when they lead to an FSCA relevant to CE-marked devices.

The vigilance guidance establishes that incident reporting for in vitro diagnostic devices (IVDs) may be comparatively difficult to implement because such devices do not generally come into contact with patients. In those cases, direct harm to patients due to IVDs may be difficult to demonstrate. Any harm is more likely to be indirect—a consequence of a medical decision or action taken on the basis of information provided by the device, such as the following:
- wrong or delayed diagnosis
- inappropriate or delayed treatment
- transfusion of inappropriate substances

The guidance gives special attention to self-test devices because with those products, the medical decision is to be made by the user or patient. The guidance establishes that inadequacies in the information and instructions for use of self-test devices may lead to harm and should be carefully reviewed.

Types of Incidents to Be Reported
Three types of incidents must be reported to the Competent Authorities:
- incidents that result in a death
- incidents that result in a serious deterioration in the state of health of a patient, user or other person
- events that might have led to death or serious deterioration in health but did not, as a result of fortunate circumstances or the intervention of healthcare personnel

The vigilance guidance states specifically that "serious deterioration in the state of health" may include life-threatening illness or injury or the permanent impairment of or damage to a body function. The same is true for cases that require medical treatment or surgery to prevent injury or permanent impairment of specific body functions.

For events that might have led to death or serious deterioration in health, the reporting duty exists if the event occurred in connection with the use of a medical device and was such that it might lead to death or serious deterioration in health if it occurs again. These events also may occur when testing or examining the device, or the Instructions for Use reveals deterioration in characteristics or shortcomings that could lead to death or serious deterioration in health.

In all cases, the guidance points out that the term "serious deterioration" cannot be conclusively defined in practice because it is subject to evaluative interpretation in each case. When doubt exists as to reporting duty, the guidance establishes that a medical practitioner must be consulted and that, in general, personnel should be predisposed to report.

Criteria for Incident Reporting
When they become aware of a situation that may be considered an incident or near incident, manufacturers are to use three basic criteria to decide whether the Competent Authorities should be notified:
- An event has occurred.
- The manufacturer's device is suspected to be a contributory cause of the incident.
- The event led, or might have led, to one of the following outcomes:
  o death of a patient, user or other person
  o serious deterioration in the state of health of a patient, user or other person

Some additional considerations must be taken into account concerning what may be a "serious deterioration in the state of health," and certain events may be considered exempt from reporting duties even though they meet reporting criteria. Section 5.13 of the vigilance guidance provides criteria for determining such exemptions; examples include:

- deficiencies in devices found by the user prior to use
- events caused by patient conditions
- adverse events related to use of the device after the stated service life or shelf life has expired
- events that did not lead to death or serious deterioration in the state of health because protection against a fault functioned correctly
- events that did not lead to death or serious deterioration in the state of health and when, within a full risk assessment, the risk of death or serious deterioration was quantified and found to be negligible
- expected and foreseeable side effects
- events described in an advisory notice
- specific exemptions granted by a Competent Authority

Manufacturers should carefully consider all circumstances when deciding whether an event should be exempt from reporting duties. All criteria used should be formally documented for possible future reference by evidence that the issue was evaluated and the rationale for the decision.

Medical Device Linked to the Incident

To trigger a reporting duty, a certain link must exist between the event and the use of the medical device. The vigilance guidance recommends that the manufacturer take certain background information into account when the link between the event and the medical device is difficult to establish. Examples of such information are:

- the opinion, based upon evidence, of healthcare professionals
- results of the manufacturer's own preliminary assessment
- evidence of previous similar incidents
- other evidence held by the manufacturer

Such a link is assumed to exist in the event of a medical device's malfunction or deterioration in characteristics or performance. Malfunction or deterioration is understood to be the failure of the device to perform its intended purpose when used in accordance with the manufacturer's instructions (e.g., an unpredicted biological effect of the device).

Omission of information or errors and inaccuracies in labelling or instructions for use also are considered sufficient grounds for establishing a possible link between the incident and the medical device.

Timeline for Initial Reporting of an Incident

Incidents are to be reported to the Competent Authority immediately, unless there is a justifiable reason for delay. The vigilance guidance establishes the maximum elapsed time from awareness of the event to notification of the Competent Authorities as two calendar days for a serious public health threat, 10 calendar days for death or unanticipated serious deterioration in state of health and 30 elapsed calendar days for other incidents.

In practice, when a death or serious deterioration is reported, the manufacturer has up to 10 days to determine whether the occurrence fulfils the reporting criteria for events. If, within that time, the manufacturer is unable to rule out a device placed on the market under its responsibility as the cause, it must inform the Competent Authorities and submit an initial vigilance report.

Similarly, when the manufacturer receives a report that a death or serious deterioration could have occurred, although fortunate circumstances or the intervention of healthcare personnel precluded death or serious deterioration in state of health relative to a device placed on the market under its responsibility and it cannot rule out the device as the cause within 30 days, it must inform the Competent Authorities and submit an initial vigilance report.

To Whom Should the Initial Report Be Sent?

In general, the report should be made to the Competent Authority in the country where the incident occurred.

In addition, national transpositions of the medical device directives may require that manufacturers inform particular Member State Competent Authorities when planning to take action in response to incidents within that Member State's territory. Manufacturers and individuals responsible for placing medical devices on the market must take this into account when applying Community-wide corrective or preventive actions.

If the manufacturer is located outside the EEA, a suitable contact point within the EEA should be provided in the initial report (European Authorised Representative).

A suggested format for the initial report is included as Annex 3 of MEDDEV 2.12/1 (Rev. 6). This document is now available on the European Commission website. Some Member States have made similar formats available on the Internet to facilitate the administrative procedure and provide specific incident reporting criteria. Also, some Member States require mandatory electronic reporting.

If the initial report is made by means other than mail or fax (e.g., telephone or email), it should be followed as soon as possible by written confirmation. The manufacturer must avoid unduly delaying the report due to incomplete information, and may include a statement to the effect that it is making the report without prejudice and does not imply any admission of liability for the incident or its consequences.

Incident Investigations

Manufacturers are expected to follow up initial incident assessments with an investigation of the surrounding circumstances. Competent Authorities may initiate their own investigations and decide to intervene in the manufacturer's investigation, especially if access to the device associated with the incident may alter it in any way that might affect subsequent analysis. If the manufacturer cannot perform the investigation, the Competent Authorities must ensure that an investigation is carried out and keep the manufacturer informed.

Involved Competent Authorities may monitor the investigation's progress. Monitoring may include requesting follow-up reports from the manufacturer on:

- how many devices are involved and where they have been sold
- the current status of the devices on the market
- how long the devices have been on the market
- details of design changes that have been made

The ability to trace medical devices' distribution is, therefore, vital to providing reliable information on the location and state of use of particular devices or batches in the event of an incident.

For incidents involving notification of more than one Competent Authority, a single coordinating Competent Authority responsible for most communications may be designated.

Following the investigation, the manufacturer should take all necessary action, including consulting with the Competent Authority and performing any recalls. The follow-up to the investigation should conclude with the manufacturer's final report to the relevant Competent Authority illustrating the investigation's outcome. Outcomes may include:

- no action
- additional surveillance or follow-up of devices in use
- dissemination of information to users (e.g., by advisory notice)
- corrective action for future production
- corrective action for devices in use
- device recall/FSCA
- cessation of device commercialisation

Additionally, the Competent Authority may take the following actions:

- gather more information by commissioning independent reports
- make recommendations to the manufacturer to improve information provided with the device
- keep the European Commission and Competent Authorities informed about recalls and other actions to be taken
- consult with the relevant NB on matters relating to the conformity assessment
- consult with the European Commission if device reclassification is necessary
- provide additional user education

- take any other action to supplement manufacturer action

Competent Authorities also may decide to disseminate information related to reported incidents. Such information may be circulated among Competent Authorities using a Competent Authority Report. Such reports are intended only for other Competent Authorities and the European Commission, and the manufacturer should be informed when they are to be issued. The MEDDEV also mentions the Global Harmonisation Task Force (GHTF) National Competent Authority Report exchange programme.

Competent Authorities and manufacturers may decide to disseminate information to medical device users. Such information should be directed to specific medical practitioners and healthcare facilities but, in exceptional circumstances, it also may be directed to the public. It is important to coordinate actions by Competent Authorities and manufacturers, especially when preparing and issuing statements to the media, to review the information's possible positive or negative impact.

Following receipt of the manufacturer's final report, the Competent Authority may close the incident file and inform the manufacturer; however, these files are retained by the Competent Authority and the incident may be reopened as a result of changing circumstances.

Field Safety Corrective Actions and Field Safety Notices

The manufacturer must notify the Competent Authority of any technical or medical reasons for a device's systematic recall or FSCA. The term "withdrawal" used in the *AIMDD* is interpreted in the same way. Removals from the market for purely commercial reasons are not included and do not require any vigilance reporting.

When implementing an FSCA, the manufacturer must issue Field Safety Notices (FSN) and send copies of the FSN to the Competent Authorities of the countries in which the FSCA is performed. The Competent Authority responsible for the manufacturer or Authorised Representative (if the manufacturer is not established in the EU) should be notified. For devices with NB involvement in the conformity assessment, the Competent Authority in the state in which the NB is located should also be notified.

Relation to Medical Device Global Vigilance

GHTF is establishing a global vigilance system. This global vigilance approach has many similarities to the European Medical Devices Vigilance System, but it also differs in several ways. For instance, the global system terminology is somewhat different (e.g., it uses the term "adverse event" instead of "incident"). In addition, in contrast to the European manufacturer-oriented reporting system, the global system is wider in scope, encompassing user reports and user errors. To promote systematic notation in global vigilance reporting, a technical specification (ISO TS 19218) is being developed to establish a coding system for adverse event reporting. The new system will facilitate global data exchange among regulatory bodies, thereby providing more-accurate reporting and identification of the involved devices and event types.

Vigilance Versus Manufacturers' Postmarket Duties

Although the processes are interrelated, medical device vigilance must be distinguished from manufacturers' postmarket surveillance duties.

Postmarket surveillance may be understood as a "proactive and reactive" process that involves detecting quality problems through review and analysis of market feedback. The system implemented by the manufacturer to obtain feedback should fulfil the requirements of EN ISO 13485, clause 8.2.1. Reviewing experience gained with medical devices in the postmarket phase is an important element of risk management. Medical device risk management should be implemented in accordance with EN ISO 14971.

Vigilance is a "reactive" process because it involves responding appropriately to reports that a medical device has caused or may cause patient harm, or that the instructions for use are inaccurate or open to misinterpretation. Vigilance procedures are expected to follow MEDDEV 2.12/1 (Rev. 6) even though, as guidance, the provisions may not be enforced by law.

Vigilance is an element of postmarket surveillance. Postmarket surveillance is a process for understanding experience with the device through systematic feedback and review of information from many sources, among them vigilance information. Vigilance is a specific procedure for communicating with Competent Authorities and acting on reported incidents appropriately. Incidents are often detected, for example, through such postmarket surveillance procedures as complaint handling.

Other Provisions for Market Surveillance and Control

The medical devices vigilance system described in MEDDEV 2.12/1 (Rev. 6) is one mechanism Competent Authorities use to control the medical devices market. Various other mechanisms foreseen in the medical device directives are intended specifically to facilitate enforcement of those provisions. Competent Authorities may develop administrative procedures for further market control in their corresponding Member States on the basis of the following regulations:

- requirements that technical documentation be made available for inspection by the Competent Authorities
- ability to extend incident reporting obligations to

include users and persons responsible for medical device calibration and servicing
- requirements for a registry containing the names and addresses of all persons responsible for placing medical devices on the market

Therefore, depending upon the Member State in question, additional requirements may be in place to enhance market control:

- licence for manufacture, import, assembly and sterilisation activities
- notification of distribution activities, sales activities and sales with individual adaptation of medical devices (e.g., hearing aids)
- regulation of publicity

These methods improve Competent Authorities' awareness of both the products being placed on the market within their territory and the individuals responsible for placing them on the market. Anomalies detected by Competent Authorities through market surveillance include:

- products bearing the medical device CE mark that are not covered by the medical device directives (e.g., borderline products with cosmetics and personal protection equipment)
- devices for which the appropriate Conformity Assessment Procedure has not been followed (e.g., Class I sterile devices without intervention by an NB)
- devices including parts that do not bear CE marking or that have been given a different intended use by a supplier than that intended by the original manufacturer
- devices whose labelling is not in the required language

A special Market Surveillance Operations Group (MSOG) has been established to improve Member States' coordination on these and other issues relating to market control.

Safeguard Clause

Market control procedures may facilitate information transmittal to Competent Authorities; this information may be used to initiate special measures in accordance with the Safeguard Clause in the medical device directives (*AIMDD* Article 6, *MDD* Article 8 and *IVDD* Article 8). Under the Safeguard Clause, Member States are obliged to take all appropriate interim measures to withdraw a device from the market, or prohibit or restrict its placement on the market, if the device, when correctly installed, maintained and used for its intended purpose, may compromise health or safety. A Member State that takes such measures is obliged to notify the European Commission; it must indicate the reasons

Table 25-2. Comparison of Safeguard Clause and Health Monitoring Measures

Concern	Safeguard Clause Mechanism	Health Monitoring Measure
Initiation of the procedures	The Member State must establish (e.g., as a result of vigilance) that a device may compromise health or safety when used as intended.	The Member State must provide sufficient evidence to support reasonable doubt that the medical device offers an adequate level of protection of health and safety.
Parties involved	The European Commission consults with the Member State that invoked the Safeguard Clause and other interested parties.	The European Commission must consult with interested parties and all Member States.
Outcome	If the European Commission confirms that the national measure is justified, Member States are informed and may adopt appropriate national measures.	If the European Commission confirms that the national measure is justified, it develops a measure that must be adopted (uniformly) throughout the Community after Regulatory Committee consultation.

for taking the actions and, if the measures are justified, the Commission informs all other Member States. This process, however, does not mean that all other Member States are obliged to adopt similar measures, even though they may be expected to do so.

Health Monitoring Measures

The *IVDD* introduced a new mechanism for Competent Authorities to use in the postmarket phase. Through health monitoring, a Member State may take any necessary and justified transitional measures relative to a given product or group of products if, to protect consumer health and safety or the public health, product availability should be prohibited, restricted or subjected to particular requirements. The Member State then must inform the European Commission and all other Member States. These health monitoring measures are intended to apply a precautionary principle. The Safeguard Clause and health monitoring measures have fundamental differences, summarised in **Table 25-2**.

An example of a measure taken in accordance with the Safeguard Clause is Germany's banning of catgut. In general, it is considered that further guidance is necessary to clarify the conditions under which Member States can use health monitoring measures.

Role of Eudamed in Market Surveillance and Vigilance

IVDD Article 12 required the European Commission and Member States to establish Eudamed—a European database to centralise the following data:
- manufacturers and their Authorised Representatives
- devices placed on the Community market
- certificates issued, suspended or withdrawn
- the vigilance procedure

Such issues as nomenclature, custom-made device inclusion or exclusion, and minor differences between the European Medical Devices Vigilance System and that proposed by GHTF have led to delays in putting Eudamed into operation. Some of the issues have been covered by ISO/TS 20225—Global Medical Device Nomenclature (GMDN) and by excluding custom-made devices from the database.

The European Commission published a decision that makes Eudamed mandatory among Member States in May 2011. It is expected that Eudamed will significantly enhance coordination between Competent Authorities regarding enforcement of the medical device directives and will be particularly relevant in facilitating communications within the European Medical Devices Vigilance System. For this reason, the vigilance module is one of the first features of Eudamed put into operation.

Summary

- Medical device manufacturers are obliged to implement postmarket surveillance procedures to understand the experience with medical devices in the postproduction phase and provide input to corrective and preventive processes.
- Information feedback and risk management are important postmarket surveillance aspects; they may be implemented in accordance with EN ISO 13485 and EN ISO 14971, respectively.
- Manufacturers are obliged to report incidents and near incidents to the relevant Competent Authorities. In some EU Member States, this reporting obligation is extended to medical device users.
- MEDDEV 2.12/1 (Rev. 6) establishes detailed

guidance and criteria for reportable incidents as well as procedures manufacturers and Competent Authorities should follow when such incidents occur.

- Vigilance reporting is obligatory when manufacturers implement medical device recalls for technical or medical reasons.
- Postmarket surveillance and vigilance are interrelated processes; each uses information from the other as input.
- Member State Competent Authorities exercise market surveillance using mechanisms to enforce implementation of medical device directives' provisions.
- Member State Competent Authorities may implement special controls and restrictions under the Safeguard Clause or as health monitoring measures.
- The Eudamed database will play an important part in facilitating regulatory data exchange among Competent Authorities, particularly concerning vigilance.

EU Medical Device National Particularities

By Caroline Freeman

OBJECTIVES

Understand the importance of national transpositions, in particular the following aspects:

❏ Languages for instructions for use and labels

❏ Notification to the Competent Authority

❏ National Provisions for Marketing, Sales and Distribution Organisations and Personnel

(Note this chapter relates primarily to "general" medical devices).

DIRECTIVES, REGULATIONS AND GUIDELINES COVERED IN THIS CHAPTER

❏ Council Directive 93/42/EEC of 14 June 1993 concerning medical devices (*Medical Devices Directive (MDD)*)

❏ Directive 2007/47/EC of the European Parliament and of the Council of 5 September 2007 amending Council Directive 90/385/EEC on the approximation of the laws of the Member States regarding active implantable medical devices, Council Directive 93/42/EEC concerning medical devices and Directive 98/8/EC concerning the placing of biocidal products on the market

Introduction

After many years of living with a variety of national requirements for the regulation of medical devices—with some countries focusing on the sterility of medical devices and others on electromedical equipment—industry welcomed the CE marking for medical devices as "the passport" to Europe. CE marking would cut across all national requirements and provide manufacturers with a single key to unlock the regulatory systems and markets of all EU Member States.

Council Directive 93/42/EEC of June 1993 concerning medical devices (*Medical Devices Directive (MDD)*) provides a definition of "medical device," a standard classification system and a clear set of conformity assessment procedures for each device class and procedures to follow to establish clinical investigations. However, scope remains for national particularities in interpreting these areas, as well as the opportunity for Member States to establish requirements in other important areas for doing business with medical devices.

A directive, while a European legal instrument, does not in itself constitute European law. The provisions of a directive come into effect only when they are transposed into the national law of each Member State. While, in principle, the model of the regulatory system, as represented by the *MDD*, should be transposed identically in each Member State, this is not always the case. The European Commission has the right and duty to review national transposition texts and, if necessary, to take action to eliminate inconsistencies. However, the practicalities are such that administrative features of the national legislation that do not constitute technical barriers to trade are allowed to remain.

This chapter deals with the following aspects of national transpositions, with the aim of clarifying some of the existing national particularities:

- use of languages for labelling and instructions for use
- notification to the Competent Authority before placing devices on the market and putting them into service

- activities and qualifications of marketing, sales and distribution organisations and personnel

Other aspects of national transpositions where variations exist, such as vigilance and procedures for initiating clinical investigations, are dealt with elsewhere in relevant chapters of this publication.

In summary, it is crucial when doing business in Europe to consider the national laws. Although the text of the directive is often used by manufacturers as the source text when working to achieve CE marking, it is essential to remember that each country is still independent and has its own national laws with which devices are required to comply.

Use of Languages for Labelling and Instructions for Use

EU Member States have the right to require the use of their national language(s) for device labels and instructions for use (IFU) when a device reaches the final user. This is stated in *MDD* Article 4.4:

"4. Member States may require the information, which must be made available to the user and the patient in accordance with Annex I, point 13, to be in their national language(s) or in another Community language, when a device reaches the final user, regardless of whether it is for professional or other use."

This clause should be examined more closely. Although it is written as a permissive statement (Member States "may", rather than "must" or "should"), almost all Member States and signatory States to the European Economic Area (EEA) do require their national language—see below for details.

The clause covers information made available to the user and the patient. It does not, therefore, specifically cover, for example, information provided in service manuals that are not intended for the patient or user.

The scope of the clause is found in *MDD* Annex I, point 13, covering information supplied by the manufacturer that is needed to use the device safely and properly, taking account of the training and knowledge of potential users, and to identify the manufacturer. Information concerning patents or country of origin would, therefore, not be covered.

While Member States would be expected to require information in their national language(s), there are one or two interesting exceptions to this for both information on labels and IFU.

The national language requirements are designed to be triggered when the device reaches the final user. This potentially allows IFU to be added at a later stage in the distribution process. It also suggests that Notified Bodies (NBs) should not concern themselves with whether products have labels and IFU in accordance with the requirements of the countries in which they are intended to be made available. However, NBs should ensure that a process and procedure are in place to ensure that translations, where required, are sufficient to ensure that the device can be used safely and properly, as per *MDD* Annex I Essential Requirement 13.1.

Member States are allowed to impose national language requirements, regardless of whether the device is for professional or other use. In some cases, guidance from Competent Authorities suggests that there is some flexibility for professional use devices.

As stated above, it is imperative to consider the relevant country's national transposition of the *MDD* when placing a product on the market. Some examples of national language requirements follow. These countries were chosen to illustrate the range of different approaches to national language requirements, and are examples only. Note also that requirements can change.

Belgium

The *MDD* is transposed in Belgium by the Royal Decree of 17 March 2009, modifying the Royal Decree of 18 March 1999 relating to medical devices. This decree was published in the *Moniteur Belge* on 27 March 2009. The national language requirement is stated as follows (this is an unofficial English translation from the French language text):

"Art. 18

§ 1. The information provided to the patient in accordance with Annex I, point 13, must at least be drawn up in the national languages.

§ 2 The information provided to professional users in accordance with Annex I, point 13, must at least be drawn up in the national language of the users, unless on a case-by-case basis, and conditional upon due justification, the users make another arrangement with the manufacturer, his authorised representative or the approved distributor of the devices. This agreement is signed by the parties concerned and held available to the Competent Authorities. It must satisfy the requirements of the General Regulation for worker protection, approved by the decrees of the Regent of 11 February 1946 and 27 September 1947."

The requirement for patient information is clear—information must be provided in the three national languages of Belgium: French, Flemish/Dutch and German.

In the case of information for professional users, it is possible in specific cases for users and manufacturers (or the Authorised Representative or distributor) to agree to supply information in either just one of these three languages or in a different language, such as English. Caution must be used, however, to ensure that an agreement made, for example, with an individual user is valid and representative for that user's healthcare establishment.

Bulgaria

A law amending the law on medical devices, published on 30 December 2008, is the national transposition of *MDD* as amended. While the *Medical Devices Law* requires that instructions for use and labels of medical devices placed on the market in Bulgaria have to be translated into the Bulgarian language, we understand from the Competent Authority that labels in English are acceptable for devices intended for professional use only.

Denmark

The *MDD* is transposed in Denmark by The Ministry of Health and Prevention's Executive Order No. 1263 of 15 December 2008 concerning medical devices. This order states that the Danish language is required for labelling and the IFU for all medical devices, regardless of the intended user's skills or profession.

According to the website of the Danish Medicines Agency's Medical Devices Department, www.medicaldevices.dk, the order "does not require that software and service manuals must be provided in Danish. However, it is the manufacturer's responsibility to define which information is necessary for the correct and safe use of the device." The guidance goes on to clarify this statement, as follows:

> **"Display, buttons and keys**
> Single words or phrases such as "Load," "Enter," "Page Down" or the like, are considered to be symbols. Symbols are not required to be translated, but must be explained in the instructions for use. If the information involves more than two words, and provides information/instruction to the user, this must be in Danish."

Finland

Article 12 of the *Law on Healthcare Products and Equipment* states, "the information accompanying the device must be in Finnish, Swedish or English, unless the information takes the form of generally known direction or warning symbols. Information intended for users or patients to ensure the safe use of the device must be in Finnish and Swedish. The instructions for use and labelling of medical devices intended for self-care must be in Finnish and Swedish."

Thus, in the case of professional use devices, there may be some latitude for providing information in English only. However, the worst-case interpretation of the text is that Finnish and Swedish are required for all information supplied with the device (even for professional use devices), if one assumes that all information provided is for the purposes of ensuring safe use. A manufacturer could make such

a decision on the basis of a risk assessment. It is clear that for self-care devices (i.e., patient use devices) both Finnish and Swedish are required.

Norway

Norway is worth a mention here since it made a significant change to its national language requirement in 2006 that caused some manufacturers to rapidly source Norwegian translations. The current national language requirement, as per Regulation 2005-12-15 no. 1690, amended and applicable from December 2010, is as follows:

> "§2-6: The information as provided for in AIMDD I no. 13, 14 and 15, IVDMDD I part B no. 8, or MDD I no. 13 shall be in Norwegian.
>
> The information can be provided with harmonised symbols, recognised codes or other similar solutions, provided that safe and correct use is ensured.
>
> For medical devices for clinical investigation, languages other than Norwegian can be used as long as this is accepted by the user, but the information which is intended for the patient must nevertheless be in Norwegian.
>
> As long as safe and correct use is ensured, the competent authority can make exceptions from the requirement for Norwegian language."

Prior to a regulation amendment made in September 2006, Norwegian was not required for IFU for professional use medical devices. However pressure from professional users, who noted that Norway was almost unique in offering this flexibility, resulted in the regulation amendment which required that all devices for professional use be supplied with IFU in Norwegian from October 2007.

Switzerland

The multilingual country of Switzerland offers some flexibility for professional use devices with some conditions.

The *Regulation on Medical Devices* was amended on 24 March 2010 to be effective from 1 April 2010. It contains very detailed information on the national language requirements:

> **"Article 7** Product information
> 1 Product information shall be in accordance with:
>   a. Classical medical devices: Annex I, Section 13 of the Directive 93/42/EEC43;
>   b. Active implantable medical devices: Annex 1, Sections 14 and 15 of the Directive 90/385/EEC;
>   c. Medical devices for in vitro diagnosis: Annex I, Section 8 of

the Directive 98/79/EC;

2 The product information must be written in all three official languages. Symbols which are contained in harmonized standards can replace wording.

3 Product information can be restricted to less than the three official languages, or be in English, provided:

   a. the medical device is supplied exclusively to professionals or where the medical device is a custom-made device or a medical device manufactured in-house;

   b. there is assurance that the user has the necessary professional and linguistic qualifications, and agrees with the language restriction;

   c. the protection of patients, users and third parties is nevertheless ensured; and

   d. effective and intended use is not jeopardized.

4 If requested, additional information shall be given to users in one of the official languages."

The conditional restriction to fewer than the three official languages of Switzerland gives some scope to manufacturers who may wish to make a limited initial introduction of a product to the Swiss market and have not yet prepared instructions for use in French, German or Italian. However, it is unlikely that the restriction will be used widely since French, German and Italian are required respectively for France, Germany/Austria and Italy.

UK

Readers may be surprised to know that the UK does not require its national language for IFU. According to the national transposition text (Statutory Instrument 2008 No. 2936, *The Medical Devices (Amendment) Regulations 2008, Consumer Protection*), information on the packaging and on any label must be in English, regardless of whether the device is for professional or other use. However, IFU can be in English or another Community language, on condition that if the instructions are not in English, any packaging, label or promotional literature carry a clear statement in English stating the language in which the instructions are given. For both patient and professional use devices, labels must be in English, but IFU can be in another EU language. The regulation thus leaves the market to decide whether or not to purchase products where the IFU is not in English, and ensures that purchasers are aware of this.

Notification to the Competent Authority Before Placing on the Market or Putting Into Service

Article 14 of the *MDD* established the principle that for certain devices (Class I devices, custom-made devices and systems and procedure packs) the person involved in placing such products on the market should provide a description of the devices to the Competent Authority of the state in which he is established. The purpose of Article 14 is to ensure that national Competent Authorities have a contact for the manufacturer and the means to know what Class I and custom-made devices are being put on the market by entities based in that country. Note that the emphasis of Article 14 is actually the registration of the person concerned. It is that person who makes his existence known to the Competent Authority and, in addition, informs the authority about the products for which he is responsible.

Article 14 was amended in 1998 and currently reads as follows:

"14 Registration of persons responsible for placing devices on the market

1. Any manufacturer who, under his own name, places devices on the market in accordance with the procedures referred to in Article 11 (5) and (6) and any other natural or legal person engaged in the activities referred to in Article 12 shall inform the competent authorities of the Member State in which he has his registered place of business of the address of the registered place of business and the description of the devices concerned.

    For all medical devices of classes IIa, IIb and III, Member States may request to be informed of all data allowing for identification of such devices together with the label and the instructions for use when such devices are put into service within their territory.

2. Where a manufacturer who places a device on the market under his own name does not have a registered place of business in a Member State, he shall designate a single authorised representative in the European Union. For devices referred to in the first subparagraph of paragraph 1, the authorised representative shall inform the competent authority of the Member State in which he has his registered place of business of the details referred to in paragraph 1.

3. The Member States shall on request inform the other Member States and the Commission of the details referred to

in the first subparagraph of paragraph 1 given by the manufacturer or authorised representative."

When added in 1998, the second paragraph of 14.2 referred only to Class IIb and III devices. It was expanded to include Class IIa devices by means of Directive 2007/47/EC. Importantly, this is a permissive clause, in that "Member States may request to be informed …" Also, the requirement refers to putting into service (rather than placing on the market), and can therefore be fulfilled by any entity, regardless of location, and is not restricted to companies having a registered place of business in a particular country.

Most countries have taken the opportunity to be notified of putting into service. Some examples of national requirements follow.

France

Article R.5211-66 pursuant to article L.5211-4 of the *Code of Public Health* provides that all data allowing identification of Class IIa, IIb and III devices must be communicated to *Agence française de sécurité sanitaire des produits de santé* (Afssaps) when they are put into service within French territory. The data to be communicated to Afssaps are: the trade description of the medical device; the name and address of the person submitting the communication; and a specimen of the medical device's labelling and IFU.

The communication must be made at the time of putting the device into service on national territory. The requirement applies to the manufacturer, the Authorised Representative or the distributor. Only one communication per device is needed.

Afssaps provides a form in both French and English that can be used for the communication. This is available at www.afssaps.fr.

Italy

The Italian Decree of 20 February 2007, updated 21 December 2009, established a new registration system for medical devices that, by allocating a registration number to each device, was intended to improve device traceability. The registration consists of two levels. The notification of medical devices to a database is mandatory for the manufacturer or the Authorised Representative situated in Italy. Entities situated outside Italy must notify Class IIa, IIb and III devices and active implantable medical devices. The next level of notification is to have the devices listed in the *Repertorio*, costing €100 per device listing (note: this fee may yet be repealed). The *Repertorio* is the list of devices available to be sold to the Italian National Health Service.

Although the *Repertorio* was introduced in phases, it has been compulsory for all devices within its scope since 5 May 2010.

The information initially required for registration was comprehensive. This requirement has since been simplified, following a challenge by the European Commission on the basis that the requirement to register Class I devices and systems/procedure kits in Italy was excessive if such devices had already been notified in the country in which the manufacturer or its Authorised Representative was based. However, the modalities for registration are burdensome, as the entity registering must gain access to the database using the online portal and a smart card. Information on the registration process is available at www.salute.gov.it/dispositivi/ and there is also a user manual.

Netherlands

The *Regulation on Medical Devices*, as amended, does not include a Competent Authority request for information on Class IIa, IIb and III devices when they are put into service in the Netherlands.

Portugal

In accordance with Article 11.1 of Decree Law no. 145/2009, manufacturers or Authorised Representatives based in Portugal that place Class I and custom-made devices on the market must notify the Competent Authority (Infarmed) of their name and address and all information necessary to identify the devices in question.

When Class IIa, IIb and III devices are put into service in Portugal, Infarmed requests extensive information including:

- name of manufacturer/Authorised Representative/distributor
- device name and type
- description and intended purpose
- Notified Body ID number
- copies of labels and IFU
- date of placing on the market or putting into service in Portugal
- certificates

Note that Class IIa devices were added to this group as a result of the transposition of Directive 2007/47/EC via Article 11.3 of Decree Law no. 145/2009. Notification must be done online and can be done in English. English language guidance is also provided at www.infarmed.pt

Spain

Article 24 of Royal Decree 1591/2009 of 16 October 2009 establishes that a manufacturer based in Spain, or the Spain-based Authorised Representative of a non-EU manufacturer, must notify the placing on the market of Class I and custom-made devices to the Competent Authority and the Agencia española de medicamentos y productos sanitarios (AEMPS). Note that prior to 21 March 2010, this notification was made to the Competent Authority in the autonomous community where the manufacturer or Authorised Representative was based.

Article 22 of the Royal Decree establishes that any person who makes a Class IIa, IIb or III device available for the first time for distribution and/or use on Spanish territory must communicate this to AEMPS at the time of making the device available.

This requirement applies to any entity, in Spain or elsewhere, putting devices on the Spanish market. The details of the communication to AEMPS are provided in Article 23.1. The communication is to be made electronically via a portal specifically established for the purpose, at www.aemps.es. Prior to making this communication, manufacturers should obtain a password from AEMPS. A fee is required for each product notification.

Activities and Qualifications of Marketing, Sales and Distribution Organisations and Personnel

Distribution is not covered by the *MDD*, with the result that national regulatory systems can include requirements relating to distribution of medical devices. This omission is likely to change in the recast of the *MDD* currently under consideration, since distributors play a key role in moving the product from the manufacturer to the final user. Currently, only a few countries specifically regulate the activities of distributors, some by means of provisions in their national *MDD* transposition text, others by means of other regulatory texts. The following are examples only.

Germany
Inspection

According to §26 of the *Medical Devices Law* (*Medizinproduktegesetz* (*MPG*)), entities in Germany that carry out activities regarding medical devices, generally including handling and/or distribution of medical devices, are subject to inspection by the authorities.

Medical Devices Advisor

The *MPG* sets out special education and training requirements for persons who advise medical circles about medical devices in a professional capacity. This is described in the *MPG* as follows:

"§31 Medical Devices Adviser

(1) Whoever informs professional circles professionally about medical devices and instructs them in the proper handling of medical devices (Medical Devices Adviser), may only practise this activity, if he has the necessary professional knowledge and experience for informing and where necessary, for the instruction in handling and use of the respective medical devices. Sentence 1 applies also to information provided over the telephone.

(2) Professional knowledge is possessed by,

1. Anyone who has successfully completed an education in a natural science, medical or technical profession, and who been trained in the respective medical devices, or

2. Anyone who has gained by means of an activity of at least one year, which in justified cases can be shorter, experience in information and where necessary in the instruction in handling of the respective medical devices.

(3) The medical device adviser is required to provide documentary evidence of the specialist knowledge to the Competent Authorities on demand. He must keep himself up to date on the respective medical devices, in order to be able to advise expertly. The employer must ensure regular training for the medical device adviser.

(4) The medical devices adviser is required to maintain written records of communications from persons belonging to professional circles regarding side effects, mutual influences, malfunctioning, technical defects, contra-indications, counterfeits or any other risks associated with medical devices and to communicate these in writing to the responsible person in accordance with [MPG] § 5 sentences 1 and 2 or their designated persons responsible for safety in writing."

Ireland

In early 2010, the Minister for Health and Children in Ireland announced a proposal to introduce legislation to regulate distributors of medical devices. Such regulation might include:

- registration of distributors with the Competent Authority
- requirements for record keeping by distributors and retailers
- requirements to ensure distributors have suitable facilities, personnel and equipment to maintain medical device quality during storage, transport and distribution
- requirements to ensure medical devices are CE marked and meet the mandatory labelling requirements when supplied
- requirements for maintaining a quality system in medical device distribution operations

Spain

Royal Decree 1591/2009 of 16 October 2009, regulating medical devices, contains the following provisions relating to distributors.

Article 26 enables the authorities to ask a manufacturer, Authorised Representative, importer or distributor to supply information about a product if there are concerns about it.

Article 26.5 places responsibility on the Spanish distributor to ensure that the product meets the decree's requirements and that the necessary information has been provided to the authorities prior to distributing the product.

Article 27 states that devices can only be stored in appropriate premises. Distribution and sales entities are subject to vigilance and inspection by the local authorities. Distributors must make a prior notification of their activity. Distribution entities must hold a documented register of all devices distributed. They must also have the services of a "*tecnico responsible*" (responsible technician), who is responsible for maintaining technical health information on the products distributed or put into service.

Other National Particularities

In addition to the above, there is much latitude in the different stages of the medical device lifecycle, from development to use, that can be regulated by national legislation. Reimbursement and purchasing schemes are specifically excluded from the scope of the *MDD*, by virtue of the directive's fourth recital, which states:

> "Whereas the harmonised provisions must be distinguished from the measures adopted by the Member States to manage the funding of public health and sickness insurance schemes relating directly or indirectly to such devices; whereas, therefore, the provisions do not affect the ability of the Member States to implement the abovementioned measures provided Community law is complied with;"

No mention is made in the directive of specific sales outlets; hence, the *MDD* does not establish any restrictions on who may dispense medical devices, although restrictions are applied to certain devices in some countries.

Postmarket servicing, credentials of service organizations and availability of spare parts are outside the scope of the *MDD*, while national requirements may exist in some jurisdictions.

Administration, enforcement and penalties are left to the discretion of the individual Member States. Knowledge and understanding of these areas are essential for doing business.

Summary

The *Medical Devices Directive* has harmonised the requirements for safety and performance of medical devices, to create a level playing field across the EU, EEA and beyond, with CE marking recognised as a sign of a safe medical device. However, manufacturers must look beyond CE marking to the national laws and regulations of the countries in which they wish to do business to ensure that they are in compliance. Successful manufacturers will familiarise themselves not only with the *MDD* and its national transpositions but also with other regulatory texts dealing with medical devices at national level. Alternatively, they can entrust themselves to the services of local experts.

EU Glossary of Terms

A

Abridged Application

An application for marketing authorisation that, based upon demonstrating essential similarity or by detailed references to published scientific literature, does not contain the results of pharmacological and toxicological tests or the results of clinical trials.

Acquis Communautaire

Usually just referred to as the *Acquis*, it is the collection of European laws to which all EU Member States must adhere.

Active Implantable Medical Devices Directive

(*AIMDD*) First EU medical device legislation; sets general requirements relating to the design, construction and CE-Marking of these devices and their accessories.

ADR

Adverse Drug Reaction

Advanced Therapy Medicinal Product

(ATMP) A medicinal product that is either a gene therapy medicinal product as defined in Part IV of Annex 1 to Directive 2001/83/EC, a somatic cell therapy medicinal product as defined in Part IV of Annex 1 to Directive 2001/83/EC or a tissue engineered product as defined in Article 2 1 (b) of the *ATMP Regulation.*

AESGP

Association Européenne des Spécialités Pharmaceutiques Grand Public, Association of the European Self-medication Industry

AIMDD

See *Active Implantable Medical Devices Directive*

Applicant

See Marketing authorisation applicant

Arbitration Rapporteur

Under the Mutual Recognition Procedure, the CHMP member appointed to prepare a report after notification by the Reference and Concerned Member States that there are serious public health issues remaining related to the product at the end of the Mutual Recognition Procedure's 90 day clarification and dialogue phase.

Assessment Report

The assessment of the medicinal product by the Reference Member State, including the reasons for its conclusions during the Mutual Recognition Procedure. During the Centralised Procedure, the CHMP prepares an assessment report released as the EPAR.

ATC

Anatomical Therapeutic Chemical Classification System (classification of drugs)

ATMP

See Advanced Therapy Medicinal Product.

B

Bibliographic Application

Also known as "well established use applications." The applicant prepares a product dossier based upon literature available in the public domain. The drug product concerned needs to have been on the market for at least 10 years. This type of application is especially important to the newer Member States as it allows them to keep their current generic products on the market where no reference product exists.

Blue Box

The area into which country-specific text is usually placed on packaging materials and leaflets for medicinal products approved via the Centralised Procedure.

C

CADREAC

See Collaboration Agreement of Drug Regulatory Authorities in European Union Associated Countries

CAPs

Conformity Assessment Procedures; see Conformity assessment

CAT

See Committee for Advanced Therapies

CE Marking

European conformity (Conformité Européenne) marking. Mandatory European marking for products falling under one of the New Approach directives (including medical devices) to indicate conformity with the essential health and safety requirements.

CEN

See European Committee for Standardization.

CENELEC

See European Committee for Electrotechnical Standardization

Centralised Procedure

Submission of a dossier to EMA to obtain marketing authorisation from the European Commission that is valid in all EU Member States. The Centralised Procedure is compulsory for orphan medicinal products; any medicinal product for human use containing an entirely new active substance; those manufactured using biotechnological processes; and medicinal products for the treatment of AIDS, cancer, neurodegenerative disorders, auto-immune diseases and other immune dysfunctions and viral diseases or diabetes. It also may be used on a voluntary basis for other innovative products. Products are assessed by the CHMP (human) and CVMP (veterinary). Individual Member States may prohibit the marketing of an approved veterinary product based upon epidemiological considerations.

CEP

Certificate of European Pharmacoepeia. See Certificate of Suitability.

Certificate of Suitability

(CEP) Certificate granted by the Certification Secretariat of the EDQM certifying that a substance's quality is suitably controlled by the relevant monographs of the European Pharmacopoeia with, if necessary, an annex appended. A CEP can be granted for active substances or excipients and for substances or preparations with risk of transmitting agents of animal spongiform encephalopathies.

CHMP

See Committee for Medicinal Products for Human Use

CIOMS

Council for International Organisations of Medical Sciences

Clinical Trials Directive

Directive setting analytical, pharmatoxicological and clinical standards and protocol requirements for clinical trials.

CMD(h)

See Coordination Group for Mutual Recognition and Decentralised Procedures (human).

CMD(v)

See Coordination Group for Mutual Recognition and Decentralised Procedures (veterinary).

CMS

See Concerned Member State

Co-decision Procedure

Procedure by which the Council of the European Union and the European Parliament—the two institutions responsible for EU legislation—adopt legislative acts. It applies to virtually all legislation regarding pharmaceutical law.

COE

See Council of the European Union

Collaboration Agreement of Drug Regulatory Authorities in European Union Associated Countries

(CADREAC) CADREAC's mission was to facilitate smooth transition of regulatory conditions in EU-associated countries to achieve regulatory standards required by *Acquis Communautaire*. Signatories of CADREAC (first phase) were state regulatory authorities for human medicinal products of countries in Central, Eastern and Southern Europe, i.e., Cyprus, Czech Republic, Estonia, Hungary, Latvia, Lithuania, Poland, Slovak Republic, Slovenia and Turkey. (See also new CADREAC)

Committeee for Advanced Therapies
(CAT) A multidisciplinary committee advising EMA, comprising the best available experts in Europe to assess the quality, safety and efficacy of ATMPs, and to follow scientific developments in the field.

Committee for Medicinal Products for Human Use
(CHMP) A committee that provides scientific advice to EMA on questions relating to the evaluation of medicinal products for Human Use. Formerly, the CPMP—Committee for Proprietary Medicinal Products.

Committee for Orphan Medicinal Products
(COMP) A committee that provides scientific advice to EMA on questions relating to the designation of "orphan drugs" for rare diseases.

Committee for Veterinary Medicinal Products
(CVMP) A committee that provides scientific advice to EMA on questions relating to the evaluation of veterinary medicinal products.

Committee on Herbal Medicinal Products
(HMPC) A committee that provides scientific advice to EMA on questions relating to herbal medicinal products.

COMP
See Committee for Orphan Medicinal Products

Competent Authority
For medicinal products, a Member State's governmental body responsible for authorising and supervising such products. For medical devices, the organisation authorised by a Member State's government to act on its behalf to ensure that all medical devices meet the essential requirements laid down in the medical device directives.

Concerned Member State
(CMS) A Member State included in a Mutual Recognition Procedure application.

Conformity Assessment
The systematic examination of evidence generated and procedures undertaken by the manufacturer, under requirements established by the regulatory authority, to determine that a medical device is safe and performs as intended by the manufacturer and, therefore, conforms to the Essential Principles of Safety and Performance for Medical Devices.

Coordination Group for Mutual Recognition and Decentralised Procedures (human)
(CMD(h)) Coordinates and facilitates the operation of the Decentralised and Mutual Recognition Procedures for medicinal products for human use.

Coordination Group for Mutual Recognition and Decentralised Procedures (veterinary)
(CMD(v)) Coordinates and facilitates the operation of the Decentralised and Mutual Recognition Procedures for medicinal products for veterinary use.

COREPER
Comité des Représentants Permanents, Committee of Permanent Representatives from Member States that advises the Council of the European Union.

Council of the European Union
Sometimes referred to as the Council of Ministers, it is the EU's main decision-making institution and final legislative authority. It comprises one representative per Member State. The representative is usually a government minister and varies depending upon the matters being discussed, e.g., the Minister for Health for pharmaceutical issues.

CTD
Common Technical Document

CVMP
See Committee for Veterinary Medicinal Products

D
Decentralised Procedure
Procedure that may be used for medicinal products for which there is no existing Marketing Authorisation in any EU Member State. The applicant can select the Reference Member State and list the Concerned Member States.

Directive
An EC decision that is binding upon EC institutions and Member States, and must be transposed into national legislation. However, the way in which it is implemented is left to the discretion of individual Member States.

DMF
Drug Master File

E
ECJ
European Court of Justice

eCTD
Electronic Common Technical Document

EDQM
See European Directorate of Quality of Medicines and Healthcare

EEA
See European Economic Area

EEC
See European Economic Community

EFPIA
European Federation of Pharmaceutical Industries and Associations

EFTA
European Free Trade Association, composed of Iceland, Liechtenstein, Norway and Switzerland.

EGA
European Generic Medicines Association

EMA
See European Medicines Agency

EN
See European Standard

Enterprise Directorate-General
Enterprise DGs are the principal administrative agencies of the European Commission. Their objective is to supply policy ideas that promote a supportive business environment for all European enterprises—including pharmaceutical companies.

EPAR
See European Public Assessment Report

Essential Requirements
Technical requirements defined in each New Approach directive (usually Annex 1) with which a product must comply to qualify for CE marking.

Essential Similarity
According to the European Court of Justice, a medicinal product is essentially similar to another product if it has: the same quantitative and qualitative composition of active substance(s); the same dosage form; and the same bioequivalence, documented by a corresponding bioavailability.

EU
See European Union

Eudralex
Compilation of EU pharmaceutical legislation and guidelines accessible from the European Commission Pharmaceuticals Unit website.

Eudravigilance
A data processing network and management system for reporting and evaluating suspected adverse reactions during the development and following the marketing authorisation of medicinal products in the European Economic Area (EEA).

European Medicines Agency
(EMA) The agency responsible for coordinating the scientific evaluation of the safety, efficacy and quality of human and veterinary medicinal products that undergo the Centralised Procedure as well as for arbitration during the Mutual Recognition Procedure. It comprises the CHMP, CVMP, COMP, CAT, HMPC, PDCO, a Secretariat, the Executive Director and a Management Board.

European Commission
The executive branch of the European Union, composed of 27 commissioners led by a Commission President. The body is responsible for proposing legislation, implementing decisions, upholding the Union's treaties and the general day-to-day operation of the EU.

European Committee for Electrotechnical Standardization
(CENELEC) EU standards body that establishes voluntary electrotechnical standards.

European Committee for Standardization
(CEN) Comité Européen de Normalisation promotes voluntary harmonisation of European technical standards across a wide range of products, processes and appliances.

European Community
The collective body formerly designated as the European Economic Community (EEC). The plural term European Communities is also widely used.

European Council
The heads of state of governments of the EU Member States, who meet regularly. It is the most senior manifestation of the Council of the European Union.

European Directorate of Quality of Medicines and Healthcare
(EDQM) Part of the administrative structure of the Council of Europe, its responsibilities include the Technical Secretariat of the European Pharmacopoeia Commission, the unit for certifying the suitability of PhEur monographs, developing the European network of the Official Medicines Control Laboratories (OMCL) and providing the secretariat for this network.

European Economic Area
(EEA) A free-trade area, in all but agriculture, comprising the Member States of the EU plus Iceland, Liechtenstein and Norway. Previously called the European Economic Space.

European Economic Community
(EEC) One of three communities created by the Treaties of Rome in 1957 to establish a common market. The 1967 merger of the EEC, Customs Union and European Atomic Energy Community created the European Communities. Precursor to the European Union.

European Federation of Pharmaceutical Industries and Associations
(EFPIA) Represents more than 2,000 pharmaceutical companies involved in research, development and manufacturing medicinal products for human use in Europe.

European Parliament
The directly elected parliamentary body of the European Union. Together with the Council of the European Union (the Council), it forms the bicameral legislative branch of the Union's institutions. The highest EU legislative body.

European Pharmacopoeia
(PhEur) Pharmacopée Européenne is a pharmacopoeia whose monographs are common to all concerned European nations.

European Police Office
(Europol) European Union law enforcement organisation that handles criminal intelligence. It assists Member States' law enforcement authorities in fighting organised crime. Established in 1992 as the European Drugs Unit to aid in controlling illegal drug-related activities.

European Public Assessment Report
(EPAR) Report on CHMP's scientific conclusion at the end of the centralised evaluation process, summarising the grounds for the CHMP Opinion on granting a marketing authorisation for a specific medicinal product. EMA makes this information available to the public after deleting commercially confidential information.

European Standard
(EN) Standards that are harmonised across the EU whose use, in theory, is voluntary. They address product health or safety aspects, as well as such other characteristics as durability, appearance, quality levels or even cultural preferences. These standards may be test methods or measurement guides.

European Union
(EU) Political body comprising 27 Members States established by the 1993 Treaty of Maastricht. It is the de facto successor to the European Economic Community founded in 1957 by the Treaty of Rome.

Expert Report
Report drawn up for a Marketing Authorisation Applicant by an expert, on the applicant's behalf, on the quality (chemical, pharmaceutical and biological documentation), safety (pharmacotoxicological) or efficacy (clinical) of a medicinal product, including a tabulation, written summary (optional) and critical discussion of the product's properties. The clinical and nonclinical Expert Report has been replaced in the Common Technical Document by the respective overviews (modules 2.4 and 2.5).

G
GCP
Good Clinical Practice

Genetically Modified Organism
(GMO) An organism in which the genetic material has been altered in a way that does not occur naturally by mating and/or natural recombination.

GLP
Good Laboratory Practice

GMO
See Genetically Modified Organism

GMP
Good Manufacturing Practice

H
HMPC
See Committee on Herbal Medicinal Products

I
ICH
International Conference on Harmonisation of Technical Requirements for Registration of Pharmaceuticals for Human Use

IFPMA
International Federation of Pharmaceutical Manufacturers' Associations

IFU
Instructions for use—applies to medical devices

In Vitro Diagnostic Devices Directive (*IVDD*)
Covers devices used in vitro to examine specimens

derived from the human body, including reagents, instruments and specimen receptacles.

INN
International Nonproprietary Name

ISO
International Organization for Standardization

IVDD
In Vitro Diagnostic Devices Directive

L
LOA
Letter of Access

M
MAA
See Marketing Authorisation Application

MAH
See Marketing Authorisation Holder

Marketing Authorisation
Authorisation to place a medicinal product on the market in a Member State issued by its Competent Authority or by EMA for the EU market.

Marketing Authorisation Application
(MAA) The application submitted to a Member State(s) for a Decentralised or Mutual Recognition Procedure or to EMA for the Centralised Procedure seeking permission to place a new product on the market.

Marketing Authorisation Holder
(MAH) The person who holds the marketing authorisation for placing a medicinal product on the market and is responsible for marketing the product. The MAH must be established in the EEA.

MDD
See *Medical Devices Directive*

MedDRA
Medical Dictionary for Regulatory Activities developed under the auspices of ICH. It is a medical terminology coding dictionary, important in the electronic transmission of adverse event reporting as well as in the coding of clinical trial data.

Medical Devices Directive
(*MDD*) Directive 93/42/EEC sets general requirements relating to the design and construction of medical devices and their accessories.

Member State
A member nation of the European Union. The EFTA States have adopted the complete *Acquis Communautaire* on medicinal products and are consequently parties to Community procedures; therefore, for the purposes of this book, the term Member State shall also include the EFTA countries.

MRA
See Mutual Recognition Agreement

MRL
Maximum residue limit

MUMS
Minor use, minor species

Mutual Recognition Agreement
(MRA) International agreement by which two or more countries agree to recognise one another's conformity assessments.

Mutual Recognition Procedure
Applicable to most conventional medicinal products, the Mutual Recognition Procedure is based upon the extension of national marketing authorisations to one or more additional Member States. Applicants may select the Reference Member State that conducts the assessment and applicable Concerned Member States where the product would be put on the market if approved. Sometimes referred to as the Decentralised Procedure.

N
New Approach Directives
The European Council established a "New Approach" for technical harmonisation and standardisation to remove technical trade obstacles within the European Union in its Decision of 7 May 1985. The New Approach serves *inter alia* as the basis for the European Council Directives for medical devices that have been issued thus far with the object of removing existing trade obstacles and achieving high unified security standards.

Notice to Applicants
(NTA) Procedures for marketing authorisation, regulatory guidelines and application dossier presentation and content for medicinal products for human use (Volume 2) and veterinary medicinal products (Volume 6). The NTA has no legal force.

Notified Body
Certification organisation (e.g., independent testing house, laboratory or product certifier) authorised by the relevant Member State's Competent Authority to perform

conformity assessment tasks specified in the medical device directives.

NTA
See Notice to Applicants

O
Official Journal
(*OJ*) *Official Journal of the European Union.* Contains details of all EU legislation, as well as draft legislation, information, notices and advertisements for public works and supplies contracts.

OJ
See *Official Journal*

OMCL
Official Medicines Control Laboratories (see EDQM)

Orphan Medicinal Products
A medicinal product that has a limited target population or treats a rare disease thus limiting its commercial and financial potential. In Europe, the *Orphan Medicinal Product Regulation* was adopted in December 1999, to stimulate the development in the EU of pharmaceuticals for the diagnosis, prevention and treatment of some 5,000 diseases that are classified as "rare" and affect not more than five in 10,000 persons in the EU.

OTC
Over-the-Counter (products available without a prescription)

P
Paediatric Committee
(PDCO) Scientific committee within EMA that assesses the content of paediatric investigation plans and adopts opinions on them in accordance with Regulation (EC) 1901/2006 as amended. This includes the assessment of applications for a full or partial waiver and assessment of applications for deferrals.

Paediatric Regulation
Regulation passed in 2006 to encourage the development and authorisation medicinal products to meet the special therapeutic needs of the paediatric population.

Patient Information Leaflet
PIL

PDCO
See Paediatric Committee

Periodic Safety Update Report
(PSUR) A periodic report, submitted at defined post-authorisation times, on the worldwide safety experience of a medicinal product.

PHARE
One of three pre-accession instruments funded by the EU to assist applicant countries in Central and Eastern Europe in preparing to join as Member States. Currently, it assists the Czech Republic, Estonia, Hungary, Latvia, Lithuania, Poland, Slovakia and Slovenia, as well as Bulgaria and Romania, which acceded in 2007. (Originally created in 1989 as Poland and Hungary: Assistance for Restructuring their Economies.)

Pharmacovigilance Working Party
(PhVWP) Reporting to the CHMP, the PhVWP facilitates coordination of Mutual Recognition Procedure product pharmacovigilance across Member States and the development of consensus on conclusions and proposed actions when differences arise between Member States.

PhVWP
See Pharmacovigilance Working Party

PIC
Pharmaceutical Inspection Convention. The PIC and the Pharmaceutical Inspection Co-operation Scheme (PIC Scheme) operate together as PIC/S.

PIL
Patient Information Leaflet

PMS
Postmarket Surveillance

POM
Prescription-only Medicine

Postmarket Surveillance
(PMS) Systematic procedure by which a manufacturer records, evaluates and reports any incidents, proactively gathering product experience in the postmarketing phase. Used as the basis for any necessary corrective actions.

PSUR
See Periodic Safety Update Report

Q
Qualified Person
A person at the Marketing Authorisation Holder's disposal who is responsible for ensuring that the quality of each batch of medicinal product is in accordance with the marketing authorisation's requirements.

R

Rapporteur and Co-rapporteur
Members of the CHMP, CVMP or COMP who assume responsibility for assessing marketing authorisation applications, community referrals and requests for orphan drug designation.

Reference Member State
The Member State whose Assessment Report is the basis for the Mutual Recognition Procedure and Decentralised Procedure.

Regulation
A legal act that is entirely and directly binding to the Member States. Unlike a directive, it does not require transposition into national law and its provisions can come into force immediately.

RMS
See Reference Member State

S

SMEs
Small and Medium-sized Enterprises

SmPC
See Summary of Product Characteristics

Summary of Product Characteristics
(SmPC) The definitive statement between the Competent Authority and the Marketing Authorisation Holder regarding the medicinal or veterinary product. The summary of product characteristics contains a description of a medicinal product's properties and the conditions attached to its use. This includes: name, composition, pharmaceutical form and strength, therapeutic indication(s), adverse reactions, contraindications, shelf-life, storage conditions and Marketing Authorisation Holder. It contains all information a prescriber/supplier needs for proper use of the medicinal or veterinary product. The content must be approved by the Competent Authority, and cannot be changed without the approval of the originating Competent Authority.

Supplementary Protection Certificate
A certificate that protects intellectual property rights following patent expiration and is available in the EU for medicinal products and plant protection products. A Supplementary Protection Certificate can come into force only after the corresponding patent expires and for a maximum of five years, to grant a product not more than 15 years of market exclusivity. It is intended to compensate the holder for the extended period required for some products to be approved.

T

Traditional Herbal Medicinal Products Directive
Requires traditional, over-the-counter herbal remedies to be manufactured to assured standards of safety and quality.

Treaty on European Union
The 1992 document that radically restructured the European Community, formally established the European Union and committed the EC to Economic and Monetary Union (EMU) by 1999 at the latest. Also known as the Maastricht Treaty.

TSE
Transmissible spongiform encephalopathies

Type I Variation
Any of the "minor" variations listed in Annex I of Regulations (EEC) 1084/2003 (formerly 541/95) and (EEC) 1085/2003 (542/95) to documentation in an approved marketing authorisation. A Type IA or Type IB variation notification must be filed with EMA for any such change.

Type II Variation
Any change to the documentation in an approved MA that is not a Type IA or Type IB Variation and is not regarded as an extension to the MA.

U

Urgent Safety Restriction
An interim change to product information in the summary of product characteristics by the Marketing Authorisation Holder concerning indications, dosage, contraindications, warnings, target species and withdrawal periods resulting from new information about a medicinal product's safe use.

V

VICH
International Cooperation on Harmonisation of Technical Requirements for Registration of Veterinary Medicinal Products

Vigilance
The adverse incident reporting requirements and system for devices.

W

WHA
World Health Assembly

WHO
World Health Organisation

WSMI
World Self-Medication Industry

Canadian
Medical Device
Regulation

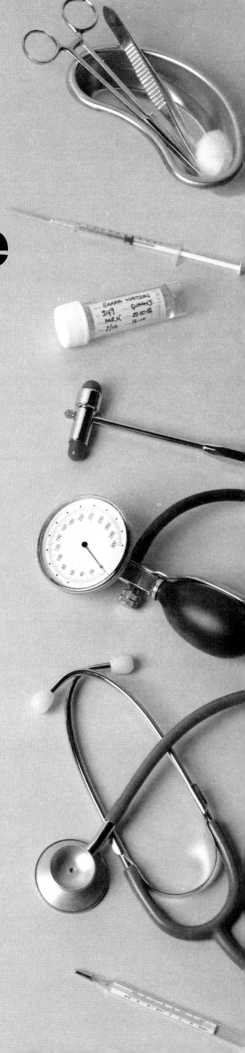

Health Canada: An Overview of the Canadian Legislative Framework

Updated by Lea Epstein, JD, LLM

OBJECTIVES

❑ Understand the mission of Health Canada

❑ Understand the organization of Health Canada

❑ Understand the legislative framework

❑ Understand the promulgation of legislation

REGULATIONS AND GUIDELINES COVERED IN THIS CHAPTER

❑ *Broadcasting Act*, 1991

❑ *Canada Health Act*, 1984

❑ Canada Labour Code

❑ *Canada Medical Act*, 1912

❑ *Canada Shipping Act*, 2001

❑ *Canadian Centre on Substance Abuse Act*, 1988

❑ *Canadian Environmental Protection Act*, 1999

❑ *Canadian Food Inspection Agency Act*, 1997

❑ *Canadian Institutes of Health Research Act*, 2000

❑ *Controlled Drugs and Substances Act*, 1996

❑ *Department of Health Act*, 1996

❑ *Emergency Preparedness Act*, 1985

❑ *Energy Supplies Emergency Act*, 1985

❑ *Excise Tax Act*, 1985

❑ *Federal-Provincial Fiscal Arrangements Act*, 1985

❑ *Feeds Act*, 1985

❑ *Financial Administration Act*, 1985

❑ *Fitness and Amateur Sport Act*, 1961

❑ *Food and Drugs Act*

❑ *Hazardous Materials Information Review Act*, 1985

❑ *Hazardous Products Act*, 1985

❑ *Immigration Act*, 2001

❑ *National Parks Act*, 2000

❑ *Nuclear Safety and Control Act*, 1997

❑ *Patent Act*, 1985

❑ *Pest Control Products Act*, 1985

❑ *Pesticide Residue Compensation Act*, 1985

❑ *Personal Information Protection and Electronic Documents Act*, 2000

- ☐ *Quarantine Act, 1985*

- ☐ *Queen Elizabeth II Canadian Research Fund Act, 1970*

- ☐ *Radiation Emitting Devices Act, 1985*

- ☐ *Statutory Instruments Act, 1985*

- ☐ *Statutory Instruments Regulations, 1985*

- ☐ *Tobacco Act, 1997*

- ☐ *Trade Marks Act, 1985*

Introduction

A century ago, most Canadians believed that it was a family's duty to look after members who were poor, unemployed, sick or old. Industrialization and the Great Depression caused this philosophy to change. The *British North America Act* gave provinces control over social welfare, including health. After World War II, both government levels saw a need for change, and the federal government agreed to pay half the cost of provincial healthcare programs. To obtain access to the federal money, each province had to ensure that its system met national standards.

Both governments are therefore responsible for assisting with the health and well-being of Canadians. The federal government enacts legislation regulating what products can be sold as drugs, how different categories of drugs (prescription, nonprescription or narcotic) are controlled and how drug abuse is avoided. Provincial governments legislate how drugs are distributed and, for certain citizens, pay for listed drugs, limited-use drug products, some nutritional products and some diabetic testing products. Provinces and territories plan, finance and evaluate the provision of hospital care, physician and allied healthcare services, some aspects of prescription care and public health.

This chapter focuses on the federal government's involvement in the healthcare of Canadians. A discussion of the organization and structure of the relevant federal department is followed by an overview of the legislative framework.

Health Canada Organization and Structure of Departments

Health Canada is the federal organization responsible for helping Canadians maintain and improve their health. In partnership with provincial and territorial governments, Health Canada provides national leadership to develop health policy, communicate health risks and promote healthy lifestyles, promote disease prevention and monitor risks related to the sale and use of drugs, food, chemicals, pesticides, medical devices and other consumer products across Canada and around the world.

Health Canada is organized into branches, each of which is responsible for a different aspect of health governance. The deputy minister and associate deputy minister of health, working with the secretariat, support the minister of health in managing these operations. See **Figure 28-1** for more information.

The Health Canada branches are broadly divided into:
- Audit and Accountability Bureau
- Chief Financial Officer Branch
- Corporate Services Branch
- First Nations and Inuit Health Branch
- Healthy Environments & Consumer Safety Branch
- Health Products and Food Branch
- Public Affairs, Consultation and Communications Branch
- Regions and Programs Branch
- Strategic Policy Branch

The agency also includes:
- Departmental Secretariat
- Legal Services
- Pest Management Regulatory Agency

Additionally, the following independent agencies are included in the portfolio of, and report directly to, the minister of health:
- Canadian Institutes of Health Research—Canada's premier federal funding agency for health research
- Patented Medicine Prices Review Board—a quasi-judicial body regulating the prices of patented medicines
- Hazardous Materials Information Review Commission—provides the trade secret protection mechanism for the Workplace Hazardous Materials Information System (The commission balances the industry's right to protect trade secrets and workers' need for accurate health and safety information about hazardous chemicals used in the workplace.)
- Public Health Agency of Canada—represents a new approach to federal leadership and collaboration with provinces and territories on public health system renewal efforts in Canada and support for a sustainable health system (The agency, headed by the chief public health officer, reports directly to the minister of health and focuses on efforts to prevent chronic diseases such as cancer and heart disease, prevent injuries and respond to public health emergencies and infectious disease outbreaks.)
- Assisted Human Reproduction Canada—regulatory agency responsible for protecting and promoting the health, safety, dignity and rights of Canadians who use or are born of assisted human

Figure 28-1
Health Canada Branches and Agencies

reproduction technologies

Some Health Canada branches are managed by assistant deputy ministers located in Ottawa, while other offices or services are independent and report directly to the deputy minister and assistant deputy minister of health. Additionally, the Regions and Programs Branch has six regional directors that represent departmental interests and provide a presence through regional offices. Health Canada maintains six regional operations throughout the provinces from coast to coast: British Columbia Region, Alberta Region, Manitoba and Saskatchewan Region, Ontario Region, Quebec Region, Atlantic Region and Northern Region. The regional offices are found under the Regions and Programs Branch (which is further comprised of the Programs Directorate and the Workplace Health and Safety Program). A more detailed account of the activities of the branches follows.

Audit and Accountability Bureau

The bureau provides independent advice and assurance to the deputy minister on the effectiveness of risk management, controls and governance processes; conducts forensic audits and investigations; and acts on disclosures of wrongdoing.

Chief Financial Officer Branch (CFOB)

CFOB is the focal point of accountability to ensure rigorous resource stewardship and management within Health Canada. CFOB provides strategic advice on the efficiency of expenditures and value-for-money, and anticipates and promotes future trends. The branch is composed of a number of directorates. The chief financial officer is also the executive for overall financial management, reporting to the comptroller general of Canada.

Corporate Services Branch (CSB)

CSB provides corporate support and services across the department in key areas:
- human resources management
- official languages
- real property and facilities management
- occupational health, safety, emergency and security management
- information technology and information management
- executive correspondence
- access to information and privacy requests/issues

CSB programs are carried out by the following directorates: Access to Information and Privacy Division, Facilities and Security Directorate, Human Resources Services Directorate, Information Management Services Directorate and the Planning and Operations Directorate.

In the regions, delivery of financial, human resources and other services is managed by the regional directors general. CSB also provides a departmental focal point for liaisons with the Treasury Board Secretariat, Public Works, Government Services Canada and other central agencies.

First Nations and Inuit Health Branch (FNIHB)

FNIHB delivers public health and health promotion services to both on-reserve and Inuit communities. It also provides drug, dental and ancillary health services to First Nations and Inuit people regardless of residence. FNIHB seeks to assist First Nations and Inuit communities to address health barriers and disease threats, and attain health levels comparable to those of other Canadians living in similar locations.

Healthy Environments and Consumer Safety Branch (HECSB)

HECSB is responsible for assisting Canadians in maintaining their health. It promotes healthy and safe living environments and reduces the harm caused by tobacco, alcohol, controlled substances, environmental contaminants and unsafe consumer and industrial products.

HECSB is responsible for:
- regulating radiation-emitting devices
- regulating consumer products, cosmetics and hazardous materials in the workplace
- regulating tobacco and controlled substances and providing drug analytical services
- defining and communicating requirements for cosmetic manufacturing, labelling, distribution and sale, and evaluating compliance
- assessing new substances and biotechnology products for regulations
- assessing and reducing environmental health risks, including noise
- promoting consumer awareness of actual and potential product-related hazards
- promoting healthy work environments and delivering occupational health and safety services
- promoting initiatives to reduce and prevent the harm caused by tobacco and abuse of alcohol and other controlled substances
- encouraging the design of safer products for the Canadian market

Health Products and Food Branch (HPFB)

The most important Health Canada branch for the regulatory field is HPFB. HPFB seeks to minimize Canadians' health risk factors while maximizing health product and food safety; promote conditions that enable Canadians to make healthy choices; and provide information to allow them to make informed decisions about their health.

HPFB's activities are carried out through offices in the

**Figure 28-2 Health Products
and Food Branch Organizational Chart**

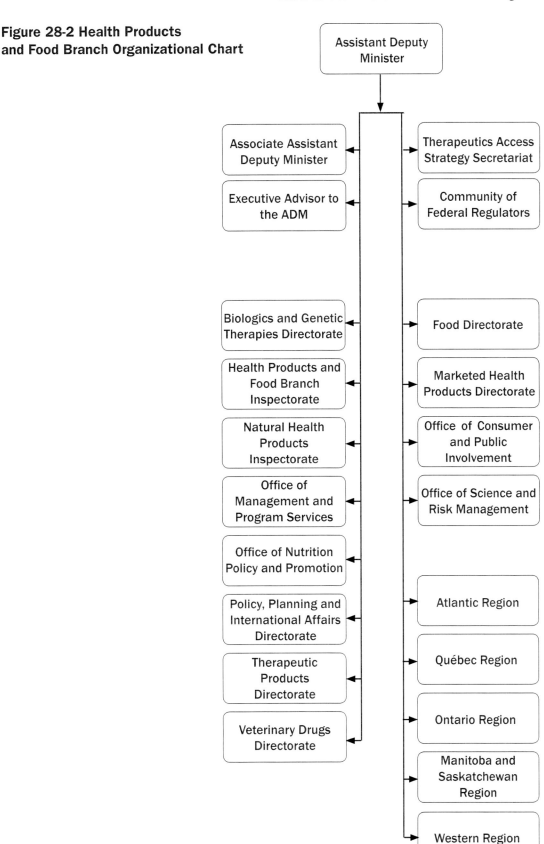

National Capital Region and five regional offices: Atlantic, Quebec, Ontario and Nunavut, Manitoba-Saskatchewan and Western (British Columbia, Alberta, Northwest Territories and Yukon). The organization of HPFB is shown in **Figure 28-2**. HPFB is divided into a number of directorates:

- The Biologics and Genetic Therapies Directorate (BGTD) regulates biological drugs (products derived from living sources) and radiopharmaceuticals for human use. BGTD reviews the evidence of safety and effectiveness provided by manufacturers to determine whether the benefits of the product outweigh its risks and whether the risks can be mitigated. BGTD then monitors the product's safety and effectiveness in concert with the inspectorate (HPFBI), the Marketed Health Products Directorate (MHPD) and the Public Health Agency of Canada (PHAC).
- The Food Directorate establishes policies, sets standards and provides advice and information on the safety and nutritional value of food. Additionally, under the *Canadian Food Inspection Agency Act,* this directorate assesses the effectiveness of the activities of the Canadian Food Inspection Agency (CFIA) related to food safety.
- The Health Products and Food Branch Inspectorate (HPFBI) is responsible for all compliance and enforcement activities across Health Canada's branches. This enables consistency of approach across the spectrum of regulated products. HPFBI engages in compliance monitoring, compliance verification and investigation, supported by establishment licensing of drugs and medical devices and laboratory analysis. The inspectorate's activities apply to all drugs and devices as defined by the *Food and Drugs Act.* These include medical devices and human drugs, natural health products, blood and blood components for transfusion, semen for assisted conception, cells, tissues, organs for transplantation and veterinary drugs.
- The Marketed Health Products Directorate ensures that HPFB programs take a consistent approach to postapproval safety surveillance, assessment of issues and safety trends and risk communications concerning all regulated marketed health products. Its activities include collecting and analyzing adverse reaction data and communicating risk assessments.
- The Natural Health Products Directorate is the regulating authority for natural health products for sale in Canada. It processes applications and submissions and grants licences for natural health products.
- The Therapeutic Products Directorate (TPD) regulates pharmaceutical drugs and medical devices for

human use. TPD reviews scientific evidence of a product's safety, efficacy and quality submitted by a manufacturer as required by the *Food and Drugs Act* and *Food and Drug Regulations.* The directorate's activities concern medical devices, clinical trials, drug submissions, patented medicines and a variety of other matters.
- The Veterinary Drugs Directorate evaluates and monitors product safety, quality and effectiveness; sets standards; and promotes the prudent use of veterinary drugs administered to food-producing and companion animals.

It is worth noting that HPFB's licensing and regulatory requirements arm is separate from its enforcement arm. HPFB's directorates focus primarily on the development and promotion of policies in each of their respective areas:
- Office of Consumer and Public Involvement
- Office of Management and Program Services
- Office of Nutrition Policy and Promotion
- Office of Paediatric Initiatives
- Departmental Biotechnology Office
- Office of the Assistant Deputy Minister
- Policy, Planning and International Affairs Directorate

Public Affairs, Consultation and Communications Branch

This branch focuses on communication and consultation with the public, and the integration of national and regional perspectives into policies and strategies.

Strategic Policy Branch

The Strategic Policy Branch focuses on developing policy responses to a range of priority issues that may affect the health of Canadians. This branch is divided into a number of directorates, each focusing on its respective subject matter:
- Applied Research and Analysis Directorate
- Health Care Policy Directorate
- Federal/Provincial Relations Division
- International Affairs Directorate
- Office of the Chief Scientist
- Office of Nursing Policy
- Policy Coordination and Planning Directorate
- Policy Development Directorate

Departmental Secretariat

The Departmental Secretariat coordinates the interface between the department's executive and political levels in such activities as parliamentary relations and ministerial correspondence and serves as a focal point for corporate planning, priorities and initiatives.

Legal Services

This organization provides legal services to the Department of Health including legal policy advice, opinions, legislative proposal development and litigation support to the minister, deputy minister, senior managers and working-level managers and officers.

Pest Management Regulatory Agency (PMRA)

PMRA is responsible for protecting human health and the environment by minimizing the risks associated with pest control products. PMRA collaborates with Environment Canada, Agriculture and Agri-Food Canada and other organizations in environmental pesticide research and monitoring, including sustainable pest management.

Relevant Acts and Regulations
Acts

The *Constitution Act* of 1867 distributes legislative power between the Parliament of Canada and the legislatures of the provinces. Areas of concern to the regulatory field, such as food and drugs, tend to fall into federal rather than provincial jurisdiction. Legislation on these topics, therefore, is created by Parliament. Parliament consists of the Crown, the Senate and the House of Commons; all three must assent to a bill for it to become an act or a statute. Bills may be introduced by members of the Senate or the House of Commons. Ministers (including the minister of health) and the prime minister also make up the Cabinet, responsible for governing, determining priorities and policies and ensuring their implementation. The *Constitution Act* requires that federal laws be enacted in both official languages (English and French) and makes both versions equally authentic.

The minister of health has total or partial responsibility for administering the following acts and their related regulations:

- *Assisted Human Reproduction Act*, 2004
- *Canada Health Act*, 1984
- *Canadian Centre on Substance Abuse Act*, 1988
- *Canadian Environmental Protection Act*, 1999
- *Canadian Institutes of Health Research Act*, 2000
- *Controlled Drugs and Substances Act*, 1997
- *Department of Health Act*, 1996
- *Financial Administration Act*, 1985
- *Fitness and Amateur Sport Act*, 1961
- *Food and Drugs Act*
- *Hazardous Materials Information Review Act*, 1985
- *Hazardous Products Act*, 1985
- *Patent Act*, 1985
- *Pest Control Products Act*, 1985
- *Pesticide Residue Compensation Act*, 1985
- *Quarantine Act*, 1985
- *Radiation Emitting Devices Act*, 1985
- *Tobacco Act*, 1997

Health Canada also is involved with or has special interest in:

- *Agriculture and Agri-Food Administrative Monetary Penalties Act*, 1995
- *Broadcasting Act*, 1991
- Canada Labour Code
- *Canada Medical Act*, 1912
- *Canada Shipping Act*, 2001
- *Canadian Food Inspection Agency Act*, 1997
- *Emergency Preparedness Act*, 1985
- *Energy Supplies Emergency Act*, 1985
- *Excise Tax Act*, 1985
- *Federal-Provincial Fiscal Arrangements Act*, 1985
- *Feeds Act*, 1985
- *Immigration Act*, 2001
- *National Parks Act*, 2000
- *Nuclear Safety and Control Act*, 1997
- *Non-Smokers Health Act*, 1985
- *Queen Elizabeth II Canadian Research Fund Act*, 1970
- *Trade Marks Act*, 1985

Regulations

Regulations addressing aspects of Health Canada's jurisdiction in more detail complement the above acts. Regulations have the force of law and set out generally applicable rules. Specific regulations promulgated from the acts listed above can be found on the Health Canada website and are discussed in subsequent chapters of this book.

Creating regulations is an extension of Parliament's power to make laws. This power is delegated through legislation to the governor in counsel, the Treasury Board, or to ministers or agencies who then make regulations accordingly.

The process of enacting regulations is governed by the *Statutory Instruments Act* (1985) and the *Cabinet Directive on Streamlining Regulation*. The *Statutory Instruments Act* establishes processes designed to ensure that regulations are made on a legally secure foundation and are accessible to the public through the *Canada Gazette*. The *Cabinet Directive on Streamlining Regulation* replaced the government of Canada's "Federal Regulatory Policy" in 2007. It establishes the requirements and policies for regulatory development process, including requiring a regulatory impact analysis as a means of ensuring that the government's regulatory activity serves the public interest. The Cabinet Directive explains that regulations are only one of several policy instruments available to the government and should be viewed as part of a mix of complementary instruments functioning together to address a public policy issue. Further guidance for the development of regulations can be found on the Regulatory Affairs Sector's website.

The power to enact regulations is granted through an

"enabling authority"—an act of Parliament—that expressly assigns such a power to certain persons or bodies. A regulation must strictly conform to the limits established by the act that authorizes it. Most legislative schemes depend upon regulations to make them work, so an act and its regulations should be developed together to ensure coherent functioning. The authority to enact regulations may be granted to the governor in council (the governor general acting on advice from the Cabinet), the Treasury Board, a minister or an administrative agency.

The development of regulations by the governor in council, for instance, involves the following steps:

1. Determine the level of impact and whether an exemption from publication is appropriate.
2. Conduct analysis and develop a Regulatory Impact Analysis Statement (RIAS), obtaining necessary concurrence.
3. Draft the regulation.
4. Justice Canada reviews the draft regulation and the RIAS and sends them to the Privy Council Office-Orders in Council (PCO-OIC), which forwards them to the Treasury Board.
5. The Treasury Board determines whether to approve for pre-publication.
6. Prepublish in *Canada Gazette* Part I.
7. Comments are received and reviewed; the regulation is revised.
8. Justice Canada again reviews the regulation and the RIAS and sends them to the PCO-OIC, which forwards them to the Treasury Board.
9. The governor in council considers the submission and determines whether to make the regulation
10. The regulation is registered and published in the *Canada Gazette* Part II.
11. Parliamentary scrutiny: as mandated by the *Statutory Instruments Act*—the Standing Joint Committee for the Scrutiny of Regulations monitors the exercise of regulatory power on behalf of Parliament to review regulations and other statutory instruments as they are made, based upon criteria that the Senate and the House of Commons approve at the beginning of each session of Parliament.

Regulations come into force on the day on which they are registered, unless a different date is specified.

Canada Gazette

New regulations created as discussed above are published in the *Canada Gazette*. The *Canada Gazette* is the official newspaper of the government of Canada, published regularly since 1841 in English and French. Section 10 of the *Statutory Instruments Act* confers the responsibility for the *Canada Gazette* on the Queen's Printer.

The *Gazette* contains public notices, official appointments, proposed regulations, regulations and public acts of Parliament from government departments and agencies. It also contains miscellaneous public notices from the private sector. Government departments and agencies, as well as entities in the private sector, may be required by law to publish notices in the *Canada Gazette*. Publication in the *Canada Gazette* serves as "official notice."

The *Gazette* is published as three parts:

- Part I is published every Saturday and contains public notices, official appointments and proposed regulations from the government as well as miscellaneous public notices from the private sector that are required to be published by a federal statute or regulation. Comments to government departments and agencies responsible for the proposed regulations can be made by professional associations and organizations as well as private individuals. The public is thereby provided with an opportunity to influence possible changes to the regulation. The contact information appears within the proposed regulations.

- Part II is published every second Wednesday and is the official notice for all regulations that are enacted, as well as other statutory instrument classes such as orders in council, orders and proclamations. Only government departments and agencies publish in Part II. The Privy Council Office coordinates regulations and other documents to be published in Part II.

- Part III is published as soon as reasonable and practical after Royal Assent and contains the most recent public acts of Parliament and their enactment proclamations. The Department of Justice determines the publication date of each issue of Part III.

Guidelines

In addition to the acts and regulations discussed above, Health Canada often presents guidelines with further information. These guidelines, guidances and policies clarify the regulations' intent and provide additional and specific details to assist industry in applying the regulations. Such guidelines do not have the force of law but can be extremely useful in interpreting the meaning of any unclear legislation.

Summary

- Health Canada is the federal organization responsible for helping Canadians maintain and improve their health.
- Health Canada is organized into branches, each of which is responsible for a different aspect of health governance, namely, Audit and Accountability

Bureau, Chief Financial Officer Branch, Corporate Services Branch, First Nations and Inuit Health Branch, Healthy Environments and Consumer Safety Branch, Health Products and Food Branch, Public Affairs, Consultation and Communications Branch, Regions and Programs Branch and the Strategic Policy Branch.

- Several independent agencies report directly to the minister of health, namely, Canadian Institutes of Health Research, Patented Medicine Prices Review Board, Hazardous Materials Information Review Commission, Public Health Agency of Canada, and Assisted Human Reproduction Canada.
- Health Canada administers many acts and regulations to promote the health and safety of Canadians.
- Guidelines may be released by Health Canada to provide clarity on the legislation and regulations.

Recommended Reading

Health Canada website, www.hc-sc.gc.ca

Department of Justice, Regulations Section. *Federal Regulations Manual*

Privy Council Office, Regulatory Affairs and Orders in Council Secretariat. *Government of Canada Regulatory Policy.* 1999. www.tbs-sct.gc.ca/ri-qr/ processguideprocessus-eng.asp

Canadian Food and Drugs Act, Regulations, Policies and Other Resources

Updated by Lea Epstein, JD, LLM

OBJECTIVES

❑ Gain an understanding of the organization of Canadian legislation regarding the Canadian *Food and Drugs Act* (F&DA) and *Food and Drug Regulations* (FDR)

❑ Understand other legislation related to the marketing of pharmaceuticals and medical devices in Canada

REGULATIONS AND GUIDELINES COVERED IN THIS CHAPTER

❑ *Access to Information Act, 1985*

❑ *Controlled Drugs and Substances Act, 1996*

❑ *Financial Administration Act, 1985*

❑ *Food and Drugs Act*

❑ *Patent Act, 1985*

❑ *Authority to Sell Drugs Fees Regulations*

❑ *Controlled Drugs and Substances Regulations*

❑ *Drug Evaluation Fees Regulations*

❑ *Establishment Licence Fees Regulations & Licensed Dealers for Controlled Drugs and Narcotics Fees Regulations*

❑ *Food and Drug Regulations*

❑ *Medical Devices Regulations*

❑ *Narcotic Control Regulations*

❑ *Natural Health Products Regulations*

❑ *Patented Medicines Regulations*

❑ *Pharmaceutical Export Certificate Fee Regulations*

❑ *Target Substances Regulations*

Introduction

Regulatory practice in Canada is primarily dominated by a single piece of legislation and its accompanying regulations: the *Food and Drugs Act* and the *Food and Drug Regulations*. The discussion below summarizes and highlights the important aspects of this act and these regulations in reference to drugs. Additional relevant legislation is discussed in context.

The *Food and Drugs Act* and *Food and Drug Regulations*
The *Food and Drugs Act*

The *Food and Drugs Act* (*F&DA*) and *Food and Drug Regulations* (*FDR*) apply to all foods, drugs (including biologics and natural health products), cosmetics and medical devices sold in Canada, whether they are manufactured in Canada or imported. The *F&DA* and *FDR* govern the sale, advertisement and labelling of foods, drugs, cosmetics and medical devices, ensuring their safety and preventing deception.

As with all other acts, the first portion of the legislation deals with certain definitions, including the following:

- "Advertisement"—any representation by any means whatsoever for the purpose of promoting directly or indirectly the sale or disposal of any food, drug, cosmetic or device
- "Analyst"—person designated as an analyst for the purpose of the enforcement of the *F&DA* under section 28 or under section 13 of the *Canadian Food Inspection Agency Act*
- "Contraceptive device"—any instrument, apparatus, contrivance or substance other than a drug that is manufactured, sold or represented for use in the prevention of conception
- "Cosmetic"—any substance or mixture of substances manufactured, sold or represented for use in cleansing, improving or altering the complexion, skin, hair or teeth, includes deodorants and perfumes
- "Device"—any article, instrument, apparatus or contrivance, including any component, part or accessory thereof, manufactured, sold or represented for use in:
  o the diagnosis, treatment, mitigation or prevention of a disease, disorder or abnormal physical state or its symptoms in human beings or animals
  o restoring, correcting or modifying a body function or the body structure of human beings or animals
  o the diagnosis of pregnancy in human beings or animals
  o the care of human beings or animals during pregnancy and at and after birth of the offspring
      This includes a contraceptive device, but does not include a drug.
- "Drug"—any substance or mixture of substances manufactured, sold or represented for use in:
  o the diagnosis, treatment, mitigation or prevention of a disease, disorder, abnormal physical state or its symptoms in human beings or animals
  o restoring, correcting or modifying organic functions in human beings or animals
  o disinfection in premises in which food is manufactured or kept
- "Food"—any article manufactured, sold or represented for use as food or drink for human beings; chewing gum; and any ingredient that may be mixed with food for any purpose whatever
- "Inspector"—any person designated as an inspector for the purpose of the enforcement of the *F&DA* under subsection 22(1) or under Section 13 of the *Canadian Food Inspection Agency Act*
- "Label"—any legend, word or mark attached to,

included in, belonging to or accompanying any food, drug, cosmetic, device or package
- "Minister"—the minister of health
- "Package"—anything in which any food, drug, cosmetic or device is wholly or partly contained, placed or packed
- "Prescribed"—prescribed by the *FDR*
- "Sell"—to offer for sale, expose for sale, have in possession for sale and distribute, whether or not the distribution is made for consideration
- "Unsanitary conditions"—such conditions or circumstances as might contaminate with dirt or filth or render injurious to health a food, drug or cosmetic

The *F&DA* contains general prohibitions regarding the advertising, labelling, packaging and sale of foods, drugs, cosmetics and devices in Canada.

The act is divided into four parts: Part I addresses food, drugs, cosmetics and devices generally, and Part II addresses administration and enforcement. Parts III and IV contain the schedules referred to in the act.

Part I of the *F&DA* begins with a general prohibition against advertising any food, drug, cosmetic or device to the general public as a treatment, preventative or cure for any of the diseases, disorders or abnormal physical states listed in Schedule A. Schedule A of the *F&DA* lists diseases, disorders or abnormal physical states that are considered not self-diagnosable—a "learned intermediary" (i.e., a physician) must interact with the patient to determine the most appropriate treatment. Examples of Schedule A diseases include alcoholism, arthritis, asthma, bladder disease, cancer and depression. The advertising of devices manufactured, sold or represented for use in the prevention of conception is similarly prohibited.

Schedule A items are permitted to be advertised to healthcare professionals but not to the general public. Some drugs are labelled and sold to the general public as a treatment for the symptoms of diseases on Schedule A (such as for treatment of the pain of arthritis) but not for the treatment of the disease itself.

Part I of the *F&DA* continues with specific requirements for foods, drugs, cosmetics and devices, set out in more detail below.

Part I
Food

The *F&DA* lays out general prohibitions concerning food that protect the safety of consumers. Food that is harmful, unfit or adulterated may not be sold, and food labels and packaging may not be false or misleading in any manner. The act further cautions that standards must similarly be preserved for imported products.

Table 29-1. Schedule D of the *Food and Drugs Act*—Biologics

Allergenic substances used for the treatment or diagnosis of allergic or immunological diseases

Anterior pituitary extracts
Aprotinin
Blood and blood derivatives, except cord blood and peripheral blood that are a source of lymphohematopoietic cells for
   transplantation
Cholecystokinin
Drugs obtained by recombinant DNA procedures
Drugs, other than antibiotics, prepared from microorganisms
Glucagon
Gonadotrophins
Human plasma collected by plasmapheresis
Immunizing agents
Insulin
Interferon
Monoclonal antibodies, their conjugates and derivatives
Secretin
Snake venom
Urokinase

Drugs

As noted above, drugs are defined broadly in the *F&DA* as any substance that may be used for the diagnosis, treatment, mitigation or prevention of a disease. The act contains four major requirements concerning drugs:

- No person shall sell or manufacture any drug that was manufactured, prepared, preserved, packaged or stored under unsanitary conditions or is adulterated.
- No person shall label, package, treat, process, sell or advertise any drug in a manner that is false, misleading or deceptive, or is likely to create an erroneous impression regarding its character, value, quantity, composition, merit or safety.
- Where a standard has been prescribed for a drug, no person shall label, package, sell or advertise any substance in such a manner that is likely to be mistaken for that drug, unless the substance complies with the prescribed standard.
- Where a standard is not prescribed in the *FDR* but is contained in a publication to Schedule B to the *F&DA*, the drug must comply with that standard.

Schedule B of the *F&DA* lists the publicized standards that are recognized in Canada. Among them are the *United States Pharmacopeia* (*USP*), the *National Formulary* and the *European Pharmacopoeia*. If the drug is not a Canadian standard drug and is not listed in a publication to Schedule B, it must meet the "professed" (labelled) standard.

The *F&DA* furthermore restricts the sale of any drug described in Schedule C or D unless the minister has indicated that the premises in which the drug was manufactured and the process and conditions of manufacture are suitable to ensure that the drug will not be unsafe for use. Schedule C includes radiopharmaceuticals and drugs, other than radionuclides, that are sold or represented for use in the preparation of radiopharmaceuticals. Schedule D includes biologics and is presented in **Table 29-1**.

The act prohibits samples of drugs from being distributed to the general public in Canada. The distribution of drug samples to physicians, dentists, veterinary surgeons and pharmacists is permitted but restricted.

Cosmetics

The *F&DA* similarly protects consumer safety and prohibits any person from selling any cosmetic that:

- "has in or on it any substance that may cause injury to the health of the user when the cosmetic is used according to the directions on the label or accompanying the cosmetic, or for such purposes and by such methods of use as are customary or usual therefore;
- consists in whole or part of any filthy or decomposed substance or of any foreign matter; or
- was manufactured, prepared, preserved, packaged or sold under unsanitary conditions."

If cosmetic standards are prescribed, the act further prohibits packaging, labelling or selling a product such that a noncompliant product may be mistaken for a cosmetic. Cosmetics are discussed in more detail in a subsequent chapter.

Devices

A device is defined in the *F&DA* as any article, instrument or apparatus that may be used for diagnosis, treatment or prevention of a disease. The *F&DA* states that no person shall sell any device that, when used according to directions or under such conditions as are customary or usual, may cause injury to the health of the purchaser or user thereof.

Additionally, no person is permitted to label, package, treat, process, sell or advertise any device in a manner that is false, misleading or deceptive, or is likely to create an erroneous impression regarding its design, construction, performance, intended use, quantity, character, value, composition, merit or safety. When a standard has been prescribed for a device, no person shall label, package, sell or advertise any article in such a manner that it is likely to be mistaken for that device, unless the article complies with the prescribed standard.

A device that is not labelled or packaged as required by, or is labelled or packaged contrary to, the regulations is deemed to be labelled or packaged contrary to the act.

Part II

Part II of the *F&DA* deals with administration and enforcement and includes sections on inspection, seizure and forfeiture, analysis, offences and punishment and exports.

A number of regulations have been enacted pursuant to the *F&DA*. In addition to the *FDR*, regulations associated with the *F&DA* include the *Cosmetic Regulations, Processing and Distribution of Semen for Assisted Conception Regulations, Medical Devices Regulations, Natural Health Products Regulations* and *Marihuana Exemption Regulations*.

The *Food and Drug Regulations*

The *FDR* is a lengthy document divided into a number of parts: Parts A (Administration), B (Foods), C (Drugs), D (Vitamins, Minerals and Amino Acids), E (Artificial Sweeteners), G (Controlled Drugs) and J (Restricted Drugs).

Part A

Part A of the *FDR* deals with administration and applies to food, drugs, devices and cosmetics. The regulations are labelled A.01.001–A.01.065. Commonly used definitions are found in Section A.01.010. For regulatory professionals, an important definition found in this section is that of "manufacturer" or "distributor:" a person, including an association or partnership, that under his or her own name or a trade design or word mark, trade name or other name sells a food or drug. A "manufacturer" can be equivalent to a distributor and does not have to be the person who makes or fabricates the product.

Other requirements set out in Part A include labelling. For example, labels may be in either English or French, except that adequate directions for use shall be in both languages if the product is available for purchase through self-selection, such as some over-the-counter (OTC) products (A.01.015). Additional language requirements under the *FDR* and other provincial and federal Canadian laws may often be applicable. A lot number on a label must be preceded by "Lot number" or "Lot No." or "Lot" or "(L)" (A.01.014). All information required to be on a label

shall be clearly and prominently displayed and readily discernible to the purchasers under the customary conditions of purchase and use (A.01.016). Finally, security packaging is generally required for drugs for human use that are mouthwashes, are for ophthalmic use or are to be inhaled, ingested or inserted into the body if they are sold in a self-selection area. Lozenges are exempted (A.01.065). Additional security packaging requirements are applicable to specific products throughout the *FDR*.

Part A of the *FDR* also deals with analysts and inspectors, importations, exports, sampling, tariff of fees (for sample analysis) and labelling of food and drugs in pressurized containers.

Part B

Part B of the regulations deals with food and is not discussed in this chapter.

Part C

Part C deals with drugs and is organized into 10 divisions:
- Division 1—General
- Division 2—Good Manufacturing Practices
- Division 3—Schedule C Drugs (Radiopharmaceuticals)
- Division 4—Schedule D Drugs (Biologics)
- Division 5—Drugs for Clinical Trials Involving Human Subjects
- Division 6—Canadian Standard Drugs
- Division 7—Sale of Drugs for the Purposes of Implementing the General Council Decision
- Division 8—New Drugs
- Division 9—Nonprescription Drugs
- Division 10 has been repealed.

The general contents of each division are discussed below.

Division 1 (General)

This division begins with regulation C.01.001 and ends with C.01.625. The basic elements of Division 1 are as follows:
- C.01.001—definitions that are used in the section
- C.01.002—list of proper names that must be used on labels in Canada in place of chemical names, e.g., acetaminophen or clofibrate
- C.01.003–013—drug product labelling requirements
- C.01.014—requirements concerning Drug Identification Numbers (DINs) (A DIN is an eight-digit number that uniquely identifies each drug product sold in Canada. A drug must be approved for sale in Canada in order to be granted

Table 29-2. Elements of GMP as Defined by the *Food and Drug Regulations*

Premises
Equipment
Personnel
Sanitation
Raw Material Testing
Manufacturing Control
Quality Control Department
Packaging Material Testing
Finished Product Testing
Records
Samples
Stability
Sterile Products

a DIN, and that DIN must be clearly specified on the label.)

- C.01.015—tablet disintegration times
- C.01.016–017—requirements for adverse drug reaction reporting (A manufacturer must inform the director (Health Canada) if any adverse drug reaction known to the manufacturer occurs.)
- C.01.021–27—limits of drug dosage; including information on maximum single and daily dosages for such drugs as acetaminophen, ephedrine and sodium salicylate, and maximum daily doses for children
- C.01.028–035—requirements concerning cautionary statements and child-resistant packages for drugs such as acetylsalicylic acid, acetaminophen and iron
- C.01.036–040—miscellaneous restrictions applicable to certain drug products or their components
- C.01.040.2—list of coloring agents permitted for use in drug products
- C.01.041–049—regulations concerning Schedule F drugs (*FD&A* Schedule F concerns prescription drugs; the list of drugs, however, is found in Schedule F of the *FDR*. Regulations C.01.041–C.01.049 are concerned with who may sell prescription drugs and under what conditions. Section C.01.044 indicates that the only advertising of Schedule F drugs that can be done to the general public includes name, price and quantity.)
- C.01.051—drug product recall reporting requirements
- C.01.061—limits of variability (i.e., a bottle of 40 or fewer tablets cannot vary from the labelled number of tablets, whereas a bottle containing more than 50 but fewer than 101 can have one unit of variance)
- C.01.071–590—specific regulations that deal with mercuric chloride tablets, aminopyrine and

dipyrone, coated potassium salts, antibiotics and chloramphenicol

- C.01.600-612—veterinary drug regulations
- C.01.625—contraceptive drugs; the regulation permits contraceptive drugs that are not listed in Schedule F to be advertised to the general public

Division 1A

Division 1A deals with Establishment Licences. Any company that fabricates, packages, labels, distributes, imports, wholesales or tests a drug must have an Establishment Licence. This requirement applies to all drug establishments other than those dealing solely with certain natural health products. Establishment Licences are issued after the Health Products and Food Branch Inspectorate is satisfied that the site has been shown to be compliant with Good Manufacturing Practices (GMPs) and must be renewed every year.

Division 2 (Good Manufacturing Practices)

This division lists GMP requirements for Canada according to the elements presented in **Table 29-2**. GMPs allow for quality assurance, ensuring that drugs are consistently produced and controlled in such a way as to meet the quality standards appropriate to their intended use. Health Canada clarifies that the basic aspects of GMP require the following:

1. Manufacturing processes are clearly defined and controlled.
2. Critical steps of manufacturing processes and significant changes to the process are validated.
3. All necessary key elements for GMP are provided, including:
   - qualified and trained personnel
   - adequate premises and space
   - suitable equipment and services
   - correct materials, containers and labels
   - approved procedures and instructions
   - suitable storage and transport
4. Instructions and procedures are written in clear and unambiguous language.
5. Operators are trained to carry out and document procedures.
6. Records are made during manufacture that demonstrate that all the steps required by the defined procedures and instructions were in fact taken and that the quantity and quality of the drug was as expected. Deviations are investigated and documented.
7. Records that enable the complete history of a lot to be traced are retained in a comprehensible and accessible form.
8. Control of storage, handling and transportation of the drugs minimizes any risk to their quality.

9. A system is available for recalling drugs from sale.
10. Complaints about drugs are examined, the causes of quality defects are investigated, and appropriate measures are taken with respect to the defective drugs and to prevent recurrence.

Division 3 (Schedule C Drugs, Including Radiopharmaceuticals)

This division is a short set of regulations dealing with licensing and labelling requirements for radiopharmaceuticals and drugs (other than radionuclides) that are intended for use in the preparation of radiopharmaceuticals.

Division 4 (Schedule D Drugs, Including Biologics)

Division 4 contains a general set of requirements, followed by specific regulations for product types as listed in Schedule D (see **Table 29-1**). Division 4 has definitions specifically dealing with "date of manufacture" and "date of issue" for biologic products:

- The date of manufacture means:
  a) the date the product passes the potency test (if there is a standard of potency)
  b) the date the animal product is removed from an animal if there is no standard of potency
  c) the date of growth cessation for a non-animal product for which there is no standard of potency
- The date of issue is the date on which the finished product is removed from cold storage with limitations of a maximum of six, 12 or 24 months after the date of manufacture, depending upon the temperature at which the drug product was stored.

Other significant provisions concerning biologics in this division include the following:

- C.04.013–014 and 016–018 contain specific directions concerning the manufacture of biologic products.
- C.04.015 indicates that, upon written request from the director, every fabricator, packager or labeller, tester or distributor and importer shall submit protocols of tests together with samples of any lot of the drug before it is sold, and no person shall sell any lot of that drug if the protocol or sample fails to meet this regulation's requirements. It is typical for Health Canada to test all drug lots before the products can be sold in Canada.
- C.04.019 indicates that the usual labelling regulations (C.01.004) do not apply to biologics and defines what is required on the label. For the most part, the labelling requirements of C.04.019 and C.01.004 overlap.
- C.04.020 states the requirements and exceptions

for the Pr symbol (denoting a prescription drug) on the labelling.
- C.04.050–136 cover regulations specific to vaccines.
- C.04.137–138 are bacteriophage regulations.
- C.04.140–190 are regulations for toxins and toxoids.
- C.04.210–219 refer to antitoxins and antisera.
- C.04.230–683 are regulations dealing with products prepared from human sources, including all blood products, insulin and anterior pituitary hormone.

Division 5 (Drugs for Clinical Trials Involving Human Subjects)

This division describes the process of applying for approval to conduct a clinical trial by filing a Clinical Trial Application. Clinical trials are generally approved 30 days after filing, unless the applicant receives a Letter of Objection. The division contains instructions as to Good Clinical Practices for Canada, appropriate labelling for the investigative trials, recordkeeping requirements, and how Health Canada may suspend trials, if necessary.

Canada follows *International Conference on Harmonisation* (ICH) guidelines very closely. ICH promotes the harmonisation of technical testing requirements for pharmaceuticals—requirements for product registration—to reduce the need for duplicate testing in different countries. Health Canada's requirements concerning adverse reactions duplicate ICH guidelines.

Division 6 (Canadian Standard Drugs)

Division 6 defines certain drugs specifically for Canada. Essentially, only conjugated estrogens and thyroid have a definition that is different from that of other jurisdictions. Other listed Canadian standard drugs simply refer to the *USP* as the standard for Canada.

Division 7 (Sale of Drugs for the Purposes of Implementing the General Council Decision)

This division concerns a program called Canada's Access to Medicines Regime, which allows eligible countries to import less-expensive generic versions of patented drugs and medical devices. The products exported under the regime meet the same rigorous requirements for safety, effectiveness and quality as those authorized for the Canadian market. Pharmaceutical products eligible for export are listed in the *Patent Act,* and include drugs to treat HIV/AIDS, malaria, tuberculosis and other diseases.

Division 8 (New Drugs)

This division provides the regulations for obtaining approval of New Drug Submissions (NDSs) and Abbreviated New Drug Submissions (ANDSs). Before a drug may be sold or advertised in Canada, an NDS or an ANDS must be filed with the minister of health, and the minister must have issued a Notice of Compliance. An ANDS is easier to file than an NDS. It may be filed when the drug in question is the pharmaceutical equivalent of the Canadian reference product, is bioequivalent to the Canadian reference product, based on the pharmaceutical and, where the minister considers it necessary, bioavailability characteristics and the route of administration and conditions of use are also equivalent to those of the reference product.

These regulations furthermore list the contents required in an application, specify when approval can be removed from a new drug, provide postmarket requirements and describe how new drugs may be sold for emergency treatment. Division 8 also presents regulations for conducting experimental studies on veterinary drugs.

Division 9 (Nonprescription Drugs)

Division 9 provides specific regulations for standard doses and labelling of acetaminophen and salicylates.

Part D

Part D of the *FDR* deals with vitamins, minerals and amino acids. As of 1 January 2004, vitamins and minerals are mostly regulated under the *Natural Health Products Regulations*. As such, most of the Part D regulations that pertain to drugs have been repealed. Part D continues to regulate the labelling of vitamins, minerals and amino acid amounts in food.

Part E

Part E of the *FDR* deals with the artificial sweeteners, saccharin and cyclamate, stating specific labelling requirements.

Part F

Part F has been repealed.

Part G

Part G concerns controlled drugs, which are listed in an accompanying schedule. The Part G Schedule is in three parts, containing amphetamines, phenobarbital and other compounds; barbiturates; and anabolic steroids, respectively. Controlled drugs are also addressed in the *Controlled Drugs and Substances Act,* discussed below.

The regulations concerning controlled drugs are stringent. For instance, only licensed dealers (other than a pharmacy or hospital) may import, produce, export or sell controlled drugs, and every import or export of controlled drugs must have a permit. All Controlled Substance Licences are site specific and must be renewed each year. Controlled drugs cannot be advertised to the general public. Very specific records of controlled drugs must be

kept separately from other records, and in a manner that permits an audit.

Controlled drugs are required to have a capital "C" in a diamond on the label.

Parts H and I

Parts H and I have been repealed.

Part J

Part J deals with restricted drugs, and describes a regime similar to that for controlled drugs for the drugs (such as amphetamines) listed in the schedule in this part. Restricted drugs are required to have "restricted drug" specified on their label.

As mentioned, in addition to the *FDR* other regulations have similarly been enacted under the *F&DA*.

The *Natural Health Products Regulations*

The *Natural Health Products Regulations* came into force on 1 January 2004. Natural health products are considered a subset of drugs, so all references to drugs in the *F&DA* also apply to natural health products. The regulations require that manufacturers submit product licence applications for natural health products; they are theoretically forbidden to sell their products until a licence has been issued. However, due to the extensive backlog of applications not yet processed by Health Canada, the Natural Health Products Directorate had maintained a policy of pursuing enforcement only in the case of high-risk products. This policy of non-enforcement was codified in August 2010 by the *Natural Health Products (Unprocessed Product Licence Applications) Regulations.*

The *Medical Devices Regulations*

As mentioned, medical devices are health or medical instruments used in the treatment, mitigation, diagnosis or prevention of a disease or abnormal physical condition. The *Medical Devices Regulations* (*MDR*) lay out the responsibilities of manufacturers of such devices in more detail. As specified in Section 2, these regulations apply to the sale, advertising and importation of medical devices, as well as to in vitro diagnostic products that may contain a drug (unless the drug is a controlled, narcotic or restricted drug).

The regulations specify the four classes of medical devices, where Class I represents the lowest risk and Class IV represents the highest risk. Rules for classification are set out in Schedule 1 of these regulations. Classification and medical devices are discussed in more detail in Chapter 30.

The *MDR* are divided into three parts: Part 2 deals with custom-made devices and medical devices to be imported or sold for special access; Part 3 applies to medical devices for investigational testing involving human subjects; and all other devices are handled under Part 1. Part 1 addresses the manufacturer's obligations, safety and effectiveness requirements, labelling requirements, the different classes of devices, Establishment Licences, complaints, problem reporting, recalls and registrations and advertising of contraceptives.

Only a person or business that holds a Medical Device Establishment Licence (MDEL) may import or sell a medical device, unless the person or business is a retailer; healthcare facility; the manufacturer of a Class II, III or IV medical device; or the manufacturer of a Class I medical device that is distributed solely through a distributor that holds an MDEL. In order to acquire an MDEL, an applicant must have systems in place for maintaining distribution records, complaint handling and mandatory problem and recall reporting.

As with other products, medical device licences are required for Class II, III and IV medical devices. Class I medical devices do not require a medical device licence but must be listed on the MDEL of either the manufacturer or the distributor.

Part 1 of the *MDR* also concerns the requirements surrounding implants—devices listed in Schedule 2 such as heart valves or pacemakers. Manufacturers of implants are required to provide two registration cards with the implant that record:

- the device name (including identification information)
- the name and address of the healthcare professional who performed the implant procedure
- the date on which the device was implanted
- the facility at which it was implanted
- patient contact information

The *Controlled Drugs and Substances Act*

Controlled drugs are categorized by the federal government as having a higher-than-average potential for abuse or addiction. Canada is a signatory to many international agreements relevant to controlled drugs, for example the *UN Single Convention on Narcotic Drugs* (1961) and the *UN Convention on Psychotropic Substances* (1971). Canadian legislation has been developed in accordance with these conventions. Controlled drugs are regulated by the *Controlled Drugs and Substances Act* and Part G and J of the *F&DA* discussed above.

The *Controlled Drugs and Substances Act* is organized in six divisions: Part I: Offenses and Punishment, Part II: Enforcement, Part III: Disposal of Controlled Substances, Part IV: Administration and Compliance, Part V: Designated Regulations and Part VI: General.

A "controlled substance" is defined as any substance included in the accompanying Schedules I, II, III, IV, V or VI. Furthermore, references to controlled substances include all synthetic and natural forms of the substance, and anything that contains or has in it a controlled substance and is intended to produce a controlled substance

or introduce it into the body. Controlled substances are assigned to the six schedules in the act:

- Schedule I—opium, codeine, morphine, cocaine and other substances
- Schedule II—cannabis resin, cannabis (marihuana), cannabidiol, nonviable cannabis seed and other substances related to cannabis
- Schedule III—amphetamines, methylphenidate, lysergic acid diethylamide (LSD), flunitrazepam, gamma-hydroxyl-butyrate (commonly known as GHB) and other substances
- Schedule IV—barbiturates, thiobarbiturates, chlorphentermine, bromazepam and other benzodiazepines and other substances
- Schedule V—phenylpropanolamine, propylhexedrine and pyrovalerone
- Schedule VI—benzyl methyl ketone, ephedrine, ergometrine, ergotamine, LSD and pseudoephedrine

The legislation goes on to lay out the law regarding possession, trafficking in, importing or producing the substances outlined in the schedules.

The *Narcotic Control Regulations*

The *Narcotic Control Regulations* are enacted pursuant to the *Controlled Drugs and Substances Act.* The regulations concern narcotics listed in an accompanying schedule such as opium, cocaine and phenylpiperidines.

Narcotics may, in certain circumstances, be prescribed as drugs. As with controlled drugs, narcotic drug manufacturers must be licensed dealers with an annual licence; imports and exports require a permit; and recordkeeping requirements are significant. *The Narcotic Control Regulations* also describe how narcotics must be packaged (a seal must be broken to open it) and how they must be transported (signatures are required and the method of transport must discourage theft). Narcotic drugs must have a capital "N" in a circle on the label.

Benzodiazepines and Other Targeted Substances Regulations

These regulations are also enacted under the *Controlled Drugs and Substances Act.* A list of targeted substances is provided in the schedule accompanying the regulations.

The regulations apply to benzodiazepines and some similar compounds. Manufacturers must be licensed dealers; import and export requires a permit; and recordkeeping requirements are significant. The difference between targeted substances and controlled or narcotic drugs is that visitors to Canada may import targeted substances for their own use from another country, but not controlled or narcotic drugs. Target substances must have a "T/M" following symbol on the label.

Table 29-3. Drug Evaluation Fees, by Submission Component

	Submission Component	Submission Type	Fee $CAN
1	Preclinical and clinical data to support a single route of administration, dosage form and condition of use.	NDS	117,000
2	Clinical data without preclinical data, or clinical data with supplementary or confirmatory preclinical data, to support a single or additional route of administration, dosage form or condition of use.	NDS, SNDS, DIN	52,900
3	Comparative (bioavailability, pharmacodynamic or clinical) data to support a single or additional route of administration or dosage form.	All types	17,200
4	Comparative (bioavailability, pharmacodynamic or clinical) data required to support each additional strength.	NDS, SNDS, ANDS, S/ANDS	2,700
5	Information and material to support: a) The removal of a drug from Schedule F to the *Food and Drug Regulations* (switch from Rx to over-the-counter). b) A new condition of use.	SNDS	52,900
6	Information and material to support the removal of a drug from Schedule F to the *Food and Drug Regulations*, same condition of use (switch from Rx to over-the-counter).	SNDS, ANDS	17,200
7	Published clinical references or other published data.	All types	2,200
8	Chemistry and manufacturing data for the medicinal ingredient of a drug (drug substance).	NDS, SNDS, ANDS, S/ANDS	11,500
9	Chemistry and manufacturing data to support a single dosage form (drug product).	NDS, SNDS, ANDS, S/ANDS	15,300
10	Chemistry and manufacturing data.	DIN	11,500
11	Published references to support a traditional herbal medicine.*	DIN	720
12	Information to support an application for a DIN.	DIN	720
13	Information establishing that a drug meets the requirements of a class monograph.	DIN	310

As of January 2004, this type of submission is replaced with a Natural Product Number submission under the Natural Health Products Regulations. To date, there have been no submission fees for NHP application submissions.

Financial Acts and Regulations

A selection of legislation is provided below concerning the cost of matters at issue in a regulatory practice. For instance, Health Canada participates in a federal government policy initiative referred to as "cost recovery." Cost recovery refers to the act of charging a fee for a qualifying government service to those who receive the service or benefit from it. Before fixing, establishing or increasing such external fees, however, Health Canada is required to consult stakeholders, determine that fees are comparable to those established in other relevant countries, establish an independent advisory panel and table a user fee proposal.

Regulations enabling government departments to participate in cost recovery are enacted pursuant to Section 19(1) of the *Financial Administration Act.* The regulations allowing Health Canada to participate in cost recovery initiatives are discussed below.

The *Drug Evaluation Fees Regulations*

These regulations, enacted pursuant to the *Financial Administration Act,* identify the fees for the components of a drug submission. **Table 29-3** is a guide for the type of

fee currently charged for different submission components (all amounts are in Canadian dollars). Current guidance documents should always be referenced immediately prior to submitting a fee.

Establishment Licence Fees Regulations and the Licensed Dealers for Controlled Drugs and Narcotics Fees Regulations

These regulations provide the fees for Establishment Licences and generally build the fee on three components: GMP inspection, laboratory analysis and controlled substances inspection.

In general, the fee increments follow the cumulative cost of the additional scope or type of activity required for different situations. The component basis for the fee schedule—which differentiates activities, categories of drugs and dosage form classes—is designed to allow a wide range of fees to accommodate the different types of firms that are subject to the licensing framework.

The laboratory analysis fee is proportional to the product analysis cost for different drug categories averaged across all firms dealing in that drug category. Different product classes (e.g., vaccines, prescription drugs) are charged varying fees in recognition of their relative risk and the resulting frequency of laboratory surveillance.

The licence fee's controlled substances component reflects the incremental cost of inspecting a site that handles controlled drugs, narcotics or both, and which, therefore, will require additional inspection time to assess security and recordkeeping practices.

Fees are based upon annual renewal. Amendments to the licence, for example, to change the type of activity or add a new drug category, will result in additional fees consistent with the additional activity required.

Drug Master File Fee Regulations

A Drug Master File (DMF) is a reference that provides drug evaluators confidential information not available to drug product manufacturers (sponsors) about the specific processes and components used in the manufacturing, processing and packaging of a drug. The DMF registration fee is $350. The fee for processing a Letter of Access is $50. These fees are based upon estimates of administrative costs, including overhead.

Authority to Sell Drugs Fees Regulations

Each year, drug manufacturers are required to complete forms confirming that the drugs continuing to be sold in Canada conform to the basic information on file at Health Canada. Associated with the completion of these forms are annual product fees, which apply to drugs that have been assigned a DIN.

Fees in Respect of the Medical Devices Regulations

Fees are charged for annual Medical Device Licences for Classes II to IV, and for MDELs. There is a provision for fee reduction based upon expected or actual sales volume.

Patented Medicines
The Patented Medicines (Notice of Compliance) Regulations

These regulations require Health Canada to maintain a "Patent Register." The Patent Register lists the patents associated with a drug for which a Notice of Compliance has been issued, if the applicant has provided that information to Health Canada with its New Drug Submission (NDS). As part of the submission filing process, the applicant requests that given patents be added to the patent list when the Notice of Compliance is issued. If a patent issues after the NDS has been filed (provided that the patent was applied for at the time of the NDS), there is a 30-day window to file the patent information.

Generic drug manufacturers agree that the Notice of Compliance will issue after the patent expires, or claim that the information on the patent list is wrong (in that there

is no patent, that the patent has expired, that the patent is not valid or that no claim for the medicine or its use is made). A generic product manufacturer must give reasons for its assessment if it claims that the patent list information is wrong, and prove that it has served notice on the person or company for whom the patent is listed.

The innovator, after receiving notice, has 45 days to apply for an order prohibiting a Notice of Compliance until after the patent's expiration. Health Canada then cannot issue the Notice of Compliance until the issue is dismissed from court, the patent expires, or 24 months elapse from the time the innovator applies for the order to prevent the Notice of Compliance from issuing.

Patented Medicines

Sections 79–103 of the *Patent Act* address patented medicines. These sections define a Patented Medicine Prices Review Board (PMPRB) and stipulate that a patentee (patent owner or licensee) must file pricing and research information with the board. The *Patent Act* also specifies that the board will determine whether the price is excessive and, if so, it can direct that the price be reduced. To offset any excessive revenues, the board can also: reduce the drug's price below what is excessive for a certain time; reduce the price of another drug of the company; or require that the company pay a penalty (which can be as much as twice the excessive revenues). In determining whether a price is excessive, the board considers the following:

- the price at which the medicine was sold in the relevant market
- the price of other medicines in the same therapeutic class in the relevant market
- the price of the medicine and other medicines in the same therapeutic class in countries other than Canada
- changes in the Consumer Price Index (published by Statistics Canada)
- drug manufacturing and marketing costs

The board is not permitted to consider the drug's research and development costs. If a price is thought to be excessive, the board may hold a hearing, which is usually public.

The patentee is required to file sales information with the board every six months and information on research and development expenditures every 12 months. Each year, the board must submit a report to the minister of health reporting the amount of money spent on research and development, the percentage of sales each company spent on research and development and a pricing information analysis. The report is given to the House of Commons and the Senate.

The Patented Medicines Regulations

These regulations specify how companies file the pricing

and research and development information. The regulations also identify the countries to which prices will be compared as France, Germany, Italy, Sweden, Switzerland, the UK and the US. For the purposes of these regulations, drugs are divided into the following three categories:

- Category 1: New Drugs—Line Extensions: For these drugs, the price is excessive if it does not bear a reasonable relationship to the average price of other DINs of the same medicine in the same or comparable dosage forms.
- Category 2: New Drugs—Breakthrough or Substantial Improvement: For these drugs, the price is excessive if it exceeds the therapeutic class comparison test and the median of the international price comparison test.
- Category 3: New Drugs—"Me Too" or Small Improvement: For these drugs, the price is excessive if it exceeds the therapeutic class comparison.

Prices can be increased each year by the same percentage as the Consumer Price Index. The price in Canada cannot be higher than the price of the same medication in the seven selected countries.

When an excessive price investigation is underway, a company can opt to take a voluntary compliance undertaking (VCU). Only the company's chairman can approve a VCU. The VCU must say what price will be charged and for how long. Also, if money needs to go back to consumers, the VCU must outline how much and when. The VCU is not an admission of guilt. VCUs are made public.

In determining the therapeutic price comparison, it is very important to make the right comparison for the comparative drug, indication and dosage. Companies prepare submissions to the PMPRB to present their view of what this selection should be. Companies also make submissions to have a drug classified as a Category 2 drug (i.e., breakthrough or substantial improvement).

Access to Information
Access to Information Act
Under the *Access to Information (ATI) Act*, every Canadian citizen and resident has the right to be provided with any record under the control of a government institution. A request for access to a record must be made in writing to the government institution controlling the record. When a request is received, the government is required to advise the person within 30 days whether the record can be released. If it can be released, the record should be provided within this time period. The time limit can be extended if there are a lot of records or a consultation is necessary, in which case the requester is notified. If the extension is more than 30 days, the information commissioner is also notified.

A fee of not more than $25 is paid when the request

is filed. Additional charges may be made for excessive copying.

Certain information is exempted from this legislation, such as information provided in confidence from a government or anything that might affect international affairs or defence. Also exempted are trade secrets of a third party that might result in material or financial loss or interfere with a contractual relationship. If the government intends to release third-party information, it will notify the third party, which can file an objection within 20 days.

Summary
- The *F&DA* and *FDR* govern the sale, advertisement and labelling of all foods, drugs, cosmetics and medical devices sold in Canada.
- The advertising of a food, drug, cosmetic or device to the general public as a treatment, preventative or cure for any of the diseases, disorders or abnormal physical states listed in Schedule A is prohibited.
- If a drug is not a Canadian standard drug and is not listed in a publication to Schedule B, it must meet the "professed" (labelled) standard.
- The sale of any drug described in Schedule C or D is restricted unless the minister has indicated that the premises in which the drug was manufactured and the process and conditions of manufacture are suitable to ensure that the drug will not be unsafe for use.
- All references to drugs in the *F&DA* also apply to natural health products and biologics.
- Manufacturers are prohibited from selling natural health products until a product licence has issued. Due to backlogs, a product licence application is sufficient to sell as published in the *Natural Health Products (Unprocessed Product Licence Applications) Regulations*.
- The *Medical Devices Regulations* specify four classes of medical devices, where Class I represents the lowest risk and Class IV represents the highest risk.
- A "controlled substance" is defined as any substance included in Schedules I, II, III, IV, V or VI of the *Controlled Drugs and Substances Act*.

Canadian Medical Device Classification and Submissions

By Laila Gurney, MSc, RAC

OBJECTIVES

❏ Understand the risk-based classification system and classification rules for medical devices and IVDDs

❏ Review the six different types of medical device applications

❏ Review medical device submissions requirements (Class II, III and IV and Private Label applications)

❏ Review medical device licence amendments

REGULATIONS AND GUIDELINES COVERED IN THIS CHAPTER

❏ *Medical Devices Regulations (MDR)*

❏ *Guidance for the Interpretation of Sections 28 to 31: Licence Application Type (GD002)* (January 1999)

❏ *Draft Guidance for the Risk-Based Classification System of In Vitro Diagnostic Devices (GD007)* (March 1998)

❏ *Preparation of a Premarket Review Document for Class III and IV Device Licence Applications (GD008)* (October 1998)

❏ *Preparation of an Application for Investigational Testing—In Vitro Diagnostic Devices (GD010)* (February 1999)

❏ *Guidance on How to Complete the Application for a New Device Licence (GD013)* (May 2008)

❏ *Guidance Document GD207: Guidance on the Content of ISO 13485 Quality Management System Certificates Issued by Health Canada Recognized Registrars* (November 2007)

❏ *Keyword Index to Assist Manufacturers in Verifying the Class of Medical Devices* (September 2006)

❏ *Draft Guidance—Keyword Index to Assist Manufacturers in Verifying the Class of In Vitro Diagnostic Devices (IVDD)* (September 2009)

❏ *Guidance Document: Recognition and Use of Standards under the Medical Devices Regulations* and the associated *List of Recognized Standards* (Revised September 2006)

❏ *Guidance for Industry: Guidance on the Regulation of Medical Devices Manufactured from or Incorporating Viable or Non-viable Animal Tissue or their Derivative(s)* (July 2004)

❏ *Guidance for Industry: Guidance for the Interpretation of Significant Change of a Medical Device* (January 2011)

❏ *Guidance Document: "Fees for the Review of Medical Device Licence Applications* (April 2011)

❑ *Guidance Document: How to Pay Fees* (February 2011)

Introduction

Medical devices are regulated by Health Canada under the *Food and Drugs Act* (*F&DA*) and the *Medical Devices Regulations* (*MDR*). The *MDR* were promulgated in 1998 and apply to the sale, advertising for sale and importation for sale or for use on individuals (other than for personal use) of a medical device or in vitro diagnostic device (IVDD).

This chapter reviews Health Canada's risk-based classification system and details the steps involved in device licensing .

Risk-based Classification

Medical devices are classified into four classes (Class I–IV) according to their potential risk, where Class I represents the lowest risk and Class IV represents the highest risk. If a medical device can be classified into more than one class, the class representing the higher risk applies.

There are four tools to assist in assessing device classification:

1. the risk-based classification system set out in Schedule 1 of the *MDR*
2. the *Keyword Index to Assist Manufacturers in Verifying the Class of Medical Devices* (*Keyword Index*)
3. the Medical Devices Licence Listing (Licence Listing)
4. the Medical Devices Bureau

It is best to begin with application of the risk-based classification system set out in the *MDR*. Part 1 of the Schedule contains rules for non-IVDD medical devices, while Part 2 contains the rules for IVDDs. The steps to be considered are discussed in more detail below.

Although not binding on the Medical Devices Bureau, the *Keyword Index* and the Licence Listing can help in determining proper classification. Both the *Keyword Index* and the Licence Listing can be searched for similar products to see how they have been classified in the past.

Please note that Health Canada is working on a keyword index for IVDDs. This document has not yet been finalized.

Non-IVDD Medical Device Risk Classification

Criteria used to determine risk class are:
- degree of invasiveness
- duration of patient contact
- affected body system
- local versus systemic effects
- energy transmission hazard
- consequences of device malfunction or failure

Classification rules set out in the *MDR* for non-IVDD medical devices are divided into four groups:

1. invasive devices are covered in rules 1–3
2. noninvasive devices are covered in rules 4–7
3. active devices are covered in rules 8–12
4. Special Rules are rules 13–16

The first step in determining the risk classification of a device is to check the Special Rules (rules 13–16). If the device in question is not described by one of these special rules, the manufacturer shall determine whether the device is invasive, noninvasive or active. Rules under all applicable categories should be reviewed and the final classification should be determined by the rule that assigns the highest risk. For example, if a device is both noninvasive and active, then rules 4–7 and 8–12 should be reviewed and the classification should be assigned based on the rule that provides the highest class. It is important to note that it is the device's intended use that ultimately determines its classification.

IVDD Risk Classification

Criteria used to determine the risk class of an IVDD include:
- its intended use and indication(s) for use (the specific disorder, condition or risk factor for which the test is intended)
- its application (screening, patient-based testing/diagnosis, monitoring, etc.)
- the technical, scientific or medical expertise of the intended user (testing laboratories vs. near-patient testing)
- the importance of the information to the diagnosis (sole determinant or one of several)

The classification of an IVDD is largely dependent upon the information provided about its intended use and indications for use. These may be derived from any part of the labelling. In cases of ambiguous labelling, the higher risk class will apply.

The classification rules set out in the *MDR* for IVDDs are grouped as follows:

1. Classification of IVDDs for use with respect to transmissible agents—Rules 1–3 apply to IVDDs used to gain information about the disease status or immune status of individuals with respect to transmissible agents.
2. Classification of IVDDs for uses other than for transmissible agents—Rule 4 applies to IVDDs that are intended to establish disease status or for patient management purposes. Rule 5 applies to IVDDs that are used for blood grouping or tissue typing.
3. Rules 6–9 (Special Rules) were developed to address specific issues related to IVDDs, such as the IVDDs used outside central laboratories.

Table 30-1. Types of Medical Device Licence Applications

Option	Applicability	Device Name	Manufacturer	Additional Requirements
System	Components intended to be used together to fulfill some or all of the device's intended function	Sold under a single name (the name of the system must appear on each component)	All components produced by the manufacturer of the system are licensed together.	Components not sold under the system name cannot be licensed with the system. Component made by another manufacturer must be licensed separately.
Medical Device Family	Group of medical devices that differ only in shape, colour, flavour or size, that have the same design, manufacturing process and intended use	The device name must appear at least in part on the label of each of the member devices.	Each component has to be made by the same manufacturer	Materials, labelling, manufacturing processes, design and performance specifications cannot be significantly different Individual device names may contain an additional descriptive phrase.
Medical Device Group	A collection of medical devices, such as a procedure pack or tray	Labelled and sold under a single name	Not required to have the same manufacturer or to be labelled with the name of the group	Devices deemed to be licensed in a medical device group cannot be sold outside the group without a single medical device license. Bulk items may be repackaged without labelling for inclusion in the group.
Medical Device Group Family	A collection of medical device groups that are made by the same manufacturer, have the same generic name specifying their intended use, and differ only in the number and combination of products that comprise each group	The device name indicated for the medical device group family must appear, at least in part, on the label of each of the member devices; individual device names may contain additional descriptive phrases.	Must be made by the same manufacturer	Licensing the groups as a family allows the manufacturer to customize medical device groups for particular hospitals or physicians, while maintaining the same generic name and intended use.
Single Medical Device	Single device	Identified with a unique name	Sold as a distinct packaged entity	Medical devices, parts or components, that cannot be assigned to a system, a test kit, a medical device family, a medical device group or a medical device group family must be licensed individually. These include components that are not made by the manufacturer of the devices or systems with which they are connected. Medical devices that are sold outside the system, group or group family must have a single medical device licence.
Test Kits	Applicable to IVDDs only Reagents or articles used together to conduct a specific test	Device names and identifiers of all constituents of the test kit must be listed on the application.	All reagents or articles produced by the same manufacturer	The kit does not include the instrumentation, such as the analyzer. Reagents and articles can be sold separately as replacement items for the kit.

Table 30-2. Required Licence Application Information

Item	Description
1. Name of the Device	As it appears on the product label. Device name indicated for a system, medical device family or medical device group family must appear, at least in part, on the label of each of the member devices. Only one name can be entered here.
2. Manufacturer Information	The name and complete mailing address of the manufacturer. In addition, provide the name, title and contact information of the manufacturer's contact person. NOTE: The name and address of manufacturer on the licence application should be the same as that on the label and on the ISO 13485:2003 QMS certificate issued from a CMDCAS recognized registrar.
3. Regulatory Correspondent Information	If a third party is preparing and submitting the MDL application and liaising on the manufacturer's behalf with the Medical Devices Bureau, then provide contact information of the regulatory person at the third party. If the manufacturer is submitting the MDL application on its own behalf, indicate "Not Applicable" in this section.
4. Invoicing Information	Check the appropriate box and provide information, if necessary.
5. Quality Management Certificate	Provide the ISO 13485:2003 (as amended from time to time) certificate number for the manufacturer as well as the name of the CMDCAS-recognized registrar. Ensure that a copy of the QMS certificate is included in the submission.
6. Attestations	Before checking each attestation, review the applicable documents to ensure that they comply with the *MDR* and that a truthful attestation is being made. The attestation section must be signed by a senior official of the manufacturer.
7. Purpose/ Intended Use	This information is used to verify that the device is properly classified by the manufacturer. Failure to supply an appropriate level of detail may result in the application being rejected. The Intended Use Statement must include the following information: • Intended purpose, indications for use and conditions for which the device is used • Patient population for which the device is intended (including age range, if applicable, and specific diagnoses) • Anatomical and physiological particulars related to the device, if applicable • Whether or not the device uses an energy source and/or energy is transferred to the patient.
8. Licence Application Type	Select the proper licence application type: Single Medical Device, Medical Device Family, Medical Device Group, Medical Device Group Family or System.
9. Place of Use	Respond to questions about home use and IVDD. If device is an IVDD, indicate whether it is used at point of care.
10. Medical Devices Containing Drugs	The section, as it stands now, will require the manufacturer to provide a Drug Identification Number (DIN) or a Natural Product Number (NPN) for devices containing drugs, as applicable. If the drug does not have a DIN or NPN, the manufacturer is required to provide a Drug Establishment Licence number (DEL). For IVDD test kits containing Controlled Substances (listed in Schedules I–IV of the *Controlled Drugs Substances Act*), a test kit number must be provided.
11. Device History	If the subject device has been subject to an Investigational Testing Authorization or Special Access, answer YES to the question and provide the applicable authorization or identification number.

As with non-IVDD medical devices, the first step for determining the risk class of IVDDs is to check the Special Rules (rules 6–9). If these do not apply, all applicable rules in the other categories should be reviewed and the rule that results in the highest classification should be used to classify the device.

For more information about the licensing of IVDDs, see Chapter 34.

Medical Device Application Type

The *MDR* describes six options for a medical device, including its components, to be deemed to be licensed following a single successful application. These options are:
- a System
- a Medical Device Family
- a Medical Device Group
- a Medical Device Group Family
- a Single Medical Device
- Test Kits (applicable only to IVDDs)

Health Canada provides six application types for licensing medical devices (**Table 30-1**). The application type should be determined based upon the marketing strategy before an application is submitted to Health Canada.

For example, a device that has multiple components may be licensed together or separately. An ultrasound system that has optional transducers and software could be licensed by the manufacturer as a System, or the main unit could be licensed as a Group and the transducers and software as a Family.

Medical Device Submissions

Under the *MDR*, no person shall import or sell a Class

Table 30-2. Required Licence Application Information Continued

Item	Description
12. Identifier of the Device	Only devices, components, parts and accessories and product codes (model, catalogue numbers and identifiers) listed on the application will be considered for licensing. Spare parts that do not represent medical devices themselves should not be listed. **Ensure that this list is accurate and complete**. Refer to Table 1 for instructions on how to provide device details for each device type. **Table 1. Completing Section 12 of Device Licence Application Forms.** **Name of Device, Components, Parts and/or Accessories as per Product Label** **Identifier for device (bar code, catalogue, model or part number)** **Device contains ≥ 0.1% w/w of DEHP (check if applicable)** **Device is manufactured from raw materials containing or derived from BPA** **Preferred Name Code** **(For HC use Only)** Single Device: enter name of device here Medical Device Group, Medical Device Family or Medical Device Group Family à enter names of constituent members System: name of System and components Provide identifiers for each of the entries in the first column. **NOTE:** According to Section 21 of the *Medical Devices Regulations*, the device identifier must appear on the device label. As such, ensure that the identifier provided under "model or catalogue number" in the above table, matches the identifier that appears on the product label. For System applications, for each of the entries in the first column, make the calculation based on the following criteria: • If the part is assembled in the finished device then the % mass is calculated using the mass of the finished device • If the part is not assembled in the finished device (infusion set or disposable tubing for example) then the % mass should be calculated based on the part alone. For a single device, device family, device group or device group family, the DEHP calculation is made based on the mass of the member device, identified in the first column. Place a check mark if the calculation results in ≥ 0.1% w/w DEHP; otherwise, leave blank. This section only applies to the entries in the first column that <u>contact the patient or patient fluids</u>. For the applicable entries, if raw materials used in the construction of the devices/components contain or are derived from Bisphenol A (BPA), place a check mark here; otherwise, leave blank. Leave blank.
13. Compatibility of Interdependent Devices	If the subject device is intended to be used with another previously licensed device by the same manufacturer, the name and licence number of the compatible device must be provided here. For compatible devices manufactured by other manufacturers, only those intended to be used (according to labelling of subject device) with subject device must be included here. **NOTE:** Devices listed in this section are already licensed separately from the subject device.
14. List of Recognized Standards Complied with in the Manufacture of the Device	Attest that the device conforms to applicable standards recognized by Health Canada (list at: http://www.hc-sc.gc.ca/dhp-mps/md-im/standards-normes/md_rec_stand_im_norm_lst_2_e.html) and provide list of applicable standards OR Attest that the manufacturer has objective evidence that the device meets an equivalent or better standard or alternate evidence of safety and effectiveness exists.
Fees	Fee calculations must be made as part of the application forms and a cheque in Canadian funds must be issued to **The Receiver General for Canada** from a **Canadian bank** for payment. Application Fees are detailed in the document *Fees For The Review of Medical Device Licence Applications*.
Authority to Disclose	The last page of the application form requires the submitter to declare whether or not he or she consents to having information regarding timing of submission provided to third parties.

II, III or IV medical device unless the device's manufacturer holds a licence or, if the medical device has been subjected to a change requiring a licence amendment, an amended device licence.

The manufacturer of a Class I medical device must hold a Medical Device Establishment license (MDEL) unless it imports or distributes solely through the holder of a MDEL (such as an importer or distributor).

In addition, manufacturers of Class II, III and IV medical devices are required to have a Quality Management System (QMS) that is certified to ISO 13485:2003 by a Canadian Medical Devices Conformity Assessment System (CMDCAS)-recognized registrar. Class II devices should be manufactured under a QMS that is certified to this standard, while Class III and IV devices should be designed and manufactured under a QMS that is certified to this standard. In addition to compliance with the ISO standard, the requirements of the *MDR* should be included in the QMS. For more information, please see Chapter 33.

A manufacturer or importer of Class II, III or IV devices may sell a medical device to a qualified investigator for investigational testing involving human subjects if the manufacturer or importer holds an investigational testing authorization. For a Class I medical device, the manufacturer has to maintain records and be prepared to provide them to Health Canada if requested.

Class III or IV custom-made devices or medical devices for special access cannot be sold or imported unless an authorization has been issued by the Medical Devices Bureau.

Who needs to apply for a device licence?

Manufacturers of Class II, III and IV medical devices are required to have a valid medical device licence (MDL) for these devices, issued by Health Canada prior to importing or selling them in Canada.

The manufacturer (as defined in the *MDR*) may submit the MDL application on its own or elect a third party (such as an importer or distributor) to do so on its behalf. If the submission responsibility is delegated, the delegate will be contacted regarding any additional information and will also receive the MDL, but the MDL will be issued in the manufacturer's name (i.e., manufacturer will be the owner of the MDL).

When is a medical device licence required?

The manufacturer of a Class II, III or IV medical device is required to apply for an MDL under the following circumstances:

1. The medical device is new and has not been previously licensed in Canada.
2. A licensed medical device has undergone a change and the change requires the licence to be amended.

Submission Content

Health Canada will release a guidance document in 2011 or 2012 that will require submissions to be provided in Standard Technical Document (STED) format. The reader should refer to that guidance document when published. This section provides guidance on submission requirements per Health Canada's current guidance document: *Preparation of a Premarket Review Document for Class III and Class IV Device Licence Applications* (GD008). It also covers content requirements for Class II applications.

Application Forms

A class-specific Health Canada application form must be completed for all MDL applications. Regardless of the class of the device, information is required on the common elements in **Table 30-2.**

Format of Submissions

It is recommended that documents be printed on 8.5" x 11" paper, be three-hole punched and placed in a three-ring binder, and a cover label be printed and applied to the binder. Only one hard copy is submitted to Health Canada. The entire submission should also be provided on CD, together with the hard copy.

All submissions must include the following elements:
- Cover letter—A brief letter describing the reason for the application (device name, risk class, device type and nature of submission: new MDL application or amendment). For device licence amendments, include MDL number to be amended.
- Class-specific application form
- Table of contents
- Labelling
- Manufacturer's ISO 13485:2003 QMS Certificate issued by a CMDCAS-recognized registrar. The QMS certificate must adhere to the following (see Health Canada *Guidance Document, GD207: Guidance on the content of ISO 13485 Quality Management System Certificates issued by Health Canada recognized Registrars*):
  o Scope should be clear and cover activities related to the device being submitted in the MDL application.
  o Name and address of manufacturer (same as the name and address of the manufacturer on the MDL application).
  o Certificate is valid and active (not expired).
  o Certificate is issued by a CMDCAS-recognized registrar.
  o CMDCAS or Canadian Medical Devices Conformity Assessment registrar appears on the certificate.
  o Standards Council of Canada (SCC) logo is present on the certificate.

Table 30-3. Class III Submission Structure

Cover Letter
Complete Application Form for Class III
Executive Summary
Table of Contents
1.   Background Information
       1.1 Device Description
       1.2 Design Philosophy
       1.3 Marketing History
2.   Summary of Safety and Effectiveness Studies
       2.1 List of Standards
       2.2 Methods of Sterilization
       2.3 Summary of Studies (can break this down into
             subsections)
       2.4 Bibliography
3.   Labelling
4.   Near Patient IVDD
5.   QMS Certificate
6.   Payment

   o   The correct standard is listed: ISO 13485:2003.
 • Payment of required fees. For more information
   refer to the Health Canada Documents "How to
   Pay Fees", and "Fees for the Review of Medical
   Device Licence Applications."

New Applications
Class II
   The Class II application form (www.hc-sc.gc.ca/
dhp-mps/md-im/applic-demande/form/licapp_demhom_
cla2-eng.php) must be completed as described above.

   The Class II application package contains only the
elements described in the section called "Format of
Submissions."

   Please note that although the *MDR* requires submission of labelling only for Class III and IV devices, Health
Canada sometimes asks for labelling to be submitted for
Class II device applications. As such, submission of labelling with Class II applications will expedite review and
avoid clock stops.

Class III
   The Class III application form (www.hc-sc.gc.ca/
dhp-mps/md-im/applic-demande/form/licapp_demhom_
cla3-eng.php) must be completed as described above. A Class
III submission should be structured as shown in **Table 30-3**.

   Items in **Table 30-3** not described under Format of
Submissions are detailed below:

Executive Summary
   Include a summary of the information to be found in
the submission with reference to the specific sections.

Background Information
 • Device Description—general description/list of
   components
   o   Indications for use
   o   General description of the device, including
       functional components—refer to labelled
       photographs, diagrams and/or drawings in this
       description.
   o   If applicable, provide a tabular comparison of
       the device with the previously licensed version
       ("predicate"). Include a reason why the changes
       were made and if they provide an advantage
       over the previous version.
   o   If applicable, briefly describe the modifications
       (comparison to predicate) made to the subject
       device, outline new features and describe
       features that are the same as those of the
       predicate device.
   o   Components, accessories and materials:
           Provide a complete list of components and
           accessories and identify those that can be
           sold separately and used with other medical
           devices, systems or units.
           Identify variants/configurations/options of
           device and their parameters/specifications.
           Identify and describe materials used in
           construction and packaging, and indicate
           whether they come into contact with the
           user or patient (reference and include in an
           appendix, biocompatibility information on
           materials that come into contact with user
           or patient).
 • Design Philosophy—describe features that allow
   the device to function as intended
   o   Overview of purposes and principles of
       operation and summary of method of use and
       operation of the device. Please note that product
       data sheets may be provided in this section for
       this purpose.
 • Marketing History—provide a summary of the
   marketing history of the device
   o   Special Access—if applicable, provide details; or
       state that it is not applicable
   o   Countries where product is sold—in tabular
       format, list by country and indicate number of
       devices sold to date
   o   Summary of reported problems, number
       reported and corrective action (e.g.,
       modifications to device)
   o   Summary of recalls and corrective actions as a
       result of a recall in countries where product has
       been sold to date

If referencing aspects of safety and effectiveness of a

predicate device, a marketing history for the predicate device should also be provided.

Summary of Safety and Effectiveness Studies

- List of Standards—A list of national or international standards complied with, in whole or in part, in the design and manufacture of the device must be provided. The Health Canada Declaration of Conformity Form should be used for this purpose.
- Health Canada publishes a list of recognized standards at: www.hc-sc.gc.ca/dhp-mps/md-im/ standards-normes/md_rec_stand_im_norm_ lst_2_e.html. If Health Canada ceases to recognize a standard or a version of a standard, conformance to it will no longer be acceptable for new MDL applications or amendments.
  - o Declaration of Conformity—If demonstrating conformance with the safety and effectiveness requirements by using recognized standards, a Declaration of Conformity[1] to the standards must be provided (www.hc-sc.gc.ca/dhp-mps/ md-im/applic-demande/form/md_doc_im_ ddc_form_e.html).
- Method of Sterilization—If the device is sold in sterile condition, provide a description of the sterilization and packaging methods used to maintain sterility. Include the sterilization process, level of sterility assurance and an attestation that the process has been properly validated. If not applicable, include this section but state that it is not applicable. Keep reports of sterility verification and validation process on record.
- Summary of Studies—Summarize how requirements of Sections 10–20 of the *MDR* have been met.
- Provide summary reports of documents required to show proof of safety and effectiveness. These may include: risk management, summary of design controls, system/design validation and verification, software validation and verification, clinical data, etc., as applicable.
- If certain aspects of safety and effectiveness cannot be demonstrated by recognized standards, data from other sources such as clinical testing, published reports or abstracts on the device must be provided. References from this section should be included in chronological order in the bibliography section of the submission.
- If safety and effectiveness are established by declaring conformity to standards that have unique pass/fail criteria, it is not required to submit summary reports of the results of these studies. The Declaration of Conformity is sufficient. If, however, a recognized standard describes a test

method but does not specify a unique pass and/ or fail criterion, supporting evidence for how this criterion was established and results of tests must be submitted as proof of safety and effectiveness.

- Software Studies—If the device contains or consists of software, as part of evidence for Section 20 of the *MDR*, the final software version number should be provided along with a description of software design and development, functional requirements, specifications, design safeguards, error checks and controls, verification and validation protocols, reports and results. Review the summary report to ensure that all criteria against which the software was tested have been met. If there are failures, an explanation should be provided as to why the failure does not affect the device's safety and effectiveness. The summary report must have a conclusion stating that the software meets all required specifications for safety and effectiveness and can therefore be released. This is also applicable to design and system validation and verification reports.
- If providing evidence of safety and effectiveness by submitting clinical data, published reports or abstracts, include the references in this section in chronological order. If this is not applicable state: "No published reports regarding the use of "Device Name" are available. Please refer to the safety and effectiveness and marketing history regarding "Device Name," respectively, for proof of safety and effectiveness."

Near-patient In Vitro Diagnostic Device

A near-patient IVDD is a device intended to be used outside a laboratory environment for home testing or point-of-care testing, such as in a pharmacy, a healthcare professional's office or at the bedside.

The manufacturer must provide a summary of investigational tests conducted on the near-patient IVDD, simulating expected conditions of use. For these tests, people representative of the intended users must follow the instructions provided in the labelling, without assistance. The application must include identification of test sites, description of the users and testing algorithm and provide a summary of the results.

Class IV

The Class IV application form (www.hc-sc.gc.ca/ dhp-mps/md-im/applic-demande/form/licapp_demhom_ cla4-eng.php, must be completed as described above.

A Class IV submission should be structured as shown in **Table 30-4**.

Please note that the difference between Class III and IV applications is that summaries of studies are provided

Table 30-4. Class IV Submission Structure

Cover Letter

Complete Application Form for Class IV

Executive Summary

Table of Contents

1.   Background Information

    1.1 Device Description

    1.2 Design Philosophy

    1.3 Marketing History

2.   Risk Assessment

3.   Quality Plan

4.   Device Specific Detailed Information

    4.1 Material Specifications

    4.2 Manufacturing Process Specifications

        4.2.1 Method of Manufacture

        4.2.2 Quality Control Activities

    4.3 List of Standards

5.   Summary of Safety and Effectiveness Studies

    5.1 Preclinical and Clinical Studies

    5.2 Process Validation Studies

    5.3 Software Studies

    5.4 Literature Studies

6.   Devices Containing Biological Material

7.   Labelling

8.   QMS Certificate

9.   Payment

for Class III devices, while full data sets and summaries are required for Class IV device applications.

Items unique to Class IV submissions are described below.

Risk Assessment as per ISO 14971

In this section, the manufacturer must provide an analysis and evaluation of the risks inherent in the use of the device, as well as measures taken to reduce risk to satisfy safety and effectiveness requirements of the *MDR*.

Note: the risk assessment report must include the identity of the person(s) or organization that carried out the risk analysis, and the method of risk analysis must be appropriate for the subject device and the level of risk involved.

Quality Plan as Described in ISO 10005

The manufacturer must provide a quality plan that specifies the quality practices, resources and sequence of activities relevant to the device. The quality plan provides a mechanism to ensure that specific requirements for the product are tied back to existing quality system processes and procedures. The manufacturer may provide a diagram to show how the quality system requirements will be met.

Device-Specific Detailed Information

- Material Specifications—For this part of the application, all components of the device must be listed and characterized. For IVDDs, chemical and biological characterization of antibodies, antigens, assay controls, substrates used to detect antigen/antibody complexes and test reagents, as applicable, is required. For non-IVDDs, details of material identification (proper identification must be provided for brand name materials) and specifications, including raw materials and components, are to be provided.
- The manufacturer may make reference to a product Master File[2] for this information. In cases where the manufacturer is referencing information that is contained in a Master File submitted by a third party, the manufacturer must enclose a letter of permission from the Master File owner indicating the extent of information that can be considered for the application.
- Manufacturing Process Specifications—In this section, a list of resources and activities that transform inputs into desired outputs should be provided. A flowchart, diagram or test description of the manufacturing steps should be provided and quality control steps should be clearly identified and described.
- In cases where multiple facilities are involved in the manufacture of the device, applicable information for each facility must be provided. If the information is identical, it should be so stated. As with Material Specifications, the Master File may be referenced in this section.
- The method of manufacture and quality control activities, as well as a description of installation and servicing, as applicable, should also be provided in this section.
  - The method of manufacture is a complete description of the methods used in, and the facilities and controls used for, the device's manufacture, processing, packaging, storage and, where appropriate, installation.
  - Quality control activities ensure that design outputs match design inputs. This section should describe quality control methods used for raw material and component acceptance, intermediate production steps and the acceptance criteria for the finished device. Sampling plans, testing and inspection methods and related acceptance criteria should be provided. In addition, a summary of the quality assurance internal audit program that addresses recordkeeping and traceability of all components from raw materials to finished

product, including procedures to ensure correct labelling should be provided. A summary of procedures for segregation, identification and storage of untested or unacceptable items, including details of the disposal and reprocessing procedures, if applicable, should also be provided.

Summary of Safety and Effectiveness Studies

- Process Validation Studies—A full description of procedures for monitoring and controlling the parameters of validated processes must be provided. For example, if the device is sterile, process validation studies for sterilization must be provided. This information must include the sterilization method, sterility assurance level (SAL), packaging used to maintain sterility and a summary of validation testing.
- Literature Studies—Copies of all literature studies (abstracts and key papers) that are used in support of safety and effectiveness must be provided, in addition to the bibliography.

Devices Containing Biological Material

If the device contains biological material (i.e., it is manufactured from or incorporates animal or human tissue or their derivative(s)), detailed information to show that measures have been taken to reduce risks associated with transmissible agents must be provided. The manufacturer should consult Health Canada's *Guidance for Industry: Guidance on the Regulation of Medical Devices Manufactured from or Incorporating Viable or Non-viable Animal Tissue or their Derivative(s)*.

Private Label Devices

The *MDR* allow the licensing of private label devices.

A private label device is identical to the original manufacturer's device except for the device name, identifier(s) and manufacturer name and address.

Although the original device is already licensed, the private label manufacturer must obtain an MDL for the private label device before sale in Canada.

The private label manufacturer does not need to have ISO 13485 certification; the manufacturer is allowed to cross-reference the original manufacturer's certificate.

The private label manufacturer's MDL will be automatically amended when the original manufacturer's MDL is amended, but the private label manufacturer must submit an amendment application to change the name of the private label device or the name or address of the private label manufacturer.

The private label manufacturer must label the private label device with its own trade name, identifier(s) and manufacturer's name and address. If it is desirable to include

the original manufacturer's name and address on the label, the following verbiage must be used: "Manufactured by: Original manufacturer's Name and Address; Manufactured for: Private Label Manufacturer's Name and Address."

The private label manufacturer must ensure that a reporting structure has been established between it and the original manufacturer to ensure that all incidents are investigated and those that result in a Mandatory Problem Report or recall are clearly communicated to allow timely reporting to Health Canada.

Medical Device Licence Amendments

An amendment to a licensed medical device is required for the following changes:

- For a Class II device, a change in medical conditions, purposes or use for which the device is manufactured, sold or represented
- For a Class III or IV device, a Significant Change[3]
- Change in device class
- Change in the manufacturer's name and/or address
- Change in the device name
- Nonsignificant change or addition/deletion of the device identifier

If an amendment application is required to be submitted, the modified device cannot be imported or sold until the licence has been amended.

Significant changes require the submission of an Application for a Medical Device Licence Amendment to Health Canada.

For nonsignificant changes, additions or deletions of identifiers, change of device name or change in manufacturer name and/or address, only a Fax-Back Amendment is required.

The MDB attempts to process Licence Amendment Fax-Back forms within seven calendar days from the date of receipt. The receipt of a MDB-signed fax-back form (note that the process has now changed such that MDB uses email instead of fax to amend the MDL) is considered to be authorization that the licence is amended and, therefore, the modified medical device can be imported and/or sold. An amended licence will be sent from MDB by mail.

Summary

- Medical devices are classified into four classes (Class I–IV) according to their potential risk, where Class I represents the lowest risk and Class IV represents the highest risk. If a medical device can be classified into more than one class, the class representing the higher risk applies.
- Criteria used to determine risk class of non-IVDD devices are: degree of invasiveness, duration of patient contact, affected body system, local versus

systemic effects, energy transmission hazard and the consequences of device malfunction or failure.

- Criteria used to determine risk class of IVDD devices include: the intended use and indication(s) for use (the specific disorder, condition, or risk factor for which the test is intended); the application (screening, patient-based testing/diagnosis, monitoring, etc.); the technical, scientific or medical expertise of the intended user (testing laboratories vs. near-patient testing); and the importance of the information to the diagnosis (sole determinant or one of several).
- The manufacturer of a Class I medical device must hold an MDEL unless it imports or distributes solely through the holder of an MDEL (such as an importer or distributor).
- Manufacturers of Class II, III and IV medical devices are required to have a valid medical device licence issued by Health Canada prior to importing or selling devices in Canada.
- Manufacturers of Class II, III and IV medical devices are required to have a QMS that is certified to ISO 13485:2003 by a CMDCAS-recognized registrar. Class II devices should be manufactured under a QMS that is certified to this standard, while Class III and IV devices should be designed and manufactured under a QMS that is certified to this standard.
- A manufacturer or importer of Class II, III or IV devices may sell a medical device to a qualified investigator for investigational testing involving human subjects if the manufacturer or importer holds an investigational testing authorization. For a Class I medical device, the manufacturer has to maintain records and be prepared to provide them to Health Canada if requested.
- Class III or IV custom-made devices or medical devices for special access cannot be sold or imported unless an authorization has been issued by the Medical Devices Bureau.

References

1. The "Declaration of Conformity" must:
   a. identify the recognized standard or standards that were met including the edition of the standard
   b. attest that all the requirements for each standard have been met, except for requirements which do not apply or deviations as noted below
      i. identify any sections or requirements of a standard that are not applicable to the device
      ii. identify any ways in which a standard has been adapted for application to

the device in question, for example, by choosing one of several acceptable test methods specified in the standard
      iii. specify any deviations from a standard, such as deviations from an international standard necessary to meet national or provincial regulations
   c. specify any differences between the device tested for conformance with a standard and the device to be marketed, and justify the use of the test results in case of differences
   d. provide the name and address of any third-party laboratory or certification body that was employed in determining conformance with a standard

2. Master File, as defined in Health Canada's *Guidance Document for Preparation of Premarket Document for Class III and IV Devices*, is a document provided by a subcontractor or manufacturer that contains specific objective evidence, for example material characterization or sterilization processing characteristics. This data is often independent of final device processing and can be referenced by many different device licence applications. If the file has been submitted by someone other than the manufacturer, permission must be granted by the file owner for each licence application using the information contained in the Master File.

3. As per the *MDR*, "significant change" means a change that could reasonably be expected to affect the safety or effectiveness of a medical device. It includes a change to any of the following:
   (a) the manufacturing process, facility or equipment
   (b) the manufacturing quality control procedures, including the methods, tests or procedures used to control the quality, purity and sterility of the device or of the materials used in its manufacture
   (c) the design of the device, including its performance characteristics, principles of operation and specifications of materials, energy source, software or accessories
   (d) the intended use of the device, including any new or extended use, any addition or deletion of a contraindication for the device and any change to the period used to establish its expiry date.
   See Health Canada *Draft Guidance for the Interpretation of Significant Change of a Medical Device*

Canadian Medical Device Postmarketing Activities

Updated by Susan K. Hamann, MS, MT(ASCP), RAC

OBJECTIVES

❑ Understand how to maintain distribution records

❑ Understand implant registration and which devices require it

❑ Understand the limitations on advertisements

❑ Understand the annual licence renewal process

❑ Become familiar with regulations governing importing and exporting medical devices

❑ Know the schedules and requirements related to establishment licences

❑ Understand how and when Health Products and Food Branch Inspectorate inspections are conducted

REGULATIONS AND GUIDELINES COVERED IN THIS CHAPTER

❑ *Food and Drugs Act*, Sections 3, 5, 9, 20, 22, 23, 37

❑ *Medical Devices Regulations*, Sections 2, 24, 27, 43, 44, 46, 48, 52, 53, 54, 55, 56, 66, 67, 68, 70, 80, 87, 89, 90, 91, 92

❑ *Draft Guidance for the Risk-based Classification System (GD006) (May 1998)*

❑ *Draft Guidance for the Risk-based Classification*

System of In Vitro Diagnostic Devices (GD007) (March 1998)

❑ *Keyword Index to Assist Manufacturers in Verifying the Class of Medical Devices (September 2006)*

❑ *Guidance for the Labelling of Medical Devices, Section 21 to 23 of the Medical Devices Regulations, Appendices for Labelling: Soft Contact Lenses and Menstrual Tampons* (June 2004)

❑ *Draft Guidance for the Labelling of In Vitro Diagnostic Devices* (June 1998)

❑ *How to Complete the Application for a New Medical Device Licence* (May 2008)

❑ *Preparation of a Premarket Review Document for Class III and Class IV Device Licence Applications* (October 1998)

❑ *Guidance for Industry: Preparation of a Premarket Review Document in Electronic Format for a Class IV Medical Device Licence Application* (December 2009)

❑ *Guidance for Industry: Preparing Premarket Application for Ultrasound Diagnostic Systems and Transducers* (June 2006)

❑ *Preparation of a Premarket Review Document for Breast Implant and Tissue Expander Applications* (February 2001)

❑ *Guidance for Industry: Guidance for the Interpretation of Significant Change of a Medical Device* (March 2003)

❑ *Guidance for the Interpretation of Sections 28 to31: Licence Application Type V.1* (January 1999)

❑ ISO 13485 and ISO 13488 Quality System Audits Performed by CMDCAS Recognized Registrars

❑ *Guidance on the Content of ISO 13485 and ISO 13488 Quality Systems Certificates Issued by CMDCAS (GD207 REV 0)* (February 2002)

❑ *Guidance on the Medical Device Inspection Program (GUI-0064)* (September 2010)

❑ *Guidance on the Acceptance of Quality System Certificates before and after January 1, 2003 (GD208/REV 0)* (February 2002)

❑ *Guidance on Medical Device Establishment Licensing* (November 2005)

❑ *Guidance for Medical Device Complaint Handling and Recalls* (September 1998)

❑ *Guidance on Mandatory Problem Reporting for Medical Devices (GUI-0059)* (January 2011)

❑ Medical Devices Special Access Programme How to Apply for Authorization to Obtain Custommade or Special Access Devices (November 2007)

❑ *Preparation of an Application for Investigational Testing—Medical Devices* (February 1999)

❑ *Preparation of an Application for Investigational Testing—In Vitro Diagnostic Devices* (February 1999)

Introduction

A medical device manufacturer's regulatory obligations continue throughout the device's lifecycle, long after the sale to a customer. The breadth of postmarketing activities affects a number of departments within a company, ranging from distribution to marketing, and is monitored by two divisions of Health Canada—the Therapeutic Products Directorate (TPD) and the Health Products and Food Branch Inspectorate (HPFBI). This chapter addresses postmarketing activities and responsibilities, with the exception of complaint and recall handling and mandatory problem reporting, which are the subject of Chapter 32.

Distribution Records

Maintaining traceability of medical devices serves to expedite the retrieval and removal of a device or contact with the device's owner, if such action is necessary, as it is with product recalls. Distribution records must contain sufficient information to permit a complete and rapid recall of the device from the market (*Medical Devices Regulations* (*MDR*) Section 53), and must be maintained in a manner that allows for their rapid retrieval (*MDR* Section 56).

The requirement to maintain adequate distribution records for each device applies only to the device's manufacturer, importer and distributor. It does not apply to a retailer or healthcare facility to which the device has been sold for use within that facility (*MDR* Section 52). The manufacturer, importer and distributor are required to maintain distribution records for the device's projected useful life or for two years after the date the device is shipped, whichever is longer (*MDR* Section 55).

Implant distribution records must also contain information submitted by the healthcare facility on the registration cards that are returned to the manufacturer (*MDR* Section 54(1)). The records must be updated as the manufacturer receives new information from the healthcare facility or the patient who received the device (*MDR* Section 54(2)).

Implant Registration

The *MDR* mandate that the manufacturer of a device that is an implant maintain more-detailed distribution records in the form of implant registration. This process is generally used for higher-risk implantable devices, where contacting the patient immediately is more crucial than for devices that pose a lower risk to the patient or user. As with distribution records, the purpose of implant registration is to enable the manufacturer to notify the patient of new information concerning the safety, effectiveness or performance of the implantable device, as well as any required corrective action.

The following medical devices are "implants" and require implant registration:
- heart valves
- annuloplasty rings
- active implantable device systems
  - all models of implantable pacemakers and leads
  - all models of implantable defibrillators and leads
  - artificial heart
  - implantable ventricular support system
  - implantable drug infusion system
- devices of human origin
  - human dura mater
  - wound covering containing human cells (*MDR* Schedule 2)

The manufacturer of an implant must include two implant registration cards with the device, written in both English and French (*MDR* Sections 66(1) and 66(3)). However the manufacturer may choose to provide four cards: two in English and two in French. The implant registration cards must contain the following information:

- manufacturer name and address
- name and address of any person designated by the manufacturer to collect implant registration information
- notice advising the patient of the implant registration cards' purpose
- statement advising the patient to notify the manufacturer of any change of address (*MDR* 66(1))

The cards must also be designed for recording the following case-specific information regarding the device, the patient and the healthcare facility:

- device name, control number and identifier, including the identifier of any medical device that is implanted as part of a system, test kit, medical device group, medical device family or medical device group family
- name and address of the healthcare professional who performed the procedure
- date on which the device was implanted
- name and address of the healthcare facility at which the implant procedure took place
- patient name and address or the healthcare facility's identification number for the patient (*MDR* Section 66(2))

This required information is recorded on both implant registration cards by a member of the healthcare facility where the implant procedure is performed. One card is given to the patient and the other is forwarded to the device manufacturer or the person designated by the manufacturer (*MDR* Section 67(1)).

Patient privacy for implant registration is addressed by the *MDR*. Patients must give written consent to allow their names and addresses to appear on the implant registration cards that are forwarded to the manufacturer or the person that the manufacturer has designated. The healthcare facility, the manufacturer and its designate are not permitted to disclose the patient's name or address or any information that might identify the patient unless disclosure is required by law (*MDR* Sections 67(2) and 67(3)).

A manufacturer may choose to use an implant registration method that differs from that described by the *MDR*. To do so, the manufacturer must receive authorization from TPD (*MDR* Section 68).

Advertisements

The *Food and Drugs Act* (*F&DA*) and *MDR* regulate the manner in which devices may be advertised. The *F&DA* defines an "advertisement" as any representation by any means for the purpose of promoting directly or indirectly the sale or disposal of any regulated product, including medical devices. As with all the activities overseen in regulatory affairs, the advertisements must be truthful (*F&DA* Section 20(1)).

A Class II, III or IV device can be advertised only if the device manufacturer holds a licence for that device or, if the device has been subjected to a change described in Section 34 of the *MDR*, an amended medical device licence (*MDR* Section 27 (a)). Unlicensed devices may be advertised in a catalogue only if there is a clear and visible warning indicating that the devices advertised are not licensed in accordance with Canadian law (*MDR* Section 27 (b)).

Schedule A Claims

As with drugs, food and cosmetics, no person is allowed to advertise any device to the general public as a treatment, preventative or cure for any of the diseases, disorders or abnormal physical states listed in Schedule A of the *F&DA* (*F&DA* Sections 3(1) and (2)). Although Section 3 of the *FD&A* prohibits claims that refer to any of the listed diseases, some claims that do not expressly mention a Schedule A disease also may violate this section, including claims referencing:

- diseases considered synonyms for or subsets of Schedule A diseases
- certain symptoms and signs of Schedule A diseases
- risk factors for Schedule A

A claim to treat, prevent or cure the "symptoms" of a Schedule A disease would be considered a claim to treat, prevent or cure the disease itself and, hence, advertisement to the general public is not allowed.

References to risk factors for listed diseases, however, can in some situations be tolerated. A label or advertisement stating that a product addresses a risk factor associated with a Schedule A disease without expressly mentioning the disease name itself may be permissible in an advertisement intended for the general public. For example, a statement such as "this product helps maintain healthy sugar levels" may not necessarily relate to diabetes and would be allowed.[1]

There are also exceptions to this rule specifically mentioned in the *MDR*. Section 24(1) allows the advertisement of a condom for the purpose of preventing the transmission of venereal disease, a Schedule A disease, so long as the advertisement and product label claim only that the condom reduces the risk of transmitting venereal disease.

Table 31-1. Type of TPD Authorization Required for the Importation of Devices for Various Uses

Type of Authorization Required for Importation	Class I	Class II	Class III	Class IV
Device licence (Section 26)	Not required	Yes	Yes	Yes
Custom or special access (Section 70)	Not required	Not required	Yes	Yes
Investigational testing authorization (Section 80)	Not required; however, the manufacturer or importer must meet the requirements of Section 81	Yes	Yes	Yes

Contraceptive Advertising

Section 3(3) of the *F&DA* also regulates advertising to the general public of any contraceptive device manufactured, sold or represented for use in the prevention of conception, except as authorized by regulation.

The exception to Section 3(3) is found in Section 24(2) of the *MDR*, which permits the advertisement of contraceptive devices, other than intrauterine devices, to the general public by any means other than by distribution of samples of the devices door-to-door or through the mail.

Advertising of Devices Authorized Only For Investigational Testing

Requirements specific to medical devices for investigational testing exist. A person can advertise such a device only if: (1) an authorization for investigational testing has been issued for that product; and (2) the advertisement clearly indicates that the device is the subject of investigational testing and cites the purpose of the investigational testing (*MDR* Section 87).

Annual Licence Renewal

Manufacturers holding medical device licences are required to confirm annually their intention to renew those device licences for the following year by submitting a renewal form to the Medical Devices Bureau before 1 November of each year. The licences are valid for a one-year period from 1 November to 31 October (*MDR* Section 43(1)).

The intent of the annual licence renewal process is to ensure that TPD has current information on devices being sold in Canada. If the information that was submitted to TPD has changed but does not result in a licence amendment, a description of such changes must be supplied to TPD at the time of annual licence renewal (*MDR* Section 43(1)).

To comply with the annual licence renewal requirement, a manufacturer needs to submit to Health Canada the following documents:

- a completed and signed renewal form
- a description of any changes to device information (not resulting in an amended licence)
- a completed fee reduction form, if the revenue from product sales is below a certain amount

The renewal form allows the manufacturer to discontinue any licences for product(s) it does not intend to sell in the following year. Failure to submit the information required for the annual licence renewal process may result in TPD's cancellation of the manufacturer's licences (*MDR* Section 43(2)).

If at any other time during the year the manufacturer discontinues the sale of a device in Canada, it is required to inform TPD within 30 days after stopping sales. TPD will cancel the licence when it receives notification (*MDR* Section 43(3)). In addition, if a new or modified quality systems certificate is issued for a licensed device, the manufacturer must submit a copy of the new or modified certificate to TPD within 30 days after it has been issued (*MDR* Section 43.1).

Importation and Exportation
Importation

The MDR applies to all medical devices imported into Canada if they are to be sold or used on humans, other than devices imported for personal use (*MDR* Section 2). A medical device can be imported into and sold in Canada only if:

- the importer or distributor holds an Establishment Licence (discussed in the next section); this requirement does not apply to a retailer, a healthcare facility, the manufacturer of a Class II, III or IV device, or the manufacturer of a Class I device if the device is distributed solely through a person who holds an Establishment Licence (*MDR* Section 44)
- the manufacturer has been issued an authorization, as required, for the specific device class or the device's specific use (see **Table 31-1**)

Exportation

The *F&DA* and *MDR* do not apply to devices manufactured for sale in a country other than Canada; however, the package must be clearly marked with the word "Export" or

Figure 31-1. Export Certificate

EXPORT CERTIFICATE FOR MEDICAL DEVICES
UNDER THE Medical Devices Regulations

I,_____ , certify that I have knowledge of all matters contained in this certificate and that

1. I am (check applicable box)
    (a) where the medical device described in this certificate is exported by a corporation
        ☐ the exporter's senior executive officer,
        ☐ the exporter's senior regulatory officer,
        ☐ the authorized agent of the exporter's senior executive officer, or
        ☐ the authorized agent of the exporter's senior regulatory officer; and
    (b) where the medical device described in this certificate is exported by an individual
        ☐ the exporter, or
        ☐ the exporter's authorized agent.

_____ (State name and address of exporter or, if a corporation, name and address of principal place of business in Canada).

2. On the _____day of , _____, a package containing_____(description of device, including serial number, model name, lot number and quantity, as applicable; if additional space required, attach as Appendix "A") is/will be consigned to _____(name and address of consignee).

3. The package is marked in distinct overprinting with the word "Export" or "Exportation".
4. The medical device was not manufactured for consumption in Canada.
5. The medical device is not sold for consumption in Canada.
6. The package and its contents do not contravene any known requirement of the law of the country of _____
_____(state country of consignee).
7. All relevant information is contained in this certificate and no relevant information has been knowingly withheld.

_____
Signature

_____
Position title

_____
Date

"Exportation" and have an accompanying certificate indicating that the package and its contents do not contravene any known legal requirement of the country to which it will be exported (*F&DA* Section 37).

The export certificate template to be used is set out in Schedule 3 of the *MDR* (*MDR* Section 89(1)) and is shown in **Figure 31-1**. To be valid, the certificate must be signed by the exporter or his or her agent. If the exporter is a corporation, the certificate must be signed by the exporter's senior executive officer in Canada or senior regulatory officer in Canada, or the authorized agent of either of these individuals. Export certificates must be accurate, and the exporter must maintain copies for a minimum of five years from the date of export in case an HPFBI inspector asks to examine them (*MDR* Sections 90, 91, 92).

Establishment Licence

Every importer or distributor of a medical device (other than for personal use) must hold an Establishment Licence, except:

- healthcare facilities
- Class II, III or IV device manufacturers (as defined in the *MDR*)
- Class I device manufacturers that sell devices solely through a person who holds an establishment licence
- retailers (*MDR* Section 44)
- persons selling only devices for investigational testing or for special access (*MDR* Section 8)
- dispensers (*MDR* Section 4)

Table 31-2. Regulatory Requirements Assessed During HPFBI Inspection of Medical Device-related Companies

Regulatory Requirement	Section of MDR	Other Guidance Documents*
Device classification	6, 7	Draft Guidance for the Risk-based Classification System (GD006) Draft Guidance for the Risk-based Classification System of In Vitro Diagnostic Devices (GD007) Keyword Index to Assist Manufacturers in Verifying the Class of Medical Devices
Safety and effectiveness	9–20	"Policy on Recognition and Use of Standards under the Medical Devices Regulations" "Policy on Safety and Effectiveness of Latex Condoms" "Interim Policy on Medical Gloves" "Draft Policy on Static Magnets Sold as Medical Devices"
Labelling	2–23	Guidance for the Labelling of Medical Devices, Section 21 to 23 of the Medical Devices Regulations, Appendices for Labelling: Soft Contact Lenses and Menstrual Tampons Draft Guidance for the Labelling of In Vitro Diagnostic Devices
Advertising of contraceptive devices	24	
Class I devices	25	
Importation, sale and advertising conditional on device licensing	26, 27	
Device license application and issuance	28–37	How to Complete the Application for a New Medical Device Licence Preparation of a Premarket Review Document for Class III and Class IV Device Licence Applications V.2 Guidance for Industry: Preparation of a Premarket Review Document in Electronic Format for a Class IV Medical Device Licence Application Guidance for Manufacturers Preparing Premarket Application for Ultrasound Diagnostic Systems and Transducers Preparation of a Premarket Review Document for Breast Implant and Tissue Expander Applications Guidance for Industry: Guidance for the Interpretation of Significant Change of a Medical Device Guidance for the Interpretation of Sections 28 to31: Licence Application Type V.1 ISO 13485 and ISO13488 Quality System Audits Performed by CMDCAS Recognized Registrars Guidance on the Content of ISO 13485 and ISO 13488 Quality Systems Certificates Issued by CMDCAS (GD207 REV 0) Guidance on the Medical Device Inspection Program Guidance on the Acceptance of Quality System Certificates before and after January 1, 2003 (GD208 REV 0)
Terms and conditions of device licences	36–37	
Establishment licensing	44–51	Guidance on Medical Device Establishment Licensing

Distribution records	52–55	
Complaint handling	57, 58a	*Guidance for Medical Device Complaint Handling and Recalls*
Recalls and notifications	58b, 63–65	
Mandatory problem reporting	59–61	*Guidance on Mandatory Problem Reporting for Medical Devices (GUI-0055)* *Guidance for Medical Device Complaint Handling and Recalls*
Implant registration	66–68	
Custom-made and special access devices	69–78	*How to Apply for Authorization to Obtain Custom-made or Special Access Devices* *Application Form for Custom-Made Devices and Medical Devices for Special Access* *The Medical Devices Special Access Programme*
Devices for investigational testing involving human subjects	79–88	*Preparation of an Application for Investigational Testing—Medical Devices* *Application for Investigational Testing Authorization* *Preparation of an Application for Investigational Testing—In Vitro Diagnostic Devices*
Export certificates	89–92	

*Current drafts.

Establishment Licences are managed by HPFBI. The purposes of establishment licensing requirements are:[2]

- to inform HPFBI of the identity of facilities that import and/or distribute devices in Canada, the identity of the device manufacturers and the classification of the devices sold
- to require establishments to provide an attestation that they have met the regulatory requirements relating to distribution records, complaint-handling, recalls and mandatory problem reporting, and have documented procedures in place, where applicable, for the handling, storage, delivery, installation, corrective action and servicing of any Class II, III or IV devices they import or distribute

Until 2011, Establishment Licences had expired annually on 31 December. Effective 1 April 2011, an Establishment Licence will no longer expire on 31 December of each year and there will be no expiry date indicated on Establishment Licences. All MDEL holders must now submit a request for an annual review by 1 April of each year to continue to hold a valid licence. A notification will be sent to licence holders by the Establishment Licensing Unit of the inspectorate prior to 1 April of each year.

When submitting an application for annual review, all relevant changes must be included in the application. Failure to do this renders the licence invalid.

The application and the fee reduction request form (if applicable) are available on Health Canada's website, www.hc-sc.gc.ca/dhp-mps/compli-conform/licences/form/ index_e.html, and can also be obtained by contacting the national HPFBI office at the following address:

Establishment Licensing Unit
Health Products and Food Branch Inspectorate
250 Lanark Avenue
Graham Spry Building – Second Floor
Address Locator 2002C
Ottawa, Ontario, K1A 0K9
Phone: +1 613 946 5141; fax: +1 613 957 4147

Completed application forms are submitted to HPFBI at the same address.

Health Canada Inspections

Further to the mandate of minimizing health risk factors and promoting informed use of food and health products, HPFBI is involved in compliance and enforcement with federal legislation to protect Canadians' health. To this end, HPFBI inspectors are authorized to carry out on-site inspections of medical device manufacturers, importers and distributors at any time (*FD&A* Sections 22 and 23). HPFBI developed a national inspection strategy for the medical device industry to assess and, where necessary, improve medical device manufacturer, importer and distributor compliance with *FD&A* and *MDR* requirements.[3]

The inspection program, launched 1 March 2004, applies to:

- Class I device manufacturers that do not hold Class II, III or IV device licences
- importers and distributors

- companies or individuals selling medical devices for investigational use or for special access,[4] unless the company has its quality systems certified to the ISO13485/13488 standards and the Canadian Medical Devices Conformity Assessment System (CMDCAS) requirements

The reason for excluding companies that hold medical device licences from the inspection program is that regulatory compliance is assessed for these companies during the licensing process by requiring them to submit an ISO13485/13488 quality systems certificate issued by a CMDCAS-recognized registrar (discussed elsewhere in this book). However, any company subject to the *F&DA* and *MDR*, including companies holding ISO 13485/13488 quality system certificates under CMDCAS, may be subject to inspections if there are any indications of noncompliance.

On-site inspections will be performed to assess the compliance of companies located in Canada. Companies located outside Canada will be required to provide documentation and records necessary for the assessment, but on-site inspections of foreign companies may take place when warranted.[5] Inspections are scheduled according to criteria such as previous compliance history and class of product handled.

The scope of the inspection will depend upon the type of inspection scheduled. There are three inspection types:

- Regular—an inspection against the applicable sections of the *F&DA* and *MDR*
- Reinspection—a follow-up inspection, performed when a company has not provided adequate evidence that it has corrected a problem of noncompliance identified in a previous inspection; the inspection focuses on but is not limited to the regulatory requirements against which the noncompliance was previously cited
- Other inspection—all other types of inspections, including targeting and surveillance of specific regulatory requirements for certain types of medical devices or specific industry sectors[6,7]

The inspectors will assess a company's compliance with the regulatory requirements based upon the medical device-related activities that take place at the company and the class of products it handles. **Table 31-2** lists the regulatory requirements, the relevant sections of the *MDR* and the guidance documents that the inspector may reference when assessing a company's compliance with the *F&DA* and the *MDR*.

Summary

- Distribution records should be accurate, include adequate information and be well maintained to facilitate prompt retrieval.

- Implant registration is required for all devices defined as "implants."
- Class II, III and IV devices can be advertised only if the manufacturer holds a licence or an authorization for investigational testing (the label must include a note on the device's investigational status).
- Advertising must not claim that the device is a treatment, preventative or cure for any of the diseases listed in *FD&A* Schedule A.
- Medical device licences must be renewed each year before the 1 November deadline.
- Depending upon the device class, specific authorization may be required before importation into Canada is allowed.
- Devices intended for export must have an accompanying export certificate.
- Persons who import or distribute medical devices (other than for personal use) must hold an Establishment Licence, which is renewed annually.
- A new inspection program for medical device manufacturers, importers and distributors was implemented in 2004.

References

1. Health Canada. *Schedule A and Section 3: Guidance Document*. Ottawa, Canada: Health Canada (February 2003).
2. Health Products and Food Branch Inspectorate, Health Canada. *Guidance on Medical Device Establishment Licensing*. Ottawa, Canada: Health Products and Food Branch Inspectorate (November 2005).
3. Health Products and Food Branch Inspectorate, Health Canada. *Inspection Strategy for Medical Device Companies*. Ottawa, Canada: Health Products and Food Branch Inspectorate (October 2003).
4. Health Products and Food Branch Inspectorate, Health Canada. *Guidance on the Medical Device Inspection Programme*. Ottawa, Ontario Canada: Health Products and Food Branch Inspectorate (March 2004).
5. Op cit 2.
6. Ibid.
7. Ibid.

Medical Devices— Canadian Complaint Handling, Problem Reporting and Recalls

Susan K. Hamann, MS, MT(ASCP), RAC

OBJECTIVES

❑ Understand the principal elements of handling medical device complaints

❑ Learn how to report medical device problems

❑ Know what is involved in the medical device recall process

REGULATIONS AND GUIDELINES COVERED IN THIS CHAPTER

❑ *Medical Devices Regulations*, Sections 57, 58, 59, 60, 61, 61.1, 63, 64, 65, 65.1

❑ *Draft Guidance for Medical Device Complaint Handling and Recalls* (September 1998)

❑ *Guidance on Investigation of Reported Medical Device Problems* (GUI-0065) (March 2011)

❑ *Medical Device Problem Reporting by Health Care Facilities, Medical Professionals and other device users* (December 2001)

❑ "Health Products and Food Branch Inspectorate Recall Policy" (POL-0016) (September 2006)

❑ *Guidance Document for Mandatory Problem Reporting for Medical Devices* (GUI-0059) (January 2011)

❑ *Guide to Recall of Medical Devices* (GUI-0054) (March 2011)

❑ *Mandatory Problem Reporting for Medical Devices—Preliminary Report Form* (FRM-0237) (January 2011)

❑ *Mandatory Problem Reporting for Medical Devices—Final Report Form* (FRM-0238) (January 2011)

❑ *Mandatory Problem Reporting for Medical Devices—Preliminary and Final Report Form (FRM-0255)* (January 2011)

❑ *User Problem Reporting for Medical Devices* (GUI-0060) (January 2011)

❑ *Medical Device User Problem Report Form (FRM-0029)* (January 2011)

❑ *Health Products and Food Branch Inspectorate Medical Devices Problem Report Form*

❑ *Guidance to Industry: How to Submit a Trade Complaint (Guide 0038)* (January 2006)

❑ *Guidance Document: How to Submit a Consumer Complaint (Guide 0044)* (January 2006)

Introduction

In a continuing effort to protect the health and safety of Canadians, Health Canada encourages medical device users to report any problems or potential problems they have identified before or after using the product. The device manufacturer or its agent (such as the importer or distributor) is often the first point of contact when the end user has had an unsatisfactory experience with the product or recognizes a problem that could make the device unsafe. Hence, the manufacturer and its agent need to have an effective process for handling such complaints, especially since some may result in mandatory or voluntary problem reporting or a device recall

Complaint-Handling

The *Medical Devices Regulations* (*MDR*) state that the manufacturer, importer and distributor must each document and implement procedures that will enable them to carry out "effective and timely" investigations of problems reported to them. In addition to these documented processes, manufacturers, importers and distributors must each maintain records of reported problems with the device, including any consumer complaints, and all actions taken in response to the reported problem or complaint. For the manufacturer, this requirement also applies to problems reported outside Canada after the device is first sold in Canada. These records and documented procedures must be readily available to the Health Canada inspector upon request.

The requirement to maintain records does not apply to retailers or healthcare facilities unless they import medical devices for resale, in which case the complaint-handling regulations would apply.

Maintenance of Records

Maintaining thorough records of problem reports and related actions is imperative because complaints implying safety and effectiveness issues may require a report to Health Canada (discussed later in this chapter).

Records must include, at a minimum, the following information:

- device identification information, including name; licence number; model or catalogue number; control, serial or lot number; and any other identification feature
- manufacturer, importer and distributor names and addresses
- detailed description of the problem or incident and the circumstances that led to the discovery of the medical device's defect or potential defect
- date the incident or problem occurred
- date the manufacturer, importer or distributor was first notified
- records of any actions related to investigation of the problem

The record of actions taken by the manufacturer, importer or distributor in response to the problems includes:

- any communications with the reporter or complainant
- evaluation of the problem or product
- any action (i.e., corrective and preventive action) taken to correct the problem or prevent its recurrence

Complaint-Handling Procedure

The *MDR* requires manufacturers, importers and distributors to have in place a written complaint-handling procedure. The complaint-handling procedure's intent is to identify activities that must occur once a problem or complaint report is received and to ensure a thorough and effective investigation. The procedure identifies the personnel involved and their roles in the investigation. It also describes how to maintain and assess records, and indicates a timeframe for the investigation's completion.

The procedure will require decisions on issues of quality and compliance and whether specific actions need to be taken, such as:

- associating a health hazard with the device
- assessing the device's conformance to any claim made by the manufacturer or importer relating to effectiveness, performance characteristics or safety and to *Food and Drugs Act* (*F&D*A) or *MDR* requirements
- developing the appropriate corrective and preventive action
- determining whether a problem report to Health Canada is required

Risk Analysis

The purpose of a preliminary risk analysis is to evaluate the available information from the complaint to determine whether the alleged defect could impact the device's safety or performance. In the complete risk evaluation, the estimated level of risk associated with the problem, determined through a thorough risk analysis, should be evaluated to determine whether it is acceptable. Any newly estimated risks may be compared with previously defined criteria for risk acceptability contained in the risk management plan for the device. Some of the factors that should be considered to determine risk level can be found in Appendix 4 of the *Guidance on Investigation of Reported Medical Device Problems*.

Risk management decisions require the following actions to be completed and documented:

- risk analysis (based on conclusions of root cause investigation and related information, e.g., manufacturing records, trend analyses)
- risk evaluation (is the risk acceptable?)
- risk control (if not acceptable, how to minimize)
- correction (recall)
- corrective action (design/manufacturing/quality system change to prevent recurrence)

- preventive action (design/manufacturing/quality system change to prevent occurrence)

Conformance to Specifications and Compliance With the Act and Regulations

The complaint investigation should examine whether:
1. The device failed to conform to any manufacturer or importer claim relating to its effectiveness, performance characteristics or safety.

or

2. The sale of the device failed to meet *F&DA* or *MDR* requirements; any existing deficiency should be documented and its potential health risk consequences assessed.

Corrective and Preventive Action

The problem investigation should determine any given situation's appropriate corrective and preventive action. A decision tree may be developed to establish what action can best resolve the problem and any other deficiency that the investigation may have unveiled. Corrective and preventive actions may include:
- increased device postmarket surveillance
- product design or manufacturing change
- device recall

Mandatory Problem Reporting

A mandatory problem report is submitted to Health Canada by the manufacturer and importer for any incident involving a medical device sold in Canada that meets all three of the basic reporting criteria of *MDR* Section 59:
1. it occurred within or outside Canada
2. it is related to a device failure or deterioration in its effectiveness or any inadequacy in its labelling or directions for use
3. it has led to a the death or serious health deterioration of a patient, user or other person, or could do so were it to recur

This requirement allows Health Canada to identify and monitor serious incidents involving medical devices and manage the risk associated with problematic devices in Canada.

Mandatory Problem Reporting

The mandatory problem report is typically filed in two parts: preliminary and final. The preliminary report proposes the timeline for this submission, and the final report is submitted when the manufacturer completes the investigation. The following sections describe the information required in preliminary and final reports.

A report of this type must be submitted to Health Canada as soon as possible after the manufacturer has decided to take action or the regulatory agency has mandated a corrective action.

Preliminary Canadian reports, however, must occur within either:
- 10 days after the medical device's manufacturer or importer becomes aware of an incident involving death or serious injury
- 30 days after the manufacturer or importer becomes aware of the incident, if death or serious injury did not occur but could do so if the incident were to recur

For a product sold or distributed in Canada, an incident occurring outside Canada must be reported only if either:
- the manufacturer has informed the regulatory agency in the country where the incident occurred that corrective action will be taken
- the regulatory agency has requested the manufacturer to take corrective action

When the decision has been made to report a foreign incident to Health Canada, regulations require that a preliminary report be submitted as soon as possible after the manufacturer has informed the foreign regulatory agency of the intention to take corrective action, or as soon as possible after the foreign regulatory agency has required the manufacturer to take corrective action. As soon as possible has been interpreted to mean 48 hours after the decision has been made.

Preliminary Mandatory Problem Report

MDR Section 60(2) describes the information required in the preliminary report (IFRD-0237):
- device's name, identifier, catalogue number and control number
- device manufacturer's and importer's names and addresses, as well as the contact information of the company representative who will respond to requests for additional information about the incident
- date the manufacturer or importer became aware of the incident (awareness date)
- incident details, including the date of the occurrence and consequences for the patient, user or other person
- name and contact information of the person who reported the incident to the manufacturer or importer
- information on other medical devices or accessories involved in the incident
- preliminary findings of the manufacturer's or importer's investigation and an assessment of the risk to patients or users
- proposed actions by the manufacturer or importer

in this investigation, the expected investigation completion timeline and, thus, the final report submission timeline
- statement indicating whether a report previously has been made regarding the device and, if so, the report's date

Final Mandatory Problem Report

After submitting the preliminary report, the manufacturer and importer must each, within the timeline described in the preliminary report, file a final report (FRM-0237) with Health Canada, which contains:
- an incident description, including the number of people who have suffered serious injury or death due to the event
- all new information since the submission of the preliminary report
- a detailed explanation of the incident's root cause and justification for the actions taken in response to the incident
- actions resulting from the investigation intended to resolve the problem and eliminate its recurrence

Mandatory problem reports may be emailed or sent by fax or postal mail. Health Canada prefers email. An automated response acknowledgement will be sent if the email includes the acronym "MDPR" in the subject line. Once the report has been received and entered into the database, a letter confirming receipt will be sent to the reporter.

Combined Preliminary and Final Reports

Use FRM-0255 if submitting a combined preliminary and final report.

Voluntary Problem Reporting

A voluntary problem report on a medical device incident or complaint is submitted to Health Canada at the reporter's discretion. These reports typically are submitted by healthcare professionals and the general public on the Medical Device User Report Form (FRM-0029)(See **Figure 32-1**).

These reports may include the following:
- actual problems that have been detected during use
- concerns about the safety of the device
- deficiencies in design, manufacturing or labelling of the device
- a contravention of a regulatory requirement, such as the sale of a device without a device licence

Recalls

A "recall" is defined as any action taken by a manufacturer, importer or distributor to take back or correct a device or to notify a device's owners of a potential defect. Stock recovery and product withdrawal are not considered recalls. A "stock recovery" is a firm's removal or correction of a product that has not been marketed or that has not left the firm"s direct control. A "product withdrawal" refers to a firm's removal from the market of a product that does not violate the *F&DA* or *MDR.*

Both the manufacturer and importer will inform Health Canada of the recall. The recall reporting requirement does not apply to a retailer or healthcare facility that uses the device.

There is no standard recall report template; however, the information required is specified in *MDR* Section 64:
- device name and identifier, including the identifier of any medical device that is part of a System, Test Kit, Medical Device Group, Family or Group Family
- manufacturer and importer names and addresses and the establishment name and address where the device was manufactured, if different from the manufacturer
- recall reason, the nature of the defect or possible defect, and the date on and circumstances under which the defect or possible defect was discovered
- risk evaluation of associated defect or possible defect
- number of affected device units that the manufacturer or importer
  1. manufactured in Canada
  2. imported into Canada
  3. sold in Canada
- period during which the affected units were distributed in Canada
- name of each person who received the affected device and the number of units sold to each
- copy of any communication issued to customers regarding the recall
- proposed recall strategy, including the start date, information about how and when Health Canada will be informed of recall progress and the proposed completion date
- proposed action to prevent the problem's recurrence
- name, title and telephone number of the manufacturer's representative or importer to contact for recall information

When the recall is completed, its results and the actions taken to prevent its recurrence must be reported to Health Canada. Medical device recall reports should be sent to the appropriate regional office. Addresses can be found in Appendix 1 of the *Guide to Recall of Medical Devices* (GUI-0054). Companies that do not know under which region of responsibility they fall, should contact the Medical Devices Compliance Unit of the Inspectorate at +1 613 957 3836.

Device manufacturers, importers and distributors are

Figure 32-1 Health Canada User Problem Report Form

Figure 25-1 Health Canada User Problem Report Form

Health Santé
Canada Canada

Health Products and Food Branch Inspectorate
Problem Reporting for Medical Devices
User Problem Report Form (FRM-0029)

User Reporter Information
Note: * The contact information in Fields 1 and 2 is essential for follow-up.

1. * Name/Title:
2. * Telephone number: (   )
3. E-mail:
4. User
      a. Name of facility:
      b. Street address:
      c. City:
      d. Province:
      e. Postal Code:
      f. Facsimile number: (   )

Medical Device Details
5. Trade/Brand Name:
6. Type of device:
      a. Model #:
      b. Catalogue #:
      c. Serial #:
      d. Lot #:
      e. Other # (specify):
7. Manufacturer's name:
      a. Street address:
      b. City:
      c. Province/State:
      d. Postal/Zip Code:
8. Distributor's/Supplier's name:
      a. Street address:
      b. City:
      c. Province/State:
      d. Postal/Zip Code:

9. Date the device was purchased (yyyy/mm):

10. How long the device was in use prior to the incident? (yyyy/mm):

11. Expiration date, if applicable (yyyy/mm/dd):

12. If implanted, give date (yyyy/mm/dd):

13. If explanted, give date (yyyy/mm/dd):

Canada

Figure 32-1

Figure 25-1

14. Device available for evaluation by Health Canada?
- □ a. Yes
- □ b. No - Disposed of by hospital/reporter
- □ c. No - Retained by hospital/reporter
- □ d. No - Returned to manufacturer on (yyyy/mm/dd):
- □ e. No - Other explanation:

Description of Incident

15. Date the incident occurred (yyyy/mm/dd):

16. Date the incident was reported to the:
- □ a. Manufacturer (yyyy/mm/dd):
- □ b. Distributor/Supplier (yyyy/mm/dd):
- □ c. Not reported. Please provide rationale why it was not reported:

17. User of device (if other than reporter)
- □ a. Health professional, specify:
- □ b. Technician, specify:
- □ c. General public/patient, specify:

18. Patient outcome attributed to incident:
- □ a. Death (yyyy/mm/dd)
- □ b. Injury
- □ c. Potential for death/injury
- □ d. Minimal/no adverse health consequences

19. Please include as much detail as is known about the incident (for example: what happened and to whom, was contamination or lack of sterility involved), or the nature of the defect:

20. Please provide any comments or additional information. This may include relevant tests/laboratory data including dates, relevant patient history, and/or therapy dates and other medical products in use at the time of the incident including dates, time to symptom onset, time of symptom duration, concomitant drugs, and de-challenge response to concomitant drugs.

21. Authorizations
- □ I authorize Health Canada to provide my contact information to the manufacturer/importer, in order to facilitate the investigation by the manufacturer/importer into my problem report.
- □ I authorize Health Canada to release the sample/specimen provided to them, to the manufacturer/importer for evaluation.

required to have documented procedures in place to carry out an effective and timely recall. The recall procedure:

- identifies all involved internal and external personnel and their functions and responsibilities
- outlines communication channels for recall execution
- helps determine the priority level and assigns a timeframe for completing a recall

The written recall procedure guides recall strategy development and ultimately helps ensure that defective or potentially defective medical devices are removed from use and that measures are taken to correct the problem effectively and in a timely manner.

Summary

- Medical device manufacturers, importers and distributors must have documented procedures for handling complaints and recalls.
- Incidents that involve the failure or deterioration in a device's effectiveness or any inadequacies in its labelling, if they have led to death or serious health deterioration of a patient, user or other person, or could do so should the problem recur, must be reported.

Canadian Medical Device Quality System Requirements

Updated by Amber Cheng, MSc and Vicky Cheng, PMP

OBJECTIVES

❑ Become familiar with how ISO 13485:2003 quality system requirements are used in the *Medical Devices Regulations (MDR)*

❑ Understand how a manufacturer complies with the medical device quality system requirements

❑ Obtain an overview of Health Canada's third-party auditing and certification process

REGULATIONS AND GUIDELINES COVERED IN THIS CHAPTER

❑ *Medical Devices Regulations*

❑ *Regulations Amending the Medical Devices Regulations (1293–Quality Systems) (May 2003)*

❑ ISO 13485:2003 (ISO 13485-03-CAN/ CSA) *Medical Devices—Quality Management Systems—Requirements for Regulatory Purposes*

❑ *ISO/TR 14969:2004, Medical Devices, Quality Management Systems: Guidance on the Application of ISO 13485:2003*

❑ *Guidance on the Acceptance of Quality System Certificates before and after January 1, 2003 (GD208/Rev0)*

❑ *Guidance on the Content of ISO 13485 Quality System Certificates Issued by Health Canada*

Recognized Registrars (GD207) (2 January 2008)

❑ ISO 13485:2003 *Quality Management System Audits Performed by Health Canada Recognized Registrars (GD210) (31 January 2007)*

❑ *Quality Management System—Medical Devices— Guidance on the Control of Products and Services Obtained from Suppliers (May 2010)*

Introduction

ISO 13485:2003 is an international quality system standard for the manufacture of medical devices. It was developed by a joint committee[1] made up of members of ISO TC 210 Working Group 1 and Global Harmonization Task Force (GHTF) Study Group 3. The objective of this committee was to write an internationally accepted, medical device-specific, quality management system (QMS) standard that could be implemented globally by medical device manufacturers. From its formation in 1999 to the present, the joint ISO-GHTF working group has been composed of interested medical device manufacturers, industry associations, regulatory bodies, technical experts and observers from Australia, Canada, China, the EU, Japan, Taiwan and the US.

ISO standards usually are adopted by an ISO member country and then republished with or without modification by that country's national standards body. Canada is a member country of ISO, and the Canadian Standards Association (CSA) is the Canadian national standards body responsible for ISO 13485:2003.

The ISO 13485:2003 standard continues to be the worldwide recognized standard for auditing a medical device QMS. The standard is similar but not identical to the US Food and Drug Administration's medical device quality system requirements, *US Code of Federal Regulations* Title 21 Part 820. It is also the EU harmonized standard for demonstrating conformance to an appropriate annex of the *Medical Devices Directive* (93/42/EEC), the *Active Implantable Medical Devices Directive* (90/385/EEC) or the *In Vitro Diagnostic Directive* (98/79/EC).

To address possible periodic changes in ISO quality system requirements that would force amendments to the *Medical Devices Regulations* (*MDR*) if the standards' text were incorporated directly into the regulations, Health Canada made the strategic decision to reference the quality system standards in *MDR* Section 32, Subsections (2)(f), (3)(j) and (4)(p). To ensure that its regulatory concerns are adequately addressed in present and future versions of ISO 13485, Health Canada actively participates in GHTF Study Group 3 and ISO TC 210 Working Group 1, which are the joint international committees responsible for writing and periodically reviewing ISO 13485.

Who Requires ISO 13485:2003 Certification?

Manufacturers of Class II, III and IV medical devices sold in Canada are required under the *MDR* to have a QMS certified under ISO 13485:2003. Device licences, licence applications and applications to amend the name or address on a licence must always be supported by a valid certificate. A certificate received by Health Canada prior to the effective date will not be accepted.

Please note that a medical device "manufacturer" is defined in the regulations as the "person who sells a medical device under their own name or under a trademark, design, trade name or other name or mark owned or controlled by the person, and who is responsible for designing, manufacturing, assembling, processing, labelling, packaging, refurbishing or modifying the device, or for assigning to it a purpose, whether those tasks are performed by that person or on their behalf." It is this manufacturer that must hold the certification.

The manufacturer's name and address on the certificate shall be the same as that used on the medical device licence and medical device label. Health Canada will not accept certificates from a manufacturer's subcontractor as evidence of compliance with *MDR* subsections 32(2)(f), 32(3)(j), 32(4)(p), 34 or 43.1. For an organization with a complex structure, multiple names, sites and ownership, the identified manufacturer bears the responsibility of complying with the *MDR*.

It is the manufacturer's responsibility to draft the initial scope statement, which consists of QMS processes including related services and device listing using generic device groups. The finalized scope statement will be subject to clarifications, audit findings and the registrar's certification decision. *Guidance on the Content of ISO 13485 Quality System Certificates Issued by Health Canada Recognized Registrars* includes the scope templates to be employed in "Appendices for Manufacturers and Registrars."

When Is ISO 13485:2003 Certification Not Required?

ISO 13485:2003 certification is not required for Class I devices or devices regulated under Parts 2 (custom-made devices) and 3 (devices for investigational testing) of the *MDR*. Importers and distributors of medical devices and manufacturers who obtain medical device licences exclusively through Health Canada's Private Label process also are not required to obtain a QMS certificate.

Manufacturers with an established ISO 13485:2003 QMS may voluntarily include Class I devices or devices regulated under Parts 2 and 3 in their QMS, but all non-medical device products must be excluded from the official scope of the ISO 13485 QMS. In special cases like this, the organization could maintain a related ISO 9001:2008 system and control all non-medical devices under the scope of this generic QMS. Currently, there is no estimation as to when a change will be made, as ISO 13485:2003 and ISO 9001:2008 did not simultaneously change. Many medical device companies continue to maintain and register for both certificates, and the requirements in their QMS satisfy the requirements for both standards.

Quality System Requirements
Class II Devices

The regulatory QMS requirement of CAN/CSA ISO 13485:2003 for Class II devices is found in subsection 32(2)(f) of the *MDR*. Subsection 32(2)(f) requires a manufacturer to submit "a copy of the quality management system certificate certifying that the quality management system under which the device is manufactured satisfies National Standard of Canada CAN/CSA-ISO 13485:03, *Medical devices—Quality management systems—Requirements for regulatory purpose,*" with a device licence application. This certificate must be issued by a third-party organization that has been formally recognized by Health Canada to audit manufacturers and must be valid at the time of submission.

In keeping with the present regulatory practice of excluding design control for Class II devices, manufacturers implementing the new ISO 13485:2003 QMS are allowed to exclude requirements in Section 7.3 Design and Development.[2] Any other exclusion must be justified on the grounds that it is not performed by the manufacturer and must be documented in the manufacturer's quality manual.

Class III and IV Devices

The regulatory QMS requirements, CAN/CSA ISO 13485:2003, for Class III or IV devices are found in subsections 32(3)(j) and 32(4)(p), respectively. The regulatory text for subsections 32(3)(j) and 32(4)(p) requires a manufacturer to submit "a copy of the quality management system certificate certifying that the quality management system under which the device is *designed and manufactured* satisfies National Standard of Canada CAN/CSA-ISO 13485-03, *Medical devices Quality management systems – Requirements for regulatory purposes*" with its device licence application. This certificate must be issued by a third-party organization that has been formally recognized by Health Canada to audit manufacturers and must be valid at the time of submission.

Incorporation of the MDR in a QMS

ISO 13485:2003 states only what a manufacturer shall do, not how the manufacturer can effectively use the standards to meet the *MDR*. However, element 4.2.1 of ISO 13485:2003 states in part that the "the quality management system documentation shall include… any other documentation specified by national or regional regulation" and "where this International Standard specifies that a requirement, procedure, activity or special arrangement be "documented", it shall, in addition, be implemented and maintained."

Because the *MDR* references ISO quality system standards and requires manufacturers to be certified to a particular standard's requirements by a qualified third-party organization, then, logically, all relevant regulation parts must somehow be included as specified requirements subject to periodic assessment in the certified QMS. These regulatory requirements must be documented in the quality manual and incorporated in the appropriate QMS sections.

For example, *MDR* Sections 59–61 contain specific, mandatory criteria for reporting problems. Therefore, a manufacturer's effective QMS would include these reporting criteria and document and implement one or more procedures for reporting device problems to the appropriate Health Canada section.

Similarly, element 8.5.1 of the standard, Improvement/General of ISO 13485:2003, states, "If national or regional regulations require notification of adverse events that meet specified reporting criteria, the organization shall establish documented procedure to such notification to regulatory authorities." Therefore, the manufacturer would address the mandatory problem-reporting criteria of Sections 59–61 by establishing documented procedures that specifically address the Canadian mandatory problem-reporting criteria and implementing a procedure for reporting device problems to the appropriate Health Canada section.

To assist manufacturers in implementing the appropriate *MDR* sections in their QMS, Health Canada has published a guidance document that provides information on how regulatory requirements can be incorporated into an ISO 13485:2003 QMS. This guidance document is *ISO 1348:2003 Quality Management System Audits Performed by Health Canada Recognized Registrars* (GD210).

ISO TC 210 Working Group 1 has also developed and published a companion guidance document to ISO 13485:2003, *Medical Devices, Quality Management Systems: Guidance on the Application of ISO 13485:2003* (Revision of ISO 14969:1999). This document is a technical report that offers up-to-date guidance on how a medical device manufacturer can implement the QMS requirements of ISO 13485:2003. It can also be used in conjunction with Health Canada's guidance document GD210 to implement applicable sections of the *MDR*.

Auditing Quality Management Systems

An audit of a QMS for 13485:2003 certification per *MDR* requirements must be undertaken by a third-party auditing body approved by Health Canada known as a "registrar."

As Health Canada may not relinquish its regulatory responsibility to third-party auditing bodies, it developed a mechanism to ensure control over all aspects of the third-party auditing process. This mechanism uses established accreditation[3] and auditing practices[4] and procedures developed by Health Canada, GHTF,[5] ISO and the International Accreditation Forum[6] (IAF) to officially recognize the competence of third-party auditors that choose to participate in the program. In North America, third-party auditing bodies are commonly called "registration bodies" or simply registrars. Health Canada's objective in accrediting and recognizing registrars is to confirm their ability to audit and certify manufacturers' QMSs while maintaining control over the audit process. Health Canada establishes confidence and control over the registrars by verifying that, among other things, each:

- is independent from the organizations being audited
- has adequate resources and procedures to perform medical device audits
- has the necessary organizational structure to perform audits and carry out independent reviews of audit reports and recommendations
- uses auditors and review personnel who have been qualified by the registrar as competent to perform their assigned tasks
- conforms to internationally developed standards and guidelines relating to the medical device auditor qualification and performing audits and certification of manufacturers

This control mechanism is called the Canadian Medical Devices Conformity Assessment System[7] (CMDCAS). A list of all formally recognized registrars can be found on the Health Canada website.[8] The significance of CMDCAS recognition is that Health Canada has, through an established process, found these registrars to be competent to issue valid certificates. These certificates confirm that a manufacturer has a QMS that meets an applicable standard's requirements and that it includes all applicable sections of *MDR* Part 1. Health Canada has updated *MDR* Sections 32.1, 32.5, 32.6 and 32.7 to regulate registrars' activities, requirements and responsibilities. The minister of health may cease to recognize a person as a registrar if he or she no longer meets the requirements of Section 32.1 or fails to comply with Section 32.3 or 32.4 (*MDR* Amendment, SOR/2009-303).

Some of the special requirements that Health Canada has imposed on CMDCAS-recognized registrars are described below.

- They must use audit teams with at least one member who has passed the Health Canada CMDCAS training course and has been qualified by Health Canada to perform these types of audits.
- They can issue ISO 13485:2003 certificates valid for a maximum of three years.
- The certificates of conformity to ISO 13485: 2003 issued must contain very specific and accurate information as stated in GD207.

Health Canada has also provided a guidance document (GD210) to registrars on how to perform ISO 13485:2003 QMS audits under the CMDCAS. The exclusion and nonapplicability of ISO 13485:2003 clauses have been reinforced in the latest revised version of GD210, for example, that manufacturers of Class II medical devices are allowed to exclude clause 7.3—Design and development from the QMS, with justification(s). Manufacturers intending to sell their products in Canada are encouraged to consult this guidance to gain a better understanding of the QMS auditing process. The QMS audits performed by Health Canada recognized registrars shall follow the general process for preparing and performing the audit described in ISO 10911.

Auditing of Suppliers or Outsourced Processes

In deciding whether to visit a supplier's facility, the registrar must consider:

i) whether the supplier has a substantial involvement with the design and/or manufacture of the medical device
ii) whether the supplier is undertaking the supply of a part, material or service that may affect conformity of the medical device with the *MDR*'s safety and effectiveness requirements

If the answer to either i) or ii) above is yes, the registrar must determine whether there is sufficient objective evidence at the legal manufacturer's location to show the supplier's competence to undertake supply of the part, material or service in relation to the medical devices that are manufactured, or designed and manufactured,

under the registered QMS. The manufacturer must always exercise control over the supplier and its products/services. Manufacturers must be able to demonstrate control over their suppliers and whether their suppliers hold any QMS registration. In May 2010, Health Canada adopted GHTF's *Quality Management System—Medical Devices—Guidance on the Control of Products and Services Obtained from Suppliers*. The principles and practices therein provide manufacturers and healthcare professionals guidance on how to control their suppliers by obtaining objective evidence throughout different phases of product realization.

Multi-site Organizations

For large companies with multiple facilities under a single QMS, the registrars may audit all sites or a sampling of locations based on processes performed at each site defined in the scope of the manufacturers' Quality Manual (*IAF guidance on the Application of ISO/IEC Guide 62, 2005*). Annex C of GD210 provides guidance on auditing multi-site organizations.

Virtual Manufacturer

An organization that acts as a "virtual manufacturer" (e.g., own brand labellers, distributors or retailers acting as manufacturers) present more of a challenge to the auditor in planning and conducting the audit because of the potential need to visit the virtual manufacturer's suppliers to collect objective evidence that the manufacturer meets applicable QMS requirements. A virtual manufacturers has the same legal responsibility for meeting the safety, effectiveness and QMS requirements as a "real" manufacturer.

An organization that acts as a regulatory correspondent and has been assigned specific regulatory activities by the manufacturer must be audited by the registrar. However, the audit might be conducted through a documentation review, phone calls or interviews, thus avoiding an on-site visit. In any case, if the registrar decides not to visit a supplier, an original equipment manufacturer (OEM) or a regulatory correspondent, the final decision and justification shall be documented and made available for review.

Nonconformities and Audit Reports

The Health Canada qualified auditor shall directly report all nonconformities following applicable requirements of ISO 13485:2003 and never directly refer to sections of *MDR*. In the case of a nonconformity where the manufacturer has not adequately addressed one or more applicable *MDR* requirements, the Health Canada qualified auditor shall determine which ISO 13485:2003 requirement has not been met, then cite the *MDR* section as objective evidence to support the nonconformity. The classifications of nonconformities can be found in FD210 Section 2.3.3. There is no special process or requirement for the closure of a major nonconformity related to an *MDR* requirement other than the 30-day requirement for a manufacturer to submit an action plan to its registrar.

Health Canada does not currently specify a format for audit reports. However, audit reports will clearly indicate that one objective is to assess QMS capability to ensure compliance with the appropriate requirements of the most recent version of *MDR* Part 1. Reports shall also clearly state that a second objective of the audit is to assess conformity with ISO 13485:2003. Health Canada expects audit reports to contain statements of conformity with respect to these objectives.

The auditor's observations and handwritten notes can be located in either the final audit report or the auditor's supporting notes that are placed in the manufacturer's file. All auditor's notes must be complete, legible, non-fading and tamper resistant over the period that the records are retained.

Amendments to QMS Certificates Issued by a CMDCAS-Recognized Registrar

Periodically, a manufacturer amends its existing quality system in a manner that can cause some or all of the information in the existing QMS certificate to be outdated. In such cases, *MDR* Section 43.1 requires the manufacturer to submit a new or modified certificate to Health Canada within 30 days of the registrar's reissue of a new or corrected certificate to the manufacturer.

Activities that would cause a registrar to modify an existing QMS certificate include, but are not limited to:
- a change in the manufacturer's name or address
- an addition or deletion of sites under the certified QMS system's control
- an expansion or reduction in registration scope
- a transition to a newer version of the QMS standard

Activities that would cause a registrar to issue a new QMS certificate to a manufacturer already holding a certificate include, but are not limited to:
- a registrar name change
- a manufacturer's transfer of its business to a new registrar
- a manufacturer's receipt of a new certificate after an earlier one was cancelled
- a registrar's change to the certificate format
- a registrar's change to its certificate tracking method

Manufacturers are required to fill out Form 202 when the certificate changes. A copy of Form 202 with the attached new or modified certificate should be mailed or faxed to the Medical Device Bureau within the required timeframe.

Summary

- As of 15 March 2006, Health Canada stopped accepting certificates of conformance to CAN/CSA ISO 13485:1998, CAN/CSA ISO 13488:1998, ISO 13485:1996 and ISO 13488:1996 with new licence applications or licence amendments.
- Class I devices are not required to be manufactured under a certified quality system.
- Class II devices are required to be manufactured under a certified QMS that meets CAN/CSA ISO 13485:2003.
- Class III or IV devices are required to be designed and manufactured under a certified QMS that meets CAN/CSA ISO 13485:2003.
- QMS certificates are valid for only three years.
- Health Canada developed the Canadian Medical Devices Conformity Assessment System to control the auditing and certification process used by third-party auditing bodies (registrars).
- Specific guidance for a manufacturer on how to incorporate the applicable sections of *MDR* Part 1 into its QMS is published in GD210, *ISO 13485:2003 Quality Management System Audits Performed by Health Canada Recognized Registrars*.
- Specific guidance on the content of a QMS certificate issued by CMDCAS-recognized registrars is published in GD207, *Guidance on the Content of ISO 13485 Quality Management System Certificates Issued by Health Canada Recognized Registrars*.

References

1. Memorandum of Understanding Between ISO TC210 and the Global Harmonization Task Force. 1999.
2. Section 1.2, Application, ISO 13485:2003, *Medical devices, Quality managements: Requirements for regulatory purposes.*
3. ISO/IEG Guide 62:1996, *Criteria for accreditation of organizations registering quality systems.*
4. ISO 19011:2002, Guidelines for quality and/or environmental management systems auditing.
5. GHTF, SG4/N28R4:2008 *Guidelines for Regulatory Auditing of Quality Management Systems of Medical Device Manufacturers—Part 1: General Requirements.* 2008.
6. IAF: *Guidance on the Application of ISO/IEC Guide 62*, latest edition.
7. "Policy on Canadian Medical Devices Conformity Assessment System (CMDCAS) to Address the Medical Devices Regulations' Quality Systems Requirement," Q90R0:2000-04-19.
8. List of registrars recognized by Health Canada under section 32.1 of the Medical Devices Regulations (MDR), December 15, 2009.

Recommended Reading

ISO 13485:2003, *Medical devices—Quality management systems—Requirements for regulatory purposes.*

ISO/TR 14969:2004, *Medical devices—Quality management systems—Guidance on the application of ISO 13485:2003.*

Medical Devices Regulations, SOR/98-282, May 7, 1998, Part 1, Sections 32(2)(f), 32(3)(j), 32(4)(p), latest consolidated version.

GD207: *Guidance on the Content of ISO 13485 Quality System Certificates Issued by Health Canada Recognized Registrars,* January 2, 2008.

GD 210: *ISO 13485:2003 Quality Management System Audits Performed by Health Canada Recognized Registrars,* 31 January 2007.

Chapter 34

Canadian In Vitro Diagnostic Device Classification and Submissions

Updated by Nancy Ruth and Merry Lane

OBJECTIVES

❏ Know the definition of an in vitro diagnostic medical device (IVDD)

❏ Become familiar with the licence application types for IVDDs

❏ Understand the risk-based classification system for IVDDs

❏ Understand the application process and content for a medical device licence for an IVDD

❏ Understand the application process and content for investigational testing for IVDDs

REGULATIONS AND GUIDELINES COVERED IN THIS CHAPTER

❏ *Medical Devices Regulations*

❏ *Guidance for the Interpretation of Sections 28 to 31: Licence Application Type* (GD002) (January 1999)

❏ *Draft Guidance for the Risk-Based Classification System of In Vitro Diagnostic Devices* (GD007) (March 1998)

❏ *Preparation of a Premarket Review Document for Class III and IV Device Licence Application* (GD008) (October 1998)

❏ *Preparation of an Application for Investigational*

Testing—In Vitro Diagnostic Devices (GD010) (February 1999)

❏ *Draft Guidance for the Labelling of In Vitro Diagnostic Devices* (GD012) (June 1998)

❏ *Guidance on How to Complete the Application for a New Device Licence* (GD013) (May 2008)

❏ *Guidance for Industry: Preparation of a Premarket Review Document in Electronic Format for a Class IV Medical Device Licence Application* (December 2009)

❏ *Draft Guidance: Keyword Index to Assist Manufacturers in Verifying the Class of In Vitro Diagnostic Devices (IVDD)* (September 2009)

❏ *Guidance on the Recognition and Use of Standards Under the Medical Devices Regulations* (Updated September 2006) and the associated *List of Recognized Standards* (Updated July 2010)

Introduction

An "in vitro diagnostic medical device" (IVDD) is defined in the *Medical Devices Regulations* (*MDR*) as a "medical device that is intended to be used in vitro for the examination of specimens taken from the body." This includes an IVDD that is a drug or contains a drug. A near-patient IVDD is one intended for use outside a laboratory for testing at home or at the point of care, including pharmacies, healthcare professionals' offices or the bedside.

Table 34-1. Format and Contents of Class III Premarket Review Document

Device Licence Application Form
Executive Summary
Table of Contents
1. Background Information
1.1 Device Description
1.2 Design Philosophy
1.3 Marketing History
2. Summary of Safety and Effectiveness Studies
2.1 List of Standards
2.2 Method of Sterilization
2.3 Summary of Studies
2.4 Bibliography
3. Labelling
4. Near-Patient In Vitro Diagnostic Devices (if applicable)
5. Quality System Requirements

Source: TPD guidance document, Preparation of a Premarket Review Document for Class III and Class IV Device Licence Applications.

IVDDs must meet the same safety and effectiveness requirements as non-IVDDs for:

- risks
- risk mitigation
- adverse effects on safety and effectiveness
- intended use
- shelf life and shipping conditions
- compatibility
- hazards
- sterility
- system effects
- software validation

Technical dossiers prepared for submission in other jurisdictions, such as the US and EU, contain substantial supporting technical and medical information for use in medical device licence applications. However, there may be some differences in Health Canada's safety and effectiveness requirements that must be addressed.

Although labelling content requirements are similar to those of the US Food and Drug Administration (FDA) and EU Clinical Laboratory Standards Institute (CLSI), differences in definition of "legal manufacturer," trademark interpretation and the nonacceptability in Canada of internationally recognized symbols in place of words, as well as French language requirements, are some of the considerations in planning for the Canadian market. Labelling for legally marketed devices in other jurisdictions is not necessarily acceptable to Health Canada.

Risk-based Classification System for IVDDs

IVDDs are classified according to risk, where Class I represents the lowest risk and Class IV the highest risk to the patient, user or population (*MDR* Schedule 1, Part 2). The level of risk depends upon the intended use, indications for use and the degree of risk associated with use. The criteria for risk classification depend upon application, expertise required of the intended user, diagnostic degree, outcome of delaying treatment or initiating treatment unnecessarily, emotional effect of diagnosis, nature of follow-up measures and public health effects (infectious agents).

- **Class I**—Minimal risk (general lab equipment and diagnostic reagents, microbiology and cell culture media)
- **Class II**—Low public health risk or moderate individual risk (not easily propagated, transmissible or a self-limiting infectious agent; not the sole determinant of diagnosis; or an erroneous result not likely to cause death or disability)
- **Class III**—Moderate public health risk or high individual risk (Community risk: test may detect a transmissible agent that causes a treatable disease; however, it may result in death or disability if not treated in a timely manner (sexually transmitted disease and nosocomial infections). Individual risk: erroneous result immediately endangers life (meningitis, septicemia). May be a critical or sole determinant in diagnosis or cause emotional stress as a result of diagnosis, such as a cancer marker.)
- **Class IV**—High public health risk: donor screening, HIV screening, hepatitis screening

Table 34-1 summarizes the rules as set out in Schedule 1, Part 2. The rules define the risk groups of test types, based upon the above criteria.

The *Draft Guidance: Keyword Index to Assist Manufacturers in Verifying the Class of In Vitro Diagnostic Devices* available on Health Canada's website is a useful tool for determining or confirming classification.

IVDD Licensing

Class I devices are regulated through the Medical Device Establishment Licence (MDEL). Class II, III and IV devices are regulated by Medical Device Licences. For more information about device and establishment licensing, see "Chapter 30 Medical Device Classification and Submissions."

Licence Application Types

IVDDs may be licensed as a Single Device, a System, a Test Kit, a Medical Device Family, a Medical Device Group or a Medical Device Group Family (*MDR* Sections 28–31). The combination of devices can reduce the number of applications needed and the administrative burden to the manufacturer and Health Canada. Where an IVDD does not meet the definition of any of the combinations below, it is licensed as a single device.

Basic required elements apply to all IVDD and non-IVDD Class II–IV medical device licence applications. Health Canada's website provides application forms specific for each class.

System

An IVDD System is an IVDD that is sold under a single name, where all components are sold under the same manufacturer and system names. Components that are not sold under the same manufacturer and system names cannot be licensed with the system. An IVDD System may consist of an analyzer and all associated test kits and reagents. If test kits in a system have different risk classifications (see below), separate system licences for each risk class that include the test kits of that class must be obtained.

Test Kits

A Test Kit applies only to IVDDs, and consists of reagents or articles used together to perform a specific test. The reagents may be sold packaged in the kit or separately, as long as they are listed on the licence application form.

Medical Device Family

This is a group of medical devices with the same intended use, differing in size, shape, colour or flavour, made by the same manufacturer using the same design and manufacturing process.

Medical Device Group

This is a medical device composed of a collection of medical devices that are labelled or sold under a single name. The devices are not required to have the same manufacturer or be individually labelled with the name of the group. However, if a device is licensed only as part of a Medical Device Group, it cannot be sold separately without a single device licence.

Medical Device Group Family

This is a collection of Medical Device Groups made by the same manufacturer, with the same generic name specifying intended use. The groups differ only in the number and combination of products in each group.

Licence Application Forms

There are some important differences to note with respect to applications for IVDDs.

IVDDs Containing a Controlled Substance

If an IVDD contains a controlled substance, as set out in Schedule I, II, III or IV of the *Controlled Drugs and Substances Act* (found on the Department of Justice website), it must have a Test Kit (TK) registration number. In order to obtain a TK registration number, the company must first hold a Controlled Substance Licence and must apply for the number prior to applying for the Medical Device Licence (MDL). This number does not have to be in hand prior to submission of the licence application but must be pending.

The application form can be found on the Health Canada website (www.hc-sc.gc.ca/hc-ps/alt_formats/hecs-sesc/pdf/substancontrol/substan/test-essai/applic-demande/test-kit-application-eng.pdf). The completed application is submitted as directed to the Evaluation and Authorization Division of the Office of Controlled Substances. It typically takes six to eight weeks to receive the TK registration number. This number must be displayed on the external label of the kit, along with any brand name of the controlled substance, prior to marketing the IVDD.

Premarket Review Document— Class III and IV IVDDs

Scientific and medical requirements for safety and effectiveness must be addressed in applications for Class III and IV MDLs. *MDR* Section 32 (Subsections 3 and 4) sets out the information needed in addition to the basic application requirements. The guidance document, *Preparation of a Premarket Review Document for Class III and IV Device Licence Applications*, specifies the expected content and format.

In addition to this guidance, *Guidance for Industry: Preparation of a Premarket Review Document in Electronic Format for a Class IV Medical Device Licence Application* describes a pilot initiative to encourage manufacturers to move toward electronic MDL submissions. Health Canada strongly recommends both IVDD and non-IVDD Class IV MDL applications be submitted electronically. The electronic format requested is not consistent with the earlier effective guidance document, but the content required is the same. This guidance is not located with the application guidance documents but is posted under Medical Devices/Activities/Announcements at www.hc-sc.gc.ca/dhp-mps/md-im/activit/announce-annonce/notice_e-form_classiv_avis-eng.php.

There are no IVDD-specific guidance documents in effect that are publically posted on the Health Canada website. A draft guidance document, *Guidance for Manufacturers of Human Immunodeficiency Virus (HIV)*

Table 34-2. Format and Content of Class IV Premarket Review Document*

```
    1.  Device Licence Application Form
        Executive Summary
        Table of Contents
        1.0  Background Information
        1.1  Device Description
        1.2  Design Philosophy
        1.3  Marketing History
    2.  Risk Assessment¹
    3.  Quality Plan
    4.  Device Specific Detailed Information
        4.1  Material Specifications
        4.2  Manufacturing Process Specifications
             4.2.1 Method of Manufacture
             4.2.2 Quality Control Activities
        4.3  List of Standards
    5.  Safety and Effectiveness Studies
        5.1  Preclinical and Clinical Studies
             5.1.1 Sensitivity/Specificity
             5.1.2 Validation of Cutoff
             5.1.3 Interference
             5.1.4 Reproducibility
             5.1.5 Stability
        5.2  Process Validation Studies
        5.3  Software Validation Studies (if applicable)
        5.4  Literature Studies
        5.5  Other Studies
    6.  Additional information for Near-Patient IVDDs (if applicable)
    7.  Device Label
    8.  Quality System Audit
```

Source: TPD guidance document GD2008, Preparation of a Premarket Review Document for Class III and Class IV Device License Applications.

Test Kits Intended to be used in the Laboratory (July 2010), which proposes changes to an earlier draft version of this document, has been posted for comment at www.hc-sc. gc.ca/dhp-mps/consultation/md-im/consult_md_gd_ hiv_im_ld_vih_draft_ebauche-eng.php. FDA's expectations tend to evolve with the rapidly changing technology, and the Medical Devices Bureau makes use of guidelines and recognized standards used by the US FDA, the EU CLSI and industry. A few of these standards are included in Health Canada's *List of Recognized Standards.* It can be useful to contact the Medical Devices Bureau for advice on the expectations for specific IVDDs, however, as dossiers of supporting safety and effectiveness information acceptable in other jurisdictions may not meet all of Health Canada's requirements.

The guidance document, *Preparation of a Premarket Review Document for Class III and IV Device Licence Applications,* gives some specifics for Class III IVDD applications and is quite detailed for Class IV IVDDs. In practice, Health Canada tends to apply many of the requirements for Class IV to Class III as well, where pertinent. The guidance indicates that licence applications for Class III and IV should be organized as shown in **Tables 34-1** and **34-2**, respectively, with the titles and numbering suggested. However, refer to the guidance on electronic submissions mentioned above for the Class IV pilot project recommendations; the format is shown in **Figure 34-1**.

The IVDD Premarket Review Document for both classes should include the application form, executive summary, detailed description of the device and packaging, design philosophy, marketing history, list of standards, details of preclinical and clinical studies, validations and near-patient studies, if applicable. For Class III applications, study summaries with interpretation and conclusions are needed; Class IV applications must include more-detailed descriptions with reports and conclusions of studies and line data from the clinical studies. Note that the Medical Devices Bureau expects characterization of clinical samples (and product antigens and antibodies) to be done with at least one Canadian licensed assay when available. Near-patient IVDD studies must simulate expected conditions of use by intended users based only upon the instructions provided in the labelling. A bibliography and any literature studies should be included. Product labelling, including instructions for use, must be submitted and a copy of the ISO 13485:2003 quality system certificate (issued by a registrar recognized under the Canadian Medical Devices Conformity Assessment System—CMDCAS) must be supplied. The guidance document provides greater detail and should be consulted for a complete description.

Figure 34-1. Electronic Folder Structure for a Premarket Review Document for a Class IV In Vitro Diagnostic Device Licence Application*

- 📁 [device name]
    - 📁 1.0 Cover Letter
    - 📁 2.0 Table of Contents
    - 📁 3.0 Administrative Information
        - 📁 3.1 Medical Device Licence Application Form and Fee Form
        - 📁 3.2 Quality Management System Certificate
        - 📁 3.3 Letter of Attestation for Electronic Copy Submission
    - 📁 4.0 Executive Summary
    - 📁 5.0 Background Information
        - 📁 5.1 Device Description
        - 📁 5.2 Design Philosophy
        - 📁 5.3 Marketing History
    - 📁 6.0 Risk Assessment
    - 📁 7.0 Quality Plan
    - 📁 8.0 Device Specific Detailed Information
        - 📁 8.1 Material Specifications
            - 📁 8.2.1 Method of Manufacture
            - 📁 8.2.2 Quality Control Activities
    - 📁 9.0 Safety and Effectiveness Studies
        - 📁 9.1 Preclinical and Clinical Studies
            - 📁 9.1.1 Sensitivity and Specificity
            - 📁 9.1.2 Validation of Cutoff
            - 📁 9.1.3 Interference
            - 📁 9.1.4 Reproducibility
            - 📁 9.1.5 Stability
        - 📁 9.2 Process Validation Studies
        - 📁 9.3 Softward Validation Studies
        - 📁 9.4 Literature Studies and Bibliography
        - 📁 9.5 Other Studies
    - 📁 10.0 Additional Information for Near-patient IVDDs
    - 📁 11.0 Device Label

Source: TPD Guidance for Industry: Preparation of a Premarket Review Document in Electronic Format for a Class IV Medical Device Licence Application.

IVDD Labelling

The labelling requirements for IVDDs include the same basic requirements for all medical devices outlined in *MDR* Section 21, and some additional requirements as in Sections 22 and 23. The "label" includes the immediate device container label, reagent and component labels and package insert. The outer label must contain the following information in either English or French:
- device name
- manufacturer name and address
- device identifier: a unique series of letters and numbers or any combination of those, or a bar code assigned by the manufacturer, which uniquely identifies the device as different from other similar devices

- control or lot number (Class III or IV device)
- units of the package contents (size, weight, volume, etc.)
- the words "sterile" and "stérile" if the device is sold in a sterile condition
- expiration date
- medical conditions, purposes and uses for which the device is sold and used
- directions for use, unless they are not required for the device to be used safely and effectively
- special storage conditions

Package inserts are necessary for most IVDDs, and must include directions for use. There is no prescribed order or

---

format for presentation of the information, but it should include the elements listed as applicable to the device:

- device name
- manufacturer name and address
- intended use (monitoring, screening, diagnosis, technology used, whether qualitative or quantitative, analyte, patient population, where the device may be used, type of specimen required, specific contraindications)
- summary and explanation (techniques, reactions, description of antibodies and antigens, purification methods)
- directions for use:
  - components provided: name, volume/quantity, nonreactive materials, maximum number of tests that can be run, directions for reagent preparation, storage instructions for opened and unopened reagents
  - list of materials required but not provided
  - list of dedicated equipment or software, including model and version numbers
  - warnings, precautions, contraindications and possible side effects (internationally recognized symbols may be used; *Guidance Document for the Labelling of In Vitro Diagnostic Devices* (GD012) contains a list of possible precautions)
  - the phrase "For in vitro diagnostic use" must be included in the directions for use
  - if the device contains biological hazards from human or animal sources, specific cautions must be used (see GD012, Section 3.2.5.2)
  - specimen collection and handling instructions, storage, patient preparation, known interferents
  - test procedure: required amount of reagents and controls, temperatures, wavelengths, sample handling, calibration information, reaction stability, quality control procedures
  - results: formulae, sample calculations
  - interpretation of results: acceptance and rejection criteria, when to retest, significance of the results, cut-off levels
  - limitations, including contraindications, personnel qualification, clinical factors that may affect results
  - expected values: range of expected values from various populations and how the range was established, using literature references if appropriate
  - disposal and handling
  - performance characteristics: must include a summary of clinical trials performed on the device (sensitivity, specificity, positive and negative predictive values, repeatability, stability, limits of detection, earliest clinical detection, etc.)
  - storage instructions
  - catalogue number or identifier
  - date of issue, revision level
  - bibliography

The insert may be provided in either English or French, but it must be available in both languages upon request of the customer or Health Canada. However, warnings and contraindications must be printed in both languages in any case.

Note that the Province of Québec language laws have additional requirements for French language labelling for all products.

Internationally recognized symbols may be used on labelling, but a legend must be included to show the meaning of each symbol used. Symbols may not be used to replace required wording.

Devices Sold Directly to Consumers

If the device is sold directly to consumers, the information listed for the label on the outer package must be visible under normal conditions of sale. Both the outer label and the instructions for use must be provided in English and French. Sales to consumers include transactions via retail establishments, mail order and the Internet.

IVDDs Used for Screening Blood Donors

Health Canada pays particular attention to labelling for IVDDs used for screening donors of blood, organs and tissues for transplantation. Intended use statements for these must specify donor screening and supporting studies submitted must include donor sample testing. The current labelling requirements are somewhat inconsistent with the guidance in GD012.

Investigational Testing for IVDDs

Clinical studies in humans using a Class I medical device, including an IVDD, may be conducted in Canada provided required records prescribed in Section 81 of the *MDR* are retained. No submission to Health Canada is needed.

Clinical studies in humans with a Class II, III or IV device, including an IVDD, which is not licensed in Canada, must be conducted under an Investigational Testing Authorization (ITA). The clinical study may be intended to obtain clinical data in support of a new licence application in Canada, or marketing authorization in another jurisdiction. An ITA is also required to collect data to extend the intended use of a device licensed in Canada. *MDR* Sections 79–88 set out the requirements for an ITA. *Preparation of an Application for Investigational Testing—In Vitro Diagnostic Devices* (GD010) describes the regulatory requirements, submission process and content.

The application for an ITA for Class II–IV IVDDs,

Table 34-3. Recommended Format for an Investigational Testing Application*

```
Application Form
    Executive Summary
    Table of Contents
    1.  Background Information
        1.1  Device Description
        1.2  Design Philosophy
        1.3  Marketing History
    2.  Risk Assessment
        2.1  Risk Analysis and Evaluation
        2.2  Previous Studies
        2.3  Alternate Treatments
        2.4  Precautions
    3.  Institutional Information
        3.1  Investigator(s)
        3.2  Name of Institution(s)
        3.3  Research Ethics Board Approval(s)
    4.  Protocol
    5.  Device Label
    6.  Investigator Agreement(s)
```

* Source: Guidance document GD010, Preparation of an Application for Investigational Testing – in vitro Diagnostic Devices.

and for a Class III IVDD that will not be used for patient management (not including a near-patient IVDD), requires the following information:

- manufacturer identification
- device identification—name and identifiers
- device risk classification
- institutional information
- clinical protocol
- device labelling—label must include device name and identifier, manufacturer's name and required English and equivalent French statements: "Investigational Device," "To be used by qualified investigators only," and "The performance characteristics of this product have not been established." Instructions for use for the investigators and/or patients and promotional/advertising should be provided.

Note that the information submitted should include a description of the device, its materials and how it is used. Sufficient information may be available in the instructions for use; if not, it could be added with the device identification.

Research Ethics Board approval must be obtained; it is submitted with the ITA for a Class III IVDD not used for patient management, but is not submitted for a Class II IVDD. Investigator names and addresses, their CVs and signed Investigator Agreements (Health Canada template or equivalent) must be retained as part of the records requirements described in *MDR* Section 81.

Class III and IV IVDDs used for patient management decisions and Class III and IV near-patient IVDDs have more-comprehensive submission requirements, in addition to the above:

- device description
- design philosophy
- marketing history
- risk assessment and risk reduction, including previous studies, alternate treatments and precautions
- investigator names, CVs and signed Investigator Agreements
- Research Ethics Board approval

See **Table 34-3** for the recommended application format.

The application form that accompanies the submitted information is included in the guidance document, along with the Investigator Agreement template and other useful information for sponsors planning a study. Applications are submitted to:

Medical Device Bureau
Therapeutic Products Directorate
Room 1605, Main Building
150 Tunney's Pasture Driveway
Tunney's Pasture
Address Locator 0301H1
Ottawa, Ontario
Canada K1A 0K9

The target review time for ITA submissions is 30 days. A study cannot begin until a Letter of Authorization has been issued by Health Canada.

Responsibilities of the manufacturer and/or sponsor during study conduct are described in *MDR* Section 88, and include mandatory problem reporting, recall, complaint handling and distribution record retention. Procedures must be in place to meet these obligations.

Summary

In vitro diagnostic devices are considered medical devices in Canada and are classified according to risk, based on rules included in the *MDR*. Class I devices are regulated through Medical Device Establishment Licences, without premarket review of specific product information, while Class II, III and IV are subject to Medical Device Licences that Health Canada issues following evaluation of the manufacturer's submitted dossier. The extent of evidence to support safety and effectiveness required by Health Canada increases in proportion to the risk of erroneous results posed to individuals and the community.

References

1. The international standard, ISO 14971:2007: *Medical Devices—Application of Risk Management to Medical Devices*, may be used to assist in performing risk analyses and assessments for IVDDs.

Recommended Reading

Medical Devices Regulations, *Canada Gazette, Part II*, 27 May 1998, Vol. 132, No. 11

Guidance for the Interpretation of Sections 28 to 31: Licence Application Type.i (GD002)

Guidance for the Risk-Based Classification System of in vitro Diagnostic Devices (GD007)

Preparation of a Premarket Review Document for Class III and IV Device Licence Application (GD008)

Preparation of an Application for Investigational Testing – in vitro Diagnostic Devices (GD010)

Guidance for the Labelling of in vitro Diagnostic Devices (GD012)

Guidance on How to Complete the Application for a New Device Licence (GD013)

Guidance for Industry: Preparation of a Premarket Review Document in Electronic Format for a Class IV Medical Device Licence Application

Chapter 35

Canadian Glossary of Terms

A

AbNDS

Abbreviated New Drug Submission (Veterinary Drugs)

Advertisement

Any representation by any means whatsoever for the purpose of promoting directly or indirectly the sale or disposal of any food, drug, cosmetic or device.

ACAA

Advisory Committee on Causality Assessment. A committee composed of independent experts in infectious diseases, public health, vaccine safety, epidemiology, pathology, neurology and paediatrics that reviews serious adverse events following immunization, such as deaths or hospitalizations to determine causality.

ADR

Adverse Drug Reaction

AHRC

Assisted Human Reproduction Canada. Federal regulatory agency responsible for protecting and promoting the health, safety, dignity and rights of Canadians who use or are born of assisted human reproduction while allowing scientific advances that benefit Canadians.

ANDS

Abbreviated New Drug Submission. Used for a generic product. The submission must meet the same quality standards as an NDS and the generic product must be shown to be as safe and efficacious as the brand-name product.

API

Active Pharmaceutical Ingredient

ASC

Advertising Standards Canada

ATI

Access to Information Act

Authorized SAR

Authorized Special Access Request

B

Batch

A quantity of drug in dosage form, a raw material or a packaging material, homogeneous within specified limits, produced according to a single production order and as attested by the signatories to the order.

BGTD

Biologics and Genetic Therapies Directorate

Bioavailability

The rate and extent of absorption of a drug into the systemic circulation.

Bioequivalence

A high degree of similarity in the rate and extent of absorption into the systemic circulation of two comparable pharmaceutical products, from the same dose, that are unlikely to produce clinically relevant differences in therapeutic effects or adverse effects, or both.

Biologics

A subset of therapeutic products made from biological starting material, including those obtained by recombinant DNA procedures.

Blinded Study

Clinical trial in which the patient (single-blind) or patient and investigator (double-blind) are unaware of which treatment the patient receives. Involves use of multiple treatment groups such as other active, placebo or alternate dose groups.

BREC
Biologics and Radiopharmaceuticals Evaluation Centre

C

CADTH
Canadian Agency for Drugs and Technologies in Health (formerly Canadian Coordinating Office of Health Technology Assessment)

Canada Vigilance Program
Health Canada's postmarket surveillance program that collects and assesses reports of suspected adverse reactions to health products marketed in Canada.

CASRN
Chemical Abstract Services Registry Number. The identification number assigned to a substance by the Chemical Abstracts Service Division of the American Chemical Society.

Category IV Monograph
Outlines the permissible conditions of use and labelling requirements, such as dose, intended use, directions for use, warnings, active ingredients and combinations thereof for nonprescription drugs. Developed for drugs that have a well characterized safety and efficacy profile under specific conditions of use.

CCDT
Canadian Council for Donation and Transplantation

CCTFA
Canadian Cosmetic, Toiletry and Fragrance Association

CDR
Common Drug Review. A single common process for reviewing new drugs to assess potential coverage under Canadian public drug benefit plans, established in September 2001 by federal, provincial and territorial health ministers.

CDSA
Controlled Drugs and Substances Act

CEDAC
Canadian Expert Drug Advisory Committee. An independent advisory body of drug therapy and evaluation professionals.

CEO Substance
Contained Export-Only Substance

CEPA
Canadian Environmental Protection Act

CERB
Centre for Evaluation of Radiopharmaceuticals and Biotherapeutics

Certificate of Manufacture
Issued by a vendor to a distributor or importer and attests that a specific lot or batch of drug has been produced in accordance with its master production document. Such certificates include a detailed summary of current batch documentation, with reference to respective dates of revision, manufacture and packaging, and are signed and dated by the vendor's quality control department.

CFIA
Canadian Food Inspection Agency

CFOB
Chief Financial Officer Branch

CHA
Canada Health Act

CIHR
Canadian Institutes of Health Research Act

CIOMS
Council for International Organizations of Medical Sciences

Clarifax
A request sent to a manufacturer by Health Canada requesting clarification during the screening and review of an application.

C&M
Chemistry and Manufacturing/Quality

CMCD
Communications, Marketing and Consultation Directorate

CMDCAS
Canadian Medical Devices Conformity Assessment System

CMIB
Compendium of Medicating Ingredient Brochures

CNSC
Canadian Nuclear Safety Commission

Combination Product
Therapeutic product that combines either a drug (biological or pharmaceutical) component and a device

component (which by themselves would be classified as a drug or a device), or a biological pharmaceutical combination, such that the distinctive nature of the two components are integrated in a single product.

Compendium of Monographs
A compilation of monographs based on natural health product ingredients.

Cosmetic
Any substance or mixture of substances manufactured, sold or represented for use in cleansing, improving or altering the complexion, skin, hair or teeth, and includes deodorants and perfumes.

CPhA
Canadian Pharmaceuticals Association

CPID
Certified Product Information Document

CPID-R
Certified Product Information Document—Radiopharmaceuticals

CPP
Certificate of a Pharmaceutical Product

CPS
Compendium of Pharmaceuticals and Specialties

CR
Central Registry

CRP
Canadian Reference Product. A marketed drug used for the purpose of demonstrating the bioequivalence of a subsequent entry drug.

CSA
Canadian Standards Association

CSB
Corporate Services Branch

CS-BE
Comprehensive Summary: Bioequivalence

CSLI Substance
A substance consumed in a chemical reaction used for the manufacture of another substance and either manufactured and consumed at the site of manufacture, manufactured at one site and transported to a second site where it is consumed, or imported and transported

directly to the site where it is consumed.

CTA
Clinical Trial Application. Submitted by sponsors prior to initiation of clinical testing in human subjects.

CTA-A
Clinical Trial Application Amendment. An application in which a manufacturer provides new information that updates a previously authorized Clinical Trial Application.

CTD
Common Technical Document. A common international format that may be used by drug sponsors to submit information supporting new drug applications to regulatory authorities for review. The US, EU, Japan, Australia and now Canada all use this format.

CTO Regulations
Safety of Human Cells, Tissues and Organs for Transplantation Regulations

CTSIF
Clinical Trial Site Information Form

D

Declaration of Equivalence
A Notice of Compliance issued in respect of a new drug on the basis of information and material contained in a submission filed pursuant to section C.08.002.1 shall state the name of the Canadian reference product referred to in the submission and shall constitute a declaration of equivalence for that new drug.

DEL
Drug Establishment Licence. A licence issued to a person in Canada to conduct licensable activities in a building that has been inspected and assessed as being in compliance with the requirements of Divisions 2 to 4 of the *FDR*.

DIN
Drug Identification Number. An eight-digit numerical code assigned to each drug product approved under the *F&DA* and *FDR*, except for Schedule C drugs (i.e., radiopharmaceuticals, kits and generators).

DIN Application
Must be filed for those products that do not meet the definition of a 'new drug.' In such circumstances, the substance for use as a drug has been sold in Canada for a sufficient time and quantity to establish that substance's safety and effectiveness for use as a drug.

DIN-HM
Drug Identification Number for Homeopathic Medicine

DMF
Drug Master File. A reference that provides information about specific processes or components used in the manufacturing, processing and packaging of a drug.

DNF
Drug Notification Form

DSL
Domestic Substances List. Comprehensive inventory of known substances in use in Canadian commerce (past and present).

DSSAP
Donor Semen Special Access Programme

DSSC
Drug Schedule Status Committee

DSTS-IA
Drug Submission Tracking System—Industry Access

DTC
Direct-to-Consumer

E
EAU
Environmental Assessment Unit

ECC
Economic Council of Canada

eCTD
Electronic Common Technical Document

EDR
Emergency Drug Release (Veterinary)

EL
Establishment Licence

ELDU
Extra Label Drug Use

EMA
European Medicines Agency (formerly European Medicines Evaluation Agency)

EP
End-use Product

ESC
Experimental Study Certificate

EUND
Extraordinary Use New Drug. Intended to treat a condition where human efficacy studies are not ethical or feasible.

F
F&DA
Food and Drugs Act

FDA
US Food and Drug Administration

FDR

Food and Drug Regulations

FNIHB
First Nations and Inuit Health Branch

G
GD
Guidance Document

Generic Drug
A medicinal product with the same active ingredient, but not necessarily the same inactive ingredients as a brand-name drug. A generic drug may only be marketed after the original drug's patent has expired.

GHTF
Global Harmonization Task Force. Comprised of five Founding Members: EU, US, Canada, Australia and Japan. Formed to encourage convergence in regulatory practices related to ensuring the safety, effectiveness/ performance and quality of medical devices, promoting technological innovation and facilitating international trade.

GMP
Good Manufacturing Practice

GLP
Good Laboratory Practice

GP
General Public

GCP
Good Clinical Practices

H
HC
Health Canada

HDE

Human Derived Excipients

HECSB
Healthy Environments and Consumer Safety Branch

HIV
Human Immunodeficiency Virus

HMIRC
Hazardous Materials Information Review Commission

HPFB
Health Products and Food Branch

HPFBI
Health Products and Food Branch Inspectorate

I
IACB
Information, Analysis and Connectivity Branch

IAF
International Accreditation Forum

IB
Investigator's Brochure. Relevant clinical and nonclinical data compiled on the investigational drug, biologic or device being studied.

ICH
International Conference on Harmonisation (participants include the EU, Japan and US; observers include Australia and Canada).

ICL
In Commerce Substance List

IMEP
Importation for Manufacturing and Export Program

INCI
International Nomenclature Cosmetic Ingredient

IND
Investigational New Drug

Informed Consent
The voluntary verification of a patient's willingness to participate in a clinical trial, along with the documentation thereof. This verification is requested only after complete, objective information has been given about the trial, including an explanation of the study's objectives, potential benefits, risks and inconveniences; alternative therapies available; and of the subject's rights and responsibilities in accordance with the current revision of the Declaration of Helsinki.

IRN
Information Request Notice

IRP
Integrated Review Process for ANDSs. Uses a team approach, comprised of Regulatory Project Managers and Scientific Evaluators to perform a comprehensive screening to evaluate the completeness of the drug submission.

ISP
Integrated System Product

ISO
International Organization for Standardization

ITA
Investigational Testing Authorization

IVDD
In vitro diagnostic device

L
Labelling
Includes any legend, word or mark attached to, included in, belonging to or accompanying any therapeutic product and is commonly understood to mean all packaging and product inserts, including the drug product monograph.

LCDC
Laboratory Centre for Disease Control

Letters of Access
Authorizes Health Canada to access related master files if they are cross referenced in the CTA/CTA-A submission.

Letter of Undertaking
A letter submitted to Health Canada by a sponsor of a drug submission prior to the issuance of a Notice of

Compliance, qualifying under the NOC/c policy. The letter must be signed by the Chief Executive Officer, or designated signing authority of the sponsor and must outline commitments to pursue postmarket activities satisfactory to Health Canada.

Lot Release Program
Provides an additional check on biologic drugs to help assure their safety for human use.

LRC
Law Reform Commission of Canada

M
MAD
Mutual Acceptance of Data. Data generated in an OECD member country in accordance with OECD Test Guidelines and Principles of Good Laboratory Practice (GLP) shall be accepted in other member countries for assessment purposes and other uses relating to the protection of human health and the environment.

MAH
Market Authorization Holder. Also referred to as sponsor or manufacturer, the MAH is the legal entity that holds the Notice of Compliance, the Drug Identification Number (DIN), the medical device licence number, the product licence number or has received approval to initiate clinical trials in Canada.

Marketing Authorization
A legal document issued by Health Canada, authorizing the sale of a drug or a device based on the health and safety requirements of the *F&DA* and *MDR*. The marketing authorization may be in the form of a Notice of Compliance (NOC) or Drug Identification Number (DIN).

Master File
A document provided by a subcontractor or manufacturer that contains specific objective evidence, for example material characterization or sterilization processing characteristics. These data are often independent of final device processing and can be referenced by many different device licence applications. If the file has been submitted by someone other than the manufacturer, permission must be granted by the file owner for each licence application using the information contained in the Master File.

MDALL
Medical Devices Active Licence Listing

MDB
Medical Devices Bureau

MDR
Medical Devices Regulations

MDRC
Medical Devices Review Committee
MDEL
Medical Device Establishment Licence

MEDEC
Medical Devices Canada

MedEffect Canada
Health Canada initiative to provide centralized access to important new health product safety information and to build awareness about adverse reactions and the importance of reporting them.

Medical Device
Any article, instrument, apparatus or contrivance, including any component, part or accessory thereof, manufactured, sold or represented for use in:
- the diagnosis, treatment, mitigation or prevention of a disease, disorder or abnormal physical state or its symptoms in human beings or animals
- restoring, correcting or modifying a body function or the body structure of human beings or animals
- the diagnosis of pregnancy in human beings or animals
- the care of human beings or animals during pregnancy and at and after birth of the offspring

Medical Device Family
A group of medical devices made by the same manufacturer, that differ only in shape, colour, flavour or size, that have the same design and manufacturing process and that have the same intended use.

Medical Device Group
A medical device comprising a collection of medical devices, such as a procedure pack or tray, sold under a single name.

Medical Device Group Family
A collection of medical device groups made by the same manufacturer, that have the same generic name specifying their intended use and differ only in the number and combination of products that comprise each group.

Medical Devices SAP
Special Access Programme. Permits healthcare professionals to access custom-made and unlicensed

medical devices for emergency use or when conventional therapies have failed, are unavailable or are unsuitable to provide a diagnosis, treatment or prevention for patients under their care.

Medical Device User Problem Report
Any account of a problem or concern involving a medical device, which is forwarded to Health Canada at the discretion of the reporter.

MHPD
Marketed Health Products Directorate

MIB
Compendium of Medicating Ingredient Brochures

MOU
Memorandum of Understanding. An agreement between Health Canada and another country's regulatory authority that allows mutual recognition of inspections.

MRA
Mutual Recognition Agreement. Legally binding, negotiated agreements between governments concerning specific regulated products.

MRL
Maximum residue level

N
NAPRA
National Association of Pharmacy Regulatory Authorities

NC
Notifiable Change

NCC
National Coordination Centre

NCE
New Chemical Entity

New Drug
Drugs that fall under Division 8 of the Canadian *FDR*. Drugs under Division 8 are those that have not been available for a long period of time and for which manufacturers must submit anNDS.

NDMAC
Nonprescription Drug Manufacturers Association of Canada

NDS
New Drug Submission. An application submitted to

TPD or BGTD requesting marketing approval for a new drug. Contains scientific information about the product's safety, efficacy and quality. It includes the results of both preclinical and clinical studies, details on the production of the drug and its packaging and labelling, and information about its claimed therapeutic value, conditions for use and side effects.

NDSAC
National Drug Scheduling Advisory Committee

NDSL
Non-domestic substances list. Comprehensive inventory of substances not on the DSL but believed to be in use in international commerce.

NHP
Natural Health Product. Vitamins and minerals, herbal remedies, homeopathic medicines, traditional medicines such as traditional Chinese medicines, probiotics and other products like amino acids and essential fatty acids.

NHPD
Natural Health Products Directorate

NHPR
Natural Health Products Regulations

NHPRP
Natural Health Products Research Program

NMI
Nonmedicinal Ingredient

NOA
Notice of Allegation

NOC
Notice of Compliance. Letter issued by HPFB concluding that a drug's benefits outweigh the risks and that the risks can be mitigated and/or managed,

NOC/c
Notice of Compliance with Conditions. Authorizes the manufacturer to market a drug on condition that the manufacturer undertake additional studies to confirm the clinical benefit.

NOC/c-QN
Notice of Compliance with Conditions Qualifying Notice. Issued by Health Canada to manufacturer indicating that the submission qualifies for an NOC,

under the NOC/c policy, and outlining the additional clinical evidence to be provided in confirmatory trials, postmarket surveillance responsibilities and any requirements related to advertising, labelling, or distribution.

NOD

Notice of Deficiency. Issued by Health Canada if the manufacturer fails to submit requested information within the required time period; there is unsolicited information; or the information is incomplete or deficient.

NOD-W

Notice of Deficiency–Withdrawal. If a manufacturer's response to an NOD is still found to be deficient, Health Canada requires the sponsor to withdraw the file from review.

NOAEL

No Observable Adverse Effects Level

NOEQ

Notice of Excess Quantity

NOMI

Notice of Manufacture or Import

NOL

No Objection Letter. Issued by Health Canada within the review period if no clinical or quality deficiencies are identified and the CTA or CTA-A is deemed acceptable.

NON

Notice of Noncompliance. Issued if HFPB finds that the submission fails to comply with the requirements set out in the *FDR*.

NON-W

Notice of Noncompliance–Withdrawal. Issued by Health Canada if the response to a NON is inadequate, indicating the company must withdraw the submission.

Notice of Decision

Outlines the authorization received and general information related to the drug.

NPN

Natural Product Number

NSN

Not Satisfactory Notice. Issued by Health Canada if significant deficiencies are identified during the review of the CTA or CTA-A.

NSN

New Substances Notification

NSNR

New Substances Notification Regulations

NS Program

New Substances Program. Consists of representatives from both Environment Canada and Health Canada. Each department conducts an assessment of the information provided to the minister in the NSN package.

O

OCDO

Office of the Chief Dental Officer

OCRR

Office of the Coordinator, Regulatory Reform

OCS

Office of Controlled Substances

OCS

Office of the Chief Scientist

OECD

Organisation for Economic Co-operation and Development

Old Drug

Drugs that fall under Division 1 of the Canadian *FDR*. These are generally older drugs that have been on the market for a number of years, often available without a prescription.

OSE

Onsite Evaluation. Preapproval inspection of a manufacturing facility by BGTD.

OPML

Office of Patented Medicines and Liaison

OPP

Office of Pesticide Programs

OPPTS

Office of Pollution Prevention and Toxics

OPRA

Office of Privatization and Regulatory Affairs

OTC

Over-the-Counter. Drugs available for purchase without a physician's prescription.

P

PAAB
Pharmaceutical Advertising Advisory Board

PAAC
Product Assessment Against Criteria

Patent Register
Listing of medicinal ingredients and their associated patents, the patent expiry dates and other related information established in accordance with the *Patented Medicines (Notice of Compliance) Regulations* (SOR/133-93 as amended).

PCERT
Preclinical and Clinical Evaluation Report Template

PCO
Privy Council Office

PD
Pharmacodynamics. Study of the reactions between drugs and living structures.

PDN

Processing Deficiency Notice

PERs
Positron-Emitting Radiopharmaceuticals

PET
Positron Emission Tomography

PHAC
Public Health Agency of Canada

Pharmacovigilance
The science and activities relating to the detection, assessment, understanding and prevention of adverse reactions or any other drug-related problem.

Phase I Study
The first of four phases of clinical trials, Phase I studies are designed to establish the effects of a new drug in humans. These studies are usually conducted on small populations of healthy humans to specifically determine a drug's toxicity, absorption, distribution and metabolism.

Phase II Study
After the successful completion of Phase I trials, a drug is then tested for safety and efficacy in a slightly larger population of individuals who are afflicted with the disease or condition for which the drug was developed.

Phase III Study
The third and last preapproval round of testing of a drug is conducted on large populations of afflicted patients. Phase III studies usually test the new drug in comparison with the standard therapy currently being used for the disease in question. The results of these trials usually provide the information that is included in the package insert and labelling.

Phase IV Study
After a drug has been approved by Health Canada, Phase IV studies are conducted to compare the drug to a competitive product, explore additional patient populations or to further study any adverse events.

PIC/S
Pharmaceutical Inspection Convention and Pharmaceutical Inspection Co-operation Scheme

PIPEDA
Personal Information Protection and Electronic Documents Act

PK
Pharmacokinetics

PLA
Product License Application

Placebo
A "dummy" preparation having no specific pharmacological activity against the patients' illness or complaint. It is administered to the control group in a controlled clinical trial to distinguish the experimental treatment's specific and nonspecific effects.

PM
Product Monograph. A factual, scientific document, devoid of promotional material, that describes the properties, claims, indications and conditions of use for a drug and that contains any other information that may be required for optimal, safe and effective use of the drug. Product monographs are submitted to HPFB as part of a new drug submission.

PM-NOC
Patented Medicines (Notice of Compliance) Regulations. Encourages investment in drug research and development by preventing competitors from infringing the patent rights of brand-name drug manufacturers while still allowing generic drugs to enter the market as soon as the patent expires.

PMPRB
Patented Medicine Prices Review Board

PMRA
Pest Management Regulatory Agency

PPHB
Population and Public Health Branch

Preclinical testing
Before a drug may be tested on humans, preclinical studies must be conducted either *in vitro* but usually *in vivo* on animals to determine that the drug is safe.

Private Label Medical Device
A medical device that is identical in every respect to a medical device manufactured by an original manufacturer and licensed by Health Canada, except that the device is labelled with the private label manufacturer's name, address and product name and identifier.

Principal Mechanism of Action
The single mechanism of action by which the claimed effect or purpose of the combination product is achieved. Used to determine whether the combination product will be subject to the *FDR* or the *MDR*.

Priority Review Status
A priority review status assigns eligible submissions a shortened review target. This status may be granted to drug submissions intended for the treatment, prevention or diagnosis of serious, life-threatening or severely debilitating illnesses or conditions where there is no existing drug on the Canadian market with the same profile; or the new product represents a significant improvement in the benefit/risk profile over existing products.

Product Monograph
A factual scientific document describing the drug. It is devoid of promotional material and describes the properties, claims, indications and conditions of use for the drug. It also contains any other information that may be required for optimal, safe and effective use of the drug.

Product Withdrawal
A firm's removal from the market of a product that does not violate the *F&DA* or *MDR*.

Protocol
A detailed plan that sets forth the objectives, study design and methodology for a clinical trial. A study protocol

must be approved by an REB before investigational drugs may be administered to humans.

PSD
Product Safety Directorate

PSEAT-CTA
Protocol Safety and Efficacy Assessment Template—Clinical Trial Application

PSUR
Periodic Safety Update Report. A standard report used internationally by regulatory authorities to systematically monitor the safety of marketed drug products and a primary source of clinical safety information concerning a given drug.

PSUR-C
Periodic Safety Update Report—Confirmatory

Q
QAP
Quality Assurance Person

QAR
Quality Assurance Report

QIS-B
Quality Information Summary—Biological

QIS-P
Quality Information Summary—Pharmaceutical

QIS-R
Quality Information Summary—Radiopharmaceuticals

QMS
Quality Management System

QOS-BS
Quality Overall Summary—Bioequivalence Study

QOS-CE
Quality Overall Summary—Chemical Entity

R
R&D Substance
Research and Development Substance. A substance undergoing systematic investigation or research, by means of experimentation or analysis other than test marketing.

Radiopharmaceutical
Pharmaceutical, biological or drug that contains a

radioactive entity. Radiopharmaceuticals are primarily used for various imaging functions but can also be used in a therapeutic capacity.

REB
Research Ethics Board
An independent group of professionals designated to review and approve the clinical protocol, informed consent forms, study advertisements and patient brochures, to ensure the study is safe and effective for human participation. It is also the REB's responsibility to ensure the study adheres to Health Canada's regulations.

Recall (for Health Products Other Than Medical Devices)
A firm's removal from further sale or use, or correction, of a distributed product that presents a risk to the health of consumers or violates legislation administered by HPFB.

Recall (*Medical Device Regulations*)
Any action taken by the manufacturer, importer or distributor of a device that has been sold, to recall or correct the device, or to notify its owners and users of its defectiveness or potential defectiveness, after becoming aware that the device may: be hazardous to health; fail to conform to any claim made by the manufacturer or importer relating to its effectiveness, benefits, performance characteristics or safety; or not meet the requirements set in the *F&DA* or *MDR*.

Reference Biologic Drug
Biologic drug authorized on the basis of a complete qualifying nonclinical and clinical data package to which an SEB is compared in studies to demonstrate similarity.

RIAS
Regulatory Impact Analysis Statement

ROD

Record of Decision

RPM
Regulatory Project Manager (TPD)

RPO
Regulatory Project Officer (BGTD)

RRR Polymer
Reduced Regulatory Requirement Polymer

S
SAbNDS
Supplemental Abbreviated New Drug Submission (Veterinary Drugs)

SAMS
Special Access Management System. An internal database listing all drugs eligible through the SAP.

SANDS
Supplemental Abbreviated New Drug Submission. This document must be filed by a manufacturer if changes are made to a drug authorized under an Abbreviated New Drug Submission (ANDS). Such changes may include method of manufacture, labelling, recommended route of administration or a new indication.

SAP
Special Access Programme. Allows practitioners to request access to drugs that are unavailable for sale in Canada. This access is limited to patients with serious or life-threatening conditions on a compassionate or emergency basis when conventional therapies have failed, are unsuitable or are unavailable.

SAR
Special Access Request. Form submitted by practitioners to request access to a SAP drug.

SBD
Summary Basis of Decision. A document that outlines the scientific and benefit/risk-based decisions that factor into Health Canada's decision to grant market authorization for a drug or medical device.

SCC
Standards Council of Canada

SDN
Screening Deficiency Notice. Issued if deficiencies are identified during screening of a drug submission.

SEB
Subsequent Entry Biologic. A biologic drug that would enter the market subsequent to, and 'similar' to an innovator product authorized for sale in Canada. A subsequent entry biologic relies in part on prior information regarding safety and efficacy that is deemed relevant due to the demonstration of similarity to the reference biologic drug.

SIPD
Submission and Information Policy Division

SG
Study Group

SLA
Site Licence Application (for Natural Health Products)

SMCE
Small Molecule Chemical Entity

SNAc
Significant New Activity. Any activity that results or may result in (a) the entry or release of the living organism into the environment in a quantity or concentration that, in the ministers' opinion, is significantly greater than the quantity or concentration of the living organism that previously entered or was released into the environment; or (b) the entry or release of the living organism into the environment or the exposure or potential exposure of the environment to the living organism in a manner and circumstances that, in the ministers' opinion, are significantly different from the manner and circumstances in which the living organism previously entered or was released into the environment or of any previous exposure or potential exposure of the environment to the living organism.

SNDS
Supplemental New Drug Submission. Must be filed by the manufacturer if certain changes are made to already-authorized products.

SNDS-C
Supplemental New Drug Submission—Confirmatory

SRL
Screening Rejection Letter. Issued if a drug is considered a new drug, and hence an NDS is required, and if a proposed ingredient is a prohibited substance, or if a statement within the product monograph is found not to reflect the submission content.

STD
Sexually Transmitted Disease

STED
Summary Technical Documentation

Stock Recovery
A firm's removal or correction of a product that has not been marketed or that has not left the direct control of the firm.

T

TAS
Therapeutic Access Strategy

TC
Technical Committee

TGAI
Technical Grade Active Ingredient

TK
Test Kit. An IVDD that consists of reagents or articles, or any combination of these, and is intended to be used to conduct a specific test.

TMA
Terms of Market Authorization

TPCC
Therapeutic Products Classification Committee. A committee appointed by the director general of TPD to develop, maintain, evaluate and recommend for approval policies, procedures and guidelines concerning the classification and review of therapeutic products as drugs, devices or combination products; and to assess submissions for combination products referred to it and determine an appropriate classification and review mechanism for the submission.

TPD
Therapeutic Products Directorate

TR
Technical Report

TSCA
Toxic Substances Control Act (US)

U

UCVB
Unknown or Variable Composition Complex Reaction Products and Biological Materials

URMULE
User Requested Minor Use Label Expansion. A necessary use expansion of a registered pest control product for which the anticipated volume of sales is insufficient to persuade a manufacturer to register the new use in Canada.

User Fees
HPFB levies three types of user fees relating to therapeutic product regulatory activities:

- a fee to evaluate the documentation submitted by a manufacturer to demonstrate a product's safety, efficacy and quality
- fees for maintaining the right to market a product
- a fee for an Establishment Licence that certifies the type of operations and category of products the establishment is authorized to handle.

V

VAAE
Vaccine Associated Adverse Event

VAAESS
Vaccine Associated Adverse Event Surveillance System

VBS
Veterinary Biologics Section

VCU
Voluntary Compliance Undertaking. A written commitment by a patentee to comply with PMPRB's guidelines, including adjusting its price to a non-excessive level and offsetting excess revenue.

VDD
Veterinary Drug Directorate

VICH
International Cooperation on Harmonization of Technical Requirements for Registration of Veterinary Medicinal Products

vNHP
Veterinary Natural Health Product

W

WG
Working Group

WHO
World Health Organization

Y

YBPR
Yearly Biologic Product Report

Japanese Medical Device Regulation

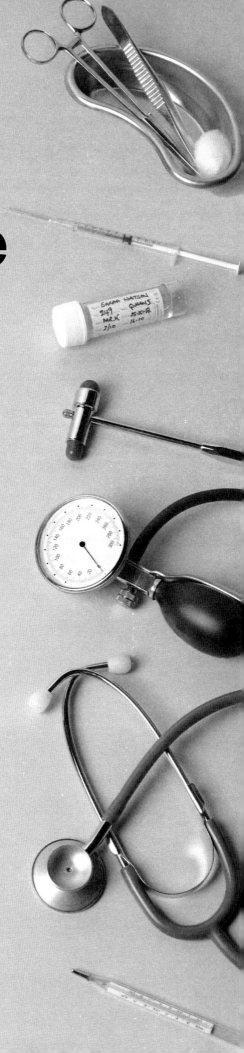

History and Regulatory Scope of Japanese Pharmaceutical Regulations

OBJECTIVES

❑ To understand how the *Pharmaceutical Affairs Law* was established and how the regulations were developed.

❑ To provide an overview of the current *Pharmaceutical Affairs Law* and to grasp the details of the most recent amendments.

RELATED LAWS AND REGULATIONS

❑ *Pharmaceutical Affairs Law* (Law No. 145 of Showa 35 (1960))

❑ *Act on Pharmaceuticals and Medical Devices Agency* (Law No. 192 of Heisei 14 (2002))

Introduction

According to one theory, the first evidence that verifies the existence of a Japanese pharmaceutical industry is in ancient documents recording that 33 drug stores in Doshomachi, Osaka submitted joint seal letters describing the regulation of "fake drugs" in 1658. Under the Tokugawa feudal system, a peaceful time without war continued for 260 years and pharmaceutical regulations were put in place under the leadership of industry. This was an unprecedented, distinct and unique style of regulation. The industry then developed into the modern Japanese pharmaceutical industry. Although the history of pharmaceutical regulations is often described based upon the existing *Pharmaceutical Affairs Law* from the 1960s onward, we believe that understanding the historic background is important in order to understand the meaning of the regulations. We have traced the history of Japanese pharmaceutical regulations, including the history of the pharmaceutical industry.

Prior to the Edo Period

The place name Doshomachi has been verified in the ancient documents of 1588. "Medicinal Products Retailers" that were the equivalent of today's pharmaceutical corporations were conducting business before the 1658 joint seal letters. Subsequently, the *Wayakushu Aratame Kaisho* facility was established in 1722 with the official approval of 124 shares in Doshomachi drug wholesalers. This facility was established for the entire industry to monitor fake drugs and distribute good products to the market. This may be considered the beginning of Good Manufacturing Practice (GMP, standards for manufacturing control and quality control) for drug products in Japan. In this way, the drug wholesale industry governed itself by actively offering its opinions in the form of joint seal letters from the companies to the Tokugawa Shogunate, the highest authority at that time. The methods used were not to regulate through laws or systems but to virtually eliminate defective products and unsuitable traders by sharing technologies and know-how among partners. Here, it should be noted that a characteristically Japanese industry-led method was used.

There were two types of medicine at that time: "*Touyakushu*" (Chinese medicine) that was imported from China, etc. and "*Wayakushu*" (Japanese medicine) that was developed and cultivated in Japan. The Chinese medicine was imported to Nagasaki, the only port where trade was permitted during the period of national isolation, where "drug wholesalers" in Doshomachi verified the purity and quantity of the medicines, and exclusively bought and sold them. Later, in 1779, all Chinese medicines were regulated and handled in Doshomachi in Osaka according to the *Chinese Medicinal Products Regulation Law*.

Table 36-1. Major Events Prior to the Edo Period

Name of Period	Events
1658	33 drug stores in Doshomachi submitted joint seal letters regarding regulations for fake drugs
1722	124 shares of drug wholesalers in Doshomachi were officially approved and the *Wayakushu Aratame Kaisho* was established
1779	Inspections of all imported medicines were conducted in Osaka according to the *Chinese Medicinal Products Regulation Law*
1791	The *Shinnokou* was organized
1799	Shares were increased to 129 due to an increase of five drug wholesaler shares

Another characteristic before the Edo period is that one could not become a large trader with a large network without obtaining a license to become a wholesaler. In other words, commercial transactions based upon business licenses for drug wholesalers were being conducted during this period, and cartels of full-time traders were established. Because the number of shares was fixed at 124, until the increase of five more shares was allowed in 1799, new entries were limited. For that reason, opportunities for the relatives or long-time employees of drug wholesalers to join a drug wholesaler through newly acquired stock was limited even if they tried to conduct business by setting up a new branch or a branch family. Therefore, the *Shinnokou* was organized in 1791. This organization allowed anyone starting a new business by setting up a new branch or a branch family to conduct similar business as drug wholesalers by joining a *kou* (social group).

There are many corporations that have been conducting business since the time of drug wholesalers, including today's Takeda Pharmaceutical Company, Mitsubishi Tanabe Pharma Corporation (Tanabe Pharma Corporation) and Ono Pharmaceutical Co., as well as those that had developed from new branches or branch families, including Shionogi & Co. Ltd. and Astellas Pharma Inc. (Fujisawa Pharmaceutical Co.). The traditional pharmaceutical traders see the history of Doshomachi since the early Edo period as their own and still maintain its traditions and its pride.

Due to the development of the money economy at the end of the 17th century, the demand for drugs rapidly increased. Because trust in Japanese medicine was eroded by the distribution of counterfeits, the representatives of drug stores in Edo, Sumpu, Kyo, Osaka and Sakai were summoned for lectures in 1772, and the *Six Points of Japanese Medicine*, which are methods and standards of inspection of Japanese medicine, were established. At the same time, *Wayakushu Aratame Kaisho* facilities were established in these five cities. The *Six Points of Japanese Medicine* can be said to be the basis for the later Japanese Pharmacopoeia, and we can see that "Quality Assurance," one of the objectives of the *Pharmaceutical Affairs Law*, has been of serious interest since that time and substantially

regulated. Noteworthy events from the Edo period are listed in **Table 36-1**.

What we would like you to understand is that, throughout the entire Edo period, various arrangements regarding drug products were being made for 300 years or more led by the industry, opinions were offered to the government, and to this day the industry has maintained the position that there ought to be regulations.

From the Meiji Period to World War II

Because ports in Yokohama and Kobe were opened to trade in 1859 and 1867, respectively, medicine manufactured in foreign countries (Western medicine) started to be imported into Japan. With the Meiji Restoration in 1867, the period of the feudal Tokugawa government shifted to the period of the new Meiji government. By the government's order in 1872, the wholesalers were dissolved, and in 1874, the Drug Sellers Association (renamed the Osaka Drug Wholesalers Association in 1894) was approved and the activities that had been carried out by the wholesalers were continued. With the emergence of modern pharmaceutical businesses in 1902, the Osaka Pharmaceutical Manufacturers Association was established, and until the economic regimentation during World War II, the industry was led by two organizations for distribution and manufacturing, respectively: the Osaka Drug Wholesalers Association and the Osaka Pharmaceutical Manufacturers Association. After World War II, associations or institutions were reorganized according to industry or region, and these continue to form the current industrial organizations. Through such processes, the pharmaceutical industry that had continued since the Edo period was differentiated into the pharmaceutical and wholesale industries, creating the basis for the manufacturing and marketing businesses regulated by the *Pharmaceutical Affairs Law*.

The Meiji period was an era when all Western medicine had to be imported, and counterfeits, imitations or other questionable products were distributed in the market. Therefore, it was an era when systems for regulating drug products and certifying doctors and pharmacists were promoted as countermeasures against such defective products. The Meiji government enacted the *Medicines Control Regulations* in 1871, and from 1874 to 1875, chemical

Table 36-2. Major Events From the Meiji Period to World War II

Name of Period	Events
1872 (Meiji 5)	Dissolution of drug wholesalers in Doshomachi
1874 (Meiji 7)	Promulgation of "medical system" and establishment of Tokyo chemical inspection site
1875 (Meiji 8)	Establishment of Osaka and Kyoto chemical inspection sites
1886 (Meiji 19)	Promulgation of the Japanese Pharmacopoeia
1889 (Meiji 22)	Promulgation of *Regulations on the sale and handling of chemicals* (pharmaceutical rules)
1914 (Taisho 3)	Promulgation of *Medicine Sales Law*
1943 (Showa 18)	Promulgation of the former *Pharmaceutical Affairs Law*

inspection institutions, which were drug testing sites, were established in Tokyo, Osaka and Kyoto, and various measures and policies, including the promulgation of the "Medical Practice System," were implemented in 1874. In 1876, the *Procedures for Pharmaceutical Licenses*, which stated that pharmaceutical businesses were under a licensing system, were promulgated. This system enabled the Meiji government to start eliminating the unfavorable situation of relying on imports for all Western medicine and promoting the development of the domestic pharmaceutical industry. Furthermore, in 1888, the Japanese Pharmacopoeia, which provides the quality standards for drug products, was established, and the *Regulations on the Sale and Handling of Pharmaceuticals* (pharmaceutical rules), which became the basis for manufacturing and marketing and the handling of drug products, were promulgated in 1889. Then, the system of the modern *Pharmaceutical Affairs Law*, including the promulgation of the *Medicine Sales Law*, was established in 1914.

In Japan, the first all-glass syringes were manufactured in 1903, and along with steel tools, medical devices with new functions were created. However, it is said that injections became common during the Taisho period (1912–26), when camphor injections became popular, and it is believed that as a result of the development of pharmaceutical technology and Western medicines, medical devices serving as delivery technologies were developed at the same time.

World War II (1939–45) was an era when the enhancement of military power for the war was the top priority. Fields such as drug products were no exception, and a *Pharmaceutical Affairs Law* including the aim of "having the right quality of pharmaceutical affairs and improving the physical strength of citizens" was promulgated in 1943. This was the so-called *War-ready Pharmaceutical Affairs Law*. All of the provisions of this law were infused with the national requirements for the enhancement of military power. Noteworthy events from the Meiji period until World War II are listed in **Table 36-2**.

From World War II to the Enactment of the Current *Pharmaceutical Affairs Law*

In a country devastated by World War II, the government and industries were also in a state of chaos. After the controlled economy of the wartime period, the Osaka Drug Wholesalers Association was dissolved in 1944 and the Osaka Pharmaceutical Manufacturers Association was integrated into a Drug Product Regulating Corporation. In 1945, after the war ended, efforts toward reconstruction were continuously made in the industry, including the establishment of the Osaka Drug Products Association (primary) and Osaka Home Medicine Cooperation (later known as the Osaka Home Medicine Association), as well as the Osaka Industrial Chemical Association and the Osaka Drug Products Wholesalers Association in 1946.

At the same time, the *Enterprise Reorganization Act* and the *Pharmaceutical Affairs Law* were newly promulgated in 1946 and 1948, respectively, but pharmaceutical businesses needed time to rebuild themselves to become modern, large businesses after the devastation caused by the war, and they continued developing laws related to pharmaceutical affairs until the current *Pharmaceutical Affairs Law* of 1960 was established. Noteworthy events from this time are listed in **Table 36-3**.

The Current *Pharmaceutical Affairs Law* and Onward
Enactment of the Current Pharmaceutical Affairs Law (1960)

After an accident in 1956 in which a professor from the University of Tokyo Faculty of Law died of penicillin shock, awareness regarding the safety of drug products rapidly increased. Due to this accident, "safety assurance" started to be recognized as an important issue along with the traditional Quality Assurance. Thus, the current *Pharmaceutical Affairs Law* was enacted in 1960, and the development of a modern system for the *Pharmaceutical Affairs Law* has continued. The details of the current *Pharmaceutical Affairs Law* at the time of its enactment are listed in **Table 36-4**.

However, soon after the law was enacted, a major

Table 36-3. Major Events From World War II to the Enactment of the Current *Pharmaceutical Affairs Law*

Name of Period	Events
1944 (Showa 19)	Dissolution of Osaka Drug Wholesalers Association Integration of Osaka Pharmaceutical Manufacturers Association into Drug Product Regulating Corporation
1945 (Showa 20)	Establishment of Osaka Drug Products Association (primary) and Osaka Home Medicine Cooperation (later known as the Osaka Home Medicine Association)
1946 (Showa 21)	Promulgation of *Enterprise Reorganization Act* Establishment of Osaka Industrial Chemical Drug Association and Osaka Former Drug Products Wholesalers Association
1948 (Showa 23)	Promulgation of the former *Pharmaceutical Affairs Law*
1960 (Showa 35)	Promulgation of the current *Pharmaceutical Affairs Law*

Table 36-4. Details of the Current *Pharmaceutical Affairs Law* (at the time of enactment in 1960)

- Established a system for quasi-drugs
- For pharmacies, manufacturing and sales, shifting the registration system to a licensing system and established licensing standards.
- For sales businesses, defined General Sales Medicinal Product Retailing, Retailing by Home Distribution and Special Sales
- Established requirements for indications of lot numbers and quantity of ingredients
- Limited advertisements of drug products for special diseases, such as cancer, and nonapproved drug products
- Separated matters associated with the identification of pharmacists (establishment of the *Pharmacists Law*)

incident that shook the basis of the pharmaceutical affairs regulatory system occurred. That was the Thalidomide Incident. Although German pediatrician Dr. Widikind Lenz had warned of the teratogenicity of thalidomide and the Gruenenthal Company decided to recall it in 1961, in 1962, the then Ministry of Health and Welfare approved products containing thalidomide in Japan. As a result, many babies were born with birth defects that were found to be drug-induced. Cases in which the side effects of a drug product had caused deformities were unknown at that time, and even in countries other than Japan, regulatory agencies mainly regulated counterfeit medicines and defective drug products.

Triggered by the Thalidomide Incident, the *Kefauver-Harris Amendment* (1962) in the US, the *Medicines Act* of 1968 in the UK, and the *Medicines Act* of 1976 in West Germany were enacted, and licensing and approval of new medicines were tightened, and systems involved in the collection of information on side effects were promoted. In Japan, the *Fundamental Principles Regarding Manufacturing Approval for Drug Products* were formulated (1967), the reporting of side effects for three years after obtaining manufacturing approval for new drug products became mandatory (1971), and GMP was formulated (1974; became a ministerial ordinance in 1980).

Fundamental Principles Regarding Manufacturing Approval for Drug Products (1967)

A major change in the character of examinations for approval in Japan was the *Fundamental Principles Regarding Manufacturing Approval for Drug Products*, issued in 1967 (**Table 36-5**). With these principles, the materials attached when applying for approval for a drug product were clarified, and professional use drugs and OTC drugs were categorized and examined. Moreover, the reporting of information on side effects for two years after obtaining approval became mandatory, contributing to the establishment of a regulatory system for medical devices. However, because it was a time when neither Good Clinical Practice (GCP) nor Good Laboratory Practice (GLP) existed, it was mandatory to publish information at academic conferences or in academic journals in order to ensure the reliability of data. This requirement continued until it was abolished when the fundamental principles were revised in 1999.

Amendment of the *Pharmaceutical Affairs Law* and Enactment of the *Adverse Drug Reaction Sufferings Relief Fund Law* (1979)

Another incident that shocked the regulatory agency during this time involved drug-induced Subacute Myelo-optic Neuropathy (SMON). Although some cases of SMON symptoms were reported sporadically during the 1960s, the cause remained unknown, and many cases were reported

Table 36-5. Details of *Fundamental Principles Regarding Manufacturing Approval for Drug Products* (1967)

- Classification of professional use drugs and OTC drugs
- Prohibition of advertisements for professional use drugs targeting the general public
- Standardization and tightening of review policy
- Mandatory reporting of side effects for at least two years after approving a new drug product for manufacture

between 1967 and 1968. For a long time, it was considered a rare disease of unknown cause until the SMON Investigation and Research Conference in 1972 concluded that it was a neurological disorder caused by chinoform agents. Chinoform agents were first developed as external medicines and then used internally. Because of the medicines' improved efficacy and the shift from short-term to long-term usage, the number of patients with SMON had increased, and these were found to be drug-induced cases. Thus, because the discovery of side effects sometimes takes a long time, the *Adverse Drug Reaction Sufferings Relief Fund Law* was established in 1979 (**Table 36-6**), and the *Pharmaceutical Affairs Law* was drastically revised at the same time (**Table 36-7**). What we learned from the SMON incident was that even well-known drugs could cause a serious incident involving safety issues depending upon how they were used (e.g., dosage form and route of administration).

In 1982, health hazards caused by defective dialyzers at 63 facilities and involving 172 people occurred in Osaka. Although manufacturers began a recall for other reasons, research and studies conducted by the National Institute of Health at that time explained that impurities in the materials and the mixing of impurities through deficiencies in the manufacturing process or manufacturing control were the causes of this incident. Taking this opportunity, there was growing debate over whether regulations should

be strengthened by introducing GMP for medical devices, which were regulated more loosely than drug products.

After the US-Japan Summit in January of 1985, the US-Japan Market-Oriented Sector Selective (MOSS) talks were held and drug products and medical devices became the target fields. Since then, a variety of systems, including evaluation processes and processes of insurance coverage recognized as non-tariff barriers, have been reviewed in order to increase transparency. Policies for the relaxation of regulations, including the introduction of policies for foreign manufacturing approval, have begun to be implemented, and the system for medical devices has been expanding in step with the pharmaceutical administration.

Amendment of the *Pharmaceutical Affairs Law* (1993)

With the amendment of the *Pharmaceutical Affairs Law* in 1993, the introduction of the Research Promotion Fund System for drug products and medical devices for rare disorders made both drug products and medical devices (known as "medical tools" at that time) specified items with exceptional utility value by item and made them eligible for priority review and subsidies (**Table 36-8**).

Table 36-6. Introduction of the Relief System for Sufferers From Adverse Drug Reactions

- Conference on the Relief System for Sufferers from Adverse Drug Reactions (1973)
- Outline of Relief System for Sufferers from Adverse Drug Reactions (1977): Provide necessary benefits to relieve sufferers from adverse drug reactions; manufacturers bear the costs and establish the fund
- Established the *Adverse Drug Reaction Sufferings Relief Fund Law* and Adverse Drug Reaction Sufferings Relief Fund. (1979)

Table 36-7. Details of Amendments of the *Pharmaceutical Affairs Law* of 1979: The First Drastic Reform Since the Enactment of the Current Law

- Established regulations regarding approval, such as making items listed on the Japanese Pharmacopeia subject to approval
- For safety assurance after approval, established laws for reexamination systems for new drugs
- Established laws for drug reevaluation systems to review efficacy and safety based on developments in science and technology
- Mandatory labeling of the expiration date of drug products and the ingredients of cosmetics, etc.
- Mandatory provision of information from manufacturers to distributors
- Mandatory notification of clinical trial plans

Table 36-8. Details of Amendments of the *Pharmaceutical Affairs Law* in 1993: Introduction of Research and Development Promotion System for Drug Products for Rare Disorders

- Mandatory provision of information from manufacturers to distributors
- Regarding intended use, added "taking necessary measures to promote research and development for drug products and medical devices with especially high demand for medical usage" to the objectives of the Pharmaceutical Affairs Law
- Systems including subsidies for priority inspections, tax breaks and experiments and research were introduced for drug products recognized as being in high demand for medical usage, including those for rare disorders
- Specific requirements for drug products, including those for rare disorders
  - The number of target patients is 50,000 or less
  - Products with exceptional usage value related to their intended end-usage
  - Possibility of development

Table 36-9. Details of Amendments of the *Pharmaceutical Affairs Law* in 1994: Safety Assurance According to the Characteristics of Each Medical Device

- Mandatory preparation and retention of records, treating cardiac pacemakers, etc. as a "specified medical device"
- Introduced reexamination and reevaluation systems for medical devices
- Consigned some evaluation operations for medical devices to a designated corporation (Japan Association for the Advancement of Medical Equipment)
- Added GMP (standards for manufacturing control and quality control) to the approval requirements for manufacturing medical devices

Amendment of the *Pharmaceutical Affairs Law* (1994)

Since that amendment, the efficacy and safety of medical devices were evaluated according to the characteristics of each medical device, and regulatory control focusing on areas from drug products to the uniqueness of each medical device was begun. In 1994, a series of amendments regarding medical devices, such as the introduction of reexamination and reevaluation systems, also were enacted (**Table 36-9**). The establishment of the Medical Devices Division at the Pharmaceutical Affairs Bureau and its specialization in policy planning for medical devices contributed to the promotion of regulatory reform.

The use of GMP for medical devices was begun in October of 1988 based on *Standards for Quality Assurance at Manufacturing Sites of Medical Devices (GMP for Medical Equipment)* (*Yakuhatsu* No. 87 of January 28, Showa 62 (1987)). The standards were issued as a ministerial ordinance in *Standards for Manufacturing Control and Quality Control of Medical Devices* enacted in June of 1994, and became effective in July of 1995 as one of the approval requirements. Compared to the process for establishing GMP for drug products in 1974 based upon a WHO advisory from 1969, implementing it as administrative guidance from 1976, and issuing it as a ministerial ordinance in 1980, the GMP for medical devices was established quickly.

Cases of improper trade involved in deliveries of pacemakers to medical institutions were uncovered in 1992 and became an issue that shocked the medical device industry. Taking this opportunity, a proposal was submitted at the

Central Social Insurance Medical Council (*Chuikyo*) in 1993 to promote appropriate costs and distribution of medical devices. As costs have become more transparent, the economic effects of medical devices have consistently been a central question for insurance administration. For this reason, characteristic utility, which is present in medical devices but not drug products, such as "making more accurate diagnoses with images" and "providing radical cures through surgery or treatment," has become clear. Also, if the profiles of utility or safety are not clarified and evaluated properly through regulatory review and approval, they will not be counted properly in the NHI reimbursement schedule. Therefore, it is believed that the importance of evaluating the utility and safety of new medical devices is growing.

Amendment of the *Pharmaceutical Affairs Law* (1996)

The incident that led to the enhancement of the examination system for new drugs and of safety measures was the Sorivudine Incident that occurred in 1993. This was an incident where death was caused when sorivudine metabolite, an antiviral drug, inhibited the metabolism of fluorouracil anticancer drugs and increased the *in vivo* concentration, thus enhancing the actions of the anticancer drugs. Soon after, some facts were uncovered indicating that the safety was not sufficiently reviewed at the developmental stage and the delivery of information from corporations to medical institutions was inadequate. The

Table 36-10. Details of Amendments of the *Pharmaceutical Affairs Law* in 1996: Safety Assurance of Drug Products

- Mandatory reporting of the side effects of investigational drugs
- Reliability assurance for application materials for approval and materials for reexamination and reevaluation
- Mandatory reporting of side effects and infectious diseases (Article 77-4-2 of the Pharmaceutical Affairs Law)
- Mandatory reporting of recalls
- Enhancement of information provision for distributors, etc. and information provision from pharmacists
- Introduction of special approval system

Table 36-11. Details of Amendments of the *Pharmaceutical Affairs Law* in 2002

- Introduction of Marketing Authorization Holder (MAH) system Risk-based classification of medical devices and introduction of review system of third party certification bodies
- Drastic review of safety policy regarding medical devices
- Reinforcement of safety assurance policies for Biological Products
- Reinforcement of postmarketing safety policies and revision of approval and license systems

Pharmaceutical Affairs Law was amended in 1996 in order to ensure safety (**Table 36-10**).

In 1997, Ministerial Ordinances on GCP, GLP and GPMSP (Good Postmarketing Surveillance Practice) for drug products went into effect and the Pharmaceuticals and Medical Devices Evaluation Center of the National Institute of Health Sciences (hereafter referred to as the Evaluation Center) was established in June of 1997. After this, a tetrapolar structure was created in which the Organization for Pharmaceutical Safety and Research conducted similarity reviews for drug products, etc., the Japan Association for the Advancement of Medical Equipment conducted similarity reviews for medical devices, the Evaluation Center conducted evaluations of new drug products and new medical devices, and the Pharmaceutical and Food Safety Bureau of the Ministry of Health, Labour and Welfare (hereafter referred to as the Office of Review Administration) conducted monitoring and was in charge of policy.

In 1999, with the relaxation of sales regulations, standards for manufacturing approval for new designated quasi-drugs were established. With the relaxation of regulations, supplement drinks containing vitamins became available at stores other than pharmacies. Due to this, GMP became a requirement for manufacturing licenses for some quasi-drugs, and the GMP for drug products was implemented as *Regulations for Manufacturing Control and Quality Control for Drug Products and Quasi-drugs.*

Amendments of the *Pharmaceutical Affairs Law* and the *Bleeding Donor Supply Service Control Law* (2002)

Infections of Creutzfeldt-Jakob Disease (CJD) caused by dried human dura mater transplantation that first occurred in the US became a global issue in countries including Japan. Although dried human dura mater has been used since import approval was granted in 1973 in Japan, an emer-

gency order for a recall was issued after the WHO advised discontinuing its use in 1997. This was an unprecedented case in which the presence of pathogenic microorganisms unimagined at the time of approval was discovered with the development of scientific technology. Problems also arose regarding the safety of Biological Products, including Bovine Spongiform Encephalopathy (BSE), which became a global issue, as well as Human Immunodeficiency Virus (HIV) and hepatitis C, which became large social issues in Japan. Against this background of drug-induced diseases, some parts of the *Pharmaceutical Affairs Law* and the *Bleeding Donor Supply Service Control Law* were amended in 2002 (**Table 36-11**).

For the *Pharmaceutical Affairs Law*, regulations on medical devices were reviewed and various regulations on Biological Products and drug products were comprehensively reviewed. In these amendments, the introduction of a system known as the Marketing Authorization Holder (MAH) System was the biggest amended part of the *Pharmaceutical Affairs Law*. Because licenses were separated between "MAH licenses" and "product approval" for manufacturing authorization holder and "manufacturing licenses" for manufacturers, it became possible to outsource the entirety of manufacturing processes that were traditionally only outsourced in part, and to outsource processes to overseas manufacturing sites. In outsourcing manufacturing processes, it became mandatory to prepare an agreement with the manufacturer and to undergo GMP and Quality Management System (QMS) inspections. It is necessary for overseas manufacturing sites to obtain foreign manufacturing accreditation (FMA). In 2004, the Pharmaceuticals and Medical Devices Agency was established and started evaluation operations for drug products and medical devices. Moreover, the implementation of risk-based approval and certification systems was begun for medical devices, and for Class II products with established certification standards, a system of certification from third party certification bodies (referred to Recognized

Certification Bodies in the terms used in the *Pharmaceutical Affairs Law*) was also established. At the same time, marketing authorization holders were designated as parties bearing sole responsibility not only for Quality Assurance at the manufacturing stage but also for postmarketing safety assurance, and their responsibilities were clarified.

For the *Bleeding Donor Supply Service Control Law*, while naming it as a law regarding securing a stable supply of safe blood products and clarifying the fundamental principles and responsibilities of the involved parties, a total reform was carried out, including the formulation of basic principles specified by the Minister of Health, Labour and Welfare, a program for promoting blood donations and plans regarding the safe supply of blood products.

References

1. Kusuri no Doshomachi Shiryokan website (http://www.kusuri-doshomachi.gr.jp/)
2. Mitsubishi Tanabe Pharma Corporation website (http://www.mt-pharma.co.jp/)
3. Pharmaceutical and Medical Device Regulatory Science Society of Japan (ed.): "Risk management for drug products based on actual cases," Jiho 2007
4. Pharmaceutical and Medical Device Regulatory Science Society of Japan (ed.): "Summary and know-how of PMS," Jiho, 2008
5. University of Tokyo website (http://www.u-tokyo.ac.jp/index_j.html)
6. Terumo Corporation website (http://www.terumo.co.jp/)
7. The Japanese Society for History of Pharmacy (ed.): "History of the Japanese Drug Industry," Yakuji Nippon Limited, 1995
8. "Commemoration of the 100th anniversary: History of the Japan Pharmaceutical Association," Japan Pharmaceutical Association, 1994

Japanese Regulatory Agencies and Organizations and the Scope of Their Supervision

OBJECTIVES

❏ To understand regulatory agencies and their organizations in Japan and the scope of their supervision.

❏ To understand the organizations within the Ministry of Health, Labour and Welfare and their major regulatory roles.

❏ To understand the organizations within the Pharmaceuticals and Medical Devices Agency and their major roles.

❏ To understand how tasks are divided between national and prefectural governments.

RELATED LAWS AND REGULATIONS

❏ Article 9 of the *National Government Organization Law* (Law No. 120 of Showa 23 (1948))

❏ Articles 43 and 57 of the *Establishment of the Cabinet Office Law* (Law No. 89 of Heisei 11 (1999))

❏ *Establishment of the Ministry of Health, Labour and Welfare Law* (Law No. 97 of Heisei 11 (1999))

❏ *Pharmaceutical Affairs Law* (Law No. 145 of Showa 35 (1960))

❏ *Pharmaceutical Affairs Law, Enforcement Ordinance* (Government Ordinance No. 11 of Showa 36 (1961))

❏ *Act on Pharmaceuticals and Medical Devices Agency* (Law No. 192 of Heisei 14 (2002))

❏ Statement of operational procedures related to relief operations of the Pharmaceuticals and Medical Devices Agency (Approved by the Minister of Health, Labour and Welfare on April 1, Heisei 16 (2004))

❏ Statement of operational procedures related to operations for reviews and safety measures of the Pharmaceuticals and Medical Devices Agency (Approved by the Minister of Health, Labour and Welfare on April 1, Heisei 16 (2004))

❏ *Pharmaceutical Affairs and Food Sanitation Council Law* (Government Ordinance No. 286 of Heisei 12 (2000))

Introduction

In Japan, it is necessary to comply with the regulations of the *Pharmaceutical Affairs Law* at all times in order to manufacture, import and sell drug products and medical devices. The government office that takes the central role in promulgating and administering regulations (henceforth referred to as "pharmaceutical affairs administration") under this *Pharmaceutical Affairs Law* is the Ministry of Health, Labour and Welfare (MHLW). MHLW conducts operations and services related to pharmaceutical affairs administration while working with the Pharmaceuticals and Medical Devices Agency (PMDA) and prefectural governments.

The roles of each of these organizations (MHLW, PMDA and prefectural governments) are: MHLW implements measures and punishments, such as approval and administrative orders; PMDA conducts operations

Table 37-1. MHLW Organization (As of 1 April 2009)

Ministry of Health, Labour and Welfare	
Minister's Secretariat	Personnel Division, General Coordination Division, Finance Division, Regional Bureau Administration Division, International Affairs Division, Health Sciences Division
Statistics and Information Department	Policy Planning Division, Vital and Health Statistics Division, Social Statistics Division, Employment Statistics Division, Wages and Labour Welfare Statistics Division
Health Policy Bureau	General Affairs Division, Guidance of Medical Service Division, Medical Professions Division, Dental Health Division, Nursing Division, Economic Affairs Division, Research and Development Division, National Hospital Division
Health Service Bureau	General Affairs Division, Specific Disease Control Division, Tuberculosis and Infectious Diseases Control Division, Environmental Health Division, Water Supply Division
Pharmaceutical and Food Safety Bureau	General Affairs Division, Evaluation and Licensing Division, Safety Division, Compliance and Narcotics Division, Blood and Blood Products Division
Department of Food Safety	Policy Planning and Communication Division, Standards and Evaluation Division, Inspection and Safety Division
Labour Standards Bureau	General Affairs Division, Inspection Division, Wages and Working Hours Division
Industrial Safety and Health Department	Policy Planning Division, Safety Division, Industrial Health Division, Chemical Hazards Control Division
Worker's Compensation Department	Worker's Compensation Administration Division, Compensation Division, Compensation Operation Division
Worker's Life Department	Policy Planning Division, Worker's Life Division
Employment Security Bureau	General Affairs Division, Employment Policy Division, Employment Development Division, Employment Insurance Division, Public Employment Service Division, Private Employment Service Division, Foreign Worker's Affairs Division, Labour Market Center Operation Office
Employment Measures for the Elderly and Persons with Disabilities Department	Policy Planning Division, Elderly Workers' Affairs Division, Disabled Workers' Affairs Division
Human Resources Development Bureau	General Affairs Division, Human Resources Development Bureau Division, Vocational Training Division, Overseas Cooperation Division
Equal Employment, Children and Families Bureau	General Affairs Division, Equal Employment Policy Division, Work and Family Harmonization Division, Part-time Work and Home Work Division, Family's Welfare Division, Child-rearing Promotion Division, Day Care Division, Maternal and Child Health Division
Social Welfare and War Victim's Relief Bureau	General Affairs Division, Public Assistance Division, Community Welfare and Services Division, Welfare Promoting Division, Planning Division of War Victims' Relief Division, Record Division
Department of Health and Welfare for Persons with Disabilities	Policy Planning Division, Welfare Division for Persons with Disabilities, Mental Health and Welfare Division
Health and Welfare Bureau for the Elderly	General Affairs Division, Long-term Care Insurance Division, Health Planning Division, Promotion Division, Division of the Health for the Elderly
Health Insurance Bureau	General Affairs Division, Employees' Health Insurance Division, National Health Insurance Division, Medical Economics Division, Actuarial Research Division

Table 37-1. MHLW Organization (As of 1 April 2009) (Cont'd.)

Pension Bureau	General Affairs Division, Pension Division, International Pension Division, Corporate Pension and National Pension Fund Division, Pension Fund Management Division, Actuarial Affairs Division
Director-General for Policy Planning and Evaluation	Counselor for Social Insurance, Counselor for Labour Policy, Counselor for Labour Relations, Counselor for Industrial Relations, Counselor for Policy Evaluation

(Affiliated institutions)

Research institutions (4): National Institute of Health Sciences, National Institute of Public Health, National Institute of Population and Social Security Research, National Institute of Infectious Diseases

National hospitals (22): National Cancer Center, National Cardiovascular Center, National Center of Neurology and Psychiatry, International Medical Center of Japan, National Research Institute for Child Health and Development, National Center for Geriatrics and Gerontology, National Hansen's Disease Sanatorium

Quarantine stations (13): Otaru, Sendai, Narita Airport, Tokyo, Yokohama, Niigata, Nagoya, Osaka, Kansai Airport, Kobe, Hiroshima, Fukuoka, Naha

Social welfare facilities (10): National Homes for Juvenile Training and Education (2), National Homes for the Blind (4), National Recuperation Homes (2), National Homes for Persons with Intellectual Disabilities, National Rehabilitation Center for the Disabled

(Councils, etc.)

Social Security Council, Health Sciences Council, Labour Policy Council, Medical Ethics Council, Pharmaceutical Affairs and Food Sanitation Council, Evaluation Committee for Independent Administrative institutions, Cancer Control Promotion Council, Central Minimum Wages Council, Labour Insurance Appeals Committee, Central Social Insurance Medical Council, Examination Committee of Social Insurance, Examination Committee for Certification of Sickness and Disability, Examination Committee for Relief Assistance

(Regional Bureaus)

Regional Bureaus of Health and Welfare: Hokkaido, Tohoku, Kanto-Shinetsu, Tokai-Hokuriku, Kinki, Chugoku-Shikoku (Shikoku Regional Bureau of Health and Welfare), Kyushu Regional Social Insurance Bureaus (47) : Each Regional Social Insurance Bureau

(External Bureaus)

Social Insurance Agency	(Internal Offices) General Affairs Department, Administration Department; (Affiliated institutions) Social Insurance College, Social Insurance Operation Center, (Regional Bureaus) Regional Social Insurance Bureau (47)
Central Labour Relations Commission	Executive Office, Regional Offices (7)

(Created based on the chart on the MHLW website) Figures in parenthesis indicate the number of facilities.

such as examinations, investigations and data analysis before an administrative measure is implemented; and the prefectural governments have the authority to grant licenses as established under the *Pharmaceutical Affairs Law* and related laws and to undertake pharmaceutical affairs administration in their jurisdictional prefectures.

For example, for the authority to grant approval and licenses for marketing of drug products, the *Pharmaceutical Affairs Law* states that: the Minister of Health, Labour and Welfare grants manufacturing and marketing approval and licenses of drug products (Approval: Articles 14 and 19-2; Licenses: Article 12), and the governor of the prefectural government handles some of the administrative matters related to approval authority for marketing authorization and all matters related to licensing authority that fall under the authority of the Minister of Health, Labour and Welfare (Article 81 and Article 80, *Enforcement Ordinance*). It is also

stated that the Minister of Health, Labour and Welfare may require PMDA to conduct all or some of the inspections necessary for evaluations of drug products (Article 14-2 and Article 27, *Enforcement Ordinance*).

This chapter discusses the organization of the regulatory agencies and their major roles, as well as how they are different from regulatory agencies in the US. This should be used as a reference for understanding not only the roles of each organization but also the differences in the systems of different countries (however, descriptions regarding drug products for animals have been omitted).

Ministry of Health, Labour and Welfare

MHLW is one of the central government ministries under the Cabinet (one office and 12 ministries) that runs the government. It is an administrative institution that was inaugurated when the Ministry of Health and Welfare and the Ministry of Labour were integrated due to the restructuring of the central government on 6 January 2001.

MHLW's duties for securing and improving the lives of citizens include the provision of aid to repatriates and war victims and survivors as well as families and relatives of nonrepatriated persons; the settling of the remaining works of the former Army and Navy; the improvement and enhancement of social welfare, social security and public health; the improvement of the working environment for laborers and the securing of employment (Article 3 of the *Establishment of the Ministry of Health, Labour and Welfare Law*).

MHLW is composed of the headquarters and external bureaus. Internal offices (Minister's Secretariat, 11 bureaus and the Director-General for Policy Planning), affiliated institutions (e.g., the Research Institution of National Institute of Health Sciences and the International Medical Center of Japan), councils (e.g., the Pharmaceutical Affairs and Food Sanitation Council) and regional bureaus acting as field agencies that handle different matters (Regional Bureaus of Health and Welfare and Prefectural Labour Bureaus) are based in the headquarters (Articles 43 and 57 of the *Establishment of the Cabinet Office Law*, and Article 9 of the *National Government Organization Law*). The external bureaus consist of the Social Insurance Agency and the Central Labour Relations Commission (**Table 37-1**).

Within MHLW, pharmaceutical affairs administration is managed primarily by the Health Policy Bureau, the Pharmaceutical and Food Safety Bureau (PFSB) and the Pharmaceutical Affairs and Food Sanitation Council. Of these bureaus, PFSB grants licenses and enforces regulations for clinical trials, evaluations and postmarketing safety measures, and the Health Policy Bureau has functions directed toward industry, such as research and development promotion, countermeasures for production and distribution and measures related to pharmaceutical prices.

Health Policy Bureau

In recent years, in response to the aging of society, changes in disease structures and stronger demands for higher quality medical services, the Health Policy Bureau plans and proposes policies to foster a high-quality, effective system for offering medical services.

The Health Policy Bureau consists of the General Affairs Division, Guidance of Medical Service Division, Medical Professions Division, Dental Health Division, Nursing Division, Economic Affairs Division, Research and Development Division and National Hospital Division. Of these, the divisions involved in drug products and medical devices are the Economic Affairs Division and the Research and Development Division, and the responsibilities of each division follow:

Economic Affairs Division

1. affairs related to the production of drug products and medical devices, the enhancement of distribution and consumption, and improvements and regulations (except those within the purview of PFSB or the Research and Development Division)
2. affairs related to the development, improvement and regulation of the Marketing Authorization Holder (MAH) system, manufacturing, marketing and leasing of drug products and medical devices (except those under the Research and Development Division)
3. affairs related to the export and import of drug products and medical devices
4. affairs regarding the arrangement and usage of medical devices (excluding medical equipment, dental materials and sanitary products) (except those under the Guidance of the Medical Service Division)
5. affairs related to the consignment of operations at hospitals, clinics and midwifery homes
6. affairs related to operational guidance for the improvement of business management at hospitals, clinics and midwifery homes
7. affairs related to clinical laboratories as stipulated in laws related to clinical laboratory technicians and health laboratory technicians

In addition, the Economic Affairs Division has the Office of Medical Devices Policy, Office of Medical Services and Senior Counselor for Distribution. The Office of Medical Devices Policy conducts the affairs of 1–4 for medical devices, and the Office of Medical Services conducts the affairs of 5–7 listed above. The Senior Counselor conducts investigations on the distribution of drug products and medical devices (including those related to cost) and affairs related to guidance (except those under PFSB) when instructed.

Research and Development Division

1. affairs related to the research and development of drug products and medical devices (except affairs under PFSB)
2. affairs related to the cultivation and production of botanical plants used for producing medicinal products
3. affairs related to the development, improvement and regulation of marketing authorization for drug products and medical devices, manufacturing, marketing, leasing and repairing businesses (limited to areas involved in research and development)
4. affairs related to the maintenance of systems related to healthcare information processing
5. affairs related to medical technology evaluations (except those under other divisions)

Moreover, the Office of Clinical Trial Promotion was established in the Research and Development Division, which conducts affairs related to the promotion of clinical trials stipulated in the *Pharmaceutical Affairs Law* (except those under the PFSB).

Pharmaceutical and Food Safety Bureau

PFSB implements measures for securing the efficacy and safety of drug products and medical devices and addresses various issues directly related to people's lives and health, such as blood products-related operations and restrictions on narcotics and stimulants.

PFSB consists of the General Affairs Division, Evaluation and Licensing Division, Safety Division, Compliance and Narcotics Division, Blood and Blood Products Division and Food Safety Division. All divisions except the Food Safety are involved in drug products and medical devices, and the affairs of each division are as follows:

General Affairs Division

1. affairs related to comprehensive management related to affairs of PFSB
2. affairs related to pharmacists
3. matters related to affairs conducted by PMDA (except those under the Evaluation and Licensing Division, Safety Division, or Compliance and Narcotics Division)
4. in addition to those listed above, matters related to affairs of PFSB not under any other division

The Office of Adverse Drug Reaction Sufferings Relief was set up in the General Affairs Division and conducts the following:

- matters related to the affairs conducted by PMDA (relief affairs for health damages caused by adverse reactions of drug products or infections via Biological Products)
- affairs related to policy for health damages caused by harmful actions of drug products and medical devices

Evaluation and Licensing Division

1. affairs related to technical guidance and supervision on the production of drug products and medical devices
2. affairs related to drug product and medical device approval and manufacturing licenses
3. affairs related to drug product and medical device reexaminations and reassessments
4. affairs related to marketing, leasing and repair work for medical devices (except those under the Health Policy Bureau)
5. affairs related to the Japanese Pharmacopoeia

6. affairs related to standards for drug products and medical devices
7. affairs related to specifications for drug products and medical devices for rare diseases
8. affairs related to the regulation of poisonous and deleterious substances (except those under the Compliance and Narcotics Division)
9. affairs related to regulations on evaluations and manufacturing, import, usage and other handling based upon environmental sanitation for chemical materials that may cause health damage or affect animal habitats
10. affairs related to regulations on household goods containing harmful substances
11. affairs related to tolerable daily intake of dioxins
12. matters related to affairs conducted by PMDA (review-related affairs)
13. affairs related to the promotion of industrial standards for medical devices and other industrial standardization

The Office of Evaluation and Licensing of Medical Devices and the Office of Chemical Hazards Control were set up in the Evaluation and Licensing Division, where the Office of Evaluation and Licensing of Medical Devices conducts the affairs of aforementioned 1–4, 6, 7, 12 and 13 for medical devices, and the Office of Chemical Hazards Control conducts the affairs of 8–11 listed above.

Safety Division

1. affairs related to planning and development for safety assurance for drug products and medical devices
2. affairs related to MAH licenses for drug products and medical devices
3. affairs related to inspections of drug product and medical device safety (except those under the Evaluation and Licensing Division)
4. affairs related to guidance and advice regarding matters involving preparing and saving records of Biological Products and specified medical devices
5. matters related to affairs conducted by PMDA (safety policy affairs)

Compliance and Narcotics Division

1. affairs related to regulations on defective and mislabeled drug products and medical devices
2. affairs related to advertisements for drug products and medical devices
3. affairs related to drug product and medical device inspections and testing
4. affairs related to pharmaceutical affairs compliance inspectors
5. affairs related to regulations on specified drugs, as stipulated in the *Pharmaceutical Affairs Law*

6. affairs related to inspectors of poisonous and deleterious substances
7. affairs related to regulations on narcotics and stimulants
8. affairs related to the duties of narcotics control officers
9. affairs related to regulations on narcotics and stimulants and international cooperation involving stimulant regulation
10. matters related to affairs conducted by PMDA (such as on-site inspections at factories manufacturing distributors of drug products and medical devices)

Blood and Blood Products Division
1. affairs related to supervision of blood collection work
2. affairs related to the promotion of blood donation
3. affairs related to ensuring proper use of blood products
4. affairs other than those listed in 2 or 3 related to securing stable supplies of blood products
5. affairs related to the enhancement, improvement and promotion of the production and distribution of Biological Products

Pharmaceutical Affairs and Food Sanitation Council

The Pharmaceutical Affairs and Food Sanitation Council is an agency for conducting evaluations, reevaluations and safety inspections of drug products and medical devices for the inquiries of the Minister of Health, Labour and Welfare.

When it was established in 1961, it was called the Central Pharmaceutical Affairs Council, but its name was changed to the Pharmaceutical Affairs and Food Sanitation Council after the Central Pharmaceutical Affairs Council and the Food Sanitation Investigation Council were integrated due to the restructuring of the central government in January 2001.

The Pharmaceutical Affairs and Food Sanitation Council is an agency set up within the headquarters of MHLW based upon the provisions of Article 11, Paragraph 1 of the *Establishment of the Ministry of Health, Labour and Welfare Law*, and organizations and committees are stipulated in the *Pharmaceutical Affairs and Food Sanitation Council Law* (Government Ordinance No. 286 of Heisei 12 (2007)). Along with two subcommittees on food sanitation and pharmaceutical affairs set up in the council, and nine divisions and four investigation committees under the Food Sanitation Commission and 16 divisions and 18 investigation committees under the Pharmaceutical Affairs Commission have been set up (**Table 37-2**).

The affairs of the council include handling matters (regulations on drug products, foods, chemical substances and household goods) under its authority based upon the

provisions of the *Pharmaceutical Affairs Law* and *Food Sanitation Law*, and the committees are comprised of a maximum of 30 people appointed from among academic experts by the Minister of Health, Labour and Welfare. A special committee will be appointed, when necessary, to investigate and discuss specific matters, and an expert committee will be appointed, when necessary, to investigate specialized matters.

Matters on which the Minister of Health, Labour and Welfare must always hear the views of the Pharmaceutical Affairs and Food Sanitary Council as important matters regarding the *Pharmaceutical Affairs Law* include:

- approval of new drug products and new medical devices
- withdrawal of approval of drug products and medical devices
- specification of Highly Controlled Medical Devices, Controlled Medical Devices, General Medical Devices and Designated Maintenance Control Medical Devices
- reassessment of drug products and medical devices

For example, materials for evaluations of new drug materials will undergo conformity assessment and reviews conducted by review specialists and outside experts (expert members) from the medical, pharmaceutical and statistical fields. After PMDA's investigations, a notification of the investigation results will be sent to MHLW and investigative deliberations will be held by the Pharmaceutical and Food Sanitary Council. If approved by the council, approval by the Minister of Health, Labour and Welfare is ultimately obtained.

Although the frequency of deliberations differs for each committee, they are typically held between four and eight times a year. In principle, the Subcommittee on Pharmaceutical Affairs convenes four times a year. In addition, the minutes of the council are published at www.mhlw.go.jp.

Comparison with the US

MHLW in Japan is an administrative organization equivalent to the Department of Health and Human Services (DHHS) in the US. Following are what are believed to be the differences between MHLW and DHHS.

- MHLW also conducts affairs related to various labor relations that are administered in the US by the Department of Labor.
- The Social Insurance Agency, which became a separate organization in the US in 1995, was set up in MHLW as an external bureau (however, in January 2010, the Social Insurance Agency was abolished and the Minister of Health, Labour and Welfare has taken responsibility for financial administration

Table 37-2. Organization of the Subcommittee on Pharmaceutical Affairs of the Pharmaceutical Affairs and Food Sanitation Council

Subcommittee on Pharmaceutical Affairs	Investigation Committees
Committee on Japanese Pharmacopoeia	———
Primary Committee for Determining Damages from Adverse Drug Reactions and Infections	———
Secondary Committee for Determining Damages from Adverse Drug Reactions and Infections	Investigation Committee for Determining Damages from Biological Products
Primary Committee on Drug Products	———
Secondary Committee on Drug Products	———
Committee on Blood-related Operations	Investigation Committee on Safety Technology Investigation Committee on Proper Usage
Committee on Medical Devices and In Vitro Diagnostics	———
Committee on Drug Product Reassessment	———
Biological Technology Group	Investigation Committee on Drug Products Using Recombinant DNA Technology for Animals
Committee on OTC Drugs	———
Committee on Cosmetics and Quasi-drugs	———
Committee on Safety of Drugs	Investigation Committee on Countermeasure Against Transmissible Spongiform Encephalopathy Investigation Committee on Safety Measures
Committee on Safety Measures for Medical Devices	Investigation Committee on Safety Measures
Committee on Poisonous and Deleterious Substances	Investigation Committee on Standards for Handling Technology Investigation Committee on Poisonous and Deleterious Substances
Committee on Safety Measures for Chemical Substances	Investigation Committee on Chemical Substances Investigation Committee on PRTR Substances Investigation Committee on Safety Measures for Household Goods
Committee on Drug Products for Animals	Investigation Committee on Biological Products for Animals Investigation Committee on Antibiotic Preparations for Animals Committee on General Drug Products for Animals Committee on Drug Product Reassessments for Animals Investigation Committee on Residual Problems of Drug Products for Animals Investigation Committee on Drug Products for Fisheries

and operations regarding public pensions based on the *Japan Pension Organization Law* (Law No. 109 of Heisei 19 (2007)) enacted in 2007, and the Japan Pension Organization was newly established as a public corporation to conduct operational affairs related to the public pension system under the direct supervision of the Minister of Health, Labour and Welfare).

- Because Japan has a universal healthcare system, an organization called the Health Insurance Bureau, which develops ideas and plans for the health insurance system and stabilizes the medical insurance system for the long term so that all people can access medical care without concern in a fully fledged aging society with fewer children in the future, has been set up in MHLW.
- Because the US adopts a federal system, various administrative services may actually differ depending upon the policies of each state.

Furthermore, the US Food and Drug Administration (FDA) is an agency belonging to HHS that conducts expert oversight, such as approval of foods, drug products, medical devices, cosmetics and animal drugs, and regulations on noncompliant products. FDA can be said to combine the Pharmaceutical and Food Safety Division of MHLW with PMDA in terms of assurance measures for drug product and medical device effectiveness and safety. The affairs of a combination of three FDA centers (Center for Biologics Evaluation and Research (CBER), Center for Drug Evaluation and Research (CDER), and Center for Devices and Radiological Health (CDRH)) are most similar to the affairs of PMDA. The number of PMDA employees is 346 in the Inspection Division and 82 in the Safety Division as of August of 2009, and the total number of employees involved in these two divisions is far less than the number of employees in FDA, which is about 2,900.

Pharmaceuticals and Medical Devices Agency

PMDA is an organization established in the *Pharmaceuticals and Medical Devices Agency Law* (*Agency Law*) based upon the Reorganization and Rationalization Plan for Special Public Corporations approved by the Cabinet in December 2001, and it integrates some of the affairs of the Organization for Pharmaceutical Safety and Research (henceforth referred to as the Pharmaceutical Organization), the National Institute of Health Sciences (henceforth referred to as the Evaluation Center), and the Japan Association for the Advancement of Medical Equipment Center (henceforth referred to as the Equipment Center) and was established in April 2004 (**Figure 37-1**).

PMDA's objectives are to provide prompt relief for health damages caused by adverse reactions to drug products or infections via Biological Products, and to conduct affairs including investigations that help to improve drug product quality, effectiveness and safety, thus contributing to the improvement of national health (Article 3 of the *Agency Law*). The major affairs can be categorized broadly into three parts: health damage relief affairs, product review affairs and safety policy affairs.

For examinations, PMDA cooperates mainly with PFSB of MHLW and conducts operations such as evaluations, investigations and data analysis for the stages from preclinical trials to postmarketing surveillance. Previously, reviews of drug products were conducted by the Evaluation Center, and consulting affairs regarding clinical trial plans were conducted by the Pharmaceutical Organization, but with the establishment of PMDA in 2004, a consistent guidance and evaluation system covering the stages from preclinical trials to approval and postmarketing was created.

In addition, the affairs of the Research and Development Division were transferred to the National Institute of Biomedical Innovation established on 1 April 2005.

Main Affairs of PMDA
Health Damage Relief Affairs
The Pharmaceutical Organization, which was PMDA's precursor, was established in 1979 as the Adverse Drug Reaction Sufferings Relief Fund and started handling affairs related to adverse drug reaction sufferings relief in May of the following year. It has added several relief systems, commissioned loan affairs and commissioned benefits affairs since that time. In addition, basic matters regarding its affairs are stipulated in business and service documents related to PMDA's relief affairs.

Relief System for Sufferers from Adverse Drug Reactions
This system provides relief benefits for health damages such as diseases or disabilities requiring hospitalization that were caused by adverse effects from pharmaceuticals prescribed at hospitals or clinics as well as pharmaceuticals purchased at pharmacies, etc., despite proper use of the products.

Relief System for Sufferers from Infections via Biological Products
This system provides relief benefits for health damages such as diseases or disabilities requiring hospitalization that were caused by Biological Products despite proper use of the products. Treatments for preventing the occurrence after infection and patients with secondary infections are also eligible for relief.

Consignment and Loan Affairs Including Healthcare Allowances for Patients With SMON
PMDA provides healthcare allowances and nursing care expenses for SMON patients for whom a settlement has been reached in court.

Commissioned Benefits Affairs Including Benefits Such as Healthcare Allowances for HIV-positive and HIV Patients
Under a commission from the Yu-ai Welfare Foundation Inc., PMDA asks HIV-positive patients infected via HIV-tainted blood products who have not yet developed AIDS to report their health conditions and

Figure 37-1. History of PMDA

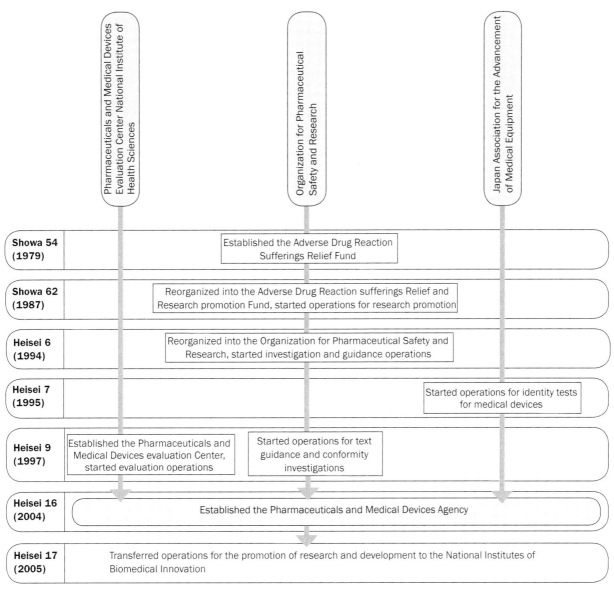

From the PMDA website

provides healthcare expenses for the purpose of preventing the onset of AIDS. PMDA also provides healthcare allowances for AIDS patients who have been infected with HIV through blood coagulation factor products and who have reached a settlement in court.

Payment of Benefits Based Upon the Law on Special Measures Concerning the Payment of Benefits to Relieve Victims of Hepatitis C Infected through Specific Concentrates and Specified Coagulation Factor XI Concentrates

PMDA provides benefits under this law.

Product Review Affairs

Examination-related affairs involve evaluating the quality, effectiveness and safety of each drug product or medical device. Examination-related affairs include face-to-face counseling, such as clinical trial counseling on materials for applications for approval in the preclinical trial stage; reliability studies that evaluate whether the details of submitted application materials are logically and scientifically reliable; and evaluations, based upon standards for current scientific technology, of the effectiveness, side effects, and quality of products submitted while considering the results of the reliability studies.

Figure 37-2. Flowchart of Operations for Safety Measures

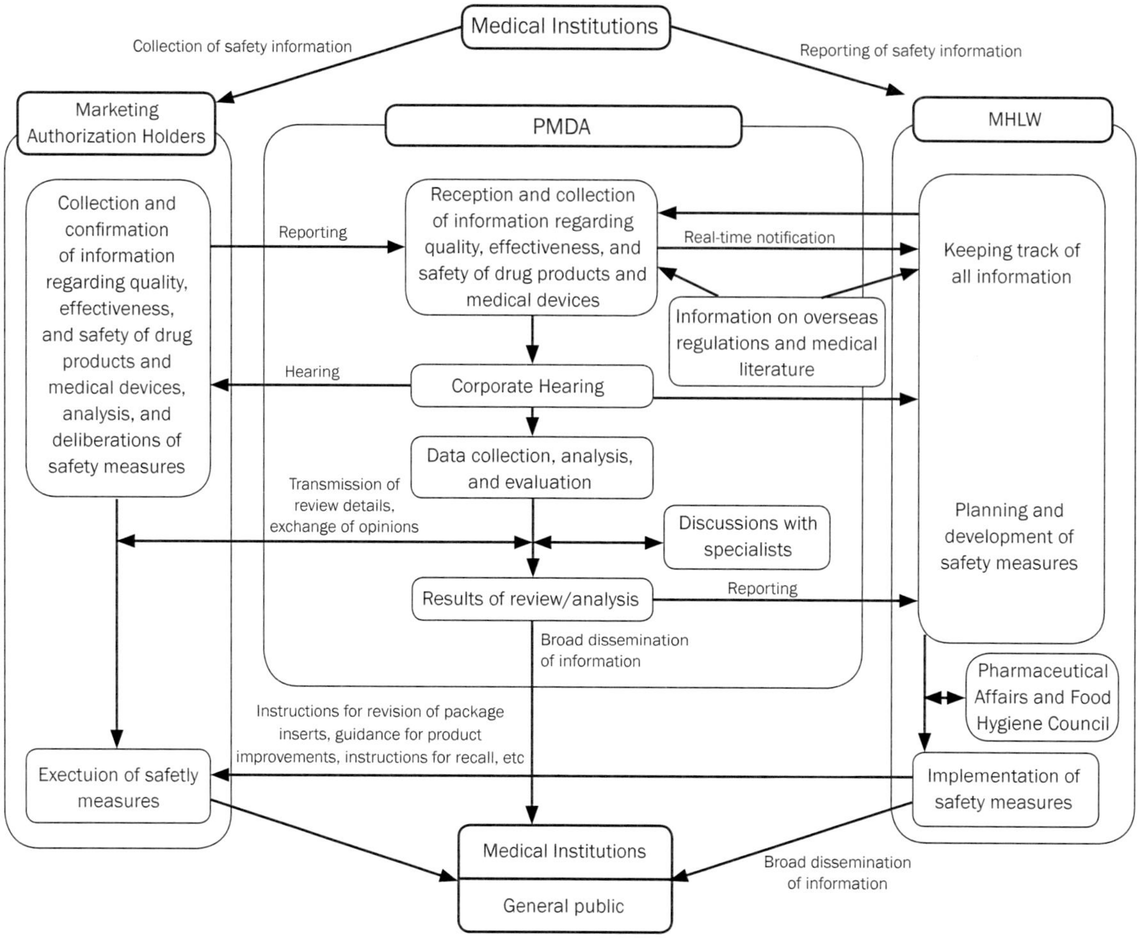

From the PMDA website

PMDA aims to conduct more reliable, prompt affairs by conducting clinical trial counseling and examinations from the preclinical trial stage through the approval stage with the same evaluation team. In addition, basic matters regarding PMDA's affairs are stipulated in business and service documents related to its product review affairs and safety policy affairs.

Face-to-face Counseling

Upon request from a clinical trial sponsor, PMDA offers face-to-face guidance and advice for clinical trials for new drug products or new medical devices as well as for clinical tests relating to reassessments and reexaminations of drug products and medical devices.

Reliability Studies

PMDA ensures compliance of materials attached to applications for approval or applications for confirmation of reexamination and reassessment with GLP, GCP and

Good Postmarketing Study Practice (GPSP) standards, and also conducts document-based investigations.

Evaluation Affairs

PMDA evaluates drug products and medical devices based upon the *Pharmaceutical Affairs Law*.

GMP/QMS Conformity Assessment Inspections

GMP/QMS Conformity Assessment inspections are conducted to inspect manufacturing facilities, processes and quality control to determine whether manufacturing sites of drug products and medical devices operate under proper management. These inspections involve not only traveling to manufacturing sites to conduct on-site inspections but also document-based inspections.

Reevaluation and Reassessment

PMDA confirms reevaluations and reassessments based upon the *Pharmaceutical Affairs Law*.

Figure 37-3. PMDA Organization (as of 1 August 2009)

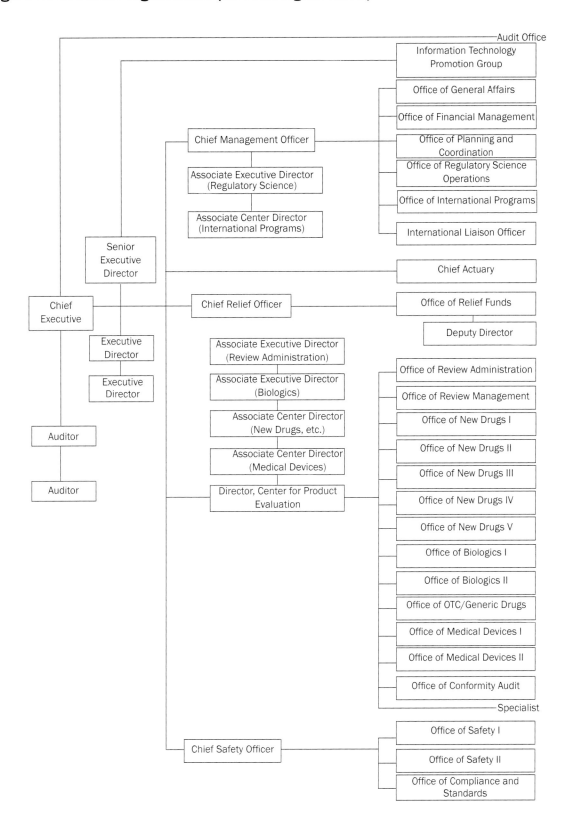

(Based upon diagrams on PMDA's website)

Table 37-3. Division of Tasks Between the State and the Prefectural Governments on Marketing Authorization, etc. for Drug Products and Medical Devices

Major Procedures	Subject	Office in Charge
1. Marketing Authorization Holder licenses (Article 12 of the Pharmaceutical Affairs Law)	Drug products, quasi-drugs, cosmetics and medical devices	Prefectural governments
2. Manufacturing licenses (Article 13 of the Pharmaceutical Affairs Law)	Drug products 1. Biological Products (except in vitro diagnostics) 2. Radioactive drug products 3. Drugs with national test certificates (Article 43, Paragraph 1 of the Pharmaceutical Affairs Law) 4. Recombinant drugs 5. Cell tissue drug products, etc.	Regional Bureaus of Health and Welfare*[1]
	6. Drug products other than those listed above	Prefectural governments
	Quasi-drugs	Prefectural governments
	Cosmetics	Prefectural governments
	Medical device 1. Biological Product category	Regional Bureaus of Health and Welfare*[1]
	2. Sterilization category 3. General category 4. Packaging, etc. category	Prefectural governments
3. Marketing and leasing businesses for medical devices	Medical devices	Prefectural governments
4. Pharmacies and drug retail businesses	Pharmacies General sales medicinal product retailing businesses Retailing by home distribution businesses	Prefectural governments
	General marketing businesses Special marketing businesses	Prefectural governments of City/Ward Mayor
5. Repairing businesses	Medical devices	Prefectural governments
6. Foreign Manufacturer Accreditation (Article 13-3 of the Pharmaceutical Affairs Law)	Drug products, quasi-drugs, cosmetics and medical devices	PMDA
7. Product approval (Article 14, Paragraph 1 of the Pharmaceutical Affairs Law)	Drug products, quasi-drugs and medical devices However, with the exception of those specified in separate announcements, etc.*[2]	PMDA
	Special cases of marketing at pharmacies	Prefectural governments
	Clean cotton, etc.	
8. Certification for marketing authorization of Specified Controlled Medical Devices (Specified In Vitro Diagnostics) (Article 23-2 of the Pharmaceutical Affairs Law)	Specified Controlled Medical Devices (Specified In Vitro Diagnostics)	Recognized Certification Body
9. Conformity assessment inspection (Article 14, Paragraph 6, Article 23-2, Paragraph 3 and Article 80, Paragraph 1 of the Pharmaceutical Affairs Law)	Refer to Table 37-4	Prefectural governments Recognized Certification body PMDA

Table 37-3. Division of Tasks Between the State and the Prefectural Governments on Marketing Authorization, etc. for Drug Products and Medical Devices (cont'd.)

Major Procedures	Subject	Office in Charge
10. Notification for marketing (Article 14-9 of the *Pharmaceutical Affairs Law*)	Drug products, in vitro diagnostics and quasi-drugs not requiring approval	PMDA
	General medical devices	
	Cosmetics	Prefectural governments
11. Notification for manufacturing drug products for export, etc. (Article 80, Paragraph 3 of the Pharmaceutical Affairs Law, Article 74, Paragraph 1 of the *Pharmaceutical Affairs Law, Enforcement Ordinance*)	Drug products, quasi-drugs, cosmetics and medical devices	PMDA
12. Notification for import of drug products for manufacturing and marketing (manufacturing) (Articles 94 and 95 of the *Pharmaceutical Affairs Law, Enforcement Regulations*)	Drug products, quasi-drugs, cosmetics and medical devices	*Kanto-Koshinetsu* or *Kinki* Regional Bureau of Health and Welfare
13. Reporting system for side effects (Article 77-4-2, Paragraph 2 of the *Pharmaceutical Affairs Law*)	Drug products, quasi-drugs, cosmetics and medical devices	MHLW

*1 Submit to the Regional Bureau of Health and Welfare through the prefectural government of the area where the manufacturing site is located.

*2 However, for Controlled Medical Devices or in vitro diagnostics for which the Minister of Health, Labour and Welfare has established standards based upon the provisions of Article 23-2 of the Pharmaceutical Affairs Law, instead of approval, certification granted by a registered certification body is necessary, and for products that do not require approval or certification, a notification for manufacturing and marketing must be sent to PMDA.

Safety Measures Affairs

PMDA aims to improve the safety and reliability of drug products and medical devices and conducts the following affairs. In addition, basic matters regarding their affairs are stipulated in business and service documents related to the product review affairs and safety policy affairs of the Pharmaceuticals and Medical Devices Agency.

- collecting, reviewing, investigating, analyzing and providing information regarding the quality, effectiveness and safety of drug products and medical devices
- responding to enquiries from consumers regarding the safety of drug products and medical devices
- providing guidance and advice to manufacturers to improve the safety of drug products and medical devices

Figure 37-2 shows a flowchart of operations for safety measures.

PMDA Organizations

PMDA consists of 22 offices, one section, and a Chief Actuary (**Figure 37-3**). An outline of the major activities of each department conducting affairs related to examinations and safety measures is shown below.

Office of Review Administration

This office coordinates product reviews and conducts affairs related to the appointment of specialist discussion committees; affairs related to fees; time accounting management; reception and management of applications and notifications related to product review affairs and affairs related to the reception and management of registration applications for the Drug Master File.

Office of Review Management

This office primarily conducts planning and development of review operations and audits. It conducts a variety of operations, including, for example, those related to: collection or management of information regarding operations for examinations; process management; process adjustments for face-to-face counseling regarding new drug products in each review administration office; arranging face-to-face counseling; and communication management with each review administration office.

Office of New Drugs I

This office confirms clinical trial notifications and adverse drug reactions of digestive system drugs, drugs for external use, immunosuppressive agents, hormonal agents, drugs for metabolic diseases and other new drug products, and also conducts necessary reviews for approval, reexamination and reevaluation.

Office of New Drugs II

This office confirms clinical trial notifications and adverse drug reactions of cardiovascular agents, anti-Parkinson's disease drugs, drugs for improving cerebral circulation and metabolism, drugs for Alzheimer's disease, drugs for genitourinary and anal use, compound agents for medical use, radioactive agents, contrast agents and other new drug products, and also conducts necessary reviews for approval, reexamination and reassessment.

Office of New Drugs III

This office confirms clinical trial notifications and adverse drug reactions of central nervous system drugs, peripheral nervous system drugs, drugs for sensory organs (except those related to inflammatory diseases), narcotics and other new drug products, and also conducts necessary reviews for approval, reexamination and reassessment.

Office of New Drugs IV

This office confirms clinical trial notifications and adverse drug reactions of anti-infective drugs, drugs for sensory organs (except those related to inflammatory diseases), drugs for respiratory organs, allergy drugs and other new drug products, and also conducts necessary reviews for approval, reexamination and reassessment.

Office of New Drugs V

This office confirms clinical trial notifications and adverse drug reactions of anticancer drugs and other new drug products, and also conducts necessary reviews for approval, reexamination and reassessment.

Office of Biologics I

This office confirms clinical trial notifications and adverse drug reactions of blood coagulation factor products and also conducts necessary examinations for approval, reexamination and reassessment as well as preliminary reviews of applications for confirmation of drug products and medical devices for gene treatment, preliminary reviews of applications for approval or confirmation based on the *Cartagena Law* (Act No. 97 of Heisei 15 (2003); *Law Concerning the Conservation and Sustainable Use of Biological Diversity through Regulations on the Use of Living Modified Organisms*) and reviews regarding the quality of antibody products.

Office of Biologics II

This office confirms clinical trial notifications and adverse drug reactions of vaccines, antitoxins and drug products for cell treatment, and conducts necessary reviews for approval, reexamination and reevaluation as well as preliminary reviews of applications for confirmation of

drug products and medical devices using cell tissue.

Office of OTC/Generic Drugs

This office conducts necessary reviews for the approval of generic drugs, OTC drugs, quasi-drugs and cosmetics, as well as investigations to confirm export certifications and confirm quality reassessments.

Office of Medical Devices I and II

These offices conduct necessary reviews for the approval of medical devices and in vitro diagnostics, necessary confirmation for reexamination and reassessment, investigations regarding clinical trial plans and investigations for face-to-face counseling and discrepancy reports during clinical trials.

Office of Conformity Audit

This office conducts material conformity investigations (investigations related to GLP, GCP and GPSP) regarding applications for approval or reexamination/reassessment of drug products and medical devices, as well investigations (on-site and document-based) regarding standards for the reliability of application materials.

Office of Safety I and II

These offices conduct operations related to the collection, management, investigation, analysis and provision of information regarding the quality, effectiveness and safety of drug products and medical devices; respond to inquiries from consumers regarding the safety of drug products and medical devices; and provide guidance and advice for manufacturers to improve the safety of drug products and medical devices.

Office of Compliance and Standards

This office grants licenses for the manufacturing of drug products and quasi-drugs and conducts inspections on conformity with standards for buildings and facilities necessary for the Foreign Manufacturers Accreditation; inspections on conformity with GMP, etc.; inspections on conformity with standards for building and facilities necessary for manufacturing licenses for medical devices and in vitro diagnostics; inspections regarding conformity with QMS, etc.; and operations regarding the general nomenclature for drug products and standards for medical devices.

Division of Tasks Between National and Prefectural Governments

From among the administrative duties under the authority of the Minister of Health, Labour and Welfare as stipulated in the *Pharmaceutical Affairs Law*, some related to the authority to grant approval for manufacturing and marketing, as well as all those related to the authority to provide licenses, are consigned to the prefectural

Table 37-4. Offices in Charge of GMP/QMS Conformity Assessment Inspections

Classification		Domestic manufacturing facilities	Overseas manufacturing facilities
Drug products	New drug products	PMDA	PMDA
	Biological Products	PMDA	PMDA
	Radiopharmaceutical products	PMDA	PMDA
	Drug products specified by the Minister of Health, Labour and Welfare based on the provisions of Article 43, Paragraph 1 of the Pharmaceutical Affairs Law	PMDA	PMDA
	Drug products using recombinant technology, cell tissue drug products, etc.	PMDA	PMDA
	Others	Prefectural governments	PMDA
Quasi-drugs	–	Prefectural governments	PMDA
Medical devices	New medical devices	PMDA	PMDA
	Cell tissue medical devices	PMDA	PMDA
	Class IV: Highly Controlled Medical Devices	PMDA	PMDA
	Class III: Highly Controlled Medical Devices	Prefectural governments	PMDA
	Class II: Controlled Medical Devices	Prefectural governments (Recognized Certification Bodies for those with certification standards)	PMDA (Recognized Certification Bodies for those with certification standards)
	Class I: General Medical Devices	Not subject to inspection	Not subject to inspection

For details regarding subject drug products and medical devices, etc. requiring conformity with GMP/QMS, please refer to Chapter 41.

governments (Article 80 of the *Pharmaceutical Affairs Law, Enforcement Ordinance*).

The division of tasks between the state (MHLW and PMDA) and the prefectural governments for the major procedures regarding the manufacturing and marketing, etc., of drug products and medical devices are shown in **Tables 37-3 and 37-4**. In addition, the details of licenses are discussed in "Chapter 39 Required Licenses," and the details of conformity investigation are discussed in "Chapter 41 Quality Manufacturing Practice (QMS) of Medical Devices and In Vitro Diagnostics."

Summary

- Pharmaceutical affairs administration in Japan is administered by MHLW, which is equivalent to DHHS in the US. PFSB deals with problems directly associated with people's lives and health through measures to ensure the effectiveness and safety of drug products and medical devices and measures for blood-related businesses and narcotics and stimulants, while the Health Policy Bureau plans and proposes policies for the realization of a high-quality, effective system for offering medical services.

- PMDA was established in 2004, enabling counseling and evaluations to be conducted at the clinical trial stage for drug products and medical devices, as well as reliability investigations on application data using a consistent system. PMDA performs its duties while coordinating closely with PFSB. In addition, PMDA is an organization comparable with the US FDA's CBER, CDER and CDRH.

- Some administrative duties regarding pharmaceutical affairs administration are delegated to prefectural governments by MHLW.

Related Notifications and Announcements

- MHLW Announcement No. 366 of Showa 45 (1945), *Types, etc. of drug products specified by the Minister of Health, Labour and Welfare based on the provisions of Article 80, Paragraph 2, Section 5 of the Pharmaceutical Affairs Law, Enforcement Ordinance*
- MHLW Announcement No. 104 of Heisei 6 (1994), *Drug Products, etc. specified by the Minister of Health, Labour and Welfare as not requiring approval for manufacturing and marketing based*

on the provisions of Article 14, Paragraph 1 of the Pharmaceutical Affairs Law

- MHLW Announcement No. 194 of Heisei 6 (1994), *Quasi-drugs requiring approval from prefectural governors*
- MHLW Announcement No. 54 of Heisei 9 (1997), *Quasi-drugs, etc. specified by the Minister of Health, Labour and Welfare as not requiring approval for marketing based on the provisions of Article 14, Paragraph 1 of the Pharmaceutical Affairs Law*
- MHLW Announcement No. 431 of Heisei 16 (2004), *Drug products specified by the Minister of Health, Labour and Welfare based on the provisions of Article 20, Paragraph 1, Sections 6 and 7 of the Pharmaceutical Affairs Law, Enforcement Ordinance, as well as Article 96, Sections 6 and 7 of the Pharmaceutical Affairs Law, Enforcement Ordinance*
- MHLW Announcement No. 112 of Heisei 17 (2005), *Specified medical devices for which the Minister of Health, Labour and Welfare has established standards based on the provisions of Article 23-2, Paragraph 1 of the Pharmaceutical Affairs Law*
- MHLW Announcement No. 120 of Heisei 17 (2005), *Specified in_vitro diagnostics for which the Minister of Health, Labour and Welfare has established standards based on the provisions of Article 14, Paragraph 1 of the Pharmaceutical Affairs Law*
- MHLW Announcement No. 121 of Heisei 17 (2005), *Specified in_vitro diagnostics for which the Minister of Health, Labour and Welfare has established standards based on the provisions of Article 23-2, Paragraph 1 of the Pharmaceutical Affairs Law*
- *Yakushokukanmahatsu* No. 0331004 of 31 March, Heisei 17 (2005), *Handling of import notification for drug products, etc.*
- *Yakushokuhatsu* No. 0706002 of 6 July, Heisei 17 (2005), *Revision of operating procedure for side effects, infectious diseases and discrepancy reports on drug products or medical devices from medical institutions, etc.*
- MHLW Announcement No. 528 of Heisei 20 (2005), *Specified medical devices for which the Minister of Health, Labour and Welfare has established standards based on the provisions of Article 23-2, Paragraph 1 of the Pharmaceutical Affairs Law*

References

1. Japan Pharmacists Education Center (ed.), *Guideline for Manufacturing and Marketing of Drug Products 2008*, Jiho, 2008
2. Japan Pharmaceutical Manufacturers Association, Pharmaceutical Information in English Task Force (ed.), *Pharmaceutical Affairs in Japan, March 2009* (free online version)
3. http://www.jpma.or.jp/about/issue/gratis/index2.html
4. PMDA, *Operation Reports of Fiscal Year of Heisei 20 (2008)*
5. MHLW website (www.mhlw.go.jp)
6. PMDA website (www.pmda.go.jp)
7. Database System of Laws of MHLW (http://wwwhourei.mhlw.go.jp/hourei/index.html)

Japanese Medical Device Nomenclature and Classification

OBJECTIVES

❏ To understand the concepts of medical device nomenclature and device classification based upon the development history of the nomenclature.

❏ To understand classification perspectives.

❏ To understand appropriate nomenclature selection methods.

❏ To understand nomenclature differences with other countries.

RELATED LAWS AND REGULATIONS

❏ Article 2, Paragraphs 4–7 of the *Pharmaceutical Affairs Law* (Law No. 145 of Showa 35 (1960))

❏ Article 1 of the *Pharmaceutical Affairs Law, Enforcement Ordinance* (Government Ordinance No. 11 of Showa 36 (1961)), and Appendix 1

❏ Ministry of Health, Labour and Welfare Announcement No. 298 of Heisei 16 (2004), *Highly Controlled Medical Devices, Controlled Medical Devices, and General Medical Devices Specified by the Minister of Health, Labour and Welfare Based on the Provisions of Article 2, Paragraphs 5 to 7 of the Pharmaceutical Affairs Law* (Amendment: Ministry of Health, Labour and Welfare Announcement No. 71 of Heisei 17 (2005); Ministry of Health, Labour and Welfare Announcements No. 174 and 317 of Heisei 19

(2007); Ministry of Health, Labour and Welfare Announcements No. 110 and 381 of Heisei 20 (2008); and Ministry of Health, Labour and Welfare Announcements No. 280, 281, 349 and 460 of Heisei 21 (2009))

Introduction

Medical devices have been marketed in many countries since before device regulations were established. Because laws are enacted based upon each country's history and culture, nomenclature unique to each country is created when existing medical devices become subject to laws and regulations. However, as medical devices are distributed globally as they are today, it is necessary to map and harmonize these devices.

In Japan, the Global Medical Device Nomenclature (GMDN)) was introduced in the revision of the *Pharmaceutical Affairs Law* to globalize and internationally harmonize the former *Medical Devices Nomenclature and Classifications* (Notice of the Director of the Pharmaceutical Affairs Bureau, *Yakuhatsu* No. 1008 of November 1, Heisei 7 (1995)). However, problems have arisen because the nomenclature was introduced as a regulatory requirement.

This chapter, by describing the background of the creation of the Japanese Medical Device Nomenclature (JMDN) to provide an understanding of its concepts, will explain the methodology for selecting the appropriate JMDN when filing an application. Furthermore, it also will describe the nomenclature systems used overseas and provide information enabling global industries to map the nomenclature used in each country within their companies.

Medical Device Definition and Classifications

Article 2, Paragraph 4 of the *Pharmaceutical Affairs Law*, defines medical devices as follows:

"In this Law, 'medical devices' refer to machinery or appliances, etc., used for the purpose of diagnosing, treating, or preventing disease in a human or animal, or for the purpose of affecting the bodily structures or functions of a human or animal, and that are specified in ministerial ordinances."

Article 1 of the *Pharmaceutical Affairs Law, Enforcement Ordinance* states that "medical devices as defined in Article 2, Paragraph 4 of the *Pharmaceutical Affairs Law* are as shown in Appendix 1," and in Appendix 1, 84 machines and appliances, six medical supplies, nine dental materials, four sanitary goods and 12 medical devices for animals are listed under the general category of medical devices. This is a product type-based categorization system, called "Type Category (*Ruibetsu*)." Although the Ministry of Health and Welfare (as it was known at the time) explained that "machines and appliances (appliances and machinery before the revision of the law)" could be further classified into those for hospitals (Type Category 1–12), those for diagnosis (Type Category 13–28), those for surgery (Type Category 29–46), those for treatment (Type Category 47–58), those for dental use (Type Category 59–70), simple medical devices (Type Category 71–83) and accessories (Type Category 84), and dental materials could be further classified between those attached inside the oral cavity (Type Category 1–5) and others (Type Category 6–9), due to changes over time, some existing medical devices cannot be recognized under these names.

In addition to the Type Categories, Highly Controlled Medical Devices, Controlled Medical Devices and General Medical Devices are defined in Article 3, Paragraphs 5–7 of the *Pharmaceutical Affairs Law*, and the nomenclature of each classification is stipulated in the so-called *Notification on Classification* (MHLW Announcement No. 298 of Heisei 16 (2004)) based upon these provisions. Although 4,044 names were defined at the time of publication of the *Notification on Classification*, currently (as of 8 January 2009), the number of names has increased to 4,050 after adding six more for new medical devices approved later.

Along with code numbers and definitions, classes based upon each nomenclature are stipulated in a notification (*Yakushokuhatsu* No. 0720022 of July 20, Heisei 16 (2004), the *Notification on Classification*). This notification includes four classes (I–IV), and Highly Controlled Medical Devices, Controlled Medical Devices and General Medical Devices fall under Classes IV and III, Class II and Class I, respectively. In practice, reviewing the notification is sufficient to identify medical devices within these four classes.

Perspectives on Classification

The JMDN is a combination of the classification rules of the GMDN and of the Global Harmonization Task Force (GHTF). The GHTF guidance document, *GHTF/SG1/N15:2006, Principal of Medical Devices Classification*, uses the word "risk" to classify four classes (Classes A–D). The terms used in ISO 14971 and their definitions are used in the GHTF guidance document, and Japan introduced risk classification based on Classes I–IV.

What, then, is a risk? According to ISO/IEC Guide 51 (1999), risk is a "combination of the probability of occurrence of harm and the severity of that harm." As indicated in the definition provided in ISO 14971, the consequences of an event can be indicated by "the probability of occurrence of a dangerous condition multiplied by the probability that the dangerous condition will lead to harm." These probabilities are generally decreasing due to the maturity and prevalence of the medical devices and the technologies used and are therefore not fixed.

However, the risk classifications of the GHTF guidance document are specific for each medical device and will not decrease. What does this mean? Unlike the above definitions, the word "risk" as used in the GHTF guidance document refers to "harm" (or "the severity of harm" according to ISO 14971). Simple mistakes in the use of words in the GHTF guidance document have resulted in distinct problems for medical device risk classification in Japan.

Some traditional medical devices have been moved into higher classifications with the introduction of the GHTF rules; it has been concluded that "risks of all medical devices are eternally unchanged and shall never decrease." This problem may be perceived as a problem of global harmonization, but for now, it is just a problem for Japan because the GHTF guidance document has not yet been introduced in other countries.

On the other hand, some medical device classifications did not comply with the GHTF rules and were changed to lower classes. For example, based on Rule 16 of the GHTF guidance document, which states that "all medical devices used for contraception or the prevention of Sexually Transmitted Diseases (STDs) are classified as Class C," "contraceptive condoms for males" would be designated as

Figure 38-1. JMDN Code System

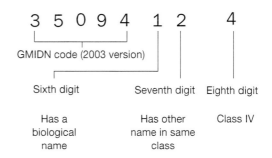

Class III, becoming a Highly Controlled Medical Device in Japan. Although GHTF has deemed the probability of harm as high, it is readily apparent that this probability has been significantly decreased through manufacturing controls. Therefore, it was decided that contraceptive condoms for males would be Class II in Japan. However, because there was no time to verify the degree of actual risks for all 4,044 devices when the JMDN was established, the GHTF rules were automatically applied, leaving some challenges for many medical devices in Japan.

Setting Method for JMDN Codes

The JMDN is based on the GMDN and uses a method known as "division" to follow the GMDN as closely as possible when creating nomenclature specific to Japan. Details of the process are described in "Process of Creation of Nomenclature" later in this chapter. This section explains the division process and how the GMDN is used in Japan. However, it is not always possible to select GMDN from the JMDN because some deleted GMDN terms are still present in the JMDN (see "Problems of the JMDN"). It should be noted that the following information is intended for explaining the relationship between the GMDN and the JMDN.

Figure 38-1 shows the JMDN code system.

Rule 1. JMDN codes are eight-digit numbers. The first five digits are the GMDN code itself (starting with the numbers 1, 3 or 4), or a number set independently in Japan (staring with the number 7). The last three digits are numbers applied independently in Japan.

Rule 2. When a nomenclature indicated by the first five digits is not divided, the last three digits are "000." For example:
- 11389000: Ophthalmic ultrasonic diagnostic imaging devices
- 37891000: Ultrasonic diagnostic probes for the esophagus
- 40767000: External ultrasonic diagnostic probes for installation
- 70014000: Ultrasonic probe covers for body surfaces

Rule 3. The final digit indicates that the class was different when the nomenclature was divided. For example:
- 35209001: Reusable blood collection needles, Class I
- 35209002: Single-use blood collection needles, Class II

In these cases, because the class was different when the nomenclature for 35209, "blood collection needles," was divided, "001" and "002" were added to the last 3 digits of

the Class I "Reusable blood collection needles" and Class II "Single-use blood collection needles," respectively.

Therefore, in principle, only the numbers 0, 1, 2, 3 and 4 are used for the final digit.
- 36957001: Probes for stimulation of body surfaces
- 36957002: Probes for subcutaneous stimulation
- 36957003: Probes for intramuscular stimulation
- 36957004: Probes for cardiac and central nerve stimulation

After publication of the Announcement, some JMDN codes and their definitions were deemed inappropriate for further use. For that reason, any JMDN codes ending with the number 9 should not be used.
- 17470009: Cuffs for vascular catheters

Rule 4. The seventh digit indicates that the class was not changed when the nomenclature was divided. For example:
- 37626010: Mobile analog general-purpose X-ray diagnostic devices
- 37626020: Mobile analog general-purpose integrated X-ray diagnostic devices

In these cases, the nomenclature of 37626, "Mobile analog general-purpose X-ray diagnostic devices," remained Class II when it was divided, and so the numbers "010" and "020" were added. In this case, 10 should always be the nomenclature upon which the division was based.

Theoretically, it can be divided into 9, from 010 to 090.
- 36387010: Refractometers
- 36387020: Refractometers with functions for subjective refraction measurement
- 36387030: Refractor/Keratometers
- 36387040: Refractor/Keratometers with functions for subjective refraction measurement
- 36387050: Refractor/Keratometers with functions for axial length measurement
- 36387060: Ref/Kerato/Tonometers

Rule 5. The sixth digit indicates nomenclature divided based upon derivation from drugs and biological products. For example:
- 10729100: Central venous catheters
- 10729200: Central venous catheters with antibacterial action
- 10729300: Central venous catheters using heparin
- 10729400: Central venous catheters using urokinase

These cases indicate that when 10729, "Central venous catheters," was divided based upon derivation from drugs or biological products, the class remained the same and therefore, 100, 200, 300 and 400 were added. In this case,

100 should always be the nomenclature upon which the division was based.

Theoretically, it can be divided into 9 segments, from 100 to 900.

In addition, it becomes "000" when a nomenclature derived from drugs or biological products exists independently, but it should be noted that nomenclatures not using these numbers may exist.

36125000: Intermittent urinary catheters
34096000: Antibacterial urinary catheters

Rule 6. When a class changes due to division but does not change based upon derivation from a biological product, a combination of the above Rules 3–5 is used.

35094012: Catheter guide wires for temporary use
35094022: Nonvascular guide wires
35094032: Catheter guide wires for peritoneal irrigation
35094103: Vascular catheter guide wires
35094203: Vascular catheter guide wires using heparin
35094114: Catheter guide wires for cardiac and central circulatory systems
35094214: Catheter guide wires for cardiac and central circulatory systems using heparin
35094124: Catheter guide wires for central nervous systems

The above are cases in which 35094, "Catheter guide wires," was divided.

Because there are nomenclatures in Classes II to IV, the numbers 2 to 4 are added as the final digit based upon Rule 3.

Because there are 3 kinds of nomenclatures in Class II, the numbers 1 to 3 are used as the seventh digit based upon Rule 4.

Because the nomenclatures in Class III are divided based upon whether they are derived from biological products, the numbers 1 and 2 are used as the sixth digit based upon Rule 5.

The numbers 1 and 2 are used as the sixth digit because the nomenclatures of Class IV are divided based upon whether they are derived from biological products, and the numbers 1 and 2 are used as the seventh digit because there are 2 types of nomenclatures for non-biologically derived products.

Selection Method for Nomenclature

When selecting an appropriate JMDN, sometimes it is not available even though the corresponding GMDN is known and being utilized. Some translation-related problems exist. In addition, there are JMDN codes to which the coding rules described above are not applied due to simple mistakes. It is necessary to consider the following points when searching for a JMDN because if there is no appropriate JMDN code, the product will be recognized as a new medical device in Japan and will require an enormous application cost and lengthy review time.

A nomenclature can be recognized as having been divided if numbers are used in the last three digits.

If an appropriate JMDN code was identified and it has a number in its last 3 digits, it is necessary to verify other divided nomenclatures by using only the first five digits because the divided nomenclatures are not necessarily listed sequentially.

In that case, keep in mind that divided nomenclatures include numbers in the sixth or seventh digit, even if only the final digit includes a number other than 0. The following are examples.

15679001: Reusable tine test needles
15679012: Single-use tine test needles
15679022: Tine test and vaccination needles

When a nomenclature includes the terms "general-purpose," "general," "single-use," "reusable," "using XX," "antibiotic" and "combination," the nomenclature search should exclude these terms.

There are also nomenclatures for kits and sets. For example, it is often assumed that most syringes are under "general-purpose syringes," but there is a total of 22 nomenclatures for syringes. Also, there are 21 nomenclatures related to urinary catheters, including "Urinary catheter implantation and urine sampling kits" and "Urine-sampling urethral catheterization kit, Ureteral stent-placement set."

Searches should be conducted using not only definitions but also Japanese and English technical terms related to the product under the Terms and Definitions.

In this case, it is necessary to increase the hit count, because identification of words with low hit counts may lead to misidentification. For example, urinary Foley catheters may not appear as a result when the search term is "urinary catheter."

Because terms in English may be different, even when the same Japanese nomenclature is used, it is necessary to verify terms with similar nomenclatures and conduct searches using multiple terms. For example, the term "clamp" is translated as "*kuranpu*" or "*kanshi*," but the original word for "*kanshi*" is "forceps" or "clamp."

16449000: Clamp, cannula (Catheter clamps)
15672000: Forceps, tonsil (Tonsil clamps)
10861002: Clamps, surgical, single use (Single-use clamps)

In addition to looking at items related to GHTF rules, *Specifically Designated Control Medical Devices Requiring Maintenance Control, and Medical Devices Requiring*

Installation Control, it is necessary to conduct comparisons with approved medical devices and confirm whether the product corresponds to the nomenclature.

Because the use of old nomenclature or Type Categories may cause misidentification, it is essential to follow the above procedures.

Background of Creation of JMDN and Future Tasks and Nomenclature in Other Countries

As previously discussed, although the JMDN is based upon the GMDN, Japan has used a method known as "division" to create its own nomenclatures. However, the JMDN still has problems that need to be resolved in the future. This section discusses the background of the creation of the nomenclature and points that need to be solved in the JMDN in the future.

Background of Creation of Nomenclature

According to the *Notification on Classification* (*Yakushokuhatsu* No. 0720022 of Heisei 16 (2004)), the *Announcement on Classification* is described as follows:

"Each nomenclature has been stipulated with reference to the Global Medical Device Nomenclature (GMDN) stipulated in the GMDN project of ISO/TC210."

"The classification rules have been stipulated based on the classification rules discussed by the Global Harmonization Task Force (GHTF)."

The origin of the *Nomenclature and Classification of Medical Devices* is the GMDN described in 1 above, and the GHTF classification rules described in 2 were incorporated for those nomenclatures. We will first explain how these were stipulated.

Trends of ISO and GMDN

Japan, the US, Europe and other regions each have their own nomenclature for medical devices. With the aim of exchanging information on medical devices (especially information related to postmarket safety) between regulatory agencies, efforts were made to integrate the nomenclatures. In 1997, the European Community (EC) and The European Committee for Standardization (CEN) launched the GMDN project to create a single nomenclature based upon the following six types of nomenclatures.

- The Universal Medical Device Nomenclature System (UMDNS) of the US Emergency Care Research Institute (ECRI, a nonprofit organization established in 1968)
- Nomenclature of US Food and Drug Administration (FDA) (21 CFR 862 to 892)
- Nomenclature of the European Diagnostic Manufacturers Association (EDMA; a diagnostic manufacturers association established in 1979)

- *Norsk Klassifisering Koding & Nomenklatur* (NKKN) of Norway
- Nomenclature of Japan (*Yakuhatsu* No. 1008 of November 1, Heisei 7 (1995)), henceforth referred to as "old nomenclature," the *Red Book*
- *ISO 9999: Technical aids for persons with disabilities. Classification and Terminology*

The budget was provided by the EC because it was a project of CEN, and the project was carried out with that budget in the US and Japan.

In Japan, the Regulatory Data Exchange System Exploratory Committee (KKS; discussed below) was organized under ISO/TC210/WG3, and actual operations were carried out by the JFMDA (as it was known at the time) by calling for experts from member organizations to participate. This project was positioned as a global "reporting system for failures of medical devices" in the committee and was presided by the Office of Promotion of Proper Use of Drug Products of the Safety Division of the Ministry of Health and Welfare.

In the GMDN project, medical devices were divided into categories from 01 to 12 and the integration of nomenclatures was conducted by each category's Device Expert Task Group (DETG). However, the issue of the old Japanese nomenclature's classification file structure had already been discussed in 1997. Although the nomenclature in Japan was to be used for implementation of the regulatory system and involved a classification file structure that included Large (*Dai*: the top tier), Middle (*Chuu*: the second tier), Small (*Shou*: the third tier), Detail (*Sai*: the forth and the lowest tier) categories (hierarchy structure), the GMDN was a project designed only for integrating nomenclatures and there was no need to use a classification file structure. Debates were held over whether or not the hierarchy structure of the Japanese nomenclature should be eliminated to make the coding structure flat. As a result, the hierarchy structure was eliminated. In other words, the nomenclatures in all categories in the *Red Book* were translated into English and they were integrated into one single category. During this process, nomenclatures in all of the Large category and Middle category were processed as "synonyms/equivalents" (where the former (nomenclatures in Large category) remain as nomenclatures but the latter (nomenclatures in the Middle category) are completely eliminated) because their definitions were too broad. This work was completed in 2000.

Regulatory Reform Trends

Based on a Cabinet decision of 31 March 2000, the statement, "In order to promote decisions over whether clinical tests are required, Japan must actively cooperate with the project for the international integration of nomenclature (GMDN)" was included in the *Three-year Plan for the Promotion of Regulatory Reform* (second revision). This second revision also states that

"Operations are being implemented sequentially, such

as applying the classification standards of the Global Harmonization Task Force (GHTF) and the Global Medical Device Nomenclature (GMDN) and enforcing the revised *Pharmaceutical Affairs Law* of April 1, Heisei 17 (2005) for the various systems involved in approval under the *Pharmaceutical Affairs Law*."

Given this background, it can be seen that the decision to establish the JMDN as "a product of integrating the GHTF classification rules into the GMDN" as discussed earlier was made within the trend of regulatory reform.

JMDN Trends

The Regulatory Data Exchange System Review Subcommittee was established in August 2000. It became known as KKS based on the initials of *Kisei*, *Kokan* and *System*. Working groups (WGs) established in each industrial association worked on translation to prepare "temporary translations" (Japanese translations) of the GMDN, setting 2001 as the first year. Specifying 8,000 nomenclatures related to medical devices from among a total of 20,000 and translating them into Japanese required a lot of professional work and effort. Unfortunately, the fact that the classification file structure of the "old nomenclature" was eliminated in 1997 was never discussed at this time.

While establishing various committees and WGs to deal with the revision of the *Pharmaceutical Affairs Law* within the Japan Medical Devices Manufacturers Association (JMED), the first Classification Review WG meeting was held in May 2002. The purposes of the meeting were to scrutinize the temporary translations prepared by the KKS and to work on adding the GHTF classification rules. The GHTF classification guidance was *SG1/N015R18: Medical Devices Classification* (Working Draft, 23 May 2002)."

SG1/N015R19 (PROPOSED DOCUMENT, 23 October 2002) began to be used for operations from November of that year. Ultimately, this version will be used to identify risk class. At this point, some of the medical devices were classified into lower classes based upon historical background considerations.

Guidelines for the addition of general nomenclature (partially cited) were issued in February 2003, and work to add Japan-specific JMDN codes began.

In the same month, the Medical Devices and In Vitro Diagnostics Group and the Medical Materials Group of the Pharmaceutical Affairs and Food Sanitary Council met jointly and accepted the establishment of the JMDN. A Public comment period regarding classification was held from March through April, while additions to the nomenclatures and revisions of definitions continued in the Classification Review WG. This was when the rule to add three-digit code numbers to JMDN codes was created.

A second round of the public comment process was held in October and November of 2004. Based upon the results, a final plan for the industry was submitted to the Pharmaceutical and Food Examination Subcommittee and resulted in promulgation of the *Announcement on Classification* in March 2005, which completed the creation of the JMDN.

The GMDN Agency handles not only requests for additions—two additions each day—but also periodically revises nomenclatures and definitions. JFMDA launched the GMDN Subcommittee under the Technical Committee in August 2005 to keep the JMDN updated. At first, the subcommittee focused on laying the groundwork for Middle categories.

As previously described, the GMDN term "category" was recognized as the Large category when creating the JMDN, but this word has been interpreted in other countries to mean "characterization." For work on the first stage until 2000, 12 categories were used. This has since grown to 16, and a limit allowing future increases up to 20 has been established. Furthermore, the Collective Terms (CTs) being created by the GMDN were misunderstood as "Middle categories" in Japan. The hierarchy utilizing CTs is intended for multiple search-system structures, which was completely different from Japan's expectation of a single, fixed-classification file structure. Therefore, the subcommittee was unable to continue work on creating a classification file structure (creating subcategories) as had been planned at the beginning. In other words, it was unable to establish groupings of the JMDN due to a lack of understanding of the concept. This had a significant impact on QMS audits, Third Party Certification Systems and the Statistical Survey of Pharmaceutical Industry Productions.

Problems With the JMDN

The JMDN gradually began to depart from its objective of harmonization with the international nomenclature for medical devices. Although it is partially harmonized with the GMDN, it became a nomenclature for medical devices unique to Japan.

The JMDN was established as a result of the complex intertwining of concepts of the ISO, GMDN and GHTF and regulatory reform, revisions to the *Pharmaceutical Affairs Law*, etc., and we now need to resolve the problems.

GMDN Concept and Intended Use of the JMDN are Different

The purpose of the GMDN project is to enable the global exchange of data on regulations (information primarily regarding postmarket safety). In fact, it was first considered as a project using a "reporting system for failures of medical devices," even by the Japanese KKS. However, based upon subsequent developments, it was positioned as a project related to the basis of regulations on medical devices. Because it was established as a regulatory requirement, GMDN's traditional flexibility has been lost.

If existing GMDN nomenclatures and definitions were not suitable for an existing product in the market, an original JMDN nomenclature was created and the definition was changed only in Japan.

The JMDN Lacks a Classification File Structure Similar to the *Red Book*

Although it was recognized from the beginning of the GMDN project that the *Red Book*'s classification file structure would be lost, opinions calling for the creation of a classification file structure based on the creation of subcategories were frequently heard. Ultimately, the JMDN created a structure in which 4,044 (at the time) nomenclatures existed in parallel at the same level. Due to the laws and regulations, QMS audits must be conducted for each of these nomenclatures (products) and a significant burden is imposed on Marketing Authorization Holders, but they cannot be used for the Statistical Survey of Pharmaceutical Industry Productions.

JMDN Cannot be Appropriately Maintained

Although deletions, additions and revisions to the GMDN nomenclatures based upon requests from registered corporations are always made and the nomenclatures are always changing, it is impossible to reflect all of these changes in the JMDN nomenclatures because the JMDN nomenclatures are stipulated in Announcements the Japanese government publishes. For example, GMDN36282, "Contraceptive, condom, male," was established as 36282000, "Contraceptive condoms for males" in the JMDN. At a later date, GMDN 36282 was deleted and six new nomenclatures were created to replace it, but the JMDN has not been changed.

There are also problems with translations. For example, GMDN code 45167, "Moxa," is translated as "*mogusa*" and is regulated as a drug in Japan. However, it is apparent that the definition of the GMDN code also includes medical devices, and it must be translated as "Moxibustion therapy device" in the JMDN. Translating a word using only a dictionary is insufficient; it is necessary to have an understanding of which medical devices distributed in the market to choose the appropriate translated nomenclature of those medical devices. It has been suggested that the mapping of words using only a dictionary is impossible because the nomenclatures of medical devices include technical terminology that has been part of each country's conventions. Using only a GMDN code when exchanging information between countries certainly leads to translation problems.

The JMDN Has Created Risk-based Nomenclatures

When introducing the GMDN in Japan, GHTF's *Principles of Medical Devices Classification* were used to classify each medical device as Highly Controlled Medical Devices, Controlled Medical Devices and General Medical Devices.

However, since the GMDN does not include the concept of risk, it was necessary to divide the nomenclatures by adding risk classifications when adding them to the JMDN.

Risk-based classification of medical devices is implemented by all regulatory agencies and it is apparent that on this point the GMDN does not fit directly into the regulations.

Nomenclatures That Use Template Terms

In the 2003 edition of GMDN, nomenclatures had not been fully created to cover all medical devices on the market at the time. Therefore, for some devices, the only choice was to use Template Terms, which normally cannot be used for identifying devices. It is obvious that nomenclatures such as "Scissors, <specify>," "Dermatome, <specify>," and "Retractor, <specify>" do not refer to specific devices. Since these Template Terms are continuously being eliminated from the GMDN, replacing them with the appropriate GMDN codes is necessary when exporting medical devices outside Japan.

The GMDN Includes Nomenclatures of Non-medical Devices

GMDN licenses are granted even to medical institutions. These medical institutions file requests for the addition of nomenclatures for inventory control, and the applicability of medical devices must be tested individually. GMDN code 10085 "Ambulance" is a well-known case, but 37424 "Laundry bag" and even 38554 "Toothbrush" are not recognized as medical devices by any regulatory agencies, and the creation of such nomenclatures is not needed. In this regard, it is desirable for the original objectives of the GMDN be re-acknowledged and for regulatory agencies to decide to limit necessary nomenclatures to medical devices.

Comparison With Nomenclature in Other Countries

Japan has adopted the GMDN and translated it into the law as the JMDN, but is this the case for other countries? Most countries mainly adopt the use of the GMDN into law without modifications because the continual amendments and additions are difficult to maintain.

Australia

The Therapeutic Goods Administration (TGA) revised the *Therapeutic Goods (Medical Devices) Regulations* of 2002 and adopted the use of the GMDN into law based on ISO 15225:2000(E). According to "1.7 Device nomenclature system codes" (Act s 41BE (3)), for Class I devices, the use of relevant template terms is stipulated when the device is not applicable to specific conditions, but problems have arisen because, as noted previously, the GMDN is moving toward eliminating template terms.

Hong Kong

The Department of Health has publicized a website for searching the GMDN, but like Japan, it uses the 2003 version. If GMDN data can be searched for free at other websites, it is important to note that such data from the fee website may not be current.

Italy

The *Ministero del Lavoro, della Salute e delle Politiche Sociali* (Ministry of Labor and of Health and of Social Policies) adopted a databank registration system for medical devices. For registration, it is necessary to identify both the *Classificazione Nazionale Dispositivi Medici* (CND, National Medical Device Classification) code, which is the Italian classification system for medical devices, and the GMDN code. The classification system in Italy has a seven-level classification file structure and seems to be updated regularly (the former *Red Book* in Japan had a five-level classification file structure). The GMDN can be selected from the system, but the frequency of revisions is unknown. There has been a trend toward the use of such databanks in various European countries, and it is necessary for us to keep obtaining the most current information on regulatory revisions.

US

The US has completed mapping the GMDN codes to the Product Codes and is moving toward adopting the GMDN. Specifically, it has been suggested that the GMDN be used for the Unique Device Identification (UDI) system.

If regulatory agencies use the GMDN as regulatory requirements, there is a need to promote an environment where the most recent data can be used at no charge. Among developing countries, there is a tendency to avoid using the GMDN because the Universal Medical Device Nomenclature System (UMDNS) of the ECRI Institute is free, and there are active debates within the GHTF to make GMDN codes available to all free of charge as well. We believe that the global harmonization of nomenclatures for medical devices will take some time. Meanwhile, it is necessary for companies to continue their efforts to map the nomenclatures used for their products to the most recent nomenclature used in the regulations in various countries.

Summary

The JMDN is basically a combination of GMDN and GHTF classifications.

The JMDN was created, based upon the GMDN, in order to globalize and internationally harmonize the old *Nomenclature and Types of Medical Devices*.

More than 4,000 codes were created, as a result of choosing the method known as the division of codes to limit deviations from the original GMDN as much as possible when creating the Japan specific nomenclature.

It is important to select the appropriate JMDN at the time of submitting an application.

Related Notifications

Yakushokuhatsu No. 0709004 of July 9, Heisei 16 (2004), *Enforcement of laws, etc. partially revising the Pharmaceutical Affairs Law and the Bleeding Donor Supply Service Control Law*

Yakushokuhatsu No. 0720022 of July 20, Heisei 16 (2004), *Enforcement of Highly Controlled Medical Devices, Controlled Medical Devices, and General Medical Devices (Announcement) specified by the Minister of Health, Labour and Welfare based on the provisions of Article 2, Paragraphs 5 to 7 of the Pharmaceutical Affairs Law and Designated Medical Devices Requiring Maintenance Control (Announcement) specified by the Minister of Health, Labour and Welfare based on the provisions of Article 2, Paragraph 8 of the Pharmaceutical Affairs Law*

Yakushokuhatsu No. 0311005 of March 11, Heisei 17 (2005), *Enforcement of matters (Announcement) partially amending the Highly Controlled Medical Devices, Controlled Medical Devices, and General Medical Devices specified by the Minister of Health, Labour and Welfare based on the provisions of Article 2, Paragraphs 5 to 7 of the Pharmaceutical Affairs Law and matters (Announcement) partially amending the Designated Medical Devices Requiring Maintenance Control specified by the Minister of Health, Labour and Welfare based on the provisions of Article 2, Paragraph 8 of the Pharmaceutical Affairs Law*

Jimurenraku of February 8, Heisei 19 (2007), *Handling of nomenclature of medical devices and in-vitro diagnostics not applicable to any general nomenclature*

Yakushokuhatsu No. 0423005 of April 23, Heisei 19 (2007), *Enforcement of Highly Controlled Medical Devices, Controlled Medical Devices, and General Medical Devices (Announcement) specified by the Minister of Health, Labour and Welfare based on the provisions of Article 2, Paragraphs 5 to 7 of the Pharmaceutical Affairs Law and Designated Medical Devices Requiring Maintenance Control (Announcement) specified by the Minister of Health, Labour and Welfare based on the provisions of Article 2, Paragraph 8 of the Pharmaceutical Affairs Law*

Jimurenraku of May 14, Heisei 19 (2007), *Partial amendments of issued notices*

Yakushokuhatsu No. 0928016 of September 28, Heisei 19 (2007), *Partial amendments of 'Enforcement of Highly Controlled Medical Devices, Controlled Medical Devices, and General Medical Devices (Announcement) specified by the Minister of Health, Labour and Welfare based on the provisions of Article 2, Paragraphs 5 to 7 of the Pharmaceutical Affairs Law and Designated Medical*

Devices Requiring Maintenance Control (Announcement) specified by the Minister of Health, Labour and Welfare based on the provisions of Article 2, Paragraph 8 of the Pharmaceutical Affairs Law

Yakushokuhatsu No. 0325003 of March 25, Heisei 20 (2008), *Addition of nomenclature of medical devices*

Yakushokuhatsu No. 0325043 of March 25, Heisei 20 (2008), *Changes in definitions of nomenclature of medical devices*

Yakushokuhatsu No. 0711001 of July 11, Heisei 20 (2008), *Addition of nomenclature of medical devices*

Yakushokuhatsu No. 0428001 of April 28, Heisei 20 (2008), *Addition of nomenclature of medical devices*

Yakushokuhatsu 0706-1 of March 25, Heisei 21 (2009), *Addition of nomenclature of medical devices*

Chapter 39

Required Japanese Licenses

OBJECTIVES

❏ To understand an overview of required licenses for handling drug products, etc. and to understand requirements for each license category and license acquirement

RELATED LAWS AND REGULATIONS

Marketing Authorization Holder/Overall

❏ *Pharmaceutical Affairs Law* (Law No. 145 of Showa 35 (1960))

❏ *Pharmaceutical Affairs Law, Enforcement Ordinance* (Government Ordinance No. 11 of Showa 36 (1961))

❏ *Pharmaceutical Affairs Law, Enforcement Regulations* (Ministry of Health and Welfare Ordinance No. 1 of Showa 36 (1961))

❏ *Ministerial Ordinance on Good Quality Practice for Drug Products, Quasi-drugs, Cosmetics, and Medical Devices* (Ministry of Health, Labour and Welfare Ordinance No. 136 of Heisei 16 (2004)) (*Ministerial Ordinance on GQP*)

❏ *Ministerial Ordinance on Standards for Post-Marketing Safety Management System for Drug Products, Quasi-drugs, Cosmetics, and Medical Devices* (Ministry of Health, Labour and Welfare Ordinance No. 135 of Heisei 16 (2004)) (*Ministerial Ordinance on GVP*)

❏ *Structures and and Facilities Requirements for*

Pharmacies, etc. (Ministry of Health and Welfare Ordinance No. 2 of Showa 36 (1961))

Manufacturing Licenses/Foreign Manufacturer Accreditation

❏ *Ministerial Ordinance on Good Manufacturing Practice for Drug Products and Quasi-drugs* (Ministry of Health, Labour and Welfare Ordinance No. 179 of Heisei 16 (2004)) (*Ministerial Ordinance on GMP*)

❏ *Ministerial Ordinance on Quality Management System for Medical Devices and In Vitro Diagnostics* (Ministry of Health, Labour and Welfare Ordinance No. 169 of Heisei 16 (2004)) (*Ministerial Ordinance on QMS*)

Introduction

The *Pharmaceutical Affairs Law* (Law No. 145) was enacted in Showa 35 (1960) for the purpose of providing regulations required for securing the quality, effectiveness and safety of drug products, quasi-drugs, cosmetics and medical devices (henceforth referred to as "drug products, etc.") and improving health and sanitation. Manufacturing, acting as a Marketing Authorization Holder (MAH) and sales, etc. of drug products, etc. cannot be conducted if compliance with the *Pharmaceutical Affairs Law* is not achieved. Penalties for violations of the *Pharmaceutical Affairs Law* are also defined in the law. This chapter provides an overview of regulations on the required licenses, etc. for acting as an MAH of drug products, etc.

In addition, a person who wishes to release products into the market must obtain approval from the Minister of Health, Labour and Welfare for each product. For details regarding applications, please refer to "Chapter

43 Applications for Medical Devices" and "Chapter 44 Applications for In Vitro Diagnostics."

Definition and Types of Licenses

Under the *Pharmaceutical Affairs Law*, a person who has not obtained approval from the Minister of Health, Labour and Welfare may not release drug products, etc. onto the market as a business (Article 12 of the *Pharmaceutical Affairs Law*). Manufacturing (including labeling and storage), sales, leasing and repair of drug products, etc. conducted as businesses are also regulated in a similar manner. Licenses include the following:

- Marketing Authorization Holder Licenses
- Manufacturing Licenses (for overseas manufacturing sites, Foreign Manufacturer Accreditation)
- Sales Licenses
- Leasing Licenses (limited to medical devices)
- Licenses for Repair Business (limited to medical devices)

Acting as the MAH refers to "manufacturing, etc. (including manufacturing outsourced to another party but not including manufacturing outsourced by others; the same applies below) or sales, leasing, or providing imported drug products (except drug products that are drug substances), quasi-drugs, cosmetics, or medical devices" (Article 2, Paragraph 12 of the *Pharmaceutical Affairs Law*). In other words, MAHs are those who develop drug products, etc., manufacture such products by themselves or outsource manufacturing to another company, and release the products onto the market. Therefore, the MAH is solely responsible for the products.

A manufacturer is a party that manufactures drug products, etc. outsourced by an MAH. Leasing and repair businesses are businesses limited to medical devices. As reference, the relationship between typical product processes and associated licenses is shown in **Figure 39-1**.

Marketing Authorization Holder (MAH) Licenses
Overview of Licenses

An MAH license is necessary to act as the MAH for drug products, etc. Importing and selling drug products manufactured abroad are also included in the actions for which the MAH is responsible.

Types of Licenses

The required licenses differ depending upon the type of products for which MAHs are responsible. These requirements are shown in **Table 39-1** (Article 12 of the *Pharmaceutical Affairs Law*). However, a person who has acquired a Type I MAH license for medical devices is considered as having also acquired both a Type II and a Type III MAH license for medical devices. A person who has acquired a Type II MAH license for medical devices is considered as having also acquired a Type III MAH license for medical devices (Article 9 of the *Pharmaceutical Affairs Law, Enforcement Ordinance*).

Therefore, a single corporation may acquire only one MAH license for medical devices. On other hand, the same corporation may acquire both Type I and Type II MAH

Figure 39-1. Product Processes and Required Licenses

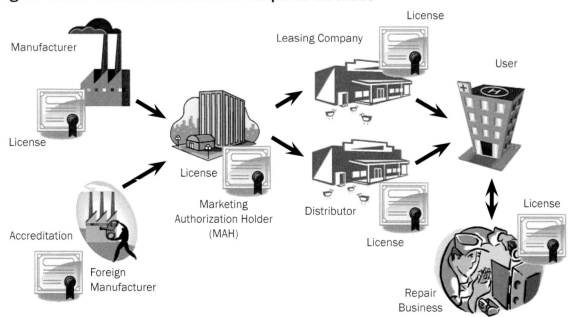

Table 39-1. Types of Marketing Authorization Holder Licenses and Corresponding Products

Type Marketing Authorization Holder (MAH) License	Type of Products That Can Be Handled
Type I MAH license for drug	Drug products specified by the Minister of Health, Labour and Welfare as stipulated in Article 49, Paragraph 1 (including prescription drugs)
Type II MAH license for drugs	Drug products other than those corresponding to the preceding paragraph (including in vitro diagnostics)
MAH license for quasi-drugs	Quasi-drugs
MAH license for cosmetics	Cosmetics
Type I MAH license for medical devices	Highly Controlled Medical Devices (Class III/IV)
	Controlled Medical Devices (Class II)
	General Medical Devices (Class I)
Type II MAH license for medical devices	Controlled Medical Devices (Class II)
	General Medical Devices (Class I)
Type III MAH license for medical devices	General Medical Devices (Class I)

licenses for drug products. Also, the same corporation may acquire multiple licenses for different types of products, such as drug products and quasi-drugs, as well as cosmetics and medical devices, etc.

Licensing Requirements

An MAH license will be granted to an applicant who meets the following personnel and organizational requirements for quality control and safety management:

There must be a general controller who supervises operations.

A quality control system that complies with the *Ministerial Ordinance on Standards for Quality Control for Drug Products, Quasi-drugs, Cosmetics, and Medical Devices* (*Ministerial Ordinance on GQP*) must be established.

A safety management system that complies with *Ministerial Ordinance on Standards for Quality Control for Drug Products, Quasi-drugs, Cosmetics, and Medical Devices"* (*Ministerial Ordinance on GVP*) must be established.

Qualifications for General Controller

The qualifications for a general controller for drug products and medical devices are as shown in **Tables 39-2** and **39-3**.

In addition, please refer to Article 85 of the *Pharmaceutical Affairs Law, Enforcement Regulations* and Paragraph 2 of the same article for the qualifications for the general controller for quasi-drugs and cosmetics.

License Applications

The governor of the prefectural government where the operations site (operations site with the main functions) supervised by the general controller has the authority to grant licenses. Applications based upon Form No. 9 of the *Pharmaceutical Affairs Law, Enforcement Regulations* are submitted to the governor. The following materials must be attached to the applications (Article 19 of the *Pharmaceutical Affairs Law, Enforcement Regulations*).

- a certificate of Corporate Registry, if the applicant is a corporation
- a medical certificate issued by a doctor stating that the applicant does not suffer from impaired mental functions (if the applicant is a corporation, the certificate would specify the board member conducting the operations; the same applies below) and is not addicted to narcotics, marijuana, opium or stimulants
- a copy of the MAH licenses, if the applicant has already acquired them
- an organizational chart, if the applicant is a corporation
- a copy of the employment contracts and other documents proving the relationship between the applicant and the general controller if the applicant is not the general controller
- documents proving that the general controller meets the provisions of Article 17, Paragraph 1 of the law
- documents describing Good Quality Practice (GQP) compliant system
- documents describing Good Vigilance Practice (GVP) compliant system

Inspections on GQP and GVP system are conducted by the prefectural government after the application is filed.

An MAH license is valid for five years. To maintain

Table 39-2. Qualifications for General Controller (Drug Products)

Drug Product to be Handled	Drug Products Specified by the Minister of Health, Labour and Welfare as Stipulated in Article 49, Paragraph 1 (Including Prescription Drugs)	Drug Products Other Than Those Corresponding to the Preceding Paragraph (Including In Vitro Diagnostics)
Legal basis	Article 17 of the *Pharmaceutical Affairs Law*	
Requirements	Pharmacist	

Table 39-3. Qualifications for General Controller (Medical Devices)

Type of Medical Device to be Handled	Highly Controlled Medical Devices (Class III/IV) Controlled Medical Devices (Class II)	General Medical Devices (Class I)
Legal basis	Article 85-3 of the *Pharmaceutical Affairs Law, Enforcement Regulations*	Article 85-4 of the *Pharmaceutical Affairs Law, Enforcement Regulations*
Requirements	A person who has completed academic studies in any of the fields of physics, chemistry, metallurgy, electricity, mechanics, pharmacology, medicine or dentistry at a university, etc. + Three years of experience in quality control for drugs and medical devices or Postmarket safety management operations	A person who has completed courses on physics, chemistry, metallurgy, electricity, mechanics, pharmacology, medicine or dentistry at an old-education-system junior high school or high school or any equivalent or higher-ranked school + Three years of experience in quality control for drug products, etc. or Postmarket safety management operations
	A person recognized by the Minister of MHLW as having equivalent or higher levels of knowledge and experience compared to the person described above	A person recognized by the Minister of MHLW as having equivalent or higher levels of knowledge and experience compared to the person described above

a license after the valid period expires, it is necessary to renew the license in advance (Article 12, Provision 2 of the *Pharmaceutical Affairs Law*, and Article 23 of the *Pharmaceutical Affairs Law, Enforcement Regulations*).

The license fees may vary by prefecture and it is necessary for the applicants to check the fees in advance.

Manufacturing Licenses
Overview of Licenses

A person who has not acquired a manufacturing license for drug products, quasi-drugs, cosmetics or medical devices may not manufacture those products as a business. Licenses shall be granted by the Minister of Health, Labour and Welfare to individual manufacturing sites according to the categories stipulated in MHLW's ordinances.

License Categories

License categories for the manufacturing of prescription drugs, in vitro diagnostics, and medical devices are stipulated in Article 26 of the *Pharmaceutical Affairs Law, Enforcement Regulations* (**Tables 39-4**, **39-5** and **39-6**).

So-called branch warehouses (*Bunchi Soko*) of manufacturing sites require "Labeling, etc. Manufacturing" licenses for conducting operations associated with the manufacturing process, including the storage of products awaiting product release determination, and storage and shipping/receiving operations after product release determination is made. It should be noted that a Manufacturing License is required, instead of "Labeling, etc. Manufacturing" license, if the prescription drugs fall into the Biological Products category (Subcategory No. 1) or Radiopharmaceutical products category (Subcategory No. 2).

Table 39-4. Categories of Manufacturing Licenses for Prescription Drugs

Article 26 (Categories of Manufacturing Licenses) of the *Pharmaceutical Affairs Law, Enforcement Regulations*		
No. 1	Biological Products	Sites for performing all or part of manufacturing processes for drug products stipulated in Article 80, Paragraph 2, Section 3A, C, and D of the law (including Biological Products, recombinant drug products, etc.)
No. 2	Radiopharmaceutical products	Sites for performing all or part of manufacturing processes for radiopharmaceutical products (excluding sites described in No. 1)
No. 3	Aseptic drug products	Sites for performing all or part of manufacturing processes for aseptic drug products (refers to sterilized drug products excluding those described in No. 1 and No. 2; the same applies below) (excluding sites described in No. 5)
No. 4	General	Sites for performing all or part of manufacturing processes for drug products other than those described in No. 1 to No. 3 (excluding sites described in the following paragraph)
No. 5	Packaging , etc.	Sites for performing only packaging, labeling or storage from among the manufacturing processes for drug products described in No. 3 and No. 4

Table 39-5. Categories of Manufacturing Licenses for In Vitro Diagnostics

Article 26 (Categories of Manufacturing Licenses), Paragraph 2 of the *Pharmaceutical Affairs Law, Enforcement Regulations*		
No. 1	Radiopharmaceutical products	Sites for performing all or part of manufacturing processes for radiopharmaceutical products
No. 2	General	Sites for performing all or part of manufacturing processes for drug products other than those described in the previous paragraph (excluding sites described in the following paragraph)
No. 3	Packaging , etc.	Sites for performing only packaging, labeling or storage from among the manufacturing processes for drug products described in the previous paragraph

Table 39-6. Categories of Manufacturing Licenses for Medical Devices

Article 26 (Categories of Manufacturing Licenses), Paragraph 5 of the Pharmaceutical Affairs Law, Enforcement Regulations		
No. 1	Minister-specified	Sites for performing all or part of manufacturing processes for medical devices specified by the Minister of MHLW and those specified by the Minister of MHLW based on the provisions of Article 43, Paragraph 2 of the law as requiring special attention for manufacturing control or quality control based on Article 80, Paragraph 2, Section 3 of the law
No. 2	Sterilization	Sites for performing all or part of manufacturing processes (referring to medical devices sterilized in the manufacturing process, excluding those described in No. 1) (excluding sites described in No. 4)
No. 3	General	Sites for performing all or part of manufacturing processes for medical devices other than those described in No. 1 and No. 2 (excluding sites described in the following paragraph)
No. 4	Packaging, etc.	Sites for performing only packaging, labeling or storage from among the manufacturing processes for medical devices described in No. 2 and No. 3

For quasi-drugs and cosmetics, please refer to Article 26, Paragraphs 3 and 4 of the *Pharmaceutical Affairs Law, Enforcement Regulations*.

Licensing Requirements

Both physical and personnel requirements must be met to acquire a Manufacturing License.

Physical Requirements

The manufacturing site's structures and facilities must comply with the *Regulations for Structures and Facilities Requirements for Pharmacies, etc.* (Article 13, Paragraph 4, Section 1 of the *Pharmaceutical Affairs Law*). Facilities subject to QMS compliance facilities must also comply with Article 24 of the *Ministerial Ordinance on QMS*.

Facilities subject to GMP compliance must also comply with the *Ministerial Ordinance on GMP*.

Personnel Requirements

Personnel requirements for Manufacturing Licenses include those related to the "applicant" and those related to the "manufacturing supervisor." For the manufacturing supervisor, it is necessary to pay attention to differences between requirements for drug products and medical devices.

Applicant

The applicant (if the applicant is a corporation, the board member conducting manufacturing-related operations) must not meet any of the disqualification clauses (Article 5, Paragraph 3 of the *Pharmaceutical Affairs Law*).

Manufacturing Supervisor
Drug Products

Unless a drug product manufacturer is a pharmacist and directly manages its production on site, each manufacturing site must have a pharmacist on site to supervise manufacturing operations. However, for drug products not requiring a pharmacist for manufacturing control, a technician who is not a pharmacist may take on this position (Article 17, Paragraph 3 of the *Pharmaceutical Affairs Law*). "Drug products not requiring a pharmacist" are the following two types, and the necessary qualifications for each are stipulated (Article 88 of the *Pharmaceutical Affairs Law, Enforcement Regulations*).

* drug products manufactured at manufacturing sites performing only powdering or chopping of crude drugs
* medical gases

Medical Devices

A medical device manufacturer must have a manufacturing supervisor (responsible engineering manager) at each manufacturing site who has met the necessary qualifications shown in **Table 39-7** (Article 17, Paragraph 5 of the *Pharmaceutical Affairs Law*, Paragraphs 3 and 4 of the *Pharmaceutical Affairs Law, Enforcement Regulations*).

Biological Products

A manufacturing supervisor must be present at each manufacturing site handling Biological Products. Please refer to *Iyakuhatsu* No. 0515017 of May 15, Heisei 15 (2003), which describes necessary qualifications.

Quasi-drugs and Cosmetics

Please refer to Article 91 of the *Pharmaceutical Affairs Law, Enforcement Regulations* and Paragraph 2 of the same article for necessary qualifications for the responsible engineering manager required at each quasi-drug and cosmetic manufacturing site.

License Applications

License applications are filed by submitting an application based upon Form No. 12 of the *Pharmaceutical Affairs Law, Enforcement Regulations* to the head of the Regional Bureau of Health and Welfare or the prefectural governor. The authority to grant manufacturing licenses for drug products (excluding Biological Products), quasi-drugs, cosmetics and medical devices resides with the governor of the prefecture where the manufacturing site is located. The head of the Regional Bureau of Health and Welfare has the authority to grant manufacturing licenses for Biological Products (also known as drug products approved by the head of the Regional Bureau of Health and Welfare). For sites that manufacture both drug products approved by the head of the Regional Bureau of Health and Welfare and other drug products, the manufacturing sites must be separated. When applying for a license from the prefectural governor, it is necessary to check the fees and payment method, which are determined based upon each prefect's regulations.

The following materials must be attached to the application (Article 25 of the *Pharmaceutical Affairs Law, Enforcement Regulations*).

* a certificate of Corporate Registry, if the applicant is a corporation,
* a medical certificate issued by a doctor stating that the applicant does not suffer from impaired mental functions (if the applicant is a corporation, the certificate would specify the board member conducting the operations; the same applies below) and that the applicant is not addicted to narcotics, marijuana, opium or stimulants
* a copy of the employment contracts and other documents proving the relationship between the applicant and the manufacturing site manager or responsible engineering manager if the applicant is not the manufacturing site manager or the responsible engineering manager
* documents proving that the manufacturing site manager is a pharmacist or a person described in Article 88 of the *Pharmaceutical Affairs Law, Enforcement Regulations*, or that the responsible engineering manager is a person described in Article 91 of the same regulations
* documents regarding structures and facilities of the manufacturing site
* lists of products to be manufactured and documents regarding the manufacturing processes
* when handling radiopharmaceuticals (except such products below an amount or concentration specified by the Minister of Health, Labour and Welfare), documents describing the types of radiopharmaceuticals and an overview of facilities necessary for handling them
* if the applicant has already acquired a manufac-

Table 39-7. Necessary Qualifications for Responsible Engineering Manager for Medical Devices

Types of Medical Devices to be Manufactured	Highly Controlled Medical Devices (Class III/IV) Controlled Medical Devices (Class II)	General Medical Devices (Class I)
Legal basis	Article 91, Paragraph 3 of the Pharmaceutical Affairs Law, Enforcement Regulations	Article 91, Paragraph 4 of the Pharmaceutical Affairs Law, Enforcement Regulations
Qualifications	A person who has completed academic studies in any of the fields of physics, chemistry, metallurgy, electricity, mechanics, pharmacology, medicine or dentistry at a university, etc.	A person who has completed academic studies in any of the fields of physics, chemistry, metallurgy, electricity, mechanics, pharmacology, medicine or dentistry at an old-education-system junior high school or high school or any equivalent or higher-ranked school
Qualifications	A person who has completed courses on physics, chemistry, metallurgy, electricity, mechanics, pharmacology, medicine or dentistry at an old-education-system junior high school or high school or any equivalent or higher-ranked school + Three years of experience in manufacturing of devices	A person who has completed courses on physics, chemistry, metallurgy, electricity, mechanics, pharmacology, medicine or dentistry at an old-education-system junior high school or high school or any equivalent or higher-ranked school + Three years of experience in manufacturing of devices
Qualifications	Five years of experience in manufacturing of medical devices + Seminar	A person recognized by the Minister of MHLW as equivalent to the above (Showa 36 (1961) Notification) At least five years of experience in manufacturing of medical devices (expected)
Qualifications	A person recognized by the Minister of MHLW as equivalent to the above	N/A

turing license under a different category, a copy of the license(s)

Foreign Manufacturer Accreditation
Overview of Accreditations and Accreditation Categories
An individual who intends to manufacture drug products, quasi-drugs, cosmetics or medical devices overseas and import them into Japan is referred to as a foreign manufacturer and must acquire a Foreign Manufacturer Accreditation (FMA) from the Minister of Health, Labour and Welfare to provide such products to the market. When an MAH intends to import foreign-manufactured medical devices, the foreign manufacturers of such products must have an FMA before acquiring approval or certification or filing notifications for the products. Although the authority

to grant FMAs resides with the Minister of Health, Labour and Welfare, the Pharmaceuticals and Medical Devices Agency (PMDA) inspects structures and facilities of overseas manufacturing sites for accreditation, and accreditation is granted to individual manufacturing sites based upon the accreditation categories. The accreditation categories for overseas manufacturing sites are the same as the categories for the manufacturing licenses discussed above (refer to Article 36 of the *Pharmaceutical Affairs Law, Enforcement Regulations*). Also, the accreditation is effective for five years, and a renewal application is necessary to maintain the accreditation.

Applications for FMA
Two copies of applications for the accreditation based upon Form No. 18 of the *Pharmaceutical Affairs Law* (to the

attention of the Minister of Health, Labour and Welfare) and a copy of applications for audit for accreditation based upon Form No. 16(2) of the *Pharmaceutical Affairs Law, Enforcement Regulations* must be submitted to PMDA (to the Chief Executive of PMDA). The following documents must be attached to these applications (Article 35 of the *Pharmaceutical Affairs Law, Enforcement Regulations*). The MAH of the products manufactured by such foreign manufacturers may handle procedures for accreditation on behalf of the foreign manufacturer. The applicant will remain the foreign manufacturer.

Attachments for Applications for Foreign Manufacturer Accreditation)

- a medical certificate issued by a doctor stating that the applicant does not suffer from impaired mental functions (if the applicant is a corporation, the certificate would specify the board member conducting the operations; the same applies below) and that the applicant is not addicted to narcotics, marijuana, opium or stimulants
- resume of the manufacturing site manager
- lists of manufactured products (products scheduled for export to Japan are acceptable) and documents regarding manufacturing processes
- documents regarding manufacturing site structures and facilities
- when handling radiopharmaceuticals (except such products below an amount or concentration specified by the Minister of Health, Labour and Welfare), documents describing the types of radiopharmaceuticals and an overview of facilities necessary for handling them
- when the country of the foreign manufacturer has systems for MAH licenses, manufacturing licenses, product approval, accreditation or equivalent systems, copies of licenses related to such systems issued by that country's government agencies

Notes:

- For corporations, medical certificates from a doctor are required for board members having the right of representation and board members handling operations, and documents clearly identifying the division of tasks of all board members with or without the right of representation must be submitted with the application. If a medical certificate from a doctor is difficult to acquire due to some unavoidable and reasonable cause in the country where an overseas manufacturing site is located, documents of self declaration may be submitted instead. However, it should be noted that cases in which it is "difficult to acquire due to some unavoidable and reasonable cause" are limited to cases with reasonable grounds,

such as cases in which acquisition of a medical certificate from a doctor in the country where the manufacturing site is located conflicts with laws and ordinances, etc.
- Although MAHs of drug products, etc. manufactured by such foreign manufacturers may handle the accreditation procedures on behalf of the foreign manufacturer, they are only permitted to do so when the foreign manufacturer has legitimate reasons for not being able to file the application and they are officially asked to do so by the foreign manufacturer. This is, however, limited to persons capable of taking responsibility for communication, etc. with the foreign manufacturer as required for the application and subsequent management for maintaining accreditation.

Applications for FMAs are submitted to PMDA. For details regarding fees, please refer to the applicable descriptions in the following PMDA website: http://www.pmda.go.jp/operations/shonin/info/fee/file/36_tesuryokiki.pdf

Sales Licenses
Overview of Licenses (Matters Regarding License Implementation) and License Categories
Drug Products
To sell or provide drug products, or to store or exhibit drug products for the purposes of sales or provision as businesses (henceforth referred to as "sales, etc."), it is necessary to acquire a license to open a pharmacy or a sales license for drug products. Sales licenses for drug products include the following three types (Article 25 of the law).
- Retail Licenses
- Retail License for Home Distribution
- Wholesale Licenses

Only individuals who have acquired a Retail License or a Retail License for Home Distribution may sell drug products to the general public. However, although pharmacies are not included within "Retail," they may still sell drug products (**Table 39-8**).

OTC drugs are classified into Type I, Type II and Type III categories based upon risks, and different regulations are in place for marketing methods, etc. based upon these categories.

Pharmacies
A pharmacy is defined as "a location where a pharmacist dispensing drugs for the purpose of sales or provision (including locations required for sales when the person establishing the pharmacy also sells drug products)" (Article 2, Paragraph 11 of the law). In pharmacies, in addition to dispensing drug product, selling drug product is also permitted. Pharmacies may handle all drug products, including

Table 39-8. Types of Sales Licenses

Types of Licenses	Specialist	Scope of Allowable Products
Pharmacies	Pharmacist	All drug products, including ethical and OTC drugs
Retailing	Pharmacist or Registered retailer	For pharmacists, all OTC drugs
Retailing by Home Distribution		For registered retailers, drug products excluding Type I drug products
Wholesale		

ethical drugs and OTC drugs. In addition, a registered retailer that is not a pharmacist may provide information to or conduct consultations with customers, etc. for selling OTC drugs categorized as Type II or Type III,

Retailing

A Retail License is necessary for selling or providing OTC drugs at stores, and each store must acquire this license.

Unlike pharmacies, drugs may not be dispensed even if a pharmacist is working at the store, and sales of drug products other than OTC drugs is not permitted (Article 27 of the law). It states that an operator who has acquired a Retail License (henceforth referred to as a "retailer") must have a pharmacist to sell or provide Type I OTC drugs and must have a pharmacist or registered retailer to sell or provide Type II and Type III drug products (Article 36-5 of the law). Therefore, Type I drug products may not be sold or provided when a pharmacist is not present at the store.

In addition, selling drug products by mail, etc. is allowed, but it should be noted that such cases are limited to Type III drug products, and an appropriate notification must be submitted to the prefectural governor before initially conducting sales by mail, etc. (Article 139-4 of the *Pharmaceutical Affairs Law, Enforcement Regulations*).

Retailing by Home Distribution

A license for retaining by home distribution is granted for sale or provision through home distribution for each prefecture having an area where such sales activity is conducted (Article 25, Section 2 of the law). In addition, retailing by home distribution is a system by which drug products are left at a potential purchaser's house in advance and the right to demand payment comes into effect only after the purchaser uses the product (referred to as "Use First Pay Later"). Qualified drug products are limited to OTC drugs compliant with standards such as not being susceptible to degradation over time (Article 31 of the law). Moreover, Type I OTC drugs may not be sold or provided when a pharmacist is not engaged in this form of the business.

Wholesale

Wholesale is defined as selling or providing drug products to: individuals who have established pharmacies;

MAHs; manufacturers or distributors; individuals who have established hospitals, clinics or treatment facilities for domestic animals; or other individuals specified by the Ministry of Health, Labour and Welfare. The general public is not eligible for such sales or provision (Article 25 of the law). Wholesale distributors may handle all drug products.

Medical Devices
Licenses for Selling (Leasing) of Highly Controlled Medical Devices

When selling, providing or leasing medical devices specified as Highly Controlled Medical Devices, which have high risks for the human body when problems occur, or Specially Designated Medical Devices Requiring Maintenance Control, which require technical knowledge or skills for maintenance and inspection, a Selling (leasing) License for Highly Controlled Medical Devices is required in addition to an MAH license for medical devices.

Notification of Marketing (Leasing) of Controlled Medical Devices

When selling Controlled Medical Devices with relatively low risks for the human body when problems occur, a "notification of selling (leasing) of Controlled Medical Devices" is required.

Selling (Leasing) of General Medical Devices

Licenses and notifications are not required.

Licensing Requirements
Drug Products
Physical Requirements

- Pharmacies (Article 1 of the *Regulations for Structures and Facilities for Pharmacies, etc.*)
  A pharmacy is a location where a pharmacist conducts operations for dispensing drugs for the purposes of sales or provision. In addition to dispensing drugs, selling drugs is also permitted at the location. Because the drug products that may be handled at a pharmacy include not only OTC drugs but also ethical drugs, a wide range of detailed requirements are specified for structures and facilities.
  Major requirements include:
    - securing sufficient ventilation

- clear separation of the pharmacy from store and residential locations
- securing minimum floor areas and lighting
- closure of the pharmacy possible when necessary
- having facilities to store handled products in a sanitary and safe manner
- meeting the exhibit requirements when selling or providing Type I drug products
- meeting the dispensary requirements and being equipped with a list of required instruments and measuring/scaling instruments for dispensing drugs

When handling radiopharmaceutical products above the predetermined quantities or concentrations, there are additional requirements such as location restrictions, main structures' specifications stipulated in the *Building Standards Law*, and the establishment of facilities or instruments for preventing contamination.

- Retailing (Article 2 of the *Regulations for Structures and Facilities for Pharmacies*)

    Although there are requirements for structures and facilities similar to those for pharmacies, there are no requirements related to the handling of radiopharmaceuticals because selling drug products other than OTC drugs is not permitted with a Retail License.

- Retailing by Home Distribution

    There are no requirements for structures and facilities because Retailing by Home Distribution is based on peddling.

- Wholesale (Article 3 of the *Regulations for Structures and Facilities for Pharmacies*)

    For wholesaler offices handling radiopharmaceuticals above the predetermined quantity or concentration, the aforementioned additional requirements for pharmacies for handling radiopharmaceuticals will be applied and the rest of the requirements are the same as those of Retailing.

*The above is an overview of the requirements for each business type. For details, please refer to the *Regulations for Structures and Facilities for Pharmacies*.

Personnel Requirements

- Pharmacies: Placement of a responsible pharmacist

    When the individual who establishes the pharmacy is a pharmacist, he or she must either manage the operation of the pharmacy, or designate a pharmacist as the responsible pharmacist, from among the pharmacists engaging in the operation, to manage the operation of the pharmacy. When the person who establishes the pharmacy is not a pharmacist, a pharmacist must be designated as the responsible pharmacist, from among the pharmacists engaging in the operation, to manage the operation of the pharmacy.

- Retailing, Retailing by Home Distribution and wholesale: Employment of pharmacist or registered distributor

    It is necessary to employ a pharmacist when handling all OTC drugs or a registered distributor when handling only Type II and Type III drug products.

    A registered distributor is a person who has passed a test for registered distributors administered by the prefectural government.

Medical Devices

To acquire a selling/leasing license for medical devices, the following physical requirements and personnel requirements must be met (Article 4 of the *Regulations for Structures and Facilities for Pharmacies*).

Physical Requirements

- Structures and facilities of sales offices must meet the following standards:
- natural lighting, illumination and ventilation are appropriate and sanitary conditions
- clearly separated from residential locations and unsanitary locations
- have facilities necessary to store products in a sanitary and safe manner

Personnel Requirements

Although a manager (a sales manager for Highly Controlled Medical Devices, etc.) must be present at the sales office, it should be noted that requirements for sales entities of Highly Controlled Medical Devices to sell the Designated Lenses for Visual Correction, etc. only are different from the requirements for sales entities of Highly Controlled Medical Devices to sell products other than the Designated Lenses for Visual Correction, etc. (Article 162 of the *Pharmaceutical Affairs Law, Enforcement Regulations*).

Entities selling Highly Controlled Medical Devices, etc. other than the Designated Lenses for Visual Correction must meet one of the following sets of requirements:

1. A person who completed the training course administered by the party who has been accredited by the Minister of Health, Labour and Welfare according to the MHLW ordinances after engaging in sales related operations for Highly Controlled Medical Devices, excluding sales related operation for the Designated Lenses for Visual Correction, etc., for at least three years

2. A person recognized by the Minister of Health, Labour and Welfare as having an equivalent or

Table 39-9. Requirements for Distributors of Only the Designated Lenses for Vision Correction From Among Highly Controlled Medical Devices

Types of Medical Devices to be Marketed/Leased	Highly Controlled Medical Devices (Class III/IV) Controlled Medical Devices (Class II)	General Medical Devices (Class I)
Legal basis	Article 162 of the *Pharmaceutical Affairs Law, Enforcement Regulations*	Article 175 of the *Pharmaceutical Affairs Law, Enforcement Regulations*
Qualifications	More than three years of experience in sales or leasing of medical devices + Basic training course + Continuing training courses	More than three years of experience in sales or leasing of medical devices + Basic training courses
	A person with equivalent or higher qualifications compared to the above (*Yakushokukihatsu* Notification No. 0628001 of June 28, Heisei 18 (2006)). a. Doctors, dentists, pharmacists b. A qualified person for General Controller for Type I MAH for Medical Devices c. A qualified person for Responsible Engineering Manager for manufacturing of medical devices. d. A qualified Responsible Engineering Manager for repair business of medical devices e. Medicinal Product Retailer. f. A person who has completed "Training Couse for Responsible Sales Administrator"	

higher level of knowledge and experience compared to the person described in (a), including the following (*Yakushokuhatsu* No. 0628001 of June 28, Heisei 18 (2007)):

- A person licensed as doctor, dentist or pharmacist
- A person qualified for general controller for Type I MAH for Medical Devices
- A person qualified for responsible engineering manager for manufacturing medical devices
- A person qualified for responsible engineering manager for a repair business of medical devices
- The applicant of the license application for Medicinal Products Retailing (Refer to Chapter 1) at the facility licensed for Medicinal Products Retailing (limited to an individual applicant) or a qualified person at the retailing facility (a person meeting the standards stipulated in Article 51 of the *Pharmaceutical Affairs Law, Enforcement Regulations*, or person who has passed the test specified in Article 28, Paragraph 2 of the *Pharmaceutical Affairs Law* and whose test results enabled the corporation to acquire a license for Medicinal Product Retailing)

- A person who has completed "Training Course for Responsible Sales Administrators," a course administered under the Accreditation System for Appropriate Medical Devices Sales Offices jointly offered by the Japan Association for the Advancement of Medical Equipment (JAAME) and the Japan Medical Instrument Industrial Association

Sales entities of Highly Controlled Medical Devices, etc. who sells only the Designated Lenses for Visual Correction must meet one of the following sets of requirements (**Table 39-9**):

1. A person who completed the training course administered by the party who has been accredited by the Minister of Health, Labour and Welfare according to the MHLW ordinances after engaging sales related operation for Highly Controlled Medical Devices for more than one year (a person who satisfies Article 162, Paragraph 2, Section 1 of the *Pharmaceutical Affairs Law, Enforcement Regulations*)
2. A person recognized by the Minister of Health, Labour and Welfare as having an equivalent or

Table 39-10. License Categories for Repair Business for Medical Devices

Repair Business for Designated Maintenance Control Medical Devices		Repair Business for Medical Devices Other Than Designated Maintenance Control Medical Devices	
Designated Maintenance Category I:	Related to medical imaging systems	Nondesignated Maintenance Category I:	Related to medical imaging systems
Designated Maintenance Category II:	Related to systems for measuring/ monitoring biological phenomena	Nondesignated Maintenance Category II:	Related to systems for measuring/ monitoring biological phenomena
Designated Maintenance Category III:	Related to devices for therapy/facilities	Nondesignated Maintenance Category III:	Related to devices for therapy/facilities
Designated Maintenance Category IV:	Related to artificial internal organs	Nondesignated Maintenance Category IV:	Related to artificial internal organs
Designated Maintenance Category V:	Related to optical devices	Nondesignated Maintenance Category V:	Related to optical devices
Designated Maintenance Category VI:	Related to physical therapy devices	Nondesisgnated Maintenance Category VI:	Related to physical therapy devices
Designated Maintenance Category VII:	Related to dental devices	Nondesignated Maintenance Category VII:	Related to dental devices
Designated Maintenance Category VIII:	Related to laboratory testing devices	Nondesignated Maintenance Category VIII:	Related to laboratory testing devices
Designated Maintenance Category IX:	Related to steel devices and domestic medical devices	Nondesignated Maintenance Category IX:	Related to steel devices and domestic medical devices

Note: Because repairing medical devices in Nondesignated Maintenance Category I with a license for Designated Maintenance Category I is not allowed, it is necessary to acquire licenses for both categories.

higher level of knowledge and experience compared to the person described in (a)

License Applications and Fees
Drug Products
- Pharmacies: Must receive clearance from the local prefectural governor.
- Retailing: The prefectural governor of the location of the store (city mayor if the store is located in a city with a healthcare center, or ward mayor in a special ward) shall grant a license to each store (Article 26, Paragraph 1 of the law).
- Retailing by Home Distribution: An application must be filed with the prefectural governor because the license is granted for each prefecture containing an area for the retailing activitiy, (Article 30, Paragraph 1 of the law). In addition, due to the fact that Retailing by Home Distribution is based upon peddling, a retail entity for Retailing by Home Distribution or persons engaged in such activity must submit their names, the areas in which the retailing activities are to be conducted, and other matters stipulated in the MHLW ordinances to the prefectural governor of the area in which the

retailing activity is to be conducted, and must carry an ID issued by the local prefectural governor.
- Wholesale: Such licenses can be acquired by submitting an application to the prefectural governor (Section 153 of the *Pharmaceutical Affairs Law, Enforcement Regulations*).

Medical Devices
- Licenses for selling Highly Controlled Medical Devices must be acquired for each office. Applications must be submitted to the governor of the prefecture where the sales office is located.
- In order to sell Controlled Medical Devices, in principle, a notification for selling Controlled Medical Devices must be submitted to local prefectural government; such notifications are free of charge.

When applying for clearance from the prefectural governor, it is recommended to check the fees, which vary between prefectures.

Table 39-11. Necessary Qualifications for Responsible Engineering Manager for Medical Device Repair Business

Types of Medical Devices to be Repaired	Designated Maintenance Control Medical Devices	Medical Devices Other Than Designated Maintenance Control Medical Devices
Legal basis	Article 188 of the Pharmaceutical Affairs Law, Enforcement Regulations	
Qualification	More than three years of experience in repair work of medical devices + Basic training and specialized training	More than three years of experience in repair work of medica devices + Basic training
Requirements	A person recognized by the Minister of MHLW as having qualifications equivalent to or higher than those described above	People recognized by the Minister of MHLW as having qualifications equivalent to or higher than those described above

Leasing Licenses

Leasing licenses apply to medical devices only, and the categories of licenses and the requirements are the same as those for a sales license.

Licenses for Repair Business

Overview of Licenses

Repair business refers to restoring broken, damaged or otherwise deteriorated parts of medical devices to their original condition and/or function (including replacing such parts). Regardless of whether there are any broken parts, such business includes overhauls for dismantling and inspection as well as the replacement of deteriorated parts when necessary, but does not include maintenance and inspection activities such as cleaning, calibration or replacement of consumable parts.

A license for repair business is not required when the activities engaged in only include referrals to a repair shop. Even when actual repair work is not conducted and all repair work is outsourced to a separate repair shop, etc., if an agreement for repairing such medical devices is signed with a medical institution, etc., the person signing the repair contract is responsible for the safety of the repaired medical devices and a license for repair business is required. In addition, modifications such as changing the specifications of medical devices are beyond the scope of repairs, and it is necessary to acquire a separate license for manufacturing medical devices (*Yakushokukihatsu* 0904-1 of September 4, Heisei 21 (2009)).

The business type of repair work is not applicable to drug products.

License Categories

When repairing medical devices, it is necessary to apply for a license for a repair business for medical devices. Licenses are divided into nine categories from I to IX as shown in **Table 39-10**, and these nine categories are further divided between medical devices other than Designated Medical Devices Requiring Maintenance Control and Designated Medical Devices Requiring Maintenance Control (*Yakushokukihatsu* No. 0331004 of March 31, Heisei 17 (2005)).

Licensing Requirements

The following physical and personnel requirements must be met to acquire a license.

Physical Requirements

Structures and facilities of business sites must comply with Article 5 of the *Regulations for Structures and Facilities for Pharmacies, etc.* (Article 40-2, Paragraph 4, Section 1 of the *Pharmaceutical Affairs Law*).

Personnel Requirements

- Applicant: The applicant (if the applicant is a corporation, the board member conducting manufacturing-related operations) must not meet any of the disqualification clauses (Article 5, Paragraph 3 of the *Pharmaceutical Affairs Law*).
- Responsible engineering manager: A responsible engineering manager meeting the necessary qualifications shown in **Table 39-11** must be placed (Article 40-3 and Article 17, Paragraph 5 of the *Pharmaceutical Affairs Law*).

License Applications

- It is necessary to acquire a license for a repair business for each relevant category for each business site conducting repair business.
- The authority to grant the licenses resides with the governor of the prefecture where the business site is located.
- It is necessary to check the fees because they vary between prefectures.

Summary

- The licenses stipulated in the *Pharmaceutical Affairs Law* must be acquired in order to import and manufacture (including labeling and storage), sell, provide and lease drug products, etc. (including exhibiting for such purposes), and conduct repair work.
- Licenses include Marketing Authorization Holder Licenses, Manufacturing Licenses, Sales Licenses, Leasing Licenses and Licenses for Repair Business, but Leasing Licenses and Licenses for Repair Business only apply to medical devices.
- Physical and personnel requirements are set for each license.
- A person who intends to manufacture drug products, etc. overseas for importing into Japan is referred to as a foreign manufacturer, and an approval for such drug products, etc. in Japan will not be granted without acquiring appropriate FMA at the foreign manufacturing sites.
- OTC drugs are categorized into Type I, Type II and Type III drug products, and the requirements for handling these drug products vary.

Related Notifications
Marketing Authorization Holder/Overall

Yakushokuhatsu No. 0922001 of September 22, Heisei 16 (2004), *Enforcement of the Ministerial Ordinance partially revising the Ministerial Ordinance and the Pharmaceutical Affairs Law, Enforcement Regulations on Good Quality Practice for drug products, quasi-drugs, cosmetics, and medical devices (Ministerial Ordinance on GQP)*

Yakushokuhatsu No. 0922005 of September 22, Heisei 16 (2004), *Enforcement of the Ministerial Ordinance partially revising the Ministerial Ordinance and the Pharmaceutical Affairs Law, Enforcement Regulations on Good Vigilance Practice for drug products, quasi-drugs, cosmetics, and medical devices (Ministerial Ordinance on GVP)*

Jimurenraku of December 24, Heisei 16 (2004), "Q&A on the enforcement of the Ministerial Ordinance partially revising the Ministerial Ordinance and the Pharmaceutical Affairs Law, Enforcement Regulations on Good Vigilance Practice for drug products, quasi-drugs, cosmetics, and medical devices" (GVP Q&A)

Jimurenraku of March 17, Heisei 17 (2005) "GQP cases (March 2005)" (GQP Q&A)

Jimurenraku of April 9, Heisei 19 (2007), "Cases related to licenses for Marketing Authorization Holder of drug products, etc."

Manufacturing Licenses/ Foreign Manufacturer Accreditation

Yakushokukanmahatsu No. 0330001 of March 30, Heisei 17 (2005), *Enactment and improvement/elimination of Ministerial Ordinances and announcements related to manufacturing control and quality control (GMP/QMS) for drug products and medical devices following enforcement of laws partially revising the Pharmaceutical Affairs Law and the Bleeding Donor Supply Service Control Law (Administrative Notice on GMP/QMS)*

Yakushokukihatsu No. 0707001 of July 7, Heisei 17 (2005), *Materials to be attached to applications for certification of foreign manufacturer for medical devices and in vitro diagnosticJimurenraku* of July 7, Heisei 17 (2005), "Q&A on materials to be attached to applications for Foreign Manufacturer Accreditation for medical devices and in vitro diagnostics"

Jimurenraku of February 14, Heisei 18 (2006), "Q&A on Foreign Manufacturer Accreditation"

Jimurenraku of July 27, Heisei 18 (2006), "Q&A on materials to be attached to applications for Foreign Manufacturer Accreditation for medical devices and in vitro diagnostics (Part 2)"

Jimurenraku of August 3, Heisei 18 (2006), "Additional delivery of Attachment 7 of 'Q&A on materials to be attached to applications for Foreign Manufacturer Accreditation for medical devices and in vitro diagnostics (Part 2)'"

Jimurenraku of October 13, Heisei 18 (2006), "GMP/QMS cases (2006 version)" (GMP/QMS Q&A)

Yakushokuhatsu No. 0330012 of March 30, Heisei 19 (2007), *Enforcement of the Ministerial Ordinance partially amending the Pharmaceutical Affairs Law, Enforcement Regulations*

Yakushokuhatsu No. 0619002 of June 19, Heisei 19 (2007), *Forms, etc. to be attached to applications for manufacturing licenses and Foreign Manufacturer Accreditation for drug products, etc.*

Yakushokushinsahatsu No. 0619004 of June 19, Heisei 19 (2007), *Handling of applications for Foreign Manufacturer Accreditation*

Sales/Leasing

Jimurenraku of March 31, Heisei 17 (2005), "Q&A on handling of sales and leasing of medical devices (Part 1)"

Yakushokukihatsu No. 0628001 of June 28, Heisei 18 (2006), *Operations, etc. for sales and leasing of medical devices related to Ministerial Ordinances, etc. partially revising the Pharmaceutical Affairs Law, Enforcement Regulations*

Jimurenraku of June 28, Heisei 18 (2006), "Q&A on handling of sales and leasing of medical devices (Part 2)"

Yakushokukihatsu 0904-No. 1 of September 4, Heisei 21 (2009), *Handling of sales and leasing of medical devices following the enforcement of laws, etc. partially revised the Pharmaceutical Affairs Law*

Repair Business

Yakushokukihatsu No. 0331004 of March 31, Heisei 17 (2005), *Operations for repair business for medical devices following the enforcement of laws, etc. partially revising the Pharmaceutical Affairs Law and the Bleeding Donor Supply Service Control Law*

Jimurenraku of April 1, Heisei 17 (2005), "Q&A on handling of repair business for medical devices"

Chapter 40

Regulatory Supervision and Inspections by the Japanese Government

OBJECTIVES

❏ To understand regulatory supervision, various inspections and their methods according to the *Pharmaceutical Affairs Law.*

❏ To understand the details of measures based upon the results of regulatory supervision and inspections.

❏ To understand postmarket corrective measures for products, such as recalls.

❏ To understand punishments for various violations.

RELATED LAWS AND REGULATIONS

❏ *Pharmaceutical Affairs Law* (Law No. 145 of Showa 35 (1960))

❏ *Pharmaceutical Affairs Law, Enforcement Regulations* (Ministry of Health and Welfare Ordinance No. 1 of Showa 35 (1961))

❏ *Ministerial Ordinance on Post-Marketing Safety Management System for Drug Products, Quasi-Drugs, Cosmetics, and Medical Devices* (Ministry of Health, Labour and Welfare Ordinance No. 135 of Heisei 16 (2004)) (*Ministerial Ordinance on GVP*)

❏ *Ministerial Ordinance on Good Quality Practice for Drug Products, Quasi-Drugs, Cosmetics, and Medical Devices* (Ministry of Health, Labour and

Welfare Ordinance No. 136 of Heisei 16 (2004)) (*Ministerial Ordinance on GQP*)

❏ *Ministerial Ordinance on Good Manufacturing Practice for Drug Products and Quasi-Drugs* (Ministry of Health, Labour and Welfare Ordinance No. 176 of Heisei 16 (2004)) (*Ministerial Ordinance on GMP*)

❏ *Ministerial Ordinance on Good Vigilance Practice and Good Quality Practice for Medical Devices and In Vitro Diagnostics* (Ministry of Health, Labour and Welfare Ordinance No. 169 of Heisei 16 (2004)) (*Ministerial Ordinance on QMS*)

❏ *Regulations for Structures and Facilities for Pharmacies, etc.* (Ministry of Health and Welfare Ordinance No. 2 of Showa 35 (1961))

Introduction

Article 1 of the *Pharmaceutical Affairs Law* states, "the purpose of this law is to improve public health and hygiene while implementing necessary regulations for ensuring the quality, effectiveness, and safety of drug products, quasi-drugs, cosmetics, and medical devices and taking necessary measures to promote research and development for drug products and medical devices with especially high demand in medical practices," and that the objectives of pharmaceutical affairs administration can be broadly divided between "ensuring the safety and effectiveness of products" and "improving public health and hygiene with the introduction of new medical technologies." This chapter explains how the *Pharmaceutical Affairs Law* is enforced and supervised while focusing on various inspections conducted for the purpose of "ensuring the safety and effectiveness of products."

Violations of the
Pharmaceutical Affairs Law

In the *Pharmaceutical Affairs Law*, marketing, etc. of mislabeled or defective drug products and medical devices (henceforth referred to as "drug products, etc.") is prohibited. Mislabeled or defective products include:

- mislabeled
  - ° drug products, etc. without legally required labeling on the product itself, container and packaging
  - ° products without prominently displayed, easily understandable descriptions
- products without a package insert containing required information
- drug products, etc. manufactured in (foreign) manu-facturing sites without an appropriate manufacturing license (accreditation)
- drug products, etc. that do not have product approvals or medical devices that are Specified Controlled Medical Devices, but do not have product certifications.
- drug products, etc. with false or misleading descriptions
- drug products, etc. with labeling describing unap-proved efficacy and effects
- drug products, etc. with labeling describing methods of use that may be harmful to health and hygiene

Enforcement and Regulatory Supervision by MHLW

To achieve the objectives stipulated in Article 1 of the *Pharmaceutical Affairs Law*, a broad-range of authority is given to the Minister of Health, Labour and Welfare and to prefectural governors. Based on Article 69 of the law, when the Minister of Health, Labour and Welfare or a prefectural governor finds it necessary to confirm whether Marketing Authorization Holders (MAHs), manufacturers, distributors (leasing entities) or repair entities comply with the provisions of the *Pharmaceutical Affairs Law* or related ordinances, they may have such MAHs submit necessary reports or have relevant office staff visit the manufacturing facilities, offices and other locations where such MAHs operate and handle medical devices to review structures and facilities of the locations as well as books, records and other items, or to ask questions of employees and other related parties.

If drug products, etc. are manufactured, sold, leased or stored for the purposes of sales or provision in violation of rules regarding prohibitions for sales, etc., administrative actions or even criminal charges will be imposed based upon the degree of the violation. These provisions are not only for MAHs but are also for all manufacturers, distributors and leasing parties. The measures are broadly divided into two categories:

- disposal of drug products, etc. that caused problem(s)
  - ° emergency order for necessary measures, including suspension of manufacturing, sales and leasing (Article 69-3 of the law)
  - ° orders for disposal, recalls, etc. of problematic drug products, etc. (Article 70 of the law)
- actions for MAHs, manufacturers, distributors and leasing parties that marketed the drug products, etc. to businesses
  - ° administrative actions
- investigation order (Article 71 of the law)
- improvement order (Article 72 of the law)
- order for replacing general controller, etc. (Article 73 of the law)
- revocation of approval, etc. (Article 74-2 of the law)
- revocation of license and temporary suspension of operations (Article 75 of the law)
- revocation of Foreign Manufacturer Accreditations (FMAs), etc. (Article 75-4 of the law)
  - ° criminal penalties such as fines and imprisonment
- Note: If the violation is heinous, a criminal pros-ecution will result in addition to administrative actions.
- Note: A business without a license will face crim-inal prosecution(s) because administrative actions cannot be taken against such business.

Inspections by the Government

Requirements for licenses to place drug products, etc. on the market include compliance with requirements such as Good Vigilance Practice (GVP), Good Manufacturing Practice (GMP) for drug products, Quality Management System (QMS) for medical devices and in vitro diagnostics and *Regulations for Structures and Facilities* as discussed in Chapter 39. Inspections are broadly categorized as follows (*Yakushokukanmahatsu* No. 1130002 of November 30, Heisei 17 (2005)):

- audits conducted to verify status of compliance for obligations associated with licenses for MAH (Article 69, Paragraph 1 of the *Pharmaceutical Affairs Law*)
- investigation conducted to identify and eliminate defective products, etc. (Article 69, Paragraph 3 of the *Pharmaceutical Affairs Law*)

Inspectors and Inspection Methods
Inspectors

Inspections for MAHs are conducted by the prefectural government, while GMP and QMS inspections for manufacturers are conducted by the prefectural government or the PMDA.

Methods for Inspections

GMP and QMS inspections are conducted based upon *Yakushokukanmahatsu* No. 1130002 of November 30, Heisei 17 (2005), Managerial Notification of the Compliance and Narcotics Division of the Pharmaceutical and Food Safety Bureau of the Ministry of Health, Labour and Welfare, *Guidance for GMP/QMS inspections*. GVP and GQP investigations are also conducted pursuant to this notification.

Inspections include processes such as advance preparation, conducting investigations, postinspection measures and guidance, the creation of inspection reports, and the delivery of reports. Specific processes for inspections are:

- Formation of inspection team
  Inspections must be led by an inspection manager who has experience in inspections and has the ability to manage inspections, with a team of two or more people, including the manager, in order to mutually complement areas of specialty and experience among the inspectors, and to ensure the safety of the inspectors.

- Formulation of an inspection plan
  The inspection manager collects and analyzes sufficient information related to the inspection and creates inspection plans while communicating with other members of the inspection team and taking into account the available resources and time.

- Advance notification of an inspection
  In principle, when conducting an inspection, an inspection notification including the following information must be provided one week prior to the planned inspection date:
  - inspectors' names, job titles and affiliations
  - purpose of the inspection
  - matters to be inspected
  - scheduled date(s) of the inspection: (year/month/day/time) to (year/month/day/time)
  - name of business subject to the inspection, etc. (for corporations, the name thereof)
  - addresses of business subject to the inspection (for corporations, the location of the main office)
  - names of manufacturing sites subject to the inspection.
  - locations of manufacturing sites subject to the inspection

- Conducting inspections and results
  In principle, inspections are conducted through the following processes.
  - obtaining understanding about the inspection (opening at the inspection)
  - confirming basic matters related to the inspection (consensual validation of inspection methods, managers, and schedules)
  - conducting inspection

- issuing feedback and observations on items identified during the inspection (When inspections are conducted over multiple days, information for the scope of the inspection conducted on that day with the schedule for the next day is provided at the end of the day. On the last day, a report on feedback and observations on the items identified is issued.)
- collecting improvement plans and reports on the results of improvements and confirming the details of the improvements (A follow-up audit may be conducted.)
- drafting a report on the results of the inspection, providing a copy of the draft report, and entering a record in the ledger (including records entered in the ledger for administrative actions specified in *Regulatory Enforcement Manual 2*)

Inspections Related to MAH Licenses

GVP Conformity Assessment Inspections

GVP is one of the MAH license requirements (Article 12-2, Section 1 of the *Pharmaceutical Affairs Law*). GVP conformity assessment inspections are conducted based upon applications for MAH licenses or applications for an MAH license renewal according to Article 12 of the *Pharmaceutical Affairs Law*.

Conformity Assessments Methods

Conformity assessment items based upon each provision of GVP must be evaluated based upon a four-level scale from A to D. For details, please refer to *Yakushokuanhatsu* No. 0303001 of March 3 Heisei 17 (2005), Directorial Notification of the Safety Division of the Pharmaceutical and Food Safety Bureau of the Ministry of Health, Labour and Welfare (henceforth referred to as "*Notification on GVP conformity assessments*") and one of the items for conformity assessments from the attachment to this notification is shown in **Table 40-1**.

Standards for Conformity Assessments, Inspection Results and Measures

Assessments for Each Item

Items identified are evaluated as having an assessment of A (compliance), B (minor deficiency), C (moderate deficiency) or D (serious deficiency) based upon the GVP conformity assessment standards and a comprehensive assessment of the audit is conducted by using these individual assessment results. The following are the criteria used for Grade A, B and C (from the *Notification on GVP conformity assessments*).

- Grade A (compliance): implemented appropriately
- Grade B (minor deficiency): although it is deemed that there is not a problem for appropriately

Table 40-1. Duties of the General Controller (Related to Article 3)

1. Whether the MAH allows the general controller to perform the following duties:
    - supervise the safety controller
    - respect the opinions of the safety controller
    - coordinate closely with the safety manager and the quality controller manager as well as other responsible people involved in operations related to placing products on the market

    (Reference items for assessment)

    ° When implementing GVP, the system must accommodate the duties of the general controller and the safety controller without a conflict.

    ° When the general controller is also serving as a manager of another function, the concurrent assignment of the positions is appropriate and the duties of the general controller are conducted appropriately.

    ° Coordination between the general controller, the safety controller and the quality controller, based upon consideration on their respective locations, is appropriate.

    ° When an entity subject to the assessment has both Type I and Type II MAH licenses for drug products, the coordination between both MAH license holders is appropriate.

implementing GVP, improvements are required to ensure appropriate implementation of GVP

- Grade C (moderate deficiency): it is deemed that there is a possibility of problems for implementing GVP appropriately, but the situation corresponds to neither Grade D (nonconformity) nor Grade B (minor deficiency) and requires improvements

Comprehensive Conformity Assessment

The comprehensive conformity status is assessed as described below by using the assessment results of A (compliance), B (minor deficiency), C (moderate deficiency) and D (serious deficiency) assessed for each item.

- Conformity: all assessment results are A
- Overall Conformity: assessment results are A and B or B only
- Improvement Required: less than half of all assessment results are C, and none are D Nonconformity: cases not applicable to any of the above

Postconformity Assessment Measures

When the comprehensive conformity assessment result is Conformity, the system for GVP conforms to the standards specified in the MHLW ordinances.

When the comprehensive conformity assessment result is Overall Conformity:

- When applying for MAH licenses: For items for which the conformity assessments for individual provisions are not A, submit specific improvement plans according to the observation and submit a report on the improvement results after they are completed. If the improvements are verified, the Conformity status is given.

- When applying for renewal of MAH licenses: For items for which the conformity assessments for individual provisions are not A, submit either a report on the results of improvements or specific improvement plans according to the observation within the effective period of the license before renewal. If the results of improvements or the improvement plans are verified as being appropriate, Conformity status is given. If an improvement plan is submitted, a report on the results of the improvements must be submitted immediately after they are completed.

When the comprehensive conformity assessment result is Improvement Required:

- When applying for MAH licenses: For items for which the conformity assessments for individual provisions are not A, submit specific improvement plans according to the observation and submit a report on the results of improvements after they are completed. If the improvements are verified, the Conformity status is given.

- When applying for renewal of MAH licenses: For items for which the conformity assessments for individual provisions are not A, submit specific improvement plans according to the observation and submit a report on the results of improvements after they are completed. If the improvements are verified within the effective period of the license, the Conformity status is given.. If improvements are not completed within the effective period of the license, the assessment result will be Nonconformity.

Table 40-2. Duties of the General Controller (Related to Article 3)

No.	Provision of the Ministerial Ordinance	Question
1	Article 3, Section 1	• Whether the MAH of drug products requires the general controller to supervise the quality controller
2	Article 3, Section 2	• In addition to the provisions of Article 11, Paragraph 2, Section 2, whether the MAH of drug products requires the general controller to determine necessary measures based on reports from the quality controller and direct the Quality Assurance department or other departments or managers involving in quality management operations to enforce such measures.

When the comprehensive conformity assessment result is Nonconformity, the GVP systems do not conform to the standards specified in the MHLW ordinances.

GQP Conformity Assessment Inspections

GQP is one of the requirements for MAH licenses (Article 12-2, Section 1 of the *Pharmaceutical Affairs Law*). GQP conformity inspections are conducted based upon applications for MAH licenses or applications for the renewal of MAH license according to Article 12 of the *Pharmaceutical Affairs Law*.

Conformity Assessment Methods

Assessments are based upon a four-level scale of A, B, C and D, with an assessment of A indicating that questions for conformity assessments based upon individual GQP provisions have been responded to appropriately. **Table 40-2** is an example of standards for conformity assessments based upon the provisions of the *Ministerial Ordinance on GQP*. For more details, please refer to *Yakushokukanmahatsu* No. 0330001 of March 30, Heisei 17 (2005), Managerial Notification of the Compliance and Narcotics Division of the Pharmaceuticals and Food Sanitary Bureau of the Ministry of Health, Labour and Welfare (henceforth referred to as "*Notification on Enforcement of Ministerial Ordinances on GMP/QMS*").

Standards for Conformity, Investigation Results and Measures
Conformity Assessment Standards

Items are assessed as having an assessment rank of A (compliance), B (minor deficiency), C (moderate deficiency) and D (serious deficiency), based upon the conformity assessment standards of the *Ministerial Ordinance on GQP*, and comprehensive assessments are conducted using the results of these individual evaluations. The criteria used for assessment ranks are:

- Rank A (compliance): GQP is implemented appropriately (including cases immediately improved on site)
- Rank B (minor deficiency): it is deemed that there are almost no effects on the quality of medical

devices, but improvement for completely implementing the standards is required
- Rank C (moderate deficiency): it is deemed that undeniable effects on the quality of medical devices exist and improvements in implementing the standards is required
- Rank D (serious deficiency): there are obvious conflicts with the standards exist

Conformity Assessments

The comprehensive conformity status is assessed as described below using the assessment results of Rank A (compliance), Rank B (minor deficiency), Rank C (moderate deficiency) and Rank D (serious deficiency), evaluated based upon the conformity assessment standards of the *Ministerial Ordinance on GQP*.

- Conformity: all assessment results are A
- Overall Conformity: assessment results are A and B or B only
- Improvement Required: less than half of all assessment results are C, and none are D
- Nonconformity: cases not applicable to any of the above

Postconformity Assessment Measures

For MAHs with Conformity status, the methods for quality control conform to the standards specified in the MHLW ordinances.

For MAHs with Overall Conformity status, a conformity status is gained by submitting, within the effective period before the following license renewal (before obtaining a license when applying for a new license), either 1) detailed reports on improvement results or 2) specific improvement plans for the items for which the conformity assessment results for each provision are determined as B. If the MAH fails to submit the documents of 1) or 2) within the period before the following license renewal, a detailed report on improvement results must be submitted within 30 days after the improvements are completed.

For MAHs with Improvement Required status, items for which the conformity assessment results for each provision are determined as B, the provisions of

Overall Conformity will be applied. For items for which the conformity assessment results for each provision are determined as C, Conformity status is granted when either 1) detailed reports on improvement results or 2) specific improvement plans are submitted and improvements are completed within the period before the following license renewal (before obtaining a license when applying for a new license). When improvements are not completed, the assessment result will be Nonconformity.

For manufacturing sites and products with Nonconformity status, the quality control methods do not conform to the standards specified in the MHLW ordinances. However, in limited cases where the items with Rank D can be immediately improved, such cases may be considered as though Rank C was granted and the requirements for Improvement Required will be applied.

Inspections Related to Manufacturing Licenses

GMP/QMS inspections are broadly divided into conformity assessment inspections based upon conformity assessment applications and investigations based upon Article 69 of the *Pharmaceutical Affairs Law* (Article 69 investigations). Even for products not requiring product approval or certification, drug products, quasi-drugs, medical devices and in vitro diagnostics to which the *Ministerial Ordinance on GMP* is applied are subject to Article 69 investigations (from the *Notification on Enforcement of GMP/QMS*).

GMP/QMS Inspections
GMP/QMS Inspectors
Drug Products (Including In Vitro Diagnostics)
GMP/QMS inspections of all foreign manufacturing sites and domestic sites for the following products are conducted by PMDA, while inspections for other drug products are all conducted by the prefectural government.

- biological products (except in vitro diagnostics), Nation-certified drugs (drugs passed the test(s) specified by the Minister of Health, Labour and Welfare) and drug products manufactured using recombinant technoldrug products using drug products manufactured using recombinant technology as ingredients
- Designated Biological Products
- drug products manufactured using technologies for culturing human or animal cells
- drug products or cell-tissue drug products using drug products manufactured using technologies for culturing human or animal cells as ingredients (drug manufacturing sites for drug products manufactured using recombinant technology, drug products using drug products manufactured using recombinant technology as ingredients, drug products manufactured using technologies for culturing

human or animal cells and drug products using drug products manufactured using drug products manufactured using technologies for culturing human or animal cells as ingredients are limited to the manufacturing sites where the Minister of Health, Labour, and Welfare has the authority to grant manufacturing licenses)

Medical Devices
QMS inspections of medical device manufacturing sites are defined as described in **Table 40-3** based on class and on the handling of products under the *Pharmaceutical Affairs Law*.

Categories of Investigations
GMP/QMS Conformity Assessment Inspections
- Preapproval conformity assessment inspections: conformity assessment inspections for applications for approval and for partial changes of approved products
- Postapproval conformity assessment audits: periodic conformity assessment audits for manufacturing of approved products, conformity assessment audits for manufacturing of imported products

Governing laws and regulations are Article 14, Paragraph 6, Article 14, Paragraph 9, Article 19-2, Paragraph 5, and Article 80, Paragraph 1 of the law.

On-site Inspections, etc. based upon Article 69 of the Pharmaceutical Affairs Law
- Routine investigations: regularly confirm compliance with the provisions of the *Ministerial Ordinance on QMS*
- Special investigations: when there is a need to confirm the status of compliance due to unforeseen circumstances (for-cause inspections)

Governing laws and regulations are based upon Article 69 of the *Pharmaceutical Affairs Law*.

Frequency and Methods of Inspection
On-site inspections are conducted approximately once every two years for each manufacturing site, and a series of inspections is conducted within the license period (five years) to cover all subsystems of GMP and QMS.

Inspection Results
GMP and QMS Conformity Assessment Results and Measures for Each Provision
GMP and QMS inspections are conducted based upon related notifications. Assessments to determine a Rank A (compliance), B (minor deficiency), C (moderate deficiency) or D (serious deficiency) for each provision

Table 40-3. QMS Investigation Classifications

	Highly Controlled Medical Devices		Controlled Medical Devices		General Medical Devices
	Cell tissue Medical Devices/Class IV	Class III	Class II		Class I
	Approval	Approval	Approval	Certification	Notification
Domestic Facilities	PMDA	Prefectural governments	Prefectural governments	(Recognized Certification Body)	Prefectural governments
Overseas Facilities (outside Japan)	PMDA	PMDA	PMDA	(Recognized Certification Body)	PMDA

For Class II products with certificatin standards, QMS Audits are conducted by Recognized Certification Bodies, and the full transition of Class II products is being considered for 2011, based upon the Action Program.

are conducted, and the conformity status is assessed based upon the following assessment standards using these evaluation results, stipulated in *Yakushokukanmahatsu* No. 1130002 of November 30, Heisei 17 (2005), *Guidance for GMP/QMS investigations.*

Improvement measures for each rank are:

- Minor deficiency (B): Specific improvement plans or reports on improvement results are submitted and the improvements are confirmed during the following inspection.
- Moderate deficiency (C): Improvements are implemented within an appropriate period (for preapproval conformity inspections, within the remaining period of the standard administrative processing period) and reports on improvement results are submitted before the date specified by the authority for the inspection.
- Serious deficiency (D): Improvements are implemented within 15 days from the date of issuance of the QMS inspection report, and detailed reports on improvement results are submitted and the improvements are confirmed by the regulator. If confirmation for the improvements is not requested , the entity receives Serious Deficiency determination and are subject to administrative actions based upon related notifications (*Yakushokuhatsu* No. 0331006 of March 31, Heisei 17 (2005)).

QMS Conformity Assessment Results and Measures

With the following judgment standards, the conformity status is evaluated using the assessment results of Rank A (compliance), B (minor deficiency), C (moderate deficiency) and D (serious deficiency) for each provision.

- Conformity: assessment results include A only
- Overall Conformity: assessment results are A and B or B only
- Improvement Required: fewer than half of all assessment results are C and none are D
- Cases not applicable to any of the above

These are based upon *Notification on Enforcement of the Ministerial Ordinance on GMP/QMS,* Chapter 4, Section 5: Standards for conformity assessments.

Standards for conformity assessments:

- Manufacturing sites and products with Conformity determination.
  Methods for manufacturing control and quality control conform to the standards specified in the MHLW ordinances.
- Manufacturing sites and products with Overall Conformity determination.
  Conformity determination is gained by submitting, within the effective period before the following license renewal (before receiving a license when applying for a new license), either 1) detailed reports on improvement results or 2) specific improvement plans for the items with Rank B assessment.
- Manufacturing sites and products with Improvement Required determination.
  For items with Rank B assessment, the provisions of Overall Conformity will be applied. For items with Rank C assessment, Conformity determination is granted when either 1) detailed reports on improvement results, or 2) specific improvement plans are submitted and improvements are completed within the period before the following license renewal

(before receiving a license when applying for a new license). When improvements are not completed, the assessment result will be nonconformity.

- Manufacturing sites and products with Nonconformity determination
Methods for manufacturing control and quality control do not conform to the standards specified in the MHLW ordinances. However, in limited cases where the items with Rank D can be immediately improved, such cases may be considered that Rank C was granted and the requirements for Improvement Required will be applied.

Conformity Assessment of Manufacturing Site Structures and Facilities

Conformity assessment of structures and facilities of manufacturing sites is conducted in a similar manner to that described in previous section.

Conformity Standards for Structures and Facilities Related to GMP and QMS

For more details, please refer to the *Notification on Enforcement of the Ministerial Ordinance on GMP/QMS* and see **Table 40-4** for conformity assessment standards for each provision of regulations for structures and facilities of pharmacies, etc. from Attachment 2 of the notification.

Conformity Inspection Results and Measures
Standards for Conformity Assessments

Items are evaluated and an assessment rank of A (compliance), B (minor deficiency), C (moderate deficiency) or D (serious deficiency) based upon the conformity standards of regulations for structures and facilities is determined. Comprehensive assessments are conducted using these results.

The approaches taken for assessment ranks are described below.

- Rank A (compliance): implemented appropriately (including cases immediately improved on site)
- Rank B (minor deficiency): it is deemed that there are almost no effects on the quality of medical devices, but requiring improvement for completely implementing the standards
- Rank C (moderate deficiency): it is deemed that there are undeniable effects on the quality of medical devices and need for improvements in implementing the standards
- Rank D (serious deficiency): obvious conflict with the standards

Conformity assessments and postconformity assessment measures are implemented according to GQP, GMP and QMS.

Voluntary Corrective Actions

The investigations described above are conducted to confirm the status of compliance with obligations associated mainly with MAH licenses and to determine whether product approval or certification should be granted. They can be positioned as inspections for systems used within manufacturing facilities. However, unexpected side effects or malfunctions caused by products may occur after marketing the product, even if such manufacturer's systems have been developed and implemented. The following is a summary of corrective actions that MAHs must proactively implement in such cases.

Postmarket measures for products are broadly divided into four categories: recalls, modifications, inventory processing and product replacement. The measures for each are defined below.

- Recalls: This refers to cases in which an MAH, etc. reclaims or "modifies" drug product, etc. that has been manufactured or placed on the market, or for which it has received product approval. However, this excludes inventory processing and product replacement. This also excludes cases in which an MAH, etc. substitutes an old product without problems in quality, effectiveness and safety when marketing a new product.
- Modifications: This refers to cases in which an MAH, etc. repairs, improves, adjusts, disposes of or monitors (including monitoring of patients) a medical device, that has been manufactured, placed on the market, or for which the MAH has received product approval, without physically moving the device to a different location.
- Inventory processing: This refers to cases in which an MAH, etc. reclaims or repairs, improves, adjusts or disposes of drug product, etc. that has been manufactured, placed on the market or for which the MAH has received product approval for but has not yet released onto the market, or drug product, etc. still under the direct control of the MAH, etc. However, this excludes such actions in cases of leasing, as when a person other than the MAH, etc. is actually using the medical device while the MAH etc. still holds the ownership, or when the medical device is stored in a location separate from the MAH for the purpose of use.
- Replacement: This refers to cases in which a business entity reclaims and replaces the products, drug product, etc. (or, for medical devices, performs repairs, modifications, adjustment, disposal or monitoring) when it is apparent that no problems in health and hygiene will occur and that similar defects in drug products other than the relevant products, including lots and a fixed range of drug products, will not occur.

Table 40-4. Structure and Facility of Manufacturing Sites of OTC Drugs (Related to Article 6)

No.	Provision of the Ministerial Ordinance	Question
1	Article 6, Section 1	Are facilities or equipment necessary to manufacture the products (including intermediate Products; the same applies below) provided at the manufacturing site?
2	Article 6, Section 2	Are facilities arranged to prevent mix-ups and contamination of products and raw materials (henceforth referred to as "products, etc." in Articles 6–10) and materials to prevent problems in ensuring flawless and appropriate operations, and to perform cleaning and maintenance easily?
3	Article 6, Section 3	Are there hand-washing facilities, toilets and changing rooms?
4	Article 6, Section 4	Does the facility conform to the following specifications? A. Light and ventilation are appropriate and sanitary B. Is clearly separated from residential locations and unsanitary locations C. Has structures or facilities for protection from dust and insects. However, this requirement does not apply for operational facilities performing manufacturing processes before final purification of products related to drug substances provided to manufacture drug products, wherein the manufacturing facilities for such manufacturing processes are enclosed structures. D. Has facilities or equipment required for the disposal of wastewater and waste. E. When handling toxic gases for a product, etc. (excluding products related to drug products specified in Ministerial Ordinances as stipulated in Article 14, Paragraph 2, Section 4 of the Law), the facilities required for the processes must be present.

The following descriptions will focus mainly on recalls.

Recalls

Recall Reports (Article 77-4-3 of the *Pharmaceutical Affairs Law*) are part of a system for promptly obtaining information regarding defective drug products, etc. and preventing the occurrence or spread of harm for health and hygiene caused by such drug products, etc. If some defect or malfunction (henceforth referred to as "defect") occurs in a drug product, etc., it is important for the MAH to review the extent of health damage that may occur, from a scientific point of view, to identify the applicable products and to conduct necessary recalls.

Basic Perspectives on Recalls

The standards below are used to determine the necessity of a recall (*Iyakuhatsu* No. 237) from the following perspectives: effectiveness and safety, specification of scope of defects and types of foreign matters and product properties.

Determination From Effectiveness and Safety Perspectives

- Conduct a recall if there are any problems in the safety of a drug product, etc. due to some defect.
- Conduct a recall if expected effects are not achieved due to problems in efficacy, etc., even if there are no safety concerns.
- Recall any drug product, etc. if the MAH, etc. is unable to clearly explain that a defect of the drug product, etc. involves no efficacy and safety problems.
- Recall any drug product, etc. that violates the *Pharmaceutical Affairs Law* or approval conditions

Determination of Scope of Defects

- When a defect occurs in a drug product, etc., recall the product if the MAH, etc. is unable to clearly explain that the defects do not affect the entire lots or product lines.
- In particular, for cases other than those meeting all of the following conditions, recall products for which it cannot be explained that the defects does not affect the entire lots or product lines.
  - It is possible to specify the root causes and processes of the occurrence of defective products.

- There are no problems in GMP when measures to prevent the recurrences of defective products are appropriately taken.
- There are no abnormalities in the quality of retention samples.
- There are no problems on GQP that affect quality.

- Even if the defect is believed not to affect entire lots or product lines, at the first occurrence, if the defect has actually been identified at multiple facilities, a recall is, in principle, conducted by considering the relationship with the defect's occurrence rate.

- For defects of medical devices not consisting of lots, such as large-sized medical devices and implantable medical devices, if similar defects are found in other related products, such groups of products are considered as lots and handled according to the procedures for recalls.

- If it can be clearly explained that similar defects will not be found in other similar products, the products are handled based upon the procedures for product replacement.

Determination on Types of Foreign Matters and Product Properties

- For drug products, make a determination while taking into account the types of drug formulation (sterile or nonsterile products) and the types of foreign matters (endogenous foreign materials such as glass pieces, exogenous foreign materials such as wood pieces or biological products such as hair and insects).

- For sterile products, in principle, the determination of whether sterility can be guaranteed with certainty is an important judgment factor, and a recall is conducted if there is contamination of exogenous foreign materials and biological products.

- For nonsterile products, a recall is conducted if there is contamination of biological products.

- The conditions for nonsterile products described above are also applicable to disposable medical devices.

Processes (From Recall Initiation Report to Completion Report)
Recall Initiation Report

For recall initiation reports, the matters to be reported are stipulated in Article 64-5-3 of the *Pharmaceutical Affairs Law, Enforcement Regulations*. In principle, the reports should be prepared as documents. However, in urgent circumstances—to prevent the occurrence or spread of the harm to health and hygiene—it is acceptable to submit a document later after reporting

an overview of the situations by fax, etc.

In addition, the following points should be noted when filing a report (Article 254 of the *Pharmaceutical Affairs Law, Enforcement Regulations*).

- For the "name and address of the party conducting a recall," enter the name of the company and a representative of the corporation, the location, the name of the person in charge of the recall and the contact information of the office at which the general controller conducts recall operations.

- For "names of drug products, quasi-drugs, cosmetics, and medical devices subject to recall," enter the nomenclature and the brand name.

- For "method of recall," provide written confirmation of the lot number, quantity and date of the shipment of the drug products, etc. subject to the recall; the scope of medical institutions/patients, etc. subject to recall (hereinafter referred to as "medical institutions, etc."); methods used to spread information regarding the recall; the scheduled date for completing the recall; and the products being received at the recall destinations.

- For "details of measures to be taken to prevent the occurrence or spread of other damages to health and hygiene," include the reasons for the recall and the scope of anticipated health damages.

Prefectural Governments' Contact With MHLW on *Recall Initiation Reports*

When a recall initiation report is prepared by an MAH, etc., the prefectural government receiving the report must immediately contact the Compliance and Narcotics Division of MHLW's Pharmaceutical and Food Safety Bureau about this matter and send copies of the documents related to the recall initiation report. However, in urgent circumstances—to prevent the occurrence or spread of the harm to health and hygiene—in which immediate delivery of the documents is difficult, copies of such documents are sent later after verbally reporting the situation.

Government Instructions to MAH, etc. Based Upon Recall Initiation Reports

When a recall initiation report is prepared by an MAH, etc., the prefectural government receiving the report must provide instructions for the following matters to the MAH, etc. as necessary.

- **scheduled recall completion date**
- **scope of** recall
- **request for periodic reports on progress** of recall
- other required matters

In addition, for details of handling related to an instruction for a recall, please refer to the *Operating manual for health risk management for drug products, etc.,* which provides an overview of operations conducted through cooperation between MHLW and PMDA and within the Pharmaceutical and Food Safety Bureau.

Communications to the Prefectural Government by MAH on Completion of the Recall

In addition to the instructions at the initiation of the recall described above, the prefectural government requires the MAH, etc. to immediately submit a written report after the recall is completed. The MAH, etc. is also required to report the details of improvement measures already taken or to be taken in the future as well as the disposal methods for the drug products, etc. recalled.

Communication From the Prefectural Government to MHLW About Completion of the Recall

When a report on the completion of a recall is prepared and submitted by the MAH, etc., the prefectural government receiving the report must immediately contact the Compliance and Narcotics Division of MHLW's Pharmaceutical and Food Safety Bureau regarding this matter and send copies of the reports on the completion of the recall.

Others

If necessary, confirm the operational status of improvement measures implemented by MAHs, etc. and the disposal status of recalled drug products, etc.

In addition to the point described above, in on-site investigations conducted for MAHs or manufacturers based on Article 69 of the *Pharmaceutical Affairs Law,* the appropriate conduct of recalls is verified based upon the following required matters.

- *Ministerial Ordinance on Good Quality Practice for Drug Products, Quasi-Drugs, Cosmetics, and Medical Devices* (MHLW Ordinance No. 136 of Heisei 16 (2004))
- *Ministerial Ordinance on standards for manufacturing control and quality control for drug products and quasi-drugs* (MHLW Ordinance No. 179 of Heisei 16 (2004)) or *Ministerial Ordinance on standards for manufacturing control and quality control for medical devices and in vitro diagnostics* (MHLW Ordinance No. 169 of Heisei 16 (2004)).

Provision of Recall Information
Basic Perspectives on Provision of Recall Information

Basic perspectives on the provision of recall information for drug products, etc. are described below.

- Disclose all recall information according to established practice.
- In addition to immediately providing the information for each MAH, etc. to the medical institution,

etc., the government actively provides the MAHs, etc. with support in providing the recall information. Appropriate measures must be taken for each individual case of recall to facilitate the collection of information by medical institutions, etc., according to the degree of occurrence of health damages or the risk of occurrence of such damages.

Following is an outline of methods for providing recall information on drug products, etc.

Classification of Recalls

Depending upon the degree of health risks caused by the product, numerical designation of I, II or III must be assigned to each individual recall:

- Class I: The use, etc. of the product may cause serious health damage or death.
- Class II: The use, etc. of the product may cause temporary or medically curable health damage, or where there is no risk of serious health damage.
- Class III: The use, etc. of the product will not cause heath damage.

Basic Classification Perspectives

- When classifying a recall, it is necessary to take a comprehensive look at possible health damage from the defective drug product, etc., including not only issues directly related to safety arising from its use (e.g., factors that may extend surgery time, etc.) but also issues related to its effectiveness, such as failure to achieve the expected effects (e.g., factors that may affect the accuracy of diagnosis).
- When determining a recall classification, start by classifying it as Class II. If there is positive information to support the concept that the product will not cause health damage, change the determination to Class III. If there is a risk for the occurrence of more serious health damage than in Class II, change the determination to Class I.
- If a determination of Class I or Class III is deemed reasonable, or if the prefectural government determines that it is reasonable to change the original classification based upon subsequent information, the Pharmaceutical Affairs Division of the prefectural government must consult the Compliance and Narcotics Division of MHLW's Pharmaceutical and Food Safety Bureau to clarify the reasons before changing the classification.

Providing Information via the Internet

To quickly provide recall information to individual medical institutions, etc., MAHs, etc. also post recall information on the Internet (a part of the PMDA website posting the information on drug products and medical devices) to quickly and broadly disseminate the information.

Preparation and Submission of Internet Materials by MAHs, etc.

When recalling a drug product, etc., materials for the Internet (henceforth referred to as "materials") must be submitted to the prefectural government immediately along with the recall reports mentioned earlier.

Materials to be Submitted

The materials must include sufficient details on the following items to make the content simple and easy to understand.

- date materials were created
- whether the recall is for a drug product, quasi-drug, cosmetic or medical device
- recall classification
- nomenclature of the product and brand name
- affected lot, quantity and shipment period
- name of MAH, etc.
- reasons for recall
- specific health damages causing concern
- recall initiation date
- efficacies and effects, or intended use, etc.
- other
- name and contact information of person in charge

Other

- In principle, one set of materials is prepared for each recalled product.
- Materials must be created in text form.
- Materials must be submitted to the prefectural government in an appropriate manner, e.g., via email or on a diskette, etc.

Transfer of Materials from the Prefectural Government to MHLW

The prefectural government must immediately transfer materials submitted by the MAH, etc., to the Compliance and Narcotics Division of MHLW's Pharmaceutical and Food Safety Bureau via email, but may also request the MAH, etc. to cooperate in transferring the materials if necessary.

Requesting Cooperation from Media Organizations
Bulletins for Media Organizations

When it is necessary to quickly and widely provide recall information for reasons of health and hygiene, even to people other than those who have acquired information from the Internet, MAHs, etc. are required to issue a press release to media organizations in the following cases to gain their cooperation.

- Class I recalls (excluding cases of drug products, etc. that do not consist of lots, when no defects are

found in other similar products and it is certain that the relevant drug products, etc. will not be used)
- Class II recalls (excluding cases in which the MAH, etc. already identified all the affected medical institutions, etc. and there is little need to provide information using media organizations)

Press Release Information

To prepare a press release, an MAH, etc., should include the same details as those specified in the materials for the Internet described earlier. In such a case, consideration must be given to using diagrams while avoiding technical terms as much as possible.

Follow-up Investigations

The need for post-recall investigations is not described specifically, but it is quite possible that such investigations may be conducted with the authority described in Article 69 of the *Pharmaceutical Affairs Law* described earlier.

Penalties, etc.

The requirements discussed above are essential to ensure the safety and effectiveness of products and to ensure the safety of patients and healthcare workers. Penalties, the severity of which depends upon the violation, are defined for parties not in compliance with these requirements. Following are lists of violations and their associated penalties.

Imprisonment for up to Three Years or a Fine Not Exceeding ¥3 Million or a Combination Thereof

- Parties violating the provisions of licenses for establishing facilities (Article 4, Paragraph 1 of the *Pharmaceutical Affairs Law*)*
- Parties violating the provisions of MAH licenses (Article 12, Paragraph 1 of the *Pharmaceutical Affairs Law*)
- Parties violating the provisions of product approval (Article 14, Paragraph 1 or 9 of the *Pharmaceutical Affairs Law*)*
- Parties violating the provisions of product certification for Designated Controlled Medical Devices (Article 23-2, Paragraph 1 or 4 of the *Pharmaceutical Affairs Law*)*
- Parties violating the provisions of Sales Licenses for drug products (Article 24, Paragraph 1 of the *Pharmaceutical Affairs Law*)*
- Parties violating provisions regarding products for retail sales (Article 27 of the *Pharmaceutical Affairs Law*)*
- Parties violating provisions regarding products for

retailing by home distribution (Article 31 of the *Pharmaceutical Affairs Law*)*
- Parties violating the provisions of Sales/Leasing Licenses for Highly Controlled Medical Devices (Article 39, Paragraph 1 of the *Pharmaceutical Affairs Law*)*
- Parties violating the provisions of licenses for repair business for medical devices (Article 40-2, Paragraph 1 or 5 of the *Pharmaceutical Affairs Law*)*
- Parties violating provisions regarding testing (Article 43, Paragraph 1 or 2 of the *Pharmaceutical Affairs Law*)*
- Parties violating provisions regarding exhibits (Article 44, Paragraph 3 of the *Pharmaceutical Affairs Law*)*
- Parties violating provisions regarding the sales of prescription drugs (Article 49, Paragraph 1 of the *Pharmaceutical Affairs Law*)*
- Parties violating provisions regarding prohibitions on sales and provision, etc. (Articles 55-2, 60, 62 and 64 of the *Pharmaceutical Affairs Law*)*
- Parties violating provisions regarding prohibitions on sales and manufacturing, etc. of drug products (Articles 56, 57, 60 and 62 of the *Pharmaceutical Affairs Law*)*
- Parties violating provisions regarding prohibitions on sales and manufacturing, etc. of medical devices (Articles 65 and 68-6 of the *Pharmaceutical Affairs Law*)*
- Parties violating orders based on the provisions of an emergency order (Article 69-3 of the *Pharmaceutical Affairs Law*)*
- Parties violating orders based on provisions regarding the disposal of noncompliant products (Article 70, Paragraph 1 and Article 76-7, Paragraph 1 of the *Pharmaceutical Affairs Law*)*
- Parties refusing, preventing or avoiding discarding and other forms of disposal based on provisions regarding the disposal of noncompliant products (Article 70, Paragraph 2 and Article 76-7, Paragraph 2 of the *Pharmaceutical Affairs Law*)
- Parties violating provisions regarding prohibitions on manufacturing, etc. of designated drug substances (Article 7-4 of the *Pharmaceutical Affairs Law*)*
- Parties violating provisions regarding prohibitions on manufacturing and importing of drug products for animals (Article 83-2, Paragraph 1, Article 83-3 or Article 83-4, Paragraph 2, and Article 83-5, Paragraph 2 of the *Pharmaceutical Affairs Law*)*

Note: * Fines not exceeding ¥100 million yen will also be imposed for corporations.

Imprisonment for up to Two Years or a Fine Not Exceeding ¥2 Million or a Combination Thereof

- Parties violating provisions regarding restrictions on sales methods, etc. (Article 37, Paragraph 1 of the *Pharmaceutical Affairs Law*)
- Parties violating provisions regarding restrictions on delivery (Article 47 of the *Pharmaceutical Affairs Law*)
- Parties violating provisions regarding prohibitions on sales and provision, etc. (Article 55, Paragraph 1 and Articles 60, 62, 64, and 68-5 of the *Pharmaceutical Affairs Law*)
- Parties violating provisions regarding hyperbole (Article 66, Paragraph 1 or 3 of the *Pharmaceutical Affairs Law*)
- Parties violating provisions for preapproval or certification (Article 68 of the *Pharmaceutical Affairs Law*)
- Parties violating orders to suspend operations based on provisions regarding the revocation of licenses (Article 75, Paragraph 1 or 3 of the *Pharmaceutical Affairs Law*)
- Parties violating provisions regarding restrictions on advertisement regarding designated deleterious substances (Article 76-5 of the *Pharmaceutical Affairs Law*)

Imprisonment for up to One Year or a Fine Not Exceeding ¥1 Million or a Combination Thereof

- Parties violating provisions regarding the management of pharmacies (Article 7, Paragraph 1 or 2 of the *Pharmaceutical Affairs Law*), retail management (Article 28, Paragraph 1 or 2 of the *Pharmaceutical Affairs Law*), management of areas in each prefecture for products marketed via home distribution (Article 31-2 of the *Pharmaceutical Affairs Law*), or office management (Article 35, Paragraph 1 or 2 of the *Pharmaceutical Affairs Law*)
- Parties violating the provisions of manufacturing licenses (Article 13, Paragraph 1 or 6 of the *Pharmaceutical Affairs Law*)
- Parties violating provisions regarding changes in the Drug Master File (Article 14-13, Paragraph 1 of the *Pharmaceutical Affairs Law*)
- Parties violating provisions regarding the placement of a general controller and a responsible engineering manager (Article 17, Paragraph 1 or 5 and Article 40-3 of the *Pharmaceutical Affairs Law*)
- Parties violating provisions regarding the placement of managers for Highly Controlled Medical Devices and Designated Maintenance Control Medical Devices (Article 39-2 of the *Pharmaceutical Affairs Law*)
- Parties violating provisions regarding restrictions on the marketing of unsealed products (Article 45 of the *Pharmaceutical Affairs Law*)

- Parties violating provisions regarding transfer procedures (Article 46, Paragraph 1 or 4 of the *Pharmaceutical Affairs Law*)
- Parties violating provisions regarding storage and exhibition (Article 48, Paragraph 1 or 2 of the *Pharmaceutical Affairs Law*)
- Parties violating provisions regarding the marketing of prescription drugs (Article 49, Paragraph 2 or 3 of the *Pharmaceutical Affairs Law*)
- Parties violating provisions regarding seals for poisonous drugs or powerful drugs (Article 58 of the *Pharmaceutical Affairs Law*)
- Parties violating restrictions and other measures stipulated in Ministerial Ordinances based on provisions regarding restrictions on advertisements of drug products for designated diseases (Article 67 of the *Pharmaceutical Affairs Law*)
- Parties violating provisions regarding manufacturing managers for biological products (Article 68-2, Paragraph 1 of the *Pharmaceutical Affairs Law*)
- Parties violating orders to suspend operations based on the provisions of an improvement order (Article 72, Paragraph 1 or 2 of the *Pharmaceutical Affairs Law*)
- Parties violating orders to suspend use of facilities based on the provisions of an improvement order (Article 72, Paragraph 3 or 4 of the *Pharmaceutical Affairs Law*)
- Parties violating orders based on the provisions of an improvement order (Article 72-4, Paragraph 1 or 2 of the *Pharmaceutical Affairs Law*)
- Parties violating orders based on the provisions of an order for changes in the general controller or responsible engineering manager, etc. (Article 73 of the *Pharmaceutical Affairs Law*)
- Parties violating orders based on provisions regarding the supervision of retailing by home distribution (Article 74 of the *Pharmaceutical Affairs Law*)
- Parties violating orders based on provisions regarding the revocation, etc. of approval (Article 74-2, Paragraph 2 or 3 of the *Pharmaceutical Affairs Law*)
- Parties violating orders based on provisions regarding inspections of products that may be designated   drugs (Article 76-6, Paragraph 2 of the *Pharmaceutical Affairs Law*)

Imprisonment for up to Six Months or a Fine Not Exceeding ¥300,000

- Parties violating provisions regarding reexaminations of new medical devices, etc. (Article 14-4, Paragraph 7 and Article 19-4 of the *Pharmaceutical Affairs Law*)
- Parties violating provisions regarding reevaluations of new medical devices (Article 14-6, Paragraph 6 and Article 19-4 of the *Pharmaceutical Affairs Law*)
- Parties violating provisions regarding records retention related to biological products (Article 68-9, Paragraph 7 of the *Pharmaceutical Affairs Law*)
- Parties violating provisions regarding records retention related to Designated Medical Devices (Article 77-5, Paragraph 5 of the *Pharmaceutical Affairs Law*)
- Parties violating provisions regarding the handling of clinical trials (Article 80-2, Paragraph 10 of the *Pharmaceutical Affairs Law*)

Fine Not Exceeding ¥500,000

- Parties violating provisions regarding notifications of discontinuance and abolishment of sales and leasing operations for Controlled Medical Devices and sales operations for drug products (Articles 10 and 38 and Article 40, Paragraphs 1 and 2 of the *Pharmaceutical Affairs Law*)
- Parties violating provisions regarding notifications of minor changes in manufacturing and product approval (Article 14, Paragraph 10 of the *Pharmaceutical Affairs Law*)
- Parties violating provisions regarding product notification (Article 14-9, Paragraph 1 or 2 of the *Pharmaceutical Affairs Law*)
- Parties violating provisions regarding changes on the entry of Drug Master File (Article 14-13, Paragraph 2 of the *Pharmaceutical Affairs Law*)
- Parties violating provisions regarding notifications of discontinuance and abolishment of MAH operations as well as repair business (Article 19, Paragraph 1 or 2 and Article 40-3 of the *Pharmaceutical Affairs Law*)
- Parties violating provisions regarding notifications of minor changes in product certification (Article 23-2, Paragraph 5 of the *Pharmaceutical Affairs Law*)
- Parties violating provisions regarding identification papers of parties engaging in retailing business via home distribution (Article 33, Paragraph 1 of the *Pharmaceutical Affairs Law*)
- Parties violating provisions regarding notifications for the sales and leasing of Controlled Medical Devices (Article 39-3, Paragraph 1 of the *Pharmaceutical Affairs Law*)
- Parties violating provisions regarding on-site inspections, etc. (Article 69, Paragraphs 1 to 3 and

Article 76-8, Paragraph 1 of the *Pharmaceutical Affairs Law*)

- Parties violating orders based on an inspection order (Article 71 of the *Pharmaceutical Affairs Law*)
- Parties violating provisions regarding inspections of goods that may be designated drugs (Article 76-6, Paragraph 1 of the *Pharmaceutical Affairs Law*)
- Parties violating provisions regarding the handling of clinical trials (Article 80-2, Paragraphs 1 and 2 and former clause of Paragraph 3 or Paragraph 5 of the *Pharmaceutical Affairs Law*)

Fine Not Exceeding ¥300,000

- Parties violating provisions regarding restrictions on the use of the name (Article 6 of the *Pharmaceutical Affairs Law*)
- Parties violating provisions regarding notifications for engaging in retailing business via home distribution (Article 32 of the *Pharmaceutical Affairs Law*)

Fines for Recognized Certification Bodies' Representatives

In addition, under the revised *Pharmaceutical Affairs Law* enacted in 2005, the responsibilities of registered certification bodies were clearly defined and stated, and if a board member or employee of such a certification body engages in any of the following violations, a fine not exceeding ¥300,000 will be imposed on that person.

- If a report based on provisions regarding the submission of reports (Article 23-5 of the *Pharmaceutical Affairs Law*) is not filed, or if a false report is filed
- If, in violation of provisions regarding the maintaining of account ledgers (Article 23-11 of the *Pharmaceutical Affairs Law*), account ledgers are not kept, entries are not made in account ledgers, false entries are made in account ledgers or if account ledgers are not saved
- If the entire operation related to certifying on conformity assessment to standards is abolished without filing a notification of discontinuance and abolishment of operations (Article 23-15, Paragraph 1 of the *Pharmaceutical Affairs Law*)
- If reports based on provisions regarding on-site inspections, etc. (Article 69, Paragraph 4 of the *Pharmaceutical Affairs Law*) are not filed or if a false report is made, or if on-site inspections based on the provisions of said paragraph are refused, prevented, or avoided, or if answers for questions based on the provisions of said paragraph are not provided without just cause or if false answers are given

Furthermore, under the *Pharmaceutical Affairs Law*,

recognized certification bodies are required to maintain financial statements in a format that allows browsing whenever necessary. Civil fines not exceeding ¥200,000 will be imposed on any party who, in violation of provisions regarding the maintaining and browsing of financial statements (Article 23-17 of the *Pharmaceutical Affairs Law*), does not maintain financial statements, etc., does not enter required items in financial statements, or makes false statements or rejects demands made under the provisions of each section of Paragraph 3 of said article without just cause.

Summary

- The objectives of pharmaceutical affairs administration are broadly divided into two categories: "ensuring the safety and effectiveness of products" and "improving public health and hygiene with the introduction of new medical technologies."
- Various authorities are granted to the Minister of Health, Labour and Welfare and to prefectural governors to achieve these objectives. One representative example is Article 69 of the *Pharmaceutical Affairs Law*.
- Inspections include audits conducted to confirm the status of compliance of duties, etc. associated with MAH licenses and investigations conducted to identify and eliminate defective and mislabeled products, etc.
- Assessment standards are set for confirming compliance with duties associated with licenses, and actions are taken based upon these assessment standards.
- When cases of manufacturing or placing the products on the market of defective and mislabeled products are identified, corrective measures, including recalls, are required.
- Administrative actions are determined by taking the details of the violation and the degree of maliciousness and the frequency of violations into consideration. Criminal penalties may also be imposed.
- Under the revised *Pharmaceutical Affairs Law* of 2005, the responsibilities of the recognized certification bodies were clearly stated, and provisions regarding penalties for board members and employees of certification bodies were established.

Related Notifications

- Ministry of Health, Labour and Welfare Enactment of March 31, Heisei 9 (1997), *Operating manual for health risk management for drug products, etc.*" (Final revision: June 29, Heisei 16 (2004))
- *Yakushokuan* No. 0303001 of March 3, Heisei 17 (2005), *Conformity assessments regarding Good*

Vigilance Practice for drug products, quasi-drugs, cosmetics, and medical devices

- *Yakushokukanmahatsu* No. 0330001 of March 30, Heisei 17 (2005), *Enactment and improvement/ elimination of Ministerial Ordinances and announcements related to manufacturing control and quality control (GMP/QMS) for drug products and medical devices following enforcement of laws partially amending the Pharmaceutical Affairs Law and the Bleeding Donor Supply Service Control Law*

- *Yakushokuhatsu* No. 0331006 of March 31, Heisei 17 (2005), *Revisions of outline of pharmaceutical inspections and guidance*

- *Yakushokuhatsu* No. 0331021 of March 31, Heisei 17 (2005), *Recalls of drug products, etc.*

- *Yakushokukanmahatsu* No. 1130002 of November 30, Heisei 17 (2005), *Guidance for GMP/QMS investigations*

Chapter 41

Quality Management System for Japanese Medical Devices and In Vitro Diagnostics

OBJECTIVES

❑ To understand the *Ministerial Ordinance on QMS* and its scope of application.

❑ To understand the differences between the *Ministerial Ordinance on QMS* and ISO13485.

❑ To understand the responsibilities of MAHs and manufacturers.

❑ To understand inspections and corrective actions.

RELATED LAWS AND REGULATIONS

❑ Article 14, Paragraph 2, Section 4 of the *Pharmaceutical Affairs Law* (Law No. 145 of Showa 35 (1960)) and said section applied *mutatis mutandis* to Article 19, Paragraph 2, Section 5 of the Law

❑ *Pharmaceutical Affairs Law, Enforcement Ordinance* (Government Ordinance No. 11 of Showa 36 (1961))

❑ *Pharmaceutical Affairs Law, Enforcement Regulations* (Ministry of Health and Welfare Ordinance No. 1 of Showa 36 (1961))

❑ *Ministerial Ordinance on Quality Management System for Medical Devices and In Vitro Diagnostics* (Ministry of Health, Labour and Welfare Ordinance No. 169 of Heisei 16 (2004)) (*Ministerial Ordinance on QMS*)

❑ *Regulations for Structures and Facilities for Pharmacies, etc.* (Ministry of Health and Welfare Ordinance No. 2 of Showa 36 (1961))

❑ *Medical Devices Specified by the Minister of Health, Labour and Welfare based on the Provisions of Article 20, Paragraph 3 of the Pharmaceutical Affairs Law, Enforcement Ordinance as Requiring Careful Manufacturing and Quality Control* (Ministry of Health, Labour and Welfare Ordinance No. 440 of Heisei 16 (2004))

❑ *Medical Devices Specified by the Minister of Health, Labour and Welfare based on the Provisions of Article 4, Section 1 of the Ministerial Ordinance on Quality Management System for Medical Devices and In Vitro Diagnostics* (Ministry of Health, Labour and Welfare Ordinance No. 84 of Heisei 17 (2005))

Introduction

Global harmonization of pharmaceutical affairs regulations was one of the objectives of the revised *Pharmaceutical Affairs Law* enacted on 1 April 2005, which led to the establishment of the Marketing Authorization Holder (MAH) system. The revision of the system was followed by the abolishment of the established GMP unique to Japan (old *Ministerial Ordinance on GMP*) and the enactment of the *Ministerial Ordinance on Quality Management System for Medical Devices and In Vitro Diagnostics* (Ministry of Health, Labour and Welfare Ordinance No. 169 of Heisei 16 (2004)) (*Ministerial Ordinance on QMS*) pursuant to ISO13485: 2003, *Medical devices—Quality management systems—Requirements for regulatory purposes.*"

The MAH system under the revised *Pharmaceutical*

Table 41-1. Conformity Assessment Inspections for Each Classification

	Classification	Domestic Manufacturing Facilities	Overseas Manufacturing Facilities
In Vitro Diagnostics	New drug products	PMDA	PMDA
	Radiopharmaceutical products	PMDA	PMDA
	Others	Prefectural Governments (for those with certification standards, Recognized Certification Body)	PMDA (for those with certification standards, Recognized Certification Body)
Medical Devices	New medical devices	PMDA	PMDA
	Cell tissue medical devices	PMDA	PMDA
	Class IV	PMDA	PMDA
	Class III	Prefectural Governments	PMDA
	Class II	Prefectural Governments (for those with certification standards, Recognized Certification Body)	PMDA (for those with certification standards, Recognized Certification Body)
	Class I	–	–

(Source: "QMS Inspections" on the PMDA website)

Affairs Law deals with "placing products onto the market" and "manufacturing" as separate activities and no longer requires products to be manufactured in manufacturer-owned factories. This allows MAHs that have obtained product approval (certification) to outsource the entire manufacturing processes to manufacturers.

However, at the same time, the *Ministerial Ordinance on QMS* was newly positioned as a set of requirements for product approval (certification), and MAHs of medical devices and in vitro diagnostics to which the *Ministerial Ordinance on QMS* was applied, as well as designated MAHs (D-MAHs), must require contract manufacturers (including foreign manufacturers) to implement QMS-compliant manufacturing and quality control for products at manufacturing sites.

Also, the *Ministerial Ordinance on QMS* requires manufacturers to undergo preapproval (pre-certification) QMS conformity inspections for each product and regular QMS conformity assessment inspections conducted every five years for each manufacturing site and to receive QMS conformity certificate from the inspection authority.

As shown in **Table 41-1**, there are different conformity assessment inspections for different products.

Each manufacturing site must receive licenses and certification for structures and facilities and stationing a responsible engineering manager at each manufacturing site. If the major parts of the structures and facilities are changed, a notification of such changes must be submitted pursuant to Article 100 of *Pharmaceutical Affairs Law, Enforcement Regulations*.

Outline and Scope of Application of the *Ministerial Ordinance on QMS*
Outline of the *Ministerial Ordinance on QMS*

The structure of the *Ministerial Ordinance on QMS* is shown in **Table 41-2**.

The *Ministerial Ordinance on QMS* specifies requirements in Chapter 37; additional standards for Biological Medical Devices in Chapter 38; and standards for in vitro diagnostics in Chapter 39. These chapters include requirements specific to Japan.

Scope of Application of the Ministerial Ordinance on QMS

Medical devices and in vitro diagnostics to which the *Ministerial Ordinance on QMS* is applied are prescribed in Article 14, Section 1 and Article 19-2, Section 1 of the *Pharmaceutical Affairs Law*, and include:
- Highly Controlled Medical Devices (Class III and IV medical devices)
- Controlled Medical Devices (Class II medical devices)
- some general medical devices (Class I medical devices specified in Ministry of Health, Labour and Welfare Ordinance No. 440 of Heisei 16 (2004))
- in vitro diagnostics

Article 4, Section 1 of the *Ministerial Ordinance on QMS* specifies that the provisions on design and development in Articles 30 to 36 of the ordinance do not apply to medical devices and related products other than "Medical devices

Table 41-2. Structure of Ministerial Ordinance on QMS

Chapter 1: General Provisions (Articles 1-3)

Chapter 2: Manufacturing and Quality Control at Manufacturing Sites of Medical Device Manufacturers

- Section 1: General Principles (Article 4)
- Section 2: Quality Management System (Articles 5-9)
- Section 3: Responsibilities of Top Management (Articles 10-20)
- Section 4: Resource Management (Articles 21-25)
- Section 5: Product Realization (Articles 26-53)
- Section 6: Measurement, Analysis, and Improvement (Articles 54-64)

Chapter 3: Manufacturing and Quality Control at Manufacturing Sites of Manufacturers Involved in Processes including Storage of Medical Devices (Articles 65-72)

Chapter 4: Manufacturing and Quality Control at Manufacturing Sites of Manufacturers of Medical Devices with Biologically Derived Materials, etc. (Articles 73-79)

Chapter 5: Manufacturing and Quality Control at Manufacturing Sites of Manufacturers of In Vitro Diagnostics (Article 80)

Attached clauses (date of enactment and transitional measures)

specified by the Minister of Health, Labour and Welfare" (Ministry of Health, Labour and Welfare Announcement No. 84 of Heisei 17 (2005)) as requiring management for design and development.

However, the provisions on design and development apply to the majority of medical devices requiring certification or approval. It is important to ensure the proper individuals are aware of the application of the provisions.

PMDA has published the principles of the scope of QMS conformity assessment inspections conducted in the manufacturing process (**Tables 41-3** and **41-4**). For updated information on QMS, please visit the PMDA website (http://www.pmda.go.jp/operations/shonin/info/iryokiki/file/ qms-j.pdf).

Facilities requiring QMS inspections and their requirements are:

- Manufacturing sites (facilities performing sterilization only): QMS inspections are not required if QMS conformity has been verified within two years
- External facilities for design and development management: QMS inspections are not required if QMS conformity has been verified within two years. Limited to the facilities engaging in principle management for design of Design Control Medical Devices.
- External testing facilities: Facilities conducting tests of particular importance for quality assurance of final products and that are not managed under the QMS of the manufacturer. Descriptions of particular importance for Quality Assurance for final products include, for example, biological indicator (BI) culture tests performed immediately after ethylene oxide gas (EtO) sterilization for sterility assurance, uniformity tests for stent-coating drugs,

and precious metal content tests for metals for dental use.

Description of the *Ministerial Ordinance on QMS* by Chapter

The content of each chapter of the *Ministerial Ordinance on QMS* is described below along with points to consider.

Chapter 1: General Provisions (Articles 1 to 3)

Chapter 1 (Articles 1-3) specifies the purpose, definitions and scope of application of the *Ministerial Ordinance on QMS*. As described below, the terminology used is different from that used in ISO13485:2003.

Chapter 2: Manufacturing and Quality Control at Manufacturing Sites of Medical Device Manufacturers

Section 1 (Article 4) specifies, in the form of general provisions, the scope of application of this chapter's requirements.

Section 2 (Articles 5-9) specifies the requirements for quality management systems. Manufacturers must establish and operate a quality management system and maintain effectiveness in accordance with the provisions of this chapter. This section describes management for the following documents and records.

- statements on quality policies and statements on quality objectives
- QMS standards
- documents required to ensure effective and planned operation of processes and management at manufacturing sites
- written procedures and records specified in this chapter
- other documents specified in laws and ordinances related to pharmaceutical affairs

Table 41-3. Principles of Licenses and Certifications of Manufacturing Sites for Medical Devices, QMS Inspections and Descriptions on Applications for Approval

	Licenses and Certifications	QMS Inspections	Descriptions on Applications for Approval
Manufacturing sites (facilities performing sterilization only)*[1]	Required	Required	Required
Manufacturing sites (facilities engaging in storage and other processes)	Required	Required	Required
Manufacturing sites (other than those described above)	Required	Required	Required
External facilities for design and development management[1,2]	Not required	Required	Required
External testing facilities[1,3]	Not required	Required	Required

1   QMS inspections are not required if QMS conformity has been verified within two years.
2   Limited to facilities engaging in principal management for the design and development of medical devices.
3   Facilities conducting tests of particular importance for Quality Assurance of final products and that are not managed under the manufacturer's QMS. Tests of particular importance for Quality Assurance for final products include, for example, BI culture tests performed immediately after EtO sterilization for sterility assurance, uniformity tests for stent-coating drugs and precious metal content tests for metals for dental use.

It is also necessary to prepare, for each product, a product master formula that details the specifications and requirements related to quality management systems. The sections on objectives in both the QMS standards and the Quality Manual under the ISO13485 would need to state "Application to the Ministerial Ordinance on QMS" as an objective.

The retention periods for documents and records are as follows. Ensure that the retention periods specified in the procedures for the manufacturing site meet the requirements of the Ministerial Ordinance on QMS.

- education and training: 5 years
- Designated Maintenance Control Medical Devices: 15 years (However, if the labeling of the effective period or expiration date ("effective period") of the medical device is required and the period calculated by adding one year to the effective period exceeds 15 years, the retention period is the effective period plus one year.)
- medical devices other than Designated Maintenance Control Medical Devices: five years (However, if the labeling of the effective period of the medical device is required and the period calculated by adding one year to the effective period exceeds five years, the retention period is the effective period plus one year.)

Section 3 (Articles 10 to 20) specifies the responsibilities of top management, covering management activities, emphasis on customers, quality policies, quality objectives, establishing plans for quality management systems, responsibilities and authorities, responsible engineering managers (management representatives as described in ISO13485:2003 and their responsibilities and authorities), internal communication, management reviews and requirements for input for management reviews.

The *Ministerial Ordinance on QMS* includes regulatory provisions. Top management and responsible engineering managers must be aware that serious noncompliance may result in administrative orders such as suspension of shipments, recalls/repairs, suspensions of operations and fines. Top management must ensure that the responsible person for the manufacturing site and other affiliates are aware of the importance of compliance with regulatory provisions and requirements concerning MAHs and other parties receiving products.

Section 4 (Articles 21–25) describes resource management, covering securing resources, employees, education and training, business management infrastructure and work environments.

Regarding education and training, manufacturers must determine the skills required for employees engaged in duties affecting product quality, execute well-planned education and training programs, and assess the effectiveness of such measures. For internal communication, top management must be aware of what is happening at the manufacturing site to determine whether there are any problems with the Plan, Do, Check, Act (PDCA) system and have a plan that allows for visual assessments and guidance on any affected processes if there are any problems with the PDCA system. Procedures and work environments must be designed not only to prevent negative impacts on quality but to improve worker safety and avoid human errors.

Section 5 (Articles 26–53) describes product realization, including:

- product realization planning

Table 41-4. Principles of Licenses and Certifications for Manufacturing-Related Facilities for Medical Devices, QMS Inspections and Descriptions on Applications for Approval

	Licenses and Certifications	QMS Inspections	Descriptions on Applications for Approval
Facilities manufacturing component parts[1]	Not required	Not required	Not required
Facilities performing processes affecting the quality, performance and safety of the final product[2,3]	Not required	Not required	Description of manufacturing conditions[4]
Facilities performing processes other than those described above	Not required	Not required	Not required

1   *If obtaining approval for a component part as a medical device, the manufacturer of the part must receive a license (certification) and undergo a QMS inspection.*

2   *Examples include heparin coating of catheters and drug coating of stents.*

3   *Provided that the facilities are properly managed through the manufacturer's QMS, in principle, QMS inspections are not required for these facilities.*

4   *It is not necessary to provide the facility name on the application, but manufacturing protocols for critical processes are required. Individuals with questions regarding how to fill in an application for approval should utilize the consultation system offered by the Office of Medical Devices.*

(Source for Tables 2 and 3: "QMS Inspections" on the PMDA website)

- clarification and reviews of product requirements
- communication with customers
- design and development planning
- design and development inputs and outputs
- design and development reviews
- design and development verification and validation
- control of design and development changes
- purchasing processes
- purchase information
- verification of purchased products
- control of production and service provision
- cleanliness control of products
- installation activities
- servicing activities
- manufacturing control for sterile medical devices
- validation of manufacturing and sterilization processes
- identification
- traceability
- product traceability for Designated Medical Devices
- product status identification
- products provided by the final product recipients
- product preservation
- management of facilities and measuring devices.

Note that securing product traceability is required for Specially Designated Medical Devices.

Risk management is an important part of product realization. Although ISO13485:2003 specifies ISO14971 as guidelines for risk management, the *Ministerial Ordinance on QMS* does not mention ISO14971. However, ISO14971 (JIS T 14971) was cited as a guideline in *Applications for product approval (certification)* during preparation of the

Essential Principles. Risk management involves studies and measures of risks related to processes all the way up to receiving the product, including receipt of manufacturing substances and component parts, manufacturing processes and transportation, as well as risks during use by customers. However, in addition to the design and development phase, it is also necessary to continue risk management in the post-market phase and to manage records and updates.

Section 6 (Articles 54–64) describes measurement, analysis and improvement, covering monitoring and measuring, analysis and improvement, feedback from product recipients, internal audits, monitoring and measurement for processes and products, product monitoring and measurement for specific medical devices, management of nonconforming products, data analysis, improvements and corrective and preventive measures.

Note that product monitoring and measurement is also described as a separate item for Specially Designated Medical Devices.

Chapter 3 (Articles 65 to 72): Manufacturing and Quality Control at Manufacturing Sites of Manufacturers Involved in Processes Including Storage, etc. of Medical Devices

In Japan, only the Japanese language may be used for labeling. This chapter provides provisions regarding manufacturing and quality control for manufacturers involved only in preparing Japanese-language labeling, packaging and storage. Although the requirements are more limited than the provisions of Chapter 2, Chapter 3 provides provisions regarding the duties of responsible engineering managers, documents related to manufacturing and quality control, manufacturing and quality control, management of nonconforming products, corrective measures, internal audits, education and training and management of documents and records.

Chapter 4 (Articles 73 to 79): Manufacturing and Quality Control at Manufacturing Sites of Manufacturers of Biological Medical Devices, etc.

These are provisions concerning manufacturers of Biological Medical Devices, etc. Chapter 4 details provisions concerning infrastructure, documents, process control, tests and examinations, education and training and management of documents and records at manufacturing sites for Specially Designated Biological Medical Devices, etc.

Chapter 5 (Article 80): Manufacturing and Quality Control at Manufacturing Sites of Manufacturers of In Vitro Diagnostics

This chapter contains provisions concerning manufacturing sites of manufacturers of in vitro diagnostics. The majority of the details apply *mutatis mutandis* to Chapters 2 and 3. Note that a drug product manufacturing manager for in vitro diagnostics corresponds to a responsible engineering manager for medical devices, but the qualifications for a drug product manufacturing manager are different than those for a responsible engineering manager.

Attached clauses

Although these clauses describe the date of enactment (1 April 2005) of the *Ministerial Ordinance on QMS* along with transitional measures, as of 2009, the ordinance has been enacted and the transitional measures are no longer in place.

Relationship Between the Ministerial Ordinance on QMS and ISO 13485:2003
Differences in Internal Systems

The *Ministerial Ordinance on QMS* requires the establishment of quality management systems at each manufacturing site, but ISO13485:2003 specifies that such systems are established for the entire organization. The following questions and answers concerning the relationship of the ordinance with ISO13485 are from the *Jimurenraku* of October 13, Heisei 18 (2006), "*GMP/QMS case studies (2006)*" (excerpts).

Question 1

Is it acceptable to be in compliance with ISO13485 instead of the provisions of Chapter 2 as well as Chapter 2 applied *mutatis mutandis* to Chapter 5 of the *Ministerial Ordinance on QMS for devices and in vitro diagnostics*?

Answer 1

No. The *Pharmaceutical Affairs Law* requires compliance with the provisions of Chapter 2 as well as Chapter 2 applied *mutatis mutandis* to Chapter 5 of the *Ministerial Ordinance on QMS for devices and in vitro diagnostics*, not ISO13485:2003.

Question 2

When preparing written procedures for manufacturers, is it acceptable to use terminology from ISO13485:2003 instead of terminology from the *Ministerial Ordinance on QMS for devices and in vitro diagnostics*?

Answer 2

In written procedures for manufacturers, terminology used in the *Ministerial Ordinance on QMS for devices and in vitro diagnostics* may be replaced with terminology from ISO13485:2003. However, note that you must document how the ISO 13485:2003 terminology corresponds with that of the ordinance in order to provide clear explanations.

Question 3

There are cases in which an MAH(s) and a manufacturer(s) have built a cross-organizational quality management system covering the relevant headquarters and multiple manufacturing sites and laboratories pursuant to ISO13485:2003 or ISO9001:2000. In such cases, can we interpret that the requirements of the *Ministerial Ordinance on QMS for devices and in vitro diagnostics* can be met by applying this quality management system to the manufacturing sites?

Answer 3

As described in Chapter 4, Section 3, Paragraph 4(3) and (4) of the Enforcement Notice, a cross-site quality management system is generally established at a manufacturing site to cover multiple products, but conformance with these provisions is, in principal, assessed for individual products at each manufacturing site. However, if the provisions of the *Ministerial Ordinance on QMS for devices and in vitro diagnostics* are met by including the outsourced process, for example, outsourced sterilization processes, the manufacturer may establish a single quality management system that covers multiple manufacturing sites. In such cases, however, it is necessary to provide a clear statement regarding the application of the system to each manufacturing site by, for example, specifying the processes that are specific to the manufacturing site. If, in addition to establishing a quality management system that covers MAH(s), the MAH conducts management review and internal audits, the relationship between the manufacturing sites and the MAH must be adequately defined in an agreement in accordance with the provisions of the *Ministerial Ordinance on GQP*.

Product Master File (*Seihin Hyojun Sho*) and Device Master Record (DMR)

Chapter 4-3, 6(11) of *Yakushokukanmahatsu* No. 0330001 of March 30, Heisei 17 (2005) specifies the following requirements for product master formulae.

- product nomenclature and brand name

Table 41-5. Terminology of *Ministerial Ordinance on QMS* and ISO 13485:2003

Ministerial Ordinance on QMS	ISO 13485:2003 (JIS Q 13485:2005)
Quality Management and Monitoring System	Quality Management System
QMS Standards	Quality manual
Kotei (Process)	Process
Kotei nyuryoku jyoho (Input)	Input
Kotei shutsuryoku jyoho (Output)	Output
Shosa (Review)	Review
Kanri kantokusha (Top management)	Top management
Product recipient	Customer
Opinion	Feedback
Responsible technician	Management representative
Naibu jyoho dentatsu (Internal communication)	Internal communication
Reviews of top management authorities	Management review
Employees	Human resources
Effectiveness	Efficacy
Business management infrastructure	Infrastructure
Validation	Validation
Verification of purchased goods	Verification of purchased products
Tsuiseki kanousei (Traceability)	Traceability
Goods of product recipient	Customer property
Storage of product	Preservation of product
Corrective actions	Corrective measures
Preventive actions	Preventive measures

- product approval (certification) number, or the number and date of a product notification for the product and the date of change application
- product specifications
- operational methods or methods of use
- design, drawings and specification or components and quantities of the product (form, composition and principles, and raw materials or component parts
- manufacturing methods and procedures
- name of exporting country for imported products, name of principal countries where the product is distributed and brand names used
- matters concerning labeling and packaging (label materials, accessories, and form of packaging)
- test and examination methods for product, manufacturing substances and component parts
- storage methods and conditions for product, manufacturing substances and component parts
- product effective period and expiration date
- product transportation methods and procedures

- product repair procedures and storage methods and maximum retention/storage periods for component parts used for repairs
- matters concerning installation and servicing activities
- matters concerning sterilization of Sterile Medical Devices
- documents describing agreements with the MAH
- specifications and test methods
- test protocols, methods and rationale of the test when stricter and more precise testing methods used for the product approvals (certifications) are used
- test protocols, methods and grounds for the test that was voluntarily developed and required for quality control
- test protocols and methods used at external testing agencies
- storage conditions and stability test results providing grounds for effective period or expiration date

Please also include classification, traceability management units and specifications and procedures for release from manufacturing sites.

Given these provisions on document control, you must specify the originator and approver of the created document and the date of creation, and in cases of revision, the originator, approver, date, details and reasons for such revisions.

The *Pharmaceutical Affairs Law* and the *Ministerial Ordinance on QMS* require overseas manufacturing sites to create a product master file for each product or include the details of the specifications in the DMR, or create a supplementary document in order to meet Japanese regulatory requirements.

Terminology

The *Ministerial Ordinance on QMS* and ISO13485:2003 (translated JIS: JIS Q 13485:2005) use different terminology (**Table 41-5**).

If the ISO (JIS) terminology is used, it is necessary to prepare a terminology table that shows the terminology of both ISO and the Ministerial Ordinance on QMS.

Other Points Regarding the *Ministerial Ordinance on QMS*
Responsibilities of MAHs and Manufacturers

The *Pharmaceutical Affairs Law* affects business categories involving coordination between manufacturers, distributors and repairers led by MAHs. Manufacturers are responsible for product manufacturing outsourced by MAHs and release the products to the MAH, not directly to sellers or distributors. Product release determination cannot be made solely by the manufacturers.

MAHs (e.g., quality controllers) make such decisions, but the decision may be made, at the discretion of and as the sole responsibility of the MAH, by a manufacturer in Japan (Article 9 of the *Ministerial Ordinance on GQP* and *Yakushokuhatsu* No. 0922001 of September 22, Heisei 16 (2004)). In such cases, a decision is made on product release from a manufacturing site located in Japan with a manufacturing license. To qualify for such decision making, the manufacturer must be a "manufacturer handling drug products (medical devices) for which all decisions related to product release have been made. The regulation does not prevent the manufacturer and MAH from working together to make a decision on product release onto the market" (*Yakushokuhatsu* No. 0922001 of September 22, Heisei 16 (2004)).

Article 10 of the *Ministerial Ordinance on GQP* (Appropriate Manufacturing and Quality Control) requires MAHs with the ultimate responsibility for the distribution, quality and safety of medical devices and in vitro diagnostics on the market to periodically check that manufacturers perform duties related to manufacturing and quality control in an appropriate and efficient manner and to document related records.

MAHs must establish agreements with manufacturers on the following matters and include the items agreed in procedures for quality control operations (Article 7 of the *Ministerial Ordinance on GQP*). It is necessary to establish agreements with the MAH before starting manufacturing duties and to perform those duties in accordance with such agreements.

- procedures covering the scope of manufacturing and other related duties (henceforth referred to as manufacturing duties) of the manufacturer, as well as related manufacturing, quality control and product release
- technical conditions regarding manufacturing methods and test and examination methods
- periodic checks by the MAH to confirm that duties related to manufacturing and quality control are performed for the manufacturing duties in an appropriate and efficient manner
- methods for quality control during transportation and product delivery (conditions, label checks, package contamination, damage checks and temperature record checks during transportation and storage)
- methods for the responsible engineering manager for advance notices to the MAH in cases in which changes to manufacturing methods or test methods, etc. are expected to affect product quality
- methods for the responsible engineering manager for swift communication to the MAH of the following information obtained regarding the product
  - information regarding suspensions of manufacturing, importation or distribution of the product and measures (e.g., recall and disposal) taken to prevent health hazards from occurring or spreading
  - other information regarding product quality
  - other necessary matters

"Other necessary matters" is a very broad statement, but MAHs and manufacturers may need agreements for more than the aforementioned requirement to ensure product quality, performance and safety. Such matters may include market information (e.g., complaints), malfunction status and information on manufacturing processes (e.g., yield rate) and raw material acceptance. However, given that the details to be provided and the methods involved may vary significantly depending upon product characteristics, appropriate matters must be specified between the MAH and the manufacturer.

"The manufacturers who are required to establish agreements with the MAHs may be either the manufacturer of a final product, a foreign manufacturer, an entity performing test, or an entity specified in the section on manufacturing methods in the product approval application (e.g., facilities performing design control)" (*GMP/QMS case studies (2006)*.

Inspections and Corrective and Preventive Actions

Inspections

Inspections are designed to assess the degree of conformity with legal provisions and customer requirements related to management systems as well as improvements and effectiveness. Inspections are generally categorized into first-party, second-party and third-party inspections according to the parties involved.

- First-party inspections: internal audits
- Second-party inspections: inspections conducted by a beneficiary of the inspected organization (e.g., inspection on supplier)
- Third-party inspections: inspections (assessments) conducted by an external (assessments) inspector (assessor) (e.g., assessment for ISO certification)

The *Ministerial Ordinance on QMS* describes inspections in terms of internal audits (Articles 19, 56, 62, 65, 66 and 70). Manufacturers must perform internal audits at set intervals to confirm whether or not the quality management system conforms to the requirements of the *Ministerial Ordinance on QMS*. Also, in procedures, manufacturers must state that these audits are to be conducted periodically and according to the plan.

Audits can also be effectively conducted on an irregular basis on certain occasions, such as prior to the release of a new product, upon quality-affecting changes to manufacturing sites and workspaces, and for checks on corrective measures such as voluntary recalls. A system must be built for supplier assessments and some of the outsourced manufacturing processes so audits can be conducted by using assessment procedures including evaluation processes and methods.

It is desirable to appoint an auditor who has a deep understanding of the *Ministerial Ordinance on QMS*, an objective view and is able to sternly point out any nonconformity. For auditor qualities, refer to the following ISO standard: ISO 19011: 2003 (JIS Q 19011:2003) *Guidelines for quality and/or environmental management systems auditing.*

Corrective and Preventive Action

Corrective and Preventive Action (CAPA) is a term used in both ISO13485 and the *Ministerial Ordinance on QMS.*

Manufacturers must take appropriate corrective actions depending upon the effects of identified nonconformities (nonconformity with the requirements of the *Ministerial Ordinance on QMS*). Such identified nonconformities include those related to the final product as well as in-process nonconformities. Corrective actions are actions that eliminate the causes of nonconformity. Nonconformities must be corrected and corrective actions must eliminate the causes.

Corrective actions must identify the causes of nonconformity, assess the need for measures to prevent nonconformity from recurring, identify and implement specific corrections, document results and review the effectiveness of corrective actions taken. The *Ministerial Ordinance on QMS* states that "written procedures for corrective actions specifying the following requirements must be prepared" (Article 63).

- review of nonconformity (including customer complaints)
- identification of causes of nonconformity
- assessment of the need for actions to prevent nonconformity from recurring
- identification and implementation of specific correction (including document updates)
- documentation of results of investigations on corrective actions as well as corrective actions taken based upon such results
- review of corrective actions taken and their effectiveness

Preventive actions refer to the elimination of potential causes of nonconformity and the prevention of such nonconformity. Risk management is one preventive action, and repeatedly asking the question "why" can lead to the identification of root causes. The *Ministerial Ordinance on QMS* states that "written procedures for preventive actions specifying the following requirements must be prepared" (Article 64).

- identification of potential nonconformity and causes
- assessment of the need for preventive actions
- identification and implementation of specific preventive actions
- documentation of results of investigations on preventive actions as well as preventive actions taken based upon such results
- review of preventive measures taken and their effectiveness

Summary

The *Ministerial Ordinance on QMS* is similar to ISO13485:2003 but is not identical.

A manufacturing site that is in compliance with ISO13485:2003 may not necessarily be in compliance with the Japanese *Pharmaceutical Affairs Law* and related laws and regulations.

Medical devices and in vitro diagnostics are important products in the treatment and diagnosis of diseases. Top management and responsible engineering managers must always work with MAHs to exercise care so product manufacturing and quality are appropriately controlled as specified in product approval (certification) in accordance with the Japanese *Pharmaceutical Affairs Law.*

Related Notifications

Iyakukan No. 69 of May 1, Heisei 10 (1998), *Guidelines for sterilization validation for medical devices*

Yakushokuhatsu No. 0330008 of March 30, Heisei 17 (2005), *Enactment and amendment or abolishment of Ministerial Ordinances and announcements related to manufacturing control and quality control (GMP/QMS) for drug products and medical devices following enforcement of the Law Partially Amending the Pharmaceutical Affairs Law and the Bleeding Donor Supply Service Control Law*

Yakushokukanmahatsu No. 0330001 of March 30, Heisei 17 (2005), *Enactment and amendment or abolishment of Ministerial Ordinances and announcements related to manufacturing control and quality control (GMP/QMS) for drug products and medical devices following enforcement of the Law Partially Amending the Pharmaceutical Affairs Law and the Bleeding Donor Supply Service Control Law*

Yakushokushinsahatsu No. 0330006 and *Yakushokukanmahatsu* No. 0330005 of March 30, Heisei 17 (2005), *Handling of applications for GMP conformity investigations*

Jimurenraku of September 9, Heisei 17 (2005), *Draft English translations of the Ministerial Ordinance on GQP, the Ministerial Ordinance on GMP for Drug Products and Quasi-drugs, the Ministerial Ordinance on QMS for Medical Devices and In Vitro Diagnostics, and Regulations for Building and Facilities*

Yakushokukanmahatsu No. 1130004 of November 30, Heisei 17 (2005) *Guidance for GMP/QMS investigations*

Jimurenraku of October 13, Heisei 18 (2006), "GMP/QMS case studies (2006)"

Yakushokukanmahatsu No. 0612008 of June 12, Heisei 19 (2007), *Handling of guidelines for radiation sterilization validation for medical devices*

References

1. Pharmaceuticals and Medical Devices Agency website, "QMS Inspections" http://www.pmda.go.jp/operations/shonin/info/iryokiki/file/qms-j.pdf

Labeling, Package Inserts, Advertisements and Sales Promotion for Japanese Medical Devices

OBJECTIVES

❑ To understand the regulatory requirements for labeling for medical devices.

❑ To understand package insert (PI) and instruction manuals.

❑ To understand an overview of advertising regulations.

❑ To understand the regulatory bodies and provisions of penalties.

RELATED LAWS AND REGULATIONS

❑ *Pharmaceutical Affairs Law* (Law No. 145 of Showa 35 (1960))

❑ *Pharmaceutical Affairs Law, Enforcement Regulations* (Ministry of Health and Welfare Ordinance No. 1 of Showa 36 (1961)), Chapter 6

❑ *Highly Controlled Medical Devices, Controlled Medical Devices, and General Medical Devices specified by the Minister of Health, Labour and Welfare based on the provisions of Article 2, Paragraphs 5 to 7 of the Pharmaceutical Affairs Law* (Ministry of Health, Labour and Welfare Announcement No. 298 of Heisei 16 (2004)) (Announcement on Classification)

❑ *Biological Products and Designated Biological Products specified by the Minister of Health, Labour and Welfare* (Ministry of Health, Labour

and Welfare Announcement No. 209 of Heisei 15 (2003))

❑ *Medical devices based on the provisions of Article 63, Paragraph 1, Section 4 of the Pharmaceutical Affairs Law* (Ministry of Health and Welfare Announcement No. 21 of Showa 36 (1961))

Introduction

Because medical devices have a variety of forms, properties and methods of use compared to drug products, it is necessary to refer to each provision of regulations specified for individual devices for the details of labeling requirements, etc. This chapter summarizes common regulations for medical devices that are the core requirements. The details of these regulations are important for users of medical devices to use the devices properly and safely, and it is imperative to understand them.

Pharmaceutical Affairs Requirements for Medical Device Labeling

Principles for labeling on medical devices include the following two requirements:
- duty to provide clear descriptions (clear descriptions in legible script) (Article 217 of the *Pharmaceutical Affairs Law, Enforcement Regulations*)
- descriptions in Japanese (Article 218 of the *Pharmaceutical Affairs Law, Enforcement Regulations*)

At the same time, it is prohibited to include the following information on products and package inserts, etc:

- false or misleading information (Article 54 of the *Pharmaceutical Affairs Law*)
- unapproved efficacies or effects (Article 54 of the *Pharmaceutical Affairs Law*)
- usage, dosages or periods of use that cause risks for health and hygiene (Article 54 of the *Pharmaceutical Affairs Law*)

Although there are some exceptions or differences in regulatory requirements according to the properties of the devices, basic items applied to medical devices are described below (refer to Chapter 6 and Chapter 7, Section 5 of the *Pharmaceutical Affairs Law* and Chapter 6 of the *Pharmaceutical Affairs Law, Enforcement Regulations*). Because medical devices have a variety of product shapes and properties, to meet the requirements for labeling, the properties of each individual device should be considered and applicable regulations should be understood. For electrical products, it may also be necessary to further indicate a Product Safety Electric Appliance and Materials mark (PSE mark) in accordance with the *Electrical Appliance and Material Safety Law*.

Items to be Described on All Medical Devices or on Immediate Containers or Packaging

- name or appellation and address of Marketing Authorization Holder (MAH)
- nomenclature
- serial number or product code
- designation of Highly Controlled Medical Devices, Controlled Medical Devices or General Medical Devices

Items to be Described on Medical Devices or on Immediate Containers or Packaging According to Device Characteristics

- content amounts, such as weight, dosage or quantity
- for Biological Products, describe as such
- expiration date
- names of foreign entities with special approval and their respective countries, as well as the names and addresses of Designated Marketing Authorization Holder (D-MAH)
- statement identifying Designated Maintenance Control Medical Devices
- statement prescribing single-use
- names and amounts of components composing dental metals

Items to be Described on Package Inserts or on Containers or Packaging for All Medical Devices

- methods for use and other precautions for use and handling

Items to be Described on Package Inserts or on Containers or Packaging According to Device Properties

- items regarding maintenance and inspection
- for Biological Products, describe as such

Package Inserts for Medical Devices

MAHs of medical devices are required to include package inserts in their products (Article 63-2 of the *Pharmaceutical Affairs Law*). The details are specified in the related notifications (*Yakushokuhatsu* No. 0310003 of March 10, Heisei 17 (2005), *Guidance for descriptions on package inserts for medical devices*, etc.) and an overview of the requirements is provided in this section. It may be difficult to include necessary information in a fixed format for package inserts due to the variety of shapes and operating principles of medical devices; in such cases, the information must be described in instruction manuals, etc.

Units of Preparation

- Prepare one type of package insert for each "approval," "certification" and "notification." However, a series of product groups may be described together (e.g., artificial joints), if combining the descriptions in a single package insert can facilitate better understanding for users, etc. In addition, if several products are included in a single approval, certification or notification and the products function by being combined, they may be described in a single package insert.
- For medical devices having accessories in addition to the main unit, package inserts for the accessories must also be prepared if the accessories are separately distributed, even if the accessories are included in the same approval, certification or notification of the medical devices. However, in this case, some descriptions could be abbreviated by describing that the accessories are used with the main unit.

Items and Orders of Descriptions in Package inserts

1. date of creation or revision
2. approval number, etc.
3. type and nomenclature, etc.
4. trade name
5. warnings
6. contraindications and prohibitions
7. shape, composition and principles, etc.
8. intended use and efficacy or effects
9. product specifications, etc.
10. operational methods or methods of use, etc.
11. precautions for use
12. clinical performance

13. storage methods and periods of use, etc.
14. precautions for handling
15. items regarding maintenance and inspection
16. approval conditions
17. packaging
18. major literature and address(es) for requesting the literature
19. name and address of MAH and manufacturers

Outline of Descriptions

1. Date of creation or revision
   Enter the date of creation or revision and the edition number. For revisions, make sure the revision history is clearly understood.

2. Approval number, etc.
   Enter either the approval number, certification number or notification number. For single-use medical devices, enter a description stating, "Reuse prohibited."

3. Type and general nomenclature, etc.
   Enter the nomenclature of the medical device; the JMDN code; whether the device is a Highly Controlled Medical Device, Controlled Medical Device or General Medical Device; whether the device is a Designated Maintenance Control Medical Device or an Installation Control Medical Device; and whether the device is a Designated Biological Product or a Biological Product.

4. Trade name
   Enter the trade name. Do not enter abbreviations or aliases. If the device is a Designated Biological Product or a Biological Product and is manufactured using recombinant technology, describe as such.

5. Warnings
   Enter items requiring caution, especially those involving risks, within the medical device's intended use. Also create sub-items and provide descriptions for warnings including "Applicable subjects (patients)," "Medical devices for combination use" and "Methods for use."

6. Contraindications and prohibitions
   Describe subjects and methods for use beyond the scope of assurance, such as design limitations and improper use of the medical device. Also create sub-items that provide descriptions for contraindications and prohibitions including "Applicable subjects (patients)," "Medical devices for combination use" and "Methods for use."

7. Shape, composition and principles, etc.
   Provide an overview using block diagrams, molecular formulae or compositions of constituent metals so the overall composition of the medical device can be easily understood. In addition,

briefly describe the principles and mechanisms for fulfilling the medical device's functions. Because there are additional requirements for specific Biological Products and Biological Products, check the original text of the notifications.

8. Intended use and efficacy or effects
   Describe the approved intended use and the efficacy or effects. For certified medical devices, describe the intended use and the efficacy or effects that have been certified. For medical devices for which a notification has been filed, describe the definitions of nomenclatures used in the Announcement on Classification regarding such devices.

9. Product specifications, etc.
   Provide brief descriptions of the performances of the products described in the Product Specifications column in the applications for approval, certifications or notifications.

10. Operational methods or methods of use, etc.
    Describe the methods for installation, assembly and use, etc. In addition, for medical devices used in combination, describe requirements for the medical devices, or describe medical devices that can be used in combination.

11. Precautions for use
    Describe general cautionary items for using the medical device. Also create sub-items and provide descriptions for cautionary items including "Applicable subjects (patients)," "Medical devices for combination use" and "Methods for use." In addition, for specific Biological Products, if parties involved in the healthcare industry dealing with specific Biological Products, such as doctors, are required to explain necessary items for effectiveness and safety as well as other items regarding proper use of such products to users of the products, describe as such.

12. Clinical performance
    Describe the clinical performance used for the application for approval, or the results of postmarket clinical studies, etc.

13. Storage methods and periods of use, etc.
    For storage methods, create sub-items and provide descriptions for the expiration (for single-use), the effective period and the expiration date (for medical devices requiring the setting of a durable period).

14. Precautions for handling
    If specific precautions for handling are detailed in standards or certificates of approval, certifications or notifications, describe those precautions. For specific Biological Broducts, provide a statement describing that parties involved in the healthcare industry dealing with specific Biological Products, such as doctors, must record the names,

addresses, etc. of the product's users and retain those records at medical institutions, etc.

15. Items regarding maintenance and inspection
For Designated Maintenance Control Medical Devices and those used multiple times, describe necessary measures for reuse (sterilization, operation and maintenance, and maintenance and inspection).

16. Conditions for approval
If specific conditions were given on the approval, describe those conditions.

17. Packaging
Describe the packaging unit.

18. Major literature and address(es) for requesting the literature
Enter the name and address of the party to whom requests for the literature should be directed.

19. Name and address of MAHs and manufacturers
Provide the name, address and telephone number of the MAH. In addition, provide the name of the manufacturer, and for medical devices manufactured at a foreign manufacturing site, the name of the country where the foreign manufacturing site is located and the manufacturer's name in English.

Related Documents Such as Instruction Manuals

For medical devices for which sufficient information cannot be provided with only package inserts, it is necessary to consider the nature of the device and create an "instruction manual" in addition to the package inserts. In this case, the following contents matched to the contents described in the package inserts should be described in the "instruction manual" if necessary.

- table of contents
- safety warnings and precautions
- overview of product and name and composition of each part and accessory
- methods of assembly and installation
- information regarding preparation before use
- general methods of use and related cautionary items
- special methods of use and related cautionary items
- information regarding processing after use
- information on medical device cleaning, changing consumable parts and storage methods
- information regarding maintenance and inspection
- information on troubleshooting
- technical specification
- descriptions and index of terminology
- information regarding safety education for parties involved in medical practice
- information regarding after-sales service and contact information

Advertising Regulations for Medical Devices

For medical devices for medical professionals, advertisements targeting the general public other than parties involved in medical practice are prohibited. In addition, even for medical devices for the general public, certain standards apply for the contents of advertisements, as is discussed later. Moreover, it is prohibited to advertise devices such as so-called health appliances as though they provide similar efficacies and effects as medical devices. The applicability of advertisements is determined mainly based upon the following three criteria (*Yakuhatsu* No. 1339 of October 9, Showa 55 (1980), *Standards for Fair Advertising Practice for Drug Products, etc.*):

- There is a clear intention to attract customers (to motivate them to make purchases).
- Brand names of Designated Drug Products, etc. (including medical devices) are clearly described.
- The information is made readily available to the general public.

Major Advertising Regulations Under the *Pharmaceutical Affairs Law*

There are three prohibitions based upon the *Pharmaceutical Affairs Law* and the notification (*Standards for Fair Advertising Practice for Drug Products, etc.*) for advertising regulations for medical devices, and the details are described in the *Standards for Fair Advertising Practice of Drug Products, etc.* The objective of these standards is "to prevent false or exaggerated advertisements (of drug products, quasi-drugs and cosmetics) and to ensure that advertisements are appropriate." It states that persons involved in advertisements of medical devices must ensure that correct information is provided to enable users to operate such medical devices properly. The three prohibitions are:

1. Prohibition of exaggerated advertisements
False or exaggerated advertisements regarding manufacturing methods, efficacies, effects or performance, and advertisements in which doctors, etc. guarantee such qualities, are prohibited. Please refer to the overview described in the *Standards for Fair Advertising Practice for Drug Products, etc.*

2. Restrictions on advertisements for the general public for medical devices for doctors
For medical devices other than those for the general public, advertisements on TV, radio, newspapers and the Internet are prohibited.

3. Prohibition of advertisements for medical devices prior to approval
Advertisements for medical devices prior to their approval are strictly prohibited. In addition, exhibitions, etc. at academic conferences are possible

so long as permission is acquired from the organizer, but the number of products and their allowable purpose are, of course, limited.

Standards for Fair Advertising Practice for Drug Products, etc.

The standards and their contents are described below. For actual examples of regulations or operational policies, please refer to the website of the Pharmaceutical Inspection Division of the Health and Safety Department of the Bureau of Social Welfare and Public Health, Tokyo (Tokyo Pharmaceutical Affairs (*Yakuji*) Index). http://www.fukushihoken.metro.tokyo.jp/joho/soshiki/anzen/yakuji/index.html.

In addition, if the advertiser operates in Tokyo, the Tokyo government provides consultations by appointment, so please check the website if necessary.

Items Related to Product Name

- Allowable name of medical devices requiring approval and certification
- Name other than approved or certified brand names or nomenclature may not be used.
- Allowable nomenclature of medical devices not requiring approval or certification
- Name other than nomenclature or brand names shall not be used. In addition, brand names shall not increase the risk of misunderstanding regarding manufacturing methods, efficacies and effects or safety.

Items Related to Manufacturing Methods

For the manufacturing methods of medical devices, etc., expressions that deviate from actual manufacturing methods or that may raise the risk of misunderstandings regarding excellence in quality shall not be used.

Items Related to Efficacies and Effects, Performance and Safety

- Allowable statements regarding efficacies and effects, etc. of medical devices requiring approval and certification
  Statements of efficacies and effects, etc. of medical devices requiring approval and certification shall not go beyond the scope of approved or certified efficacies and effects, etc. In addition, statements that especially emphasize only certain approved or certified efficacies and effects, etc. and lead to misunderstandings that the product is used for specific diseases shall not be used.
- Allowable statements regarding efficacies and effects, etc. of medical devices not requiring approval or certification
  Statements regarding medical devices not requiring

approval shall not go beyond the scope recognized in medicine and pharmacology.

- Allowable statements regarding raw materials, shapes, compositions and dimensions
  False statements regarding raw materials, shapes, compositions and dimensions, as well as advertisements using inaccurate statements, etc. that may raise the risk of misunderstanding on efficacies and effects or safety, shall not be used.
- Allowable statements regarding dosage and administration
  Regarding dosage and administration, advertisements that may raise the risk of misunderstanding regarding efficacies and effects or safety, that use statements beyond the approved scope for medical devices requiring approval and certification, or that use statements beyond the medically recognized scope or inaccurate statements, etc. for medical devices not requiring approval shall not be used.
- Prohibition of statements guaranteeing efficacies and effects or safety
  Regarding the efficacies and effects or safety of medical devices, statements indicating specific efficacies and effects, etc. or safety and guaranteeing their reliability shall not be used.
- Prohibition of superlative statements on efficacies and effects or safety or similar expressions
  Superlative statements or similar statements regarding efficacies and effects or safety shall not be used.
- Allowable statements regarding degree of expression of efficacies and effects
  Statements regarding quick-acting or sustainable properties of medical devices shall not go beyond the medically recognized scope.
- Prohibition of claims not recognized as the original efficacies and effects, etc.
  Regarding the efficacies and effects of medical devices, advertisements that may raise the risk of misunderstanding regarding efficacies and effects, etc. by claiming efficacies and effects not recognized as the product's original efficacies and effects shall not be used.

Restrictions on Advertisements That May Raise the Risk of Promoting Excessive Consumption or Improper Use of Medical Devices

Advertisements that may raise the risk of promoting excessive consumption or improper use of medical devices shall not be used.

Restrictions on Advertisements for Medical Devices for Doctors

1. For medical devices used by parties involved in

medical practice that may cause harm to health and hygiene if used by the general public, with the exception of those involving no concern of use by the general public, advertisements targeting the general public other than parties involved in medical practice shall not be used.

2. For medical devices provided for the purpose of being used by parties involved in medical practice, such as doctors, dentists and acupuncturists, that may cause harm to health and hygiene if used by the general public, with the exception of those involving no concern of use by the general public, the same restrictions described in the above paragraph 1 shall be applied.

Restrictions on Expressions Regarding Efficacies and Effects in Advertisements for the General Public

For diseases that are generally considered incurable without diagnosis or treatment conducted by doctors or dentists, statements indicating that such diseases can be cured without such diagnosis or treatment shall not be used for advertisements for the general public other than parties involved in medical practice.

Items Regarding Precautions for Use and Handling to be Appended or Added to Advertisements of Drug Products, etc.

When advertising medical devices that require special precautions for use and handling, such items or notes for precautions for use and handling should be appended or added.

Restrictions on Libelous Advertisements Against Products of Other Companies

Regarding the quality, efficacies and effects and safety, etc. of medical devices, libelous advertisements against a competitor's products shall not be used. (In addition, caution is required as some comparisons of facts, such as product performance, may be considered libelous advertisements).

Endorsements From Parties Involved in Medical Industry

Advertisements in which parties involved in the drug industry, hairdressers, beauticians, hospitals or clinics, or public offices, schools or organizations that may considerably influence the views of others regarding the efficacies and effects, etc. of drug products, etc., designate, authorize, recommend, instruct or select and use the product shall not be used.

Restrictions on Advertisements With Prizes and Gifts, etc.

- Advertisements for medical devices or corporations

using methods promoting the gambling spirit, such as excessive prizes and gifts, etc., shall not be used.
- As a rule, advertisements indicating that medical devices shall be granted as prizes or gifts shall not be used.
- Advertisements indicating that medical devices shall be exchanged for medical device containers or packaging shall not be used.

Restrictions on Expressions Causing Discomfort and Anxiety

Advertisements for medical devices using statements that may increase the risk of causing discomfort or anxiety and fear shall not be used.

Handling of Advertisements on Sponsored Programs on Television and Radio

- Performers shall not mention or imply the quality, efficacies and effects or safety of specific medical devices in sponsored programs on television or radio or at cinemas or theatres, etc.
- Particular caution is required to ensure that false information on medical devices is not provided in sponsored programs for children on television and radio.

Restrictions on Expressions Regarding Use of Medical Devices as Beauty or Health Appliances

Advertisements that promote easy use of medical devices for consumers by promoting the use of the devices as beauty or health appliances shall not be used.

Guarantee of Integrity of Medical Devices

In addition to the contents specified in the previous clauses, advertisements that may significantly damage the integrity or the reputation of a medical device shall not be used.

Regulatory Government Offices and Penalties

The government regulatory agencies directly involved in advertisements and indications of medical devices are the governments of the respective prefectures where businesses are located. Penalties are summarized in Article 11 of the *Pharmaceutical Affairs Law*. If products do not satisfy the legal requirements for indications, voluntary recalls are usually conducted.

In addition, a fine between ¥1–2 million or imprisonment for one to two years will be imposed as penalties on the MAH of the product.

Summary

- Labeling for medical devices is required on labels, package inserts and immediate containers. Labeling must be described clearly in legible script and in Japanese. In addition, package inserts, advertisements and promotional materials must properly reflect the contents of approval, certifications and licenses.

- For medical devices for doctors, advertisements targeting the general public are prohibited.
- Advertisements of unapproved medical devices are prohibited.
- If the regulations on indications and advertisements are violated, penalties for the operators may result and product recalls, etc. may be required.

Related Notifications

- *Yakukan* No. 309 of October 30, Showa 39 (1964), *Labeling of patents*
- *Yakuhatsu* No. 1136 of December 15, Showa 45 (1970), *Handling of acupressure devices*
- *Yakukan* No. 28 of February 2, Showa 47 (1972), *Scope of efficacy of medical apparatus*
- *Yakuhatsu* No. 1339 of October 9, Showa 55 (1980), *Standards for fair advertising practice for drug products, etc.*
- *Yakukanhatsu* No. 121 of October 9, Showa 55 (1980), *Standards for fair advertising practice for drug products, etc.*
- *Yakukan* No. 62 of November 5, Showa 51 (1976), *Handling of medical devices (vibrators)*
- *Yakuhatsu* No. 127 of February 13, Heisei 1 (1989), *Presentation of unapproved medical devices at exhibitions, etc.*
- *Jimurenraku* of February 13, Heisei 1 (1989), *Presentation of unapproved medical devices at exhibitions, etc. (Q&A)*
- *Yakukan* No. 56 of October 19, Heisei 4 (1992), *Advertisements for devices for generating medical materials*
- *Iyakukan* No. 104 of December 25, Heisei 9 (1997), *Handling of combination drug products, etc.*
- *Jimurenraku* of December 25, Heisei 9 (1997), *Handling of combination drug products, etc.*
- *Iyakukan* No. 60 of March 31, Heisei 10 (1998), *Advertisements for drug products, etc.*
- *Iyakukan* No. 148 of September 29, Heisei 10 (1998), *Applicability of advertisements for drug products, etc. under the Pharmaceutical Affairs Law*
- *Iyakuhatsu* No. 968 of November 5, Heisei 10 (1998), *Handling of advertisements for drug products, etc.*
- *Jimurenraku* of November 5, Heisei 10 (1998), *Operations of inspections and guidance regarding advertisements for drug products, etc.*
- *Iyakukan* No. 65 of June 30, Heisei 11 (1999),

Handling of provision of information for recruiting subjects for clinical trials
- *Iyakukanmahatsu* No. 50 of January 31, Heisei 13 (2001), *Handling of provision of information for recruiting subjects for clinical trials*
- *Iyakushinhatsu* No. 139 and PFSB/CND Notification No.123 of February 27, Heisei 13 (2001), *Handling of nasal washers*
- *Iyakushinhatsu* No. 0206001 and *Iyakukanmahatsu* No. 0206001 of February 6, Heisei 14 (2002), *Handling of bleaching materials for tooth surfaces using peroxide*
- *Iyakuhatsu* No. 0328009 of March 28, Heisei 14 (2002), *Partial amendments of standards for fair advertising practice for drug products, etc.*
- *Yakushokuhatsu* No. 0720022 of July 20, Heisei 16 (2004), *Enforcement of Highly Controlled Medical Devices, Controlled Medical Devices, and General Medical Devices (announcement) specified by the Minister of Health, Labour and Welfare based on the provisions of Article 2, Paragraphs 5 to 7 of the Pharmaceutical Affairs Law and Designated Maintenance Control Medical Devices (announcement) specified by the Minister of Health, Labour and Welfare based on the provisions of Article 2, Paragraph 8 of the Pharmaceutical Affairs Law*
- *Yakushokuhatsu* No. 0310003 of March 10, Heisei 17 (2005), *Guidance for descriptions on package inserts for medical devices*
- *Promotion Code of the Medical Devices Industry* (enacted 28 January 1997 by the Japan Federation of Medical Devices Associations, final revision on 15 March Heisei 17 (2005)) (Voluntary industrial regulations)

References

- Compliance Division, Pharmaceutical Affairs Bureau, Ministry of Health and Welfare and Pharmaceutical Affairs Division, Bureau of Public Health, Tokyo Metropolitan Government (eds.), *Facts on Advertisements for Drug Products and Cosmetics, etc. (1994),*" Jiho, 1994
- Pharmaceutical Inspections Study Group (ed.), *Facts on Advertisements for Drug Products and Cosmetics, etc. (Supplement for 2002)*, Jiho, 2002

Chapter 43

Japanese Applications for Medical Devices

OBJECTIVES

❏ To understand the scope of medical devices.

❏ To understand the product review process for each medical device classification.

❏ To understand the process from application to approval.

❏ To understand the complete set of documents for applications for approval.

RELATED LAWS AND REGULATIONS

❏ *Pharmaceutical Affairs Law* (Law No. 145 of Showa 35 (1960))

❏ *Pharmaceutical Affairs Law, Enforcement Ordinance* (Government Ordinance No. 1 of Showa 36 (1961))

❏ *Pharmaceutical Affairs Law, Enforcement Regulations* (Ministry of Health and Welfare Ordinance No. 1 of Showa 36 (1961))

❏ *Highly Controlled Medical Devices, Controlled Medical Devices, General Medical Devices specified by the Minister of Health, Labour and Welfare based on the provisions of Article 2, Paragraphs 5 to 7 of the Pharmaceutical Affairs Law* (Ministry of Health, Labour and Welfare Announcement No. 298 of Heisei 16 (2004)) (Announcement on Classification)

❏ *Designated Medical Devices for which the Minister of Health, Labour and Welfare has Established Standards Based on the Provisions of Article 23-2, Paragraph 1 of the Pharmaceutical Affairs Law* (Ministry of Health, Labour and Welfare Announcement No. 112 of Heisei 17 (2005))

Introduction

This chapter describes the stipulated procedures for each medical device classification for marketing medical devices regulated by the *Pharmaceutical Affairs Law*, as well as the reviews conducted in the process from application to approval or certification.

What are medical devices?

In Article 2, Paragraph 4 of the *Pharmaceutical Affairs Law*, medical devices are defined as "machinery or appliances, etc. used for the purpose of diagnosing, treating or preventing disease in a human or animal, or for the purpose of affecting the bodily structures or functions of a human or animal, and that are specified in Ministerial Ordinances." Medical devices' intended use is the same as those of drug products, and they are defined as products with differing configurations.

Compared to drug products, there is greater variety in configurations, methods of use and raw materials. Familiar diagnostic devices include thermometers and blood pressure monitors as well as large magnetic resonance imaging (MRI) and computed tomography (CT) devices or film for image diagnosis.

Medical devices for therapy or treatment include a variety of products, including disposable devices to be used only once, such as syringes and needles and urinary, digestive and vascular tubes; electronic medical equipment, such

Table 43-1. Differences in Product Reviews by Classification

Classification	Regulatory Path	Review Body
I: General Medical Devices	No approval or certification required (Notification/Self-certification)	N/A
II: Controlled Medical Devices	Product Certification (Products compliant with certification standards)	Recognized Certification Body
III: Highly Controlled Medical Devices	Product approval from Minister of Health, Labour and Welfare	PMDA
IV: Highly Controlled Medical Devices		

as artificial respirators, anesthetic machines and heart-lung machines; and implantable pacemakers and artificial hearts. The degree of invasiveness to patients also varies.

Medical devices also include those used for the purpose of prevention, such as oral cleaning kits and other dental devices related to preventing cavities. Elastic panty horses used for the purpose of reducing or preventing hemostasis in the limbs are also medical devices.

Recently, autologous cultured epidermises that consist of actual cells have also been approved as medical devices.

Overview of Premarket Product Review Systems
Product Review Systems by Medical Device Classification

Parties wishing to market a medical device must receive an approval or a certification by going through reviews for each product, or must go through these processes by filing a notification. Under the revised *Pharmaceutical Affairs Law* implemented in April 2005, a risk-based classification system was introduced for medical devices (Ministry of Health, Labour and Welfare Announcement No. 298 of 2004, *Yakushokuhatsu* No. 0720022 of July 20, Heisei 16 (2004)). The product reviews shown in **Table 43-1** are implemented according to these classifications.

The product reviews involve confirming the safety and effectiveness of each medical device, as well as whether appropriate systems for manufacturing control and safety management are in place. In order to manufacture and market such a medical device, regardless of its class, it is necessary to acquire Marketing Authorization Holder (MAH) licenses (Article 12, Paragraph 1 of the *Pharmaceutical Affairs Law*). However, there are different classes of MAH licenses. A Type III MAH license for medical devices is required for handling only general medical devices, a Type II MAH license for handling Controlled Medical Devices, and a Type I MAH license for handling Highly Controlled Medical Devices.

Comparison With Product Review Systems in Foreign Countries

As in Japan, product reviews of medical devices in other

countries or regions are handled differently depending upon the medical device's classification. Because the Japanese medical device classification rules refer to the GHTF rules, the Japanese classifications closely resemble those used in Europe, upon which the latter are based.

Product reviews for marketing authorization in Japan include quality management system (QMS) conformity inspections for manufacturing sites, which are similar to the product review system of Premarket Approval Original (first application of a PMA filing) in the US.

In the US, Class I and some Class II products are handled under General Controls and notification and Class II products are handled under Special Controls, specifically an application (premarket notification) known as a 510(k). The product premarket notifications are reviewed for any substantial equivalence with existing medical devices and given clearance by the US Food and Drug Administration (FDA). For Class III devices (equivalent to Class IV and some Class III devices in Japan), product reviews are conducted based upon PMA applications. For Original PMAs, an on-site Quality System Regulation (QSR) inspection is conducted for manufacturing sites based on QSR and Good Manufacturing Practice (GMP) requirements, and if there are no problems, approval is ultimately granted.

In the EU, document reviews for products are only conducted for Class III (equivalent to Class IV in Japan) and for Class IIa and IIb. After being reviewed as the first product in a certain category, products under the same category are only confirmed in the annual Conformity Assessment Surveillance. All of these products are reviewed by a third party organization known as a "Notified Body."

Product Notification System

For general devices (with the exception of those clearly different from existing medical devices), a product notification is submitted for each product to PMDA (Article 14, Paragraphs 9 and 10 of the *Pharmaceutical Affairs Law*). The items in the notification form are as shown in **Table 43-2**, and additional proposals are attached (Article 70 and Form No. 39(3) of the *Pharmaceutical Affairs Law, Enforcement Regulations*). Because the details of each item

Table 43-2. Product Notification Items

• Type of marketing authorization holder license	• Product specifications
• License number and date of marketing authorization holder license	• Operational methods or methods of use
• Medical device classification	• Manufacturing methods
• Names (general nomenclature, brand name)	• Storage method and shelf life
• Intended use and its efficacy or effects	• Manufacturing sites of the product
• Shape, structure and principles	• Manufacturing sites of the raw materials
• Raw materials or component parts	• Remarks

From Form No. 39(3) of the Pharmaceutical Affairs Law, Enforcement Regulations.

in the forms are substantially similar, please refer to the section on applications for approval.

Product Certification System

In April 2005, a Third-party Certification System was introduced based upon Article 23, Paragraph 2 of the *Pharmaceutical Affairs Law.* Under this system, instead of by the government, "Recognized Certification Bodies," stipulated in Article 23, Paragraph 2 of the *Pharmaceutical Affairs Law,* are contracted to conduct product reviews and confirmations of conformity with Essential Requirements (described below) for specified devices for which the Minister of Health, Labour and Welfare has established standards. The standards are also referred to as "Conformity Assessment Standards for Certification," and medical devices subject to these standards are specified in an announcement from the Ministry of Health, Labour and Welfare (Ministry of Health, Labour and Welfare Announcement No. 112 of Heisei 17 (2005)). Because the medical devices are specified as Controlled Medical Devices (Class II), they are referred to as "Specified Controlled Medical Devices." In addition, because those devices are reviewed for conformance to the certification standards, they are also referred to as "certification products."

Recognized certification bodies apply for registration with the Minister of Health, Labour and Welfare and renew their registration every three years. Requirements for registration include: (1) compliance with ISO/IEC Guide 62/65, (2) independence from marketing authorization holders and (3) nonapplicability of applicant disqualification clauses.

When an MAH applies for product certification with a recognized certification body, the recognized certification body assesses conformity to the certification standards and QMS. If the product under application is not in compliance with the certification standards, Article 2-2, Paragraph 23 of the *Pharmaceutical Affairs Law* says the recognized certification body must not grant certification, and so the medical device must apply for product approval instead of certification. If certification is granted, this is reported to

PMDA. After certification, periodic follow-up audits are conducted by the recognized certification body.

The certification standards comprise the nomenclature of the medical device, the Japanese Industrial Standards (JIS) as technical standards, the intended use and the efficacy or effects. In addition to the certification standards, a checklist for confirming conformity to "Essential Requirements" stipulated based upon the provisions of Article 41, Paragraph 3 of the *Pharmaceutical Affairs Law* has also been formulated and released.

As of 1 April 2009, conformity assessment standards for certification have been enacted for 413 types of devices. Further, based upon the "Action Program for Accelerating Review Process of Medical Devices" released by MHLW in December 2008, deliberations are underway with the aim of placing, as a rule, all controlled devices under a certification system by the end of Fiscal 2011.

Product Approval System
Application for Product Approval

Based upon Article 14 of the *Pharmaceutical Affairs Law,* Highly Controlled Medical Devices, as well as Controlled Medical Devices (Class II products with no certification standards) and new medical devices, etc. for which a nomenclature has not been determined, must receive approval from the Minister of Health, Labour and Welfare for each product before marketing. When filing an application for product approval for a Specified Controlled Medical Device that does not conform to the certification standards, it is necessary to describe how the device does not conform to the relevant certification standards in the Remarks field of the application for approval and to attach information explaining the nonconformity.

PMDA conducts product reviews for approval based upon the provisions of Article 14, Paragraph 2 of the *Pharmaceutical Affairs Law,* and the Minister of Health, Labour and Welfare grants approval by referring to the results of the review by PMDA.

The MAH submits an application for product approval to PMDA and attaches information and supporting data proving that the device's efficacy and safety have been demonstrated based upon Article 40, Paragraph 1 of the *Pharmaceutical Affairs Law, Enforcement Regulations.*

On 1 April 2009, the submission categories were reconsidered and modified to "New medical devices," "Improved medical devices" and "Generic (*Kohatsu*) medical devices." A device that has approval standards and conforms to those standards is defined as a "Generic (*Kohatsu*) medical device (with approval standards, no clinical data)." For details regarding the handling, etc. of submission categories, please refer to *Yakushokuhatsu* No. 0327006 and *Yakushokukihatsu* No. 0327001 of March 27, Heisei 21 (2009).

Process up to Approval

Product approval reviews include assessments of the efficacy and safety (document-based review), conformity assessment of the application materials (reliability studies) and QMS conformity assessment inspections of the manufacturing sites (**Figure 43-1**). After the MAH submits an application to PMDA, in tandem with the product reviews (Office of Medical Devices I and II), reliability study (Office of Conformity Audit) and QMS conformity inspections based upon the application for the inspection are conducted (Office of Compliance and Standards of PMDA, or prefectural government).

New Medical Devices and Review Process Thereof

"New medical devices" refers to devices with clearly different structures, purposes of use, efficacies, effects or performance from those of devices that have already been approved (excluding those for which the reexamination period stipulated in Article 14-4, Paragraph 1, Sections 1 and 2 has not passed; henceforth referred to as "approved medical devices"), (*Yakushokuhatsu* No. 0327006 of March 27, Heisei 21 (2009)).

New medical devices undergo PMDA review, and then the Medical Devices and In Vitro Diagnostics Subcommittee of the Pharmaceutical Affairs and Food Hygiene Council discusses whether approval should be granted, after which a report is submitted to the Committee on Pharmaceutical Affairs of the Pharmaceutical Affairs and Food Hygiene Council. For medical devices with substantial novelty compared to approved medical devices, further discussion is conducted in the Pharmaceutical Affairs Committee.

The overall product review processes from application to approval are shown in **Table 43-3**.

Figure 43-1. Review Process with PMDA

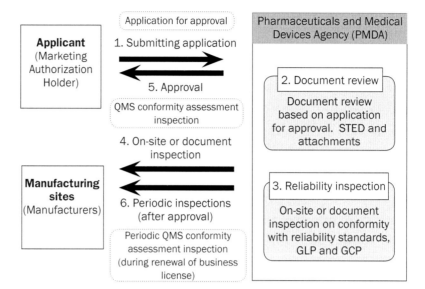

QMS inspections and reliability studies are conducted in tandem with product reviews of the confirmation stage to the assessment stage.

Since Fiscal 2009, performance goals have been set under the Action Program for accelerating the review process. For traditional review products, a reduction of seven months in the review period by Fiscal 2013 is being targeted by setting goals of 14 months of the total review period from application to approval and seven months each for the government and the applicant (median values in approval cohorts hereafter). For a product that is eligible for Priority Review, goals of 10 months for the total review period, six months for the government and four months for the applicant have been set as a goal for Fiscal 2013.

What are Generic Product Reviews?

In April 2009, product reviews of generic devices were introduced. The reviews of generic medical devices are to assess efficacy and safety by indicating equivalence with existing products and were introduced to streamline reviews.

"Generic medical devices" are medical devices recognized as having identical structures, intended use, efficacies, effects and performance as existing medical devices. In other words, they refer to devices that have substantially equivalent structures, intended use, efficacies, effects and performance as existing medical devices (*Yakushokuhatsu* No. 0327006 of March 27, Heisei 21 (2009)).

When filing an application for approval of a generic device, the areas of difference (henceforth referred to as "differences") compared to existing medical devices must be clarified to explain how the device is substantially equivalent (*Yakushokukihatsu* No. 0327004 of March 27, Heisei 21 (2009)).

Table 43-3. Process From Application to Approval for New Medical Devices

Confirmation Stage	• Application for approval (PMDA reception)
	• First interview (presentation)
	• (Specialist discussion (conducted in cases in which it is necessary to clarify review policies))
	• Delivery of main homework questions
Assessment Stage	• Responses from applicant regarding the questions
	• Specialist discussion
	• Delivery of inquiries related to specialist discussion
Approval Stage	• Responses from applicant regarding the inquiries
	• Preparation of review report
	• Substitution
	• Notification of review results
	• Medical Devices and In Vitro Diagnostics Subcommittee
	• Enactment (approval)

Whether a device is determined to be in the generic medical device category is based upon the following:

- The basic structure and principles are substantially equivalent with those of approved medical devices.
- With the exception of any specific operational procedures, etc. to the device itself, the area of use, basic techniques of use and operating procedures are substantially equivalent.
- The intended use and efficacy or effects are substantially equivalent to those of approved medical devices.
- The fact that the differences do not affect quality, efficacy or safety can be confirmed based upon established and publicly known test methods (except animal tests (other than biological safety tests pursuant to JIS T 0993) or clinical trials) used for approved medical devices, or based upon other findings.
- As an overview, it is generally deemed that the risks of the product under application are equivalent to those of approved medical devices based upon the results of design verification and validation.

In other words, when the differences between approved medical devices and the product under application are clarified and the differences do not exceed the scope of existing medical devices, the submission category of generic medical device is applicable. The target review period for generic medical devices in Fiscal 2013 is four months for the total review period from application to approval, three months for the government review and one month for the applicant.

Improved Medical Devices

In April 2009, the category of "Improved medical devices" was introduced. Improved medical devices are medical devices that are neither new devices nor generic ones. In other words, the term refers to devices that are not so novel as to receive an instruction for reexamination, but do not have substantially equivalent structures, intended use, efficacies, effect or performance as existing medical devices (*Yakushokuhatsu* No. 0327006, *Yakushokukihatsu* No. 0327001 of March 27, Heisei 21 (2009)). When the application is filed with clinical data as attachments related to the descriptions of differences from approved medical devices, the application is categorized as "Improved medical device (with clinical results);" applications with no attachments of clinical data are categorized as "Improved medical device (no approval standards, no clinical results)." Depending upon the contents of the application, expert panel meetings may be held.

The target review period for improved medical devices (with clinical results) for Fiscal 2013 is 10 months for the total review period from application to approval, six months for the government review and four months for the applicant, or, for improved medical devices (no clinical results), six months for the total review period, four months for the government review and two months for the applicant.

Essential Requirements, etc.
Essential Requirements

The "Essential Requirements" are the "Essential Requirements of Safety and Performance of Medical Devices (Essential Principles)" and were devised based upon GHTF's Essential Requirements, which recommend international harmonization for regulatory systems for medical devices. GHTF proposes the acceptance of the Summary Technical Document (STED), which is a template for materials that includes considerations of the Essential Requirements for legal amendments or enactments, as well as explanations of conformity to the Essential Requirements. The details of STEDs will be described later.

In Japan, it was announced as *Standards for medical devices designated by the Minister of Health, Labour and Welfare based on the provisions of Article 41, Paragraph 3 of the Pharmaceutical Affairs Law* (Announcement No. 122 of March 29, Heisei 17 (2005)), which stipulates basic requirements for the quality, efficacy and safety of all medical devices. Therefore, when filing an application for marketing authorization (approval or certification), demonstration of conformity to the Essential Requirements is required.

The Essential Requirements are composed of the general requirements of Chapter 1 (Articles 1–6) and the design and manufacturing requirements of Chapter 2 (Articles 7–16). Until 31 March 2008, only Chapter 1 was applied, but full-scale enforcement began on 1 April 2008.

If there are any appropriate specifications, standards, etc. to show the conformity to each of the provisions of the Essential Requirements, it is possible to utilize and show them, but if there are any other reasonable methods, it is not necessarily required to conduct the tests and reviews stipulated in particular specifications, standards, etc. If there are no specifications, standards, etc. to which to refer, it is necessary to describe the test methods, etc. used for proving conformity to the Essential Requirements and to explain how the obtained test results can demonstrate conformity to them.

For medical devices, etc. not requiring approval or certification (Class I), when filing a notification of the marketing authorization, the MAH must confirm conformity with the Essential Requirements.

The following are excerpts from the Essential Requirements.

Chapter 1: General Requirements
Article 1 (Design)
Design and manufacturing shall be implemented so that, in cases of proper use, no harm shall be caused to the patient's clinical state or safety and no damage shall be caused to a user or third party's safety or health.

Article 2 (Risk Management)
Safety must be ensured based upon the latest technologies. Moreover, hazardous risks must be managed so that remaining risks related to various hazards may be determined to be within an acceptable scope.

Article 3 (Performance and Functions of Medical Devices)
Medical devices must successfully exhibit the intended performance and must be designed, manufactured and packaged so they may perform the functions of a medical device.

Article 4 (Product Lifecycle)
If a medical device is operated under normal usage conditions and appropriately maintained within the scope of the product lifecycle, the performance and functions must not be adversely affected to a degree causing threats to the health and safety of patients, users and third parties.

Article 5 (Transportation and Storage, etc.)
A medical device shall be designed, manufactured and packaged so that if it is transported and stored under conditions in accordance with instructions and information from the manufacturing distributor, etc. and used based on the intended methods of use, its performance and functions will not deteriorate.

Article 6 (Effectiveness of Medical Devices)
A medical device's intended effectiveness shall exceed potential failures.

Chapter 2: Requirements for Design and Manufacturing
Article 7 (Chemical Properties, etc. of Medical Devices)
This article specifies caution regarding the chemical, physical and biological properties of a device.

Article 8 (Prevention of Microbial Contamination, etc.)
Infections and microbial contamination should be eliminated or reduced.

Article 9 (Manufacturing and Environmental Properties)
Risks should be eliminated or reduced through risk management.

Article 10 (Considerations for Measurement or Diagnostic Functions)
This article describes appropriate cautions and guarantees for medical devices or in vitro diagnostics having diagnostic or measurement functions.

Article 11 (Protection Against Radiation)
Appropriate levels of radiation and reduction of patient radiation exposure should be secured.

Article 12 (Considerations for Active Medical Devices)
This article sets requirements for medical devices or in vitro diagnostics connected to energy sources or equipped with energy sources.

Article 13 (Considerations for Mechanical Hazards)

This article discusses protection against mechanical risks.

Article 14 (Considerations for Medical Devices Supplying Energy)

This article describes protection against risks posed to patients by supplied energy or substances used in medical devices.

Article 15 (Considerations for Self-inspection Medical Devices)

This article presents protective measures for risks posed to patients by medical devices and in vitro diagnostics for self-inspections or equipment for self-medication

Article 16 (Performance assessments)

All data collected for conducting performance assessments of medical devices must be collected according to laws and regulations related to pharmaceutical affairs, and clinical trials must be conducted according to the *Ministerial Ordinances on GCP*.

Approval Standards

There are two types of approval standards, which include *Standards regarding quality, etc. of medical devices, based upon Article 42, Paragraph 2 of the Pharmaceutical Affairs Law* based upon the MHLW announcement, and the approval standards based upon notifications from the director of MHLW's Pharmaceutical and Food Safety Bureau. These were prepared so that the product review can be accelerated by confirming compliance with those standards and, as of November 2009, approval standards had been prepared and used for six products under the MHLW announcements and 38 products under the notifications from the director of the Pharmaceutical and Food Safety Bureau.

Unlike other submission categories, application fees for the category "Generic medical device (with approval standards)" are relatively inexpensive.

Approval standards are those related to medical devices to be used for product reviews by confirming conformity to them. As of November 2009, standards had been prepared and used for 38 products.

The submission category for a product to conform to the approval standards is "Generic medical device (with approval standards, no clinical results)."

Approval standards are comprised of technical standards and Essential Requirements formulated based upon international standards, etc., and are stipulated for products not required for attachments regarding clinical trial results. The standards are mainly composed of the following items:

- Scope of the standard
  - Subject medical devices are specified using their nomenclature.
- Technical standards

- Based upon relevant JIS, ISO/IEC, FDA guidance, etc., performance, functions, effectiveness, etc. are stipulated.
- Intended use and efficacy or effects
- The intended use and efficacies or effects subject to standards are limited.
- Checklist for conformity to the Essential Requirements

A checklist for confirming conformity with the *Standards for medical devices specified by the Minister of Health, Labour and Welfare based on the provisions of Article 41, Paragraph 3 of the Pharmaceutical Affairs Law* (Ministry of Health, Labour and Welfare Announcement No. 122 of Heisei 17 (2005)) has been prepared.

In addition, products subject to approval standards are limited to the range of existing medical devices (generic medical devices) for which clinical trials are not required.

For details on certification standards, please refer to the section on "Product certification system" in this chapter.

Reliability Studies

Based upon the latter clauses of Article 14, Paragraph 3 of the *Pharmaceutical Affairs Law*, when materials regarding a medical device's quality, effectiveness and safety are attached, the reliability of the application materials must be ensured based upon Article 43 of the *Pharmaceutical Affairs Law, Enforcement Regulations*.

Reliability studies are conducted to determine whether materials attached to applications (materials of applications for approval or materials of applications for reexamination and reassessment) have been collected and prepared in accordance with the standards stipulated by the Minister of Health, Labour and Welfare, which are the GLP for medical devices (Ministry of Health, Labour and Welfare Ordinance No. 37 of March 23, Heisei 17 (2005), *Ministerial Ordinance on Standards for Good Laboratory Practice for Safety of Medical Devices*), GCP for medical devices (Ministry of Health, Labour and Welfare Ordinance No. 36 of March 23, Heisei 17 (2005), *Ministerial Ordinance on Standards for Clinical Trials for Medical Devices*), GPSP for medical devices (Ministry of Health, Labour and Welfare Ordinance No. 38 of March 23, Heisei 17 (2005), *Ministerial Ordinance on Standards for Good Postmarketing Study Practice and Clinical Practice for Medical Devices*) and the following *Reliability Standards for Application Materials (Article 43 of the Pharmaceutical Affairs Law, Enforcement Regulations)*:

- The materials must be accurately prepared based upon results obtained in investigations or tests conducted for the purpose of preparing the application materials.
- If investigation results, test results, etc. raising doubt over the quality, effectiveness or safety of the

medical device under application are found, studies and assessments must be conducted regarding the relevant investigation results, test results, etc., and the results must be described in the application materials.

- Supporting materials providing the basis for the application materials must be stored until the date of an action granting or withholding approval under the regulations of Article 14 of the law. However, this need not apply if it is recognized that storage is significantly difficult due to the nature of the materials.

Application for Product Approval
Items Described in Applications for Approval

The format of an application for product approval (Form No. 22(3) of the *Pharmaceutical Affairs Law, Enforcement Regulations*) is shown in **Figure 43-2**.

The items described in each field of the application for product approval are determined based upon the following. For details, please refer to *Yakushokuki* No. 0216001 of February 16, Heisei 17 (2005).

Product Category Field

Describe the product category according to Appendix 1 of the *Pharmaceutical Affairs Law, Enforcement Ordinance.* Determine the applicability under each classification by referring to the attachments of *Yakushokuhatsu* No. 072022 of July 20, Heisei 16 (2004), *Enforcement of Highly Controlled Medical Devices, Controlled Medical Devices, and General Medical Devices specified by the Minister of Health, Labour and Welfare according to the provisions of Article 2, Paragraphs 5-7 of the Pharmaceutical Affairs Law (Announcement), and Designated Maintenance Control Medical Devices specified by the Minister of Health, Labour and Welfare according to the provisions of Article 2, Paragraph 8 of the Pharmaceutical Affairs Law (Announcement) (Notification on Classification).*

If multiple categories are applicable to the product, enter the category of the medical devices classified as having the highest risk among those products, and if there are multiple medical devices categorized as having the highest risk, enter the category determined based upon the main performance.

Name (Nomenclature/Trade Name) Field

Determine and enter the nomenclature based upon the definitions in the attachment to the *Notification on Classification*. If there is no applicable nomenclature at the time of application, leave the field blank, and in the Remarks field of the application, describe an overview of the medical device (around 300 characters) and describe which of the classification rules in the *Notification on Classification* are likely to apply.

The trade name shall not raise the risk of misunderstandings regarding the medical device's performance, etc.

and possible harm to health and hygiene, and shall be respectful. Moreover, names indicating other end-usages shall not be recognized. In principle, a single name is used for a single item, but if an application is filed for a single item with multiple names based upon valid reasons, explanatory materials shall be attached to the application. In this case, it is necessary to file an application for product approval for each trade name.

Intended Use and Efficacy or Effects Field

For the intended use of the product, provide adequate descriptions of the intended patients and disease names, the situations of use, the expected effects, etc. Describe the efficacy or effects as necessary.

Shape, Structure and Principles Field

Provide concrete and detailed descriptions regarding the outer shape of the medical device, its structure, each composition unit, electrical specifications, the functions, etc. of each part and details regarding products. For the principles for meeting the device's intended use, provide a description using a block diagram, etc. for electronic medical equipment. If there are supplementary functions, describe the details thereof.

Raw Materials or Component Parts Field

Accurately describe raw materials, etc. so as to clarify their corresponding relationships with the details described in the Shape, Structure and Principles field, and articulate the specifications. However, for parts or materials that do not come into contact (either directly or indirectly) with blood, biological fluids, mucous membrane, etc. and do not greatly affect performance, a simple description is sufficient. For descriptions of raw materials, it is preferable that the descriptions be made with reference to the *Jimurenraku* (Medical Device Review No. 19).

For human or animal tissue or products derived from such tissue, consider the possibility of infections caused by pathogens and set necessary specifications for raw materials. In particular, provide details regarding methods for selecting donors and animals, reviews of viruses, inactivation methods, etc.

For raw materials derived from cows, etc., describe the country of origin, region, processing method and, as necessary, information regarding Transmissible Spongiform Encephalopathy (TSE) materials along with other items required from the perspective of securing quality and safety.

For raw materials derived from humans or animals, describe the derivation, details of donor screening and other items required from the perspective of securing quality and safety.

Product Specifications Field

From the perspectives of quality, safety and effectiveness, describe items that do not fall under Shape, Structure

Figure 43-2. Form for Application for Premarket Approval (Form No. 22 (3) (Items Related to Article 38))

Application for Premarket Approval for Medical Devices

Revenue Stamp

Classification		
Name	General nomenclature	
	Trade name	
Intended use and efficacy or effects		
Shape, Structure, and Principles		
Raw materials or component parts		
Product specifications		
Operational methods or methods of use		
Manufacturing method		
Storage method and shelf life		

Manufacturing site of product to be manufactured and marketed	Name	Location	License classification or Certification classification	License number or Certification number

Manufacturing site of raw materials	Name	Location	License classification or Certification classification	License number or Certification number

| Remarks | |

Based on the above information, we hereby file this application for approval for the manufacturing and marketing of medical devices.

[Date]

Address (Location of head office in case of a corporation)

Name (Name or name of representative in case of a corporation)

To: the Minister of Health, Labour and Welfare

and Principles from among the product's required design specifications. These details are primarily obtained during the design verification stage and guarantee the quality, effectiveness and safety of the product being manufacturing and marketed, and specifications, etc. required from the perspectives of quality, safety (including physical, chemical and biological safety) and effectiveness (performance, functions) are set.

If no specifications or standards can be cited to be referred to, test methods also must be set. In this case, include important specifications, etc. requiring confirmation during the manufacturing process.

Operational Methods and Methods of Use Field

Describe operational methods or methods of use sequentially and in an easy-to-understand manner using diagrams, etc. as necessary. For unsterilized products that require sterilization before use, describe as such along with sterilization methods and sterilization conditions (including agents, gases, etc.).

Table 43-4. Items Described in Each Attachment

A. Materials regarding background of origin or discovery, and status of use overseas, etc.	1. Materials regarding background of origin or development 2. Status of use overseas 3. Comparison with similar medical devices
B. Materials regarding setting of specifications	1. Materials regarding specifications and setting of specifications
C. Materials regarding stability and durability	1. Materials regarding stability and durability
D. Materials regarding conformity with standards stipulated in Article 41, Paragraph 3 of the Law	1. Materials regarding declarations of conformity to Essential Requirements 2. Materials regarding conformity to Essential Requirements
E. Materials regarding performance	1. Materials regarding tests corroborating performance and safety 2. Materials regarding tests corroborating efficacy 3. Materials regarding tests corroborating methods of use
F. Materials regarding risk analysis	1. Materials regarding systems for implementing risk analysis 2. Materials regarding important hazards
G. Materials regarding manufacturing methods	1. Materials regarding manufacturing processes and manufacturing facilities 2. Materials regarding sterilization methods 3. Materials regarding quality control
H. Materials regarding clinical trial results	1. Materials regarding test results of clinical trials 2. Investigation plans (proposals) regarding records of use, etc. of new medical devices

If a product is used in combination with other products, describe operational methods including the devices to be used in combination. For medical devices to be resterilized and used repeatedly, describe as such along with resterilization methods.

Manufacturing Method Field

In principle, descriptions should cover all aspects from the process of receiving parts to the process of shipment determination. The scope of processes to be described shall be that in which manufacturing and quality control are implemented in the quality system for the product (however, from the receiving process onward, if some processes are outsourced to another manufacturing site, include the contracted manufacturing site). For sterile medical devices, describe sterilization methods, etc. Also describe the names and locations, etc. of operators performing design verification and the test sites of external testing institutions.

In cases of manufacturing using raw materials derived from humans or animals, describe methods for processes for inactivating or eliminating bacteria, fungi, viruses, etc. during the manufacturing process along with other required items from the perspective of securing quality and safety.

For perspectives regarding the scope of manufacturing sites that must be described in applications for approval, please refer to the PMDA website.

Storage Method and Shelf Life Field

As necessary, describe specific storage methods required to ensure product quality and stipulate shelf life for products in which the quality deteriorates over time. If a product's shelf life exceeds three years, it need not be described.

Regarding storage method, for products requiring storage under specific conditions, such as a dark and cool location, in order to prevent transformation and deterioration, etc., describe the storage method and conditions.

Manufacturing Site of Product Field

For the operations site conducting the manufacturing processes described in the Manufacturing Method field, provide the manufacturing site name and location, manufacturing license and certification numbers, and license and certification categories. If a manufacturing license or certification for the manufacturing site is under review, indicate as such.

Manufacturing Site of Raw Materials Field

For manufacturing sites of raw materials, etc. for medical devices registered in a master file (limited to cases in which a manufacturing license for the medical device or certification for the manufacturing site is required for manufacturing a registered item), describe the manufacturing site location, etc.

Remarks Field

Include the following details in the Remarks field.

- Indicate whether it is a Highly Controlled or Controlled Medical Device.
- Specify classification based upon the *Notification on Classification*.
- If the product is a Designated Maintenance Control Medical Device, describe as such.
- For products containing biological or equivalent materials, describe as such.
- For medical devices manufactured using recombinant technology, describe as such.
- If the product is for single-use, describe as such.
- If the product contains new raw materials, describe as such.
- If multiple nomenclatures are included, include all corresponding nomenclatures.
- If it is a kit product, describe as such.
- If an application is for a product that is eligible for Priority Review, describe as such.
- If multiple parties are filing applications jointly due to joint development, describe as such along with the names of joint applicants.
- Attach package inserts (proposals).
- Provide the clinical trial notification number, and if clinical trial consultation at PMDA was used, note this.
- Provide MAH license numbers of the applicant, license categories and locations of main operations sites or, if licenses are under review, describe as such (including locations of main operations sites).
- Note the submission category based upon notifications issued by the director (*Yakushokuhatsu* No. 0327006 of March 27, Heisei 21 (2009)) and notifications on fees (*Yakushokukihatsu* No. 0327001 of March 27, Heisei 21 (2009)).
- If an application for product approval has been filed for a product that does not conform to certification standards, explain that the product is not in conformity and attach materials describing the nonconformance items.
- If there is no applicable nomenclature at the time

of application, provide an overview of the medical device (around 300 characters) and explain what section of the *Notification on Classification* rules is likely to apply to the product.

- If the product under review is used in the manufacturing process of another product as part of another medical device, describe as a "medical device that may be used exclusively for manufacturing."
- Attach photographs clearly showing the product's exterior appearance.
- Explain the need for an application for conformity investigation of manufacturing sites and specify the intended destination for submitting application.

Items Described in Package Inserts

For materials to be attached to applications for approval, based upon Article 40 of the *Pharmaceutical Affairs Law, Enforcement Regulations*, the materials noted in **Table 43-4** are required. For details, please refer to *Yakushokuki* No. 0216001 of February 16, Heisei 17 (2005).

The scope of materials to be attached to applications for approval according to the submission category is as shown in **Table 43-5** (*Yakushokuhatsu* No. 0327006 of March 27, Heisei 21 (2009)).

A. Materials Regarding Background of Origin or Discovery and Status of Use Overseas, etc.

1. Materials regarding background of origin or development

    Provide a simple and chronological description of the background starting from the idea of developing the medical device to its clinical application so that the history and development of the technology can be understood. Describe the background of development of the medical device in relation to this first background.

2. Status of use in foreign country

    Describe the status of use, etc. overseas (including the country of manufacture for medical devices manufactured overseas). If there is a record of use, also describe the status of any reported failures (failure types, frequencies, etc.). If an application for approval of partial changes is filed for an product for which approval has already been granted, also describe the status of use and the status of occurrence of failures in Japan in a similar manner.

3. Comparison with similar medical devices

    For principles and properties, etc., such as materials regarding comparative studies, etc. with other similar medical devices, describe the new aspects and improved aspects of the medical device as well as the results of comparisons of differences or equivalence with

Table 43-5. Scope of Materials to be Attached to Applications for Manufacturing and Marketing Approval

Application category		A Development			B Specifications	C Stability	D Conformity with standards		E Performance			F Risk analysis		G Manufacturing			H Clinical	
		1	2	3	1	1	1	2	1	2	3	1	2	1	2	3	1	2
New medical devices, etc.	Class IV, Class III or II	R	R	R	R	D	R	R	R	D	D	R	R	R	D	R	R	R
Improved medical devices	Class IV, Class III or II (With clinical data)	R	R	R	R	D	R	R	R	D	D	R	R	R	D	R	R	N
Improved medical devices	Class IV, Class III or II (No approval standards, no clinical data)	R	R	R	R	D	R	R	R	D	D	R	R	R	D	R	N	N
Generic medical devices	Class IV, Class III or II (No approval standards, no clinical data)	R	R	R	R	D	R	R	R	D	D	R	R	R	D	R	N	N
Generic medical devices	Class IV, Class III or II (With approval standards, no clinical data)	N	D	R	R	D	R	R	R	D	D	R	R	R	D	R	N	N

R: Attachment required; N: Attachment not required; and D: Determined for individual medical devices.
(Note: Medical devices with approval standards that do not comply with the approval standards are categorized as either Improved medical devices "with clinical data" or "no approval standards, no clinical data," or Generic medical devices with "no approval standards, no clinical data," and the categorization is determined for each individual device.)

existing similar medical devices.

B. Materials Regarding Setting of Specifications

1. Materials regarding specifications and setting of specifications

    For product specifications, prepare materials about how each product specification was set, how test methods were selected, and how test conditions and standard values were determined. In addition, explain why the set product specifications are sufficient for securing the effectiveness, safety and quality of the product under application.

C. Materials Regarding Stability and Durability

1. Materials regarding stability and durability

    For products for which stability has not yet been sufficiently confirmed, perform tests of stability and other changes over time during storage under actual storage conditions and harsh conditions, and set an appropriate storage method and effective period based upon the results. When considering the use of acceleration test results for setting the effective period, refer to *Yakushokuki* No. 0905001 of September 5, Heisei 20 (2008) (*Setting of Effective Periods and Stability Tests for Medical Devices*) and the administrative notice dated August 5, Heisei 21 (2009) (Q&A).

    For medical devices undergoing radiation sterilization, both those sterilized with the maximum exposure dose described in the materials regarding manufacturing method (radiation dosage equivalent to worst-case scenario) and those sterilized under sterilization conditions (e.g., radiation dosage, time) with twice the effect, attach information regarding the properties immediately after sterilization and after six or more months (excluding those with a shelf life of less than six months) as well as information about material deterioration in strength tests, etc. However, this need not apply if findings regarding material deterioration are already known.

    For medical devices to be resterilized and used repeatedly, take into account the use environment and include comments regarding durability during repeated sterilization under the sterilization conditions.

D. Materials Regarding Conformity With Standards Stipulated in Article 41, Paragraph 3 of the Law

1. Materials regarding declarations of conformity with Essential Requirements

Attach self-declaration forms indicating that the product is in conformity with the Essential Requirements, that the product is manufactured in accordance with regulations for manufacturing control and quality control for medical devices, and, for products with approval standards and that are under application as a product in compliance with the approval standards, that the product is in conformity with the approval standards.

2. Materials regarding compliance with Essential Requirements
   - application for products in conformity with approval standards
   - materials proving conformity with approval standards as well as Essential Requirements prepared for each indicated nomenclature based upon the checklist for conformance to the Essential Requirements
   - applications for medical devices with no approval standards and medical devices not in conformity with approval standards

    In order to prove the medical device's conformity with the Essential Requirements, attach a list of specifications and standards used and test methods, etc. established independently, and explain the validity of the specifications and test methods, etc. used.

    Even if there are no appropriate specifications or standards for the medical device, if there are specifications, etc. that can be used as references, such standards, etc. may be used as references. In this case, it is necessary to explain the validity of the specifications, etc. used in order to prove conformity with the Essential Requirements.

E. Materials Regarding Performance

1. Materials regarding tests corroborating performance and safety
2. Materials regarding tests corroborating efficacy
3. Materials regarding tests corroborating methods of use

    Attach materials regarding tests conducted in order to confirm conformity with the Essential Requirements and review and confirm the validity of their design to corroborate performance, safety, efficacy and methods of use, etc., as well as test results.

    For medical devices for measurement that are used in reviews and diagnosis, etc., attach materials regarding performance, such as measurement scope, sensitivity, specificity and reproducibility (if there are specific in vitro diagnostics to be used together with analysis equipment, provide descriptions with considerations of the performance of the in vitro diagnostics).

F. Materials Regarding Risk Analysis

1. Materials regarding systems for implementing risk analysis

    Refer to JIS T 14971 *Medical Devices: Application for Medical Devices for Risk Management* and attach materials providing an overview of risk management systems and their status of implementation.

2. Materials regarding important hazards

    • For the medical device under application, attach materials that summarize, in tabular form, risk analyses and risk reduction measures for hazards for which MHLW has demanded safety measures (including hazards related to similar medical devices and hazards with relevance to the medical device under application).

    • In addition, if serious hazards are observed as a result of performing risk analysis with reference to JIS T 14971, attach materials that summarize, in tabular form, the results of risk analyses and risk reduction measures performed for those hazards.

G. Materials Regarding Manufacturing Methods

1. Materials regarding manufacturing processes and manufacturing facilities

    In principle, provide descriptions of all aspects from the process of receiving parts to the process of shipment determination.

    The scope of processes to be described shall be the scope in which manufacturing and quality control are implemented in the quality system for the product (however, from the receiving process onward, if some processes are outsourced to another manufacturing site, include the contracted manufacturing site). Also provide the names of those who performed design and its verification and the names and locations, etc. of test sites of external testing institutions.

2. Materials regarding sterilization methods

    For sterile medical devices, attach declaration forms regarding implementation periods for sterilization validation as well as sterilization parameters.

3. Materials regarding quality control

    For each manufacturing process, describe the quality inspection items to be implemented.

H. Materials Regarding Clinical Trial Results

1. Materials regarding clinical trial test results

    For basic policies regarding the scope of

medical devices for which applications require attachment regarding clinical trial test results, please refer to *Yakushokukihatsu* No. 0804001 of August 4, Heisei 20 (2008), *Required scope of clinical trial data regarding medical devices.*

    • Clinical trials are required if it is not possible to assess a medical device's clinical effectiveness and safety based only upon nonclinical tests, such as animal tests, or existing references, etc., and it is necessary to submit materials regarding clinical trial results.

    • Because the need for materials on clinical trial test results is determined comprehensively, based upon the properties of each individual medical device, equivalence with existing medical devices and the test results of nonclinical tests, etc., if necessary, PMDA's clinical assessment consultation or presubmission consultation services may be used for making such determinations.

    For medical devices with clearly different performance, structure, etc. compared to existing medical devices (new medical devices), in principle, it is necessary to submit materials regarding test results of clinical trials.

2. Investigation plans (proposed) regarding records of use, etc. of new medical devices

    For new medical devices, refer to PMDA Notification No. 133 of July 26, Heisei 7 (1995) and attach investigation plans (proposed) regarding records of use, etc. of the new medical device.

Summary Technical Document

To promote timely access to international markets, Summary Technical Documents (STEDs) have been discussed by GHTF as a method for summarizing premarket requirements designed to be accepted by various countries as materials for premarket reviews. Currently, additional data and information are required based upon each country's unique premarket requirements. In Japan, STEDs were introduced with the enforcement of the revised *Pharmaceutical Affairs Law* in April 2005.

Table 43-6 shows the improved medical devices requiring clinical trial results forms, as well as the items described in STED overviews of materials for new medical devices (*Yakushokukihatsu* No. 0216001 of February 16, Heisei 17 (2005)).

Table 43-6. Items Described in STED Overviews of Materials

1. General overview of article (General Information)

  1.1 Overview of article

  1.2 Background of origin or discovery and background of development

  1.3 Status of use in foreign countries

2. Essential Requirements and conformity with Essential Requirements

  (Essential Requirements and evidence of conformity)

  2.1 List of reference specifications

  2.2 Essential Requirements and evidence of conformity

3. Information regarding device (Device description)

  3.1 General information

  3.2 Raw materials

  3.3 Product specifications

  3.4 Storage method and shelf life

  3.5 Comparison with similar medical devices

4. Overview of design verification and validation documents
(Summary documents of preclinical design verification and validation)

  4.1 General information

    (1) Declaration of compliance with standards

  4.2 Overview of validation of device design

    4.2.1 Tests corroborating device safety

    (1) Physical and chemical properties

    (2) Electrical safety and electromagnetic compatibility

    (3) Biological safety

    (4) Radiation safety

    (5) Mechanical safety

    (6) Stability and durability

    4.2.2 Tests corroborating device performance

    4.2.3 Tests corroborating device efficacy

    4.2.4 Tests corroborating methods of use of device

  4.3 Test results of clinical trials

    (1) Clinical trial results

    (2) Summary of clinical trial results

    (3) Other

5. Labeling

  5.1 Package Insert (proposed)

  5.2 Labels (proposed)

6. Risk analysis

  6.1 Systems for implementing risk analysis

  6.2 Important hazards

7. Manufacturing information

  7.1 Information regarding manufacturing processes and manufacturing facilities

  7.2 Information regarding sterilization methods

  7.3 Information regarding quality control

Details of Items described in STED (for Cases With Clinical Trials)

Methods of compiling STEDs differ between generic medical devices and other medical devices (new medical devices, improved medical devices).

For generic medical devices, descriptions of differences with approved products are important, and in this format, differences are clarified and the product's applicability as a generic medical device is described based upon the development and design concepts described in section 1.2. It is not necessary to describe parts that overlap items for applications for approval. For details regarding generic medical device (no approval standards), please refer to *Yakushokukihatsu* No. 0327004 of March 27, Heisei 21 (2009), *Points to consider when preparing attachments for applications for manufacturing approval for generic medical devices.*

For generic medical devices (with approval standards), in this format, the attached materials are edited into the STED format and conformity with the approval standards is described. For details regarding products with approval standards, please refer to *Yakushokuki* No. 0401003 of April 1, Heisei 17 (2005).

STEDs for new medical devices as well as improved medical devices with clinical results are described below, with reference to *Yakushokuki* No. 0216003 of February 16, Heisei 17 (2005). For further detail, please refer to the notification. For details regarding principles for preparing overviews of materials for new medical devices and improved medical devices, as well as principles for preparing attached materials for generic medical devices (no approval standards), please refer to the PMDA website.

STED for New Medical Devices and Improved Products With Clinical Study

1. General overview of the product
1.1 Overview of the product
   In addition to describing an overview of the product, attach color photographs or distinct color printouts for confirming the outer appearance and dimensions.

Overview of Product

1	Classification		
2	Name	Nomenclature	
		Trade name	
3	Class		
4	Applicant name		
5	Intended use and efficacy or effects		
6	Structure and principles		
7	Operational methods or methods of use		
8	Remarks		Date of application: Submission category: Description of novelty:

1.2 Background of origin or discovery and background of development
   (1) Provide descriptions with the following basic tone: "When and where the product was developed, by whom, based on what ideas, what triggered development, and the purposes of subsequent product development, the details of deliberations, and the results. Ultimately, effectiveness and safety were sufficiently confirmed based on such and such data, and the product is useful in such and such manner."
   (2) For each process (establishment of design requirements, preparation of documents regarding design results, reviews of design results, design verification, validation and changes in design during development process), describe how deliberations proceeded. At the same time, describe all items required for assessing the quality, durability, reliability, safety, efficacy or effects, performance, utility value, etc. of the medical device being developed. Also describe problems encountered during the development

process, and if changes were made to plans, describe the details and reasons as well as the validity of measures taken.
   (3) Describe the period when nonclinical tests and clinical trials were started as well as the basis for deciding on transitions from nonclinical tests to clinical trials. If processes were advanced in a manner differing from conventional methods used for similar medical devices, describe the differences and their validity.
   (4) Describe problems encountered during the development process, and if changes were made to plans, describe the details and reasons as well as the validity of measures taken (e.g., if there are significant differences with the intended use, subject patients, and product specifications, etc. of the introducing country).
   (5) Regarding each test for design verification and validation, provide diagrams of the background of development that chronologically describe the starting dates and end dates.
   (6) If medical devices with identical structures and principles as the medical device under application but of a different model, energy output, site of application, intended use, etc. are being developed, also provide an overview of such devices.

1.3 Status of use in foreign countries
   (1) Regarding licenses and status of use in foreign countries, provide a list organized by country of the latest available information on licenses and the number of countries where the device is used, the names of the main license-granting countries and countries where the device is used, trade names (original language), dates of licenses, dates of starting use, approximate amounts of annual use, purposes of use, efficacies or effects and methods of use. Provide similar descriptions for products under application for licenses. If a PMA approval/510(k) clearance has been granted by FDA, provide the approval/clearance numbers for all products included in the application.
   (2) Provide a list describing an overview of the occurrence status of defects and malfunctions reported in overseas use, including the types and frequencies of defects and malfunctions.
   (3) If the product is not being used in the exporting country, explain the reasons.
   (4) For its descriptions, be sure to clarify the dates

of the surveys and periods subject to the surveys.

(5) Appropriately report any changes made to the described items of (1) to (3) after preparing the overview of the attached materials. In particular, if a determination regarding clearance is made at a key country processing an application, or if changes are made to the frequency of important device defects and malfunctions believed to have a relatively high probability of endangering life, swiftly provide a written report to PMDA's Office of Review Management. Regarding other aspects of the status of the occurrences, provide revisions with the latest information each time the relevant materials are revised.

(6) If an application for approval of partial changes is being filed for a product for which premarket approval has already been granted, also describe the status of use and the status of occurrence of defects and malfunctions in Japan in a similar manner.

2. Essential Requirements and conformity to the Essential Requirements

This field is for indicating conformity to the *Standards for medical devices specified by the Minister of Health, Labour and Welfare based on the provisions of Article 41, Paragraph 3 of the Pharmaceutical Affairs Law* (Ministry of Health, Labour and Welfare Announcement No. 122 of Heisei 17 (2005)), known as the Essential Requirements, stipulated as standards for ensuring the appropriate nature, quality, and performance of medical devices based on Article 41, Paragraph 3 of the *Pharmaceutical Affairs Law*.

2.1 List of reference standards

Provide a list of standards used for indicating conformity to the Essential Requirements along with sources (titles, etc.), years of publication, standard numbers, etc. At the same time, be aware that although descriptions of laws, ordinances and notifications are not necessary, they may be identified, and descriptions regarding risk analyses and quality systems are not required.

2.2 Essential Requirements and evidence of conformity

Using the checklist for conformity to the Essential Requirements, explain the conformity of each item with the Essential Requirements.

Also explain the validity of the specifications and standards used for indicating conformity to the Essential Requirements and the conformity thereof. If there are no specifications, standards, etc. to refer to, describe test methods, etc. for proving conformity with the Essential Requirements and explain how the

obtained test results can demonstrate the conformity to the Essential Requirements.

3. Device description
3.1 General information
(1) Explain how the device under application corresponds to the nomenclature described in the Name field of the application for approval.
(2) Regarding the device's intended purposes of use, describe details that are consistent with those described in the appendix of the application for approval, Intended use and efficacy or effects.
(3) Ensure that descriptions regarding applicable patients and diseases, patient selection criteria and contraindications and prohibitions match the details described regarding contraindications, etc. in the Information For Use (proposed).
(4) Copy the configuration diagram and the functional characteristics of each part of the device from the Shape, Structure and Principles field of the appendix of the application for approval.
(5) For electronic medical equipment, copy the principles of the device, including the operational principles, from the Shape, Structure and Principles field of the appendix of the application for approval.
(6) Describe the device's operating methods based upon the Operating methods or methods of use field of the application for approval.

3.2 Raw materials
Copy the details described in the Raw materials or component parts field in the application for approval.

3.3 Product specifications
(1) Describe the specifications of the device described in the Product specifications field of the application for approval.
(2) Describe why the established product specifications are necessary and sufficient for securing the effectiveness, safety and quality of the product under application based upon considerations of the Essential Requirements and other reference standards. If appropriate domestic or overseas standards are used, describe the scientific validity of using such standards. Also, with reference to current standards of scientific and technical knowledge, describe the rationale for determining that the test items that have been established are necessary and sufficient.

(3) If any specifications that would normally be established for similar medical devices are not being set, describe the relevant reasons and rationale.

3.4 Storage method and shelf life
(1) If a storage method and shelf life have been described in the application for approval, refer to the items described in the Storage method and shelf life field of the application for approval and describe the validity, etc. of the storage method and shelf life.

3.5 Comparisons with similar medical devices
(1) Regarding effectiveness, safety and product characteristics, etc., conduct a comparison with approved medical devices that are similar in terms of composition and principles or are clinically similar and provide a description focusing on points of difference. Also consider clinical usefulness when providing descriptions.
(2) For comparisons with similar existing medical devices, select devices that are similar in terms of intended use, product specifications and methods of use, etc. and, using the latest available package inserts, prepare a list including the nomenclature, trade names, dates of approval, intended use, efficacies or effects and, if necessary, structure and principles, raw materials, product specifications and methods of use or operating methods. For the comparative items, select appropriate items according to the properties of the medical device. Carefully consider setting comparative items for structure and principles, raw materials and product specifications. Also describe sources, etc. of materials being compared.
(3) Keep in mind the following when preparing the list described in (2).
1. If there are multiple similar medical devices, describe them sequentially starting with the most recent date of approval, certification or notification.
2. For devices for which reexamination and reassessment have been completed, also describe the date of reexamination and reassessment.
3. If a controlled clinical trial (including blind studies) using comparative devices is conducted, when preparing the list, in principle, describe the medical devices used as comparative devices after the medical device under application, and in the Remarks field, describe the type of controlled clinical trial conducted and describe that the device is a comparative device.

4. Overview of design verification and validation documents
For summaries of design verification and validation, in principle, provide a "General Overview" chapter for each item and include a summary of all testing related to the item along with remarks by the applicant. After the General Overview, provide an overview of the test methods and test results of each test related to the item and also provide additional required remarks. In this instance, use tables and diagrams as much as possible.

4.1 General items
4.1.1 Declaration of conformity to specifications
Describe the details of the self-declaration form stating that the product has been manufactured in conformance with the Essential Requirements and regulations for manufacturing control and quality control for medical devices, and include the self-declaration form as a separate attachment. The self-declaration form shall state that the product under application is in conformity with the Essential Requirements, standards stipulated in *Ministerial Ordinances on QMS* and approval standards of the product (in cases of conformity with the standards).

4.2 Overview of validation of device design
Prove conformity with specifications used to describe the rationale for indicating conformity with the Essential Requirements, for example by proving conformity with JIS T 0993-1 (*Biological assessment of medical devices—Part 1: Assessments and tests*), JIS T 0601-1 (*Electronic medical equipment—Part 1: General requirements for safety*) and specifications for radiation safety and other types of safety. Also describe the tests (excluding clinical trials) indicated as the basis for conformity with the Essential Requirements. The main points to be considered for these descriptions are described in sections 4.2.1 onward for your reference.
If conformity with the standards has been confirmed by either an agency certified by a certified body as a member of the International Accreditation Forum (IAF) as being in compliance with the general functional requirements for test sites and calibration agencies (ISO 17025) stipulated by the International Organization for Standardization, or an agency granted registration (henceforth referred to as "JNLA registration") under Article 57, Paragraph 1 of the *Industrial Standardization Law* (Law No. 185 of Showa 24 (1949)), it may be stated as such herein.

Even for devices in conformity with the specifications, if the device is labeled with new indications etc., clinical data or performance tests, etc. are required. At this time, it is necessary to prove conformity with the specifications used in the descriptions as the rationale to show the conformity with the Essential Requirements, and it is necessary to describe the tests, etc. (excluding clinical trials) indicated as the rationale for conformity with the Essential Requirements in sections 4.2.1 onward.

4.2.1 Tests corroborating device safety

(1) As an "executive summary"of this section, for tests corroborating safety, prepare a list indicating test items, test methods, test results, testing laboratories and attachment numbers, etc., and provide an overview for each test. Also, with reference to current level of scientific and technical knowledge, describe the rationale for determining that the test items conducted are necessary and sufficient for assessing the product safety.

(2) In the executive summary of this section, also discuss the relationship between the test results corroborating safety and the product specifications of the application. Further, if necessary, also describe the clinical positioning and characteristics of the product based upon the comparisons with similar medical devices.

(3) Next, prepare a list of the method and results for each test, and provide summaries along with descriptions of necessary discussions. Whenever possible, describe test results using tables and figures.

4.2.1.1 Physical and chemical properties

As an executive summary, provide an overview of testing items and relevant test results regarding the physical and chemical properties of the product. When setting testing items for medical devices utilizing dental material or polymeric materials, refer to the following and set the appropriate testing items with careful consideration on the properties of the device.

When properties of the blending ingredients affect the nature of the medical device, depending on the properties of the materials, discuss the chemical structure, infrared absorption, ultraviolet absorption, atomic absorption, melting point, boiling point, durability, hardness, color tone, effluent, surface properties, etc.

For materials in which the properties of constituting ingredients affect the nature of the medical device:

- Depending upon the properties of the materials, describe the chemical structure, infrared absorption, ultraviolet absorption, atomic absorption, melting point, boiling point, durability, hardness, color tone, effluent, surface properties, etc.

For dental materials:
- Refer to "Basic ideas on physical, chemical and biological tests necessary for applications for approval for dental materials" to set the items.

For electronic medical equipment:
- In some cases, it is possible to omit a description by stating, "Because this product uses general electrical parts and the constituting ingredients, etc. do not affect the properties of the medical device, a description of this item shall be omitted."

4.2.1.2 Electrical safety and electromagnetic compatibility

(1) As an "executive summary," for tests conducted on electric safety and electromagnetic compatibility, prepare a simple list of test items, methods and test conditions, specifications, testing laboratories, each attachment number, etc. and provide an overview for each test.

(2) Also, with reference to the current level of scientific and technical knowledge, describe the rationale for determining that the test items conducted are necessary and sufficient for assessing electrical safety and electromagnetic compatibility.

(3) If a test that is normally conducted for similar medical devices has not been conducted, explain why the test has not been done in the executive summary.

(4) Next, prepare a list of methods and results for each test, and provide summaries along with descriptions of necessary discussions.

(5) Keep in mind the following when entering descriptions for each test.
1. If additional tests have been conducted in the development process, describe the reason and background.
2. For tests that are inconsistent with the test methods stipulated in JIS T 0601-1 (*Electronic medical equipment—Part 1: General requirements for safety*), or, for tests regarding electromagnetic compatibility, JIS T 0601-1-2 (*Electronic medical equipment —Part 1: General requirements for safety— Section 2: Electromagnetic compatibility: Requirements and tests*), describe the

inconsistent parts, the reasons for the
inconsistencies and the validity of the test.

4.2.1.3 Biological safety

(1) As an "executive summary" of this section, for
tests conducted regarding biological safety,
prepare a simple list of test items, methods
and results (positivity, negativity, IC_{50} values,
histopathological review results, etc.), testing
laboratories, attachment numbers, etc. and
provide an overview for each test.

(2) Also, with reference to the current level of
scientific and technical knowledge, describe the
rationale for determining that the test items
conducted are necessary and sufficient for
assessing biological safety.

(3) If a test that is normally conducted for similar
medical devices has not been conducted, explain
the reasons in the executive summary.

(4) Next, prepare a list of the methods and results
for each test, and provide summaries along with
descriptions of necessary discussions.

(5) Keep in mind the following when entering
descriptions for each test.
1. Describe the required findings and
assessments, etc. for each test.
2. Discuss the validity of animal test models
in relation to the clinical use of the device.
3. If additional tests have been conducted in
the development process, explain the reason
and background.
4. For tests that are inconsistent with
Iyakushin 0213001 of February 13, Heisei
15 (2003), *Basic policies for biological tests
required for applications for manufacturing
(import) approval for medical devices*, or
Yakushokukihatsu No. 0831002 of August
31, Heisei 19 (2007), *Basic policies for
physical, chemical, and biological tests
required for applications for approval for
dental materials*, describe the inconsistent
parts, the reasons for the inconsistencies
and the validity of the test.

(6) For electronic medical equipment that is not
intended to come into contact with blood or
biological fluids, etc., it may be stated that
"Because this product does not come into
contact with blood or biological fluids, etc.,
descriptions for this item will be omitted."

4.2.1.4 Radiation safety

(1) As an "executive summary" of this section for
tests conducted regarding radiation safety,
prepare a simple list of test items, methods and

conditions, specifications, testing laboratories,
attachment numbers, etc. and provide an
overview of each test. Also, with reference
to current level of scientific and technical
knowledge, describe the rationale for determining
that the test items conducted are necessary and
sufficient for assessing radiation safety.

(2) If a test that is normally conducted for similar
medical devices has not been conducted, explain
the reason in the executive summary.

(3) Next, prepare a list of the methods (samples,
measurement methods and acceptance criteria
or allowable deviations, etc.) and results for
each test, and provide summaries along with
descriptions of necessary discussions.

(4) Keep in mind the following when entering
descriptions for each test.
1. Provide indications regarding conformity
with laws and ordinances related to medical
devices, such as Chapter 4, Section 2
of the *Medical Service Law, Enforcement
Regulations* (Ministry of Health and Welfare
Ordinance No. 50 of Showa 23 (1948)).
2. If additional tests have been conducted
in the development process, describe the
reason and background.
3. For tests that are inconsistent with tests
with stipulations in standards related to
individual medical devices, describe the
inconsistent parts, the reasons for the
inconsistencies and the validity of the test.

(5) For electrical medical equipment that does not
emit radiation, a description stating, "Because
this product is not a device that emits radiation,
descriptions for this item shall be omitted," may
be used.

4.2.1.5 Mechanical safety

(1) As an "executive summary" of this section, for
tests conducted on mechanical safety, prepare
a list of test items, methods and conditions,
specifications, testing laboratories, attachment
numbers, etc. and provide an overview for each
test. Also, with reference to the current level
of scientific and technical knowledge, describe
the rationale for determining that the test items
conducted are necessary and sufficient for
assessing mechanical safety.

(2) If a test that is normally conducted for similar
medical devices has not been conducted, explain
the reasons in the executive summary of this
section.

(3) Next, prepare a list of the methods (samples,
measurement methods and acceptable values

or allowable deviations, etc.) and results for each test, and provide summaries along with descriptions of necessary discussions.

(4) Keep in mind the following when entering descriptions for each test.

1. If additional tests have been conducted in the development process, describe the reason and background.

2. For electronic medical equipment, for tests that are inconsistent with test methods stipulated in JIS T 0601-1 (*Electronic medical equipment—Part 1: General requirements for safety*), describe the inconsistent parts, the reasons for the inconsistencies and the validity of the test.

4.2.1.6 Stability and durability

(1) As an "executive summary" of this section, provide an overview of the results of tests conducted on stability or durability (including items regarding material deterioration due to sterilization for radiation sterilized medical devices) as well as discussions such as the need to set storage methods and shelf life. Also, with reference to the current level of scientific and technical knowledge, describe the rationale for determining that the test items conducted are necessary and sufficient for assessing stability.

(2) Next, for each test (long-term storage tests, acceleration tests, stress tests, etc.), prepare an overview of the test conditions, measurement items and storage periods in list form and summarize the test methods and results while also describing necessary discussions.

(3) Also describe the rationale for setting the test methods.

(4) If an application is filed in the middle of a long-term storage test, describe as such.

(5) For medical devices designed to be resterilized and used, also comment on the effects of such sterilization

(6) If an acceleration test is used, describe discussions regarding whether assessments for the test are possible with an acceleration test and whether appropriate acceleration conditions were used. For details regarding setting effective periods of medical devices as well as stability tests, please refer to *Yakushokukihatsu* No. 0905001 of September 5, Heisei 20 (2008), *Setting of effective periods and stability tests for medical devices*, and the Administrative Notice of August 5, Heisei 21 (2009), *Q&A regarding setting of effective periods and stability tests for medical devices*.

(7) Also consider surface treatment and coating.

(8) If a test has been omitted based upon the use of raw materials identical to those used in approved products, for each raw material, describe the trade name and approval number, etc. of each approved product being used as a precedent.

(9) If the "Storage Method and Shelf Life" field of the application is blank, explain the reason.

4.2.2 Tests corroborating device performance

(1) As an "executive summary" of this section, for tests corroborating performance, prepare a list including test items, methods and results, testing laboratories and attachment numbers, etc., and provide an overview for each test.

Also, with reference to the current level of scientific and technical knowledge, describe the rationale for determining that the test items conducted are necessary and sufficient for assessing performance.

(2) For the executive summary, also discuss the relationship between the test results corroborating performance and the product specifications of the application. Further, if necessary, also describe the clinical positioning of the device and characteristics based upon comparisons with similar medical devices.

(3) Next, prepare a list of the methods and results for each test and provide summaries along with descriptions of necessary discussions.

(4) Whenever possible, describe test results using tables and figures.

4.2.3 Tests corroborating device efficacy

(1) As an "executive summary" of this section, for tests corroborating efficacy and those regarding action mechanisms, prepare a list of test items and methods, methods of use (dosage and administration), periods of use, comparative devices, test results, testing laboratories, attachment numbers, etc. and provide an overview for each test. Also, with reference to the current level of scientific and technical knowledge, describe the rationale for determining that the implemented test items are necessary and sufficient for assessing efficacy.

(2) In the executive summary, in addition to describing the process of studies on mechanisms of action, also consider the relationship between the results of tests corroborating efficacy and tests regarding action mechanisms on one hand and the efficacies and effects of the application on the other. Further, if necessary, also describe

the clinical positioning of the device and characteristics based upon comparisons with similar medical devices.

(3) Next, prepare a list of the methods and results for each test, and provide summaries along with descriptions of necessary discussions.

(4) Whenever possible, describe test results using tables and figures.

(5) If a test is omitted based upon reasons such as having efficacies identical to those of existing medical devices, prepare an item in the STED and clearly describe the validity of such omission.

4.2.4 Tests corroborating methods of use of device

If the methods of use are the same as existing method, descriptions are not required.

(1) As an "executive summary" of this section, for tests providing the basis for establishing methods of use, prepare a list of test items and methods, methods of use (dosage and administration), test results, testing laboratories, attachment numbers, etc., provide an overview for each test, and describe the rationale for establishing the methods of use, dosages, etc.

Also, with reference to the current level of scientific and technical knowledge, describe the basis for determining that the implemented test items are necessary and sufficient for assessing methods of use.

In addition, if necessary, consider the relationship with failures of the medical device.

(2) Next, prepare a list of the methods and results for each test and provide summaries along with descriptions of necessary discussions.

(3) Whenever possible, describe test results using tables and figures.

(4) If a test is omitted based upon reasons such as the methods of use being identical to those of existing medical devices, prepare an item in the STED and clearly describe the validity of such omission.

4.3 Test results of clinical trials

For applications for approval for medical devices, if the clinical effectiveness and safety cannot be assessed based only upon the results of nonclinical tests, such as performance tests and animal tests, or existing references, etc., it is necessary to attach the results of clinical trials.

For details regarding the required scope of materials on test results of clinical trials of medical devices, please refer to *Yakushokuki* No. 0804001 of August 4, Heisei 19 (2008), *Required scope of clinical trial data regarding medical devices.*

When attaching clinical trial results, summarize the details by referring to the following.

(1) As an "executive summary," for clinical trials that have been conducted, prepare a list of test types (comparative clinical, general clinical, etc.), subjects, numbers of cases, methods of use (dosage and administration), review and follow up items, periods of use, clinical trial periods, names of representative institutions, attachment numbers, etc., and provide an overview for each test along with necessary discussions.

(2) If a test has not been conducted using test methods normally used for similar medical devices, explain the reasons and give the rationale for determining that the quality, effectiveness and safety of the device could be appropriately assessed based upon only the clinical trials that have been conducted.

At the same time, also consider the following.

(1) If clinical trials have been omitted, prepare an item in the STED and explain the validity of such omission.

(2) If the results of clinical trials for products other than the product under application are used for assessment, explain the validity of doing so.

(3) Regarding the handling of test results of clinical trials conducted overseas, refer to the following notifications and Q&A and explain how the requirements for acceptance are met.

• *Yakuhatsu* No. 479 of March 31, Heisei 9 (1997), *Handling of clinical trial data for medical devices conducted overseas*

• *Yakushokukihatsu* No. 0331006 of March 31, Heisei 18 (2006), *Handling of test results of clinical trials for medical devices conducted overseas*

• *Jimurenraku* of June 23, Heisei 18 (2006), *Q&A regarding 'Handling of test results of clinical trials for medical devices conducted overseas'*

(4) If assessments have been omitted, the items of section 4.3.1 onward are not required.

4.3.1 Clinical trial results

(1) For each test, prepare an overview of test methods (test objectives, test types, subject selection criteria, exclusion criteria, numbers of cases, methods of use, periods of use, follow up periods, combination therapies, review/follow up items and periods, assessment methods/ standards, principal clinical investigators, names of representative institutions, numbers of institutions, test periods, etc.) and test results as a list, and describe the rationale for setting the

subject selection criteria, exclusion criteria and methods of use (dosage and administration), breakdowns of case compositions (numbers of subject cases for safety assessments and effectiveness assessments, etc.), reasons and breakdowns of cases of discontinuation, dropout, and protocol deviation, patient backgrounds (sex, age, inpatient/outpatient status, primary disease, severity before use, duration of disorder, complications, period of use, dosage, etc.), stratified analyses (if necessary), test results (detailed descriptions of results regarding effectiveness and safety) and conclusions. For these descriptions, use tables whenever possible.

For device defects, prepare a list of frequencies of occurrence by test and by defect type, a list of frequencies of occurrence by background factor and defect type, a list of defects (cases) (describe case details, courses and comments from attending physicians), etc., and provide a summary of the status of defect occurrences and relevant measures and courses. For clinical trial results, prepare a list of abnormal variations in clinical review values by test, a list of cases of abnormal variations in clinical review values and an appropriate diagram of abnormal variations in clinical review values showing the variations, and provide summaries. If there are any cases of severe defects or death, etc., prepare a table of cases including the courses, etc., and consider the relationship with the clinical trial equipment by including determinations made by physicians.

(2) If a controlled trial has been conducted, for the descriptions of section (1), also describe the reasons for selecting the comparative devices.

(3) Attach a list of cases.

4.3.2 Summary of clinical trial results

(1) Summary of effectiveness: Prepare a list regarding effectiveness by test and by background factor and describe conclusions.

(2) Summary of safety: Summarize the results of tests on safety described in the item for clinical trial results and describe conclusions.

(3) If assessments have been omitted, the items of section 4.3.1 onward are not required.

(4) If necessary, also provide summaries of clinical trial results and references, etc. from other countries for reference.

5. Labeling

5.1 Package Insert (proposed)

(1) Describe the package insert (proposed) and the rationale for the settings.

(2) For products corresponding to medical devices categorized under Class IV, medical devices categorized under Class III that are implanted or placed on the body surface and products believed to have a relatively high probability of endangering life if a malfunction occurs, describe the package insert used in major countries in particular, and enter remarks by the applicant based upon comparative reviews with package insert used in Japan. If important precautions included in the package insert used overseas are not described in the package insert used in Japan (or vice versa), explain the reasons.

(3) For parts of the package insert reflecting cautionary items, etc. as a result of risk analysis, clearly state that they are countermeasures for risks.

(4) Describe the "Intended use and efficacy or effects" of the package insert (proposed) in a box, and describe the rationale for the settings based upon summaries of the results of tests corroborating efficacy and performance and clinical trial results.

(5) Describe the "Operating methods or methods of use" of the package insert (proposed) in a box, and describe the rationale for the settings based upon summaries of the results of tests corroborating the methods of use and performance and clinical trial results.

(6) In the package insert (proposed), describe warnings and contraindications as well as precautions for use in a box, and for each item, describe the basis for the settings based upon the results of nonclinical tests and clinical trials.

5.2 Labels (proposed)

Using a table, delineate details required to be displayed on products as the legally required descriptions.

6. Risk analysis

This field is for describing overviews of risk management activities implemented for the medical device under application.

Basically, this field is for the (main) "manufacturer" or "person performing design control" listed in the "Manufacturing Method" field of the application to provide an overview of the implemented risk management activities by referring to JIS T 14971 (*Medical devices—Application of risk management to medical devices*) or the original text of this specification, ISO 14971 (*Medical devices— Application of risk management to medical devices*). If necessary, the applicant (MAH) must check the details and consider entering additional comments.

6.1 Systems for implementing risk analysis

In this field, clearly describe the specifications referred to by the manufacturer or the person performing design control.

6.1.1 Items regarding organizational systems for risk management

In this field, provide a simple overview of the organizations and documents upon which risk management activities were based at the manufacturing sites, etc. at which risk management was implemented.

6.1.2 Status of implementation of risk analysis

In this field, in addition to entering the person (department) in charge of risk management, using tables, etc., provide simple descriptions of the status of implementation of each step involved in risk management.

6.2 Serious hazards

6.2.1 Hazards for which MHLW has demanded safety measures

In this field, if there are hazards related to the medical device under application (including hazards involving similar medical devices) for which MHLW has required safety measures, use a table to provide simple descriptions of the results of risks analyses regarding such hazards as well as, if necessary, descriptions of implemented risk reduction measures. If a voluntary inspection notification, etc. related to the relevant product is issued after design and development, or if domestic notifications in Japan cannot be easily browsed for a medical device designed and manufactured overseas, even if risk management for design and development has already ended, it becomes necessary to review this item again. With considerations of the results of risk management activities implemented by the MAH (or manufacturer) during design and development, conduct an appropriate review and use a table to provide a simple description of the details.

6.2.2 Results of risks analyses and risk reduction measures for serious hazards

In this field, specify hazards for which, based upon the results of risk assessments made as part of risk management activities implemented during

design and development, it has been determined that risk control (risk reduction measures) is necessary, and also use a table to provide a simple description of the details of the reduction measures and their effects.

This field is not for describing all hazards specified in risk analysis but for describing reduction measures implemented for hazards determined to be "unacceptable risks" based upon risk assessments.

7. Information regarding manufacturing
7.1 Information regarding manufacturing processes and manufacturing facilities

Describe the processes starting with receiving component parts, etc. ("component parts, etc." as stipulated in Article 2, Paragraph 2 of the *Ministerial Ordinance on QMS* for medical devices) to the process of product release.

For the component parts, etc., stipulate procedures, etc. for ensuring compliance with requirements related to purchased goods. If the purchased goods are not inspected based upon those procedures, etc., or if the purchased goods correspond to Appendix 5 of the *Pharmaceutical Affairs Law, Enforcement Regulations*, also describe the manufacturing process of those component parts, etc. However, for component parts, etc. registered based upon Article 14-11, Paragraph 1 of the *Pharmaceutical Affairs Law* (henceforth referred to as "registration under the Master File System"), a description of the manufacturing site of such component parts, etc. is sufficient.

(1) For in-process inspections and final inspections of the products, describe the inspection items for each process.

*Describe parameters of testing and receiving inspections that have been set for guaranteeing the product specifications.

(2) For products for which the quality or properties, etc. of the products differ depending upon the manufacturing conditions, describe the manufacturing conditions for processes having a significant effect on the quality and safety of the medical device under application.

*For example, ceramic products.

(3) For sterile medical devices, describe sterilization methods. For processes involving work in a controlled clean environment (cleanrooms, etc.), describe as such.

(4) In information on manufacturing facilities, while ensuring correspondence with process flowcharts, describe the names, locations, license or certification numbers and license or certification categories related to the main

manufacturer of the medical device listed in the application for approval as well as, if applicable, sterile medical devices manufacturers, cell/tissue medical devices manufacturers and labeling, etc. manufacturers.

*For facilities performing processes affecting the quality, performance or safety of the final product, although it is not necessary to enter the facility's name, it is necessary to describe the manufacturing conditions, etc. for important processes. (e.g., heparin coating of catheters or drug coating of stents)

(5) When an external testing facility is used, describe the inspection items conducted as well as the facility's name and location.

(6) Enter the name and location of the main operations site performing design of the medical device and describe the relationship with the applicant (including overviews of agreement details).

(7) If approval is granted based upon an understanding that the component parts of the medical device may be distributed as single product, and if the manufacturing method and quality inspection items of the component parts differ from those described above, it is necessary to provide separate descriptions.

(8) When including a product approved or certified as a medical device based upon a component part alone, or a product for which a notification for marketing authorization has been filed, in locations indicating the component part, describe the name of the MAH of the component part, the location of the main operations site, the MAH license number and approval/certification numbers, and the trade name and product name.

7.2 Information regarding sterilization methods

(1) Provide an overview of each validation supporting the establishment of the sterilization

conditions and describe sterilization conditions such as sterilization parameters. Also, with reference to the current level of scientific and technical knowledge, describe the rationale for determining that the implemented test items are necessary and sufficient for assessing sterilization.

*Attach declaration forms regarding test periods of sterilization validation as well as sterilization parameters.

(2) For tests that are inconsistent with the sterilization validation standards, etc., describe the inconsistent parts and explain the reasons for the inconsistencies as well as the validity of the test.

(3) If raw materials derived from bovine sources, etc. are used, describe the country of origin, region, processing method and, as necessary, information regarding TSE materials as well as other necessary items from the perspective of securing quality and safety. For raw materials derived from humans or animals, describe the derivation; the details of donor screening, methods for processes for inactivating or eliminating bacteria, fungi, viruses, etc. during the manufacturing process; and other required items from the perspective of securing quality and safety. Also, clarify the validity of the origin (including the details of donor screening) and describe tests on validation of methods for eliminating or inactivating viruses and other pathogens during the manufacturing process.

7.3 Quality control

In information about quality control, describe the purpose of inspections and an overview of procedures for the inspection items indicated in the manufacturing process in section 7.1, and then describe the relationship of each item with the product specifications set in the application for approval.

Table 43-7. Types of Procedures for Changes

Type of Change Application	Type of Changes
Normal Application for Changes	Changes Other Than Those Described Below
Accelerated application for changes	Those stipulated in notifications, etc. as being promptly examined and processed Example: • Application for changes for the sole purpose of extending the shelf life • Application for changes for additions or changes to manufacturing sites
Application for specific changes	Changes within a specific scope (as of November 10, 2008) • Changes affecting only raw materials of parts/components coming into contact with tissue and blood • Changes affecting only sterilization methods, methods of determining sterilization doses, or methods of sterilization validation
Notification of minor changes	Changes with no effect on product quality, effectiveness or safety. Must be submitted within 30 days after the change.
No procedures required	If it is conclusively determined that there is no direct relationship with effectiveness or safety and that the equivalence of the nature of the medical device is not diminished, no specific procedures are required.

Changes in Approval Conditions

If changes are made to approval (certification) conditions, procedures for changes based upon an application for approval (certification) of partial changes (henceforth referred to as "partial change application") or a notification of minor changes is necessary. Based upon the details of the changes, assess the effects on effectiveness and safety and select the appropriate procedure. Because the effects of such changes on effectiveness and safety differ depending upon the product, it is necessary to refer to *Yakushokukihatsu* No. 0216001 of February 16, Heisei 17 (2005), *Yakushokukihatsu* No. 1023001 of October 23, Heisei 20 (2008), and other related notifications and perform the appropriate actions for changes. If the actions for changes regarding the product under application with PMDA are unclear, we recommend taking advantage of the Simple Consultations offered by PMDA.

For products for which a product notification is required, it is necessary to file notifications of changes for items corresponding to applications for changes as well as items corresponding to the notifications of minor changes.

Table 43-7 is a summary of the types of procedures.

Application for Approval (Certification) of Partial Changes

For applications for partial changes for approved products, refer to Article 4 ("Other"), Paragraph 3 of *Yakushokukihatsu* No. 0216001 of February 16, Heisei 17 (2005) and file an application using Form No. 23(3) of the *Pharmaceutical Affairs Law, Enforcement Regulations*. For applications for partial changes for certified

products, use Form No. 65(1) in a similar manner. When making changes, complete only the field for the item being changed (e.g., for changes to raw materials, the "Raw Materials or Component Parts" field) and in the "Remarks" field, specifically describe the reasons for the changes and the details of the changes using a table comparing the old and new details.

For applications for partial changes filed for the sole purpose of extending the shelf life after approval, processing is accelerated when "㊂" ("circle storage") is written in red ink on the application and the necessary test results forms, etc. are attached.

Changes and Additions to Manufacturing Sites

If the details of the changes are limited to changes and additions to manufacturing sites, and if an application for partial changes is required for items other than medical devices using recombinant technology, cell tissue medical devices and specific Biological Products, the application procedures are processed promptly. For more details, please refer to *Yakushokushinsahatsu* No. 1210003 and *Yakushokukanmahatsu* No. 1210007 of December 10, Heisei 19 (2007).

Application for Specific Changes

This new system indicated in *Yakushokukihatsu* No. 1110001 of November 10, Heisei 20 (2008), *Acceleration of procedures related to specific changes for medical devices*, is a system for conducting prompt reviews for applications for partial changes within a specific scope. This system was influenced by the US FDA's Real Time Review system and provides consultations on procedures for changes in order to conduct advance consultations with PMDA regarding the sufficiency of application materials. When the application materials are completed based upon the consultation records of the consultations on procedures for changes, an official application for approval is filed. The target administrative processing period after the application for approval is filed is two months from the time the documents required for reviews are completed, excluding the period required for reliability studies.

When this system was first introduced, it was limited to changes to raw materials only or changes to sterilization methods only, but there are plans to look into expanding its scope of application in the future.

Minor Changes

According to the stipulations of Article 14, Paragraph 10 and Article 23-2, Paragraph 5 of the *Pharmaceutical Affairs Law*, when minor changes are made to approved conditions, a notification of minor changes is submitted. The scope of application of notifications of minor changes is stipulated in Article 47 of the *Pharmaceutical Affairs Law, Enforcement Regulations*, and "items that may affect the quality, effectiveness, and safety of a product" are excluded. For each individual determination, it is necessary to respond by referring to Appendix 1 of *Yakushokuki* No. 1023001 of October 23, Heisei 20 (2008).

No Procedures Required

When it is conclusively determined that the details of changes have no direct impact on effectiveness or safety and do not diminish the equivalence of the nature of the medical device, actions for changes to approved conditions are not required. For changes within the scope of specific examples listed in Appendix 2 of *Yakushokuki* No. 1023001 of October 23, Heisei 20 (2008), notifications for minor changes and applications for approval (certification) of partial changes are not required.

Summary

- In order to market a medical device, procedures including applications for approval, applications for certification and notifications are required, and these procedures differ according to the product's classification.
- When marketing a Highly Controlled Medical Device (Class III, IV), an application for product approval is filed with PMDA.
- When marketing a Designated Controlled Medical Devices (Class II), an application for product certification is filed with a Recognized Certification Body. For Controlled Medical Devices with no certification standards and medical devices that are Designated Controlled Medical Devices that do

not conform to certification standards, an application for product approval is filed with PMDA.
- When marketing a General Medical Device (Class I), a product notification is submitted to PMDA.
- When filing an application for approval (certification), it is necessary to attach a Summary Technical Document (STED).
- Even for medical devices that have been approved, etc., if the product is marketed after making partial changes, it is necessary to follow the procedures for changes, such as applications for changes.

Related Notifications

- *Yalkuki* No. 133 of July 26, Heisei 7 (1995), *Investigations regarding records of use of new medical devices*
- *Yakuhatsu* No. 479 of March 31, Heise 9 (1997), *Handling of clinical trial data for medical devices conducted overseas*
- *Yakuki* No. 60 of March 31, Heisei 9 (1997), *Standards for the basis of setting sterilization doses for radiation sterilization of medical devices*
- *Iyakukanhatsu* No 69 of May 1, Heisei 10 (1998), *Guidelines for sterilization validation for medical devices*
- *Iyakushinhatsu* No. 0213001 of February 13, Heisei 15 (2003), *Basic policies for biological tests required for applications for manufacturing (import) approval for medical devices*
- *Yakushokuhatsu* No. 072022 of July 20, Heisei 16 (2004), *Enforcement of matters (announcement) partially amending the Highly Controlled Medical Devices, Controlled Medical Devices, and General Medical Devices specified by the Minister of Health, Labour and Welfare based on the provisions of Article 2, Paragraphs 5 to 7 of the Pharmaceutical Affairs Law and matters (announcement) partially amending the Designated Maintenance Control Medical Devices specified by the Minister of Health, Labour and Welfare based on the provisions of Article 2, Paragraph 8 of the Pharmaceutical Affairs Law (Notification on Classification)*
- *Jimurenraku* of November 15, Heisei 16 (2004), *Delivery of the report of the international harmonization study on methods of assessing the effectiveness and safety of medical devices in medical device reviewss No. 19, 'Descriptions of raw materials in applications for manufacturing (import) approval for medical devices*
- *Yakushokukihatsu* No. 0216001 of February 16, Heisei 17 (2005), *Points to consider for applications for approval for medical devices*
- *Yakushokukihatsu* No. 0216003 of February 16,

Heisei 17 (2005), *Procedures for preparing STEDs for applications for approval for medical devices*

- PFSB/CND Notification No. 0330001 of March 30, Heisei 17 (2005), *Enactment and improvement/elimination of Ministerial Ordinances and announcements related to manufacturing control and quality control (GMP/QMS) for drug products and medical devices following enforcement of laws partially amending the Pharmaceutical Affairs Law and the Bleeding Donor Supply Service Control Law*

- *Yakushokukihatsu* No. 0401003 of April 1, Heisei 17 (2005), *Points to consider when preparing attached materials for applications for approval for medical devices under application in compliance with approval standards*

- *Yakushokukihatsu* No. 0331006 of March 31, Heisei 18 (2006), *Handling of test results of clinical trials for medical devices conducted overseas*

- Administrative Notice of June 23, Heisei 18 (2006), *Q&A regarding 'Handling of test results of clinical trials for medical devices conducted overseas*

- *Yakushokukihatsu* No. 0831002 of August 31, Heisei 19 (2007), *Basic policies for physical, chemical, and biological tests required for applications for approval for dental materials*

- *Yakushokushinsahatsu* No. 1210003, *Yakushokukanmahatsu* No. 1210007 of December

10, Heisei 20 (2008), *Acceleration of procedures related to changes and additions to manufacturing sites for medical devices and in_vitro diagnostics*

- *Yakushokukihatsu* No. 0804001 of August 4, Heisei 20 (2008), *Required scope of clinical trial data regarding medical devices*

- *Yakushokukihatsu* No. 0905001 of September 5, Heisei 20 (2008), *Setting of effective periods and stability tests for medical devices*

- *Yakushokukihatsu* No. 1023001 of October 23, Heisei 20 (2008), *Procedures for partial changes to medical devices*

- *Yakushokukihatsu* No. 1110001 of November 10, Heisei 20 (2008), *Acceleration of procedures related to specific changes for medical devices*

- *Yakushokuhatsu* No. 0327006 of March 27, Heisei 21 (2009), *Applications for approval for medical devices*

- *Yakushokukihatsu* No. 0327001 of March 27, Heisei 21 (2009), *Points to consider for applications for approval for medical devices following partial amendments of the Cabinet Order for fees related to the Pharmaceutical Affairs Law*

- *Yakushokukihatsu* No. 0327004 of March 27, Heisei 21 (2009), *Points to consider when preparing attached materials for applications for approval for generic medical devices*

- *Jimurenraku* of August 5, Heisei 21 (2009), *Q&A regarding setting of effective periods and stability tests for medical devices*

Japanese Applications for In Vitro Diagnostics

OBJECTIVES

❏ To understand the positioning of regulations on in vitro diagnostics in Japan.

❏ To understand that in vitro diagnostics regulations are based upon risk (system for applications for manufacturing and marketing approval).

❏ To understand an overview of pharmaceutical applications according to risk classification as well as specific points to consider in the application process.

RELATED LAWS AND REGULATIONS

❏ *Pharmaceutical Affairs Law* (Law No. 145 of Showa 35 (1960))

❏ *Pharmaceutical Affairs Law, Enforcement Ordinance* (Government Ordinance No. 11 of Showa 36 (1961))

❏ *Pharmaceutical Affairs Law, Enforcement Regulations* (Ministry of Health and Welfare Ordinance No. 1 of Showa 36 (1961))

❏ *Regulations for Structure and Facilities for Pharmacies* (Ministry of Health and Welfare Ordinance No. 2 of Showa 36 (1961))

❏ *Ministerial Ordinance on Good Quality Practice for Drug Products, Quasi-drugs, Cosmetics, and Medical Devices* (Ministry of Health, Labour and Welfare Ordinance No. 136 of Heisei 16 (2004)) (*Ministerial Ordinance on GQP*)

❏ *Ministerial Ordinance on Good Vigilance Practice for Drug Products, Quasi-drugs, Cosmetics, and Medical Devices* (Ministry of Health, Labour and Welfare Ordinance No. 135 of Heisei 16 (2004)) (*Ministerial Ordinance on GVP*)

❏ *Ministerial Ordinance on Quality Management System for Medical Devices and In Vitro Diagnostics* (Ministry of Health, Labour and Welfare Ordinance No. 169 of Heisei 16 (2004)) (*Ministerial Ordinance on QMS*)

❏ *Specified In Vitro Diagnostics for which the Minister of Health, Labour and Welfare has Established Standards Based on the Provisions of Article 14, Paragraph 1 of the Pharmaceutical Affairs Law* (Ministry of Health, Labour and Welfare Announcement No. 120 of March 29, Heisei 17 (2005))

❏ *Specified In Vitro Diagnostics for which the Minister of Health, Labour and Welfare has Established Standards Based on the Provisions of Article 23-2, Paragraph 1 of the Pharmaceutical Affairs Law* (Ministry of Health, Labour and Welfare Announcement No. 121 of Heisei 17 (2005))

❏ *Standards for In vitro Diagnostics Established by the Minister of Health, Labour and Welfare Based on the Provisions of Article 42, Paragraph 1 of the Pharmaceutical Affairs Law* (Ministry of

Table 44-1. Market Size for In Vitro Diagnostics

Fiscal Year	In Vitro Diagnostics (For Professional Use)	General Test Drugs	Total
1998	246,185	3,555	249,740
1999	249,908	2,914	252,822
2000	266,560	2,612	269,172
2001	280,082	2,220	282,302
2002	284,379	2,224	286,603
2003	288,579	2,475	291,054
2004	281,842	2,044	283,886
2005	286,415	2,323	288,738
2006	293,517	1,830	295,347
2007	297,220	2,006	299,226

(Research by the Japan Association of Clinical Reagents Industries (www.jacr.org.jp))
(Units: millions of yen)

Health, Labour and Welfare Announcement No. 126 of Heisei 17 (2005)) (Essential Principles)

Introduction

In the medical field, in vitro diagnostics play an important role in the diagnosis of diseases and monitoring, etc. for treatment. But because they are characterized by the application of various technologies and rapid technological improvements, there was a demand for efficient handling of in vitro diagnostics under the *Pharmaceutical Affairs Law. Yakuhatsu* No. 662 of June 29, Showa 60 (1985), *Handling of In Vitro Diagnostics* and *Yakushin* 1 No. 5 of July 15, Showa 60 (1985), *Handling of In Vitro Diagnostics for Approval Applications,* clarified the scope of in vitro diagnostics and measures were taken to simplify and streamline the administrative handling of evaluations. In the revision of the *Pharmaceutical Affairs Law,* based upon Law No. 96 of Heisei 14 (2002), regulations were established that took into consideration international harmonization, such as the adoption of risk-based classification, the *Ministerial Ordinance on QMS for devices and in vitro diagnosis* (Ministry of Health, Labour and Welfare Ordinance No. 169 of Heisei 16 (2004)), Essential Principles (Ministry of Health, Labour and Welfare Announcement No. 126 of Heisei 17 (2005)) and nomenclature.

Background of In Vitro Diagnostics
Definition of In Vitro Diagnostics

In Article 2, Paragraph 13 of the *Pharmaceutical Affairs Law,* in vitro diagnostics are defined as "drug products used exclusively for the purpose of diagnosing diseases and are not directly used in the body of a human or animal."

In Article 2, Paragraph 1, Section 2 of the *Pharmaceutical Affairs Law,* drug products are defined as "items used for the purpose of diagnosing, treating or preventing disease in a human or animal, and that are not machinery or appli-

ances, dental materials, medical supplies or sanitary goods (hereinafter referred to as "machinery and appliances, etc.") (excluding quasi-drugs)." Based upon the understanding that diagnostic drugs used outside the body correspond to the items that "are not machinery or appliances, dental materials, medical supplies or sanitary goods" described in this text, they have been considered drug products and handled as drug products. However, this created a large discrepancy with other countries, where such diagnostic drugs are handled as "Medical Devices (MD)" or "In Vitro Diagnostic Medical Devices (IVD-MD)." According to the *Pharmaceutical Affairs Law* amendment of 2002, such diagnostic drugs were still legally positioned as drug products but subject to regulations similar to medical devices in consideration of international consistency. In vitro diagnostics for humans and in vitro diagnostics for animals are under the jurisdiction of MHLW and the Ministry of Agriculture, Forestry and Fisheries, respectively.

Furthermore, according to its definition in the *Law Concerning the Examination and Regulation of Manufacture, etc. of Chemical Substances* (Law No. 334 of Showa 48 (1973)), "reagents" are "chemical substances used for detecting or assaying a substance through a chemical process, for experiments for synthesizing substances, or for measuring the physical properties of a substance" (Article 3, Paragraph 1, Section 3), and there are various types of reagents. In vitro diagnostics are also referred to as reagents for clinical tests, but unlike general chemical reagents and research reagents, they are subject to the regulations of the *Pharmaceutical Affairs Law.*

Market Size

The market size in Japan for in vitro diagnostics (for professional use) and general test drugs (for OTC use) over the 10 years, 1998–2007 is shown in **Table 44-1**.

The global market for in vitro diagnostics and laboratory

Table 44-2. Classification Perspectives

Classification	Class	Perspective
Low risk	Class I	From among in vitro diagnostics with a relatively low risk for diagnostic information and for which the accuracy of information is believed to have a relatively low effect on life support compared to Class III, those that have standard reference materials for calibration and are indicated in an MHLW Announcement as involving easy self-inspection. Examples: glutamate pyruvate transaminase (GPT), glutamate oxaloacetate transaminase (GOT), alkaline phosphatase (ALP), glucose, lactate dehydrogenase (LDH), hemoglobin A1c (HbA1c), immunoglobulin G (IgG), cholesterol,and estradiol
Low risk	Class II	In vitro diagnostics with a relatively low risk for diagnostic information and for which the accuracy of information is believed to have a relatively low effect on life support compared to Class III, and in vitro diagnostics for OTC use. Examples: Fibrinogen degradation products (FDP) morphological examinations of blood cells such as hematocrit (Ht) and measurements of autoimmunity such as anti-Sm antibodies
Others	Class III	In vitro diagnostics with a relatively high risk for diagnostic information and for which the accuracy of information is believed to have a large effect on life support. Examples: Diagnostic drugs for cancer and infectious diseases such as HIV and HCV, diagnostic drugs for genes such as nucleic-acid amplification testing (NAT) and bacteriological examinations

testing devices in 2006 is said to have been approximately ¥4 trillion. The market in Japan for in vitro diagnostic reagents (in vitro diagnostics and test reagents) and laboratory testing devices is approximately ¥450 billion, constituting approximately 11% of the global market.

Classification of In Vitro Diagnostics

The classification of in vitro diagnostics is similar to that of medical devices in that it is a risk-based classification, but unlike the classification of medical devices, which considers cases of side effects and failures of their functions, this classification focuses on risks related to diagnosis. First, in vitro diagnostics are categorized based upon whether the risks for diagnostic information are relatively low, and those with a relatively low risk for diagnostic information are further categorized into two groups. An overview is shown in **Table 44-2**.

Currently, classifications for each nomenclature have been established for all in vitro diagnostics marketed domestically within Japan based upon *Yakushokuhatsu* No. 0401031, *Nomenclature of In Vitro Diagnostics* (April 1, Heisei 17 (2005)). In this notification, Class I includes 131 products, Class II includes 345 products and Class III includes 243 products.

Nomenclature for In Vitro Diagnostics

The nomenclature for in vitro diagnostics under the *Pharmaceutical Affairs Law* has been established based

upon the notification of the Pharmaceutical and Food Safety Bureau of the Ministry of Health, Labour and Welfare (*Yakushokuhatsu* No. 0401031 of April 1, Heisei 17 (2005)). Classifications, etc. (test items, codes, definitions) for each nomenclature have also been established and regulations are implemented according to these. The nomenclature has been established, with reference to GMDN, for in vitro diagnostics marketed domestically within Japan. For specific nomenclature, etc., please refer to *Yakushokuhatsu* No. 0401031 of April 1, Heisei 17 (2005).

Overview of the Marketing Authorization Holder (MAH) System
Procedures for Approval Applications, etc. by Classification

When an in vitro diagnostic is manufactured (including outsourced manufacturing) and released to the market (released by the MAH), application procedures for approval, certification or notification must be followed for each individual product. These procedures differ depending upon the class to which the product under application belongs. An overview of the necessary procedures and standards for each class is shown in **Table 44-3**.

Further, regardless of the classification, an MAH license is required for marketing in vitro diagnostics as is required for drug products and medical devices.

As a rule, Class I in vitro diagnostics require only a

Table 44-3. Classification and Necessity of Approval

Class	For Medical Use	For OTC Use	Conformity Standards, etc.
Class I	Approval not required (notification for marketing)		Standard Essential Principles QMS Standard Reference Materials for Calibration
Class II	Third Party Certification (certification for marketing)	Same as for Medical Use	Standard Essential Principles QMS Certification Standards
Class III	Ministerial Approval (approval for marketing)		Standard Essential Principles QMS Approval Standards

notification. The "Certification" field for Class II is for products (specified in vitro diagnostics) with stipulations in the certification standards (standards stipulated in announcements based on Article 23, Paragraph 2, Section 1 of the *Pharmaceutical Affairs Law*) As is the case with medical devices, the Third Party Certification System is used whereby compliance with the standards is confirmed by a "Recognized Certification Body." These certification standards and products are stipulated in Ministry of Health, Labour and Welfare Announcement No. 121, *Specified In Vitro Diagnostics for which the Minister of Health, Labour and Welfare has Established Standards Based on the Provisions of Article 23-2, Paragraph 1 of the Pharmaceutical Affairs Law* (Heisei 17 (2005)).

However, even for Class I products, the procedures differ depending upon compliance with the standards. The procedures depending upon compliance with the standards, etc. as well as the relationships of examining authorities are shown in **Table 44-4**.

However, regardless of class, all radioactive in vitro diagnostics require an approval from the Minister of Health, Labour and Welfare, and applications are submitted to PMDA (*Yakushokukihatsu* No. 0511001 of May 11, Heisei 18 (2006)).

Moreover, for new products with no approved precedents on the Japanese market, the classification at the time of the application has been set as "to be determined," because the classification, etc. for the product will not be set until the review by PMDA is completed. Moreover, even after the classification is determined, the procedure for an approval is still used for the product until an MHLW Announcement for the new list of the products applicable to certification standards is issued.

Approval for Marketing

Approval for marketing in vitro diagnostics includes reviews of the effectiveness and safety, etc. of the in vitro diagnostic in the application (intended use, form/

composition/principles, product specifications, methods of use, etc.) as well as review of the production method and management system, and approval for each product is granted by the Minister of Health, Labour and Welfare. These materials have to be those for which ethics, scientific validity and reliability have been established based upon academic standards in the fields of medicine, pharmacology, etc. (including Essential Principles) at the time of submission, and must provide sufficient evidence to prove the in vitro diagnostics' quality, effectiveness and safety. Moreover, the manufacturing site must comply with standards for manufacturing control and quality control (QMS), and the in vitro diagnostics must be manufactured under appropriate quality control and safety management systems. The reviews of the application for the product approval are conducted by PMDA.

Certification for Marketing

For specified in vitro diagnostics for which the Minister of Health, Labour and Welfare has established standards based upon the provisions of Article 23-2, Paragraph 1 of the *Pharmaceutical Affairs Law* (Ministry of Health, Labour and Welfare Announcement No. 121 of Heisei 17 (2005); henceforth referred to as "Specified in vitro diagnostics"), reviews are conducted by a Recognized Certification Body accredited by MHLW. The standards of the reviews are the same as for approved products, but the reviews focus on compliance with certification standards (equivalence with existing in vitro diagnostics) and QMS compliance.

Additionally, in order to become a Recognized Certification Body, it is necessary to apply for accreditation with the Minister of Health, Labour and Welfare and meet the following accreditation requirements. As of February 2009, there were eight Recognized Certification Bodies allowed to review in vitro diagnostics.
- compliance with ISO/IEC Guide 62/65
- independence from MAHs
- no applicability of disqualification clauses

Table 44-4. Submission Categories From the Perspective of Compliance With Standards

Class	Compliance With Standards	Procedures	Reviewing Authority
Class I	Compliance	Notification	No Review (Submission to PMDA)
	Noncompliance	Application for Approval	PMDA
Class II	Compliance	Application for Certification	Recognized Certification Body
	Noncompliance	Application for Approval	PMDA
Class III	Compliance	Application for Approval	PMDA
	Noncompliance		
	No standards		
To Be Determined	New items		

Notification for Marketing

For specified in vitro diagnostics for which the Minister of Health, Labour and Welfare has established standards based upon the provisions of Article 14, Paragraph 1 of the *Pharmaceutical Affairs Law* (Ministry of Health, Labour and Welfare Announcement No. 120 of Heisei 17 (2005)), applications for approval and certification are unnecessary and marketing may be conducted by submitting a marketing notification (*Yakushokukihatsu* No. 0331006 of March 31, Heisei 17 (2005)). However, if the product is not compliant with the standards, or if the measurement principles and analytical sensitivity, etc. clearly differ from those of existing in vitro diagnostics, an application for approval is necessary.

Manufacturing License

In order to market in vitro diagnostics, it is necessary to have a Type II Marketing Authorization Holder (MAH) License for Pharmaceuticals. To obtain an MAH license, it is necessary to first obtain a business entity ID code and then an application can be made for a MAH license. The prefectural governor holds the authority to issue such licenses. For applications for MAH licenses, it is necessary to appoint a general controller (a pharmacist), a quality controller and a safety controller, and to establish a system conforming to the *Ministerial Ordinances on GQP* and *Ministerial Ordinances on GVP*. Moreover, for manufacturing sites to manufacture the product, it is necessary to obtain a manufacturing license (or Foreign Manufacturers Accreditation (FMA)). Manufacturing licenses shall be "granted by the Minister of Health, Labour and Welfare for individual manufacturing sites according to the categories stipulated in ordinances of the Ministry of Health, Labour and Welfare." Categories for manufacturing sites for in vitro diagnostics include the following three categories.

1. sites for performing all or part of manufacturing processes for radiopharmaceuticals

2. sites for performing all or part of manufacturing processes for non-radiopharmaceuticals (excluding sites described in 3, below

3. sites for performing only packing, labeling or storage from among the manufacturing processes for drug products described in 2, above

Process From Application to Approval

The development steps, from conducting exploratory studies to obtaining approval (certification) are shown in **Figure 44-1**.

Application for Approval

As described previously, an approval is granted after reviews are conducted on the product's effectiveness and safety and its manufacturing method and management systems. An overview of an application for approval is described with a focus on descriptions provided on the application for approval.

Submission Categories

The submission categories for approval are as follows. Caution is required as the materials to be attached to the application differ depending upon the submission category (*Yakushokuhatsu* No. 0216004 and *Yakushokukihatsu* No. 0216005 of February 16, Heisei 17 (2005)).

- New item: product for attempting to detect or measure a new item
- Products outside approval standards: Class III in vitro diagnostics with no stipulations in the approval standards; applicable products at this time include items for human immunodeficiency virus (HIV), hepatitis C virus (HCV), hepatitis D virus (HDV), human T-lymphotropic virus (HTLV) and genetic testing of pathogens, as well as items for human genetic testing
- Products meeting approval standards: products

Figure 44-1. Steps From Exploratory Study to Marketing

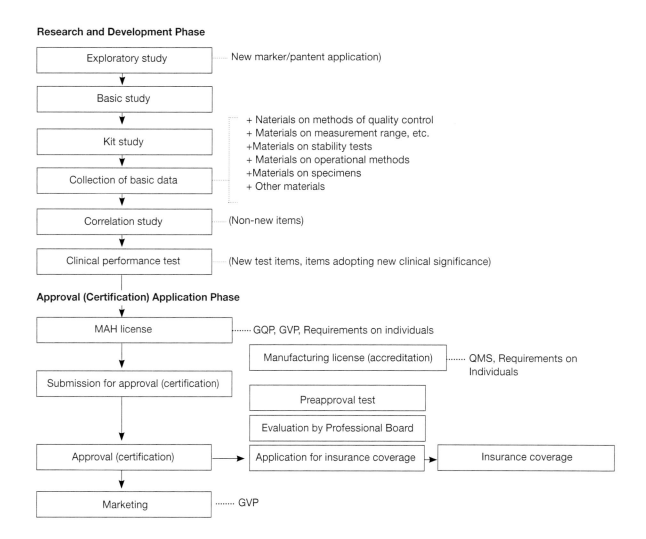

Research and Development Phase

Exploratory study ········ New marker/pantent application)

Basic study

Kit study ······· + Naterials on methods of quality control
+ Materials on measurement range, etc.
+Materials on stability tests
+ Materials on operational methods
+Materials on specimens
+ Other materials

Collection of basic data

Correlation study ········ (Non-new items)

Clinical performance test ········ (New test items, items adopting new clinical significance)

Approval (Certification) Application Phase

MAH license ········ GQP, GVP, Requirements on individuals

Manufacturing license (accreditation) ········ QMS, Requirements on Individuals

Submission for approval (certification)

Preapproval test

Evaluation by Professional Board

Approval (certification) → Application for insurance coverage → Insurance coverage

Marketing ········ GVP

---

with stipulations in the approval standards and that conform to the approval standards
- Nonconforming products: products with stipulations in the approval standards, certification standards (standards based upon Article 23-2, Paragraph 1) or standards not requiring approval or certification (standards based upon Article 14, Paragraph 1) and that do not conform to those standards

Further, for radioactive in vitro diagnostics, an application for approval is required even for products conforming to the certification standards or the standards not requiring approval or certification (*Yakushokukihatsu* No. 0511001 of May 11, Heisei 18 (2006)).

Approval Standards

Products described in the Pharmaceutical and Food Safety Bureau Notification *Enactment of approval standards for in vitro diagnostics* (*Yakushokuhatsu* No. 0622006 of June 22, Heisei 17 (2005)) correspond to the products under category 3 previously mentioned in Submission Categories, and the specific details of those products are as follows. For further details, please refer to *Yakushokuhatsu* No. 0622006 of June 22, Heisei 17 (2005).

Reagents for Detection

When a comparison is conducted with a control in vitro diagnostic or detection method and then, the detection results for identical specimens for the comparative product (or detection method) and the product under application

---

Table 44-5. Details and Scope of Materials to be Attached to Applications for Approval

Attachment	Items of the Attachment	Details of the Items of the Attachment	Scope of Materials to be Attached to Applications for Approval			
			New items	Products Outside Approval Standards	Nonconforming products	Products Meeting Approval Standards
A. Background of origin or discovery and status of use overseas, etc.	1. Background of origin or discovery and status of use overseas, etc.	1. History of the development 2. Status of domestic and overseas use 3. Significance for clinical diagnosis	R	R	R	N
	2. Descriptions of product under application	1. Measurement method (measurement principles, assay procedures and methods for determination) 2. Information on ingredients involved in reaction system 3. Descriptions of similarities with existing in vitro diagnostics	R	R	R	N
B. Setting specifications	1. Methods of quality control		R	R	R	D
	2. Measurement range, etc.		R	R	R	N
	3. Setting reference substances for calibration		R	R	R	D
	4. Compliance with Essential Principles	1. Declarations of compliance with Essential Principles 2. Compliance with Essential Principles	R	R	R	R
C. Stability	Establishing storage conditions and shelflife		R	R	R	R
D. Performance	1. Performance	1. Spiked recovery test 2. Dilution test	D	D	D	N
	2. Operation		R	D	D	N
	3. Specimen	1. Tests regarding reaction specificity	R	R	R	N
	4. Correlations with existing in vitro diagnostics	1. Tests regarding data on correlations with existing in vitro diagnostics	N/A	R	R	R
	5. Tests using seroconversion panels, etc.		D	D	D	D
E. Risk analysis	Risk analysis	1. Risk analysis implementation systems	R	R	R	R
		2. Important hazards	R	R	R	R
F. Manufacturing methods	Manufacturing processes and manufacturing facilities		R	R	R	R
G. Clinical performance test results	Clinical performance test results		R	D	D	D

R: Attachment required; N: Attachment not required at the time of submission (should be readily available for PMDA's future inquiries); D: Determined for individual in vitro diagnostics; N/A: Not applicable

Figure 44-2. Application for Approval

Revenue Stamp	**Application for Approval for In Vitro Diagnostic**	

Name	Nomenclature	
	Brand name	
Intended Use		
Form, Structure and Principles		
Components involved in reaction system		
Product specifications		
Assay procedures or methods of use		
Manufacturing method		
Storage conditions and shelf life		

Manufacturing site of the product to be marketed	Name	Location	Category of License or Accreditation	Number of License or Accreditation

Manufacturing site of active drug substances	Name	Location	Category of License or Accreditation	Number of License or Accreditation

Remarks	

Based on the above information, we hereby file this application for approval for the in vitro diagnostics.

[Date]

Address (Location of head office in case of a corporation)

Name (Name of corporation and name of representative in case of a corporation)

To: the Minister of Health, Labour and Welfare

(Form No. 22 (2))
(items related to Article 38))

are summarized in an appropriate table, the calculated agreement rate of the two must be 90% or higher.

Test Method
- Test Operator
  - Testing is conducted by the applicant or is outsourced to another testing institution, etc. The test operator (or test supervisor) writes a statement and signs documents showing test results.
- Number of specimens and selection method
  - As a rule, 100 or more specimens that have been appropriately collected using normal methods and appropriately stored are tested. However, this rule need not apply if the clinical performance can be properly assessed or if the subject disease is extremely rare.
  - As a rule, 50 or more specimens are used for the fewer of the positive or negative specimens, and the specimens are selected by including some near the concentration used for clinical determination (cut-off value, etc.). However, this rule need not apply if the subject disease count or the specimen type of the disease is extremely rare, or if it is difficult to confirm whether specimens are near the clinical concentration. In addition, semi-quantitative reagents and bacteria identification reagents should follow this method.

Reagents for Measurement

When a comparison is conducted with a control in vitro diagnostic or measurement method and the measurement results for identical specimens for the comparative product (or measurement method) and the product under application are plotted on an X-axis and a Y-axis, respectively, to obtain the correlation coefficient and regression line of the measurement values, the correlation coefficient must be 0.9 or higher and the slope of the regression line must be 0.9–1.1.

Test Method
- Test Operator
  - Testing is conducted by the applicant or is outsourced to another testing institution, etc. The test operator (or test supervisor) writes a statement and signs documents showing test results.
- Number of specimens and selection method
  - As a rule, 100 or more specimens that have been appropriately collected using normal methods and appropriately stored are tested. However, this rule need not apply if the clinical performance can be properly assessed or if the subject disease is extremely rare.
  - The concentrations of the specimens shall be distributed across the entire measuring range and specimens are selected by including some near

the concentration used for clinical determination (standard value, cut-off value, etc.). However, this rule need not apply if the subject disease count or the specimen type of the disease is extremely rare.

Comparative Products

For the subject in vitro diagnostic, an approved or certified in vitro diagnostic that is actually used in clinical practice and has good performance in areas such as reproducibility from the perspective of current levels of technology should be selected. For the approved (certified) in vitro diagnostic used as the control, if there are multiple products, as a rule, two or more products are selected as the controls. If there are multiple measurement methods, two or more types of in vitro diagnostics are selected as the control in order to evaluate multiple measurement methods. For semi-quantitative reagents, the scope of the indicated values must match. If the "y"-intercept of the regression line of a reagent for measurement greatly deviates from 0, it is preferable not to use it as the control. Further, if there is a standard detection or measurement method adopted by public agencies (WHO, etc.), standard-setting organizations (Joint Committee for Traceability in Laboratory Medicines (JCTLM), Clinical and Laboratory Standards Institute (CLSI), Japanese Committee for Clinical Laboratory Standards (JCCLS), etc.) or related academic societies, etc., as a rule, the result of that detection or measurement should be used as the control.

Details and Scope of Attachments

The details and scope of the attachments for applications for approval are shown in **Figure 44-5** (*Yakushokuhatsu* No. 0216004 of February 16, Heisei 17 (2005)).

Points to Consider When Developing Applications for Approval

Applications for approval are made by submitting an application (**Figure 44-2**) according to Form No. 22 (2) as stipulated in Article 38 of the *Pharmaceutical Affairs Law, Enforcement Regulations*. Points to consider for items described in each column in an application are as follows (*Yakushokukihatsu* No. 0216005 of February 16, Heisei 17 (2005)).

Name Field
Nomenclature
- Accurately describe the nomenclature and classification code. Furthermore, if there is no nomenclature, describe an overview (overview of measurement items and the clinical significance of the in vitro diagnostic in around 300 characters) of the relevant in vitro diagnostic in the Remarks field.
- For applications for products capable of simultaneously measuring multiple items, etc., list all relevant general nomenclature and classification code numbers.

Brand Name

- As a rule, products may be named without restrictions, but care should be taken to avoid misunderstanding and confusion on the part of users, and names that lower the products' dignity or that are excessively exaggerated should be avoided.

Intended Use Field

Describe the measurement specimen (specimen type), measurement item (analyte (measurand)) and whether it is for detection (for qualitative tests) or measurement (for quantitative or semi-quantitative tests). Use a format such as, "Aids the diagnosis of..." when describing the clinical significance.

Form, Structure and Principles Field

Make simple and concise entries so that the nature of the product under application can be understood.

Component Reagent

- Describe the name of the component reagent.
- If the form or structure of the reagent does not affect performance, describe the dosage form (e.g., liquid drug).
- If there are multiple standard solutions, describe a number or identification mark along with the name to indicate that there are multiple reagents.

Form

- If the form or structure of the reagent affects performance, provide a graphic representation of the form and structure. If the size does not affect performance, it does not have to be described. If the form and structure are not graphically represented, attach a photograph showing the appearance of the product to the Remarks field.

Principles

Provide a simple description of the measurement principles, including "components involved in the reaction system." However, for measurement principles that are commonly known in academic societies, etc., it is sufficient to describe the name of the measurement principle.

Ingredients Involved in Reaction System Field

- Describe the names of component reagents containing ingredients involved in the reaction system.
- Describe the ingredients involved in the reaction system and their quantity or content amount.
  - Quantities may be described by expressing quantities per bottle or per measurement unit. A range may also be used, as long as the performance can be verified. If the component reagent is a freeze-dried product and is described as such,

the indicated concentration at the time of use is sufficient. If the quantities or content amounts differ within the scope of the expressed range, or if there are different ingredients that are not involved in the reaction system (e.g., preservatives) and the performance is identical, a single application may be used.

- If antibodies (antiserum) are used, describe the name of the animal species from which they are derived in *katakana* and clearly describe whether they are monoclonal antibodies or polyclonal antibodies. For monoclonal antibodies, describe the name of the producing cells.

Product Specifications Field
Methods of Quality Control

- Describe the quality control methods for the final product. If items other than sensitivity tests, accuracy tests and simultaneous reproducibility tests are set, describe the basis for the settings, such as the reasons for setting that item and the reasons for selecting the test method.
- If, within a single item, two or more types of specimens (e.g., blood serum and urine) are used, describe the performance of each if the performance differs.
- If a reference material is used, describe the details of that reference material (including its origin).

Examples

As examples, for quantitative reagents, describe the measuring range using a representative model, and for qualitative reagents, describe the minimum detectable sensitivity limit.

Assay Procedures or Methods of Use Field

Divide preparative procedures for reagents and test solutions from assay procedures and provide simple descriptions so an overview of the methods of use can be understood. Further, if the method of specimen collection or storage affects the measurement results and particular caution is required, describe the specimen collection or storage method.

Preparative Procedures for Reagents and Test Solutions

- Describe the preparative procedures for all reagents. For reagents to be used without preparation, state "Use without preparation."

Assay Procedures

- Describe standard assay procedures. If a device is used for measurement, describe necessary assay items from the perspective of the reagent so that the reaction process can be understood.

- For specimens and reagents, describe specific amounts. Further, ranges and relative fluid volumes may be described so long as performance can be guaranteed.
- For measurement wavelength, describe a specific value. If the measurement wavelength differs depending upon the device, a range may be used within the scope of which measurements have been verified.
- For qualitative items, describe the method of judgment (cut-off values, etc.).

Manufacturing Method Field

If full details cannot be described in the Manufacturing Method field, use the phrase, "See attachment," in this field and provide an attachment. Examples of described items and points to consider include the following:

Kit Composition

- Describe the name of the reagent composing the kit. For component reagents containing ingredients involved in the reaction system, describe all of the ingredients involved in reactions. For component reagents that do not contain ingredients involved in the reaction system, instead of describing individual ingredient names, it is sufficient to describe, for example, "Prepared using a buffering agent, etc."
- For each component reagent of a kit product, if the reagent is distributed separately or manufactured as a supplementary reagent, describe it as such.

Manufacturing Process

- Describe the manufacturing process and provide information on the site where the product is manufactured, etc. in an easy-to-understand manner using a process flowchart, etc.
- For component reagents containing ingredients involved in the reaction system, describe all processes, from the receipt of raw materials or intermediate products, etc. used in the final container-filling process to the process of product release determination, in a flowchart, etc.
- For component reagents that do not contain ingredients involved in the reaction system, describe all processes, from the receipt of the component reagent to the process of product release determination, in a flowchart, etc.
- If the form or structure of a container affects performance, include a description of the process of receiving the container in the flowchart.

Names and Addresses of Manufacturers

- Describe information on the manufacturing sites performing each process (name and location, as well as license and certification numbers if licenses and certification have been obtained). Also describe the information in the flowchart in an easy-to-understand manner.

Operator Performing Design Control

- If the party who designed the product is the applicant and its site has the main function, describe as such. If not, describe the name of the individual or corporate name of the operator who performed design control.

External Testing Institutions

- If in-process tests are outsourced to an external testing laboratory, describe the name and location of the outsourced testing laboratory for each relevant process. Moreover, describe which processes involve test items that are outsourced.

Storage Conditions and Shelf Life Field

Set optimal storage conditions and shelf life based upon stability test results. For stability, although it is possible to set the storage conditions and shelf life by using an extrapolated test, etc., the shelf life should be set to reflect actual practice by taking into consideration the product's properties and distribution period.

Further, if different settings are established for each component reagent, describe the storage method and shelf life for each and set the storage method and shelf life for the kit.

Manufacturing Site of Product to be Marketed Field

Describe the manufacturer name and location, manufacturing license (certification) number and license and classification category of the operations site performing the manufacturing process for the product.

Manufacturing Site of Active Drug Substances Field

Make an entry if a drug substance, etc. registered in the Drug Master File System is used. There are currently no applicable in vitro diagnostics.

Remarks Field

- Describe the type of MAH, the MAH license date, license number, license category and the location of the operations site having the majority of the operational functions.
- Describe the submission category for approval (new product, product outside approval standards, product meeting approval standards or nonconforming product). If an application for approval is being filed for a product that does not conform to the certification standards or the standards not

requiring approval or certification, explain why the product does not conform to the relevant standards.

- If the product is a radioactive in vitro diagnostic, describe it as such.
- If stability testing is continuing, describe as such.
- If the product is one subject to preapproval testing, describe it as such.
- If the product has been manufactured using recombinant DNA technologies, describe "Recombinant DNA technologies used."
- If there are any accessories, describe them along with the details.
- Explain whether there is a request for insurance coverage and the requested category.
- Respond "Yes" regarding the inclusion of a package insert (draft) and attach the draft.
- In the Form, Structure and Principles field, if the form and structure are graphically represented, attach a photograph showing the appearance of the product.

Overview of Attachments

Entries in the attachments (**Table 44-5**) must be in Japanese. If the attached materials are not in Japanese, attach a translation of an overview (in this case, also submit the original source file). If any materials were deemed unnecessary for the product, explain the decision. For each test included in each attachment, describe the testing location, the test supervisor, the test period, etc. and include a signature and statement from the test operator or person preparing the attachments.

A. Materials Regarding Background of Origin or Discovery and Status of Use Overseas, etc.

1. Materials describing the background of origin or discovery and status of use overseas, etc.
   a. Describe the history of the discovery of the product, the status of domestic and overseas use, and the significance for clinical diagnosis.
   b. Describe the background starting from the purpose of development to the discovery of the item's clinical significance as a diagnostic based upon various submitted literature and materials.
   c. If the product is being sold overseas, describe the status of use overseas.
   d. Regarding the significance for clinical diagnosis, provide a simple description of the usefulness based upon data from foreign data/material and domestic data/material, etc. For new items, provide a comparison with existing measurement items and diagnoses and describe the relative positioning of the product.

2. Materials regarding descriptions of products under application
   Provide simple, easy-to-understand descriptions for each of the following items regarding novelty and characteristics, etc.
   - measurement method (measurement principles, assay procedures and methods for determination)
   - descriptions of similarities with existing in vitro diagnostics (if the product is not categorized as a new item, explain why it is not applicable to the new item category.)

B. Materials on Setting of Specifications

1. Materials on methods of quality control
   a. Describe the actual measurement values from tests performed based upon methods of quality control that you established. When establishing items other than sensitivity tests, accuracy tests or simultaneous reproducibility tests, explain the reasons for establishing that item.
   b. Actual measured values require three or more lots, with three or more measurement results per lot. For double measurements, count each double measurement performed as a single measurement.
2. Materials on measuring range, etc.
   a. For reagents for measurement (quantitative), describe the measuring range (upper limit and lower limit values).
   b. For reagents for detection (qualitative), describe test results on minimum detectable sensitivity (limit of detection).
3. Materials on setting reference substances for calibration
   Describe the details of reference substances for calibration or standard substances (including the origins of each), the basis for the settings and the composition, purity and concentration or titer.
4. Materials on compliance with Essential Principles
   a. Attach materials proving compliance with the Essential Principles prepared based upon the checklist for compliance with standard Essential Principles.
   b. If there are no suitable specifications or standards for the relevant in vitro diagnostic, perform necessary tests and explain the validity of the settings of the adopted tests.
   c. Attach self-declaration forms.
   For products with Essential Principles and approval standards, if an application is filed based upon the product's compliance with the approval standards, explain how the product is in compliance with the approval standards and has been manufactured in compliance with the regulations for manu-

facturing control and quality control for in vitro diagnostics.

- For products outside approval standards or non-conforming products, explain how the product has been manufactured in compliance with the Essential Principles and with regulations for manufacturing control and quality control for in vitro diagnostics.
- Declarations must be made by the CEO or the general controller.

C. Materials on Stability (*Yakushokukihatsu* No. 1023-1 of October 23, Heisei 21 (2009))

1. Materials on setting storage conditions and shelf life
   a. The test should be performed until the expiration date under the established storage method.
   b. The test items should be those stipulated in the quality control methods.
   c. Set the shelf life based upon the measurement results for three or more lots, with two more measurements per lot, measured at three or more time points including the starting time.

D. Materials on Performance

1. Materials on performance
   a. For measurement (quantitative) items for which solutions can be prepared at a fixed concentration using pure substances, etc., attach the results of a spiked recovery test.
   b. For measurement (quantitative) items, perform a dilution test.
2. Materials on assay procedures
   a. For products involving manual methods, attach test results on important reaction conditions (reaction time, etc.).
   b. If special attention is required for the method of specimen collection, describe the rationale for the method of specimen collection.
3. Materials on specimens
   Attach materials on reaction specificity (effects of coexisting substances, cross-reactivity, nonspecific reactions, effects of inactivation, effects of anticoagulants, etc.).
4. Materials on correlations with existing in vitro diagnostics (other than new items)
   a. Refer to the notifications regarding the approval standards and prepare materials on correlations.
   b. For products not conforming to the approval (certification) standards or to the standards not requiring approval (certification), explain the reasons for nonconformance.
5. Materials on tests using seroconversion panels, etc.
   For products for which seroconversion panels,

etc. are available and a review of such panels, etc. is required, attach the test results.

E. Materials on Risk Analysis

1. Materials on risk analysis implementation systems and materials regarding important hazards
   a. Refer to JIS T 14971 and provide an overview of the company's internal risk management system and the status of its implementation.
   b. For risk analysis, explain that the expected risks are acceptable relative to the clinical usefulness.
   c. For hazards for which MHLW, etc. has demanded safety measures, use a tabular format to summarize the risk analysis for that hazard and risk mitigation measures that have been implemented.
   d. If significant hazards are identified as a result of risk analysis, use a tabular format to summarize the risk analysis for that hazard and risk mitigation measures that have been implemented.
2. Materials on ingredients contained in component reagents (for ingredients derived from human blood)
   Attach test results that rule out the presence of HBV and HIV along with test results for HCV.

F. Materials Regarding Manufacturing Methods

1. Describe all manufacturing processes.
2. Describe the manufacturing process and quality test items in a process flowchart along with information (the following three items) on the manufacturing site performing that process.
   a. name of manufacturing site
   b. location of manufacturing site
   c. license/certification numbers, if licenses and/or certification have been obtained
   d. If an application for a license or certification is being processed, state as such.
3. If the manufacturing process is performed at multiple manufacturing sites, etc., provide descriptions so that the relationships of those sites can be understood.
4. For each quality test item, describe the objectives of the test, an overview of the test and its relationship with the product specifications.
5. If a quality test is outsourced, describe which test item of which manufacturing process is outsourced along with the following information.
   a. outsourced test items
   b. name and location of the contractor
   c. name and location of test site
6. Describe the name, location, etc. of the operator and operations site performed design control.

G. Materials on Results of Clinical Performance Tests

For new items and products outside approval standards, etc. with new significance for clinical diagnosis, describe the clinical performance test results providing the basis for the new significance for clinical diagnosis.

1. Facilities and number of specimens shall include (as a rule) two or more facilities and 150 or more specimens (including those in the normal range). For the number of specimens, this rule need not apply if a statistical analysis is possible and a sufficient clinical analysis can be conducted.
2. When preparing materials, the following items may be considered:
   a. target disease or clinical condition
   b. reference interval (standard values)
   c. cut-off values (for products used for detection)
   d. true positive rate and true negative rate in relation to disease
   e. ROC analysis
   f. effects of abnormal specimens (hemolysis, milky fluid, jaundice, etc.) on measurement results
   g. effects of drugs
   h. others
3. If results from clinical performance tests conducted overseas are used, consider the effects of racial differences, etc. between Japanese and foreign subjects on the in vitro diagnostic's performance and clinical significance.

Evaluation by Professional Board

Evaluation by a Professional Board is held on reviews of products requiring such discussions (new items, products outside approval standards, some nonconforming products, and products questioned by the reviewing authority) by designating external specialists from an expert committee who work in fields corresponding to the product under review. Discussions may be held via written communication or via a face-to-face conference.

If questions arise regarding new items or data, raw data (clinical performance test data, testing agreement, test protocol, etc.) may be checked.

Preapproval Tests

For in vitro diagnostics important to public health, the advisability of product specifications is determined through a review conducted by the National Institute of Infectious Diseases (NIDD) after submitting the application for approval (*Yakushokukihatsu* No. 0909001 of September 9, Heisei 17 (2005)).

Applicable Test Items
- products comply with the antibody standards for blood type determination
- test items regarding blood transfusion: syphilis, HBV (only for products targeting genes and HBs antigens), HCV, HDV, HIV, HTLV
- particularly important test items for public

health: HAV, rubella virus, chlamydia trachomatis (only for products targeting genes and antigens)

Application

Submit one original copy of the application for approval for in vitro diagnostics, as well as four duplicate copies and three copies of the attachments. When filing an application, affix a revenue stamp for the preapproval test fees, in addition to applicable application fee. Regarding the attachment, add the following materials.
- for imported products, the package insert used in the exporting country
- if a measuring instrument is a exclusive device, the device's specifications and the advisability of temporarily bringing the device into NIDD
- other necessary materials requested by NIDD (e.g., data on reproducibility between operators, reproducibility between measurement days, reproducibility between lots and clinical performance tests)

Determination of Implementation of NIDD Tests

The applicant is notified when the preapproval test at NIDD is deemed to be necessary by the NIDD after evaluation. Upon receiving the notification, the applicant submits tested products (as a rule, three lots) to NIDD.

Fees

Fees related to in vitro diagnostics as of 1 April 2009 are shown in **Table 44-6** as reference.

Time Clock

The standard administrative processing period for new applications for in vitro diagnostics is six months.

As a rule, the standard administrative processing period for applications for approval of partial changes to the approval conditions (partial-change application) is also six months. However, applications for changes involving only the shelf life or changes or additions to manufacturing sites only are expeditiously processed in three months.

Partial-Change Application, Notification of Changes

Generally, when a change is made to an approval condition, depending upon the details of the changes, the following procedures are necessary.

Changes Requiring a New Application for Approval

These are non-minor changes affecting ingredients and quantities involved in reaction systems, as well as performance, etc.

Table 44-6. Application Fees (Units: ¥)

Category		Fees		
		PMDA	State	Total
In vitro diagnostic (no approval standards)		584,100	43,200	627,300
In vitro diagnostic (with approval standards)	Basic	282,900	23,500	306,400
	Series addition*	60,300		60,300 × number of added composition products

Fees for series application (number of composition products = n): 282,900+23,500+60,300 × (n-1)

Changes Requiring an Application for Approval of Partial Changes (Partial-Change Application)

As a rule, these are changes that do not diminish the nature of the in vitro diagnostic. Examples include:

- changes in brand name (changes other than those require a notification of changes)
- changes made to maintain uniformity in brand names due to modifications, etc. in corporate identity
- addition of clinical significance
- addition of specimen types, etc.
- changes in form or structure affecting performance
- changes in performance tests
- changes in measurement wavelengths
- changes in storage conditions and shelf life, etc.

Changes Requiring Notification

These are minor changes with no effect on product performance. Notifications must be made within 30 days after the changes. Examples include:

- changes in brand name due to changes in business names and trademarks
- changes in a component reagent's name only (no changes in details)
- changes in ingredient names only
- changes in reagents' preparative procedures
- increases and decreases of the number of the processes in manufacturing methods

Changes Not Requiring an Application for Changes or Notification, etc.

Applications for changes or notifications are not required for extremely minor changes with no effect on product performance.

Series Applications

What is a series?

If multiple measurement items (products) are combined to be used as one in medical institutions, those with a recognized clinical necessity may be registered as a single product of an in vitro diagnostic.

For example, the following products correspond to an in vitro diagnostic series.

- paper reagents (e.g., paper reagents for urine tests)
- plate reagents (e.g., plate reagents for serum allergen measurements)
- cultures or disks (e.g., culture sets for identification and susceptibility, drug susceptibility disks)
- reagents or film for autoanalyzers (e.g., reagents for serum autoanalyzers)

Handling of Series Applications, etc.

Although it was previously possible to file an application for approval for a series of products as a single product, because approval, certification or notification is granted according to classification under the revised *Pharmaceutical Affairs Law*, separate procedures should be performed for each category of approval, certification or notification (henceforth referred to as "category of approval, etc.") for each composition product composing the series product under the same nomenclature and brand name (series name). This means that for one series of products, series applications, etc. should be filed separately for each category of approval, etc.; however, they could be handled together as one series. The series products for which approval, certification or notification has been obtained, each individual product composing the series product (henceforth referred to as "composition product") may be marketed individually or in combinations (*Yakushokukihatsu* No. 0221001 of February 21, Heisei 19 (2007)).

Application for Certification

As explained under Certification for Marketing above, applications for approval for designated in vitro diagnostics are filed to a Recognized Certification Body. Reviews will focus on compliance with certification standards and compliance with QMS (*Yakushokukihatsu* No. 0331033 and *Yakushokukihatsu* No. 0216010 of March 31, Heisei 17 (2005)).

Certification Standards

Specified in vitro diagnostics are announced in Ministry of Health, Labour and Welfare Announcement No. 121 of Heisei 17 (2005). In addition to the certification standards described in this announcement, details of materials indicating compliance with certification standards are described in *Yakushokuhatsu* No. 0331033 of March 31, Heisei 17 (2005), and the handling of these certification standards is described in the Pharmaceutical and Food Safety Bureau Notification, *Enactment of certification standards for in vitro diagnostics* (*Yakushokuhatsu* No. 0622004 of June 22, Heisei 17 (2005)). The specific details are as follows. For further information, please refer to the notification.

Reagents for Detection

When a comparison is conducted with a control in vitro diagnostic or detection method and the detection results for identical specimens for the comparative product (or detection method) and the product under application are summarized in an appropriate tabular format, the calculated concordance rate of the two must be 90% or higher.

Test Method

- Test Operator

  Testing is conducted by the applicant or is outsourced to another testing institution, etc. The test operator (or test supervisor) writes a statement and signs documents showing test results.
- Number of specimens and selection method
  - ○ Generally, 50 or more specimens that have been appropriately collected using normal methods and appropriately stored are tested, but this rule need not apply if the performance can be properly assessed or if the subject disease is extremely rare.
  - ○ As a rule, 25 or more specimens are used for the fewer of the positive or negative specimens, and the specimens are selected by including some near the concentration used for clinical determination (cut-off value, etc.) in order to assess the performance properly. However, this rule need not apply if the subject disease count or the specimen type of the disease is extremely rare, or if it is difficult to confirm whether specimens are near the clinical concentration.

Reagents for Measurement

When a comparison is conducted with a control in vitro diagnostic or measurement method and the measurement results for identical specimens for the comparative product (or measurement method) and the product under application are plotted on an X-axis and a Y-axis, respectively to obtain the correlation coefficient and regression line of the measurement values, the correlation coefficient must be 0.9 or higher and the slope of the regression line must be 0.9–1.1.

Test Method

- Test Operator
  - ○ Testing is conducted by the applicant or is outsourced to another testing institution, etc. The test operator (or test supervisor) writes a statement and signs documents showing test results.
- Number of specimens and selection method
  - ○ Generally, 50 or more specimens that have been appropriately collected and stored using normal methods are tested. However, this rule need not apply if the clinical performance can be properly assessed or if the subject disease is extremely rare.
  - ○ The concentrations of the specimens shall be distributed across the entire measuring range, and specimens are selected by including some near the concentration used for clinical determination (standard value, cut-off value, etc.) in order to properly assess the performance. However, this rule need not apply if the subject disease count or the specimen type of the disease is extremely rare.

Comparative Products

For the subject in vitro diagnostic, an approved or certified in vitro diagnostic that is actually used in clinical practice and has good performance in areas such as reproducibility from the perspective of current levels of technology should be selected. For the approved (certified) in vitro diagnostic used as the control, if there are multiple products, as a rule, two or more types are selected as the control. If there are multiple measurement methods, two or more types of in vitro diagnostics are selected as the control in order to evaluate multiple measurement methods. If the y-intercept of the regression line of a reagent for measurement is greatly deviated from 0, it is preferable not to use it as the control. Further, if there is a standard detection or measurement method adopted by public agencies (WHO, etc.), standard-setting organizations (JCTLM, CLSI, JCCLS, etc.) or related academic societies, etc., as a rule, that detection or measurement method should be used as the control.

Details and Scope of Attachments

The details and scope of materials to be attached to applications for certification are shown in **Table 44-7** (*Yakushukuhatsu* No. 0331033 and *Yakushokukihatsu* No. 0331010 of March 31, Heisei 17 (2005)).

Points to Consider When Developing Applications for Certification

The points to consider for applications for certification are the same as those for applications for approval. However, it is not necessary to describe the clinical significance in the Intended Use field.

Overview of Attachment

The attachments for applications for certification are the same as those for approval (**Table 44-8**) in general. However, the details of a self-declaration form attached as

Table 44-7. Details and Scope of Materials to be Attached to Applications for Certification

Attached Material	Items of the Attached Material	Details of Item of Attachment
A. Overview of the product	Materials describing product under application	• Measurement method (measurement principles, assay principles, and methods for determination) • Information on ingredients involved in reaction system • Descriptions of similarities with existing in vitro diagnostics (descriptions stating that new items do not apply)
B. Setting specifications	Compliance with Essential Principles	• Self-declaration forms (conformity with certification standards and QMS regulations) • Materials proving compliance with Essential Principles (checklist for compliance with standard Essential Principles)
C. Stability	Setting of storage conditions and shelf life	Setting of storage conditions and shelf life
D. Performance	Correlations with existing in vitro diagnostics	Correlations with existing in vitro diagnostics
E. Risk analysis	• Risk analysis implementation systems	Risk analysis implementation systems and status of implementation
	• Important hazards	Summary of the results of risk analyses and risk mitigation measures for hazards for which safety measures have been demanded by MHLW, etc.
		Summary of the results of risk analyses and risk mitigation measures for important hazards
		Ingredients contained in component reagents (for human-derived ingredients, tests ruling out HBV and HIV, and test results for HCV)
F. Manufacturing methods	Manufacturing processes and manufacturing facilities	Manufacturing processes and manufacturing facilities

a material on compliance with Essential Principles are as follows.

Include descriptions of compliance with Essential Principles and the relevant certification standards, as well as the fact that manufacturing is implemented in compliance with manufacturing control and quality control regulations for in vitro diagnostics.

Declarations must be made by the CEO or the general controller.

Fees

The review fees vary between Recognized Certification Bodies and the method taken for the QMS audit also makes significant difference in the fees. It is recommended that the applicant contact a Recognized Certification Body to clarify the cost in advance.

Time Clock

Because each Recognized Certification Body stipu-

lates its standard administrative processing periods, it is recommended to confirm these periods in advance.

Partial–change Application, Notification of Changes

Policies for changing certification items are basically the same as policies for changing approval items, but keep in mind that additions of clinical significance require a new application for approval, not a partial-change application.

Notification for Marketing

As described previously, products not requiring applications for approval or certification simply require a notification for marketing. As of 31 March 2009, 131 such items have been specified.

Items Not Requiring Approval

Items not requiring approval include in vitro diagnostics listed in the table attached to Ministry of Health, Labour and Welfare Announcement No. 120 of March 29,

Heisei 17 (2005), *Specified in vitro diagnostics for which the Minister of Health, Labour and Welfare has established standards based on the provisions of Article 14, Paragraph 1 of the Pharmaceutical Affairs Law,* that are either calibrated using standard reference materials for calibration or calibrated using a standard measurement method stipulated by an organization, etc. listed in the announcement. However, these standards do not apply if the measurement principles, detection sensitivity, etc. clearly differ from those of existing in vitro diagnostics.

Points to Consider When Developing Notifications for Marketing

The points to consider for developing notifications for marketing are the same as those for applications for approval. However, it is not necessary to describe the clinical significance in the Intended Use field.

Fees

Fees are not required for notifications.

Summary

- Although in vitro diagnostics are legally considered drug products, they are subject to regulations similar to medical devices in consideration of international harmonization.
- With a focus on risks for diagnosis, each nomenclature is classified among three classes (Classes I, II and III).
- In order to legally market in vitro diagnostics, it is necessary to obtain a Type II MAH license for drug products. Moreover, reviews for approval are conducted by PMDA after submitting certain attachments and completing procedures for applications for approval.
- As with applications for approval, for applications for certification, attachments are submitted to a Recognized Certification Body and reviews are conducted regarding conformity with certification standards and conformity with QMS.
- For specified in vitro diagnostics for which the Minister of Health, Labour and Welfare has established standards and that conform to those standards, applications for approval or certification

are not required and a notification for marketing is sufficient.

Related Notifications

- *Yakushokuhatsu* No. 0216004 of February 16, Heisei 17 (2005), *Applications for manufacturing and marketing approval for in vitro diagnostics*
- *Yakushokukihatsu* No. 0216005 of February 16, Heisei 17 (2005), *Points to consider for applications for manufacturing and marketing approval for in vitro diagnostics*
- *Yakushokuhatsu* of March 31, Heisei 17 (2005), *Applications for manufacturing and marketing certification for in vitro diagnostics (Bureau Notification on IVD Certification Applications)*
- *Yakushokukihatsu* No. 0331006 of March 31, Heisei 17 (2005), *Handling of notifications for manufacturing and marketing for in vitro diagnostics*
- *Yakushokukihatsu* No. 0331010 of March 31, Heisei 17 (2005), *Points to consider for applications for manufacturing and marketing certification for in vitro diagnostics*
- *Yakushokuhatsu* No. 0401031 of April 1, Heisei 17 (2005), *General nomenclature of in vitro diagnostics*
- *Yakushokukihatsu* No. 0616001 of June 16, Heisei 17 (2005), *Checklist for compliance with standard essential principles for specified in vitro diagnostics*
- *Yakushokuhatsu* No. 0622004 of June 22, Heisei 17 (2005), *Enactment of certification standards for in vitro diagnostics*
- *Yakushokuhatsu* No. 0622006 of June 22, Heisei 17 (2005), *Enactment of approval standards for in vitro diagnostics*
- *Yakushokukihatsu* No. 0909001 of September 9, Heisei 17 (2005), *Handling of preliminary tests for manufacturing and marketing approval for in vitro diagnostics*
- *Yakushokukihatsu* No. 0511001 of May 11, Heisei 18 (2006), *Handling of in vitro diagnostics that are radioactive drug products*
- *Yakushokukihatsu* No. 0221001 of February 21, Heisei 19 (2007), *Handling of series applications, etc. for in vitro diagnostics*
- *Yakushokukihatsu* No. 1023-1 of October 23, Heisei 21 (2009), *Handling of materials regarding safety to be attached to applications for manufacturing and marketing approval and applications for manufacturing and marketing certification for in vitro diagnostics*

Chapter 45

Japanese Glossary of Terms

Accreditation

Process of certifying competency, authority or credibility by an official, recognized authority such as a professional organization or government entity

Acquired Immune Deficiency Syndrome (AIDS)

Final and most serious stage of HIV disease, which causes severe damage to the immune system; caused by HIV

Adverse Drug Reaction Sufferings Relief Fund Law

Enacted 1979; Provides financial assistance for individuals affected by adverse drug reactions or infections from biological products

Agency

Administrative division of a government or government entity

Application

Request for regulatory clearance of a medical product

Approval

Action by regulatory agency on applications, uses, aspects of pharmaceuticals or medical devices

Barrier

Legislation, regulation, tax/fee or other element that prevents or delays items from reaching the marketplace

Bleeding Donor Supply Service Control Law

Law to enforce adequate use of human blood, prevent health hazards caused by drawing blood for blood products, and to protect blood donors

Biological products

Derivations of living organisms, manufactured for preventing, diagnosing, treating or curing diseases in humans or animals, certified by a regulatory authority

Biologics

Drug products and medical devices made from biologically derived materials (genes, proteins, cells and tissues) or relying on biological functions allowed to act as biologically functional molecules; facilitate or control actions of such molecules; contribute to regeneration/restoration or replacement of living cells, tissues, etc.; require special measures to prevent health hazards such as infections

Biosimilars (Follow-on biologics)

Officially approved new versions of innovator biopharmaceutical products; many not approved

Blood products

Component of blood collected from a donor for use in a blood transfusion

Bovine Spongiform Encephalopathy (BSE)

Brain disease caused by biological product from cows that became global safety issue, known as Mad Cow Disease

Branch warehouses
Buildings where operations associated with the manufacturing process, including the storage of products awaiting product release determination, and storage and shipping/receiving operations after product release determination is made are conducted; may or may not be physically located within the same lot of the manufacturing sites for the final products, but require Labeling, Manufacturing, etc. licenses

Cabinet Legislation Bureau
Examines legislative bills before they are brought before Cabinet meetings

Catheter
Tube inserted into vein, artery or other tubular element of the body to control, direct or measure activity, strength, condition

Characteristic utility
Feature of medical devices (not drug products)—usefulness or purpose, i.e., "making more accurate diagnoses with images," "providing radical cures through surgery or treatment"

Chinoform agents
Derivative of 8-hydroxyquinoline derivative used as topical anti-infective, intestinal antiamoebic and vaginal trichomonacide; first developed as external medicines, then used internally; oral version banned worldwide after found to cause/contribute to subacute myelo-optic neuropathy

Classification/Class
Category or type of medical products

Clinical trial
Tests conducted in regulated conditions to develop and collect safety and efficacy data for health interventions (e.g., drugs, in vitro diagnostics, and medical devices)

Codes
Regulations for local public organizations, determined at meetings of such organizations; established within scope of laws and ordinances

Common Technical Document (CTD)
Five modules developed as template for attachments to application materials

Compliance
Agreement or conformity with regulations, industry practices, laws and other aspects of quality control, safety, etc.

Conformity Assessment Inspections
Conducted to inspect manufacturing facilities, processes and quality control to determine whether manufacturing sites operate properly; both onsite and document-based

Contraindications
Conditions suggesting that a drug, medical device or other item should not be used for certain patients or diseases

Contributions
Payments by MAHs to cover required safety measures operations

Corrective and Preventive Action (CAPA)
Appropriate moves to respond to safety, nonconformity and other issues

Creutzfeldt-Jakob Disease (CJD)
Degenerative neurological disorder that is incurable and invariably fatal; most common of the transmissible spongiform encephalopathy diseases found in humans

Cuff
Device that wraps around the patient's arm or other extremity to measure blood pressure or used to hold catheter in place

Defects
Faults, errors or problems

Deficiencies
Lacks, problems leading to failure to function as expected, or deviations from approval conditions

Dialyzers
Medical devices used to perform dialysis—cleansing blood by removing blood from artery, purifying it and returning it to a vein

Diet
Governing entity that represents the people of Japan

Dosage

Amount of medication/pharmaceutical given to patients

Dosage form

Way in which medications are given to patients—pill, tablet, capsule, intravenous

Doshomachi

Place where "Medicinal Products Retailers" or drug wholesalers conducted business before Japan's 1658 joint seal letters

Drug Product Regulating Corporation

Integration of Osaka Drug Wholesalers Association and Osaka Pharmaceutical Manufacturers Alliance

Drug Wholesalers Association

Formed in 1874; replaced by Osaka Drug Wholesalers Association, 1894; replaced in turn by Osaka Pharmaceutical Manufacturers Association, 1902

Edo Period

Period of Japanese history ruled by shoguns of Tokugawa family, 1603–1868

Efficacy

Producing a desired result; level of function or effectiveness at which drugs are administered or medical devices used

Enterprise Reorganization Act

Promulgated 1946; intended to provide corporations with assistance for rebuilding businesses destroyed by World War II and promoting continuing prosperity after World War II

Essential Requirements (of Safety and Performance of Medical Devices)

Based on international harmonization for regulatory systems

Ethical drugs

Pharmaceuticals that must be used under the direct management and guidance of doctors or pharmacists; prescription drugs

European Community (EC)

Economic and political union of 27 member states located primarily in Europe; committed to regional integration; common coin/currency: the Euro

Flexible disks

Floppy computer disks

Food and Drug Administration (FDA)

US government agency responsible for safety of foods and drugs, products and devices

Foreign Manufacturer Accreditation (FMA)

Formal permission granted by MHLW to manufacturers located outside Japan to perform manufacturing activities for products intended for distribution on the Japanese market

Foundation work

Early research that can be used as basis of new studies

General controller

Person required for an MAH responsible for the entire operation of product release onto Japanese market; supervises quality controller on quality related issues and safety controller on safety issues of the product

Generic Products Reviews

Assess efficacy and safety by indicating equivalence with existing products; introduced to streamline reviews

Global Medical Device Nomenclature (GMDN)

Naming convention introduced to globalize and internationally harmonize the former Medical Devices Nomenclature and Classifications

Good Clinical Practice (GCP)

Set of rules established based upon lessons learned from the past, including various scandals and crises; global standard for conducting clinical trials for drug products and medical devices; based on Declaration of Helsinki and dating back to Hippocratic Oath

Good Laboratory Practice (GLP)

Standards or code of conduct as specified in MHLW Ordinances to ensure quality of data from nonclinical tests

Good Manufacturing Practice (GMP)
Standards for manufacturing control and quality control for drug products

Good Quality Practice (GQP)
One of the requirements for MAH licenses, involving quality and safety assurance responsibilities of parties engaging in product realization processes

Good Vigilance Practice (GVP)
One of the MAH's responsibilities to assure product safety in postmarket phase; certain products require establishment of a safety management department

Government Ordinance
Requirements that have more specific contents than laws, decided by the Cabinet

Guidance/Guidance Document
Directions or directives on how a product, drug or device is to be used, classified, monitored, etc.

Harmonize
Equalize standards across countries in response to increasingly global nature of pharmaceutical industry and products/devices

Health Policy Bureau
Passes and proposes policies to foster a high-quality, effective system for offering medical services; umbrella for General Affairs Division, Guidance of Medical Service Division, Medical Professions Division, Dental Health Division, Nursing Division, Economic Affairs Division, research and Development Division, National Hospital Division

Heisei
Current era in Japan; began January 8, 1989

Hippocratic Oath
"First, do no harm;" ancient Greek guiding principle for medical profession

Human Immunodeficiency Virus (HIV)
Cause of AIDS

Impurities
Imperfections in medications, pharmaceuticals

Infection
Disease or condition caused by microscopic organisms

Injections
Way of administering medications or fluids by plunging needle into patient's skin or vein; became common in Japan during Taisho period

Inspection team
Group of professionals responsible for assessing state of regulatory compliance at manufacturing and other sites relative to producing, labeling, packaging and otherwise handling medical products

Inspection plan
Plan for conducting inspections by companies, regulatory agencies or third parties which are granted inspection authorities by the regulatory agencies to assess state of regulatory compliance to requirements for safety and quality of medical products

Institutional Review Board (IRB)
Independent body that determines whether proposed clinical trials: are scientifically and ethically acceptable; are conducted suitably from subjects' perspective; protect subjects' human rights and promote safety assurance and welfare

International Standards Organization (ISO)
Global entity that manages, sponsors, establishes standards to ensure safety and harmony among products, professions and countries

Inventory
Stock or stockpile of products for which product release determination was already given and awaiting distribution or sale

In vitro
Outside the living body, in an artificial environment, such as in vitro fertilization

In vivo
Experimentation using a whole, living organism

Japanese Medical Device Nomenclature (JMDN)
Naming convention for medical devices adopted by Japan and tied to GMDN

Japanese Pharmacopoeia

Provides quality standards for drug products; established 1888

Joint seal letters

Letters signed by multiple medicinal products distributors in 1600s to request that the Japanese government promulgate appropriate regulations on pharmaceutical products

Kanpo

Government bulletin issued every weekday, used to announce and disseminate laws and ordinances to the public (similar to US *Federal Register* and the *Official Journal of the European Union*)

Kit Products

Combinations of drug products and medical devices, including special containers, or two or more drug products in a single dosage form to reduce burden and prevent contamination by bacteria or foreign-matter

Law

Enacted by a Cabinet meeting and promulgated by being published in *Kanpo*

License

Permit/permission to act in a given way—to market or sell a drug or device for specified uses in specified regions, countries, etc., granted for pharmaceuticals by Minister of Health, Labour and Welfare to individual manufacturing sites according to MHLW categories (can be for retail sales, home distribution, etc. or for leasing of medical devices)

Malfunction

Failure to perform as expected

Manufacturing

Producing medical products, such as drugs, in vitro diagnostics or medical devices; sterilization, packaging, labeling and storage of products are also recognized as manufacturing activities

Marketing Authorization Holder (MAH)

The company or individual licensed by MHLW to be responsible for distribution of a product; compliance with Good Quality Practice (GQP) and Good Vigilance Practice (GVP) is required

Medical device

Product used for medical purposes in patients, in diagnosis, therapy or surgery; machinery or appliances, etc., for diagnosing, treating or preventing disease in humans or animals, or to affect bodily structures or functions of a human or animal; range from tweezers, scalpels and contact lenses to diagnostic imaging equipment; are categorized into classes and have risk-based regulations

Medicines Control Regulations

Enacted by Meiji government, 1871; regulations aiming at identifying and removing fake medicines and their distributors

Meiji Period

Timeframe when all Western medicine had to be imported into Japan and counterfeits, imitations and other questionable products were distributed in the market; systems for regulating drug products and certifying doctors and pharmacists promoted as countermeasures against defective products

Messages

Notifications, administrative notices—forms for documents describing interpretations and operational policies for laws and ordinances; usually issued central government to prefectural governments

Metabolism

Process or rate at which the body breaks down the substances of life

Ministerial Ordinance

Issued in administrative affairs to enforce a law or government ordinance

Ministry of Health, Labour and Welfare (MHLW)

Government agency in Japan with the central role of promulgating and administering regulations under the *Pharmaceutical Affairs Law*; conducts operations and services related to pharmaceutical affairs administration; works with Pharmaceuticals and Medical Devices Agency (PMDA)

Multi-site studies

Clinical and nonclinical investigations held in various locations

Narcotics

Drugs that dull the senses

Nomenclature

Naming convention for drugs and devices

Non-tariff barriers

Restrictions on trade across borders, such as non-dumping measures and countervailing duties

Notification

Announcement published by a regulatory agency, such as MHLW, mainly intended for internal communication within the agency including local offices; describes details on interpretation of the regulations and Q&As; shared with industry associations

Online Public Bulletin

Internet version of *Kanpo*

Over-the-counter (OTC) drugs

Pharmaceuticals that are sold without a prescription; may have originally been prescription drugs

Pacemaker

Electrical device that stimulates or steadies a person's heartbeat; focus of improper trade deliveries uncovered in 1992; led to proposal at Central Social Insurance Medical Council, 1993, to promote appropriate costs and distribution of medical devices

Package Insert

Printed information in A4 size enclosed in packaging for drugs, medical devices and related items

Penalty

Punishment, such as fine, for violation of law or regulation

Pharmacy

Art, practice or profession of preparing and dispensing drugs; location where a pharmacist dispenses drugs for sale or provision

Pharmaceutical Affairs and Food Sanitation Council

Agency that conducts evaluations, reevaluations and safety inspections of drug products and medical devices in response to inquiries of Minister of Health, Labour and Welfare, established 1961

Pharmaceutical and Food Safety Bureau

Implements measures for securing efficacy and safety of drug products and medical devices; address issues related to life and health—blood products-related operations, restrictions on narcotics and stimulants

Pharmaceutical Affairs Laws

Law regulating businesses related to drugs, in vitro diagnostics, quasi-drugs, medical devices, and cosmetics in Japan. Modern era began 1914; current version established 1960, revised many times, including 1979, 1994, etc. Established system for quasi-drugs; shifted registration system for pharmacies, manufacturing and sales to licensing system and established licensing standards; established requirements for labeling of lot numbers and quantity of ingredients; restriction on advertisements of drug products for special diseases (cancer) and nonapproved drug products; separated matters associated with identification of pharmacists; established *Pharmacists Law*. The most recent revision shifted the regulatory scheme to focus on marketing authorization instead of manufacturing activities; created a solely responsible party (Marketing Authorization Holder); allowed companies to outsource entire manufacturing processes to anywhere in the world.

Pharmaceutical industry

The industry that produces medicinal products

Pharmaceuticals and Medical Devices Agency (PMDA)

Established 2004; integrates activities of Organization for Pharmaceutical Safety and Research, National Institute of Health Sciences, Japan Association for the Advancement of Medical Equipment Center; provides prompt relief for health damages caused by adverse reactions to drug products or infections via biological products; conducts investigation to improve drug product quality, effectiveness and safety

Pharmacists Law

> One*Pharmaceutical Affairs Law*-related law stipulating duties and responsibilities of pharmacists

Poisonous drugs

> Pharmaceuticals that have strong toxicity and could cause death; must be labeled as "Poison" on container or package in white letters on black background with white borders

Powerful drugs

> Pharmaceuticals that are lower levels of toxicity; must be labeled as "Powerful" on container or packaging in red letters on white background with red borders

Prescription drugs

> Medications ordered by a licensed physician or other medical professional qualified and licensed to do so

Principal investigator

> Doctor or dentist responsible for conducting clinical trials at medical institutions; lead a team of subinvestigators and contributors, implement trial in compliance with GCP and institution's stipulated procedures

Product Certification System

> Third-party process under which Recognized Certification Bodies, rather than government, conduct product reviews and confirm conformity with Essential Requirements for certain devices

Product release

> Action taken by the MAH on a *Pharmaceutical Affairs Law*-regulated product for marketing, leasing or provision in Japan

Promotion code for ethical drugs

> Voluntary industry standards for implementing fundamental principles of code of practice for pharmaceutical industry

Quality controller

> Person appointed by a general controller to manage quality aspect of products

Quality Management System (QMS)

> Organizational structure, procedures, processes and resources needed to implement quality management

Quasi-drugs

> 371 drugs that could previously only be purchased at drug stores in Japan, deregulated in 2010 and now available at shops such as convenience stores

Reagent

> Substance that participates in or causes a chemical reaction

Reassessment System

> Process for reviewing quality, effectiveness and safety of approved drug products, based upon current academic standards in medicine and pharmaceuticals

Recalls

> Actions to remove products from the market in the wake of problems or crises such as defects and safety issues in medical products

Red Book

> Collection of nomenclatures in all categories (in Japanese); replaced by JMDN

Reexamination System

> Fixed period of four to 10 years after MAH obtains approval for new drug product when records of use and quality, effectiveness and safety are reviewed and reconfirmed

Regulation

> Rule dealing with procedure; order issued by an executive authority of a government, has the force of law

Regulations on the Sale and Handling of Pharmaceuticals

> Pharmaceuticals rules; basis for manufacturing and marketing, handling of drug products; promulgated 1889

Regulatory agency

> Government entity that issues and/or oversees standards and other aspects of regulations

Regulatory Review and Approval

> Process by which products are reviewed and approved

Reliability studies

> Conducted to determine whether materials attached to applications have been collected and prepared in accordance with MHLW standards

Replacements

Items that take the place of products, drugs or devices that have been reclaimed as a result of a recall or other concern

Responsible engineering manager

Person responsible for supervising manufacturing operations at the manufacturing facility; different from management representative defined by ISO 13485; required for a manufacturing license; a plant manager is typically recognized as the responsible engineering manager at a manufacturing facility outside Japan

Retail

Sale/sell at profit over wholesale price

Risk

Possibility of causing a dangerous condition; combination of probability of occurrence of harm and severity of such harm

Route of administration

Method by which medications are delivered or given to patients

Safety assurance

Became important aspect of industry after university professor died of penicillin shock in1956

Safety controller

Person appointed by a general controller to be responsible for safety aspect of products; responsible for safety management group

Safety management information

Details required so that drug product and related items are used properly

Selection Method

Way of choosing how a drug, product or device will be named or classified

Sexually Transmitted Disease (STD)

Conditions or illnesses passed between people through sexual contact or activity

Short-term tests

Tests occurring over brief periods using widely accepted routine techniques, such as for acute toxicity or mutagenicity, melting point, vapor pressure, distribution coefficient, explosibility; designed to simplify and increase efficiency of duties and include quality assurance, test plans and final report

Showa

"Period of enlightened peace"; era of Japanese history corresponding to reign of Emperor Shōwa (Hirohito), December 25, 1926–January 7, 1989

Side effects

Any effect of a drug, chemical, or other medicine that is in addition to its intended effect, especially an effect that is harmful or unpleasant

Sorivudine metabolite

Antiviral drug that inhibits metabolism of fluorouracil anticancer drugs and increases concentration in vivo, which enhances actions of the anticancer drugs; 1993 incident led to safety concerns

Standards for Quality Assurance at Manufacturing Sites of Medical Devices

Standards enacted 1987; effective 1995

Standard Operating Procedures (SOPs)

Pattern or template of processes to ensure good clinical, laboratory and other practices, as well as consistency and reliability in testing, research and development

Subacute Myelooptic Neuropathy (SMON)

Incidents of drug-induced effects reported sporadically in 1960s; considered rare disease of unknown cause 1972 conference concluded it was neurological disorder caused by chinoform agents

Summary Technical Document (STD)

Template for summarizing premarket requirements for medical devices for acceptance by various countries as materials for premarket reviews

Syringes
> Device used to inject liquids (including blood) or medications into, or withdraw them from, the body; originally all-glass; manufactured beginning in Japan in 1903

Taisho period
> 1912–26, when camphor injections became popular; beginning of development of medical devices as delivery technologies

Tariff
> Tax or other limit on goods that move across political boundaries such as borders

Template
> Standard pattern or format for documentation

Touyakushu
> Chinese medicine

Transgenics (animals and plants)
> Drugs derived from animal or plant proteins; not yet in practical application in Japan

US-Japan Market-Oriented Sector Selective (MOSS)
> Talks held after US-Japan Summit (see next item) to identify target fields such as drug products and medical devices; followed by variety of systems to increase transparency (evaluation processes, insurance coverage)

US-Japan Summit
> Talks held in January 1985 to facilitate business between the US and Japan; continued in the form of MOSS Talks (see previous item)

Validation
> Proof or confirmation, produced through approved or specified procedures/processes

Voluntary Corrective Actions
> Steps a company may take on its own—before being forced to comply by legal avenues—to fix problems in quality, consistency, conformity, safety of medical products

War-ready Pharmaceutical Affairs Law
> Provisions infused with national requirements to enhance military power

Wayakushu
> Japanese medicine

Wholesale
> Selling or providing drug products in bulk and/or at cost to individuals with established pharmacies, hospitals, clinics or treatment facilities

Working Group
> Small division of larger entity or association, focusing on specific task

World Health Organization (WHO)
> Public health arm of the United Nations